Introduction to Web Interaction Design

With HTML and CSS

Introduction to Web Interaction Design

With HTML and CSS

Michael Macaulay

CRC Press
Taylor & Francis Group
Boca Raton London New York

CRC Press is an imprint of the
Taylor & Francis Group, an **informa** business

A CHAPMAN & HALL BOOK

CRC Press
Taylor & Francis Group
6000 Broken Sound Parkway NW, Suite 300
Boca Raton, FL 33487-2742

Printed on acid-free paper
Version Date: 20170407

International Standard Book Number-13: 978-1-1389-1185-7 (Paperback)

Library of Congress Cataloging-in-Publication Data

Names: Macaulay, Michael, author.
Title: Introduction to Web interaction design : with HTML and CSS / Michael Macaulay.
Description: Boca Raton, FL : CRC Press, [2017] | Includes bibliographical references.
Identifiers: LCCN 2016031177| ISBN 9781138911857 (pbk. : acid-free paper) | ISBN 9781317432814 (web pdf) | ISBN 9781317432807 (epub) | ISBN 9781317432791 (mobipocket/Kindle) | ISBN 9781315692333 (master)
Subjects: LCSH: Web sites--Design. | Web site development. | Human-computer interaction. | Computer software--Human factors.
Classification: LCC TK5105.888 .M25 2017 | DDC 006.7--dc23
LC record available at https://lccn.loc.gov/2016031177

Visit the Taylor & Francis Web site at
http://www.taylorandfrancis.com

and the CRC Press Web site at
http://www.crcpress.com

Printed and bound in the United States of America by Sheridan

Contents

Part II   CSS

Part III   Web Design Principles and Practices

Part IV   Web Development Process

Preface

About This Book

Much of what is in this book can be found on the Web in one form or another, but not together in one place and not in as concise and structured manner that enhances learning as in this book. The book introduces the basic Web technologies, design principles and processes, and management practices used in Web design as well as how to use all of them in the designing and building of a working interactive website that is easy to use and accessible to those with disability. There are ample examples on how all commonly used HTML elements, attributes, and CSS properties are used and design guidelines about best practices. There are also ample theoretical and practical exercises to ensure continued involvement and interest of the reader in the topics introduced, and all that is required to do the exercises or implement the examples are a Web browser and a text editor such as Notepad on Windows, TextEdit on Mac, or Gedit on Linux. For further reading and newer materials, Web addresses for the relevant sources are also provided to enable readers to check the sources for updated materials.

A companion website is available at www.routledge.com/cw/Macaulay which contains code snippets, interactive exercises and further reading and resources.

Target Audience

This book is intended for:

- Those with no prior knowledge of Web design who wish to learn how to design and build websites of professional quality.
- Someone who already knows how to design and build a website using Web tools, such as content management systems, e-commerce platforms, or blogging software, that allow him or her to build websites without the knowledge of coding, but wants more control over the design offered.

Structure of This Book

This book is divided into four parts: HTML (HyperText Markup Language), CSS (Cascading Style Sheets), Web Design Principles and Practices, and Web Development Process.

Part I: HTML

This part presents chapters that introduce the functionalities supported by HTML. It shows how to use them to add various elements to a page, including text, links, lists, tables, forms, images, audio, video, and animation. It also shows how to use them to structure the content of a Web page, such as into headings, sections, paragraphs, and quotations.

Part II: CSS

This part explains the role of CSS in the styling and layout of Web pages, and the chapters introduce the functionalities that CSS supports such as the control of the font, size and style of text, color of elements, arrangement of elements, and the use of images for background.

Part III: Web Design Principles and Practices

This part comprises chapters on the fundamental principles of visual design and their applications to Web design. It discusses how these principles can enhance the aesthetics of a design, and also the role of aesthetics in user-satisfaction as well as in how usable users judge a website to be and its credibility; all of which play important roles in user experience and acceptance.

Part IV: Web Development Process

This part presents chapters that deal with the stages of Web design and development and how they are managed to ensure the smooth running and timely completion of a project. An extra chapter is also included that presents various useful practical information, including how scripts are used with CSS to realize more advanced interactive designs, how various other common Web-programming languages are used with HTML, and how to set up a Web server on a home computer to try them out.

Author

Michael Macaulay, PhD, is a freelance educator, developer, and user-experience designer and evaluator. Formerly, he was a senior lecturer and course director for multimedia courses at London South Bank University, United Kingdom. He earned his PhD in 2000 in the effects of human–computer interaction and multimedia in learning from Loughborough University, United Kingdom. In the past, he had also been a computer systems administrator, computer systems programmer and analyst, and desktop publisher.

1

The Internet and the Web

1.1 Introduction

It is useful to know a little about the technical aspects of the Internet and the Web in order to better understand the various terminologies used in this book and also how what you produce will generally work. If you find that something is too technical in this chapter, you can skip it and then come back to it when you feel more comfortable with the subject or feel the need to know it.

1.2 Learning Outcomes

After studying this chapter, you should:

- Be aware of the basic anatomy of the Internet and the Web and terminologies.
- Know how the Web works.
- Be aware of the technologies required to create different types of websites.

1.3 Fundamentals of the Internet and the Web

The **Internet** is the technological framework on which the Web, also known as **World Wide Web** (WWW), runs. It is a global network of interconnected computer networks that comprises millions of different types of networks, such as home, private, academic, business, public, and government networks, linked through various types of connection technologies, such as fiber optic cable and wireless. The Web is only one of the applications that the Internet supports. Other applications include e-mail, telephony, and file sharing.

Central to how computers or devices on the Internet communicate with each other and send data around are the relationship between them and the system they use to communicate with each other. There are broadly two models of relationship: client-server model and peer-to-peer model. In the **client-server** network model, one computer is the **server** and the others are **clients**. The clients request data from the server and the server provides the data to clients. In contrast, a **peer-to-peer** network is one in which all computers have equal responsibilities; that is, every computer in the network works as both a server and a client. In essence, the snippets of a single file are distributed across the computers of multiple users, so that when there is a request for the file, it is compiled from these sources. This is the model that file-sharing services, such as Freenet, typically use.

In order for the computers on the Internet to communicate successfully, the Internet uses a **suite of protocols**, the most important of which, as of time of writing, are Transfer Control Protocol (TCP) and Internet Protocol (IP). **IP** is used for transmitting packets of data from one computer to another, using the computers' unique addresses, and **TCP** is used to verify the accuracy of the data being transmitted. **Internet protocol suite** is often generally referred to as **TCP/IP**.

The unique address of a computer on the Internet, or indeed any network, is known as **IP address**, and it is the unique number that makes it possible to identify a computer on the Internet. The original IP address format, known as **IPv4**, is a four-part number written, for example, as 208.132.59.234. However, the enormous growth of the Internet has led to the introduction of **IPv6**, which is a six-part number. To make an IP address easy to remember, it is normally associated with a name, called **domain name**, for example, bbc.co.uk. Like any protocol, Internet protocols impose rule and order on how things are done. Basically, they specify rules and encoding specifications for sending data from one computer to another. Without these protocols, it would be impossible for so many computers to communicate successfully at the same time. It would be like having no queues at a crowded supermarket.

In contrast to the Internet, the Web is a system that enables files on various servers to be linked to each other. This is made possible through a technology known as **hypertext**, invented by Ted Nelson. The term refers to both the technology and the principle that enables the linking of a text element to another on a computer. It makes it possible to construct a dynamic information network by using **hyperlinks**, so that when a text is clicked, for example, with a mouse, it leads a user to another textual piece of information. When different types of media objects, such as text, images, sound, and video, are linked together instead of just text, the concept is referred to as **hypermedia**. Figure 1.1 shows an illustration of a basic hypermedia system. It shows documents containing hyperlinks to other documents and media objects. The documents and media objects could be on the same Web server or on different ones that are miles apart.

A hypermedia system can be made to behave in different ways. For example, clicking a hyperlink could open a document or a media file to which it is linked; and the document and media could both be on one computer or on separate computers located far apart. These computers are known as **Web servers**. They are powerful computers that run special programs and are permanently connected to the Internet. Although, in theory, people can have their website on their own Web server at home, it is usually not practical for various reasons, such as cost. Therefore, only big companies usually have their own Web servers. For everyone else, it is more practical to use **Web hosting services**. These are companies that own and maintain big powerful Web servers and charge a fee to host people's websites on them. For mere surfing of the Web, no more than an **Internet service provider** (IPS) is required. An Internet service provider essentially connects you to the Internet; however, some also provide Web hosting.

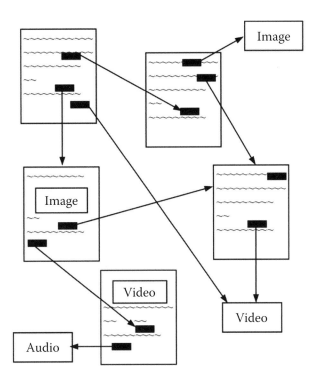

FIGURE 1.1   An illustration of a hypermedia concept.

The files on Web servers are usually accessed using a **Web browser** (technically known as **Web client**). Popular Web browsers include Internet Explorer, Microsoft Edge, Firefox, Chrome, Safari, and Opera. Technologies, such as Web browsers, that render files into Web pages in one form or another are generally referred to as **user agents**. For each file or document (i.e., **resource**) on a Web server, there is a unique address, known as Uniform Resource Locator (**URL**) or **Web address**, which describes its location. You may also come across the terms **URI** and **URN**. The relationship between these terms is clarified further shortly in the NOTE box. The format of a URL is as follows:

$$URL = protocol + IP\ address\ of\ server$$

$$+\ location\ of\ file\ on\ server$$

The syntax is: **protocol://host.domain [:port]/path/filename**

Therefore, the URL for a file situated on a Web server on the Internet might be written as shown in Figure 1.2.

In the example, the name of the file is "bolts.html." It is located in the "bits" folder (or directory), which itself is in the "products" folder on a server called "example.com," which is a WWW server (i.e., a Web server). HyperText Transfer Protocol (**HTTP**) is the protocol used by the Web for data communication, and 80 is the port that the browser typically uses to establish connection with a Web server, and assumed, so it is

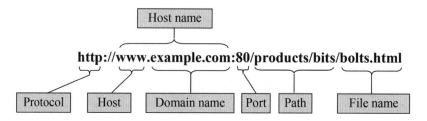

FIGURE 1.2   The anatomy of a URL or Web address.

normally omitted when an address is specified. In order to access a file on a Web server, a user would typically enter the Web address in a Web browser, click a link to it on a Web page that is already opened, or choose it from the bookmark, which is a list of previously stored visited Web addresses.

NOTE: URI versus URL versus URN

A Uniform Resource Identifier (URI) is a sequence of characters that identifies a resource, typically over a computer network such as the World Wide World. When information is included in a URI, such as a protocol (e.g., http://), that makes the location of a resource more specific, the URI is also known as a Uniform Resource Locator (URL). Therefore, for example, "example.com" is a URI, whereas "http://example.com" is a URL. A Uniform Resource Name (URN) is another type of URI. It is the name that identifies a resource and is rarely used.

How the browser delivers a requested file depends on the type of file. If it is a Web page, it is automatically displayed as a Web page, but if it is another type of file, such as a Word document, you may be given various other options, such as the option to save or open it. For files that are not Web pages, the browser may use other types of software, which are categorized as plug-ins and helper applications. A **plug-in** is embedded within a Web page, while a **helper application** is separate from the browser and operates independently of it, once the browser initiates it. Different types of files require different types of plug-ins or helper applications.

Although the Web is still most commonly accessed via desktop and laptop computers as of time of writing, it is increasingly accessed via a wide range of mobile devices, such as tablets and mobile phones, the capabilities and screen sizes of which vary widely. In addition, the Web is accessed by a wide range of people, including those with disabilities. The implication of this is that in order to reach as many people as possible, a website needs to be created in a way that allows viewing on a variety of devices and supports **assistive technologies**, which are the technologies that people with disabilities use to access Web pages. A common example is the **screen reader**, used by blind and visually impaired people to read out the contents of a Web page. Indeed, in many countries, some types of websites are required by law to be accessible to those with disabilities.

1.4 How the Web Works

When a user that is connected to the Internet types a website address in the browser or clicks on a link to the address, in order for the browser to know the location (i.e., IP address) of the Web server hosting the site and so be able to connect to it and request the site, it connects to the nearest **Domain Name System** (DNS) server to request the IP address. A **DNS server** (or **name server**) is a computer that manages a huge database that stores and maps domain names (Web addresses) to IP addresses, and there are many such servers located all over the world on every continent. They are basically like phonebooks. If the DNS server does not have the requested IP address, it requests it from another DNS server, which requests it from yet another one if it too does not have it, and so on, until options run out. If the IP address is found, it is sent to the browser. The browser uses it to connect to the Web server that hosts the required website and requests it. The Web server sends it and the browser displays it. Figure 1.3 shows an illustration.

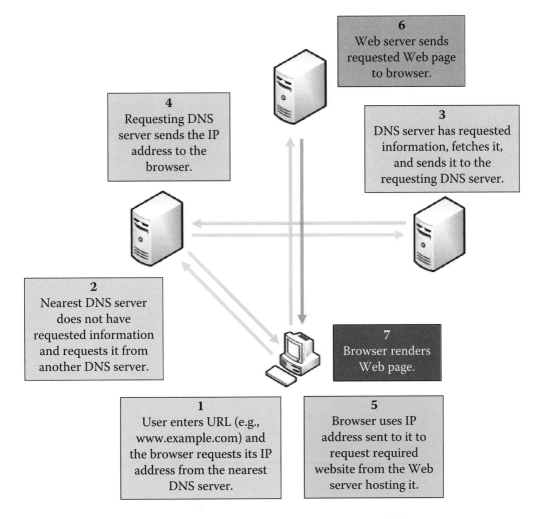

FIGURE 1.3 An illustration of what happens when a user requests a Web page.

1.5 Requirements for Creating Websites

Different types of websites require different levels of complexity in their creation, and level of complexity determines the range of languages necessary. Some languages are easy to learn and use, while others are relatively difficult. Most websites use HyperText Markup Language (**HTML**) and Cascading Style Sheets (**CSS**), because they are responsible for the look and feel of a page. In the case of **static websites** (i.e., websites in which content is not generated dynamically, such as personal websites), these two technologies are usually all that is required.

For **dynamic websites** containing a lot of interaction, it is usually necessary to use an additional technology known as **JavaScript**, which is a programming language that is typically run on the browser side. For more complex dynamic websites that require the storing and retrieval of users' data, such as e-commerce and dating sites, the use of a database is necessary, and so is the use of programming, to help the Web server carry out complex decision-making processes at the backend. Typically used programming languages include PHP, ASP.Net, Java, and Ruby. Of course, these languages in the end are still used to generate HTML and CSS, which the browser then uses to structure and style what it displayed on the screen. Most Web development authoring tools, which are **graphical user interface** (GUI) tools, allow you to use all these languages. An example is Dreamweaver.

For the types of websites that are updated regularly but do not necessarily involve a lot of interaction, programming is typically not required. They are often built using tools such as Web content management systems (WCMSs), e-commerce software, and blogging tools. These tools allow the creation of websites through simply selecting design templates and options for various pre-defined functionalities. Again, what they output and send to the browser are HTML and CSS.

1.6 Useful Info

1.6.1 Web Links

Internet and Web: en.wikipedia.org/wiki, internetsociety.org, webopedia.com, internetlivestats.com, and howstuffworks.com

1.6.2 Free Software

Multiple download sites can be found for the following software by doing a search:

Web authoring tools: Google Web Designer (*Cross Platform*), Mobirise Website Builder (*Win, Mac*), ToWeb (*Cross Platform*), KompoZer (*Cross Platform*), OpenElement (*Win*).

HTML editors: Coffee Free HTML Editor (*Cross Platform*), Komodo Edit (*Cross Platform*), PageBreeze (*Win*), Bluefish (*Cross Platform*), Brackets (*Cross Platform*), BlueGriffon (*Cross Platform*), PSPad (*Win*), SynWrite (*Win*).

CMS: WordPress (*Cross Platform*), Joomla (*Cross Platform*), Drupal (*Cross Platform*), SilverStripe (*Cross Platform*), CushyCMS (*Cross Platform*), Frog CMS (*Cross Platform*), Concrete (*Cross Platform*), Radiant CMS (*Cross Platform*), MODx (*Cross Platform*), TYPOlight CMS (*Cross Platform*), ExpressionEngine (*Cross Platform*).

Part I

HTML

2

Introduction to HTML

2.1 Introduction

HyperText Markup Language (HTML) is the standard markup language for creating Web pages. Although, the knowledge of HTML is, in theory, not necessary to create Web pages, because there are tools that allow you to do this without having to write any code, knowing HTML enables you to customize or refine outputs from these tools, where necessary. Naturally, to be a serious Web designer, the knowledge of HTML could be considered a mandatory skill.

2.2 Learning Outcomes

After studying this chapter, you should:

- Understand the concept of producing a Web page from an HTML document.
- Be familiar with the basic structure of an HTML document.
- Know how to create an HTML document with a text editor and render it in a Web browser.

2.3 About HTML

Imagine that you have a hand-written document that you want typed out and you do not know how to type or have access to a typewriter, but you know a typist. You would probably annotate (or markup) the document to show how you want it structured and styled, using an agreed convention between you and the typist, and then give the hand-written document to the typist to type. This is the basic principle behind how the Web page creation works, except that in the case of Web page creation, the document to be structured and styled is not hand-written but produced with a computer, the convention used to mark up the document is HTML, the Web browser is the typist, and the finished document is a Web page. Therefore, given an HTML document that is properly marked up, the Web browser parses it and produces the intended Web page. In the past, HTML was used for both the structuring and styling of a document, but this practice is now obsolete. The need for more flexibility and efficiency in the way Web pages are create and maintained has since led to limiting HTML's role to just structuring a document, while CSS is used for styling and scripting or programming languages are used for more complex functionalities.

HTML is a collection of elements that are used to define various parts of a document, such as header, footer, heading, and body of text. Essentially, when a document is parsed, the browser creates a hierarchal representation of the elements in it, known as a **document object model** (DOM), and it is this model that enables the document to be properly rendered into a Web page. The model also enables the use of scripting languages, such as JavaScript, to manipulate the elements of a page to create dynamism. How JavaScript is used with HTML is discussed in Chapter 22.

An HTML element comprises a **start tag** and a **closing tag**, except an empty element, which comprises only a start tag and therefore encloses no content. A **start tag** comprises a left angle bracket (<), the name of the element, and a right angle bracket (>); a **closing tag** comprises a left angle bracket (<), a forward slash (/), the name of the element, and a right angle bracket (>). This is illustrated in Figure 2.1.

An element can also take **attributes**, which provide extra information about how to treat the contents of the element. An attribute comprises two parts: an **attribute name** and a **value**, which are separated by "=". The **value is enclosed in quotation marks**. Attributes are **placed in the start tag**. Figure 2.2 shows an illustration.

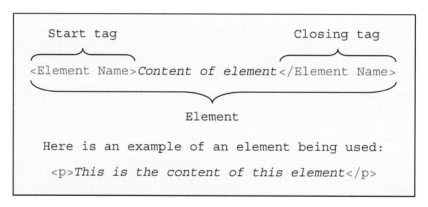

FIGURE 2.1   The structure of an HTML element.

```
                        Attribute
                   ╭──────────────╮
<Element name Attribute name="Value">Content of element</Element name>
        An example of an element being used with an attribute:
 <p title="first line">The attribute gives a title to this element</p>
  An example of an element being used with more than one attribute:
   <p id="vase" class="art">The attributes identify and classify this
                        element</p>
```

FIGURE 2.2   How attributes are used with an element.

Some attributes can only be used with some elements, while some are **global attributes**, which means that they can be used with any element. Commonly used global attributes include `title`, `id`, and `class`. These attributes are used in various examples given in this book. The `title` attribute is used to provide extra information about an element. If the element is displayed, then the value of the attribute is usually displayed when the cursor is over the element. The `id` attribute is used to give an identity that is unique in a document to an element, and `class` is used to identify a group of elements as being different from others, using a name. The same class name may be assigned to multiple elements, and vice versa. **Where an element belongs to multiple classes, the class names are space-separated**. For instance, in Figure 2.2, if the element that belongs to the "art" class also belongs to "modern" class, then the value of class attribute will be "art modern."

In addition to attributes that transform the contents of elements, there are others that represent the events generated by various HTML elements, such as **global events attributes** (generated by any element), **window events attributes** (generated by window objects), **form events attributes** (generated by form elements), **keyboard events attributes** (generated by keyboard activities), **mouse events attributes** (generated by mouse activities), and **media events attributes** (generated by media playback activities). All of these attributes are used in conjunction with a scripting language, typically JavaScript, to produce dynamic interaction with the user. Although HTML5 is not case-sensitive, it is good practice to always use uppercase and lowercase consistently for better understanding of a code.

NOTE: Representation of HTML elements

When the functions of elements are formally introduced and defined, the formats `<element name>`...`</element name>` (e.g., `<p>`...`</p>`) or `<element name>` (e.g., `<base>`) are used. The former means that the element can contain content between the tags, while the latter means that it is an **empty element** and cannot have content and can only take attributes.

2.3.1 The Structure of an HTML Document

An HTML document comprises two main parts: **header section** and **body section**, and they are defined by the `<head>` and `<body>` elements, respectively. The whole HTML document is defined by the `<html>` element. In addition, an HTML document typically starts with a **document type declaration**, which specifies that the document is an HTML document. In HTML5, it is `!DOCTYPE html`. Figure 2.3 shows the basic structure template of an HTML document.

An element that is inside another one is known as a **child element** of that element and the outer element is known as the **parent** or **containing element**. This means that the `<head>` and `<body>` elements are both child elements of the `<html>`

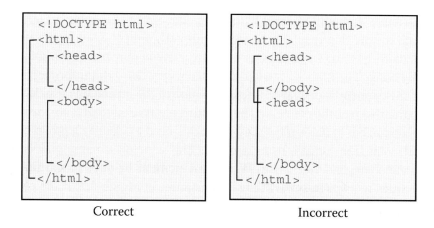

Correct   Incorrect

FIGURE 2.3   The basic elements used to structure an HTML document.

TABLE 2.1

The Primary Elements for Structuring an HTML Document

Element	Function
`<!DOCTYPE html>`	Specifies that a document is an HTML document.
`<html>...</html>`	Specifies the start and end of an HTML document.
`<head>...</head>`	Specifies the start and end of the document header section.
`<body>...</body>`	Specifies the start and end of the body of the document.

element. In Figure 2.3, notice the difference between the correct and incorrect nesting conventions. Correct nesting is necessary for a code to work properly, meaning that if an element starts inside another element, it must also end inside that element. Also, notice the vertical alignment of the start and end tags of each element and the indentation of child elements. Although doing these things are not necessary to make a code work correctly, they are good practice, as they make it easier to read and understand what a code does. Indentation of lines is possible because the Web browser renders only one space by default. This means that irrespective of the number of consecutive spaces put between words, this will be rendered as one space. This is known as **white space collapsing**. Table 2.1 describes the functions of the elements used in the illustration.

2.3.1.1 The Contents of the Head Section

The HTML elements placed in the head section (i.e., in the `<head>` element) are meta-related elements, in that they provide **metadata** (i.e., data that provide information about other data). More specifically, they provide information about a document, including information about other documents that they need (if relevant). The information is only for the browser and is not displayed in the browser window. These elements typically include `<title>`, `<meta>`, `<base>`, `<link>`, `<style>`, and `<script>`. The `<style>` element is used to embed CSS rules and discussed under CSS accordingly. The `<script>` element is used to embed or link to an executable script, such as JavaScript, and is introduced in Chapter 22 where it is more relevant, such as under Flash video in Chapters 7 and 22. The rest of the elements are discussed here.

2.3.1.1.1 `<title>...</title>`

The `<title>` element allows you to define the title of a Web page, which is displayed in the bar at the top area of the browser. Figure 2.4 shows how to use it, and Figure 2.5 depicts the result. Title description is one of the pieces of information used by search engines to index Web pages; therefore, making it reflect closely the content of a page improves the chances of search engines ranking the page highly (i.e., placing it as near to the top as possible of their search results). This ensures that the page can be found by those looking for the type of information it provides. Ideally, it should be the same as the main heading for a page. The practice of doing things to ensure high search engine ranking for a page is known as **search engine optimization** (SEO), and more about it is discussed later under other page features used for realizing it, such as page description, image description, headings, and link text. It is also discussed in Chapter 21 in relation to how it is affected by how mobile-friendly a layout is and in Chapter 26 in relation to its evaluation.

```
HTML
<!DOCTYPE html>
<html>
  <head>
    <title>I am the title</title>
  </head>
  <body>
  </body>
</html>
```

FIGURE 2.4 How elements are used in the `<head>` element and the result.

Page title

I am the title

FIGURE 2.5 Result of Figure 2.4.

CHALLENGE 2.1

Visit a few websites, navigate through the pages, and see how closely their titles match the headings and what the page is about.

2.3.1.1.2 <base>

The <base> element allows you to define the **base URL** (Uniform Resource Locator) for relative paths specified in a document. URL, as explained in Chapter 1, is the description of the location of a resource (e.g., document or media) on the Internet. Once a base URL is defined, any relative URL specified in the body section of a document is appended to its end to describe the full URL. This saves having to specify absolute paths (i.e., full paths) for all links. **Only one base element may be used** in a document, and it must have either an href attribute, a target attribute, or both. In the example in Figure 2.6, the href attribute defines the base URL, which means that the value of the **src** attribute in the <img> element (i.e., settee.jpg, which is an image filename) is appended to its end to derive the full path, "**http://www.example.com/images/settee. jpg**," which is the location of settee.jpg. The <img> element is used to display images and is discussed fully in Chapter 6. The value of the target attribute (i.e., _ blank) specifies that the image file should be displayed in a new browser window or tab.

Other possible values for the target attribute and their functions are listed in Table 2.2. These values are sometimes called **browsing context** names or keywords. This is because they describe the environment in which a document object is presented.

```
HTML
<head>
   <base href="http://www.example.com/images/" target="_blank">
</head>
<body>
   <img src="settee.jpg">
</body>
```

FIGURE 2.6 Example use of the <base> element and the href and target attributes.

TABLE 2.2

The Values for the target Attribute

Attribute's Value	Function
_blank	Opens a linked document in a new window or tab.
_self	Opens a linked document in the current window. This is default.
_parent	Opens a linked document in the parent frame.
_top	Opens a linked document in the top-level frame (i.e., whole window).

CHALLENGE 2.2

If in the example in Figure 2.6, the value of the `href` attribute is "http://www.example.com/" and the "settee.jpg" file is still in the same location, how would you write the value of the `src` attribute?

2.3.1.1.3 `<link>`

The `<link>` element allows a document to be linked to resources external to it. Table 2.3 lists the attributes that it supports, and Figure 2.7 shows how the element is used with the commonly used ones.

TABLE 2.3

Common Attributes Used with the `<link>` Element

Attribute	Function
href	Specifies the location and name (i.e., address) of the linked resource.
type	Specifies the content type of the linked resource, which is also known as **MIME type** (or **Internet media type**), a standard identifier used on the Internet for indicating the type of data that a file contains. MIME stands for "Multipurpose Internet Mail Extensions."
rel	Specifies **link type**, that is the relationship of the linked resource to the current document. There are many link types, and more than one of them can be specified in a space-separated list (e.g., "alternate stylesheet"). The most commonly used is **stylesheet.**
title	You met this global attribute earlier. When used with **stylesheet** link type, its value is listed as a style option for users to choose under the style sub-menu of the View menu of some browsers.
media	Specifies the media type to use to present the linked document (e.g., screen, print, and speech). The value must be a media query (discussed in Chapter 21).
hreflang	Specifies the language used in the text of the linked document. It is only advisory and is used only when the href attribute is used.
sizes	Specifies the sizes of icons contained in the linked document. It is used only if the rel attribute contains the **icon** link-type value. The values it takes are: any (which says that an icon can be scaled to any size) and a **space-separated list of sizes** in the format **width × height** (e.g., 12 × 12). Each size must be available.

(Continued)

TABLE 2.3 (*Continued*)

Common Attributes Used with the `<link>` Element

Attribute	Function
`crossorigin`	Specifies how an element handles cross-domain requests if it supports it. Most popular browsers support cross-domain communication. The mechanism known as **Cross-Origin Resource Sharing** (CORS) allows cross-domain requests, which used to be restricted by browsers, to be made from within scripts, so that, for example, one domain (e.g., example.com) can access data, such as an image, from another domain (e.g., takeit.com). The attribute takes two values: anonymous (which allows sharing, but with no exchange of user credentials, e.g., via cookies) and user-credentials (which allows the exchange of user credentials).

```
HTML
<head>
  <link href="style.css" rel="stylesheet" type="text/css">
</head>
```

FIGURE 2.7   Example use of the `<link>` element and the `rel` and `type` attributes.

In the example, the linked resource is a document and "style.css" specifies its location and name. In this case, the location is specified implicitly as a **relative address** (i.e., relative to the location of the current document). It essentially says that the "style.css" file is in the same folder as the document that is linking to it. The other type of address is an **absolute address**, in which full path is specified. The difference between the two is explained in Figure 2.8.

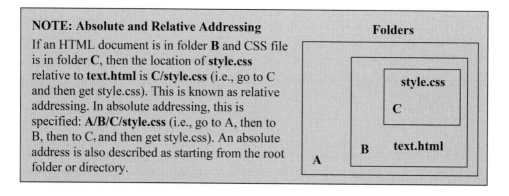

NOTE: Absolute and Relative Addressing   **Folders**

If an HTML document is in folder **B** and CSS file is in folder **C**, then the location of **style.css** relative to **text.html** is **C/style.css** (i.e., go to C and then get style.css). This is known as relative addressing. In absolute addressing, this is specified: **A/B/C/style.css** (i.e., go to A, then to B, then to C, and then get style.css). An absolute address is also described as starting from the root folder or directory.

FIGURE 2.8   Explanation of absolute and relative addressing.

Back to the example in Figure 2.7, the relationship of "style.css" to the current document is specified as "stylesheet," and "text/css" says that its content is CSS code. More than one `<link>` element can be used in a document, for example, for specifying multiple stylesheets. See "Methods of specifying CSS rules" in Chapter 8.

CHALLENGE 2.3

If an HTML file named "index.html" is located in a folder called "home" and a CSS file called "main_styles.css" is located in a subfolder of the subfolder of the folder, write a `<link>` element code to place in the head section of the HTML file that points to the CSS file.

2.3.1.1.4 `<meta>`

The `<meta>` element allows you to describe various kinds of information about a document that cannot be described using other meta-related elements, such as `<title>`, `<link>`, and `<base>`. The kinds of information it can be used to describe range from those used by search engines in ranking their search results to those about the creator of a document and the technologies, such as software, used to create the document. The element uses four attributes: `name`, `http-equiv`, `content`, and `charset`, which are combined in different ways to describe different kinds of metadata. Table 2.4 lists the functions of these attributes and the commonly used values.

While the `charset` attribute can be set alone, when either `name` or `http-equiv` is used, the content attribute must also be used in a **name-value pair** fashion. Essentially, the property to be defined is specified by the value of the `name` or `http-equip` attribute, and the value to give to the property is specified by the value of the `content` attribute. When the `http-equiv` attribute is used, a `<meta>` element is known as a **pragma directive**, which is an instruction to the compiler; a compiler is a computer language that interprets one computer language into another. Figure 2.9 shows examples of the various ways you can use the `<meta>` element and its attributes.

In the example, `charset` says that the character encoding used for the page is UTF-8. **Character encoding** is the allocation of a unique code to a character, using a **character set**. The technique predates computers, or the Internet and the Web, and goes back, for example, to the use of **Morse code** for telegraphing messages. The first internationally accepted character-encoding system to be used in computers was the American Standard Code for Information Interchange (**ASCII**) encoding standard, which is adequate for encoding all the characters in English text. Because it was unsuitable for non-English languages in its original form, various variants were later developed for different languages, leading to compatibility problems. To streamline everything, **Unicode**, a multilingual character set, was developed, and UTF-8 is one of the Unicode Transformation Format (UTF) standards for encoding the characters. It is also currently the most commonly used standard for the Web. Alternatives include UTF-16 and UTF-32. Knowing the character encoding used for a Web page enables the browser to correctly display the textual content of the page. Figures 2.10 and 2.11 demonstrate this. The default character encoding for HTML5 is UTF-8.

TABLE 2.4

Defined Attributes for the `<meta>` Element

Attribute	Function	Commonly Used Values
name	Defines a property name.	author (specifies creator of Web page), description (provides a 155-character maximum description of a page that is useful for SEO), robots (specifies whether or not search engine should index page), language (provides the natural language used), and keywords (defines keywords for a page).
http-equiv	Defines an HTTP header property that is used as an alternative to the response header sent with an HTML document by the Web server.	For example content-type (specifies MIME type), default-style (specifies the default stylesheet to use), refresh (specifies document refresh interval), pragma and cache-control (specify whether or not a page should be cached, and expires (specifies when a cached page should expire and a new version downloaded).
content	Specifies the value associated with the http-equiv or name attribute.	Depends on the value of http-equiv or name attribute. See Figure 2.5.
charset	Specifies character encoding.	Character set (e.g., UTF-8).

```
<head>
  <meta charset="UTF-8">
  <meta name="keywords" content="HTML, CSS, Web design">
  <meta name="description" content="Interaction design with
  Web languages">
  <meta name="author" content="Joe Bloggs">
  <meta name="robots" content=noindex>
  <meta name="robots" content=nofollow>
  <meta http-equiv="expires" content="Fri, 21 Aug 2015 23:59:59
  GMT">
  <meta http-equiv="pragma" content="no-cache">
  <meta http-equiv="cache-control" content="no-cache">
  <meta http-equiv="refresh" content="15">
  <meta http-equiv="refresh" content="3;url=
  http://www.newsite.com">
</head>
```

FIGURE 2.9 How the attributes of the `<meta>` element are used.

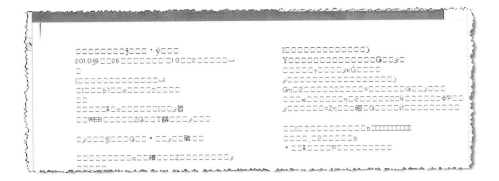

FIGURE 2.10 A Japanese page without correct encoding system.

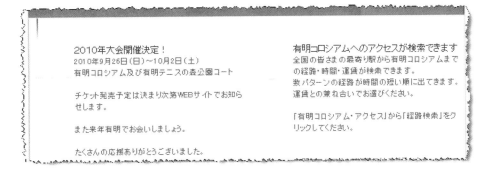

FIGURE 2.11 The same page as Figure 2.10 but with correct encoding system.

Back to the example in Figure 2.9, the value, `keywords`, gives the words that people might use to find the page; `description` says what the page is about and is used by search engines; `author` provides the name of the page creator; the first `robots` says search engines should not add page to their search results and the second `robots` says that it is all right to index page, but the pages to which the page is linked should not be indexed; `expires` says that page should be removed from the browser's cache at the specified date, which must be in the format shown, although "0" could be used to specify now, meaning that the page will not be cached at all and a new version is downloaded every time; `pragma` and `cache-control` say not to cache page; and the first `refresh` says to reload the page after 15 seconds and the second `refresh` says to redirect user to "http://www.newsite.com" after 3 seconds.

NOTE: Text in the `<head>` **element**

Although text placed in the head section, but not in meta-related elements, is displayed as if it has been placed in the `<body>` element, content should not be placed there.

CHALLENGE 2.4

In what type of Web application do you think it would be necessary to refresh the page as frequently as a few seconds and why?

2.3.1.2 The Contents of the Body Section

The contents of a Web page are placed in the body section (i.e., inside the `<body>` element), and in order for them to be displayed in a structured manner (i.e., with headings and sections), they must be marked up with appropriate HTML elements. Therefore, for example, if a body of text is inserted in the `<body>` element but without markup, it will simply be displayed without structure. This means that in addition to HTML document's structure, there is Web page structure (i.e., how the contents placed in the `<body>` element are displayed in the browser window).

Although different HTML elements can be used to mark up content to achieve the desired page structure, the recommended practice is to use **structural markup**, which basically means to use HTML elements that describe only the purpose of their contents and leave the appearance to be decided by the browser. For example, instead of using an element to make text bold in order to give it emphasis, an element that says to give it emphasis should be used. It is then left to the relevant user agent to render the text and give it emphasis in whatever way possible. For example, a Web browser might very well display the text in bold or in a different contrasting color, and a non-visual user agent, such as a screen reader, might express the emphasis in a way that is aurally appropriate. This means that the elements used for page structuring should be able to convey both visual and semantic meaning. **Semantic meaning** enables user agents to recognize an element as what it is intended to represent and renders its content in the most useful way to the user. This is especially useful because it makes contents more accessible to users with disability who use assistive technologies.

In theory, the structure of a typical Web page comprises the header, navigation menu, main content, one or more sidebars, and the footer. Whereas it was not possible in older versions of HTML to define these design components in a way that also conveyed semantic meaning, because there were no dedicated layout HTML elements to define them, HTML5 provides these elements and more. Figure 2.12 shows the difference between how layout used to be defined in older versions of HTML (typically HTML 4.01) and how HTML5 layout elements are used to do the same thing. In the HTML 4.01 example, each `<div>` element used to create a container and the `id` attribute used to give it a unique identity. The `<div>` element will be discussed further shortly with other generic HTML container elements.

Table 2.5 shows the applications of layout elements, and Figures 2.13 and 2.14 show them in use and the rendered result.

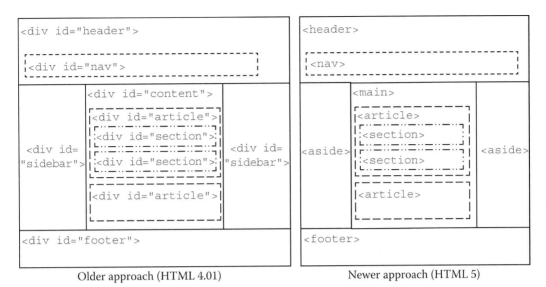

| Older approach (HTML 4.01) | Newer approach (HTML 5) |

FIGURE 2.12   Comparison between how page layout components might be defined.

TABLE 2.5

HTML5 Layout Elements and Their Functions

Element	Function
`<header>... </header>`	Used for the header of a page or the header of an `<article>` or `<section>` element.
`<footer>... </footer>`	Used for the footer of a page or the footer of an `<article>` or `<section>` element.
`<nav>...</nav>`	Used to contain the primary navigation menu.
`<article>... </article>`	Used to contain a self-contained piece of content that can be used or syndicated independently, for example a news item or a blog post.
`<section>... </section>`	Used to group related content or divide an article into different sections, with each having its own heading.
`<aside>... </aside>`	Used inside an `<article>` element to contain content that is related to the article but is not central to its overall meaning, for example a pull-quote. It is also used outside the `<article>` element to contain content that is related to the entire page, for example links to other sections, a search facility, and recent posts or tweets.
`<main>... </main>`	Used to contain content that is unique to a page and is not repeated on other pages. For example, it should not include header content, sidebars, or the footer.

(Continued)

TABLE 2.5 (*Continued*)

HTML5 Layout Elements and Their Functions

Element	Function
`<hgroup>...` `</hgroup>`	Used to group headings, so that they can be treated as one.
`<figure>...` `</figure>`	Used to contain a self-contained unit of content that is referenced from the main flow of the document and can be positioned away from the flow without changing the meaning of the document. It is used in conjunction with the `<figcaption>` element when the content has a caption. The element is intended to be used to mark up, for example, diagrams, images, graphs, videos, code examples, and supporting text.
`<figcaption>...` `</figcaption>`	Used to contain the caption for a `<figure>` element.

```
<body>
  <header>
    I am in the header element
    <nav>
      I am in the nav element
    </nav>
  </header>
  <main>
    I am in the main element
    <article>
      I am in the article element
      <section>
        I am in the section element
      </section>
      <figure>
        I am in the figure element
        <figcaption>
          I am in the figcaption
          element
        </figcaption>
      </figure>
    </article>
  </main>
  <aside>
    I am in the aside element
  </aside>
  <footer>
    I am in the footer element
  </footer>
</body>
```

FIGURE 2.13   Example of how the HTML5 layout elements is used.

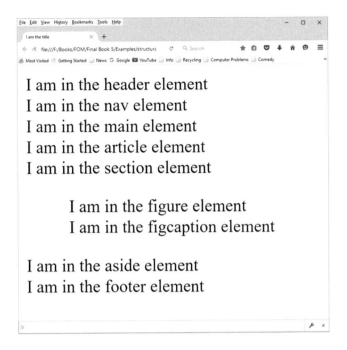

FIGURE 2.14 Result of Figure 2.13.

In Figure 2.14, notice how the rendered elements are not laid out. The only bit of structuring included is with the `<figure>` element, which, by default, is displayed with default margins (space) around it. What this shows is that in order to create a page layout, such as the one illustrated earlier in Figure 2.12, the layout elements need to be positioned and styled accordingly. They need to be given, for example, dimensions, border, and background color, all of which is done using CSS. Indeed, even though the browser might recognize the HTML layout elements for what they are, without the text descriptions in the example, it would have been impossible to know that they are there, since they are essentially containers.

CHALLENGE 2.5

Sketch the structure for the home page of your personal website on paper and then write the HTML code to describe the structure, using HTML5 layout elements and indenting the code as appropriate to make it easy to read.

2.3.1.2.1 Block-Level and Inline Elements

Once the general layout of a page is established with the layout elements, the contents of each element (e.g., text, lists, links, tables, and images) need to be structured in order for the desired visual page design to be achieved, and this is done using various other elements, which can be either block-level or inline elements. **Block-level elements** (or block elements) are elements that always start on a new line, and **inline elements** are those that always start on the same line. Figure 2.15 shows an illustration. Whether an element is a block-level element or an inline element will be noted when it is introduced later.

Figure 2.16 shows a block-level element and an inline element in use, and Figure 2.17 depicts the result. Notice in the rendered page that the content of the block-level element starts on a new line, while that of the inline element follows the existing text (i.e., the second "This content is not marked up") on the same line. The element used to create the heading (i.e., <h3>) is explained shortly.

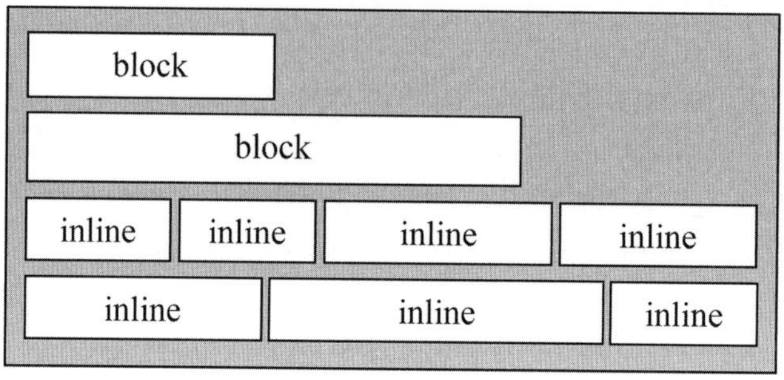

FIGURE 2.15 Representation of block-level and inline-level elements.

```
<body>
  <h3>Block-level and inline elements</h3>
  This content is not marked up.
  <div>This content is in a block element.</div>
  This content is not marked up.
  <span>This content is in</span><span>an inline element.</span>
</body>
```

FIGURE 2.16 An example usage of block-level and inline elements.

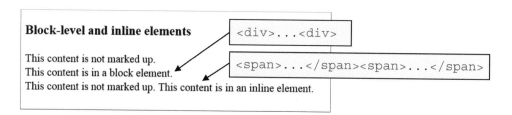

FIGURE 2.17 The rendered result of Figure 2.16.

CHALLENGE 2.6

Write an HTML code that does what the following statements describe:

> This text is in a div element.
> This text is in a span element inside a div element.
> This text has no markup, but this part is in a span element.

2.3.1.2.2 *Grouping Elements and Content*

Elements are also typically grouped within the layout elements. This is done to enable the same operation to be applied to contents or elements in unison and can be at block or inline level. For example, a number of paragraphs (block-level elements) or some words on a line (inline elements) may be grouped to enable, for example, the same color to be applied to them. **Block-level grouping** is typically done with the <div> element, while **inline grouping** is done with the <span> element. Figure 2.18 shows example of usage, and Figure 2.19 shows how the code is rendered. The <style> element is used to include CSS in an HTML document, which is discussed fully later, under CSS in this book. The element is used here to only show the effects of grouping. The <p> element is also discussed shortly. In the first <div> element, notice how the two lines in it are given the color specified for the element (i.e., blue), and how the <span> element is used to give only some of the words on a line a specific treatment. The second <div> element illustrates a block-level element being used to group together inline elements, in which all the content of the <div> element is given blue color, after which the content of <span> element is made red.

```
<h3>Block-level and inline grouping</h3>
<div style="color:blue">
  <p>This content is in a div element.</p>
  <p>This content is in the same div element.</p>
</div>
<span style="color:blue">This content is in a span
 element,</span>
<span>and this content is in the next span element.</span>
<div style="color:blue">
  <span style="color:red">This content is in a span element
   in a div,</span>
  <span>and this content is in the next span element in the
   same div.</span>
</div>
```

FIGURE 2.18   Grouping block-level and inline HTML elements.

Block-level and inline grouping

This content is in a div element.

This content is in the same div element.

This content is in a span element, and this content is in the next span element.
This content is in a span element in a div, and this content is in the next span element in the same div.

FIGURE 2.19   The result of Figure 2.18.

CHALLENGE 2.7

Write an HTML code to create a content that is rendered the same way as below, using the elements and attributes used in Figure 2.18:

> Roses are red,
> Violets are blue.
> But these are not the only things that are red or blue.

NOTE: About the remaining HTML elements

The rest of the HTML elements used to mark up content do not fall neatly into clear categories as the layout elements just discussed, since the same elements can be used with different types of contents and in different contexts. However, the functions of most elements can be explained by how they are used with text. Therefore, elements used with different types of contents and in different contexts are presented under text and the more context-specific elements are discussed under the relevant media object types (e.g., image and video) and context.

NOTE: Brief history of HTML

HTML, whose development has been handled since 1996 by World Wide Web Consortium (**W3C**), has evolved over many years and spans several versions, including HTML, HTML 2.0, HTML 3.0, HTML 3.2, HTML 4.0, HTML 4.01, and, the latest as of time of writing, HTML5. At the point HTML reached version 4.01, it was rewritten in XML to extend it to produce XHTML 1.0. XHTML 2.0, which was not backward compatible with HTML 4.01 or XHTML 1.0, was supposed to supersede both but was dropped because of considerable opposition to its goals. At the same time, another group, called Web Hypertext Application Technology Working Group (**WHATWG**), which considered XHTML 2.0 unsuitable for creating essential dynamic Web applications, such as forums and e-commerce site, was working on a project that was later adopted by W3C under the name of HTML5. HTML5 is more compatible with HTML 4.01 and XHML 1.0 than XHTML 2.0 and adds new functions. The commonly used of these new functions are discussed in this part of the book.

2.3.2 Creating a Web Page

At this point, it is useful to show how to create an HTML document and render it into a Web page, so that you can use the knowledge in trying out the examples presented in this book. How to create a Web page varies according to the type of tool used. Tools are generally categorized under text editors, HTML editors, WYSIWYG (What You See Is What You Get) HTML editors, and Web content management systems. When using text editors or plain HTML editors, HTML code needs to be typed or pasted into the editor. HTML editors typically color code elements, attributes, and values differently in order to distinguish between them and make the reading of a document easier. In a WYSIWYG HTML editor, you can type in code, in which case, the editor immediately renders the code to show the design, or you can enter content directly, as in a word processor, in which case, the editor automatically creates the corresponding code.

Web content management systems (WCMSs) are like more elaborate versions of WYSIWYG HTML editor. They typically do not require you to enter HTML code to create a Web page; this is done behind the scene by the system. The author usually needs to select one of the available page design templates, complete various forms, import contents onto pages, and specify parameters. Editors that behave in a similar way as a word processor are also usually provided to enter and style text, add links, and insert images. The codes produced by the systems can, of course, also be edited. WCMSs are suitable for wide range of Web applications, including blogs, forums, web stores, photo galleries, and wiki, and commonly used ones include WordPress, Drupal, and Joomla. The tools are available for all major platforms, such as Windows, MAC OS, and Linux, and there are free ones. Here, only how to create a page by using a text editor is discussed.

2.3.2.1 Creating a Web Page with a Text Editor

Whatever the computer platform (PC, Mac, or Linux), the steps followed to create a Web page with a text editor are generally the same:

1. You open the editor and type the HTML code in it. Different computer platforms have their own native text editor. For example, Windows has Notepad and MAC has TextEdit. There are also various free text editors on the Web. How a text editor is opened depends on the relevant operating system, but it usually can be opened in the same way as any other application.

2. Once HTML code is typed or pasted into the editor, you save it with **.html** extension in the desire folder. Therefore, assuming that the name of the file is "index," the name typed in the dialog for saving would be "index.html." In windows, it may also be necessary to select **All Files** from the **Save as type** drop-down menu in the dialog to prevent .txt from being appended to the end of the specified file name. It is useful to note that HTML editors are used in the same way.

3. Once the HTML file is saved, it can be opened as a Web page in a Web browser in various ways. One is by right-clicking it and choosing the preferred browser from the context menu; another is by going to the File menu of the browser, selecting Open, navigating to the file in the Open window, selecting it, and clicking the Open button.

NOTE: Looking at the code for other Web pages

One of the best ways to learn HTML is to study other authors' code, and the most accessible way of doing this is by studying the codes for the page on the Web. This is possible because every browser allows you to view the source code for the currently opened page. This can usually be achieved via the menu, but the exact procedure varies between browsers. For example, in Internet Explorer, it is **View>Source,** and in Firefox, it is **Tools>Web Developer>Page Source**. However, page source can also be accessed in most browsers by right clicking a page and choosing the option to view it from the menu that appears.

CHALLENGE 2.8

Search the Web for a Web page that is not too complex, and open the source code for the page, as described in the NOTE box above, and then, copy the code (e.g., via pressing Ctrl + A to select all the code and Ctrl + C to copy). Then, paste and save the file with a .html extension. Next, open the file in a browser. You will see that what is displayed does not look like the original page. This is because the resources used by the page, such as CSS and images files, are not available on your computer.

2.4 Useful Info

2.4.1 Web Links

HTML specifications: w3.org/TR/html51, w3.org/standards

Web development documents: webplatform.org

Accessibility: w3.org/WAI/tutorials, webaim.org

HTML5 support testing: html5test.com

HTML tutorials (*Here are just a few free tutorial sites on HTML and other Web languages*): w3.org/wiki, html5rocks.com, sitepoint.com, w3schools. com, codecademy.com, quackit.com, developer.mozilla.org/en-US/docs/ Web tutorialspoint.com, whatwg.org, htmlgoodies.com, htmldog.com, htmlcodetutorial.com, echoecho.com, learn.shayhowe.com, html.net, tizag.com, html-5-tutorial.com

3

Text

3.1 Introduction

Text is the most commonly used element to communicate on the Web, and one of the factors central to its ability to communicate effectively is how well it is structured. This chapter presents the HTML elements that can be used to accomplish this.

3.2 Learning Outcomes

After studying this chapter, you will know about HTML elements used to do the following:

- Describe the structure of the content of a Web page (e.g., with headings and paragraphs).
- Create superscript and subscript text, such as the text used in mathematical formula.
- Provide semantic information about content.
- Give some content more importance, emphasis, or relevance than others.
- Create definitions, quotations, citations, abbreviations, and small prints.
- Show edited content, so that people can see the information that has been changed.
- Display computer code and preformatted text and provide details about the author and publication of a Web page.
- Hide information until user requires it, and create dialog boxes and drop-down menus.
- Include special character, such as HTML characters, and extra white space in content.
- Provide language information and text directionality for content and create ruby text.

3.3 Headings

HTML provides six levels of headings, which are represented by <h1>, <h2>, <h3>, <h4>, <h5>, and <h6> elements. The contents of the elements are displayed in different sizes and in bold. The content of <h1> is displayed in the largest size and that of <h6> in the smallest size. <h1> is used for main headings, <h2> for sub-headings, <h3> for sub-subheadings, and so on. Although the displayed sizes may vary between browsers, the relationship between them is still maintained. The default text size set by users can also affect the displayed sizes of these elements. Figure 3.1 shows how the headings' elements are used, and Figure 3.2 depicts the rendered result.

```
HTML
<body>
  <h1>This a level 1 heading</h1>
  <h2>This a level 2 heading</h2>
  <h3>This a level 3 heading</h3>
  <h4>This a level 4 heading</h4>
  <h5>This a level 5 heading</h5>
  <h6>This a level 6 heading</h6>
</body>
```

FIGURE 3.1   Example usage of the headings elements.

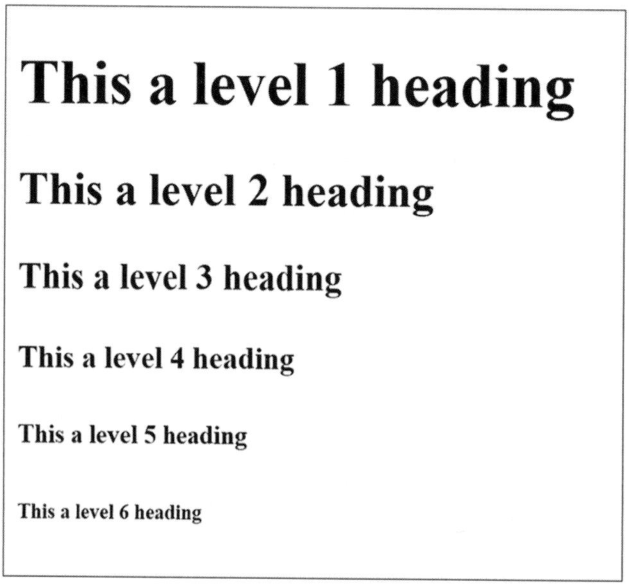

This a level 1 heading

This a level 2 heading

This a level 3 heading

This a level 4 heading

This a level 5 heading

This a level 6 heading

FIGURE 3.2   The result of Figure 3.1 in a browser.

3.3.1 Headings in Design

The use of different levels of headings creates a **visual hierarchy of importance**, which aids in the scanning and navigation of content. It essentially gives structure to a page, thereby helping users determine how to navigate it. Using headings effectively involves breaking up content and organizing it logically and predictably at the appropriate levels, so that one level leads as seamlessly as possible to the next. This means that the hierarchy should be meaningful. Ideally, a page should start with level 1, which might be the main heading, and no level should be skipped. Figure 3.3 shows an example structure.

The styling of headings should not be achieved through any means other than through marking them up with the heading elements, as the elements hold specific meanings that user agents (e.g., browsers and screen readers) recognize and use to treat their contents accordingly. This ensures that people who do not use the mouse, such as blind users, who can only use the keyboard and the screen reader, can navigate easily from one heading to the next.

Like page title, headings are one of the pieces of information used by search engines to index Web pages, and so, they should closely reflect content. They should also be **short and meaningful** in order to help improve text scanability. Figure 3.4 illustrates the visual hierarchy that can be created by breaking up text into sections and by using section headings. Notice how even without visible text, the breaks and the contrast in the right image seem to create a vision of structure and order.

- Heading Level 1
  - Heading Level 2
    - Heading Level 3
    - Heading Level 3
      - Heading Level 4
      - Heading Level 4
  - Heading Level 2
    - Heading Level 3
    - Heading Level 3
  - Heading Level 2
    - Heading Level 3
      - Heading Level 4
    - Heading Level 3

FIGURE 3.3 Example of headings' structure.

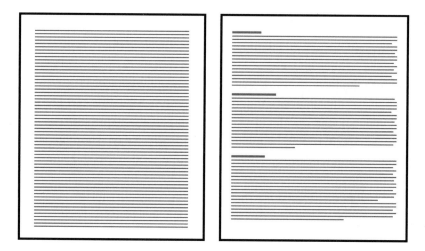

FIGURE 3.4   Illustration of the effects of heading levels.

CHALLENGE 3.1

Write the HTML code to implement the example hierarchical structure shown in Figure 3.3.

NOTE: Headings and accessibility

Headings play a very important role in the easy navigation of content by screen reader users, in that they allow users to easily skip from heading to heading and go to the desired part of a page, without having to go through the entire document. Most screen readers are capable of reading out a list of headings and allow users to go from heading to heading. This means that using headings properly when designing a page can make the page more accessible.

3.4 Paragraphs

Paragraphs are defined with the `<p>` element, which you have already seen in some examples in Chapter 2. To create a paragraph of text, the text is enclosed between the tags of the element. Since it is a **block-level element**, its content is always placed on a new line by default. Some space is also placed between it and the element directly above and below. Figures 3.5 and 3.6 illustrate how it is used and show its effect.

```
HTML
<h2>Paragraphs</h2>
<p>A paragraph comprises one or more sentences that deal
   with a topic or idea and always starts on a new line.</p>
<p>Paragraphs are essential for punctuating running text.
   They are used to divide text into smaller, logical, and
   more easily digestible blocks of text, with the aim of
   organizing information in a way that helps engage the
   reader.</p>
```

FIGURE 3.5   Example usage of the paragraph element.

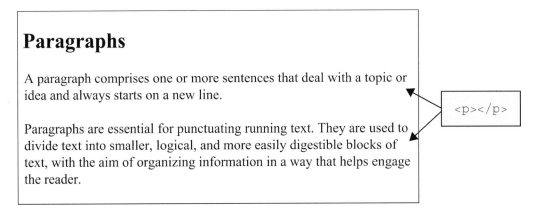

FIGURE 3.6   The result of Figure 3.5 in a browser.

3.4.1 Paragraphs in Design

Paragraphs are used for dividing a body of running text into smaller, logical, and more easily digestible blocks of text, with the number of ideas per paragraph typically limited to one. How they are styled varies widely, depending on the look and feel that is being communicated. Typical layout features used to achieve various paragraph styles include **indent** (which is the nudge to the right of the first line of the paragraph that is not the first paragraph), **outdent/hanging indent** (which is the nudge to the right of every line in a paragraph, except the first one), **initial** (which is the first letter of the first word in a paragraph when it is larger than the rest of the text), and a **space** (which is the space between paragraphs). Figure 3.7 illustrates these features, which are achieved using CSS. How to do this is shown in Chapter 14.

As shown in the illustration, first-line indents or outdents and spaces are used to delimit (separate) paragraphs, while initial is used just for decoration. Although first-line indent is most commonly used in printing, space is the most common in Web design. Unlike in printing, there are no rigid rules in Web design for styling paragraphs, and any of those illustrated in the figure, and more, are used. However, the typical default style used by browsers is to present content in paragraphs that are separated by space and are left-aligned.

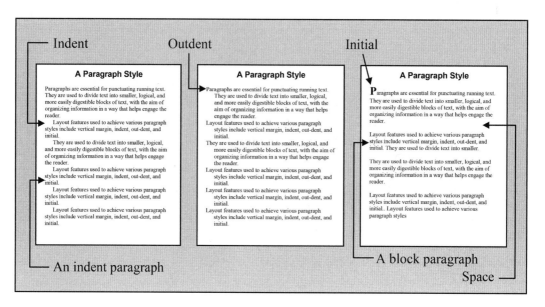

FIGURE 3.7   Common features of paragraph styles.

CHALLENGE 3.2

As you may know, the `<p>` element, like the `<div>` element, is a block element, which means that they both start on a new line. However, you should not use one in place of the other, because they have different semantic meanings to user agents. To compare the visual differences between the two, enter the following HTML code in a text editor and render it.

```
This text is followed by a paragraph element.
<p>This content is in a block element.</p>
This text is followed by a div element.
<div>This content too is in a block element.</div>
```

3.5 Line Breaks, Thematic Breaks, and Comments

The elements used for line breaks and theme breaks are `<br>` and `<hr>`, respectively, and the element used for adding comments is `<!--...-->`. The `<br>` element allows you to insert a line break (i.e., carriage return) and is especially useful for producing line break in text (such as addresses and poems), where block-level elements like `<p>` and `<div>` are not suitable, because they insert additional space between lines. The `<hr>` element was formerly used to simply draw a horizontal line to separate contents to, for example, visually convey to users a change of topic (such as in an article) or a change of scene (such as in a narration). However, now, it also carries corresponding semantic meaning in HTML5, which is referred to as a **paragraph-level thematic break**. This means that user agents are also able to recognize the meaning and render it as appropriate.

```
HTML
<h2>Line breaks, Theme breaks, and Comments</h2>
<!--This part explains the use of the line-break element in
    paragraph-->
<p>This content is in a paragraph element,<br>and the line-break
    element is used to place this part of it on a separate
    line.</p>

<!--This part explains the use of the theme break element-->
<hr>

<!--This part explains the use of the line break element in
    div-->
<div>This content is in a div element,<br>and the line break
    element is used to place this part of it on a separate
    line.</div>
```

FIGURE 3.8   Line break, horizontal rule, and comment elements in use.

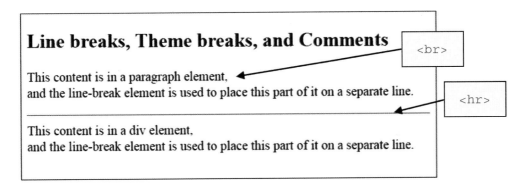

FIGURE 3.9   The result of Figure 3.8 in a browser.

In contrast, the `<!--...-->` element does not affect or display anything and is only used to annotate HTML code to make it easy to understand what different parts do. Adding comments to describe what various parts of a code do is good practice for the benefits of both authors and others who might have to work with the code at a later date, for example, for the purpose of maintenance. Figures 3.8 and 3.9 illustrate how these three elements are used and show their effects.

3.5.1 Specifying Word-Break Opportunities

In addition to specifying where a line must break, using the `<br>` element, it is possible to specify where the browser may break a line, even when its line-breaking rules do not support it. This is specified by using the `<wbr>` element. This is especially useful for preventing a long word or expression, such as URL, from being wrapped to the next line even when most of it fits into the current line, leaving a big gap as a result. Figure 3.10 shows example of its usage, and Figure 3.11 depicts the result.

```
HTML
<h3>Word-break opportunity</h3>
<p>This is
a.very.long.sentence.that.will.not.break.unless.instruction.
is.given.to.do. so.</p>
<p>This is
a.<wbr>very.<wbr>long.<wbr>sentence.<wbr>that.<wbr>will.
<wbr>not.<wbr>break.<wbr>unless.<wbr>instruction.<wbr>is.
<wbr>given.<wbr>to.<wbr>do.<wbr>so.</p>
```

FIGURE 3.10   Example usage of the `<wbr>` element.

Word-break opportunity

This is
a.very.long.sentence.that.will.not.break.unless.instruction.is.given.to.do.so.

This is a.very.long.sentence.that.will.not.break.unless.instruction.is.given.to.
do.so.

FIGURE 3.11   The result of Figure 3.10.

Notice that in the first paragraph, the joined sentence is wrapped to the next line in its entirety, while in the second paragraph, it is wrapped based on the points specified with the `<wbr>` element.

NOTE: Other ways of breaking words

Where to break a line can also be specified by using CSS. Ways of doing this are shown in Chapter 10 in Section 10.3.2, under "Handling content overflow."

CHALLENGE 3.3

Where would you insert line and theme breaks in the following and why?
    "Orange is a fruit of the citrus species. It is a hybrid between pomelo and mandarin. It is very old. For example, sweet oranges were mentioned in Chinese literature in 314 BC. Banana is an edible fruit that is botanically classified as a berry and is produced by several kinds of large herbaceous flowering plants. Plantains are a type of banana. The universe, according to Wikipedia, is all of time and space and its contents. It includes planets, stars, galaxies, the content of intergalactic space, the smallest sub-atomic particles, and all matter and energy."

3.6 Superscript and Subscript

Superscript and subscript present information in certain ways that make it more easily understandable and are useful for communicating some specific types of information. A **superscript** is text that is higher and often smaller than the main text. It is used for suffixes of dates (such as in 21st June) and in mathematics for representing the power to which a number is raised (such as in 2^{10}). A **subscript**, in contrast, is text that is lower and also often smaller than the main text. It is used in a number of different representations, such as chemical formulas (such as in CO_2), mathematical expressions (such as in $\log_{10}$), and footnotes. The HTML elements used to create them are <sup> and <sub>, respectively. Figure 3.12 shows how they are used, and Figure 3.13 depicts the result.

```
HTML
<h2>Superscript and Subscript</h2>
<p>The 21<sup>st</sup>century is from 2001to 2100.</p>
<p>The result of 10<sup>3</sup>is 1000.</p>
<p>The chemical formula for sulfuric acid is H<sub>
    2</sub>SO<sub>4</sub>.</p>
```

FIGURE 3.12 Example usage of the <sup> and <sub> elements.

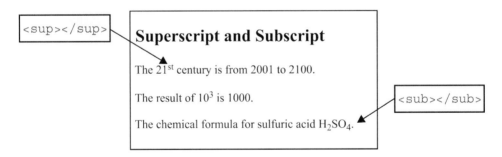

FIGURE 3.13 The rendered result of Figure 3.12.

CHALLENGE 3.4

Write the HTML code to display the content below, at least the chemical equation:

The universe is about 91 billion (28 × 10^9) light-years wide and still expanding. Inside it, many chemical reactions are going on all the time, some of which we understand and can represent with equations. For example, the following chemical equation shows what happens when methane (CH$_4$) burns in oxygen (O$_2$):
$$CH_4 + 2O_2 = CO_2 + 2H_2O$$

3.7 Importance, Emphasis, and Relevance

In a body of text, it is often necessary to make certain words or phrases look different from others for various reasons, because, for example, they are more important and you want to draw attention to them, just different, or related. The elements used to achieve goals like these are `<strong>`, `<em>`, and `<mark>`, respectively. The `<strong>` element **gives text strong importance**. Browsers typically render its content in bold. The `<em>` element **gives text stress emphasis**, and its content is typically displayed in italic type. It can be nested. When nested, each level of nesting indicates a greater level of emphasis, each of which is conveyed differently by a user agent. The `<mark>` element is **used to highlight text** to indicate its relevance to a context. This can be, for example, in the form of highlighting the instances of a search term in search results. Figure 3.14 shows how these elements are used, and Figure 3.15 depicts the rendered result.

Like with all HTML elements that have specific meanings, the `<strong>` or `<em>` elements should not be used for any purposes other than specifying importance and emphasis, respectively, as user agents will interpret this wrongly. For example, they should not be used to simply make text bold or italic. Also, the `<b>` element (which makes text boldfaced) and `<i>` element (which makes text italic) should not be used for giving importance or emphasis, as they have no semantic meaning and therefore are not recognized as conveying these meanings by user agents. However, you can use the elements where some part of text only needs to be presented in a different way from the rest and without any additional meaning, such as to attract attention. For example, the `<b>` element can be used for summary, keywords, and product names in a body of

```
HTML
<h2>Importance, Emphasis, and Relevance</h2>
<p>When considering your options, it is<strong>crucial</strong>
    to think of the consequences.</p>
<p>I <em>believe</em>in the need to address air pollution.</p>
<p>The mark element is used to <mark>highlight</mark>text that
    is relevant to a context.</p>
```

FIGURE 3.14   Example usage of the strong, emphasis, and highlight elements.

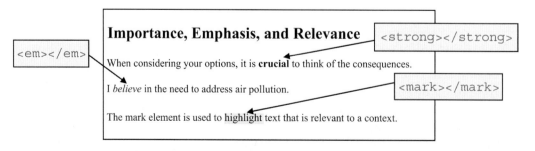

FIGURE 3.15   The result of Figure 3.14 in a browser.

```
HTML
<h2>Boldface and Italic type</h2>
<p>Each <b>keyframe</b> of in animation is important.</p>
<p>The Latin name for clove-tree is <i>Caryophyllus
   aromaticus</i>.</p>
```

FIGURE 3.16 Example usage of the bold and italic elements.

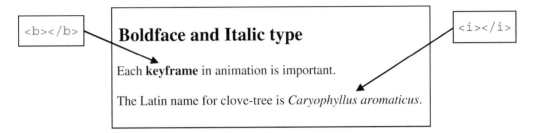

FIGURE 3.17 The result of Figure 3.16.

text (e.g., review) and the `<i>` element can be used for differentiating text such as foreign words, technical terms, and names of edifices (such as ships and buildings) from the rest. Figure 3.16 shows example usage, and Figure 3.17 depicts the rendered result.

Just like the `<b>` or `<i>` elements should not be used to communicate importance, emphasis, or relevance, **underlining should not be used**, as this can be problematic in a number of ways. For example, underlined words can be confusing and frustrating to users, because they can be mistaken for links. The `<u>` element, which was used for underlining in earlier HTML, is not supported by HTML5. However, CSS provides means of underlining text, but this is only for the purpose of decoration. This is appropriately discussed in Chapter 14.

CHALLENGE 3.5

For which of the following would you use `<strong>`, `<em>`, `<b>`, or `<i>` in a body of text?

- The new name for a process.
- The name of a body organ.
- A word that forcefully instructs.
- The name of a ship.
- The English name for a rare plant.
- The word "Warning!"
- A phrase to which you want people to pay attention.

3.8 Quotations and Citations

Quotations and citations are typically displayed in a way that differentiates them from the rest of the text. HTML provides elements that automatically do this. The two commonly used elements for quotations are <blockquote> and <q>, and the one used for citations is <cite>. Table 3.1 gives the functions of these elements, and Figures 3.18 and 3.19 illustrate how they are used and show the effects.

TABLE 3.1

Elements for Quotations and Citations

Element	Function
<blockquote>... </blockquote>	Used for block quotes (i.e., those that take up many lines), and its content is usually indented by the browser; however, the element should not be used for indenting. The URL for the source of the quote can be included by using the cite attribute.
<q>...</q>	Used for inline shorter quotes. Its content is usually enclosed in quotation marks.
<cite>...</cite>	Used to represent the reference to a creative work and must include the title of a work (e.g., book, paper, film, and song) or the name of the creator. Its content is usually rendered in italic type.

```
HTML
<h2>Quotations and Citations</h2>
<blockquote cite="www.goodreads.com/work/quotes/3275794-to
    -kill-a-mockingbird">
    <p>They're certainly entitled to think that, and they're
        entitled to full respect for their opinions... but before
        I can live with other folks I've got to live with myself.
        The one thing that doesn't abide by majority rule
        is a person's conscience.</p>
</blockquote>
<p>As Oscar Wilde said,<q>Be yourself; everyone else is
    already taken.</q></p>
<p>In the words of <cite>Oscar Wilde</cite><q>Be yourself;
    everyone else is already taken.</q></p>
<p><cite>Fly Fishing</cite>, by J.R. Hartley</p>
```

FIGURE 3.18   The block quotation and quote elements in use.

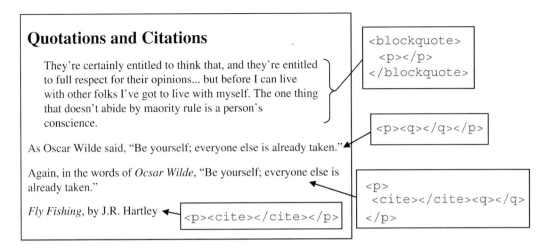

FIGURE 3.19 The result of Figure 3.18.

CHALLENGE 3.6

Why should you not use the `<cite>` element to make text italic type?

3.9 Definitions and Abbreviations

The elements used for creating definitions and abbreviations are `<dfn>` and `<abbr>`, respectively. The `<dfn>` element is used to identify the term to be defined, while the definition of the term is placed outside the element. The content of the element (i.e., the term) is usually rendered in italic type by browsers. The `<abbr>` element is used to identify an abbreviation, while the description of the abbreviation is provided with the `title` attribute. This description is usually displayed as a pop-up by browsers when the cursor is on the abbreviation. In some browsers, such as Firefox, the abbreviation may also be underlined with a dashed or dotted line. The element should be used instead of the obsolete `<acronym>` element. Figure 3.20 shows how these elements are used, and Figure 3.21 shows the result.

```
HTML
<h2>Definitions and Abbreviations</h2>
<p><dfn>The World Wide Web</dfn>, commonly known as the Web,
    is an information system of interlinked hypertext/hypermedia
    documents that runs on the Internet.</p>
<p>The 44th president of the <abbr title="United States of
    America">USA</abbr> is Barack Obama.</p>
```

FIGURE 3.20 Example usage of the definition and abbreviation elements.

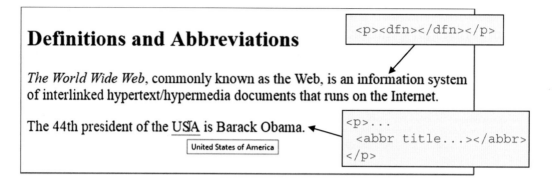

FIGURE 3.21   The rendered result of Figure 3.20.

CHALLENGE 3.7

Even though the content of the `<dfn>` element is rendered in italic, why is it not right to use it to simply make text italic or to use other elements, such as the `<em>` element, that make text italic in its place?

3.10 Small Text

Small (or fine) prints and side comments on a page, such as disclaimers, copyrights, licensing information, and legal restrictions, should not be achieved by reducing the size of font, using CSS, as this gives them no semantic meaning, which means that they will not be recognized as such by user agents. In order to give them semantic meaning and therefore make the meaning accessible to more users, the `<small>` element, which makes text small, should be used. It is important to note that the element should not be used for main texts, such as multiple paragraphs and a whole page, as these are not side comments to a page; rather, it should be used for short runs of text. Figure 3.22 shows how it is used, and Figure 3.23 depicts the rendered result. Small text may also be marked up as important by using the `<strong>` element.

```
HTML
<h3>Small text</h3>
<p>Call us on 0001 012343330 <small>(£1.99 for
    1 minute)</small></p>
<p>Single license: £299 <small>(VAT not included)</small>
<p>Group license: £539 <small>(VAT not included)</small>
<p>Thank you for downloading our software. We hope you enjoy
    experimenting with it. <small>(Disclaimer: Please note that
    we are not liable for any loss of data due to the use of
    the software)</small></p>
<p><small>Copyright © 2007-2015 Wild Tango Ltd.</small></p>
```

FIGURE 3.22   Example usage of the small text element.

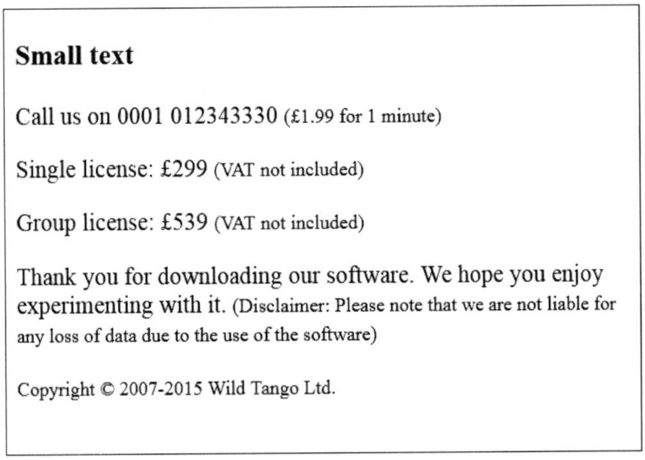

Small text

Call us on 0001 012343330 (£1.99 for 1 minute)

Single license: £299 (VAT not included)

Group license: £539 (VAT not included)

Thank you for downloading our software. We hope you enjoy experimenting with it. (Disclaimer: Please note that we are not liable for any loss of data due to the use of the software)

Copyright © 2007-2015 Wild Tango Ltd.

FIGURE 3.23   The result of Figure 3.22.

CHALLENGE 3.8

Why should you not reduce font size to achieve small text instead of using the `<small>` element?

3.11 Text Edit

Sometimes, it is useful to show both old and new content together in order to communicate some types of messages more effectively. This is done, for example, when you want to show people what the previous information was, whether for comparison (as in when showing price cuts in sales) or cross-checking (as in when people might be looking for the old information). The elements used to do this are `<ins>`, `<del>`, and `<s>`. Table 3.2 shows the functions of the elements. Figure 3.24 shows their usage, and Figure 3.25 depicts the result.

TABLE 3.2

Insert, Delete, and Strikethrough Elements

Element	Function
`<ins>...</ins>`	Inserts a span of text and underlines it. Again, the `<u>` element should not be used for this, as it is obsolete.
`<del>...</del>`	Deletes a span of text, which is usually indicated with strikethrough text.
`<s>...</s>`	Renders text with a line through it (i.e., strikethrough text).

```
HTML
<h2>Text modification</h2>
<p>The speaker for the event will be <del>James
    Bloggs</del> <ins> Henry Bloggs</ins></p>
<p>The speaker for the event will be <s>James Bloggs</s>
    Henry Bloggs</p>
```

FIGURE 3.24   Example usage of the insert, delete, and strikethrough elements.

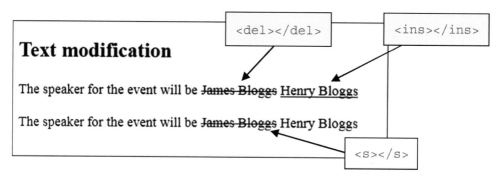

FIGURE 3.25   The result of Figure 3.24.

It is useful to note that even though both the `<del>` and `<s>` elements draw a line through their text content, user agents interpret each according to its meaning. A screen reader, for example, will say which it is, so that a blind user can understand.

CHALLENGE 3.9

Write the HTML code to produce the following:

SAVE 50%
Was £18
Now £9

3.12 Displaying Computer Code and Output

Text relating to computer input and output codes are displayed using a set of elements designed for the purpose, which usually renders the text in the browser's default **monospaced font**. This is a font in which letters and characters occupy the same amount of space. It is different from variable-width fonts, such as the one used in this text, in which the widths of letters vary. The elements include `<code>`, `<samp>`, and `<kbd>`, which are listed in Table 3.3. Figure 3.26 shows how they are used, and Figure 3.27 depicts the result.

TABLE 3.3

Elements Used for Computer Input and Output

Element	Function
`<code>...</code>`	Used to display a fragment of computer code in monospace font.
`<samp>...</samp>`	Used to present sample output from a computer program in monospace font.
`<kbd>...</kbd>`	Used to present required user input in monospace font.

```
HTML
<h2>Display of computer code and output</h2>
<p>This is normal text.<code>This is computer code.</code> This
   is normal text.</p>
<p>This is normal text.<samp>This is sample text.</samp> This
   is normal text.</p>
<p>Type the following command: <kbd>insert</kbd><br>Then press
   Enter.</p>
```

FIGURE 3.26 The code, sample, and keyboard input elements in use.

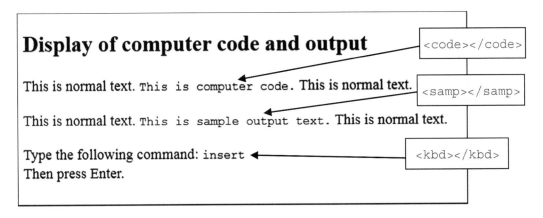

FIGURE 3.27 The result of Figure 3.26.

CHALLENGE 3.10

Which of the following elements would you use to present the sequence required to perform a word-processing task: `<code>`, `<kbd>`, or `<samp>`?

3.13 Displaying Preformatted Text

Sometimes, it is useful to display text the way you have formatted it. The `<pre>` element allows you to do this. It supports global attributes, and the content can be styled using CSS. It is a block-level element, and its content is rendered by default in **monospace font**, with leading space preserved and a margin of about 1 em added at the top and bottom edges. Figure 3.28 shows how the element is used, and Figure 3.29 depicts the result.

```
HTML
<body>
  <h1>Preformatted text</h1>
  <p>Lorem ipsum dolor sit amet, consectetur adipiscing elit.
    Aenean rhoncus ipsum...
    <pre>
        In neque quam, pretium vitae neque vitae,
          tincidunt dignissim augue. Proin dui leo,
          tempus non nisl nec, maximus pulvinar lorem.
        Mauris convallis ipsum ac ullamcorper venenatis.
    </pre>
    Praesent feugiat varius urna, id convallis turpis
    efficitur vel. Integer et ipsum...</p>
</body>
```

FIGURE 3.28   Example usage of the `<pre>` element.

Preformatted text

Lorem ipsum dolor sit amet, consectetur adipiscing elit. Aenean rhoncus ipsum sem, nec euismod libero porttitor eu. Nulla ut urna a ligula tincidunt condimentum quis sit amet diam. Morbi sed magna odio. Nam non ultricies eros. Phasellus sagittis, ipsum sed laoreet fermentum, lacus velit tincidunt lacus, ut dignissim ipsum tellus nec mi.

```
    In neque quam, pretium vitae neque vitae,
      tincidunt dignissim augue. Proin dui leo,
      tempus non nisl nec, maximus pulvinar lorem.
    Mauris convallis ipsum ac ullamcorper venenatis.
```

Praesent feugiat varius urna, id convallis turpis efficitur vel. Integer et ipsum metus. Pellentesque id lectus rutrum ante bibendum facilisis ut a neque.Cras vehicula lobortis justo. Ut congue dapibus odio, in cursus nisl consectetur quis. Aenean volutpat volutpat vehicula. Phasellus tempor purus sed commodo posuere.

FIGURE 3.29   The result of Figure 3.28.

Notice in the example that the content of the `<pre>` element is as it is in the HTML source. Also, notice that the element is inside the `<p>` element. However, it does not have to be; the text above and below it can be in separate `<p>` elements. Moreover, note that even though the `<code>`, `<kbd>`, and `<samp>` elements are, by default, rendered in monospace font, they should not be used in place of the `<pre>` element, as the element is recognized by user agents to have a specific meaning and is treated appropriately.

CHALLENGE 3.11

Use the `<pre>` element in the same body of text as the `<code>`, `<kbd>`, and `<samp>` elements to compare the outputs.

3.14 Authors' Details and Publication Dates

The elements used for providing authors' details and the publication time for a page are `<address>` and `<time>`. The `<address>` element is used to provide contact information and nothing else, and its content is usually rendered in italics. The `<time>` element is used to present time in a 24-hour format, date, and time. In reality, anything can be put in the element (i.e., between the tags), and this will be rendered verbatim. However, to include machine-readable information, the `datetime` attribute must be used. This information is essentially designed for use by user agents in, for example, scheduling users' calendar, rather than to provide information directly to users, so it is not visibly rendered by browsers. Figure 3.30 shows how the elements and attributes are used, and Figure 3.31 depicts the rendered result.

Notice that the value of the `datetime` attribute is not displayed, since it is only for use by the user agent. The way it is formatted is to use the complete or precise time format. However, the use of imprecise dates is also permitted. For example, "2015" is read as Year 2015, "2015-12" is read as December 2015, "12-25" is read as 25 December of any year, and "2015-W15" is read as Week 15 of 2015.

```
HTML
<h3>Author's details, Dates, and Times</h3>
<address>
   Our address is:<br>
   Monar Publishing House<br>
   1004 London Avenue<br>
   London<br>
   W33 9NN<br>
   United Kingdom
</address>
<p>The lecture is on: <time datetime="2015-05-15 14:00">
   5th May 2015 at 2pm</time>.</p>
```

FIGURE 3.30 The example usage of the address and time elements.

Author's details, Dates, and Times

Our address is:
Monar Publishing House
1004 London Avenue
London
W33 9NN
United Kingdom

The lecture is on: 5th May 2015 at 2pm.

FIGURE 3.31   The result of Figure 3.29.

CHALLENGE 3.12

Why is the `<br>` element used in the `<address>` element in the example to place the address lines on separate lines, instead of the `<p>` or `<div>` element, since these elements too begin on a new line?

3.15 Providing Hidden Additional Information

Sometimes, it is desirable to provide additional information but have it hidden, so that it is displayed only when users want it. HTML provides the `<details>` element, with which this can be done. The `<summary>` element can be used with this element to provide a visible heading for it, which, when users click, reveals the hidden content. Figure 3.32 shows how the elements are used, and Figures 3.33 and 3.34 depict the effect in the Chrome browser.

```
HTML
<body>
  <h2>Details and summary</h2>
  <details>
    <summary>Click for more info</summary>
    <p>This information is only revealed because it has been
       requested. This...</p>
  </details>
</body>
```

FIGURE 3.32   Example usage of the `<details>` and `<summary>` elements.

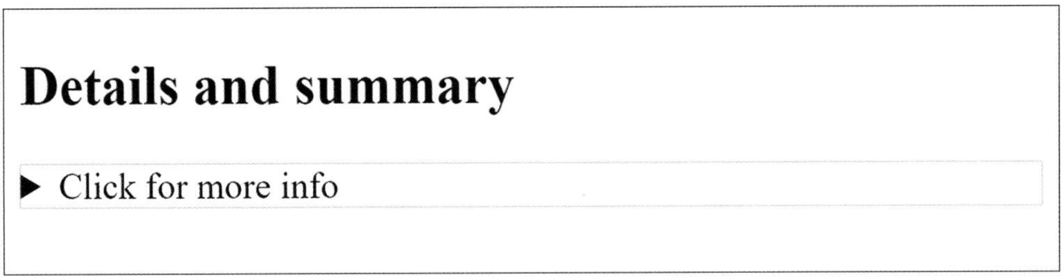

Details and summary

▶ Click for more info

FIGURE 3.33 The result of Figure 3.32 before clicking.

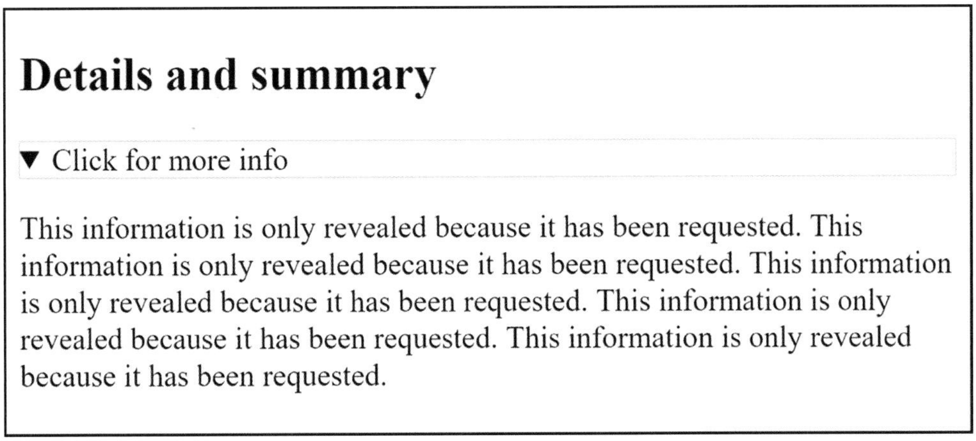

Details and summary

▼ Click for more info

This information is only revealed because it has been requested. This information is only revealed because it has been requested. This information is only revealed because it has been requested. This information is only revealed because it has been requested. This information is only revealed because it has been requested.

FIGURE 3.34 The result of Figure 3.32 after clicking.

In the example, the `<details>` element contains the hidden text and the `<summary>` element provides the heading for the element. If the `<summary>` element is not used, the name of the element is used for the heading.

CHALLENGE 3.13

Implement the example, but without the `<summary>` element, to see what happens. Also, can you think of an example of when you might use the technique of hiding text until it is requested in a document, and say what the pros and cons of the technique are?

3.16 Displaying a Dialog Box

HTML provides the `<dialog>` element for displaying content in a dialog box (or **modal window**) that can also be made interactive, typically using JavaScript. The element takes the `open` attribute, which says to display the box and make it active. When the attribute is not specified, the box is not displayed. A form can also be integrated in

```
HTML
<body>
  <dialog open>
    <p>Hello to you from thebox!</p>
    <button>Close</button>
  </dialog>
</body>
```

FIGURE 3.35   Example usage of the `<dialog>` element.

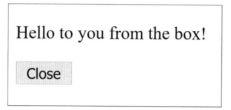

FIGURE 3.36   The result of Figure 3.35.

the element, so that the form is displayed inside it. How to create forms is explained in Chapter 5. Figure 3.35 shows how the element is used, and Figure 3.36 depicts the result. The `<button>` element is used to display a button for the user to use to close the dialog box. However, scripting is needed to make it perform this function. The `<button>` element is also discussed further in Chapter 5.

CHALLENGE 3.14

In the example, what difference would it make if the message is not placed in a `<p>` element and when it is placed in a `<div>` element?

3.17 Menu Bar and Drop-Down Menus

Menu bars and drop-down menus are common features in Web design. Traditionally, implementing them requires the use of CSS and/or scripting. However, HTML now provides elements that make this more straightforward. The downside is that, as of time of writing, they are yet to be supported by any of the major browsers. These elements are `<menu>` and `<menuitem>` and are typically used in combination with other elements, such as the `<button>` element. The `<menu>` element is used to specify the menu bar, and the `<menuitem>` element is used to specify the menu items on the drop-down menu. The `<button>` element, which again is introduced more fully in Chapter 5, is used for interactivity. Figure 3.37 uses part of the example given in the W3C draft specification to explain how these elements are intended

```
HTML
<button type="menu" menu="filemenu">Products</button>
<menu id="filemenu" type="popup">
  <menuitem label="New...">
  <menuitem label="Open...">
  <menuitem label="Save">
</menu>
```

FIGURE 3.37 Example usage of the `<menu>` and `<menuitem>` elements.

to work together. It should display a menu bar that contains a single button (i.e., a menu) that has a "File" label, which when clicked displays a drop-down menu that lists three menu items ("New...," "Open...," and "Save..."). In order to make something happen when a menu item is clicked, other attributes are used on each `<menuitem>` element to specify an action. No doubt, when the elements are supported and it is clear how they work, there will be ample examples on the Web.

NOTE: Other ways of creating drop-down menus

The drop-down menu described in Figure 3.37 can be achieved through combining list elements or the `<button>` element and the CSS properties that are used for controlling the display and positioning of elements. List elements are introduced in Chapter 4, the `<button>` element in Chapter 5, properties for displaying elements in Chapter 10, and those for positioning in Chapter 12.

3.18 Displaying Special Characters

Sometimes, it is necessary to include HTML characters, such as <, > and &, in a page. This may be, for example, because you are building an HTML tutorial Web page. In order to ensure that the browser does not interpret the characters as HTML code, **character entity references** or **numeric character references** (also known as **escape characters** or **escape codes**) are used. These references also enable characters that are not available on the computer keyboard, such as copyright symbol, to be displayed in a Web page. **Character entity references** are case-sensitive and take the format &name;. Therefore, a left-angled bracket, for example, is written as < and a right-angled bracket is written as >. This means to output <html>, for example, <html> is written.

Numeric character references are specified in decimal or hexadecimal numbers; however, decimal numeral system is the most commonly supported by browsers. The decimal numeral system is a system of counting in 10s, while the hexadecimal numeral system is a system of counting in 16s, in which after counting from

0 to 9, the rest of the count is done with letters (i.e., A to F). Therefore, a count from 0 to 16 is **0–9 A–F**, that is, **0 1 2 3 4 5 6 7 8 9 A B C D E F**. In decimal numeral system, numeric character references take the format &#number;, and in hexadecimal numeral system, they take the format &#xnumber;. For example, the copyright symbol, ©, is "©" in **decimal** and "©" in **hexadecimal** numeral system (which is also the **Unicode**). Because not all typefaces support all character references, it is important that one that supports the required characters is used. Table 3.4 lists a range of characters. For more references, you can do a quick search for "Character entity references" on the Web, and the Unicode codes for various characters can be found at **unicode.org/charts**. Figure 3.38 shows how

TABLE 3.4

A Range of Examples of Special Characters and Their Entity and Decimal References

Character Name	Special Character	Entity	Decimal	Hex/Unicode
Non-breaking space	(This is a space)			&#x00A0
Less than	<	&lt;	&#60;	&#x003C
Greater than	>	&gt;	&#62;	&#x003E
Ampersand	&	&amp;	&#38;	&#x0026
Quotation mark	"	&quot;	&#34;	&#x0022
Apostrophe	'	&apos;	&#39;	&#x0027
Yen sign	¥	&yen;	&#165;	&#x00A5
Euro sign	€	&euro;	&#8364;	&#x20AC
Cent	¢	&cent;	&#162;	&#x00A2
Copyright sign	©	&copy;	&#169;	&#x00A9
Registered sign	®	&reg;	&#174;	&#x00AE
Trademark sign	™	&trade;	&#8482;	&#x2122
Black spade suit	♠	&spades;	&#9824;	&#x2660
Fraction one half	½	&frac12;	&#189;	&#x00BD
Fraction one quarter	¼	&frac14;	&#188;	&#x00BC
Fraction three quarters	¾	&frac34;	&#190;	&#x00BE
Sum	Σ	&sum;	&#8721;	&#x2211

```
HTML
<h3>Special characters</h3>
<div>
   Copyright symbol: &copy; &#169; &#xA9;<br>
   Yen sign: &yen; &#165;<br>
   Pound sign: &pound; &POUND;<br>
   Registered sign: &reg; &#174;<br>
   HTML start tag: &lt;html&gt;<br>
   HTML close tag: &lt;/html&gt;<br>
</div>
```

FIGURE 3.38 Example usage of special characters.

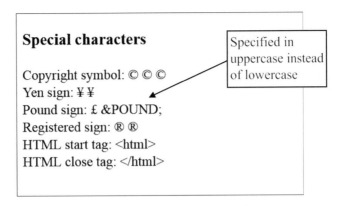

FIGURE 3.39   The result of Figure 3.38.

the references are used, and Figure 3.39 depicts the rendered output. Notice how in the output, &POUND is not converted to the pound sign. This is because it is in all uppercase, when it should actually be in all lowercase.

CHALLENGE 3.15

Write an HTML code to display the following content as it is:

Item Price: €59.99
<div id="character">
Gigabyte > Kilobyte < Megabyte

3.18.1 Non-Breaking Spaces

As mentioned in Chapter 2, the Web browser collapses multiple consecutive spaces to one by default when it renders an HTML document. This means that irrespective of how many consecutives spaces you put between words, this will be rendered as one space. In order to have more than one space rendered, the **non-breaking space entity** ( ) has to be used for each space required. Figure 3.40 shows how this is done, and Figure 3.41 depicts the result.

```
HTML
<h3>Non-breaking spaces</h3>
<p> This line has no non-break spaces at the beginning.</p>
<p>     This line has 5 non-break
   spaces at the beginning</p>
```

FIGURE 3.40   Example usage of the non-breaking space entity.

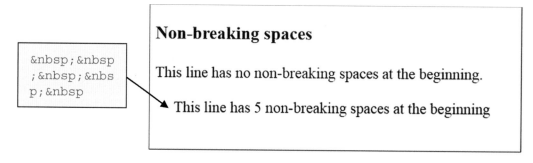

FIGURE 3.41   The result of Figure 3.40.

CHALLENGE 3.16

Write an HTML code to display the content within the quotes:

"**Fill in the blanks**:
The browser only displays   space.
Browsers and screen readers are types of   agents."

3.19 Language Information and Text Directionality

Specifying the language in which a document is written and text direction (e.g., left to right and right to left) are essential in ensuring that the browser renders the document correctly and as intended. This is one aspect of the internationalization of documents, in that it makes documents accessible to as many international users as possible. The attributes primarily used accomplish these tasks are the `lang` and `dir` attributes.

3.19.1 `lang`

The `lang` attribute specifies the base language of the attribute values and content of an element. It is intended to make browsers render a Web page meaningfully, based on the accepted usage for a specified language. It is **inherited**, and the value it takes is a **language code** that represents a natural language. A language code comprises a **primary code** and a possible **sub-code**. The primary code is a two-letter code that represents a language abbreviation, and the sub-code represents a country code. In the language code "`en-US`," for example, "`en`" is the primary code and represents English, and "`US`" is the sub-code and represents USA. The entire language code means US version of English. Most languages require only the primary code. Common primary codes include `fr` (French), `it` (Italian), `de` (Germany), `nl` (Dutch), `es` (Spanish), `el` (Greek), `pt` (Portuguese), `ja` (Japanese), `zh` (Chinese), `ru` (Russian), and `he` (Hebrew). Relevant language codes can be found in **IANA Language Subtag Registry** at iana.org. Figure 3.42 shows examples of how the attribute is used.

```
HTML
<html lang="en">
 <head>
   <title>A multilingual page</title>
 </head>
 <body>
   This part is interpreted as English...
   <p lang="fr">This paragraph is interpreted as French...</p>
   <p>This part is also interpreted as English, because no
      language is specified to override English</p>
   <p>This part is also interpreted as English<em lang="de">but
      this part is interpreted as German</em>and this part is
      interpreted as English again...</p>
 </body>
</html>
```

FIGURE 3.42 Example usage of the `lang` attribute.

Notice in the example that the `lang` attribute is used on the `<html>` element and then on the child elements, as necessary. You should always use the attribute on the `<html>` element, not on the `<body>` element, to ensure that the text inside the `<head>` element is covered.

3.19.1.1 Benefits of Using the `lang` Attribute

Providing language information in your document has several benefits. It allows you to provide language-dependent styling and behavior. Situations in which providing language information in your content is helpful include:

- Helping search engines identify words, based on users' language preferences.

- Helping speech synthesizers, such as screen readers, pronounce words properly.

- Assisting the browser in making decisions on language-dependent matters, such as where to place hyphens; where to place line breaks; how to justify; when to convert the case of letters; and which font variants, quotation marks, ligatures, and spacing to use.

- Helping in the checking of spelling and grammar, for example, of the user's input.

- Helping you to set different styles for different languages in a multilingual document. You can see example of this in Section 14.9.4 of Chapter 14.

CHALLENGE 3.17

Using the `lang` attribute on the `<head>` and `<body>` elements instead of using it on the `<html>` element will not work; True or False? Give reasons for your answer.

CHALLENGE 3.18

If you have a phrase in a paragraph that is in a different language from the one used in the rest of the paragraph, how do you isolate it, so that you can specify its language code and also give it a different color?

3.19.2 `dir`

The order in which browsers display text depends on the **base direction** set for, or inherited by, the element that contains it. The attribute used to set base direction is the `dir` attribute, and the values it takes are `ltr` (left to right), `rtl` (right to left), and `auto` (which leaves it to the user agent to decide). The default is `ltr`. It is **inherited** and can be overridden. It is useful to note that the attribute does not actually affect the order in which the characters of text are displayed, but it affects only the order of the words. It only helps, in combination with other processes, determine how the browser handles the display of text. In some cases, it only visually aligns text left or right.

The way the determination of text direction works in browsers is that each character in **Unicode** (introduced in Chapter 2) has a directionality property associated with it. Some characters are designated as `ltr` (left to right) and others as `rtl` (right to left). In addition, Unicode provides the **Unicode bidirectional** (bidi) algorithm, which is used to display these characters, using their directionality properties. Browsers, by default, determine the direction in which to display a sequence of characters (e.g., a word), using the bidi algorithm, and do this automatically, independently of the current base direction. For example, for a sequence of Latin characters, it displays one after the other from left to right, and for a sequence of Arabic or Hebrew characters, it displays one after the other from right to left. Therefore, the word "forward" in English, for example, is displayed from left to right, while the same word in Arabic is displayed from right to left.

This means that the base direction set with the `dir` attribute is used only to determine the direction in which the words are displayed. Basically, it makes the word that is displayed first in left-to-right direction display last in right-to-left direction, and vice versa. Incidentally, the bidi algorithm can be turned off, using the `<bdo>` element (or **bidirectional override element**), which overrides the current directionality properties of characters. Sometimes, it is necessary to do this when the algorithm does not produce the desired result. This usually happens when different languages are mixed in the same text. The use of the `dir` attribute is mandatory for the `<bdo>` element. Another element that can be used to resolve problems from mixing languages is the `<bdi>` element (or **bidirectional isolation element**), which can be used to isolate text that needs to be formatted differently from the surrounding text. However, this element is not supported by all major browsers. An alternative way of resolving the same issue is to use an inline element (such as the `<span>` element) to isolate the relevant text and then use the `dir` attribute. Figures 3.43 and 3.44 show some examples of how these attributes and elements are used and the effects.

```
HTML
<body>
  <h3>Text directionality</h3>
  <p>This text uses the default dir value of ltr.</p>
  <p dir="ltr">This text uses specified dir value of ltr.</p>
  <p dir="rtl">This text uses specified dir value of rtl.</p>
  <p>חיים הוא מסתורין W3C!</p>
  <p dir="rtl">חיים הוא מסתורין W3C!</p>
  <p>"Life is a W3C mystery!" in Hebrew is חיים הוא מסתורין W3C!</p>
  <p>"Life is a W3C mystery!" in Hebrew is
      <bdo dir="rtl">חיים הוא מסתורין<bdi>W3C</bdi> !</bdo></p>
  <p><bdo dir="rtl">The result of wrongly overriding the bidi
  algorithm.</bdo></p>
</body>
```

FIGURE 3.43   Examples of how the dir attribute and <bdo> element are used.

Text directionality

This text uses the default dir value of ltr.

This text uses specified dir value of ltr.

.This text uses specified dir value of rtl

חיים הוא מסתורין W3C!

חיים הוא מסתורין W3C!

"Life is a W3C mystery!" in Hebrew is חיים הוא מסתורין W3C!

"Life is a W3C mystery!" in Hebrew is חיים הוא מסתורין W3C!

.mhtirogla idib eht gnidirrevo ylgnorw fo tluser ehT

FIGURE 3.44   The result of Figure 3.43.

In the example, the content of the first <p> element is displayed using the default ltr base direction. In the second, specifying ltr does not make a difference. In the third, rtl starts the text from the right. In the fourth, the Hebrew text is not displayed from the right, as it should be, because the default ltr base direction is used. Note that the bidi algorithm still ensures that the characters of each word are displayed correctly. In the fifth <p> element, specifying rtl makes the text display correctly from the right. In the sixth, two different languages are displayed using default base direction. This makes the Hebrew text to display improperly from right to left. In the seventh, the <bdo> element overrides the bidi algorithm for the Hebrew text and sets the base direction to rtl. The <bdi> element is also used to isolate W3C to ensure that it is displayed from left to right, since it is English. In the eighth `<p>` element, the `<bdo>` element is used to override the bidi algorithm and set the direction to `rtl`, even though the correct direction for displaying the text is from left to right.

NOTE: Document language

You should always specify the language of a document, using, for example, the `lang` attribute, where the `dir` attribute is used, as this can further enhance the correct display of text.

NOTE: The `dir` attribute and tables

The `dir` attribute can also be used to specify the flow of columns in a table. For example, when `dir="rtl"` is used on the `<html>` element, the content of table cells is aligned to right, the content of each cell flows from right to left, and so do the columns.

CHALLENGE 3.19

What does the `dir` attribute do in relation to the characters in a word, and why is it not necessary to specify it for text that is displayed from left to right?

CHALLENGE 3.20

In terms of their effects on the direction of text, what are the differences between the `dir` attribute and the `<bdo>` element?

3.20 Ruby Text

Ruby text is the term that is commonly used to describe a run of text that appears alongside another run of text that is known as the **ruby base text** to annotate or provide pronunciation guide to that run of text. It is typically placed above or to the right of the base text but can also be placed below or to the left. An example is shown in Figure 3.45, rendered in Microsoft Edge, in which ruby text is used to provide the pronunciation of the Chinese characters. The translation in, for example, English, could also be given instead of, or with, pronunciation.

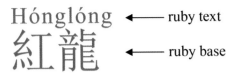

FIGURE 3.45 Illustration of ruby text.

Ruby text is usually smaller and thinner than the base text, and its use is especially common in East Asian text, such as Chinese, Japanese, and Korean (CJK) text. The elements used to implement it are listed in Table 3.5.

The elements in the table can be combined in various ways to produce the same result. For example, each pair of `<rb>` element and the corresponding `<rt>` element can be placed in `<ruby>` elements, or a sequence of `<rb>` elements and a sequence of corresponding `<rt>` elements can be placed in the same `<ruby>` element. Some examples of usage are presented next.

TABLE 3.5

Ruby Elements

Element	Function
`<ruby>...</ruby>`	Specifies that ruby text is being used. Essentially, it creates an association between the ruby base text and the ruby text and is known as the **ruby** element.
`<rb>...</rb>`	Specifies the ruby base text and is known as the **ruby base** element. It can contain one or more ruby base characters.
`<rt>...</rt>`	Specifies the ruby text to be associated with the corresponding ruby base text and is known as the **ruby text** element. It can contain one or more ruby characters.
`<rp>...</rp>`	Used to add ruby parentheses that are used to enclose ruby text, so that it can be ignored by browsers that do not support it. It is known as the **ruby parenthesis** element and can contain only left or right parenthesis.
`<rbc>...</rbc>`	Used to contain or group multiple `<rb>` elements and is known as the **ruby base container** element. It does not work well in major browsers as of time of writing.
`<rtc>...</rtc>`	Used to contain or group multiple `<rt>` elements. All `<rt>` elements in it are displayed on the same line. It is known as the **ruby text container** element and is supported only by Firefox as of time of writing.

3.20.1 `<ruby>`, `<rb>`, `<rt>`, and `<rp>`

Figure 3.46 shows how the `<ruby>`, `<rb>`, and `<rt>` elements are used, and Figure 3.47 depicts the result, using the Chinese text for "Red Dragon is Alive!" The base text is in simplified Chinese, while the ruby text gives the traditional Chinese equivalence.

In Figure 3.46, notice that there are equal numbers of `<rb>` and `<rt>` elements in the `<ruby>` element. Each `<rt>` element is associated with the corresponding `<rb>` element and is displayed above it or to the right of it. However, in Figure 3.47, notice that some ruby characters are missing above some base characters. This is because the ruby characters are the same as the corresponding ruby base characters, and it is redundant to show them twice. In cases where there is no ruby character for a ruby base, an empty `<rt>` element must still be included in order to ensure correct matching between the base and ruby characters. It is also worth noting that a space can be put between the characters by having a space between the `<rb>` elements or having them on separate lines.

```
HTML
<body>
  <h3>Ruby text</h3>
  <ruby>
    <rb>红</rb><rb>龙</rb><rb>是</rb><rb>活</rb><rb>过 </rb>
      <rb>来</rb><rb>了</rb><rb>!</rb>
    <rt>紅</rt><rt>龍</rt><rt>是</rt><rt>活</rt><rt>過</rt>
      <rt>來</rt><rt>了</rt><rt>!</rt>
  </ruby>
</body>
```

FIGURE 3.46   Example usage of `<ruby>`, `<rb>`, and `<rt>`.

Ruby text

紅 龍　　過 來
红 龙 是 活 过 来 了!

FIGURE 3.47   Result of Figure 3.46.

NOTE: Base text without the `<rb>` **element**

You can also specify base text without using the `<rb>` element, as shown below:

```
<ruby>红<rt>紅</rt>龙<rt>龍</rt></ruby>
```

or as shown below, although there will be spaces between the base-ruby character pairs in this case.

```
<ruby>红<rt>紅</rt></ruby>
<ruby>龙<rt>龍</rt></ruby>
```

Figure 3.48 shows the same code as in Figure 3.46, but with the `<rp>` element used to add parentheses to enclose the `<rt>` elements, so that browsers that do not support ruby text can ignore them. Notice how this is done (shown in bold). The left parenthesis is added with `<rp>(</rp>`, and the right parenthesis is added with `<rp>)</rp>`. The code produces the same result as Figure 3.47, in browsers that support ruby text.

```
HTML
<body>
  <h3>Ruby text</h3>
  <ruby>
    <rb>红</rb><rb>龙</rb><rb>是</rb><rb>活</rb><rb>过</rb>
      <rb>来</rb><rb>了</rb><rb>!</rb>
    <rp>(</rp><rt>紅</rt><rt>龍</rt><rt>是</rt><rt>活</rt>
      <rt>過</rt><rt>來</rt><rt>了</rt><rt>!</rt><rp>)</rp>
  </ruby>
</body>
```

FIGURE 3.48   Using the `<rp>` element to enclose `<rt>` elements.

CHALLENGE 3.21

In Figure 3.46, what will be displayed if the ruby markup is not used?

CHALLENGE 3.22

In the examples, what will happen if the `<rb>` elements are placed on different lines?

CHALLENGE 3.23

The `<span>` element can be used in place of the `<rb>` element. Given this, replace the `<rb>` elements in Figure 3.46 to see the effect. Also, can you think of the pros and cons of using either element?

CHALLENGE 3.24

Using Figure 3.46 as guide, create the following with ruby elements.

3.20.2 `<rbc>` and `<rtc>`

Apart from its use for containing `<rb>` elements so that they can be treated as one, the `<rbc>` element seems useful for little else as of time of writing. Even then, its use for containing `<rb>` elements can cause alignment problem with ruby text. On the other hand, being able to group `<rt>` elements with the `<rtc>` element makes it possible to provide more than one set of ruby text for the same base text, with the ruby texts stacked on top of the other. This means that you could, for example, provide more than one type of information for the same base text, such as pronunciation and meaning in another language. Figure 3.49 shows how the element is used, and Figure 3.50 shows the effect. It adds another layer of ruby text to provide pronunciation guide.

```
HTML
<body>
  <h3>Ruby text container</h3>
  <ruby>
    <rb>红</rb><rb>龙</rb><rb>是</rb><rb>活</rb>
        <rb>过</rb><rb>来</rb><rb>了</rb><rb>!</rb>
    <rtc>
      <rt>紅</rt><rt>龍</rt><rt>是</rt><rt>活</rt>
          <rt>過</rt><rt>來</rt><rt>了</rt><rt>!</rt>
    </rtc>
    <rtc>
      <rt>Hóng</rt><rt>lóng</rt><rt>shì</rt><rt>huó</rt>
          <rt>guò</rt><rt>lái</rt><rt>le</rt><rt>!</rt>
    </rtc>
  </ruby>
</body>
```

FIGURE 3.49   Example usage of the `<rtc>` element.

Ruby text container

Hóng lóng shì huó guò lái   le
红　龍　　　　過 來

红龙是活过来了！

FIGURE 3.50   Result of Figure 3.49.

CHALLENGE 3.25

In the example in Figure 3.49, use the `<rbc>` element to see its effect in a browser that supports ruby text, such as Firefox.

NOTE: Positioning and aligning ruby text

It is possible to specify the position and alignment of ruby text relative to the ruby base, using CSS properties. The properties are introduced in Chapter 14.

3.21 Acquiring Text for Use

There are various ways to obtain text for use in Web design, all of which allow text to be created and the characteristics to be manipulated. Here are some of the commonly methods used:

- **Text can be typed in directly** into the relevant development tool. It may also be created first in a text editing or word processing program and then cut and pasted into the relevant development tool.
- **Printed text can be scanned or photographed** and an Optical Character Recognition (OCR) program can then used to convert the printed text image into digital text and saved in the desire format. All major operating systems, such as Windows, Mac, and Linux, provide such a program and the help information for using it. Free programs, as well as professional ones, are also available on the Web.
- **Speech can be converted to text** by using speech-recognition technology, which involves a program that converts words spoken into a microphone into

text. Recorded speech audio files can also be converted in this way. Most operating systems offer this functionality too.

- **Handwriting can be converted to text** by using a digital pen (or stylus) to write on a digitizing tablet, as if writing on a paper, and the writing can be converted to text by using handwriting-recognition software. Again, most operating systems offer this functionality.

3.22 Useful Info

3.22.1 Web Links

HTML specifications: w3.org/TR/html51, w3.org/standards

Web development documents: docs.webplatform.org

Accessibility: w3.org/WAI/tutorials, webaim.org

HTML5 support testing: html5test.com

HTML tutorials (*Here are just a few free tutorial sites on HTML and other Web languages*): w3.org/wiki, html5rocks.com, sitepoint.com, w3schools. com, codecademy.com, quackit.com, developer.mozilla.org/en-US/docs/ Web tutorialspoint.com, whatwg.org, htmlgoodies.com, htmldog.com, htmlcodetutorial.com, echoecho.com, learn.shayhowe.com, html.net, tizag. com, html-5-tutorial.com, docs.webplatform.org, developers.google.com, webdesignermag.co.uk

4

Lists, Tables, and Links

4.1 Introduction

Traditionally, lists and tables are essential tools in print media for imposing structure on content. Their application in Web design is no different. They can also be combined with links, especially lists, to extend their application. This chapter discusses the HTML elements used to create them.

4.2 Learning Outcomes

After studying this chapter, you will know about HTML elements used to do the following:

- Create different types of lists.
- Describe the structure of tables and populate them with data.
- Define links to other parts of the same page, other pages within the same site, and external pages.

4.3 Lists

HTML allows you to create three different types of lists:

- **Unordered lists**, which are lists in which items begin with bullet points.
- **Ordered lists**, which are lists in which items start with numbers or alphabets and are in numeric or alphabetical order. Naturally, this is used only where the order of list items matters to meaning.
- **Definition lists**, which are lists made up of terms and the definitions for each of the terms.

The general principle that underlies how any of these lists is created is to first specify type of list and then the items of the list. Table 4.1 lists the relevant elements.

TABLE 4.1

The List Elements

Element	Function
`<ul>...</ul>`	Defines an unordered list.
`<ol>...</ol>`	Defines an ordered type of list.
`<li>...</li>`	Defines a list item for an unordered or an ordered list.
`<dl>...</dl>`	Defines a definition list.
`<dt>...</dt>`	Defines a definition term for a definition list.
`<dd>...</dd>`	Defines a definition description for a definition term.

Figure 4.1 demonstrates how the elements are used, and Figure 4.2 shows the rendered result. It is useful to know that lists are indented by browsers by default, and all the elements are block-level elements. In addition, the list elements add space at the top and bottom by default and the size of the space is about the default font size used by the browser.

```
HTML
<h2>Unordered List</h2>
<ul>
  <li>First unordered list item</li>
  <li>Second unordered list item</li>
</ul>

<h2>Ordered List</h2>
<ol>
  <li>First ordered list item</li>
  <li>Second ordered list item</li>
</ol>

<h2>Definition List</h2>
<dl>
  <dt>The first term</dt>
    <dd>First term definition description</dd>
  <dt>The second term</dt>
    <dd>Second term definition description</dd>
</dl>
```

FIGURE 4.1   Example usage of all the list elements.

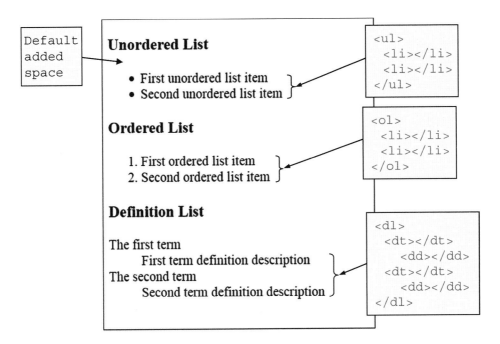

FIGURE 4.2   The result of Figure 4.1.

CHALLENGE 4.1

State the type of list that you would use for the content in the following document in order to communicate it effectively and explain why? Then, write an HTML code to implement it.

> **Creating a Web page**
> The basic steps for creating a Web page using a text editor are:
> 1. Open the text editor.
> 2. Type in the code.
> 3. Save the file with .html extension and open it in a browser.
> The end!

4.3.1 Common List Attributes

The `<ol>` element can take a number of attributes to influence numbering or lettering of the list items. The most commonly used attributes are the `start` attribute, which specifies the start value for numbering or lettering items, and the `type` attribute, which specifies the kind of marker to use for numbering or lettering, which must be `1`, `a`, `A`, `i`, or `I`. Figure 4.3 shows both attributes in use, and Figure 4.4 depicts the result.

```
HTML
<h3>Common list attributes</h3>
<h4>List 1 Part 1</h4>
<ol>
  <li>First ordered list item</li>
  <li>Second ordered list item</li>
  <li>Third ordered list item</li>
</ol>
<h4>List 1 Part 2</h4>
<ol start="4">
  <li>First ordered list item</li>
  <li>Second ordered list item</li>
  <li>Third ordered list item</li>
</ol>
<h4>A different list</h4>
<ol type="A">
  <li>First ordered list item</li>
  <li>Second ordered list item</li>
  <li>Third ordered list item</li>
</ol>
```

> start="4" specifies to start numbering from "4"

> type="A" specifies to order list by using uppercase Latin letters

FIGURE 4.3   Example usage of start and type attributes.

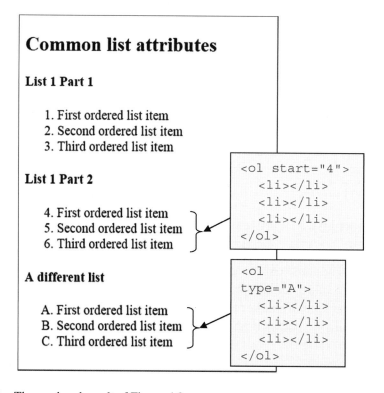

FIGURE 4.4   The rendered result of Figure 4.3.

Note that the `type` attribute should be used only where the type of marker plays an important role, such as in legal documents, where items are referred to from elsewhere in a document by their number or letter; otherwise, the CSS `list-style-type` property, which is used to specify list-item markers, should be used, since specifying list-item markers is considered styling in Web design. List-item markers for the `<ul>` element can also be changed using this property. For example, it can be used to specify custom bullets points made from images. The property is discussed more fully in Chapter 17.

4.3.2 Nested Lists

Sometimes, it is necessary to create nested lists, which are lists that have lists as list items. To achieve this, a list element is simply placed in a list-item element. Figure 4.5 shows how this is done in the unordered and ordered lists, and Figure 4.6 shows the result. Notice that in the nested ordered list, the `type` attribute is used to specify lowercase lettering. As mentioned earlier, if specifying marker type is just to order a list and the items are not to be referenced, then CSS should be used.

```
HTML
<h3>Nested Unordered List</h3>
<ul>
   <li>First item</li>
     <ul>
        <li>First item, first sub-item</li>
        <li>First item, second sub-item</li>
     </ul>
   </li>
   <li>Second item</li>
   <li>Third item</li>
</ul>

<h3>Nested Ordered List</h3>
<ol>
   <li>First item</i>
     <ol type="a">
        <li>First item, first sub-item</li>
        <li>First item, second sub-item</li>
     </ol>
   </li>
   <li>Second item</li>
   <li>Third item</li>
</ol>
```

FIGURE 4.5 Example of nested unordered and order lists.

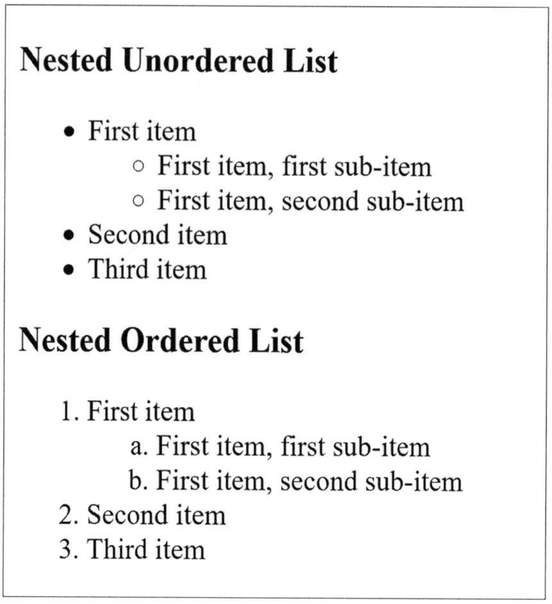

Nested Unordered List

- First item
  - First item, first sub-item
  - First item, second sub-item
- Second item
- Third item

Nested Ordered List

1. First item
   a. First item, first sub-item
   b. First item, second sub-item
2. Second item
3. Third item

FIGURE 4.6   The rendered result of Figure 4.5.

CHALLENGE 4.2

Write the HTML code to insert another list after the first list item in the second-level list of both the unordered and ordered lists in the example to see how the browser handles a three-level list by default.

4.4 Tables

Various types of information benefit from being presented by using a table. Tables are especially crucial for representing complex data, such as stock reports and time tables. The typical properties of a table are illustrated in Figure 4.7, all of which can be represented using HTML, except width, height, cell padding, cell spacing, and various other types of styling, which are defined by using CSS.

Table 4.2 describes the HTML table elements used for defining the structural properties of a table.

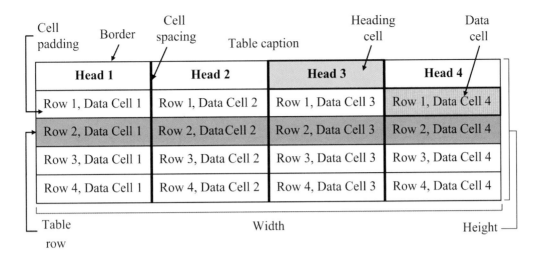

FIGURE 4.7 The typical properties of a table.

TABLE 4.2

Some Commonly Used Table Elements

Element	Function
`<table>...</table>`	Creates a table.
`<caption>...</caption>`	Defines a table caption, which is like the title.
`<th>...</th>`	Defines a cell as a header for a group of column or row cells.
`<tr>...</tr>`	Defines a row in a table, and tr stands for table row.
`<td>...</td>`	Defines a cell in a table row of a table, and td stands for table data.
`<colgroup>...</colgroup>`	Defines a group of columns.
`<col>`	Defines a column and is usually in a `<colgroup>` element. Note that it is an empty element.
`<thead>...</thead>`	Defines a block of rows that define the head of the columns of a table.
`<tbody>...</tbody>`	Defines the set of rows that form the body for a table.
`<tfoot>...</tfoot>`	Defines a set of rows that summarize the columns of a table.

4.4.1 Basic Tables

4.4.1.1 `<table>`, `<caption>`, `<th>`, `<tr>`, *and* `<td>`

The table, caption, table heading, table row, and table data elements are common to almost any table, as they describe the essence of a table. For this reason, they are being discussed together. Figure 4.8 shows how they are used, and Figure 4.9 shows the table that is created.

As you should be able to see in the example, everything about a table goes between the opening and the closing tags of the `<table>` element and the contents of every row are placed inside the `<tr>` element. The contents can be table headings or table data, as well as information about the table, such as caption, included by using the `<caption>` element.

```
HTML
<h2>A basic table</h2>
<table summary="This table provides the inventory of fruits in
     stock">
 <caption>Fruits Inventory</caption>
 <tr>
   <td></td>
   <th>Item</th>
   <th>Bought</th>
   <th>Sold</th>
   <th>Balance</th>
 </tr>
 <tr>
   <td>1.</td><th>Apples</th><td>300</td><td>200</td><td>100</td>
 </tr>
 <tr><td>2.</td><th>Bananas</th><td>250</td><td>150</td>
     <td>100</td></tr>
 <tr><td>3.</td><th>Grapes</th><td>400</td><td>200</td>
     <td>200</td></tr>
</table>
```

FIGURE 4.8   Example usage of table elements.

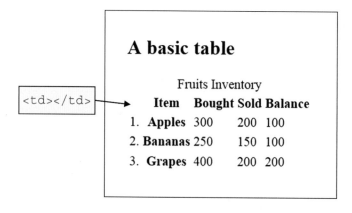

FIGURE 4.9   The rendered result of Figure 4.8, with and without border.

Caption may be made strong or emphasized, using the `<strong>` or `<em>` element, and should not be wider than a table's width to avoid being clipped. The `summary` attribute is usually used to provide additional information about a table. Although browsers do not display the information, providing the information **improves accessibility**, because it is used by user agents that do not render HTML into visual information, such as screen readers, to adequately inform visually impaired users.

Notice that even **when a cell is empty**, an empty `<td>` element is still used to represent it; otherwise, the table will not look properly when put together. Also notice that the contents of the `<th>` elements are displayed in bold. They are also displayed in the middle of the cell. Using the `<th>` element for headings (instead of using the `<td>` element and making the contents bold manually through CSS) is especially good practice, as user agents, such as screen readers, recognize the element and are therefore able to render it in the way that best communicates the contents of a table to the user. The element also enables pages to be indexed more effectively by search engines. In the example, there are both **row headers** (i.e., apples, bananas, and grapes) and **column headers** (i.e., item, bought, sold, and balance).

CHALLENGE 4.3

Write the code for creating the following table. You can ignore the border, since it is supposed to be implemented by using CSS.

Date	Event	Venue
4th September	Arts Exhibition	James Hall
5th September	Film Noir	Dome Theater
6th September	Dance	James Hall

4.4.1.2 Columns' Grouping

As introduced in Table 4.2, the element used to group columns is the `<colgroup>` element. When used, it should be placed after caption but before any other table element. It can either contain `<col>` elements (each of which can represent one or more columns) or take the `span` attribute, but not both. The `<col>` element, too, may take the `span` attribute. The attribute specifies the number of consecutive columns spanned by an element. Figure 4.10 shows how the `<colgroup>` and `<col>` elements are used together, and Figure 4.11 shows how the `<colgroup>` element is used without the `<col>` element. Both produce the same result, shown in Figure 4.12. In both examples, the `span` attribute specifies to group the next two columns and give the group a class name of "first_two", which is then used to make the group's background color gray by using CSS. The next `<colgroup>` or `<col>` element specifies to give the next column the class name of "next_col", which is used to make column's background color yellow. Note that the colors have been used here to only show the effects of the grouping elements. How this is done is shown in Chapter 17 under Section 17.4.

```
HTML
<h3>Columns grouping</h3>
<table>
 <colgroup>
   <col span="2" class="first-two">
   <col class="next_col">
 </colgroup>
 <tr>
   <th>ID_No</th>
   <th>Name</th>
   <th>Age</th>
   <th>Height</th>
 </tr>
 <tr><td>10001</td><td>James Normal</td><td>28</td>
     <td>6ft 1in</td></tr>
 <tr><td>10002</td><td>Amanda Holmes</td><td>24</td>
     <td>5ft 6in</td></tr>
</table>
```

FIGURE 4.10   Example usage of the `<colgroup>` element with the `<col>` element.

```
HTML
<h3>Columns grouping</h3>
<table>
  <colgroup span="2" class="first_two"></colgroup>
  <colgroup class="next_col"></colgroup>
  <tr>
    <th>ID_No</th>
    <th>Name</th>
    <th>Age</th>
    <th>Height</th>
  </tr>
  <tr><td>10001</td><td>James Normal</td><td>28</td>
      <td>6ft 1in</td></tr>
  <tr><td>10002</td><td>Amanda Holmes</td><td>24</td>
      <td>5ft 6in</td></tr>
</table>
```

FIGURE 4.11   Example usage of the `<colgroup>` element without the `<col>` element.

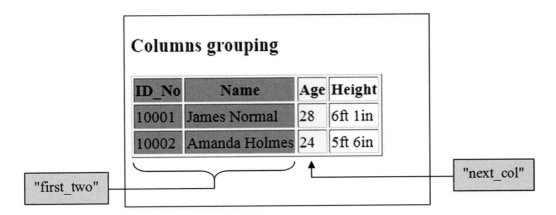

FIGURE 4.12 The result of Figures 4.10 and 4.11.

CHALLENGE 4.4

Create the following table and group the columns that have the same color. Again, you don't need to implement the border.

Name	Height	Weight	BMI	Hours of exercise	Calories burnt
Robert	6ft	15st	28.5	1	600
Laura	5ft 7in	10st 2lb	22.2	0.50	250
Denise	5ft 4in	9st	21.6	1	500

4.4.2 Table Cells' Merging

4.4.2.1 `<rowspan>` *and* `<colspan>`

The merging of table cells is crucial in extending the application of tables beyond just using them to present basic information. In HTML, this is achieved with the `rowspan` and `colspan` attributes in the `<th>` and `<td>` elements. Figure 4.13 shows how it is done, and Figure 4.14 depicts the rendered result.

In the example, notice that the table has a border. This has been done by using CSS, and it is necessary to use it at this point to show the effects of `rowspan` and `colspan`, which otherwise will not have been apparent without a border. In the **first table row element**, the first `rowspan` attribute specifies that the cell should span one column (the default) and two rows; the `colspan` specifies that the cell should span one row (the default) and two columns. Like the first, the second `rowspan` specifies to span one column and two rows. In the **second table row element**, the two `<th>` elements are used to put content in the second row of the table, which has only two columns, bearing in mind that the first cells of the first and fourth columns belong to the first row. The last two `<tr>` elements are used to fill the cells of the remaining rows, as normal.

```
HTML
<h3>Table cells merging<h3>
<table>
  <caption><em>Obesity statistics</em></caption>
  <tr>
    <td rowspan="2"></td>
    <th colspan="2">Average</th>
    <th rowspan="2">Obese <br> %</th>
  </tr>
  <tr>
    <th>Age</th>
    <th>Weight</th>
  </tr>
  <tr><th>Males</th><td>45</td><td>13st</td><td>41%</td></tr>
  <tr><th>Females</th><td>35</td><td>11st</td><td>33%</td></tr>
</table>
```

FIGURE 4.13   Example usage of rowspan and colspan attributes in cells merging.

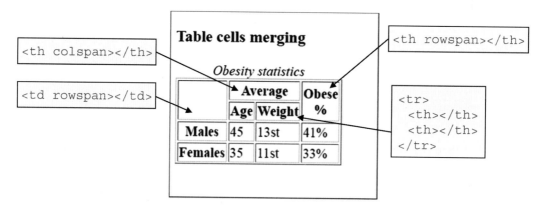

FIGURE 4.14   The result of Figure 4.13.

CHALLENGE 4.5

Write the HTML code for the table below. You can again ignore the border. The centering of the content of the data cells is left as another exercise in Chapter 17, after the property for centering content has been introduced.

Introduction to Web Design				
Academic Session 2015/2016				
	No. of Years	Courses	Weeks	Project
Day	1	Mixed	13	Yes
Evening	2	Mixed		
Enjoy the unit!				

4.4.3 Long Tables

4.4.3.1 `<thead>`, `<tbody>`, *and* `<tfoot>`

Long tables can make it difficult to use a table and also make it inaccessible to users with disability who use assistive technologies, such screen readers. For example, when a table is longer than what can fit into one screen and scrolling is required, the header usually disappears, making it difficult to figure out what goes under which column. The elements intended to solve problems caused by long tables are `<thead>`, `<tbody>`, and `<tfoot>`. However, as of time of writing, the functionality of these elements is yet to be implemented enough in most browsers to fully realize the goals for which they have been designed. Their functions have been described in Table 4.2, and Figure 4.15 shows how they can be used.

The effects of the `<thead>`, `<tbody>`, and `<tfoot>` are not usually visible; therefore, the code in Figure 4.15 will produce just an ordinary table, similar to the one in Figure 4.9. This is because these elements merely enable a table to be divided into header, body, and footer parts. It is recommended when the elements are used and a table is very long that the `<tfoot>` element is placed before the `<tbody>` element to enable the browser to render the footer before all rows of data are received, which can take time. When the elements are used, it is possible for users to scroll through the body of a table independently of the

```
HTML
<h3>Long table</h3>
<table>
 <caption><em>Fruits Inventory</em></caption>
 <thead>
   <tr>
     <td></td>
     <th>Item</th>
     <th>Bought</th>
     <th>Sold</th>
     <th>Balance</th>
   </tr>
 </thead>
 <tbody>
   <tr><td>1.</td><th>Apples</th><td>300</td><td>200</td>
       <td>100</td></tr>
   <tr><td>2.</td><th>Bananas</th><td>250</td><td>150</td>
       <td>100</td></tr>
   <tr><td>3.</td><th>Grapes</th><td>400</td><td>200</td>
       <td>200</td></tr>
   ...
 </tbody>
 <tfoot>
   <tr><td></td><td>Total</td><td>4050</td><td>5550</td>
       <td>4800</td></tr>
 </tfoot>
</table>
```

FIGURE 4.15 Example usage of the `<thead>`, `<tbody>`, and `<tfoot>` elements.

header and footer. With a long table, it may also be possible to have the header and the footer printed on every page of data, instead of just on the first and last pages, respectively.

4.4.4 Tables and Accessibility

Even when tables look well structured to the eyes, assistive technologies can still interpret their contents inaccurately, causing problems for visually impaired users. For example, screen readers might read out their contents in the wrong order. This is especially likely when tables are complex, are simple but have unusual structure, or are created by using unusual practices. Providing information about the relationship between table cells is one of the ways in which the problem is minimized, and the attributes most commonly used to achieve this are `scope`, `id`, and `headers`. The `scope` attribute can be used by itself, while `id` and `headers` must be used together.

4.4.4.1 The `scope` Attribute and Accessibility

The `scope` attribute is used for defining the scope of a header (i.e., the cells that are affected by a header). It defines whether the header defined in the `<th>` element is for a row, column, or a group of rows or columns. Situations in which using it is recommended include when the header of a table is not in the first row or column and where a data cell that is marked up with the `<td>` element is used as a header. The attribute takes any of the four values: `col`, `row`, `rowgroup`, or `colgroup`. Table 4.3 describes their function, and Figure 4.16 shows how they are used.

TABLE 4.3

The Values Taken by the `scope` Attribute

Scope Attribute Value	Function
col	Means that the header applies to all the cells in the same row as the element.
row	Means that the header applies to all the cells in the same column as the element.
rowgroup	Means that the header applies to all remaining cells in the row group to which header belongs, which are either to the left or to the right of the `<th>` element; however, it is to the right by default, since **table directionality** is left to right by default. Different table directionality can be specified by the value of the `dir` attribute in the `<table>` element. It is a global attribute, whose value can be "ltr" (i.e., left to right, and the default), "rtl" (i.e., right to left), or "auto" (i.e., the browser decides, based on content).
colgroup	Means that the header applies to all remaining cells in the column group to which header belongs.

```
HTML
<table summary="This table provides the inventory of fruits
 in stock">
 <caption>Fruits Inventory</caption>
 <tr>
   <td></td>
   <th scope="col">Item</th>
   <th scope="col">Bought</th>
   <th scope="col">Sold</th>
   <th scope="col">Balance</th>
 </tr>
 <tr>
   <td>1.</td><th scope="row">Apples</th><td>300</td>
   <td>200</td><td>100</td>
 </tr>
 <tr>
   <td>2.</td><th scope="row">Bananas</th><td>250</td>
   <td>150</td><td>100</td>
 </tr>
 <tr>
   <td>3.</td><th scope="row">Grapes</th><td>400</td>
   <td>200</td><td>200</td>
 </tr>
</table>
```

FIGURE 4.16 Example usage of the scope attribute to aid accessibility.

Notice that the code in the example is the same as that in Figure 4.8, except for the addition of the scope attribute to the cell of each row that is a header (but not in the first column) and the cells of the first row that are headers. Basically, as a general rule, all <th> elements and <td> elements that act as headers should have a scope attribute. The attribute does not affect the appearance of a table, so the code in the example produces the same result as in Figure 4.9.

4.4.4.2 *The* id *and* headers *Attributes and Accessibility*

As introduced in Chapter 2, the id attribute is a **global attribute** used to give a unique identity to an element. The headers attribute, on the other hand, is used to associate one or more header cells with a table cell. Its value must correspond to the id attribute of the <th> element with which it is associated. When multiple values are specified, the **values are space-separated**, each value again corresponding to the id attribute of the <th> element with which it is associated. The technique is usually suitable for the situation when the use of the scope attribute is not enough to describe the relationships between table headers and data cells, such as when data cells are associated with more than one row and/or column header. Figure 4.17 shows how the attributes are used together, and Figure 4.18 shows the created table. Notice that as with the scope attribute, the id and headers attributes do not affect the display of a table.

Again, note that the border has been added by using CSS, and this has been done just to make the table clearer to see. In the **first table row element**, the <th> elements are

```
HTML
<h2>Accessibility, id and headers</h2>
<table>
 <tr>
  <th rowspan="2" id="c">Coursework</th>
  <th colspan="2" id="t">Tests</th>
  <th colspan="2" id="e">Exams</th>
 </tr>
 <tr>
  <th id="t1" headers="t">1</th>
  <th id="t2" headers="t">2</th>
  <th id="e1" headers="e">1</th>
  <th id="e2" headers="e">2</th>
 </tr>
 <tr>
  <td headers="c">20%</td>
  <td headers="t t1">10%</td>
  <td headers="t t2">10%</td>
  <td headers="e e1">30%</td>
  <td headers="e e2">30%</td>
 </tr>
</table>
```

FIGURE 4.17 Example usage of `id` and `headers` attributes to aid accessibility.

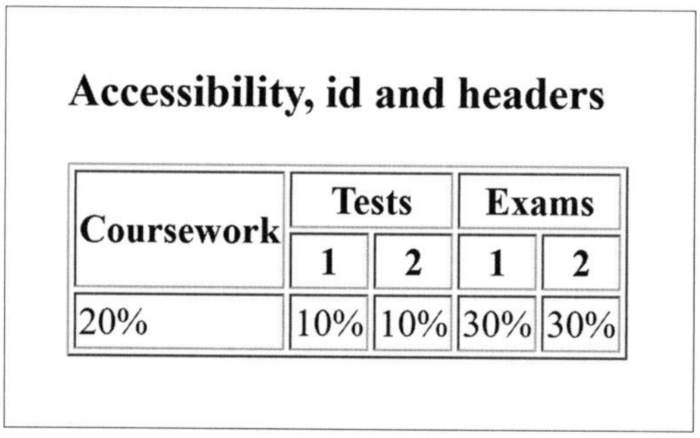

Accessibility, id and headers

Coursework	Tests		Exams	
	1	2	1	2
20%	10%	10%	30%	30%

FIGURE 4.18 The rendered result of Figure 4.17.

given `c`, `t`, and `e` identities, respectively. In the **second table row element**, each `<th>` is given an `id` and is also associated with the corresponding `<th>` element defined in the first `<tr>`, using the `headers` attribute. In the **third table row element**, the `headers` attribute is used to associate each `<td>` element with the appropriate `<th>` element.

CHALLENGE 4.6

Add `id` and `headers`, as appropriate, to the example in Figure 4.13 to make the table more accessible.

> **NOTE: Designing tables**
>
> Tables are ideal for presenting specific values intended for easy and efficient access and comprehension. However, in order for them to perform these functions effectively, they need to be designed properly in a way that is logical and aesthetically pleasing. Guidelines on how to achieve these are presented in Chapter 17, where how to style tables is discussed.

4.5 Links

Links, technically known as **hyperlinks**, are the very essence of the Web, because they are the feature that enables interconnection between pages and browsing, without which the Web would be non-existent. The common types of links are as follows:

- Linking from a page to another website.
- Linking from a page to another page on the same website.
- Linking from a part of a page to another part on the same page.
- Linking from a page to a specific part of a page on another website.
- Linking from a page to an e-mail program to start a new message.

The element used to create all these types of links is the `<a>` element (known as **anchor element**). The element **defines an anchor** but not the hyperlink; the hyperlink reference attribute, `href`, and a value (which must be a URL) are required to do this, as shown in Figure 4.19. The content between the opening and the closing tags is what is turned into a hyperlink.

In the example, the text "Click here for BBC" is made a link, so that when it is clicked, the Web browser fetches the document "index.html" from the local hard disk cache, if a copy has been cached (saved), or requests it from the Web server at the location "http://www.bbc.co.uk" and displays it. By default, a new page replaces the current one in the browser window, unless the browser is instructed to display the new page in a new window, using the `target` attribute, which was introduced in Chapter 2.

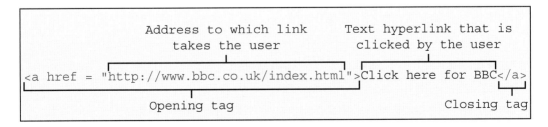

FIGURE 4.19   The structure of the HTML code for a hyperlink.

4.5.1 Linking to Another Website

When linking to a website, the link typically points to the home page (i.e., it is the URL of a website's root directory on a Web server that is typically specified); the URL of a specific document is not usually specified. When a link points to the root directory, the Web server usually serves the document **index.html** by default, which is the home page. Figure 4.20 shows how this is done, and Figure 4.21 depicts the result.

Where a link is inside text, as opposed to when used in a main menu, in order to enhance accessibility, **link text should be meaningful** enough to convey its purpose on its own and out of context. If this is not possible, any additional description providing the context for the link should be placed close to the link (e.g., in the same sentence or paragraph), such that it is easy for users to identify without moving focus from the link. A good example and a bad example are shown in the NOTE box that follows.

```
HTML
<h3>External links</h3>
<p>Popular links:</p>
  <ul>
    <li><a href="http://www.movies.com">Movies</a></li>
    <li><a href="http://www.fishing.com">Fishing</a></li>
    <li><a href="http://www.yogalessons.com">Yoga lessons</a></li>
    <li><a href="http://www.youtube.com">YouTube</a></li>
  </ul>
```

FIGURE 4.20   Example usage of the `<a>` element for external links.

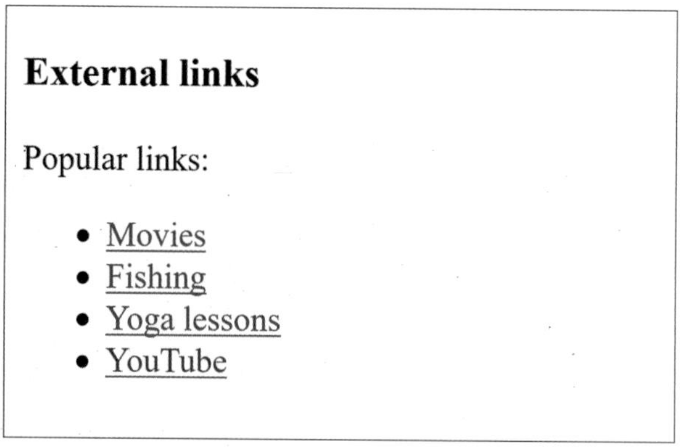

External links

Popular links:

- Movies
- Fishing
- Yoga lessons
- YouTube

FIGURE 4.21   The result of Figure 4.20.

NOTE: Examples of good and bad link texts

Good: "See the Information page to know more about…"
Not ideal: "To know more, click here to go to the Information page"
Poor: "Click here for more."

CHALLENGE 4.7

Create the menu links in Figure 4.21 but without using the list elements to produce the following:

External links

.Popular links:

- Movies
  Fishing
  Yoga lessons
  YouTube

CHALLENGE 4.8

Write the HTML code to display the content between the quotes in the paragraph below, linking the word "Earth" to https://en.wikipedia.org/wiki/Earth.

"The Solar System is made up of the Sun and the objects that orbit it. One of these objects is the planet known as Earth, which is where we live."

4.5.2 Linking to Another Page on the Same Website

Linking a page to another page on the same website is similar to linking to another website, except that you do not need to specify an absolute address. Figure 4.22 shows how it is done. Notice the relative addresses. It means that all the files are in the same directory (folder) as the page displaying the links. See Chapter 2 for explanation of absolute and relative addresses. The main advantage of using relative addressing is that an entire site can be built on a local computer and then uploaded to a Web server for hosting,

```
HTML
<h3>Within-site links</h3>
<ul>
   <li><a href="index.html">Home</a></li>
   <li><a href="features.html">Features</a></li>
   <li><a href="support.html">Support</a></li>
   <li><a href="download.html">Download</a></li>
   <li><a href="about.html">About us</a></li>
   <li><a href="store.html">Store</a></li>
</ul>
```

FIGURE 4.22 Example usage of the `<a>` element for within-site links.

without having to make any adjustments after uploading, as long as the relationships between the locations of the pages are maintained.

4.5.3 Linking to Another Part on the Same Page

Linking to another part of the same page is known as **within-page linking** and uses the same underlying principle as linking to a whole page, except that the points to which to link first have to be identified, after which the anchor element is used to link to them. The points are identified by using the id or name attribute.

4.5.3.1 *Using the* id *Attribute*

Figure 4.23 shows how the id attribute is used to link within page, and Figure 4.24 shows the rendered result. The three sections to navigate to are identified as **"instruction_video," "situation_video,"** and **"scripted_video."** The <a> element is then used to create links to the three sections from the menu at the top of the page, as well as to the start of the page from each section. Notice that the value of each href attribute starts with a # symbol, followed by the value of the id attribute of the element (i.e., section) to which to link. Using the # symbol alone for the value

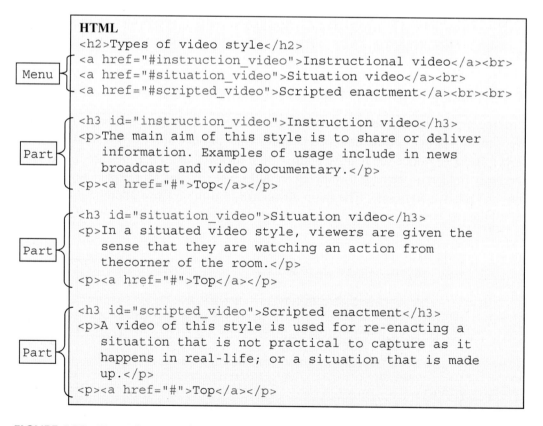

```
HTML
<h2>Types of video style</h2>
<a href="#instruction_video">Instructional video</a><br>
<a href="#situation_video">Situation video</a><br>
<a href="#scripted_video">Scripted enactment</a><br><br>

<h3 id="instruction_video">Instruction video</h3>
<p>The main aim of this style is to share or deliver
    information. Examples of usage include in news
    broadcast and video documentary.</p>
<p><a href="#">Top</a></p>

<h3 id="situation_video">Situation video</h3>
<p>In a situated video style, viewers are given the
    sense that they are watching an action from
    thecorner of the room.</p>
<p><a href="#">Top</a></p>

<h3 id="scripted_video">Scripted enactment</h3>
<p>A video of this style is used for re-enacting a
    situation that is not practical to capture as it
    happens in real-life; or a situation that is made
    up.</p>
<p><a href="#">Top</a></p>
```

Menu { ... }

Part { ... }

Part { ... }

Part { ... }

FIGURE 4.23 Example usage of id attribute for within-page links.

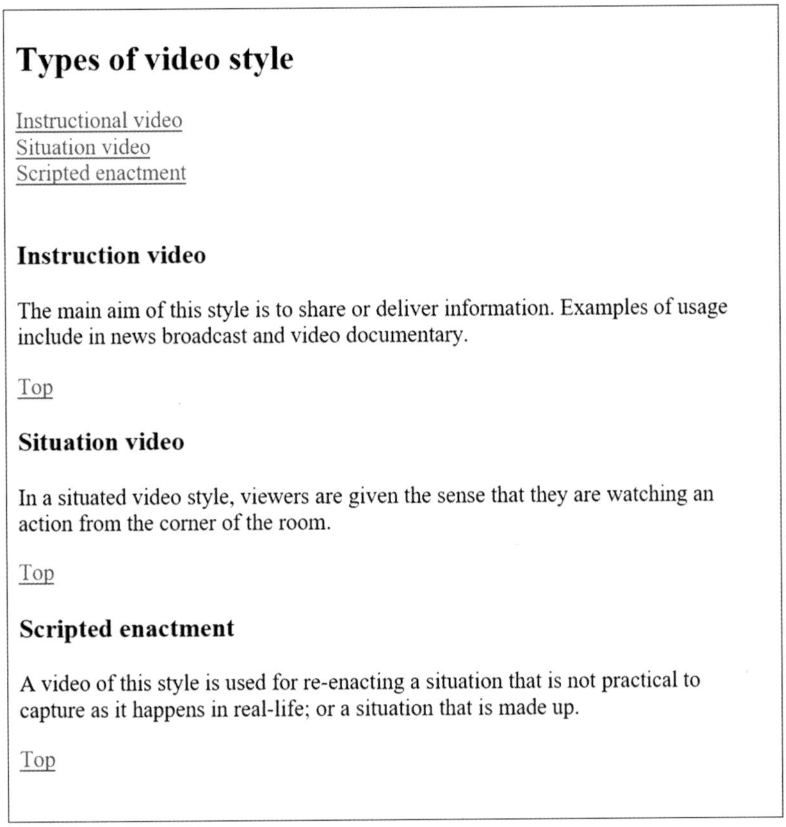

Types of video style

Instructional video
Situation video
Scripted enactment

Instruction video

The main aim of this style is to share or deliver information. Examples of usage include in news broadcast and video documentary.

Top

Situation video

In a situated video style, viewers are given the sense that they are watching an action from the corner of the room.

Top

Scripted enactment

A video of this style is used for re-enacting a situation that is not practical to capture as it happens in real-life; or a situation that is made up.

Top

FIGURE 4.24 The result of Figure 4.23 in the browser.

of the `href` attribute means to link to the start of the current page. An empty string (e.g., `href=""`) or just `href` without any value can also be used.

CHALLENGE 4.9

Implement the code in Figure 4.23, but leave out the # symbol from value of the `href` attributes that specify the destination section to see what happens.

4.5.3.2 *Using the* name *Attribute*

To use the `name` attribute to link within a page, you use the attribute with the `<a>` element to create anchors at the points to link to (i.e., the start of the page and the start of each of the three sections). Then, you use the `<a>` element again with the `href` attribute to create the necessary hyperlinks, again starting the `href` attribute's value with the # symbol, followed by the value of the `name` attribute of the `<a>` element (i.e., section) to which to link. This code is shown in Figure 4.25. Notice that no content is placed between the opening and closing tags of the `<a>` elements used to define the named anchor points to which to link. This is because it is not necessary.

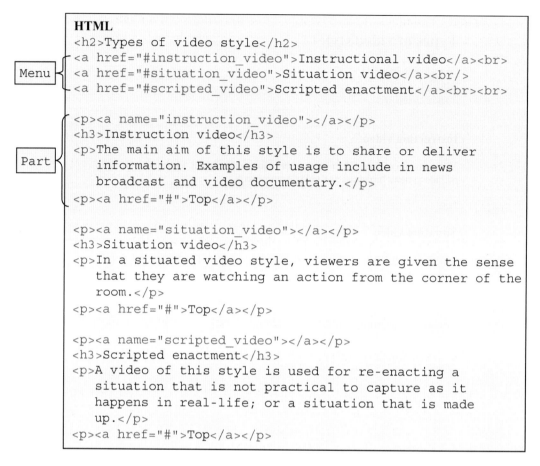

```
HTML
<h2>Types of video style</h2>
<a href="#instruction_video">Instructional video</a><br>
<a href="#situation_video">Situation video</a><br/>
<a href="#scripted_video">Scripted enactment</a><br><br>

<p><a name="instruction_video"></a></p>
<h3>Instruction video</h3>
<p>The main aim of this style is to share or deliver
   information. Examples of usage include in news
   broadcast and video documentary.</p>
<p><a href="#">Top</a></p>

<p><a name="situation_video"></a></p>
<h3>Situation video</h3>
<p>In a situated video style, viewers are given the sense
   that they are watching an action from the corner of the
   room.</p>
<p><a href="#">Top</a></p>

<p><a name="scripted_video"></a></p>
<h3>Scripted enactment</h3>
<p>A video of this style is used for re-enacting a
   situation that is not practical to capture as it
   happens in real-life; or a situation that is made
   up.</p>
<p><a href="#">Top</a></p>
```

Menu { (bracket on left of menu links)

Part { (bracket on left of instruction video part)

FIGURE 4.25   Using the name attribute for the example in Figure 4.23.

CHALLENGE 4.10

What will happen if the name attributes in the example are on the header elements instead of being on the <a> elements, and what is the problem with this, if any?

4.5.3.3 *Within-Page Links in Web Design*

The use of within-page links is generally discouraged for various reasons. One, according to the NN Group, is that it **violates the mental model that users have of the way a hyperlink should behave**, and so, it can confuse them. This model is that a link leads to a new page that is displayed from start, and the Back button takes users to the previous page. However, the use of within-page links can be less confusing if it is made clear to users what to expect when they click them. One way in which this can be done is to have link description say where a link leads, for example, "for more, click to go to the relevant section." Also, there are situations where within-page links are acceptable, such as when the sections of a page are summarized at the top of the page, with links leading directly to the sections. Examples of these types of situations include when presenting alphabetized lists, frequently asked questions (FAQs), and a page that has a table of contents at its start that leads to sections in the page, such as those shown in Figures 4.23–4.25.

NOTE: Accessibility application

The principle of linking from the top of a page to other parts of the page can be useful in making a page more accessible to screen reader users by including a "Jump to Main Content" link at the top of the page, so that it is one of the first things that screen reader users hear or users that use only keyboard encounter when using the tab key. The link enables users to skip long list of navigation menu and go directly to the main content. The link can also be hidden (made invisible), so that it does not interfere with the aesthetics of a design from the viewpoint of sighted users. This is done by using CSS, and how it is done is discussed under "Absolute positioning" in Chapter 12.

4.5.4 Linking to a Specific Part on Another Page

Linking to a specific part of a page on a website can be achieved with the same technique as used for linking to a specific part on the same page, as long as the part or section to be linked to on a page has a unique identification and it is known. All that is required is to add the identifier to the end of the link to the page. The URL can be relative or absolute. If the page in on the same website, then relative URL can be used, but if the page is on another website, it has to be absolute. For example, if the URL for a page is "http://www.example.com/glossary.html" and the section to link to is identified as "instruction_video," using the `id` or `name` attribute, the link to the section would be written in one of the following ways:

```
<a href=http://www.example.com/glossary.html#instruction_
   video>Instruction video</a>
<a href="glossary.html#instruction_video">Instruction
   video</a>
```

NOTE: Link to part of another page in design

Users should not be dumped in the middle of a new page without an indication of where they are. The part to which they are directed should have a clear heading that is visible, without the need to scroll up or down to see it. This can be done, for example, by using a named anchor above the header element that contains the heading, as shown in Figure 4.25.

4.5.5 Linking to an E-Mail Program

When a hyperlink points to an e-mail program, the user's e-mail program is opened with a new message addressed to the specified e-mail address. To achieve this, the `<a>`

```
HTML
<h3>Email link</h3>
<p>Email me at:<a href="mailto:joe@example.com">
    joe@example.com</a><p>
<a href="mailto:customer@example.com">Email us</a>
```

FIGURE 4.26 Examples of how e-mail links are created.

> ## Email link
>
> Email me at: joe@example.com
>
> Email us

FIGURE 4.27 The result of Figure 4.26 in the browser.

element is also used, except that the value of the `href` attribute starts with `mailto:`, followed by the e-mail address to which you want the message to be sent. Figure 4.26 shows how it is done, and Figure 4.27 depicts the result. When the link is clicked by the user, the default e-mail client (program) on his or her computer is opened.

CHALLENGE 4.11

Which of the above two approaches do you think is more efficient and why?

4.6 Useful Info

4.6.1 Web Links

HTML specifications: w3.org/TR/html51, w3.org/standards

Web development documents: docs.webplatform.org

Accessibility: w3.org/WAI/tutorials, webaim.org

HTML5 support testing: html5test.com

HTML tutorials (*Here are just a few free tutorial sites on HTML and other Web languages*): w3.org/wiki, html5rocks.com, sitepoint.com, w3schools. com, codecademy.com, quackit.com, developer.mozilla.org/en-US/docs/ Web tutorialspoint.com, whatwg.org, htmlgoodies.com, htmldog.com, htmlcodetutorial.com, echoecho.com, learn.shayhowe.com, html.net, tizag. com, html-5-tutorial.com, docs.webplatform.org, developers. google.com, webdesignermag.co.uk

5

Forms

5.1 Introduction

On-line forms are an essential means of collecting information from users, and most websites require the completion of a form for one purpose or another. They are basically the screen version of traditional paper forms, and most of the features commonly used in paper forms translate well into screen forms. Like paper forms, they can be of any size, but they also incorporate other features, such as buttons, drop-down list, and buttons, and can be interacted with in various ways, including via mouse, digital pen, and touch. This chapter introduces the various elements used to build a Web form.

5.2 Learning Outcomes

After studying this chapter, you will:

- Be aware of how form submission works and the role of the `<form>` element.
- Understand how form elements are used and the types of controls that they display.
- Be aware of the guidelines for ensuring a well-designed accessible form.

5.3 Form Element

Forms are used to collect information from users and vary widely in size and purpose. For example, it could contain just a single text field for the input of a search term to search the Web, two fields for taking the username and password to login to a site, or many types of inputs for collecting information about a user during registration. Every form, no matter how basic or complex, includes a button for the user to use to submit the form to the Web server for the processing of the entered information. The way the process works is illustrated in Figure 5.1.

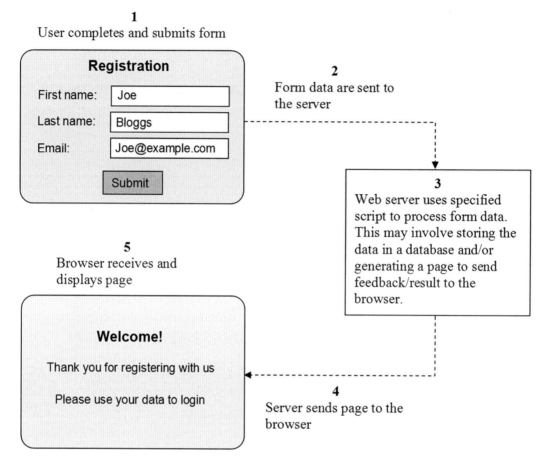

1
User completes and submits form

2
Form data are sent to the server

3
Web server uses specified script to process form data. This may involve storing the data in a database and/or generating a page to send feedback/result to the browser.

5
Browser receives and displays page

4
Server sends page to the browser

Registration

First name: Joe

Last name: Bloggs

Email: Joe@example.com

Submit

Welcome!

Thank you for registering with us

Please use your data to login

FIGURE 5.1   A basic illustration of how forms are handled.

The `<form>` element is the element that is used to hold all the various elements that are used to describe the features of a form. The elements used to collect input are known as **form controls**. A control must have a name. The information entered by the user is associated with this name, and both are sent by the browser to the Web server as a **name-value** pair. For example, in the illustration in Figure 5.1, if the names given to the controls are **fname**, **lname**, and **email**, respectively, then the name-value pairs sent would be **fname=Joe**, **lname=Bloggs**, and **email=joe@example.com**. The `<form>` element allows these pairs to be sent to the Web server through the use of the `action` and `method` attributes. The `action` attribute allows you to specify the URL of the script to use by Web server to process the data, and the `method` attribute allows you to specify how the data should be packaged and sent to the Web server. The two possible methods are **GET** and **POST**, each of which is suitable for different situations.

With the **GET method**, the pairs are added to the end of the URL specified in the `action` attribute, separated by "?," with the pairs joined using "&." Therefore, if, for example, the specified URL is "http://www.test.com/register.php," then what is sent will be: `http://www.test.com/register.php?fname=Joe&lname=Bloggs&email=joe@example.com`

Situations for which the GET method is well suited include when the amount of collected data is small and is going to be used for searching a database. It is not suitable for a lot of data, because it supports only 1024 characters. It should also not be used for sensitive information, because people can easily hack into it. It also does not support binary data, such as image files and Word documents.

With the **POST method**, the pairs are sent via what are called **HTTP headers**. The pairs are joined in the same way as in the GET method, that is, by using "&." The method is suitable for all the uses described above, for which the GET method is unsuitable. Figure 5.2 shows how the `action` and `method` attributes are used with the `<form>` element.

In addition to the `action` and `method` attributes, the `<form>` element supports other attributes that are commonly used. Table 5.1 lists them, starting with the two already mentioned.

```
HTML
<form method="post" action= "http://www.test.com/register.php">
  <!--Form control elements go here -->
</form>
```

FIGURE 5.2 Using the `action` and `method` attributes with the `<form>` element.

TABLE 5.1

Common Attributes Supported by the `<form>` Element

Form Element Attributes	Function
action	Specifies the URL of the script to use to process submitted form data.
method	Specifies the method to use to send submitted form data. Value can be `get` or `post`. Or, it can be `dialog`, when integrating the `<form>` element in the `<dialog>` element introduced in Chapter 3.
name	Specifies a unique name for a form.
enctype	Specifies how form data should be encoded and is applicable only to the POST method. Accepted values are `application/x-www-form-urlencoded` (the default), `multipart/form-data` (used for forms that contain files, binary data, and non-ASCII data, such as glyphs), and `text/plain`.
target	Specifies where to display the response to form submission. Acceptable values are `_blank`, `_self`, `_parent`, and `_top`, all of which were introduced in Chapter 2, under the `<link>` element.

(Continued)

TABLE 5.1 (*Continued*)

Common Attributes Supported by the `<form>` Element

Form Element Attributes	Function
accept-charset	Specifies the character encoding to use for submission. Accepts a space- or comma-separated list of character encodings.
novalidate	Specifies that form should not be validated and used with no value. The same result can be achieved using the `formnovalidate` attribute on a `<button>` or `<input>` element. These elements are discussed fully later in the chapter. The default is for a form to be validated.
autocomplete	Specifies whether or not browser should remember values entered previously by the user and use the best match to automatically complete an input or offer them as options as the user starts to complete the input. The values taken are `on` and `off`.

5.4 Form Controls

Forms can generally be boiled down to containing four categories of controls: those for **inputting text**, those for **making selections**, those for **uploading files**, and those for **starting an action**. Table 5.2 lists the controls that can be used to achieve these goals, all of which are discussed in this section.

5.4.1 `<input>`

The `<input>` element is the most commonly used in forms, because it is used to display different types of controls. It is an inline element, which means that the `<br>` element or a block-level container element (e.g., `<div>` or `<p>`) must be used to go to a new line. It takes many attributes. The most important is the `type` attribute, as it specifies input `type` and the type of control interface that is displayed, which includes **text-input field**, **radio button**, **checkbox**, and **drop-down menu**. Other attributes specify the behavior of these controls. Although there are many input types, their usage is based on the same principle, using the following format:

```
<input type="value">
```

Different sets of attributes are used with different input types. Some are mandatory, and others are optional. They will be introduced, as necessary, as the input types are presented.

TABLE 5.2

Form Controls and Elements Used with Them

Form Controls	Function
`<input>`	Defines a form control for user input.
`<button>...</button>`	Defines a button.
`<textarea>...</textarea>`	Defines a form control for multi-line *user text input.*
`<select>...</select>`	Used to create a drop-down list.
`<datalist>...</datalist>`	Used to create a drop-down list that suggests possible values from a range of values, based on what the user types in.
`<option>...</option>`	Defines an option in a select or datalist list.

Elements Used with Controls	Function
`<label>...</label>`	Used to associate a label with a control.
`<output>...<output>`	Used to display the result of a calculation or user action.
`<progress>...<progress>`	Used to display the completion progress of a task.
`<meter>...<meter>`	Used to display a level within a range.
`<optgroup>...</optgroup>`	Used to group options on a drop-down list.
`<fieldset>...</fieldset>`	Used to group controls. Also, it encloses them in a border.
`<legend>...</legend>`	Used to display a caption for the content of its parent `<fieldset>` element.
`<keygen>`	Although this element was introduced in HTML5, it has been deprecated and will no longer be supported by browsers, so its use is discouraged.

5.4.1.1 *Input Types for Collecting Text*

There are input types for collecting plain text as well as input types for collecting numeric data and formatted text, such as time and date, and most of them display an editable text-input field, into which the user can type. Some of them also have additional control features, such as increment-decrement and/or drop-down menu buttons, to help user input. To better explain them here, they are presented in the categories of those used for plain text input, those for entering numbers, and those for entering time and date data.

5.4.1.1.1 *Input Types for Collecting Plain Text*

The input types introduced here are typically used to collect short text inputs from a user, such as personal details and search terms, which basically can consist of any character; however, you can also make them collect only certain types of characters and in a specific order. Table 5.3 lists their names and functions.

All the input types in Table 5.3 support the same set of attributes, except the **hidden-input type**, which supports only `name` and `value`. Table 5.4 lists the attributes and their functions.

TABLE 5.3

Text-Input Type Values

Input Type	Function
text	Displays a single-line plain text box for text input.
password	Displays a single-line text box for text input and displays input as dots.
email	Displays a single-line text box.
url	Displays a single-line text box
tel	Displays a single-line text box
search	Displays a single-line text box.
hidden	Creates and hides an element from the user. Used to hold values for use by Web designer or developer.

TABLE 5.4

Attributes Supported by Input Types That Display Text Fields

Attribute	Function
name	Specifies a unique name for element.
value	Specifies the default value for element.
size	Specifies the length (in characters) of text-input field. Default is 20.
minlength	Specifies the minimum number of characters allowed in a text field.
maxlength	Specifies the maximum number of characters allowed in a text field.
pattern	Specifies an expression (a format) that user's input must match. When used, you should include a `title` attribute to describe the pattern.
placeholder	Gives an instruction or an example to user about what to enter in a text field.
readonly	Specifies whether or not users can edit a text field.
spellcheck	Specifies to check element's spelling and grammar. The values that it takes are `true` (which means to check), `false` (which means not to check), and `default` (which means to use a default value, such as the `spellcheck` value set for the parent element).
list	Specifies the `id` value on a `<datalist>` element with which to associate element.

(Continued)

TABLE 5.4 (*Continued*)

Attributes Supported by Input Types That Display Text Fields

Attribute	Function
required	Specifies that user must provide input for a control.
disabled	Specifies to disable a control, so that it is not responsive to user action.
autocomplete	Specifies whether or not browser should remember values entered previously by the user and use the best match to automatically complete a field or offer them as options as the user starts to complete the field. Typical values taken are on and off.
autofocus	Specifies to give input focus to a form control when a form loads.
autosave	Used to specify a unique category name for the search history saved by the browser for a **search-input type** field.
inputmode	Specifies which type of input mechanism (typically type of virtual keyboard) to display. It is used to display the type of keyboard that is most useful to the user for entering text into a control. It is especially useful for touch-screen devices, such as mobile phones. Values supported include verbatim, latin, latin-name, latin-prose, full-width-latin, kana, kana-name, katakana, numeric, tel, email, and url, each of which displays different type of keyboard.
multiple	Specifies whether the user is allowed to enter more than one value, and it can be specified by itself, without a value (instead of multiple="multiple"). It only applies to the **email-input type** (and **file-input type**, discussed later).

Figure 5.3 shows how the types in Table 5.3 are used, along with the commonly used attributes in Table 5.4. Figure 5.4 shows the result.

In the example, notice that all the input types have a similar format. The attributes used to perform the functions are described in Table 5.4. The **Username** and **Password** fields have been completed for the purpose of demonstration. The non-letter characters displayed in the **password-input type** field are automatic and for the purpose of preventing others from knowing what the user types. The required attribute ensures that a form is not allowed to submit until the user has completed the input for the element that has it. Notice that it does not have any value. The longhand is required="required", which is unnecessary. Since the attribute does not usually provide any visual cues until after a form has been submitted and the browser has prompted that a control must be completed, it can be useful to include some visual means of informing users of the controls that must be completed, so that they know beforehand. For example, the background or border of a field could be made with a

```
HTML
<h3>Form text input</h3>
<form>
  <p>Please complete the form below:</p>
  <p>Username:<input type="text" name="uname" required></p>
  <p>Password:<input type="password" name="password" required></p>
  <p>Email:<input type="email" name="email"
        placeholder="e.g., joe@example.com" required></p>
  <p>Phone:<input type="tel" name="phone"></p>
  <p>Personal URL:<input type="url" name="url" size="25"
  maxlength="35"></p>
  <p>Search:<input type="search" name="term" value="bolts"></p>
  <p><input type="hidden" name="subject" value="registration"></p>
</form>
```

FIGURE 5.3   Example usage of plain text-input types.

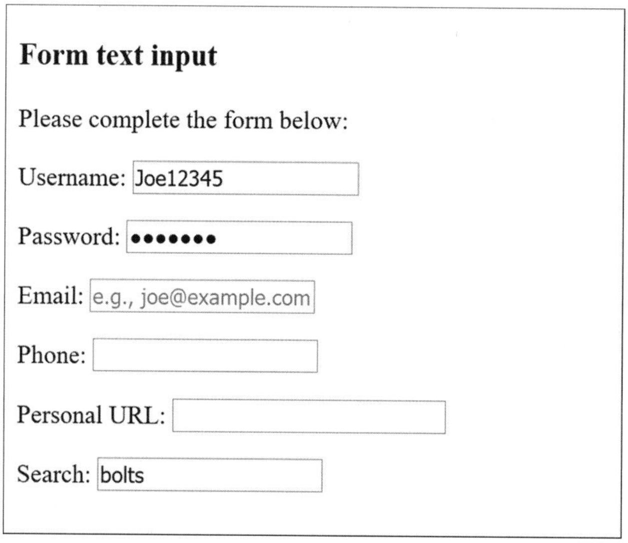

Form text input

Please complete the form below:

Username: Joe12345

Password: ●●●●●●

Email: e.g., joe@example.com

Phone:

Personal URL:

Search: bolts

FIGURE 5.4   Rendered result of Figure 5.3.

different color from those of other controls. This is achieved using CSS, and how it is done is explained in Chapter 17.

The use of the `required` attribute is a part of a process known as **form validation**, which involves checking a submitted form to ensure that all the required inputs have been completed and the inputs are of the correct type and/or format. It is an important process, because it ensures the integrity of submitted form data. Traditionally, this was done using client-side JavaScript scripting. However, HTML now has attributes to help with the process. One of them is the `required` attribute. Another is the `pattern` attribute. Although the attribute is not used in the example, it can be useful for ensuring that users

```
HTML
<form>
  Enter product code (XXX999999):
  <input type="text" name="product" pattern="[A-Za-z]{3}[0-9]{6}"
    title="Three upper- or lower-case letters followed by six
    digits.">
</form>
```

FIGURE 5.5 Example usage of the `pattern` attribute.

enter certain types of information, such as e-mail address, correctly. It is easy to specify. However, deriving the correct **regular expression** (also called **regex**) to specify can be difficult, because it involves mathematics. Figure 5.5 shows an example being used.

The expression is used to verify that user input comprises three upper- or lowercase letters, followed by six digits. The content of the `title` attribute in the code is displayed when the cursor hovers over the text field. If the user enters an input whose format does not match the pattern, the browser immediately prompts him or her to re-input the data and also reminds him or her of the correct format. Using the attribute with `email` and `password` input types can be especially useful for ensuring that correct e-mail formats are inputted and that the passwords chosen by users are varied and complex and therefore difficult to guess by hackers. To ensure password complexity, users are compelled to include a wide variety of combinations of lower- and uppercase letters, numbers, and characters. The explanation of how regular expressions are formulated is beyond the scope of this book. However, there are useful expressions on the Web. It is not important to understand how they work to be able to use them. You only need to know what they do.

Refer to Figure 5.3 and notice the text in the **email field**, which is placed there with the `placeholder` attribute. It is temporary and disappears the moment the field receives focus or the user starts to type into it. Next, notice that the **Search text field** is filled with the word "bolts" by default. This is the effect of specifying the `value` attribute in the **search-input type**. In contrast, the **hidden-input type** does not display anything. It simply creates a **name-value pair**, "subject=registration," which is sent to the server when the form is submitted and used by the relevant script for decision making. An example of how the input type is used is when the same script is used to process more than one form. Giving different hidden values to each form makes it possible for the script to identify which form has been submitted and process it accordingly. Finally, notice that the fields in the example are not vertically aligned. This is done using CSS and is dealt with in Chapter 17.

CHALLENGE 5.1

To see the effect of the pattern attribute, include it in the example in Figure 5.3 and then use the regular expression "[a-z0-9._%+-]+@[a-z0-9.-]+\.[a-z]{2,3}$" as its value to check the e-mail field. Remember to include the `title` attribute.

5.4.1.1.2 Input Types for Collecting Numbers

The input types for collecting numbers are `number` and `range`. As of time of writing, only some browsers support these input types. They include Firefox, Opera, and Chrome. Both input types support the same attributes as text-input types listed earlier in Table 5.4, except `size`, `maxlength`, `pattern`, and `placeholder`. Table 5.5 lists the extra ones that they support.

5.4.1.1.2.1 Input Type: `number`   The **number-input type** displays a single-line text field for the user to enter a number directly and also provides increment and decrement buttons, with which a number can be specified. Figure 5.6 shows how it is used, and Figure 5.7 depicts the result. The `min` and `max` attributes specify the range of numbers allowed; the `value` attribute sets the initial number as 0; and the `step`

TABLE 5.5

Attributes Supported by Input Types for Collecting Numbers

Attribute	Function
min	Specifies the minimum numeric value allowed. It can also be used for date value.
max	Specifies the maximum numeric value allowed. It can also be used for date value.
step	Specifies increment and decrement values when a control button is clicked.

```
HTML
<h3>Form number input</h3>
<form>
  <p>Please enter quantity required:</p>
  <input type="number" name="quantity" value="0" min="0" max="100"
  step="3">
</form>
```

FIGURE 5.6   Example usage of number-input control.

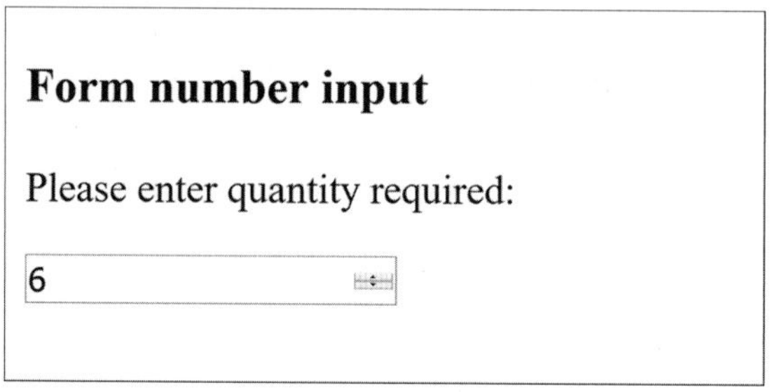

FIGURE 5.7   Rendered result of Figure 5.6.

attribute specifies that every click of the button should increase or decrease the value in the text field by 3.

CHALLENGE 5.2

Can you think of a type of Web application in which the number control is applicable?

5.4.1.1.2.2 Input Type: range   The **range-input type** displays a slide control for inputting an integer (whole) number, as opposed to decimal number. Figure 5.8 shows how it is used, and Figure 5.9 depicts the result. As in the previous example, the min and max attributes specify the range of numbers covered by the slide and the value attribute sets the initial number as 0.

The **disadvantage of the range-input type** is that it does not display any number. However, this functionality can be added using additional elements and attributes. Figure 5.10 shows an example of how to do this, and Figure 5.11 depicts the result. The <output> element is responsible for displaying the numbers, and its initial content is set as 0. In the <input> element, the min and max attributes specify the range of numbers covered by the slide; the **value** attribute sets its initial number as 0; and the oninput form event attribute says that when an input is made (i.e., when

```
HTML
<h3>Form range input</h3>
<form>
    <p>Please enter quantity required:</p>
    <input type="range" name="quantity" value="0" min="0" max="100">
</form>
```

FIGURE 5.8   How the range-input type is used.

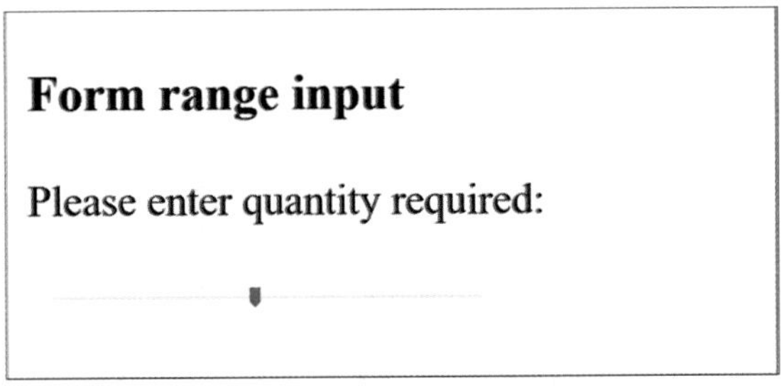

Form range input

Please enter quantity required:

FIGURE 5.9   Rendered result of Figure 5.8.

```
HTML
<h3>Form range input with values</h3>
<form>
  <p>Please use slide to enter quantity:</p>
  <output name="quantity">0</output>
  <input type="range" name="slideInput" min="0" max="100"
   value="0"oninput="quantity.value=slideInput.value">
</form>
```

FIGURE 5.10 Adding numbers display with the `<output>` element.

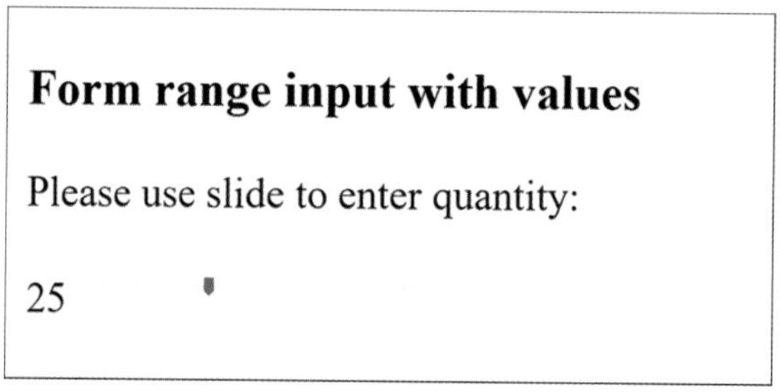

Form range input with values

Please use slide to enter quantity:

25

FIGURE 5.11 Rendered result of Figure 5.10.

the slide is moved), the value of the element bearing the name "quantity" should be replaced with the value of the one bearing the name "slideInput." A **form event attribute**, as you may recollect from Chapter 2, is an event generated by a form element when its state changes.

In the previous example, the number displayed cannot be edited. However, it is possible to make it editable and also link it to the slide, so that the user can use either of the two to make an input. This can be done by **combining the range-input type with the number-input type**. Figure 5.12 shows an example, and Figure 5.13 depicts the result. In the number-type `<input>` element, the `oninput` attribute specifies that when the user enters a number in the box, the value of the range-input type should be replaced with that of the number-input type. The reverse happens with the `oninput` attribute in

```
HTML
<h3>Form range and number inputs</h3>
<form>
  <p>Please enter quantity in field or with slide:</p>
  <input type="number" name="numberInput" min="0" max="100"
   value="0" oninput="slideNumber.value=numberInput.value">
  <input type="range" name="slideNumber" min="0" max="100"
   value="0" oninput="numberInput.value=slideNumber.value">
</form>
```

FIGURE 5.12 Combining editable number field with the `<output>` element.

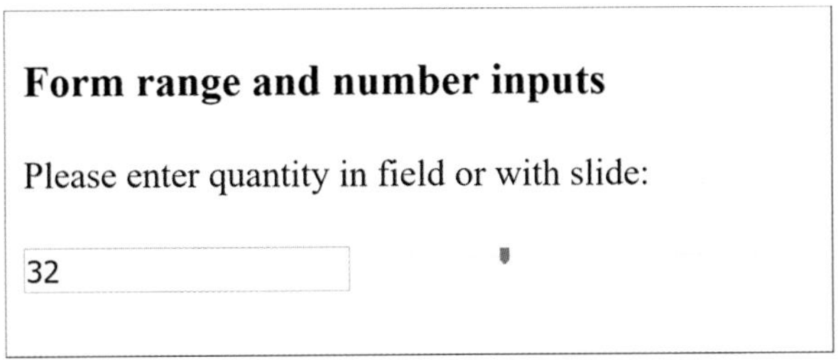

Form range and number inputs

Please enter quantity in field or with slide:

32

FIGURE 5.13   Rendered result of Figure 5.12.

the range-type `<input>` element when the slide is moved. All other attributes play the same roles, as described in the previous example.

CHALLENGE 5.3

Can you think of a situation in which the number control is applicable? Also, how would you change the text box in the example to a non-editable field?

5.4.1.1.3 Input Types for Collecting Time and Date

Like the number-input type, the category of input types for collecting time and date provides appropriately formatted text fields for users to make direct input and also provides additional button controls for choosing options. The relevant input types are `time`, `date`, `datetime-local`, `month`, and `week`. The input types support the same attributes as the **number-input types**, namely, `min`, `max`, and `step`. If the `min` or/and `max` attributes are specified, controls display only dates or times that satisfy the specified limits, and the increment or decrement button increments or decrements them only according to the specified `step` value when clicked.

5.4.1.1.3.1 Input Type: `time`   The **time-input type** displays a text box and a control for setting time. Figure 5.14 shows how it is used, and Figure 5.15 depicts the result. To use the control displayed, the user clicks the relevant time component and types in a value or uses the up and down arrows.

```
HTML
<h3>Form time input</h3>
<form>
   <p>Please enter time:<input type="time" name="time"></p>
</form>
```

FIGURE 5.14   Example usage of the time-input type.

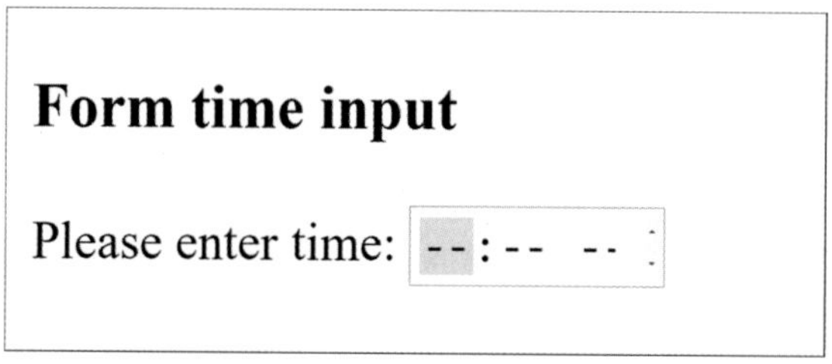

Form time input

Please enter time: `--` : `--`   `--`

FIGURE 5.15   Rendered result of Figure 5.14.

CHALLENGE 5.4

In which situations you might use the time control?

5.4.1.1.3.2 Input Type: `date`   The **date-input type** displays a single-line format-ted text box and a drop-down calendar for setting date. The input format allowed by the text field depends on the date convention of the region of the world of the user. Figure 5.16 shows how it is used, and Figure 5.17 depicts the result. To use the con-trol displayed, the user, like with the **time-input type** control, clicks the relevant date component and types in a value or uses the up and down arrows. Various other arrows allow you to navigate to the required month and year.

```
HTML
<h3>Form date input</h3>
<form>
   <p>Please enter date:<input type="date" name="date"></p>
</form>
```

FIGURE 5.16   Example usage of the date-input type.

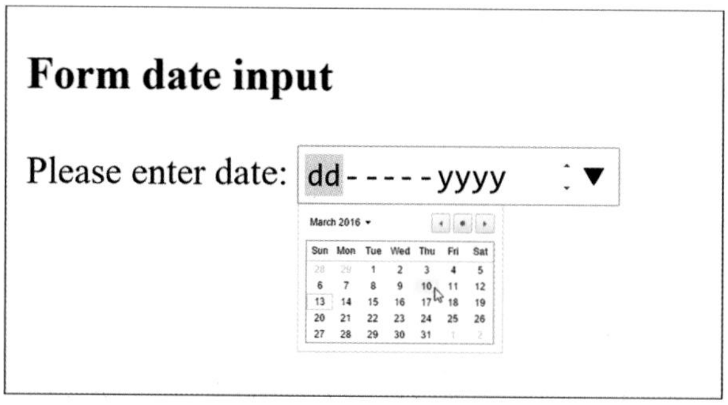

Form date input

Please enter date: `dd - - - - - yyyy`   `▼`

| March 2016 ▾ | | | | ◂ | ▪ | ▸ |

Sun	Mon	Tue	Wed	Thu	Fri	Sat
28	29	1	2	3	4	5
6	7	8	9	10	11	12
13	14	15	16	17	18	19
20	21	22	23	24	25	26
27	28	29	30	31		

FIGURE 5.17   Rendered result of Figure 5.16.

CHALLENGE 5.5

Implement the example and experiment with the control. Do this in different browsers, if possible, for comparison. Also, use the `min` and `max` attributes to see the effect, using the earlier example under the **number-input type** as guide.

5.4.1.1.3.3 Input Type: `datetime-local`   The **datetime-local-input type** displays a text box and a date and time control for setting local date and time. Figure 5.18 shows how it is used, and Figure 5.19 depicts the result. The control displayed allows you to choose a date by clicking the downward arrow to display the calendar and then clicking a day on it. The time is entered by clicking the hour, minutes, or seconds component and by using the arrows to set the values. It is worth noting that HTML also specifies a **datetime-input type**, which is intended for setting global date and time, including time zone information. However, it is not, as of time of writing, supported by any major browser.

```
HTML
<h3>Form date and time input</h3>
<form>
  <p>Please enter date and time:</p>
  <p>Date and time:<input type="datetime-local"
   name="localdatetime"></p>
</form>
```

FIGURE 5.18   Example usage of the datetime-local-input type.

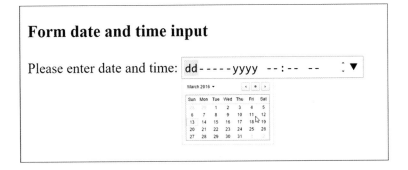

FIGURE 5.19   Rendered result of Figure 5.18.

CHALLENGE 5.6

Implement the example and interact with the features and then suggest in which type of application you might use the control. Also, using the earlier example under the **number-input type** as guide, experiment with the `min` and `max` attributes for possible applications.

5.4.1.1.3.4 Input Type: `month`   The **month-input type** displays a formatted text box and a month-and-year control for setting month and year. Figure 5.20 shows how it is used, and Figure 5.21 depicts the result. The control allows you to choose a month by clicking the downward arrow to display a calendar and then clicking the next or previous arrow to navigate to the desired month. Alternatively, you could click the button that displays all the months, to choose one.

```
HTML
<h3>Form month input</h3>
<form>
  <p>Please enter month:<input type="month" name="month"></p>
</form>
```

FIGURE 5.20   Example usage of the month-input type.

FIGURE 5.21   Rendered result of Figure 5.20.

CHALLENGE 5.7

Implement the example and interact with the features and then suggest in which type of application you might use the control. Again, using the earlier example under the **number-input type** as guide, experiment with the `min` and `max` attributes to get a better idea of how you might apply them effectively in a design.

5.4.1.1.3.5 Input Type: week   The **week-input type** displays a text box and a week-and-year control. Figure 5.22 shows how it is used, and Figure 5.23 depicts the result. The displayed control allows the user to choose the date by clicking the downward arrow to display a calendar. Different Web browsers display the control differently.

```
HTML
<h3>Form week input</h3>
<form>
  <p>Please enter week and year:<input type="week"
  name="week"></p>
</form>
```

FIGURE 5.22 Example usage of the week-input type.

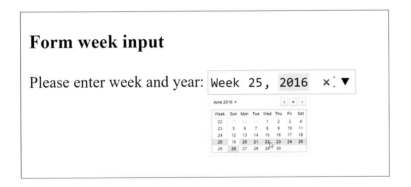

FIGURE 5.23 Rendered result of Figure 5.22.

CHALLENGE 5.8

Implement the example and interact with the features in different browsers. Also, suggest in which type of application the control might be useful.

5.4.1.2 Input Types for Offering Options

These input types allow you to provide users with options, from which they can choose. The two input types used for this are `radio` and `checkbox`. Table 5.6 lists the attributes that they support.

5.4.1.2.1 Input Type: `radio`

The **radio-input type** displays a radio button and is used when you want users to choose only one from a set of options. Once a button is selected, it cannot be unselected by clicking it. It can only be unselected by clicking another button. This ensures that only one option can be chosen as answer to a question, and it is the values of the `name` and `value` attributes of the chosen option that are **used to create the name-value pair** that is sent to the server. This also means that radio buttons are not suitable when users are allowed to not choose an option. Figure 5.24 shows how the input type is used, and Figure 5.25 depicts the result.

In the example, notice that all the elements have the same name. This is because only one response is recognized for the question. It is worth noting that it may not always be a good idea to use the `checked` attribute, as it might cause some users to think that they have made

TABLE 5.6

Attributes for Radio Button and Checkbox

Attribute	Function
name	Specifies a unique name for element.
value	Specifies the default value for element.
form	Specifies the `id` value on the form with which to associate element.
disabled	Specifies to disable control, so that user cannot interact with it. It can be specified by itself, without a value (instead of `disabled="disabled"`).
autofocus	Specifies that element should be given focus when page is loaded. It can be specified by itself, without a value (instead of `autofocus="autofocus"`).
required	Specifies that element must be given an input.
checked	Specifies to select an `<input>` element by default.

```
HTML
<h3>Radio buttons</h3>
<form>
    Please choose one:<br>
    <input type="radio" name="salutation" value="Mr" checked>Mr
    <input type="radio" name="salutation" value="Mrs">Mrs
    <input type="radio" name="salutation" value="Miss">Miss
    <input type="radio" name="salutation" value="Ms">Ms
    <input type="radio" name="salutation" value="Dr">Dr
</form>
```

FIGURE 5.24 Example usage of the radio-input type.

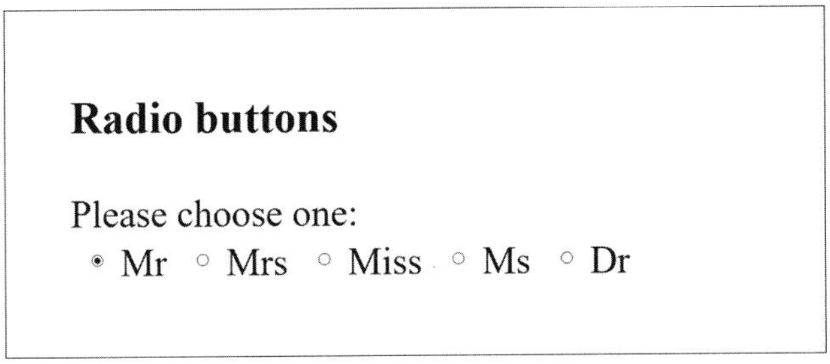

Radio buttons

Please choose one:
⦿ Mr ○ Mrs ○ Miss · ○ Ms ○ Dr

FIGURE 5.25 Rendered result of Figure 5.24.

a selection, even though they have not. This is because it is often easy to overlook things at a glance. In the case of the example, the consequence might be someone whose title is "Mrs" submitting the default response (i.e., "Mr"). Leaving all buttons unchecked makes it more unlikely that users will miss at a glance that they have not completed a question.

CHALLENGE 5.9

Implement the example in Figure 5.24 but with buttons arranged vertically.

CHALLENGE 5.10

For which of these would you use radio buttons?

- Please select your favorites.
- Please choose your gender.
- Do you agree with the terms and conditions?
- Please choose one.
- Please choose.

5.4.1.2.2 *Input Type:* `checkbox`

The checkbox-input type displays a checkbox that allows users to select or deselect it and is best for when you want users to be able to choose any number of options from a set of options per question. The values of only the checked checkboxes are sent to the server. The value of each checkbox is combined with the name to create a name-value pair for each option and sent to the server. Figure 5.26 shows how the input type is used, and Figure 5.27 depicts the result.

Notice that like with radio buttons, all the checkboxes for the question have the same value for the `name` attribute; however, more than one option can be selected. As long as the values of the `value` attributes are different, this is all right, since the **name-value pair** for each option will be different. From the viewpoint of the author who might write a script to process the form data, the common name identifies a question and the values of the `value` attributes identify the options associated

```
HTML
<h3>Checkboxes</h3>
<form>
  Which of these do you commute with? </br>
   <input type="checkbox" name="commute"
    value="tube" checked> Tube
   <input type="checkbox" name="commute"
    value="train" checked> Train
   <input type="checkbox" name="commute" value="car"> Car
   <input type="checkbox" name="commute"
    value="motorcycle"> Motorcycle
   <input type="checkbox" name="commute"
    value="bicycle"> Bicycle
   <input type="checkbox" name="commute"
    value="walking" checked> Walking
</form>
```

FIGURE 5.26   Example usage of the checkbox-input type.

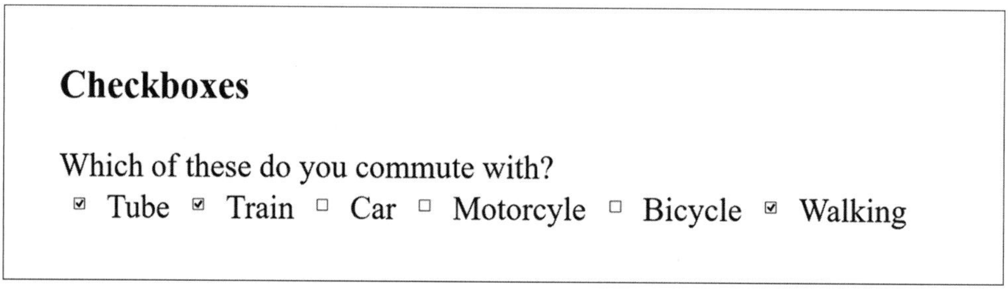

Checkboxes

Which of these do you commute with?
☑ Tube ☑ Train ☐ Car ☐ Motorcyle ☐ Bicycle ☑ Walking

FIGURE 5.27   Rendered result of Figure 5.26.

with it. In addition, notice that there is space between each box and its label. This is because there is space in the code between each < input > element and its label.

CHALLENGE 5.11

For which of these would you use checkboxes?

• Please select your favorites.
• Please choose your gender.
• Do you agree with the terms and conditions?
• Please choose one.
• Please choose.

5.4.1.3 Input Types for Starting an Action

These input types allow you to provide a push button that users can click or press to initiate an action. The action can be predetermined ones, such as the submission of a form, or it can be the execution of a script to perform a specific task. The relevant input types are submit, reset, button, image, file, and color.

5.4.1.3.1 *Input Type:* submit *and* reset

The submit-input and reset-input types are presented together, because they are typically used together. The **submit-input type** displays a push button, which when clicked or pressed makes the browser start the process of packaging and sending the information entered into a form by a user to the Web server. The input type supports usual attributes but also some that relate to forms and their submission. Indeed, the attributes perform similar functions as those listed earlier in Table 5.1 for the <form> element. For example, the formaction attribute does the same thing as the action attribute in Table 5.1. Table 5.7 lists them and their function.

TABLE 5.7

Attributes for Submit and Reset Buttons

Submit Attributes	Function
name	Specifies a unique name for element.
value	Specifies the default value for element.
disabled	Specifies to disable control, so that user cannot interact with it. It can be specified by itself, without a value (instead of disabled="disabled").
form	Specifies the id value of the <form> element with which to associate element. It allows you to place <input> elements anywhere within a document and not just within the <form> element.
autofocus	Specifies that element should be given input focus when page is loaded. It can be specified by itself, without a value (instead of autofocus="autofocus").
formaction	Specifies the URL for the script to use to process submitted form data, for example formaction=http://www.test.com/register.php. This is the same as using action="http://www.test.com/register.php" with the <form> element.
formmethod	Specifies the method to use to send form data to server, for example formaction="get". This is the same as using method="get" with the <form> element.
formnovalidate	Specifies that form is not to be validated, for example formnovalidate. This is the same as using novalidate with the <form> element.
formenctype	Specifies file encoding type, for example formenctype="text/plain". This is the same as using enctype="text/plain" with the <form> element.
formtarget	Specifies where to display the response to a form submission, for example formtarget="_blank". This is the same as using target="_blank" with the <form> element.

Like the submit-input type, the **reset-input type** displays a push button, but when clicked or pressed, it clears user's inputs and resets all the controls of a form to their default values. Unlike the submit-input type, it supports only the `name`, `value`, `disabled`, `autofocus`, and `form` attributes. Figure 5.28 shows how both input types are used, and Figure 5.29 depicts the result.

```
HTML
<h3>Form submit and reset buttons</h3>
<form>
  <input type="submit" value="Submit">
  <input type="reset" value="Cancel">
</form>
```

FIGURE 5.28   Example usage of submit- and reset-input types.

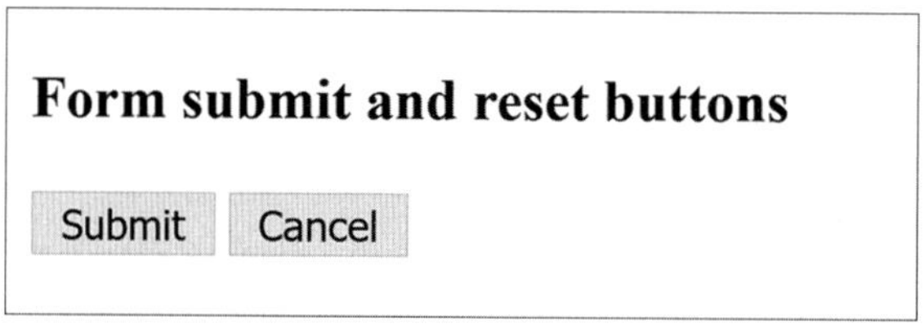

Form submit and reset buttons

Submit   Cancel

FIGURE 5.29   Rendered result of Figure 5.28.

CHALLENGE 5.12

Add the necessary things to the code in Figure 5.28 to produce the form below:

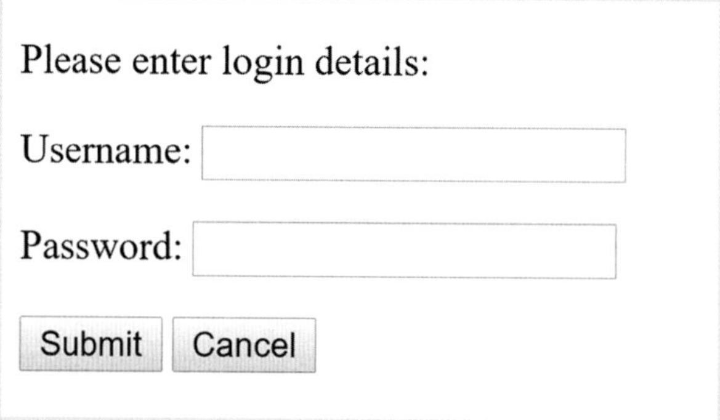

Please enter login details:

Username:

Password:

Submit   Cancel

5.4.1.3.2 Input Type: image

The **image-input type** allows you to specify an image to be used as a submit button. It supports the same attributes as listed in Table 5.7 for **submit**- and **reset**-input types, as well as the image-specific ones listed in Table 5.8. Figure 5.30 shows how the input type is used, and Figure 5.31 depicts the result.

TABLE 5.8

Attributes for Image Button

Attribute	Function
src	Specifies the URL of the image to use.
width	Specifies the width of image.
height	Specifies the height of image.
alt	Specifies the alternative text to use to describe image. It is essential for accessibility.

```
HTML
<h3>Form image button</h3>
<form>
  <p>Please enter login details:</p>
  <p>Username:<input type="text" name="uname" required></p>
  <p>Password:<input type="password"
   name="password" required></p>
  <input type="image" src="submit.png" width="148" height="32"
   alt="submit button">
</form>
```

FIGURE 5.30 Example usage of the image-input type.

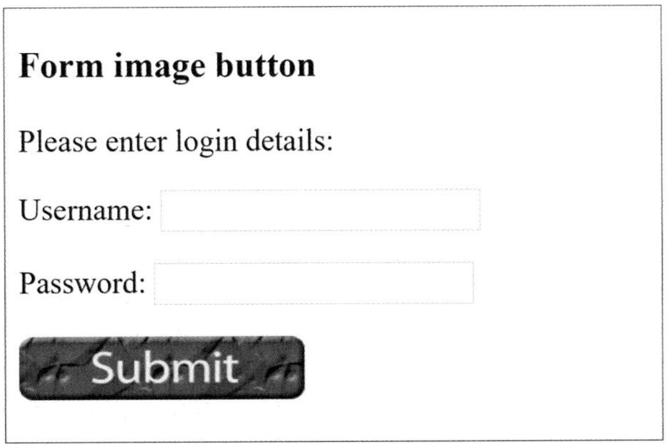

FIGURE 5.31 Rendered result of Figure 5.30.

The actual size of the image used in the example was 200 × 50 pixels and was reduced to 148 × 30 pixels. It is **good practice to create an image that is as close as possible in size to the one required**. This is because the process of reduction can cause problems, such as making the text on the image too small to be legible. If the image specified is not found, a visual predetermined by the browser is displayed instead. This can be just text or a box with text in it.

Unfortunately, unlike the **submit**- and **reset**-input types that perform predetermined functions when activated, the image-input type needs to be told what to do when it is activated, and this is typically done using the `onclick` event attribute (which generates an event each time the element on which it is used is clicked) and the **submit()** JavaScript function (which submits a form when it is called). For example, adding `onclick="submit();"` to the `<input>` element in Figure 5.28 says to submit the form when the element (i.e., the image button) is clicked.

NOTE: Image button accessibility

To make an image accessible to the visually impaired, it is necessary to provide the text alternative that describes it. To make a functional image (i.e., an image used for a specific function, such as one used as a button or link), text alternative should describe its functionality instead of its appearance. More about image accessibility is discussed in Chapter 6.

CHALLENGE 5.13

Try the example in Figure 5.30 but without providing the correct location for the image, and see what happens in different browsers.

5.4.1.3.3 *Input Type:* `button`

Like the reset-input and submit-input types, the **button-input type** displays a push button but with no predetermined behavior. This means that like with the **image-input** type, you need to specify the function to perform when it is activated. Doing this again involves using the `onclick` event attribute and the **submit()** JavaScript function. The attributes that the input type supports are `name`, `value`, `disabled`, `form`, and `autofocus`. Figure 5.32 shows how the input type is used, and Figure 5.33 depicts the result.

The `onclick` attribute in the code specifies that when the `<input>` element is clicked to execute the JavaScript function called `alert()`, which displays the text between the quotes in an alert box. Different browsers display the box in different ways. Firefox was used in the example, in which when the "Show Message" button was clicked, the window changed to gray to indicate its current role as background and the box is displayed on top.

```
HTML
<h3>Form action button</h3>
<form>
  <input type="button" value="Show Message" onclick="alert
    ('This message is displayed using a JavaScript function.')">
</form>
```

FIGURE 5.32   Example usage of the button-input type.

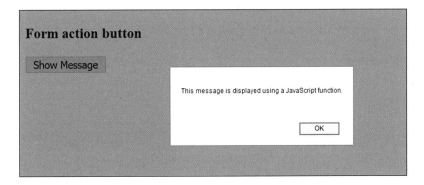

FIGURE 5.33   Rendered result of Figure 5.32.

CHALLENGE 5.14

Try the code by using different types of browsers to see the differences in rendering.

5.4.1.3.4 *Input Type:* `file`

The **file-input type** displays a single-line text field and a browse button to allow users to select files for uploading. However, it does not provide a control for the actual uploading; this is done using the **submit-input type**, which you have already read earlier in this chapter. Any time a website allows you to browse and select a file on your computer for upload, it is likely that it is the input type that is being used. The attributes supported are listed in Table 5.9. Figure 5.34 shows how the input type is used, and Figure 5.35 depicts the result.

The control in the example is from Internet Explorer. Different browsers display different designs of control. In Firefox, Chrome, or Opera, the text field is usually not as clear to see as of time of writing. Clicking the field or the button of the control displays a dialog box, with which the user can navigate to the required file or files. The `accept` attribute specifies that the file types expected are **jpeg** and **png** image files, and the `multiple` attribute specifies that many files can be selected for upload. Typically, selecting multiple files involves first selecting one and then holding down the Shift, Control, or Command key while selecting others.

TABLE 5.9

Attributes for the File-Input Type

Attribute	Function
name	Specifies a unique name for element.
value	Specifies the default value for element.
disabled	Specifies to disable control, so that user cannot interact with it. It can be specified by itself, without a value (instead of disabled="disabled").
form	Specifies the id value of the <form> element with which to associate element. It allows <input> elements to be placed anywhere within a document and not just within the <form> element.
autofocus	Specifies that element should be given focus when page is loaded. It can be specified by itself, without a value (instead of autofocus="autofocus").
required	Specifies that element must be given an input in order form to be submitted. It can be specified by itself, without a value (instead of required="required").
multiple	Specifies whether the user is allowed to upload more than one file. It can be specified by itself, without a value (instead of multiple="multiple").
accept	Specifies the file types that are accepted.

```
HTML
<h3>Form file upload control</h3>
<form>
  <p>Select file:</p>
  <input type="file" name="imagefile" accept="image/jpeg,
  image/png" multiple>
</form>
```

FIGURE 5.34 Example usage of the file-input type.

FIGURE 5.35 Rendered result of Figure 5.34.

CHALLENGE 5.15

Add a submit button to the example that will serve to upload the selected file.

5.4.1.3.5 *Input Type:* `color`

The **color-input type** allows you to display a color well (i.e., color picker), which allows a user to select a color for an element. Table 5.10 lists the attributes that it supports. Figure 5.36 shows how the input type is used, and Figure 5.37 depicts the result.

The code in the example displays a color button, which when clicked displays the color picker. The **hexadecimal value** (or **hex code**) of the color selected is what is stored and sent to the server. In theory, it is as if the user has entered the value into a text-input field.

TABLE 5.10

Attributes for Color-Input Type

Attribute	Function
name	Specifies a unique name for element.
value	Specifies the default value for element.
disabled	Specifies to disable control, so that user cannot interact with it. It can be specified by itself, without a value (instead of disabled="disabled").
form	Specifies the id value of the <form> element with which to associate element. It allows <input> elements to be placed anywhere within a document and not just within the <form> element.
autofocus	Specifies that element should be given input focus when page is loaded. It can be specified by itself, without a value (instead of autofocus="autofocus").
autocomplete	Specifies whether or not browser should remember values entered previously by the user and use the best match to automatically complete a field or offer them as options as the user starts to complete the field. The values taken are on and off.
list	Specifies the id value on a <datalist> element with which to associate element.

```
HTML
<h3>Form color picker</h3>
<form>
  Please select color:<input type="color" name="user_color">
</form>
```

FIGURE 5.36 Example usage of the color-input type.

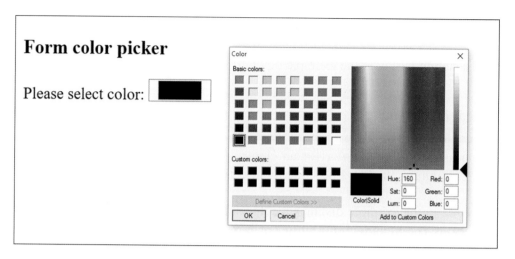

FIGURE 5.37   Rendered result of Figure 5.36.

CHALLENGE 5.16

In what type of Web application would you need to use the color-input type, and why could you not just ask users to enter the hex code or name of the color that they want in a text-input field?

5.4.2 Multipurpose Button

5.4.2.1 `<button>...</button>`

Like some of the action-button input types introduced earlier (i.e., submit, reset, and button), the `<button>` element is used to display a button. It is a multi-purpose element for creating buttons and is intended to give authors more flexibility and creative control over the appearance of buttons. For example, text can be easily combined with an image on a button to give it more meaning. Table 5.11 lists the attributes the element

TABLE 5.11

Attributes for `<button>` Element

Attribute	Function
name	Specifies a unique name for element.
value	Specifies the default value for element.
disabled	Specifies to disable control, so that user cannot interact with it. It can be specified by itself, without a value (instead of disabled="disabled").

(Continued)

TABLE 5.11 (*Continued*)

Attributes for `<button>` Element

Attribute	Function
`form`	Specifies the `id` value of the `<form>` element with which to associate element.
`type`	Specifies type of button. Possible values include `submit` (which submits form data to server), `reset` (which resets controls to their initial values), and `button` (which allows behavior to be specified through scripts). If the attribute is not specified, the behavior of the button is set to `submit`.
`autofocus`	Specifies to give input focus to the button.
`formaction`	Specifies the URL for the script to use to process submitted form data, for example `formaction=http://www.test.com/register.php`. This is the same as using `action="http://www.test.com/register.php"` with the `<form>` element.
`formenctype`	Specifies file encoding type to use for form data, for example `formenctype="text/plain"`. This is the same as using `enctype="text/plain"` with the `<form>` element.
`formmethod`	Specifies the method to use to send form data to server, for example `formaction="get"`. This is the same as using `method="get"` with the `<form>` element.
`formnovalidate`	Specifies that form is not to be validated, for example `formnovalidate`. This is the same as using `novalidate` with the `<form>` element.
`formtarget`	Specifies where to display the response to a form submission, for example `formtarget="_blank"`. This is the same as using `target="_blank"` with the `<form>` element.

supports, and Figures 5.38 and 5.39 show how the `type` attribute is used with the element and the result.

Notice the use of the `<img>` element and the associated attributes to add and size the green and red oval images. They have been used here to only demonstrate the use of the `<button>` element and are discussed more fully in Chapter 6. The `<button>` element creates a **submit-type button** and displays its content on it, and the `<img>` element adds the image. The use of the `alt` attribute is important to make the button accessible, as it provides the text for the screen reader to read out. The sizes of the actual images were 24 × 24 pixels and created with transparent background in Photoshop.

```
HTML
<h3>Form button element</h3>
<form>
    <button type="submit"><img src="green_button.png"
      width="12" height="12">Start</button>
    <button type="submit"><img src="red_button.png"
      width="12" height="12">Stop</button>
</form>
```

FIGURE 5.38   Example usage of the `<button>` element.

FIGURE 5.39   Rendered result of Figure 5.38.

CHALLENGE 5.17

What additional information do the images on the buttons in the example provide, and which types of application do you think would benefit from these kinds of buttons?

CHALLENGE 5.18

Implement the example by using your own images and then specify the wrong locations for the images. Also, omit them altogether and see what happens.

5.4.3 Multiple Lines Text Input

5.4.3.1 `<textarea>...</textarea>`

The `<textarea>` element allows you to display a control that allows users to enter multiple lines of plain text, as opposed to the single line allowed by the text-input types discussed earlier. Table 5.12 lists the attributes that it supports, and Figures 5.40 and 5.41 show how it is used and also show the result.

In the example, the `dirname` attribute is used only to explain how it works. It changes nothing, because it specifies the default directionality setting. It works as follows: when the form is submitted, its value, together with the directionality setting for the element, is sent as a name-value pair to the server. This means that the name-value pair sent for setting directionality is `comment.dir=ltr`. The directionality value "ltr" means left to right, which is the default. Directionality can be set using the `dir` attribute, a global attribute. The other value it takes is `rlt` (right to left).

TABLE 5.12

Attributes for `<textarea>` Element

Attribute	Function
name	Specifies a unique name for element.
value	Specifies the default value for element.
maxlength	Specifies the maximum number of characters allowed in a text field.
minlength	Specifies the minimum number of characters allowed in a text field.
rows	Specifies the number of lines to show. Default is 2.
cols	Specifies the number of characters per line to show. Default is 20.
disabled	Specifies to disable control, so that user cannot interact with it. It can be specified by itself, without a value (instead of disabled="disabled").
form	Specifies the id value of the `<form>` element with which to associate element. It allows `<input>` elements to be placed anywhere within a document and not just within the `<form>` element.
autofocus	Specifies that element should be given focus when page is loaded. It can be specified by itself, without a value (instead of autofocus="autofocus").
autocomplete	Specifies whether or not browser should remember values entered previously by the user and use the best match to automatically complete a field or offer them as options as the user starts to complete the field. The values taken are on and off.
required	Specifies that element must have an input. It can be specified by itself, without a value (instead of required="required").
placeholder	Gives an instruction or an example to user about what to enter in a text field.
readonly	Specifies whether or not users can edit a text field.
spellcheck	Specifies to check element's spelling and grammar. The values that it takes are true (which means to check), false (which means not to check), and default (which means to use a default value, such as the spellcheck value set for the parent element).
wrap	Specifies whether or not inputted text should be wrapped when submitted. Its value can be soft (which means it is not to be wrapped) or hard (which means it is to be wrapped). If hard is specified, then the dirname attribute must be used to specify at which character to apply wrapping.
dirname	Specifies a name to be used to send directionality value of an element to the server. It is useful for extending accessibility to those who read and write from right to left.

```
HTML
<h3>Form textarea control</h3>
 <form>
    <p>Please give us your comments below:</p>
    <textarea rows="5" cols="60" name="comments"
     dirname="comment.dir"></textarea>
</form>
```

FIGURE 5.40   Example usage of the `<textarea>` element.

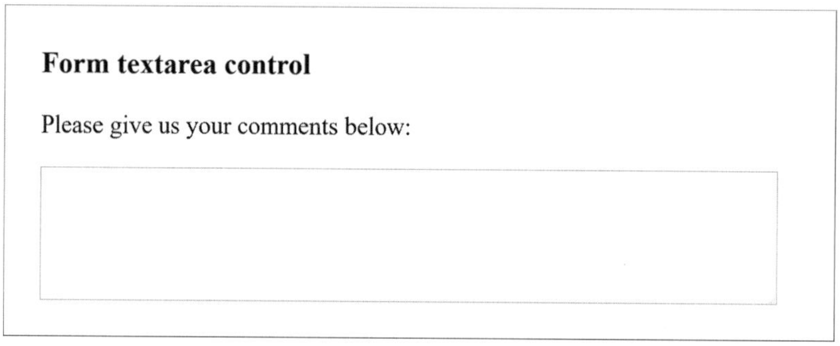

Form textarea control

Please give us your comments below:

FIGURE 5.41   Rendered result of Figure 5.40.

CHALLENGE 5.19

What is the basic difference between the textarea control and the controls for the text-input types?

5.4.4 Drop-Down List

5.4.4.1 `<select>...</select>`

The `<select>` element is used to display a drop-down list, from which a user can choose one. Each item of the list is created using the `<option>` element, and the items are grouped using the `<optgroup>` element. Table 5.13 lists the attributes supported by the `<select>` element.

Table 5.14 lists the attributes that the `<option>` element allows. Of the attributes, the `<optgroup>` element supports only the label and disabled. Figure 5.42 shows how a drop-down list is created using these elements.

In the example, notice the nesting convention (indicated with the left brackets). It is important to get this right if the list is to work correctly. Figure 5.43 shows the drop-down list after the down arrow has been clicked to activate it. Notice that the values of the `label` attributes on the `<optgroup>` elements are automatically given emphasis. When the form is submitted, the value of the `name` attribute on the `<select>` element is attached to the value of the `value` attribute on the `<option>` element to create the name-value pair that is sent to the server.

TABLE 5.13

Attributes for `<select>` Element

Attribute	Function
name	Specifies a unique name for element.
size	Specifies the number of options to show. Default is 1.
multiple	Specifies to allow one or more options to be selected. It can be specified by itself, without a value (instead of `multiple="multiple"`).
required	Specifies that element must be given an input. It can be specified by itself, without a value (instead of `required="required"`).
autofocus	Specifies that element should be given focus when page is loaded. It can be specified by itself, without a value (instead of `autofocus="autofocus"`).
disabled	Specifies to disable control, so that user cannot interact with it. It can be specified by itself, without a value (instead of `disabled="disabled"`).
form	Specifies the id value on the form with which to associate element.

TABLE 5.14

Attributes for `<option>` Element

Attribute	Function
value	Specifies a value for option.
label	Specifies a label for option.
selected	Specifies to select option by default. It can be specified by itself, without a value (instead of `selected="selected"`).
disabled	Specifies to disable control, so that user cannot interact with it. It can be specified by itself, without a value (instead of `disabled="disabled"`).

```
HTML
<h3>Form multiple select</h3>
<form>
  Please select your favorite movie:
  <select name="fav_movie">
    <optgroup label="Sci-Fi">
      <option value="startrek">Star Trek</option>
      <option value="starwars" selected>Star Wars</option>
    </optgroup>
    <optgroup label="Animation">
      <option value="shrek">Shrek</option>
      <option value="toystory">Toy Story</option>
    </optgroup>
  </select>
</form>
```

FIGURE 5.42 Example usage of the `<select>` element.

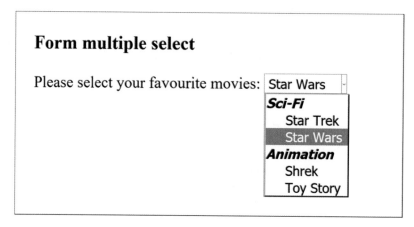

FIGURE 5.43   Rendered result of Figure 5.42.

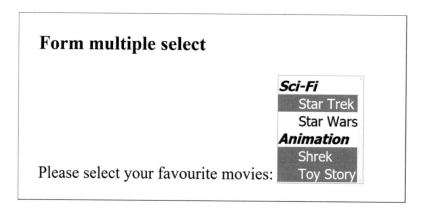

FIGURE 5.44   Using the multiple attribute with the `<select>` element.

The `<select>` element also supports the selection of multiple options when the `multiple` attribute is used on it. The value of the `size` attribute can be set high to show many or all the options at once in order to make this easier. Figure 5.44 shows the result of the same code in Figure 5.42 but with the `multiple` attribute specified and the `size` attribute set to 6. Users can select more than one option by holding down a modifier key (e.g., Shift or Ctrl in Windows and Command or Option in Mac) while clicking the options. In the example, three options are selected. However, the use of **multiple select menus is not recommended** because of the difficulty in using them. For example, many people may not know how to use modifier keys. It may be better to use checkboxes where users are allowed to make multiple selections.

CHALLENGE 5.20

Render the code in Figure 5.42 and experiment with the `multiple` and `size` attributes to see the effects. Also, notice that the list is displayed upward. Place the select control under the prompting text, on a separate line instead of placing it on the same line, and see how this behavior changes.

5.4.4.2 `<datalist>`...`</datalist>`

Like the `<select>` element, the `<datalist>` element creates a drop-down list, but it works in a different way. It works in combination with the text-type `<input>` and `<option>` elements, so that what is typed inside the text field determines the options displayed on the drop-down list. The element takes no special attributes; it takes only global ones, such as `id`. Figure 5.45 shows how it is used, and Figure 5.46 depicts the result.

In the example, when the user clicks, double clicks, or starts typing in the text-input field, the drop-down list is displayed, from which the user can choose one. If it is a long list and the desired item is not visible, then, as the user starts typing the desired word, the items are narrowed down to those that match the most to what is currently typed. However, for the element to work properly in this way, the value of the `list` attribute on the `<input>` element must match the value of the `id` attribute on the `<datalist>` element, which is "browsers" in this case.

```
HTML
<h3>Datalist</h3>
<form>
  Enter your favorite browser:
  <input type="text" name="favBrowser" list="browsers">
  <datalist id="browsers">
    <option value="Internet Explorer">
    <option value="Firefox">
    <option value="Chrome">
    <option value="Safari">
    <option value="Opera">
  </datalist>
</form>
```

FIGURE 5.45 Example usage of the `<datalist>` element.

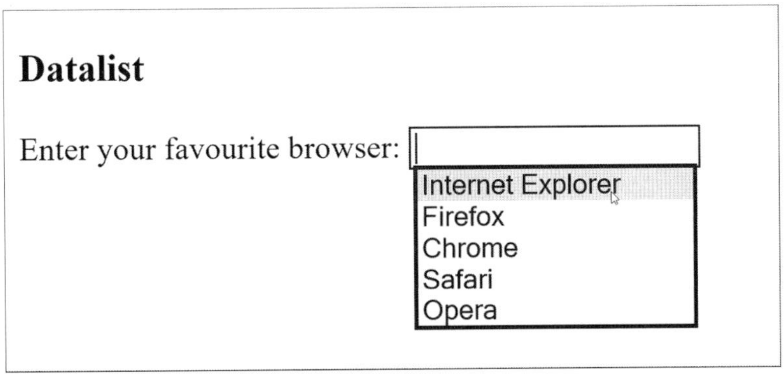

FIGURE 5.46 The result of Figure 5.45.

CHALLENGE 5.21

Implement the example and make the text box appear under the label instead of making it appear to its right. Also, interact with it to see how it works to better understand how to use it.

5.4.5 Showing Task Progress

5.4.5.1 `<progress>...</progress>`

The `<progress>` element allows you to display a control to show the progress of a task. The display is static and shows only a snapshot rather than a continuous display. In order to create a dynamic display, a script will have to be used to display snapshots at intervals. The specific attributes that it supports are `value` (which specifies the amount of task completed) and `max` (which specifies the total amount of task available to do). Figure 5.47 shows how the element is used, and Figure 5.48 depicts the result.

```
HTML
<h3>Form progress element</h3>
<form>
  <p>Progress:<progress value="30" max="100"></p>
</form>
```

FIGURE 5.47 Example usage of the `<progress>` element.

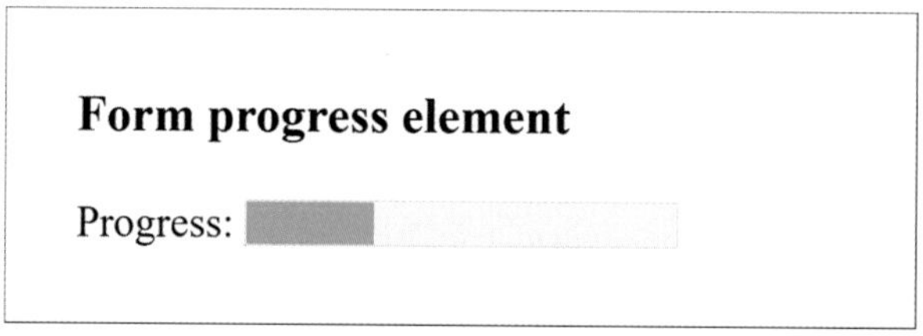

FIGURE 5.48 Rendered result of Figure 5.47.

CHALLENGE 5.22

For which of the following would you use the `<progress>` element and why?

- The number sold from stock of an item.
- Time-based information.
- State of stock of an item.
- Provide information about how full a theater is.
- The sales of tickets for a concert.

5.4.6 Displaying Measurement

5.4.6.1 `<meter>...</meter>`

The `<meter>` element is used to display a control that shows a gauge. Note that its function is different from that of the `<progress>` element and should be seen as displaying a measure of fullness, emptiness of capacity, speed, and so on. Table 5.15 lists the attributes that it supports, while Figures 5.49 and 5.50 show how it is used and also depict the result.

TABLE 5.15

Attributes for `<meter>` Element

Attribute	Function
value	Specifies the measurement.
min	Specifies the lower limit of the range for the meter.
max	Specifies the upper limit of the range for the meter.
low	Specifies the point that marks the upper limit of the "low" part of the meter.
high	Specifies the point that marks the lower limit of the "high" part of the meter.
optimum	Specifies the optimum position for the meter.

```
HTML
<h3>Form meter element</h3>
<form>
  Voter turnout: <meter value=0.45></meter><span> 45%</span>
</form>
```

FIGURE 5.49 Example usage of the `<meter>` element.

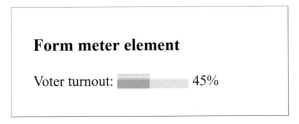

FIGURE 5.50 Rendered result of Figure 5.49.

CHALLENGE 5.23

For which of the following would you use the `<meter>` element?

- The number sold from stock of an item.
- Measure of sales.
- State of stock of an item.

5.4.7 Outputting Calculation Result

5.4.7.1 `<output>...<output>`

The `<output>` element is used to display the result of a calculation. However, the use of JavaScript is necessary to use it. To address this, HTML5 also includes the **valueAsNumber** property of JavaScript, which returns a string as a number and is relatively straightforward to use. Table 5.16 lists the attributes supported by the element. Figure 5.51 shows how the element is used, and Figure 5.52 depicts the result.

The example shows two numbers being added together, as each is inputted by the user. The **number-input type** (discussed earlier) is used to collect each number, and the `<output>` element displays the content of the value of the `name` attribute (i.e., "sum"). The `oninput` event attribute on the `<form>` element takes care of the addition of the numbers and the placing of the result in "sum." The equation says to take the values stored in "a" and "b," use the `valueAsNumber` function to change each to a number,

TABLE 5.16

Attributes for `<output>` Element

Attribute	Function
name	Specifies the name for element.
for	Specifies in a space-separated list the `id` values of elements used in a calculation.
form	Specifies the `id` value on the form with which to associate element.

```
HTML
<h3>Form output element</h3>
<form oninput="sum.value = a.valueAsNumber + b.valueAsNumber">
  <p>Please enter date:</p>
  <input id="a" name="a" type="range" step="any"> +
  <input id="b" name="b" type="number" step="any"> =
  <output name="sum" for="a b"></output>
</form>
```

FIGURE 5.51   Example usage of the `<output>` element.

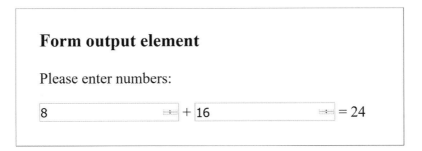

FIGURE 5.52   Rendered result of Figure 5.51.

add the numbers together, and then make the result the value of the element named "sum." Notice the **dot convention**. This is the convention used in object-oriented programming to specify to access what is stored in a variable or apply a function to it.

CHALLENGE 5.24

Write a code that displays the result of three numbers inputted by the user, the first two of which are added together and the total multiplied by the third.

5.4.8 Labeling Form Controls

5.4.8.1 `<label>...<label>`

In the examples shown so far, form controls have been labeled by simply placing text before them. However, this is limiting in various ways. For example, it makes it difficult to isolate them for styling, and since such labeling has no semantic meaning, it is not recognized by assistive technologies used by people with disabilities, making a form inaccessible to these users. The `<label>` element is designed to solve this problem and allows a label to be associated with a control. Table 5.17 lists the attributes that it supports.

The `<label>` element can be used with or without the `for` attribute and can be wrapped around just the label of a form element or the label and the element. Figure 5.53 shows typical usage, and Figure 5.54 depicts the result.

Notice that all the approaches produce the same type of labeling. In the code, numbers **1** and **2** show just the `<label>` element used, first to encapsulate the label and second to encapsulate both the label and the `<input>` element. Numbers **3** and **4** use the same principles but with the addition of the `for` and `id` attributes. This is known as the **label reference technique**, because the `id` attribute is used to

TABLE 5.17

Attributes for `<label>` Element

Attribute	Function
for	Specifies the control with which to associate label.
form	Specifies the form with which to associate label.

```
HTML
<h3>Form label element</h3>
<form>
  Please enter details:
  <p><label>Username:</label><input type="text"
     name="uname"></p>                              ①
  <p><label>Password:<input type="password" name="password">
     </label></p>                                    ②
  <p><label for="email">Email:</label><input type="email"
     name="email" id="email"></p>                   ③
  <p><label for="phone">Phone:<input type="tel" name="phone" ④
     id="phone"></label></p>
</form>
```

FIGURE 5.53   Example usage of the `<label>` element.

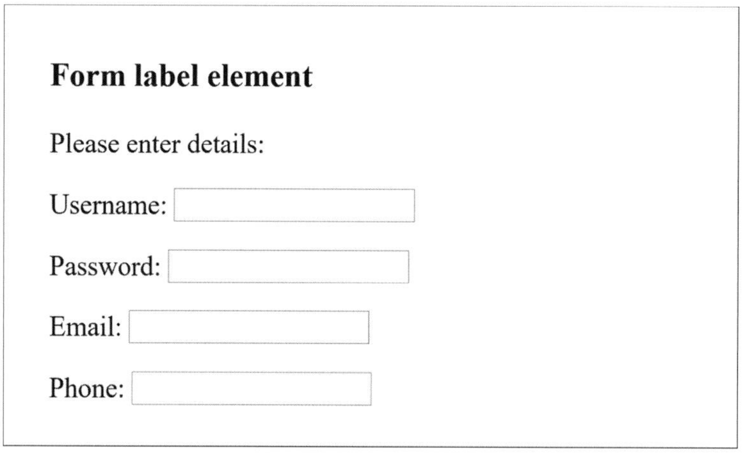

Form label element

Please enter details:

Username: _____

Password: _____

Email: _____

Phone: _____

FIGURE 5.54   Rendered result of Figure 5.53.

associate the `<input>` element with the `<label>` element. Since an `id` is unique in a form, only one label can be associated with a form control. While all the four approaches are compatible with assistive technologies and are supported by HTML specification, number **3** is most commonly used, because it allows for the label to be styled separately and is consistent with how other types of controls are labeled.

In some cases, the purpose of a form control may be clear enough, such that adding a label will create redundancy visually. An example is a text field that has a search button next to it. In such cases, although label is still added to make the control accessible to assistive technologies, it is made invisible by hiding it by using CSS. An alternative is to use the `aria-label` attribute, which provides a label to identify a form control to assistive technologies but does not provide the information visually. Figure 5.55 shows how the attribute is used, and Figure 5.56 depicts the result. Although the `title` attribute can also be used for this, it is not supported by some screen readers and assistive technologies.

```
HTML
<h3>Form aria-label</h3>
<form>
  <input type="text" name="search" aria-label="Search">
  <button type="submit">Search</button>
</form>
```

FIGURE 5.55 Example usage of the `aria-label` attribute.

Form aria-label

FIGURE 5.56 Rendered result of Figure 5.55.

5.4.8.2 Labeling and Accessibility

In addition to the point just made about labels and accessibility, there are other guide-lines, especially regarding the placement of labels in relation to form controls. Although there are no strict rules, the best practice is to **follow popular placement convention**. This ensures that a form is not confusing to use and is accessible. For form controls that display text fields and select boxes, the convention is to place labels above them or to the left, depending on various factor. For example, visually impaired users and mobile phone users benefit from placing them above, because this reduces the width of a form and therefore the need for horizontal scrolling. For radio buttons and checkboxes, it is typical to place labels to the right.

NOTE: Accessibility

- If an image, such as an asterisk, is used in front of the label of a required control, then the `<label>` element should encapsulate it.
- Form buttons (e.g., **submit-input** and **reset-input** types and `<button>` element) do not require additional accessibility information. The value of the `value` attribute used with the `<input>` element and the content of the `<button>` element provide the necessary information for the screen reader.
- When an **image-input type** is used for a button, the `alt` attribute should be used with the `<input>` element to provide accessibility information.
- If a form control is not labeled, because it is apparent visually, then a hidden label should be considered.

CHALLENGE 5.25

Why is the following poor labeling practice for accessibility?

```
<label>Select ice cream flavor
    <select name="flavor">
        <option>Vanilla</option>
        <option>Chocolate</option>
        <option>Strawberry</option>
    </select>
</label>
```

CHALLENGE 5.26

How would you label the following to make it accessible? (*Hint*: label each item separately):

```
<div>Select ice cream flavor</div>
<ul>
  <li><input type="checkbox" id="a1"
      value="vanilla">Vanilla</li>
  <li><input type="checkbox" id="a2"
      value="chocolate">Chocolate</li>
  <li><input type="checkbox" id="a3"
      value="strawberry">Strawberry</li>
</ul>
```

5.4.9 Grouping Form Controls

5.4.9.1 `<fieldset>...</fieldset>/<legend>...</legend>`

The `<fieldset>` element groups together a set of controls and draws a border around them. The `<legend>` element adds caption to the border to describe the content of the group. While the `<legend>` element has no native attributes, the `<fieldset>` element takes the three attributes listed in Table 5.18. The **legend**

TABLE 5.18

Attributes for `<fieldset>` Element

Attribute	Function
name	Specifies the name for element.
disabled	Specifies to disable control, so that user cannot interact with it. It can be specified by itself, without a value (instead of `disabled="disabled"`).
form	Specifies the `id` value on the `<form>` element with which to associate element.

should be brief and descriptive, especially because screen readers usually read it out for each control in the fieldset. Figure 5.57 shows the element in use, and Figure 5.58 depicts the result.

```
HTML
<h3>Form fieldset</h3>
<form>
  <p>Please complete the form below:</p>
  <fieldset>
    <legend>Personal Info</legend>
    <p><label for="uname">Username:</label><input type="text"
       name="uname" id="uname"></p>
    <p><label for="password">Password:</label>
       <input type="password" name="password" id="password"></p>
    <p><label for="email">Email:</label><input type="email"
       name="email" id="email"></p>
    <p><label for="phone">Phone:</label><input type="tel"
       name="phone" id="phone"></p>
  </fieldset>
</form>
```

FIGURE 5.57   Example usage of the `<fieldset>` element.

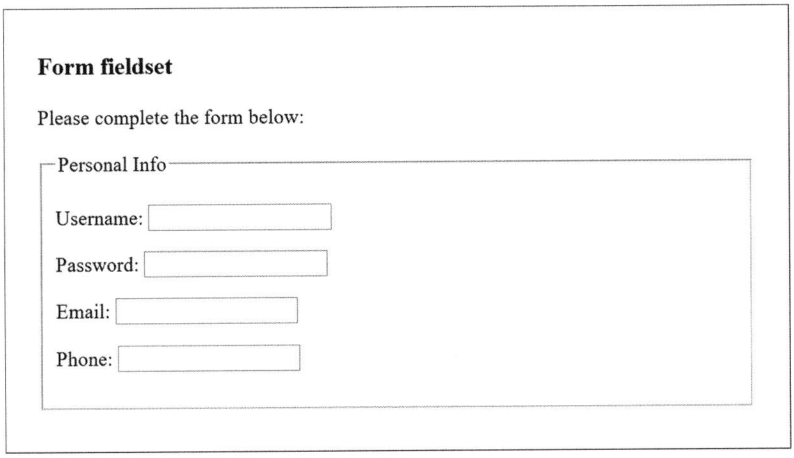

FIGURE 5.58   Rendered result of Figure 5.57.

CHALLENGE 5.27

What would happen if the `<legend>` element is used without the `<fieldset>` element?

5.4.10 An Example Form

Some of the form controls introduced so far are brought together in Figure 5.59 to produce an example of a typical form. Figure 5.60 shows the result. Notice that the text

```
HTML
<h3>Forms</h3>
<form>
  <p>Please complete the form below:</p>
  <fieldset>
    <legend>Personal Info</legend>
    <label for "fname">First name:</label><input type="text"
    name="fname" id="fname" required></label><br>
    <label for="lname">Last name:</label><input type="text"
    name="lname" id="lname"><br>
    <label for="email">Email:</label><input type="email" size="25"
    maxlength="35" name="email" id="email" placeholder=
    "e.g., joe@example.com"><br>
    <label for="url">Your personal URL (if any):</label>
    <input type="url" name="url" id="url"><br>
    <input type="radio" name="sex" value="male" id="sex1">
    <label for="sex1">Male</label>
    <input type="radio" name="sex" value="female" id="sex2">
    <label for="sex2">Female</label><br>
  </fieldset>
  <fieldset>
    <legend>Other Info</legend>
    Which of these do you own?<br>
    <input type="checkbox" name="car" id="own1">
    <label for="own1">Car</label>
    <input type="checkbox" name="bike" id="own2">
    <label for="own2">Bike</label>
    <br>
    <label for="fav_movie">Favorite Movie:</label>
    <select name="fav_movie" id="fav_movie">
     <optgroup label="Sci-Fi">
       <option value="startrek">Star Trek</option>
       <option value="starwars">Star Wars</option>
     </optgroup>
     <optgroup label="Animation">
       <option value="Shrek">Shrek</option>
       <option value="toystory">Toy Story</option>
     </optgroup>
    </select>
    <br>
    <label for="info">Extra info:</label><br>
    <textarea rows="4" cols="35" name="info" id="info">
    </textarea><br>
  </fieldset>
  <input type="submit" value="Submit">
  <input type="reset" value="Cancel"><br>
</form>
```

FIGURE 5.59   The <form> element and associated elements and attributes.

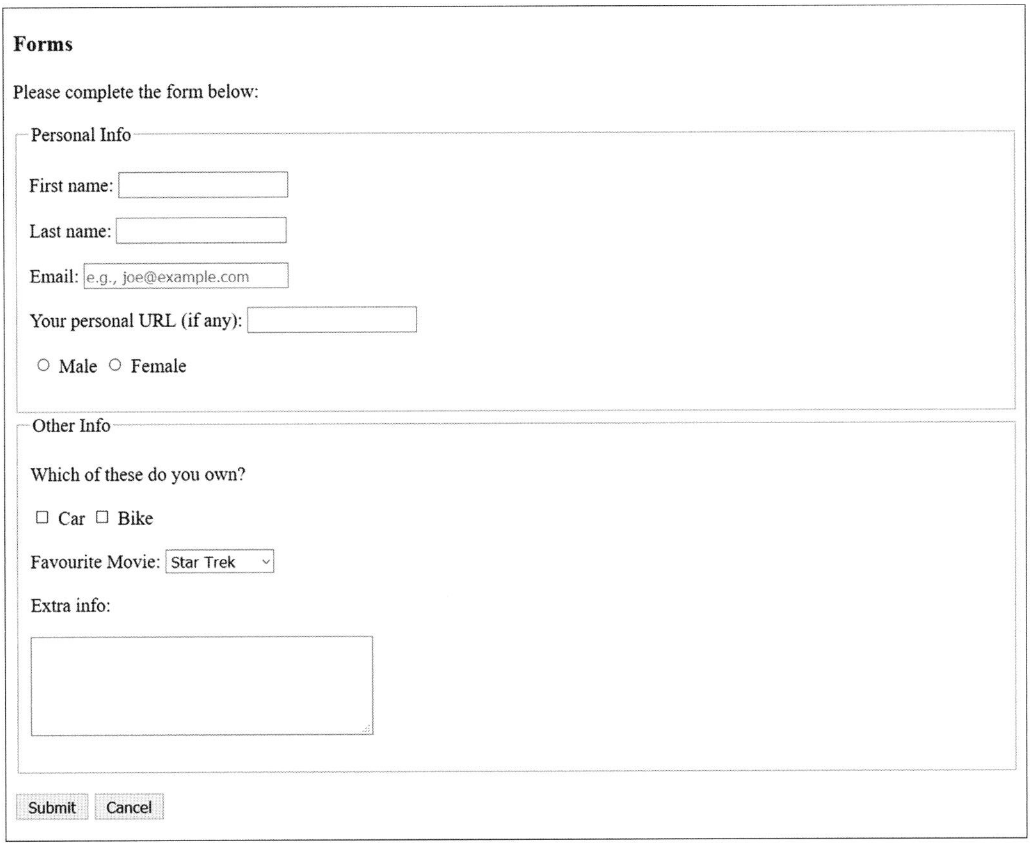

FIGURE 5.60 The code in Figure 5.59 rendered in a browser.

input fields are not properly aligned vertically. In order for a form to look professional and be easy to use, these fields should be properly aligned. This is done using CSS, and how this is done is explained in Chapter 17.

CHALLENGE 5.28

Insert appropriate markup in the code in Figure 5.59 to create line space between the controls, so that the form looks more spacious.

NOTE: Form in a dialog box

As mentioned in Chapter 3, a form can be integrated into a dialog, so that when the form is submitted, it disappears with the dialog. This is done by placing the `<form>` element in the `<dialog>` element and by using the value of `"dialog"` with the `method` attribute of the `<form>` element (thus: `method:"dialog"`).

5.5 Form Design Guidelines

Forms should be aesthetically pleasing and easy to use in order to make interaction with them a good experience. The following are some guidelines on how these goals can be achieved:

- **Related fields should be grouped together** and arranged in a logical order, such as by enclosing them in a box or by using the same color, with each group having a meaningful title. The form itself should have a meaningful title.
- **Layout should be visually appealing,** with ample use of white space and properly aligned fields.
- The **size of fields should match or be longer than the size of data** to be entered, so that what users enter does not disappear into the left or right edges of the box, making it hard for them to follow what they are entering.
- **Only really important questions should be asked**; for example, asking for salutation is not always necessary.
- If possible, **each field should be validated immediately after it is completed** and correction should be requested, if necessary.
- **Users should be allowed to enter numbers**, such as phone and credit card numbers, in flexible formats, as requiring a strict format can create problems for some users, particularly the elderly.
- **Compulsory fields should be clearly marked**, such as with an asterisk, which may be in a contrasting color, typically red. However, too many compulsory fields can be discouraging, so fields should not be mandatory unless they are really necessary. Asking for users' addresses, for example, is likely to discourage them; e-mail is often adequate.
- **Keyboard focus should be set to the first field** when the form is displayed, as this minimizes total number of clicks. Also, if possible, when a field receives focus, information should be provided on the type of data required for the field.
- **It should be possible to change any entry at any point** before a form is submitted, and how to submit a form should be clearly indicated.

5.6 Useful Info

5.6.1 Web Links

HTML specifications: w3.org/TR/html51, w3.org/standards

Web development documents: docs.webplatform.org

Accessibility: w3.org/WAI/tutorials, webaim.org

HTML5 support testing: html5test.com

HTML tutorials (*Here are just a few free tutorial sites on HTML and other Web languages*): w3.org/wiki, html5rocks.com, sitepoint.com, w3schools. com, codecademy.com, quackit.com, developer.mozilla.org/en-US/docs/ Web tutorialspoint.com, whatwg.org, htmlgoodies.com, htmldog.com, htmlcodetutorial.com, echoecho.com, learn.shayhowe.com, html.net, tizag. com, html-5-tutorial.com, docs.webplatform.org, developers.google.com, webdesignermag.co.uk

6

Images

6.1 Introduction

Images have functions in almost everything we do that involves communication. Next to text, they are perhaps the most prevalent form of communicating content on the Web. Not only this, they have an indispensible role in the aesthetic appeal and the theme setting of Web pages. This chapter introduces the HTML elements used to add images, as well as design principles that guide effective use of images in Web design.

6.2 Learning Outcomes

After studying this chapter, you should:

- Know how to add single and multiples images, including image maps, to a Web page by using HTML.
- Know how to embed another document, such as an interactive direction map, in a Web page.
- Be aware of the main types of images and file formats used in Web design.
- Be aware of guidelines for using images in Web design.
- Be aware of different ways of acquiring images for use in your design.

6.3 Adding Images with HTML

An image can be added to a Web page in two main ways. It can be embedded in the current page, or a link that points to its location can be provided. In the latter case, the image is usually displayed in a page by itself. Irrespective of whether an image is embedded or linked to, it can be used as an **image map**. This is an image that contains **hotspots** (clickable areas), which when clicked result in an event occurring, such as taking the user to a different destination to provide more information. Linking to an image is achieved using the `<a>` element, introduced in Chapter 4, and embedding one is achieved using the `<img>` element.

Traditionally, only one image source could be specified using the element, but by combining it with newer elements, such as `<source>` and `<picture>`, and with

TABLE 6.1

Elements for Incorporating Image in a Web Page

Element	Function
`<img>`	Embeds an image.
`<source>`	Used to specify multiple media sources. It represents nothing when used alone.
`<picture>…<picture>`	A container that allows multiple image sources to be specified, from which one is chosen to use with the contained `<img>` element.
`<canvas>…</canvas>`	Used to draw graphics by using scripting (typically JavaScript).
`<svg>…</svg>`	Used to embed an SVG element in HTML.
`<map>…</map>`	Defines an image map.
`<area>…</area>`	Defines a region inside an image map.

newer attributes, such as `srcset` and `sizes`, it is now possible to specify **multiple image sources**, from which the browser can choose the one that is best suited for a user situation, depending on the user's device screen pixel density, zoom level, and, possibly, other factors, such as network properties. If-conditions, known as **media conditions**, can also be used to help the browser determine which images to use and when to use them, as explained later. Multiple images that are provided to the browser to choose from are generally termed **responsive images**, and the technique is a response to the need to have images that are compatible with **responsive Web design**, discussed later in Chapter 21. Table 6.1 lists the main elements used for embedding an image in a page, including those used to embed an image map.

6.3.1 `<img>`, `<source>`, and `<picture>`

The `<img>`, `<source>`, and `<picture>` elements can be combined in different ways and used with various combinations of attributes to specify either a single image source or multiple image sources. The typically used attributes and their functions are listed in Table 6.2.

TABLE 6.2

Attributes Used with Elements Used to Embed Image

Attribute	Function
src	Specifies the URL of image resource. It is **obligatory**.
height	Specifies height of image in pixels (px).
width	Specifies width of image in pixels (px).
alt	Specifies **alternative text** (or **alt text**) description of image. This is the text that is displayed when image cannot be found, is not in a supported file format, or is not yet downloaded.

(Continued)

TABLE 6.2 (*Continued*)

Attributes Used with Elements Used to Embed Image

Attribute	Function
longdesc	Used to provide URL to a file that contains longer description about an image when short text alternative is not adequate. It is not supported by major browsers as of time of writing.
srcset	Used to specify images to use in different situations (e.g., for small screens and HD displays). It specifies a single **image URL**; a comma-separated list of strings, each string containing **an image URL** and an optional **width descriptor** that is the width of image, in pixels, followed by "w" (e.g., 640w); or a **pixel density descriptor** that is a positive floating number, followed by "x" (e.g., 1.5x). The **width descriptor** lets the browser intelligently select the best image, based on screen width, and the **pixel density descriptor** lets the browser select the best image, based on device pixel density. If no pixel density descriptor is specified, 1x is used. The attribute usually renders **fixed-size** images, except when used with the w descriptor.
sizes	Specifies a single **width descriptor** (e.g., sizes="150vw") or a single media-condition-width-descriptor pair (e.g., sizes="(max-width: 800px) 150vw"). It can also specify a comma-separated list of media-condition-width-descriptor pairs, with the **media condition** omitted in the last item (e.g., sizes="(max-width: 640px) 60vw, (max-width: 340px) 100vw, 50vw"). The last item is used as **fallback**. Although the vw (**viewport width**) unit is normally used, other length units (e.g., px) can also be used. The attribute is required when the srcset attribute is used with width descriptors.
media	Used to specify the condition under which an image source is used (e.g., media="(min-width: 600px)"). It is valid only in a <source> element that is a child of the <picture> element.
type	Specifies **MIME type** (or content type) of the specified image (e.g., type="image/jpeg").

6.3.1.1 *Specifying a Single Image Source*

Although responsive image technique is the future in Web design, if a page is not required to adjust to suit different user situations, then just specifying a single image source is adequate. Also, if a page is required to adjust but the images being used are vector-based images, such as **Scalable Vector Graphics** (SVG), a single source can be used. This is because vector-based images can scale to different sizes, as necessary, without depreciation in quality or a change in file size. A single image source can be specified using just the `<img>` element and the `src` attribute. Figure 6.1 shows how this is done and the use of other relevant attributes. Figure 6.2 shows the result.

In the example, the `src` attribute specifies the image to embed (which is "yacht.jpg") and says that it is inside a folder named "images" that is inside the folder containing the HTML document. The `alt` and `longdesc` attributes perform the functions described in Table 6.2. Using the `alt` attribute also **contributes to accessibility**, because the text is what screen readers and other assistive technologies read out to visually impaired users. For this reason, it is important for alternative text to be an **accurate but concise description** of the content of the relevant image. It should not be a list of keywords (known as "**keyword stuffing**") designed to trick search engines, as this could get your website blacklisted (i.e., blocked by search engines). **For image used only for decoration, no description is required**, but the attribute should still be specified with nothing between the quotes (thus: `alt=" "`).

```
HTML
<h2>Image element</h2>
<img src="images/yacht.jpg" alt="A yacht race" title="A
  flotilla of yachts at the start of a racing regatta.
  "longdesc="yacht_race_desc.html" width="500" height="336">
```

FIGURE 6.1 Example usage of the `<img>` element.

FIGURE 6.2 Rendered result of Figure 6.1. (Image from www.freeimages.co.uk.)

The `title` attribute, which is a **global attribute**, provides additional description for the image and is usually displayed when cursor hovers over an image, as shown in the rendered example. However, the attribute should not be used for essential information, since you cannot rely on everyone having access to it, because not every user uses a mouse and some browsers may not display it.

The `width` and `height` attributes specify the rendered size of the image. Rendered image size can also be specified using CSS. Both approaches have advantages and disadvantages. Most importantly, specifying size by using attributes enables faster download and more orderly rendering of a page. It also prevents layout from having to be reflowed multiple times as the page loads. This is because text usually downloads faster than images and the browser by default does not know the size of an image. The result of this is that when the attributes are not used, text finishes downloading, the browser displays it, and then moves it around to fit in the image when the image finishes downloading, resulting in an untidy rendering process. In contrast, when the `width` and `height` attributes are specified and the browser encounters them, it reserves the right amount of space for the image and displays the text accordingly, so that when the image finishes downloading, it fits it in, without having to move the text significantly around. On the other hand, specifying size by using CSS (discussed in Chapter 15) allows for size to be controlled dynamically and also overrides whatever size is specified, using the `width` and `height` attributes.

NOTE: Another way of adding an image

It is worth noting that images can be added to a page in a way that does not require the browser to make a separate request for it, which is what happens when you link to an external image. This is done by embedding the image data directly in the code for the Web page, using the **Base64 encoding** and **data URI scheme**. Essentially, an image file is encoded in base64 and the data URI scheme used to include the encoded data. Base64 is a technique of representing binary data in ASCII (i.e., characters). The example below shows how this can be used for Figure 6.1, showing only a tiny part of the base64 data.

```
<img
  src="data:image/jpeg;base64,/9j/4AAQSkZJRgABAgEBLAEsAAD/
  4RAjR..."
  alt="A yacht race" title="A flotilla of yachts at the start
  of a racing regatta."
  longdesc="yacht_race_desc.html" width="500" height="336">
```

Although using this method reduces the number of requests to the server, the amount of base64 data generated is typically much larger than that of the corresponding image file, which by itself can affect download performance. So, the method is usually used for small images, such as image sprites. Base64 encoders can be found on the Web.

NOTE: More on image accessibility

- When **multiple images** are used together to represent a single piece of information, such as when multiple images of a star are used to represent rating, **only the text alternative of one of the images, typically the first, should describe the information**. The `alt` attributes of the others should be empty (i.e., `alt=" "`). This is so that the screen reader does not repeat the description for every image, thereby confusing and annoying users.
- When **complex images**, such as diagrams, illustrations, maps, and charts, are used, the **text alternative should be used to convey only a summary** of what the image represents. A link is then placed next to or underneath the image to a long description. **If the long description is on the same page**, then, instead of a link, its location can be included in the text alternative. The `aria-describedby` attribute can also be used with the `<img>` element instead, in order to indicate where the long description is located on the same page. Its value should be the id of the element (e.g., `<p>` element) that provides the description.

CHALLENGE 6.1

Which of the following is a better use of alternative text for an image of a garden covered in snow, and why? Also, can you write a better one?

```
<img src="image/garden.jpg" alt="Garden">
<img src="image/garden.jpg" alt="My garden in winter">
```

CHALLENGE 6.2

What is the difference between how the browser renders alt text and the `title` attribute, and which is more valuable for accessibility?

CHALLENGE 6.3

If the image in the example was in a folder named "hobbies" that is inside a folder named "images" that is inside the one containing the HTML document, how would you write the value of the `src` attribute?

CHALLENGE 6.4

Assuming the file names of the following two images of a star,  are "full_star.png" and "empty_star.png", write a code that displays the rating below, making the text alternative "Item rating: 3 out of 5 stars.":

★★★☆☆

CHALLENGE 6.5

In CHALLENGE 6.4, which of the five star images that form the rating should carry the alternative text that describes the function of the images, and why? Also, if your answer is that only some of the images should carry the function description, what should the `alt` values for other images be?

6.3.1.2 Making an Image a Link, and Linking to an Image

Making an image clickable is an essential Web design practice and is done using the `<a>` element, which is the same element used to turn text into a hyperlink. The element and how the `href` attribute is used on it to create a link were discussed in Chapter 4. Figure 6.3 shows how this is done, and Figure 6.4 depicts the result.

In the example, notice that the entire `<img>` element, including all its attributes, is placed between the tags of the `<a>` element, just as is done to create text links. Also, notice that the cursor has changed shape to indicate that the image is clickable. Incidentally, the type of cursor shape to display can be specified using CSS. How this is done is shown in Chapter 17. The text link under the image links to the same image but displays it in a separate window when clicked. The first `<br>` element is used to place the link on a separate line, and the second to create an extra line. This is necessary, since `<img>` and `<a>` are inline elements and do not start on a new line.

```
HTML
<h2>Image link</h2>
<a href="http://www.w3c.org"><img src="images/yacht.jpg"
 width="500" height="336" alt="A yacht race image"
 title="A flotilla of yachts at the start of a racing
 regatta."></a>
<br><br>
<a href="images/yacht.jpg">A yacht race</a>
```

FIGURE 6.3   Using the `<a>` element to make an image a link and link to an image.

FIGURE 6.4 Rendered result of Figure 6.3. (Image from www.freeimages.co.uk.)

CHALLENGE 6.6

How can you achieve the same goal achieved with the `<br>` elements in the example without using the elements?

NOTE: Functional image accessibility

A functional image is one that is used to perform a specific function, such as linking to a destination and starting an action. To make the purpose of a functional image accessible to visually impaired users, the **text alternative should describe the function rather than the image**. For instance, in the example in Figure 6.3, "See a yacht race image" makes the image link more accessible than "An image of a yacht race."

6.3.1.3 Containing and Captioning Images Properly

Traditionally, the `<img>` element would be placed in the `<p>` or `<div>` element in order to be able to treat it as a self-contained unit. However, these elements are not semantically related to images. The `<figure>` container element, introduced in Chapter 2, was designed to address this. It allows images or a combination of media elements to be contained and treated as a separate unit. The `<figcaption>` element is intended to be used to add caption to the container. Figure 6.5 shows how the elements are used, and Figure 6.6 depicts the result.

```
HTML
<figure>
  <h2>Containing images</h2>
  <img src="images/car_tunnel.jpg" width="500" height="336"
   alt="A car in a tunnel" title="A car driving through a
   traffic tunnel.">
  <figcaption>
     A car driving through a traffic tunnel.
  </figcaption>
</figure>
```

FIGURE 6.5   Example usage of `<figure>` and `<figcaption>`.

Containing images

A car driving through a traffic tunnel.

FIGURE 6.6   Rendered result of Figure 6.5.

CHALLENGE 6.7

In the code example, why is the `<h2>` element placed inside the `<figure>` element and not outside of it?

6.3.1.4 Specifying Multiple Image Sources

In order to specify multiple image sources (i.e., **responsive images**), the `<picture>` and `<source>` elements need to be used with the `<img>` element, together with various combinations of the `srcset`, `sizes`, `media`, and `type` attributes. Situations in which it is necessary to use responsive images are known as **use cases**. More than one situation can occur together, in which case each situation is addressed. The commonly recognized use cases and how to specify responsive images for them are discussed here.

6.3.1.4.1 Specifying for Different Device Pixel Ratios

A device display screen is made up of many tiny dots called **pixels**. Device pixel ratio is the ratio of the number of these **physical screen pixels** to a **CSS pixel**, while CSS pixels are pixels used to specify lengths of elements in CSS. The difference between the two pixel types is that the size of a device pixel is typically fixed, while that of a CSS pixel is variable and can be smaller or larger than a device pixel. For example, if an image that has a width of 200 px is zoomed in, it takes up more device pixels; however, the number of CSS pixels remains the same (i.e., 200) and the CSS pixels only expand as necessary. High-resolution screens usually contain multiple device pixels per CSS pixel. Device screen pixels are explained further later in the chapter. Providing multiple images based on device pixel ratio is sometimes called **resolution switching** and is necessary in situations where different users might have different technology-based circumstances. For example:

- Users' devices might have different physical screen sizes, usually measured diagonally.
- Users might have screens with different pixel densities (i.e., pixels per inch).
- Different zoom levels might be used.
- Screen orientation might be different (e.g., landscape and portrait).
- Network conditions (e.g., speed) might be different. This helps prevent the download of unnecessarily large images for slow systems.

To specify multiple images to deal with the above situations, the `<img>` element is used with the `src` and `srcset` attributes, along with the x descriptor. Figure 6.7 shows how this is done.

```
HTML
<img src="images/yacht-400.jpg"
    srcset="images/yacht-600.jpg 1.5x,
            images/yacht-800.jpg 2x"
    alt="A yacht race"
    title="A flotilla of yachts at the start of a racing
           regatta."
    longdesc="yacht_race_desc.html"
    width="400" height="268">
```

FIGURE 6.7 Specifying responsive images for device-pixel-ratio use case.

In the example, the browser selects any of the image sources specified in the `src-set` attribute, using the specified pixel density descriptors (`1.5x` and `2x`), also known as **display density descriptors**. Essentially, on displays with 1.5 device pixels per CSS pixel, the image with `1.5x` pixel density is used, and on those with 2 device pixels per CSS pixel, the image with `2x` pixel density is used. This means that browsers on devices with **high-PPI** (pixels per inch) screens select a high-resolution image (i.e., one with `1.5x` or `2x`) and other browsers select a normal (`1x`) image. Where no `x` descriptor is specified, it is assumed to be `1x`. If a browser does not support the `srcset` attribute, it uses the image source specified in the `src` attribute as fallback. Newer browsers that support `srcset` attribute usually use the source as one of the options and use it as if specified with a `1x` descriptor. How `x` descriptors work in relation to image dimensions is that if the normal-resolution image is 400 × 268 and `1x`, then the image specified with `1.5x` should be 600 × 402 and the image with `2x` should be 800 × 536. Notice that the naming of the image files matches the `x` descriptors' values. This is only good practice to avoid confusion and does not affect anything.

CHALLENGE 6.8

Implement the example and vary the width of the browser to see the behavior of the image.

CHALLENGE 6.9

If the dimensions of an image that you want to use with `1x` descriptor are 500 × 325 px, what should be the dimensions for the `1.5x` version?

6.3.1.4.2 *Specifying for Different Viewport Sizes*

Providing multiple images for different viewport sizes is necessary in situations where different users might have devices that have different viewport widths. For example, a banner might be required to span the width of the viewport, whatever the size of the viewport, or an image might need to be sized to fit the width of differently sized columns. To specify responsive images to deal with these situations, the `<img>` element is used with the `src`, `srcset`, and `sizes` attributes, together with the w (width) descriptor. Figure 6.8 shows how this is done.

In the example, the `sizes` attribute specifies that image should take up 100% of the width of the viewport. The `srcset` attribute provides the image sources from which to choose, along with their width descriptors (i.e., widths), and the `src` attribute specifies the fallback image when none of the options are suitable. The browser uses this information and various other factors to determine the best image source to select, and the selected image is displayed and scaled up or down to fit the full width of the viewport.

```
HTML
<img sizes="100vw"
    srcset="images/yacht-200.jpg 200w,
            images/yacht-400.jpg 400w,
            images/yacht-800.jpg 800w,
            images/yacht-1600.jpg 1600w"
    src="images/yacht-400.jpg"
        alt="A yacht race">
```

FIGURE 6.8   Specifying responsive images for viewport-size-based use case.

CHALLENGE 6.10

Ensuring that you have created the necessary versions (shown in the example) of the same image, implement the example and experiment with the width of the browser. Also, experiment with the value of the `sizes` attribute to see the effect.

6.3.1.4.2.1 Specifying for Different Viewport Sizes Using Media Condition
Figure 6.9 shows how **media condition** is used to specify the viewport widths at which different images should be used. These specified widths are called **image breakpoints** and are different from the **breakpoints for responsive layouts**, discussed later in Chapter 21.

In the example, the `sizes` attribute specifies that if the browser window's width is 480 CSS pixels or less to make image take up 100% of the viewport width; if it is not, but is 800 CSS pixels or less, to make image take up 70%; and if it is neither of the two (i.e., if it is wider than 800px), to make image take up a width equal to the value specified by the last item, which is 600px. When a media condition is true, the browser uses the associated rendered size (i.e., 100 or 70 vw) and the width descriptors in the `srcset` attribute to determine which image source to select. The selected image is then scaled up or down to occupy the specified percentage of the viewport. In basic terms, the code says that the wider the width of the browser, the less the percentage of it that should be taken up by the image.

```
HTML
<img sizes="(max-width: 480px) 100vw, (max-width: 800px) 70vw,
            600px"
    srcset="images/yacht-200.jpg 200w,
            images/yacht-400.jpg 400w,
            images/yacht-800.jpg 800w,
            images/yacht-1600.jpg 1600w"
    src="images/yacht-400.jpg"
    alt="A yacht race">
```

FIGURE 6.9   Specifying responsive images for viewport-size-based use case, using media condition.

> **NOTE: Using CSS to calculate width**
>
> It is worth noting that image width can be specified using the CSS `calc()` function, which lets the browser calculate it dynamically, based on viewport width. The function is discussed more fully in Chapter 10.

> **NOTE: Responsive image breakpoints generators**
>
> It may be useful to know that there are free tools on the Web for determining breakpoints for responsive images. An example is **responsivebreakpoints.com**, which allows you to upload a file, from which breakpoints are determined and the generated responsive images and markup are provided for download. Again, more about breakpoints is discussed in Chapter 21.

CHALLENGE 6.11

Try out the example by using the images that you used in the previous challenge and experiment with the width of the browser to see the effects of the media conditions. Also, experiment with the values of the `sizes` attribute to see the effect.

6.3.1.4.3 Specifying for Different Image Contents

Providing multiple images that have varying content is necessary in situations where different users might want to change the content or aspect ratio of an image to ensure that it is displayed in the best way, based on the size of a page or a screen. For example, the same image can be shown full size on large screens, showing everything contained in it, or it can be zoomed in and cropped on smaller screens to show only important parts. Providing multiple images for purposes such as these is known as **art direction**. To specify responsive images to solve such use case, the `<picture>` element and the `<source>` element, together with the `media` attribute, are used. Figure 6.10 shows how this can be achieved.

```
HTML
<picture>
   <source media="(min-width: 720px)"
    srcset="images/yacht-fullshot.jpg">
   <source media="(min-width: 512px)"
    srcset="images/yacht-midshot.jpg">
   <img src="images/yacht-closeshot.jpg" alt="A yacht race">
</picture>
```

FIGURE 6.10   Specifying responsive images for image-content-based use case.

In the example, the browser selects the first `<source>` element and evaluates the condition in the `media` attribute. If it is true, it chooses the image source in the corresponding `srcset` attribute. If the condition is false, the browser goes to the next `<source>` element and does the same thing. If all the conditions in the `<source>` elements are false, the image source in the `<img>` element is used. This means that if the browser's width is 720 px or more, "`images/yacht-fullshot.jpg`" is selected; if the width is 512 px or more, "`images/yacht-midshot.jpg`" is selected; otherwise, "`images/yacht-closeshot.jpg`" is selected.

Notice that the dimensions of the images are not specified. They need to be specified, so that the browser can allocate space for the images before they are downloaded and so prevent multiple reflowing of layout during page rendering. To provide the dimensions, CSS properties and **CSS media queries** (or **media conditions**) are used, and how to do this is explained in Chapter 15. Also, to provide the dimensions for old browsers that do not support the `<picture>` element, the `width` and `height` attributes can also be used on the `<img>` element.

CHALLENGE 6.12

Try out the example. To do this, open a full-shot image in an image editor program such as Photoshop, then scale and crop it accordingly to produce the mid-shot and close-shot images, and use them as in the code.

6.3.1.4.3.1 Specifying for Different Image Contents and Device Pixel Ratios   It is possible to have situations where, in addition to solving for differences in image content, there is the need to solve for device pixel ratio. In such cases, images provided in different widths are also provided in different pixel densities. Figure 6.11 shows an example of how this is done.

The `<source>` element in the example says that if the browser window's width is 1024px or wider, to use one of the image sources in the `srcset` attribute used on it, based on the screen pixel density and other factors the browser deems relevant. This means that the high-resolution images (i.e., those with `2x` and `3x`) are used for high-resolution

```
HTML
<picture>
  <source media="(min-width: 1024px)"
          srcset="images/yacht-fullshot.jpg,
                  images/yacht-fullshot-2x.jpg 2x,
                  images/yacht-fullshot-3x.jpg 3x">
  <img src="images/yacht-closeshot.jpg" alt="A yacht race"
       srcset="images/yacht-closeshot-2x.jpg 2x,
               images/yacht-closeshot-3x.jpg 3x">
</picture>
```

FIGURE 6.11   Specifying responsive images for content and pixel ratio use case.

screens and the normal-resolution images are used for standard-resolution screens. If the width of the browser window is less than 1024 px, one of the image sources specified in the `<img>` element is used. Again, the high-resolution images are used for high-resolution screens and the normal-resolution images are used for standard-resolution screens.

CHALLENGE 6.13

Assuming that you want to display a 640 × 480 image named "large-field.jpg" on screens that are 1024 CSS pixels wide or more and a smaller 320 × 240 image named "small-field.jpg" on screens that are 1023 CSS pixels wide or less, write an HTML code to implement this.

6.3.1.4.4 Specifying for Different Image File Formats

When the browsers of different users are likely to support different image file formats, it might be necessary to provide images in multiple file formats. You might, for example, want to offer a not-so-popular format that is smaller in file size and has better quality (in case a user's browser supports it) and a more popular format that has a poorer quality. This is done using the `type` attribute. Figure 6.12 shows an example of how this is done.

In the example, each `srcset` attribute specifies an image source and the `type` attribute specifies its MIME type. The browser goes through each `<source>` element and selects the first one that specifies an image whose format it supports. If it supports none of them, it selects the format specified in the `<img>` element. Notice how the `<figure>` and `<figcaption>` elements are used. They have the same effect as in when specifying a single image, such as shown earlier in Figure 6.6.

```
HTML
<figure>
  <picture>
    <source srcset="images/yacht.webp" type="image/webp">
    <source srcset="images/yacht.jxr" type="image/vnd.ms-photo">
    <source srcset="images/yacht.jp2" type="image/jp2">
    <img src="images/yacht.jpg" width="500"
      height="336" alt="A yacht race">
  </picture>
  <figcaption>
    A yacht race in progress.
  </figcaption>
</figure>
```

FIGURE 6.12 Specifying responsive images for image-format-based use case.

CHALLENGE 6.14

Would the example work correctly if the `<picture>` element is not used and why?

6.3.2 `<canvas>...</canvas>`

The `<canvas>` element allows you to draw graphics on the fly. This enables the creation of dynamic images, such as the ones necessary in games, generation of graphs, and other images in real time. The attributes that it supports are `width` and `height`. Figure 6.13 shows how it is used. The example creates a canvas that is 150 × 150 pixels in size and has a unique identification of "oneCanvas." The fallback statement is displayed if a browser does not support the element. Note that because the element is just a container element, it does not display anything on its own, so the code does not display anything. How it is combined with JavaScript to display images is discussed in Chapter 22.

6.3.3 `<svg>...</svg>`

The `<svg>` element makes it possible to add to a Web page a type of image known as **vector image** (discussed more fully later in this chapter), which is created using coordinates. The element is useful for creating basic images on the fly but requires the understanding of a different type of markup language called SVG, which is beyond the scope of this book. Figure 6.14 shows how it is placed in an HTML document, and Figure 6.15 depicts the result. In the example, the SVG `<svg>` element defines

```
HTML
<body>
 <h3>Canvas element</h3>
 <canvas id="oneCanvas" width="150" height="150">
   Your user agent does not support the HTML5 canvas element.
 </canvas>
</body>
```

FIGURE 6.13 Example usage of the `<canvas>` element.

```
HTML
<body>
 <h2>SVG element</h2>
 <svg width="400" height="400">
   <rect x="30" y="10" width="250"
     height="250" rx="20"
     style="fill:#2111C0; stroke:#000000;
     stroke-width:2px;" />
   <rect x="90" y="70" width="250"
     height="250" rx="20"
     style="fill:#E10000; stroke:#000000;
     stroke-width:2px;" />
 </svg>
</body>
```

Description of rectangles

FIGURE 6.14 Example usage of the `<svg>` element.

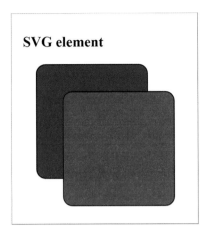

FIGURE 6.15   The result of Figure 6.14.

the image, the `width` and `height` attributes define the size, and the SVG `<rect>` elements define the rectangles and their sizes.

6.3.4 `<map>...</map>` and `<area>...</area>`

As mentioned earlier, the `<map>` and `<area>` elements are combined with the `<img>` element to create **image mapping**. To be able to use these elements to create image maps, they need to be combined with various attributes. Table 6.3 lists them and their functions.

   Image mapping has many applications. It is especially useful for providing information about different areas represented on a geographical map that would be impractical to put on the map. Essentially, an image map enables geometric areas placed on an image to be associated with hyperlinks. Creation of an image map involves the following:

1. **Declaring and naming of map**, using the `<map>` element with the `name` attribute.
2. **Creating the hotspot regions**, using the `<area>` element with the `shape` and `coords` attributes. The coordinates of shapes are typically difficult to work out. However, there are now various tools on the Web for doing this.

TABLE 6.3

Attributes Used in Image Mapping

Attribute	Function
name	Specifies a unique name for element.
href	Specifies the URL (address) of the destination of a link.
shape	Defines the type of shape to be created in an image map.
coords	Defines the x-y coordinates for the shape to be created.
usemap	Used with the `<img>` element to specify the name of the image map to use with an image to produce an image map.

A search for "image mapping" should reveal some of them. They allow an image to be uploaded and hotspots to be drawn on it, after which the x-y coordinates are generated, based on the top-left corner of the image being 0,0. Some also generate the image-map HTML code.

3. **Linking of the hotspots to the desired destinations** (files), using the `href` attribute.

4. **Associating the map with an image** containing areas and labels that correspond to the hotspots, using the `usemap` attribute. This, in principle, is like superimposing the hotspot shapes on the image.

Figure 6.16 gives a rough illustration of the components of an image map, and Figure 6.17 shows part of the code for implementing an image map.

In the example, the first `<area>` element creates a hotspot shape of the London region, which when clicked takes users to another page that provides information about the region. The second `<area>` element does the same for the Northeast region, and all the other regions (i.e., hotspot shapes) are created in the same way, all of which are enclosed within the `<map>` element. In the `coords` attributes, the first two numbers specify the x-y coordinates of the first point of the shape being created, and the next two numbers specify the x-y coordinates of the second point, and so on.

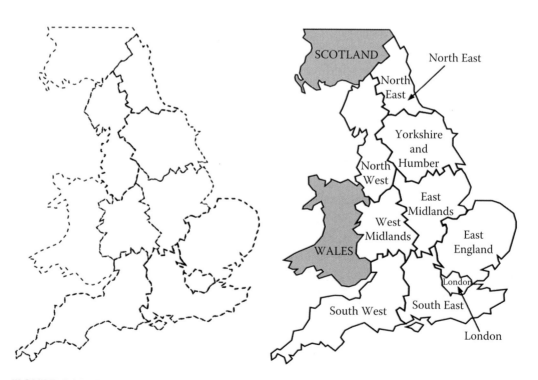

FIGURE 6.16 Map of hotspot shapes (left) and the image (right) with which it is combined to produce a clickable image.

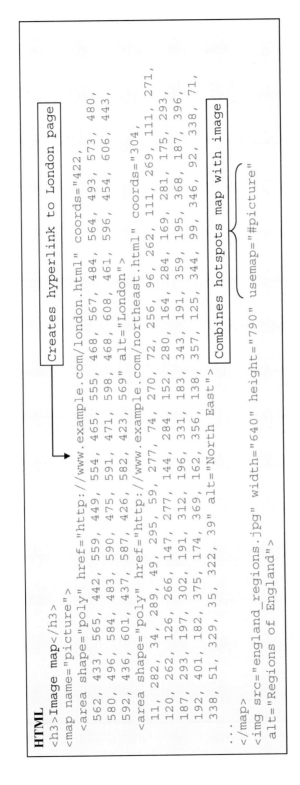

HTML

```
<h3>Image map</h3>
<map name="picture">
<area shape="poly" href="http://www.example.com/london.html" coords="422,
    562, 433, 565, 442, 559, 554, 465, 555, 468, 567, 484, 564, 493, 573, 480,
    580, 496, 584, 483, 590, 475, 591, 471, 598, 468, 608, 461, 596, 454, 606, 443,
    592, 436, 601, 437, 587, 426, 582, 423, 569" alt="London">
<area shape="poly" href="http://www.example.com/northeast.html" coords="304,
    11, 282, 34, 289, 49, 295, 59, 277, 74, 270, 72, 256, 96, 262, 111, 269, 111, 271,
    120, 262, 126, 266, 147, 277, 144, 284, 152, 280, 164, 284, 169, 281, 175, 293,
    187, 293, 197, 302, 191, 312, 196, 331, 183, 343, 191, 359, 195, 368, 187, 396,
    192, 401, 182, 375, 174, 369, 162, 356, 138, 357, 125, 344, 99, 346, 92, 338, 71,
    338, 51, 329, 35, 322, 39" alt="North East">
...
</map>
<img src="england_regions.jpg" width="640" height="790" usemap="#picture"
    alt="Regions of England">
```

Creates hyperlink to London page

Combines hotspots map with image

FIGURE 6.17 Example usage of image-mapping elements.

NOTE: The `<object>...</object>` **element**

The `<object>` element, too, can be used for adding images and image mapping. For example, the line `<img src="images/yacht.jpg" alt="A yacht race">` can be written as:

```
<object data="images/yacht.jpg" type="image/jpeg"> </object>
```

The line `<img src="england _ regions.jpg" width="340" height="790" alt="Regions of England" usemap="#picture">` in Figure 6.13 can be written as:

```
<object data="england _ regions.jpg" type="image/jpeg" width="640"
height="790" usemap="#picture">Regions of England</object>
```

The element can also be used to add dynamic media objects, such as video and audio, as shown in Chapter 7.

NOTE: Types of image mapping

There are two types of image mapping: **client-side** and **server-side** image mapping. Client-side image mapping is the one described here and the one that is recommended, for performance reasons. In **client-side** image mapping, when a hotspot is clicked, it is the Web client that deals with it. In contrast, in **server-side** image mapping, coordinates of the point clicked on an image by the user are sent to the server for the request to be dealt with, which can result in extra work for the server and the slowing of browsing.

NOTE: Image map accessibility

To ensure the accessibility of an image map, alternative text should be included for the entire map to describe the overall context for the set of links and for each clickable area to describe the destination of the link or purpose. Notice how this is done in the example.

CHALLENGE 6.15

Using an online image map generator to generate the necessary coordinates, create an image map that comprises two circular hotspots on an image of your choice, so that when each is clicked, the user is taken to different sites. Also, apart from the type of application shown in the example, how else can you use image mapping in Web design?

6.4 Document Embedding

In addition to allowing linking to other Web pages, HTML5 allows another Web page to be displayed inside a Web page and browsed independently. The element used for achieving this is the `<iframe>` element.

6.4.1 `<iframe>...</iframe>`

The `<iframe>` element is an inline element that allows content to be embedded in a page and interacted with by the user in various ways. Embedding content in this way is useful for embedding interactive applications, such as Google map. Commonly supported attributes are listed in Table 6.4. Figure 6.18 shows how it is used to embed interactive Google map, and Figure 6.19 depicts the result.

Obtaining the value for the `src` attribute required going to https://maps.google.co.uk and searching for London. Next, when the map for London was displayed, the three-line menu icon at the top-left corner of the map was clicked to display a drop-down list, from which "Share or embed map" was chosen. Next, in the dialog that appeared, the "Embed map" option was chosen and the code for embedding the map was copied and

TABLE 6.4

The HTML5 Attributes for the `<iframe>` Element

Attribute	Function
src	Specifies the URL for the page to be embedded.
width	Specifies the width of the frame.
height	Specifies the height of the frame.
name	Specifies a name for the frame.
seamless	Specifies that frame should be displayed in a way that makes it seem a part of the main page. For example, no scrollbars are shown. A value does not need to be specified; or "seamless" or "" may be specified (e.g., seamless="seamless" or seamless="").
sandbox	Specifies to disallow (or allow, if disallowed) certain features. The value may be empty (which means to apply all default restrictions, including disallowing plug-ins, form submission, scripts execution, links to other documents, and content to be treated as being from its original source), or the value may be a **space-separated list of keywords** that remove restrictions, including allow-forms, allow-scripts, allow-top-navigation, and allow-same-origin.
srcdoc	Specifies the content for the frame. If supported by the browser, it overrides what is specified in src. It is expected to be used with the seamless and sandbox attributes.

```
HTML
<body>
  <h3>iFrame Element</h3>
  <iframe width="400" height="300"
   src="https://www.google.com/maps/embed?
   pb=!1m18!1m12!1m3!1d158858.182370726!2d0.10159865000000001
   !3d51.52864165!2m3!1f0!2f0!3f0!3m2!1i1024!2i768!4f13.1!3m3
   !1m2!1s0x47d8a00baf21de75%3A0x52963a5addd52a99!2sLondon!5e0
   !3m2!1sen!2suk!4v1437373289145">
   <p>This browser does not support iframes<p>
  </iframe>
</body>
```

FIGURE 6.18   Example usage of the `<iframe>` element.

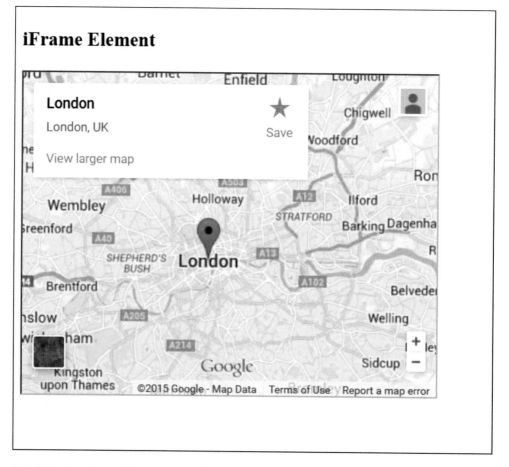

FIGURE 6.19   The result of Figure 6.18.

used, as shown in the example. Note that the code generated by the site, as of time of writing, has some attributes that are no longer supported by the `<iframe>` element and should therefore be removed.

CHALLENGE 6.16

Write an HTML code for embedding the Google map for where you are. Also, in what type of application would you use a map like this?

6.5 Types of Images

Being aware of the makeup of the types of images used in Web design can be useful in understanding why they have the properties that determine how they are used. The images shown so far are known as **two-dimensional images** (2D images). They are 2D images because they are represented in only two dimensions, width and height. They are the most used images in Web design and fall into two categories, **bitmapped** and **vector** images.

6.5.1 Bitmapped Images

Bitmapped images, also known as **raster images**, are made up of tiny dots called **pixels**. In Web design, you might refer to these pixels as **CSS pixels**, as mentioned earlier. The image of the "H" in Figure 6.20 gives an illustration. It is made up of both the white background and the "H," which are inseparable.

Representing images in pixels inevitably produces properties that can be used to describe bitmapped images. These properties revolve around how many pixels are there

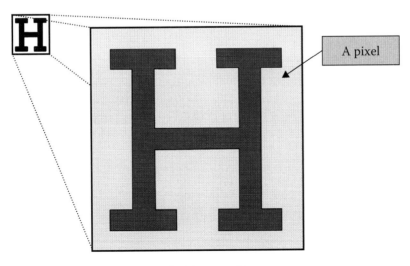

FIGURE 6.20 A graphical illustration of a bitmapped image.

in an image or specific area of it. They influence image quality and therefore have design implications. The three main properties are **image resolution, pixels per unit length**, and **color depth**.

6.5.1.1 *Image Resolution*

Image resolution describes how many pixels an image has, and it is specified in two ways. One is as pixel dimensions, and the other is as megapixels. **Pixel dimensions** are the width and height of an image in pixels. For example, 800 × 600 means that an image has width and height of 800 and 600 pixels, respectively. The term **megapixels**, on the other hand, describes the total number of pixels in an image and is expressed in megapixels. It is typically used for specifying the maximum resolution that a digital camera can produce and is the product of the width and the height of an image, in pixels. For example, a black and white image with a pixel dimension of 800 × 600 is about 0.48 megapixels (i.e., 480,000 pixels). A higher image resolution produces a bigger image when displayed or printed. Figure 6.21 shows an illustration. The design implication is that images that are too big for the screen, even when intended to be the only element on the screen or page; this often compels vertical and horizontal scrolling in order to view all parts of the image, essentially compromising user experience.

Pixel dimension should be determined when creating an image in order to prevent significant resizing later. Failing this, the usual practice is to, at least, create images of larger pixel dimensions than needed and then reduce and sharpen them in a graphics program, if necessary. Making small pixel dimensions bigger is much like trying to spread fewer than enough pixels over a larger area, which the computer responds to by, for example, creating "fake pixels," based on the values of original pixels, to make up for missing ones, resulting in a poorly defined image. This technique of using "fake pixels," or pixels with estimated values, is known as **image interpolation**, and there are various ways of achieving it. Figure 6.22 demonstrates the effects of image enlargement. The general practice is to not reduce size to the point where an image is

320 × 240 image   800 × 600 image

FIGURE 6.21   The same image with different pixel dimensions displayed in the same Web browser on a 1152 × 864 screen. (Image from www.freeimages.co.uk.)

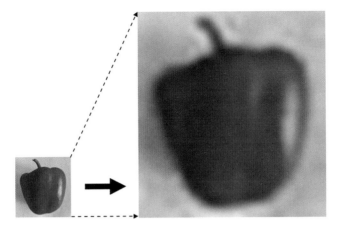

FIGURE 6.22 The effects of significant enlargement on image quality.

so small that important details are no longer discernible or, in the case of enlargement, to gradually increase size (e.g., by 10% each time) to the point where an image starts getting blocky or blurry.

6.5.1.1.1 About Image Resizing

If images must be resized, then necessary things need to be done to preserve as much of the original characteristics as possible. There are a number of ways to achieve this. A graphics program, HTML, or CSS may be used to specify the desired size. The image may also be cropped. When an image is sized by specifying new dimensions, a possible by-product that holds relevance in image display quality is **image aspect ratio** (IAR), which is the width of an image divided by its height, or the ratio of width to height. The aspect ratio of an image is established from the starting width and height when the image is created, and width and height are specified in various ways, depending on how the image is created. For an image created with a graphics program, width and height are among the parameters specified for a new document. For a scanned image, they are the dimensions of the document that is scanned, but they may also be specified. For example, if the size of the document scanned or the dimensions set is 5×3 inch and scanning resolution is 300 pixels per inch (ppi), then the aspect ratio of the image created is:

$$= (\text{width} \times \text{resolution}):(\text{height} \times \text{resolution}) =$$

$$(5 \times 300):(3 \times 300) = 1500:300 = 5:3$$

The aspect ratio of an image must be retained; otherwise, distortion can occur, as shown in Figure 6.23.

In contrast, **when images are cropped**, there is no aspect ratio problem, because a new aspect ratio is created when an image is cropped, which means that cropping can also be used to change an image's aspect ratio. Image cropping is the trimming off of the edges of an image, and it is typically done in a graphics editor. The only

Original   Elongated   Squashed

FIGURE 6.23   An original image and images produced by resizing it incorrectly.

issue with cropping is that it may adversely reduce the scope of an image, because some important details at the edges that complement the main elements in the image may be removed.

However, cropping could also be used deliberately for this purpose in order to remove unwanted details from an image and better focus on the important elements. In such a case, an image may first be enlarged and then cropped, or vice versa. Figure 6.24 shows an example. Notice the difference in presence, focus, and aspect ratio.

Original image   Enlarged and cropped image

FIGURE 6.24   Enlarging and cropping an image to focus on a specific part. (Image from www. freeimages.co.uk.)

6.5.1.2 *Pixels per Unit Length*

Pixels per unit length (or **pixel density**) describes the number of pixels per unit length and is also, confusingly enough, referred to as resolution in some context. In English-speaking countries, the pixels per unit length most commonly used is **pixels per inch** (ppi), followed by **pixels per centimeters** (ppcm). Although it is a measure more commonly used to describe the quality of a display device, it is actually a more definite indicator of quality in bitmapped images than in pixel dimensions or megapixels. For example, if you are told that an image has a resolution of 72 ppi, this immediately conveys the sense of how densely packed pixels are in the image and therefore what quality to expect. On the other hand, if you are told that an image has a resolution of 398×265 pixels, or 0.10 megapixels, there is no indication of pixel density. In order for these values to make more sense in terms of quality, it would be necessary to know the physical dimensions of the image, so as to judge how densely packed the pixels are and therefore how much details are represented in the image.

Like aspect ratio, **the ppi value of an image is determined at the point of creation**. It affects the pixel dimensions of the image and the number of pixels that the image contains. For example, a 4×6 inch photograph scanned at 100 ppi will result in a bitmapped image that has a ppi value of 100, pixel dimensions of 400×600, and a total pixel number of 240,000 (i.e., 400×600). On the other hand, the same photograph scanned at 300 ppi will produce an image that has a 300 ppi value and a total pixel number of 2,160,000 (i.e., 1200×1800). The ppi specified when an image is created is usually saved with it. This is why it is sometimes referred to as **embedded resolution**. Generally, the choice of ppi depends on how an image will be outputted, since ppi affects image display and printing differently.

6.5.1.2.1 *PPI and Displayed Image Quality*

Incidentally, when an image is intended for display on a monitor screen, ppi affects quality only indirectly. This is because **monitors do not display images in pixels per inch** but based on pixel dimensions; that is, a 300×400 pixel image with 100 ppi, for example, is displayed on a standard-resolution screen with 300 pixels across and 400 pixels down. This means that no matter what ppi is used to create an image, it will not necessarily affect its display quality. To demonstrate, a 5×4 inch document scanned at 72 ppi and 300 ppi will produce images with pixel dimensions of 360×288 (i.e., $[72 \times 5] \times [72 \times 4]$) and 1500×1200, respectively, which will be different in size when displayed, as shown in Figure 6.25, in which the two images are displayed together in a Web browser. This basically means that when an image is displayed on the screen, ppi only affects the size at which it is displayed, not the quality. Naturally, zooming can then be used to increase or decrease the size of the image.

So, what ppi should be used when creating images for Web design? Although computers and other devices used to access websites generally have ppi that is higher than 72 ppi, there is no logical reason to produce images intended for screen display at anything more than 72 ppi, since higher ppi will only result in larger files. However, it is a different matter when images are intended to be printed.

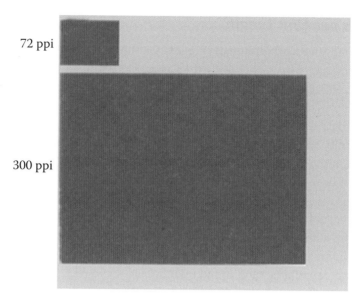

FIGURE 6.25 The relationship between the images of the same document scanned at 72 and 300 ppi.

6.5.1.2.2 PPI and Printed Image Quality

In contrast to its effects on displayed images, ppi affects the quality of printed images directly. So, typically, what looks good on screen may not look good when printed. This is because printers generally print based on **dots per inch** (dpi) and also at a much higher resolution than computer monitors. Modern printers, for example, commonly have a resolution of 600 dpi and higher. This means that an image needs to be 600 ppi or more to ensure good quality when printed. If the resolution of an image is much lower than a printer's resolution (say a 72 ppi image is outputted on a 600 dpi printer), then the printed image will be either too small in size or not detailed enough to be considered good quality.

Generally, higher ppi values ensure better-quality printed images with finer details and subtler color transitions. The implication of this is that if images are intended to be printed, then it is important to ensure that they are produced using high enough ppi/dpi values. It is also important to know that a **low-quality (low-ppi) image cannot be improved by printing it at a higher dpi**. Increasing print resolution will only make pixels larger, resulting in pixelation. Likewise, once an image is created, increasing its ppi in a graphics program will not necessarily improve its quality. This means that where you want an image to be available both for screen viewing and printing, then separate versions should be provided.

CHALLENGE 6.17

What will be the dimensions of a 3000 × 2000 pixels image on the screen when displayed on a 72 ppi monitor?

6.5.1.3 *Color Depth*

To better understand the meaning of color depth, it is useful to know how color is produced on a device screen. A color display screen is made up of tiny dots called **pixels**, each of which can be made to produce any of many colors at a time by mixing three different colors in varying degrees. Each color component is represented with a number of bits, and **color depth** (also known as **bit depth** or **pixel depth**) is the total number of bits used to represent the three color components. Color depth is also referred to as **bits per pixel** (bpp), even **bytes per pixel** (**bpp**), and it determines the number of distinct colors available to use for a pixel as well as the color quality of an image. For example, 24-bit color depth (known as **true color**), which provides 16,777,216 colors theoretically produces better color quality than 8-bit color depth, which provides 256 colors. In theory, the higher the color depth, the more accurately the colors of an image can be represented, and therefore, the more realistically rich colors can be represented. Of course, the file size is also bigger. Figure 6.26 shows the same photograph represented with different color depths. Notice the depreciation in color quality and the **posterization effect** (i.e., the banding of colors in different areas) as color depth drops to 4-bit

24-bit 8-bit

4-bit 1-bit

FIGURE 6.26 An illustration of the effects of color depth.

and 1-bit. Although, in theory, 24-bit produces better quality than 8-bit, in reality, the difference is usually not visible.

Some technologies used for creating images, such as scanners, offer higher color depths than 24-bit, such as 32-bit and 48-bit, but these are unlikely to produce any discernable benefits, since humans are capable of differentiating only between about 10 million colors, most, if not all, of which are covered by 24-bit color depth. Also, humans are not very good at distinguishing between close variations of the same color, unless they are placed close to each other. However, higher color depths can be useful, because the extra bits can be used for other functions. For example, in 32-bit color depth, 8 bits are used, each for the red, green, and blue color components (or **channels**) and the extra 8 bits for an **alpha channel** (or **transparency channel**). An alpha channel specifies which parts of an image should be transparent and by how much. Its value ranges from 0 to 255. When it is set to 0, the specified area of an image is fully transparent, and when set to 255, it is fully opaque. The channel is usually controlled with the **opacity** feature in graphics-editing programs and is usually specified as a value between 0% and 100% or between 0 and 1.0. The alpha channel has an important role in the production of images.

6.5.2 Vector Images

Unlike bitmapped images, vector images are not made up of pixels. Rather, they are made up of **geometric objects** (known as **geometric primitives**), such as points, lines, curves, and shapes, each of which can be defined in terms of a series of connecting points and/or mathematical expressions. A line, for example, is produced by connecting two points and a curve is produced by a mathematical equation. Figure 6.27 shows an illustration of how an "H" might be represented.

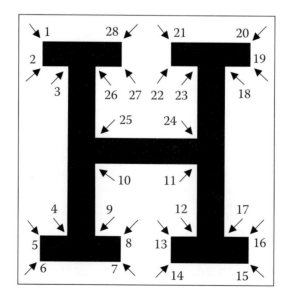

FIGURE 6.27   An illustration of the principle of vector graphic representation.

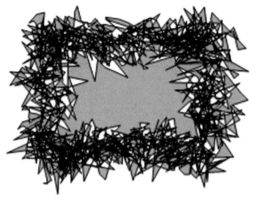

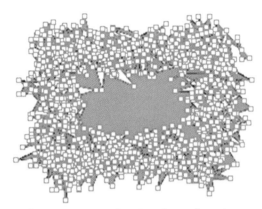

A complex vector image   The same image showing the node points

FIGURE 6.28   A demonstration of the makeup of a vector image.

Looking at the figure, it is easy to imagine that a more complex vector graphic would comprise many more points, as shown in Figure 6.28. The figure shows a relatively complex vector graphic, which is actually one object created by connecting many points (**node points**).

Storing only the coordinates of the objects and a few other properties that make up vector images means that vector image files are **seldom large in size**, making the method an effective way of producing good-quality digital images that are small in size. Also, because they are stored as a series of coordinates, they can be scaled, translated, and deformed easily by simply manipulating the node points. This means that they are **very scalable** (i.e., they can be enlarged without loss of image quality). Furthermore, their **quality is independent of display device resolution**, meaning that they can look good on displays of any resolution. Also, being small in size particularly makes vector images "Internet friendly," in that they download fast. Figure 6.29 shows examples of vector images. Image "A" is made up of many curves and color fills, and image "B" is a good example of how vector graphics can be used to create complex, highly detailed, and artistic graphics. The image, which is a digital reproduction of Alponse Mucha's F. Champenois Imprimeur-Éditeur, is made up of numerous curves, shapes, shades, and effects, using a tool called Gradient Mesh, which allows the easy manipulation of curves.

Some of the performance benefits of vector images are reduced by the fact that they still typically have to be saved in bitmapped file formats in order to use them on Web pages. An alternative to doing this is to save them in a vector-based format, such as SVG, mentioned earlier. SVG is both a vector graphics language and a file format, such that when a vector graphic is saved, it is also saved in the language, which a browser is then able to translate into a vector image and display. However, the use of SVG is not yet widespread, as of time of writing.

Another alternative to saving vector images as bitmapped is to save them in Flash file format, SWF, which is another vector-based format. However, a Web browser needs a plug-in in order to be able to display a vector graphic saved in the format. Furthermore, the popularity of the format has decreased, and this is unlikely to change, going into the future.

(a)   (b)

FIGURE 6.29   Some 2D vector graphics. (a) is from www.free-clip-art.com, and (b) is by Yukio Miyamoto. (Image from www.bekkoame.ne.jp/~yukio-m/intro/index.html.)

NOTE: Vector or raster?

- Vector images are usually ideal for geometric shapes (e.g., icons, logos, and illustrations).
- Raster image formats are suitable for complex scenes, such as photographic image, where there are a lot of shapes and details.

6.5.3 Image File Formats and Image File Size

Irrespective of how images are created, be it via photography, scanning, or graphics programs, they are stored as image files in specific formats and there many image file formats. These formats provide different features and are suitable for different types of images. While some formats are designed to store all the data that make up an image, others are capable of making an image file size smaller. This is necessary because image file can be large, especially bitmapped image files. The technique of reducing file size in computing is known as **data compression**. Some formats are designed to reduce file size without affecting the quality of what the file produces. This is known as **lossless compression**. Other formats are designed to allow the reduction of quality, if necessary. This is known as **lossy compression**. Image file formats combine both techniques in various ways to achieve their specific characteristics, and graphics production programs typically allow compression parameters to be set for any format that offers compression. Image file formats also offer other features, such as transparency, that make them suitable for different situations. Table 6.5 lists some formats used on the Web, some of which are more commonly used than others.

TABLE 6.5

Main Properties of the Image File Formats

Format	MIME type	Bitmap/ Vector	Lossless/ Lossy	Animation	Transparency
GIF (.gif)	image/gif	Bitmap	Both	Yes	Yes
JPEG (.jpeg, .jpg)	image/jpeg	Bitmap	Both	No	No
JPEG2000 (.jp2, .jpx)	imge/jp2	Bitmap	Both	Yes	Yes
JPEG XR (.jxr, .hdp, .wdp)	image/jxr, image/ vnd.ms-photo	Bitmap	Both	Yes	Yes
OpenEXR (.exr)	Image/x-exr	Bitmap	Both	Yes	Yes
PDF (.pdf)	application/pdf	Both	Both	Yes	Yes
PNG (.png)	image/png	Bitmap	Lossless	No	Yes
SVG (.svg)	image/svg+xml	Vector	None	Yes	Yes
SWF (.swf)	application/ x-shockwave-flash	Vector	Lossless	Yes	Yes
WebP (.webp)	image/webp	Bitmap	Both	Yes	Yes

NOTE: Most commonly used formats and their applications

The HTML standard does not specify the image file formats that are supported, so different browsers support different formats. The most commonly used formats that are also supported by all major browsers are JPEG, GIF, and PNG.

- **JPEG** is used for photographs and images that have many different colors and shades, even black and white photographs.
- **GIF** is used for simple illustrations, images with limited number of colors or blocks of colors, such as logos and icons that use flat colors (i.e., colors with no, for example, gradient, highlighting, and depth), and images containing text. It is not well suited for images with more than 256 colors.
- **PNG** is used for similar purposes as GIF but has wider applications. For example, it can also be used for photographs; however, it produces larger files than JPEG.

Information on browser support for other formats listed in Table 6.5 can be found on various websites dedicated to the topic, such as caniuse.com.

Given that high-quality images produce very large files, it is often necessary to **balance file size against quality** when producing images for Web design, because large files can cause performance problems, such as long download time. It is no good, for example, if images are of very high quality and pages take frustratingly long times to display, as most users will probably not be prepared to wait. Similarly, it is no good to compress an image to the point that degradation is visible, as this might compromise the information being communicated and/or user experience. Figure 6.30 shows the same image with different compression levels and their effect on quality and file size. Notice the visible degradation in 75% and 99% compressions.

To help with size-quality balancing, image production programs, such as Photoshop, typically provide information about the size of the file generated by an image and also how long it will take to transmit the file over a range of Internet connection speeds. However, while this information is readily available when using these programs, it can be useful to know how to calculate image file size and transmission time for when, for example, you are doing initial designing on paper and/or have no access to a suitable program. After all, just because we have calculators does not mean that we should not know how to add, in case calculators are not available.

Uncompressed: 165 K	50% Compression: 10.8 K
75% Compression: 3.4 K	99% Compression: 1.8 K

FIGURE 6.30 An illustration of the effects of compression on quality and file size. (Image from www.freeimages.co.uk.)

6.5.4 Calculating File Size Generated from Scanned Documents

An A4 (i.e., 8.5 × 11 inches) document scanned at 300 ppi and 24-bit color depth will generate an image file size of 25.25 MB. This can be calculated by multiplying the area of the document in square inches by the number of pixels per square inch to get the total number of pixels in the image, multiplying by the number of bits per pixel to get the total number of bits, and then dividing by 8 to get the number of bytes, thus:

$$\text{Document Image File Size} =$$

$$((\text{height} \times \text{width}) \times \text{PPI}^2 \times \text{color depth})/8$$

Using the formula for the above example gives:

$$\text{File size} = \left((8.5 \times 11) \times (300 \times 300) \times 24\right)/8$$
$$= 25{,}245{,}000 \text{ bytes}$$
$$= 25{,}245{,}000/1000 = 25{,}245 \text{ KB}$$
$$= 25{,}245/1000 = 25.25 \text{ MB}$$

CHALLENGE 6.18

Assuming that you want to include a 4 × 5 inch image in an application and, because the image is also going to be printed, you need to scan the image at 600 ppi and 24-bit color depth, calculate the possible size of the image.

6.5.5 Calculating File Size Generated from Digital Camera

An image captured with a digital camera with pixel dimensions of 640 × 480 px at 24-bit color depth produces a file size of 0.92 MB. This is calculated by multiplying the total number of pixels by the number of bits per pixel to get the total number of bits and then dividing by 8 to get the number of bytes, thus:

$$\text{Image File Size} = (\text{pixel dimensions} \times \text{color depth})/8$$

Using the formula gives:

$$\text{Image File Size} = \left((640 \times 480) \times 24\right)/8$$
$$= 921{,}600 \text{ bytes}$$
$$= 921{,}600/1000 = 921.60 \text{ KB}$$
$$= 921.60/1000 = 0.92 \text{ MB}$$

CHALLENGE 6.19

What is the file size, in gigabytes, produced by a digital camera when you take a photograph with 1600 × 1200 px dimension at 32-bit color depth?

6.5.6 Calculating File Transmission Time

Given an Internet connection of 56.6 kilobits per second (kbps), a file that is 22.25 MB in size will take about 59 min to transmit. This can be calculated by dividing the size of the file by connection or transmission speed. Both must be in the same unit, such as bits, kilobits, bytes, and megabytes. The speed of 56.6 kbps is the slowest that people use to connect to the Internet. The following formula can be used to calculate transmission time:

$$\text{Transmission Time} =$$
$$\text{size of file/lowest transmission speed}$$

Before using the formula, all values are converted to the same unit. In this case, file size is converted to the unit of the transmission speed, that is, **kilobits**. To do this, 25.25 MB is simply multiplied by 1000 twice to convert it to bytes, then multiplied by 8 to convert to bits, and then divided by 1000 to convert to kilobits. This is written as $(25.25 \times 1000 \times 1000 \times 8)/1000$, which gives 202,000 kilobits.

Using the formula gives:

$$\text{Transmission Time} = 202,000 \text{ kilobits}/56.6 \text{ kbps}$$
$$= 3568.91\,\text{s} = (3568.91/60)\text{min} = 59.48\,\text{min}$$

CHALLENGE 6.20

A 20.25 MB image is embedded in Web page. Assuming that the size of the other contents of the page is insignificant, determine how long it will take to transmit the page over 2 Mbps and 100 kbps connections, respectively.

6.6 Guidelines for Effective Use of Images

The most useful function of images is their ability to instantly and effectively communicate either single or collective visual information. For example, when we look at a picture, most of the time, we immediately get an impression of what it is. Even when we cannot immediately figure out what the picture says, the time it takes to do this is often much less than the time it would have taken if the details of the picture were described in text. Graphics are also quite versatile, in that they can be used to communicate various types of information. They can be used to **communicate reality or a concept**, to **create specific moods**, or to simply **beautify**. However, in order to achieve these goals, images need to be used correctly.

6.6.1 Decorative Images

The **use of graphics for decorative purposes should be minimized**, as they can place unnecessary burden on the download time of a page and are not appreciated by most users, anyway. Studies, for example, by the NN Group, which specializes in user experience, have shown that users generally pay attention to only those images that carry relevant information, such as photos of real people (not stock photos of models) and products, while ignoring decorative graphics. In particular, large graphics should not be used for decorative purposes, because whatever benefits they offer are likely outweighed by the performance problems that they are likely to cause.

The most common **decorative use of images is as background**. When an image is used for background, it should match the mood or context of a design; otherwise, it may create conflict and distraction. For example, a background image consisting of different-color balloons suits a page providing information about a party than one that is providing information about a funeral. Even when background image is relevant and complements a design theme, it should not be so overwhelming that it gets in the way of the content being delivered. This is unprofessional and particularly unacceptable in learning applications, given that focus is especially required during learning. To prevent background graphics from interfering with the content of a page, they should be subdued or toned down. Figure 6.31 shows some examples.

Another common technique used to prevent background image from overwhelming content is to place the content in a plain color box on the background, as shown in Figure 6.32. However, this can look a bit messy, confusing, and distracting sometimes, especially when users have to scroll through the content. Also, the background can keep attracting the eyes from the periphery.

An overwhelming background   A subdued background

FIGURE 6.31 A demonstration of the effect of overwhelming background image and a possible solution. (Image from www.freeimages.co.uk.)

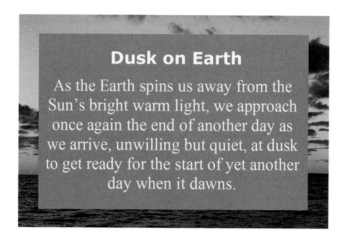

FIGURE 6.32 Preventing background from compromising legibility.

6.6.2 Large Images

The **automatic display of large images** should be avoided, even when they are relevant, because they can take too long to download and display completely. Instead, use thumbnails to introduce the images. If users then want to see the larger versions, they can click as required. For a thumbnail to be easy to be interpreted and therefore be effective for making a choice, it needs to contain useful information. However, this can sometimes be difficult to achieve, because neither of the two methods commonly used for creating thumbnails (i.e., scaling and cropping) produces completely satisfactory result. **Scaling** produces the smaller version of an entire picture but may be too crowded to convey clear and useful meaning, while **cropping** produces a clearer and more detailed image but with too many useful parts cropped off. The recommended approach, called **relevance-enhanced image reduction**, is to combine the two methods, so that the thumbnail is clear and also includes enough contexts to be meaningful. A more specific recommendation by Jakob Nielsen is that in order to produce a thumbnail that is 10% of the original image, the image is first cropped to 32% of its original size and then the result is scaled down to 32% of itself. So, assuming that the original image is 100×100 px, then cropping it to 32% gives 32×32 px (i.e., [32/100]*100 px), and scaling this down to 32% of itself gives an image that is roughly 10×10 px (i.e., [32/100]*32 px).

6.6.3 Images with Text

Where an image is used to support text or text is used to support an image, it is essential, especially in learning materials where comprehension is critical, that they are closely synchronized, so as to minimize the load on short-term memory. This prevents people from doing extra cognitive work to connect the two, as would be the case when they are far apart. In Figure 6.33, for example, the illustration on the left requires someone to look at a number on the image and then search out the matching item on the list underneath while holding the number in short-term memory, making it harder to construct the imagery that is vital for comprehension. However, the illustration on the right simply requires one glance, and because all the materials are together, constructing the imagery is easier.

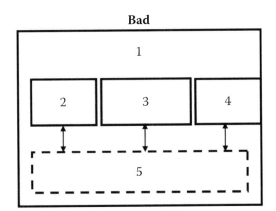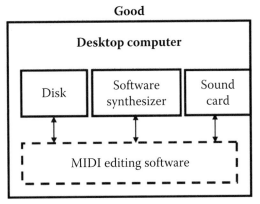

1. Desktop computer
2. Disk
3. Software synthesizer
4. Sound card
5. MIDI editing software

FIGURE 6.33   Two ways of using images with text.

FIGURE 6.34   Another way of annotating an image. (Image from Flagstaffotos.)

When it is not feasible to place annotations on an image, connecting one element to the other directly, using something like a pointing line, as illustrated in Figure 6.34, can provide a reasonable compromise.

CHALLENGE 6.21

Given the guidelines provided earlier under HTML, how would you make these types of images accessible to the visually impaired?

6.6.4 Images and Captions

Caption should be provided with every image used to present content, either underneath it or in a body of text that is relevant to it, if used to complement a story. Figure 6.35 shows part of the photo gallery of the website of a yearly tennis competition, in which

FIGURE 6.35 Example of image being delivered without a description.

this principle was not applied when the page was active. A series of images were simply presented, along with navigational aid that allowed linear or nonlinear navigation of the images. Although the images used as part of the background required no labeling, those used for content would have benefited from a brief description placed, for example, at the bottom. This would, no doubt, save those who did not know the player from wondering who she was and who she was playing at that moment.

NOTE: Quick image usage guidelines

When images are used on a Web page, they should:

- Be of good quality (i.e., clear and with discernible details).
- Be relevant.
- Be instantly recognizable.
- Communicate information, unless abstract and used, for example, for background.
- Set the right mood.
- Complement the color scheme of a design.
- Not be large or too many, as this slows down the download of a page and ruins user experience.
- Fit the color palette; otherwise, the colors of an image may not be accurately rendered.

6.7 Acquiring Images for Use

There are various ways to acquire the graphics needed for a design, each of which has design situations for which it is most suitable. However, irrespective of the method used, the principle of having them in the right format, right pixel dimensions, and right resolution persists in order for them to be able to fit well into the intended design. The most common acquisition methods include stock images, graphics editors, photography, image scanning, and the use of coding.

6.7.1 Stock Images

For non-unique graphics requirements, stock images are a common option to consider. There are both free and commercial stock images of various categories and qualities available on the Web. Some are free for both private and commercial use, while license needs to be purchased to use some stock images commercially or for specific purposes. A license may be for unlimited use (as in the case of royalty-free stock images) or for just one-time use (as in the case of rights-managed stock images), or there might be other terms involved.

6.7.2 Graphics Editors

Vector graphics editors or bitmap graphics editors maybe used to create images. **Vector graphics editors** (drawing programs) allow the composition and editing of vector images, which can be saved in a variety of vector formats, such as SVG, EPS, PDF, VML, and WMF, or in bitmapped formats. They are better for line art or line drawing, which includes logos, sharp-edged illustrations (such as cartoons and clip arts), logos, technical illustrations, and diagrams. Drawing skill is of course necessary. Popular programs used among professionals include Illustrator and CorelDraw. Popular free ones include Inkscape, and these are sufficient for beginners. **Bitmap graphics editors** (image editing programs) allow the painting and editing of pictures and save them as bitmap formats, such as GIF, JPEG, PNG, and TIFF. They are most suitable for retouching and manipulating photographs and creating photo-realistic images, which are typically images that are made up of many slightly different colors. The most popular of these editors among professionals is Photoshop, which has a cheaper version called Photoshop Element. Free ones include GIMP and RawTherapee. Online editors are also available. Some are listed at the end of this chapter.

6.7.3 Photography

This is an easier method of acquiring images than drawing or painting them, in that it mostly requires pointing a camera and capturing an image; however, taking some types of photographs requires expertise, in using both the right camera settings and techniques. There are two main types of cameras: point-and-shoot and digital single-lens reflex (DSLR) cameras. **Point-and-shoot** cameras are compact and easy to operate.

Although mobile phone cameras are a type of point-and-shoot cameras, some may not produce images that are as good as dedicated point-and-shoot cameras, such as in low-lighting conditions. In contrast, **DSLR** cameras are larger and more complex to operate but take better pictures.

In addition to using the right settings and techniques, there is also the matter of using the right lighting setup to get the right mood. This usually involves using a combination of lights of different intensity placed at different angles and distances to the subject. The most common lighting scheme is **three-point lighting**. Naturally, shots from a camera can also be manipulated in graphics editors to correct imperfections or to create effects. This is certainly necessary when producing **high-dynamic-range (HDR) images**. Production of HDR images typically involves combining differently exposed shots of the same scene (sometimes known as **bracketed photos**) and manipulating the properties of the resulting single image, such as color saturation, luminosity, contrast, and lighting. Bracketed photos are typically produced using **auto-exposure bracketing** (AEB) in cameras to capture three or more shots in sequence, using different exposures.

HDR images are images intended to be expressive and communicate something that is closer to what is seen in reality, such as the blurry yet sparkling points of light that the teary eyes see when looking at an illuminated high-contrast scene at night, something that a camera, for example, is not capable of capturing. They are used to create this type of realism, and more, including extreme and surreal visuals and typically high contrast and vibrancy.

6.7.4 Image Scanning

This is another easy way to acquire images; however, the images have to exist first in a physical form, whether on paper or on any other surfaces. Image scanners are typically hand-held or flatbed. **Hand-held scanners** are portable but more difficult to operate in that they are prone to shaking, which produces poor-quality images. **Flatbed scanners** are fixed, and using them requires simply laying an image on their glass surface and operating accordingly. Various image properties, such as scanning resolution (i.e., ppi) and contrast, can be set to ensure that the desired image quality is achieved. The use of 300 ppi is common for images intended for screen display.

Because standard image scanners do not produce good-quality images from **film negatives and slides**, these are scanned using a special type of scanner. They can be as easy to use as placing a negative in a carrier that they come with and feeding it into the scanner. Typical scanning resolution is much higher than that for normal scanning and ranges from 3000 to 4000 ppi.

6.7.5 Web Coding Languages

Web coding languages allow some types of graphics to be created procedurally and used in ways that are not possible with images created with non-procedural methods, in that the images are created dynamically. This means that images can be generated and changed in real time, making them suitable, for example, for generating graphics such as graphs, charts, and maps on the fly, based on, for example, continually changing data supplied by users. The most commonly used Web-specific languages are HTML, SVG, and JavaScript; however, general-purpose languages, such as C++, are also used. The main disadvantage of using coding languages to create images is that programming skill is required and the process can be time-consuming when complex images are involved.

6.8 Useful Info

6.8.1 Web Links

HTML specifications: w3.org/TR/html51, w3.org/standards

Web development documents: docs.webplatform.org

Accessibility: w3.org/WAI/tutorials, webaim.org

HTML5 support testing: html5test.com

HTML tutorials (*Here are just a few free tutorial sites on HTML and other Web languages*): w3.org/wiki, html5rocks.com, sitepoint.com, w3schools.com, codecademy.com, quackit.com, developer.mozilla.org/en-US/docs/Web tutori- alspoint.com, whatwg.org, htmlgoodies.com, htmldog.com, htmlcodetutorial. com, echoecho.com, learn.shayhowe.com, html.net, tizag.com, html-5-tutorial. com, docs.webplatform.org, developers.google.com, webdesignermag.co.uk

Free images: freeimages.co.uk, freedigitalphotos.net, vecteezy.com

Placeholder images: lorempixel.com

Online graphics editors: ipiccy.com, pixlr.com, sumopaint.com

Image optimization guidelines: developers.google.com/web/fundamentals/ performance

Online image optimizers: jpeg-optimizer.com, www.imageoptimizer.net, opti- mizilla.com

Responsive Image Breakpoints generator: responsivebreakpoints.com

Responsive images community group: responsiveimages.org

6.8.2 Free Software

Multiple download sites can be found for the following software by doing a search:

Image editing: GIMP (*Cross Platform*), Seashore (*Mac*), Paint.NET (*Win*), Pinta (*Cross Platform*), Artweaver Free (*Win*).

Image viewing and basic editing: Zoner Photo Studio 14 FREE (*Win*), FastStone (*Win*), InfanView (*Win*).

Image organization: Picasa (*Cross Platform*), iPhoto (*Mac*), Irfanview (*Win*).

Raw image data editing: Ufraw (*Mac, Linux*).

HDR imaging: Photomatix Essential (*Win*), Picturenaut (*Win, Mac*), Luminance HDR (*Cross Platform*), FDRTools Basic (*Win, Mac*), Essential HDR Community Edition (*Win*), Portable Fusion (*Win*).

Image noise remover: Noiseware Community Edition (*Win*), NDNoise (*Win*).

Mosaics generator: AndreaMosiac (*Cross Platform*).

Poster printer: PosterRazor (*Win, Mac*).

7

Audio, Video, and Animation

7.1 Introduction

Audio, video, and animation are introduced together because they are dynamic media, which are media that change continuously with time. These media are generally added to a Web page by using similar principles. This chapter presents the various methods and elements used to add them to a Web page.

7.2 Learning Outcomes

After studying this chapter, you should:

- Know how to add audio, video, and animation to a Web page by using suitable methods and HTML elements.
- Be aware of the most suitable file formats and codecs to use to avoid browser compatibility problems, especially in relation to audio and video.
- Know of necessary design issues and considerations involved in using audio, video, and animation in Web design.

7.3 Delivering Dynamic Media

Dynamic media is incorporated in a Web page in the same two main ways images are, which are through **hyperlinking** and **embedding**. When a dynamic media is linked to, the browser uses a **helper application**, which is separate from a Web page, to play it, and when it is embedded, it plays within the page, typically using a **plug-in**. Both delivery methods can be accomplished using HTML elements. It is also possible to combine HTML with Flash technologies to deliver dynamic media, but this is discouraged, as the use of Flash technologies for delivering media on the Web is all but obsolete. For this reason, how to add Flash media objects to a Web page is not discussed in detail in this text. Tutorials on this can be found at the website for Adobe Flash (now known as Animate CC).

Although adding dynamic media to a Web page can be as straightforward as adding a static image, an important practical thing to know is that the result is not always predictable, as different browsers and hardware (such as PC, Mac, iPhone and iPad) do not all support the same technologies. For example, the newer HTML elements (i.e., `<audio>` and `<video>`) do not work in old browsers and not all media file formats are supported by every browser. Because of these incompatibilities, delivering dynamic media successfully on a Web page requires extra considerations in order to ensure that a media file works on as many systems as possible. Often this means using multiple methods to deliver the same file as well as providing the same media in different file formats. How this is done for audio, video, and animation, using HTML, is dealt with here.

7.4 Audio

The HTML elements used to add audio to a Web page are the `<a>` element (used to link to audio) and the `<audio>`, `<embed>`, or `<object>` element (used to embed audio).

7.4.1 Linking to Audio

The `<a>` element is used to link to an audio file the same way as it is used to link to any other type of file. Figures 7.1 and 7.2 show how it is used and depict the result. Clicking the link opens a helper application, a media player in this case, to play the specified audio file. The advantage of playing audio with a helper application, as opposed to a plug-in, is that the audio continues to play when users navigate to a different page.

```
HTML
<h3>Linked Audio</h3>
<a href="sound.mp3">Listen to audio with helper application</a>
```

FIGURE 7.1 Example usage of the `<a>` element.

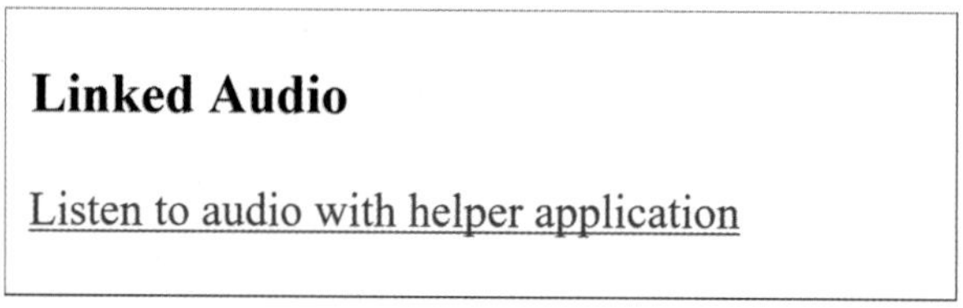

> **Linked Audio**
>
> Listen to audio with helper application

FIGURE 7.2 Rendered result of Figure 7.1.

CHALLENGE 7.1

In Figure 7.1, where is the audio file located in relation to the code. Also, in what situation is linked audio more appropriate than embedded audio?

7.4.2 Embedding Audio

In contrast to linked audio, which uses help application, embedded audio uses plug-in that is integrated into a page. It cannot be moved, and if the user navigates away from the page to another one, it stops. As already mentioned, the element used to embed audio is the `<audio>`, `<embed>`, or `<object>` element.

7.4.2.1 `<audio>...<audio>`

The `<audio>` element is optimized specifically for embedding audio. The specific attributes supported are listed in Table 7.1. Figure 7.3 shows a basic use of the element, and Figure 7.4 depicts the result. The content between the `<audio>` tags is the message that is displayed when a browser does not support the `<audio>` element and is known as **fallback content**.

TABLE 7.1

Attributes for the `<audio>` Element

Attribute	Function
src	Specifies URL of audio source.
controls	Specifies whether or not to display a control. A value is not necessary.
volume	Specifies volume of audio. It takes a range of 0.0 (silent) to 1.0 (loudest).
muted	Specifies the default state of audio stream. A value is not necessary.
autoplay	Specifies to start playing automatically. A value is not necessary.
loop	Specifies whether to repeatedly play audio. A value is not necessary.
mediagroup	Specifies to group multiple audio sources.
preload	Used with a large file to suggest how it should be loaded when page loads. Value can be "none" (which means not to buffer the file in preparation for playback), "metadata" (which means storing only information about the file), and "auto" (which leaves decision to the browser and is the default).
buffered	Provides information on time ranges of buffered audio. It is typically used with scripting.

```
HTML
<h3>Embedded audio</h3>
<audio src="audio/sound.mp3" controls>
   Your Web browser does not support HTML audio element.
</audio>
```

FIGURE 7.3 Example usage of the `<audio>` element.

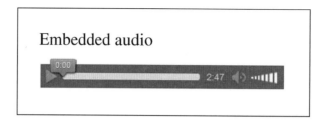

FIGURE 7.4   Rendered result of Figure 7.3.

CHALLENGE 7.2

Write a code that includes the `autoplay`, and `loop` attributes to see how they work.

The `<audio>` element can also be combined with the `<source>` element to provide multiple audio sources, from which the browser chooses the most suitable. The element is also used with other dynamic media elements, such as `<video>`. The attributes that it supports are listed in Table 7.2. Figure 7.5 shows how it is used. The code produces the same result as Figure 7.4.

TABLE 7.2

Attributes Used with the `<source>` Element When Adding Audio

Attribute	Function
src	Specifies URL of the source.
type	Specifies the type of the source. It helps the browser to determine whether it can play a file before loading it. Value is a string that identifies a valid **Internet media type** (or **MIME type**). Optional **codecs parameters** can also be added to specify how exactly the source is encoded.

```
HTML
<h3>Embedded audio</h3>
<audio controls>
    <source src="audio/sound.aac" type='audio/mp4;
    codecs="mp4a.40.2"'>
    <source src="audio/sound.oga" type="audio/ogg">
    <source src="audio/sound.mp3" type="audio/mpeg">
    Your Web browser does not support HTML audio element.
</audio>
```

FIGURE 7.5   Example usage of the `<audio>` with the `<source>` element.

When the browser encounters the `<audio>` element in the code example, it goes through the list of `<source>` elements and plays the first one that it can. If it cannot find any format that it supports, it displays the message, if the browser supports this. Notice that the audio sources specified in the `<source>` elements are the same, except for the values of the `type` attributes, which specify a different media type for each source. The **codecs parameters** specified with the `codec` attribute on the first `<source>` element specify the exact codec used to encode the source. A **codec** (derived from the two words: **co**mpressor and **dec**ompressor) is the technology used to compress (encode) and decompress (decode) digital data file or stream.

When specified, codecs parameters are one of the values of the `type` attribute and need to be in double quotes, while all the values of the attribute are enclosed in single quotes. Specifying the parameters can make the job of the browser easier, in that they help the browser determine whether or not it can play a file without first having to load it. However, if parameters are used, it is important that they are correct; otherwise, the browser will generate an error, even if it can play the specified file. On the other hand, if the parameters are not specified, the browser will load the file as normal and discover that it supports the file and play it. The full list of codecs parameters can be found on the Web. Table 7.3 lists some of the commonly used codecs parameters for audio.

TABLE 7.3

Common Media Types and Codecs Parameters Used for Audio on the Web

Media File Description	Extension	Internet Media Type	Codecs Parameters
PCM audio in WAV container	.wav	audio/wav	1
MP3 audio	.mp3	audio/mpeg	mp3
Vorbis audio in Oga/Ogg container	.oga, .ogg	audio/ogg	vorbis
Low-complexity AAC or AAC+ audio in MP4 container	.mp4, .m4a, .aac	audio/mp4	mp4a.40.2

CHALLENGE 7.3

What would happen in Figure 7.5 if "sound.aac" can be found but the value of the `codecs` attribute does not match its encoding? Also, what would happen if none of the audio files can be loaded?

CHALLENGE 7.4

What types of errors in a code can cause an audio file not to load?

7.4.2.2 `<embed>`

The `<embed>` element is used to embed an external application (typically a plug-in) or an interactive content. Although it is more commonly used to embed video or animation, it can also be used to embed audio. The attributes that it supports are listed in Table 7.4. Figures 7.6 and 7.7 show how the element is used and depict the result.

TABLE 7.4

Attributes Used with the `<embed>` Element

Attribute	Function
src	Specifies the URL for resource.
type	Specifies the Internet media type of source.
width	Specifies the length of the displayed content (e.g., media player).
height	Specifies the height of the displayed content (e.g., media player).

```
HTML
<h3>Audio with embed element</h3>
<embed src="sound.mp3" type="audio/mpeg" width="250" height="30">
```

FIGURE 7.6   Example usage of the `<embed>` element.

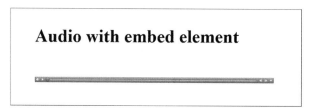

FIGURE 7.7   Rendered result of Figure 7.6.

CHALLENGE 7.5

The `width` and `height` attributes on the `<embed>` element determine how much of the control is displayed. Experiment with the attributes to see their effects. Also, what are the possible applications of such flexibility?

7.4.2.3 `<object>...</object>`

Like the `<embed>` element, the `<object>` element is used to embed external content, and it is also more commonly used for video or animation than for audio. Table 7.5 lists the attributes supported, and Figures 7.8 and 7.9 show how it is used and also depict the result. Like with the `<embed>` element, the `width` and `height` attributes determine how much of the control is displayed.

TABLE 7.5

Attributes Used with the `<object>` Element

Attribute	Function
data	Specifies the URL of content. At least one data must be specified.
type	Specifies the Internet media type of content.
width	Specifies the length of the displayed content or player.
height	Specifies the height of the displayed content or player.
name	Specifies browsing context (e.g., _blank, _self, _parent, and _top). See `target` attribute in Chapter 2.
usemap	Specifies a hash-name reference to a map element to associate the object.
form	Specifies the value of the id attribute on the `<form>` element with which to associate the element.

```
HTML
<h3>Audio with object element</h3>
<object data="sound.mp3" width="220px" height="50px"></object>
```

FIGURE 7.8 Example usage of the `<object>` element.

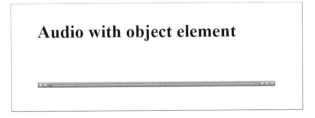

FIGURE 7.9 Rendered result of Figure 7.8.

In order to specify parameters for the `<object>` element, the `<param>` element is used inside it. The attributes that it supports are `name` (which specifies the name of parameter) and `value` (which specifies the value of the parameter). Figure 7.10 shows how to use the element. The code produces the same result as Figure 7.9. The only difference is that the audio does not start playing automatically when the page loads, because the "`autoplay`" parameter is specified and its value is set to "`false`."

```
HTML
<h3>Audio with object element</h3>
<object data="sound.mp3" width="250px" height="50px">
  <param name="autoplay" value="false">
</object>
```

FIGURE 7.10 Example usage of the `<param>` element with the `<object>` element.

CHALLENGE 7.6

Write a code that combines the `<object>` and `<embed>` elements to deliver the same file to see what happens.

7.4.3 Audio in Web Design

In order to be able to use audio effectively in Web design, several factors need to be considered, including appropriateness of use, file format compatibility, quality, and size of file. The roles of these factors are discussed here.

7.4.3.1 Audio File Formats and Audio File Size

Like image files, audio files can be large, and the size generated is directly related to quality. The sound that we hear is converted into the form that can be stored in the computer by converting it to electrical signal, taking many samples of it at regular intervals per second, giving each sample a value, and storing it as digital data. In theory, the more samples taken per second and the larger the number of bits used to represent each sample, the more the produced digital audio is a true representation of the original sound; in other words, the better the quality. The number of samples taken per second is known as **sampling rate**; it is measured in terms of samples or cycles per second, or **Hertz** (Hz). For example, 10,000 samples/sec is 10,000 Hz or 10 kilohertz (10 kHz). The number of bits per sample is known as **sampling resolution** (or **bit depth**) and is specified, for example, as 16-bit, meaning that the value assigned to each sample is determined using 16 bits. In theory, this means that the same audio sampled (or digitized) at 44.1 kHz and 16-bit will produce a better quality than if it were sampled at 22.05 kHz and 8-bit.

Unfortunately, high-quality audio produces large file sizes, and without the means of reducing them, it would be impractical to freely use audio on the Web, as we do today; Internet connection bandwidths (i.e., connection speeds) will simply not be able to cope. This is why audio files, like image files, require compression when used on the Web. The following calculations demonstrate the file size that digital audio can generate.

7.4.3.1.1 Audio File Size

File size generated when 3 min of music is digitized at CD quality, which is audio digitized at 44.1 kHz and 16-bit in stereo (i.e., 2 channels), is:

File Size = (sampling rate × bit depth × duration in seconds × number of channels)/8

$$= (44.1 \text{ kHz} \times 16\text{-bit} \times 3 \text{ min} \times 2 \text{ channels})/8$$

$$= [(44.1 \times 1000 \text{ Hz}) \times 16 \times (3 \times 60 \text{ s}) \times 2]/8 = 31,752,000 \text{ bytes}$$

$$= [31,752,000/(1000 \times 1000)] \text{MB} = 31.75 \text{ MB}$$

Dividing by 8 converts the amount in bits to bytes. To convert bytes to kilobytes, you divide by 1000; to convert kilobytes to megabytes, you divide by 1000; and so on.

CHALLENGE 7.7

What is the size, in megabytes, of the file generated by a 3-minute mono audio sampled at 22.05 kHz and 8-bit bit depth?

Although the quality of audio can be described in terms of sampling rate and bit depth, it is **bitrate** (or bit-rate) that is usually used to describe it; bitrate is the amount of bits processed, generated, or delivered per second. Higher sampling rates and bit depths naturally produce higher bitrates. The higher the bitrate, the higher the quality of an audio. The bitrate for CD, which is a standard for audio quality, for example, is 1.4 Mbps (i.e., 1.4 megabits per second). How this is derived is shown in the NOTE box.

NOTE: Explanation CD audio bit rate

Given that audio CD is sampled at 44.1 kHz at 16-bits resolution in stereo, the number of bits generated per second is:

= *samples per second* × *bits used per sample* × *number of channels*
= 44,100 samples per second × 16 bits × 2 channels
= 1,411,200 bits per second = 1,411,200/(1000 × 1000) = 1.4 Mbps

---

CHALLENGE 7.8

What is the bitrate of a 22.05 kHz 8-bit audio?

7.4.3.1.2 Audio File Formats

There are many audio file formats, and many of them support at least a codec, which, like with images, could be **lossless** (designed to retain original quality) or **lossy** (designed to reduce quality to reduce size). Lossy formats typically reduce file size more significantly than lossless formats. For example, some lossy formats, such as MP3, are capable of reducing CD-quality audio (i.e., 1.4 Mbps bitrate) to about 192 kbps, without discernible quality loss. **The main advantage of lossy file formats is that they allow you to balance quality against size**. The most commonly used formats on the Web are listed in Table 7.6.

TABLE 7.6

Commonly Used Audio Formats

File Format	Compression	Sample Rate	Bit Depth/Bit Rate	Common Usage
AAC (e.g., .aac, m4a, .mp4, and .3gp).	Standardized lossy compression scheme and format.	8–96 kHz (MPEG-2) 8–192 kHz (MPEG-4 HD-AAC).	Up to 256 kbps per channel. Supports variable bitrate (VBR).	Used in several audio codecs for almost any application or device in which audio is delivered, including on 3GP mobile phones as .3gp, which is .mp4 optimized for phones. Quality of 128 or 192 kbps is adequate for most applications. It is supported by all major browsers.
Ogg/Vorbis (.ogg and .oga)	Open source multimedia lossy container format.	None officially specified; set by encoder.	None officially specified; set by encoder. It supports VBR.	Typically used with Vorbis audio codec. Quality rivals that of other popular formats', but less supported.
MP3 (.mp3)	De facto standard lossy codec and format.	8–48 kHz.	8–320 kbps. It supports VBR.	Very popular for delivering audio. 128 kbps is often adequate for most applications. It is supported by all major browsers.
Opus (.opus)	Standardized open source lossy codec used with OGG format.	8–48 kHz.	6–510 kbps. Supports VBR.	Used for interactive delivery of voice over the Internet. It is suitable for music also and is successor to Speex.
Windows Media Audio (.wma).	Lossy and lossless codec and format.	8–96 kHz.	Up to 24 bits. It supports ABR and VBR.	Typically, WMA 9 Voice 22.05 kHz 8-bit mono is used for voice and Internet radio; 24–96 kbps for stereo; and 128–256 kbps for 5.1 channel.

7.4.3.2 Guidelines on Effective Use of Sound

The ways in which sound is used in Web design depend on the type of Web application. For example, in games and kids-learning applications, different types of sounds are used, including speech, music, and sound effects. On the other hand, an academic website is unlikely to use any sound or sound in the same way as used in games. For the majority of websites that do not use sound for the purpose of communicating specific messages, the use of sound is usually limited to music. The problem is that when not used to communicate specific messages, it is easy to misuse sound or use it in ways that make Web content inaccessible to people with disabilities, particularly the visually impaired. Some guidelines for use are presented here.

7.4.3.2.1 Automatic Starting of Sound

Sound should not start automatically, whether when users arrive at a page, after they have been there for a while and are in the middle of browsing, or when an object or area receives focus, such as when the cursor is over it. This is because users generally do not appreciate this, especially as they then have the added task of turning the sound off if they do not like it. Even when the means of turning the sound off are provided, it can be difficult to figure them out if not designed properly. It can especially be more difficult for users with disabilities who use assistive technologies and can only interact with a Web page by using the keyboard.

- If you must start sound automatically when users enter a page, then the control to turn it off should be provided and it should be near the beginning of the page, where it can be easily found. The control should be clearly labeled, keyboard-operable, and located early in the tab and reading order, so that it is quickly and easily encountered by users using assistive technologies (e.g., screen reader).
- If you must start sound automatically when an object or area receives focus, such as when the cursor is over it, you should provide a notice when focus reaches the object or area, such as through a pop-up or a callout, to say what to do to listen to the sound. Such pop-up or callout should disappear immediately after focus leaves the object or area and should not require users to click it, for example, to make it disappear, as this would require users to do something unnecessary that they would rather not be asked to do.
- If sound must be used to announce a message on entry into a page, it should play for no more than 3 s and should stop automatically. This is particularly useful for users who use screen readers, for whom other sounds can make it difficult to hear the screen reader, even if the screen reader informs them about how to control the sound or where to find the control.

7.4.3.2.2 Let Users Decide

Ideally, users should be given the courtesy of being the ones that control the use of sounds in Web content. They should be the ones that decide whether or not to start a sound. Again, this is especially beneficial for users who use screen readers, as it allows them to decide when turning on a sound will not interfere with the output of the screen reader. The option to choose can be in the form of a button that says, for example, "Turn sound on," which after it has been activated and the sound is playing should change to "Turn sound off". The option can also be in the form of a link to the relevant audio file.

7.4.3.2.3 When Multiple Sounds Are Involved

When a sound, such as music or the background sound of a scene, is behind a speech, the sound should be 20 decibels (dB) quieter (i.e., about four times quieter) to allow the speech to be heard clearly and understood. Doing this is particularly useful for preventing situations where people with hearing problems find it difficult to understand a speech when other sounds are simultaneously playing. Decibel is a measure of sound level, and applications used to create audio generally use it.

7.4.3.2.4 When Narrations Are Involved

If a narration is used in Web content, a text version should also be provided, as narration can be difficult for international users to understand for various reasons, such as accent and poor audio quality. Providing a text version gives these users time to figure out meanings and even check words in the dictionary.

CHALLENGE 7.9

Apart from when music is used as background to a speech, in what situations do you think the use of multiple sounds might be necessary?

7.4.4 Acquiring Audio for Web Design

Like with other media types, there are various ways to acquire audio for use in Web design, each of which is suitable for various types of projects. The most common acquisition methods are discussed here, which include stock audio, ripping tracks from discs, digitizing tracks from vinyl records, and creating them from scratch.

7.4.4.1 Stock Audio

As with stock images, there are both free and commercial stock audios of various categories and qualities available on the Web that can be used for non-unique audio requirements in a project. Categories range from different types of music to various non-musical types of sounds, including natural and artificial ones. Some are free for both private use and commercial use, as long as they are not reproduced for sale, whereas license needs to be purchased to use some for commercial or other specific purposes. A license may be for unlimited use (as in the case of royalty-free stock audios), which means that they may be used for any purpose and modified as required, without permission. A license may also be for just one-time use (as in the case of rights-managed stock audios), or there might be other terms involved. Some of the websites that provide commercial stock images also provide audio.

7.4.4.2 Ripping Tracks from Discs

Audios can be obtained by ripping (extracting) them from audio CDs or DVDs and then converting them to the desired format, either to directly use in an application or to import into a Digital Audio Workstation (DAW), which is the software used for audio recording, editing, and processing, for further processing or for combining with other audio and/or MIDI tracks. The main media players provide the feature for ripping tracks from CDs, including Windows Media Player, QuickTime, and iTunes. Examples of ripping software for Linux include K3b for KDE desktop and Sound Juicer for GNOME. Although major platforms have not yet, as of time of writing, provided functions for ripping audio from DVDs, there are cheap and free programs available for doing this, and to use them requires little more than opening a DVD from the program, selecting the titles or chapters to be ripped, and specifying the required quality parameters (such as sampling rate and bit rate), output format, and volume. However, there are typically issues of intellectual property involved when using this method. This matter is discussed later in this chapter.

7.4.4.3 Digitizing Tracks from Vinyl Records

Sometimes, the most suitable audio is only available on some old vinyl records. Sound tracks from vinyl records are analog signals and therefore need to be converted to digital audio. There are various ways in which this is done. For example, the analog output from a turntable player (or from the amplifier used to amplify its signal) is fed to the line input of a computer's sound card or an audio interface connected to the computer, and a DAW is used to record the resulting digital audio to mono or stereo tracks. Modern turntables designed specifically to help convert vinyl record tracks to digital tracks provide USB interface for connecting directly to the computer. In some cases, these turntables also provide special software for managing and automating the process. As with ripping, copyright issues are typically involved when using this method. Again, this matter is discussed later in this chapter.

7.4.4.4 Creating Audio from Scratch

Creating audio for a project from scratch is the most difficult and, perhaps, the most expensive, because it requires bringing together various components and resources, not least time. It also requires more skills than other methods to get the desired sound, depending on various factors, such as what is being produced. If what is being produced is just a basic sound, such as the sound of a knock, then this is less difficult than producing a musical piece that contains multiple instruments and vocals.

While a high-quality multi-track production would typically require going to a professional recording studio, good-quality music can also be produced in a modest home studio with minimum cost, given that there are free and inexpensive DAWs that are capable of producing good-quality sound and come with decent-sounding virtual instruments plug-in, such as piano, synthesizer, and drums, and even **audio effects** plug-ins, various types of which are also available for free on the Web. The standard types of

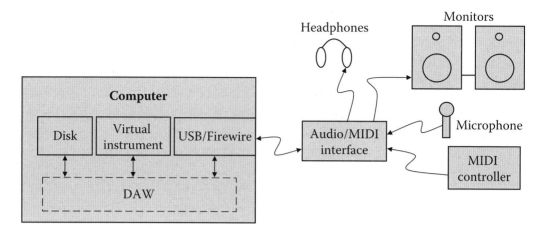

FIGURE 7.11   A basic computer-mediated sound-recording setup.

audio effects used in audio production are discussed later in the chapter. Other recording tools, such as microphone, speakers, headphones, and MIDI keyboard or any other type of MIDI controller, can also be acquired at relatively cheap prices. Figure 7.11 shows an example of an audio and MIDI recording setup.

Most modern DAWs are relatively easy and intuitive to use. Where the aim is to produce music, then some composing talent is necessary; how this is done depends on technique. For example, if all that the production is going to involve is the use of audio and/or MIDI loops, then only the talent to recognize the desire loops and combine them creatively is needed, whereas if tracks are going to be created from scratch, then the talent to compose tunes is certainly more crucial. Loops are short ready-made audio samples or MIDI patterns that can be used in tracks, instead of recording or creating them from scratch. The samples could be of anything from guitar riffs to drum parts, and the MIDI patterns are MIDI data designed to be used to play specific virtual instruments.

Whatever approach is used, producing a musical piece with multiple tracks typically involves creating the individual audio or MIDI tracks by recording them or by using loops, or both. Where live instruments are not available, such as in a small studio, the practice is to first create the instrument tracks as MIDI tracks and then convert them to audio later, when satisfied with them. Typically, the drums are done first, then the bass guitar, and then everything else one at a time, including vocals. The resulting audio tracks are then edited and processed, as desired, using audio effects and various types of processing, after which they are finally mixed down into a stereo (two-track) piece that is ready to be used in an application.

7.5 Video

Video is commonly delivered on a Web page by using hosted video services or adding it to a Web page, each of which has advantages and disadvantages in terms of the ease with which they can be achieved and the flexibility that they offer.

7.5.1 Adding Video via Hosted Video Services

This is the most in the straightforward way of adding video to a Web page. There are several video hosting services, the more popular of which are YouTube, Vimeo, and Metacafe. These services allow users to upload videos and provide the procedure to follow and the necessary HTML codes for accessing the videos from a Web page. The advantages of using them are that they provide players that are widely supported by browsers, automatically encode videos into suitable formats, and are typically free, as they get their money from adverts. The disadvantages include making uploaded videos available on their site instead of on your site only (whether or not you like it), using video quality that is not appropriate for content, and having restrictions in terms of video content, for example, videos may not be allowed to carry adverts.

7.5.2 Adding Video to Web Page

This involves hosting video on the same Web server that hosts the Web page in which the video is embedded. Although this involves more work and may even cost more, for example, in terms of paying for more bandwidth, it provides better control of what is delivered. Like other types of media, video is added to a Web page by linking and embedding, and linking is done by using the `<a>` element and embedding with the `<video>`, `<embed>`, or `<object>` element.

7.5.2.1 Linking to Video

The `<a>` element is used to link to a video file in the same way as it is used to link to any other file. Figures 7.12 and 7.13 show how it is used and also depict the result. As normal, clicking the link opens a media player to play the specified file. As with audio, the advantage of this is that the player is separate from the Web page, and so, it continues playing even if the user navigates to another page, as opposed to an embedded plug-in that stops.

```
HTML
<h3>Linked video</h3>
<a href="video/video.mp4">Watch the video with a helper
  application</a>
```

FIGURE 7.12 The `<a>` element linking to a video file.

Linked video

Watch video with a helper application

FIGURE 7.13 Rendered result of Figure 7.12.

CHALLENGE 7.10

Describe a situation in which you would consider linking to a video useful to the user?

7.5.2.2 Embedding Video

Like embedded audio, embedded video uses plug-in that is an integral part of a Web page. As noted earlier, the elements used to embed video is `<video>`, `<embed>`, or `<object>` element.

7.5.2.2.1 `<video>...</video>`

Just like the `<audio>` element is optimized for embedding audio, the `<video>` element is designed for embedding video in a page. The specific attributes that it supports are listed in Table 7.7, and Figures 7.14 and 7.15 show a basic use of it and depict the result. The content between the `<video>` tags is the message that is displayed when a browser does not support the element and is known as **fallback content**.

Notice that it is the poster ("garden.jpg") that is displayed in the example, not the video. The poster can also be used to display messages to users, such as "Please wait, media downloading ... ." It could also be a short animation to entertain while the video loads. Other image file formats that are commonly used for poster include PNG and GIF.

TABLE 7.7

Attributes Supported by the `<video>` Element

Attribute	Function
src	Specifies URL of video source.
width	Specifies the width of video.
height	Specifies the height of video.
poster	Specifies the URL for an image to display while no video is available.
controls	Specifies whether or not to display a control. A value is not necessary.
muted	Specifies the default state of audio stream. A value is not necessary.
autoplay	Specifies to start playing automatically. A value is not necessary.
loop	Specifies whether to repeatedly play video. A value is not necessary.
mediagroup	Specifies to group multiple video sources.
preload	Used with large files to suggest how a file should be loaded when page loads. Value can be "none" (which means not to buffer or store video in preparation for playback), "metadata" (which means buffering only metadata, i.e., information, about video), and "auto" (which leaves decision to the browser and is the default).

```
HTML
<h3>Embedded video</h3>
<video src="video/video.mp4" width="320" height="240" poster=
  "garden.jpg" controls>
    Your Web browser does not support HTML video element.
</video>
```

FIGURE 7.14   Example usage of the `<video>` element.

FIGURE 7.15   Rendered result of Figure 7.14.

CHALLENGE 7.11

In the code, where is the location of the poster image ("garden.jpg") relative to the HTML file? Also, where is it best kept and why?

Again, like the `<audio>` element, the `<video>` element can be combined with the `<source>` element to provide to the browser multiple choices of video file formats and encoding standards. This improves the chances of a browser finding a file format that it supports and therefore increases the chances of the video being accessed by as many users as possible. The attributes that it supports are listed in Table 7.8. Figure 7.16 shows how it is used with a code that produces the same result as Figure 7.15.

In the code, the first value of the codecs parameters is the one for the video and the second value is the one for the audio component. Note that like with the `<audio>` element, where codecs parameters are specified, they are one of the values of the `type` attribute and need to be in double quotes, while all the values of the attribute are enclosed in single quotes. Again, like with the `<audio>` element, it is worth knowing

TABLE 7.8

Attributes Supported by the `<source>` Element

Attribute	Function
src	Specifies the URL for the source.
type	Specifies the type of the source. It helps the browser determine whether it can play a file before loading it. Value is a string that identifies a valid **Internet media type**. Optional **codecs parameters** can also be added to specify how exactly the source is encoded.

```
HTML
<h3>Embedded video</h3>
<video width="320" height="240" poster="garden.jpg" controls>
  <source src="video/video.mp4" type='video/mp4; codecs=
  "avc1.42E01E, mp4a.40.2"'>
    <source src="video/video.ogv" type='video/ogv; codecs=
    "theora, vorbis"'>
    <source src="video/video.webm" type='video/webm; codecs=
    "vp8, vorbis"'>
    Your Web browser does not support HTML video element.
</video>
```

FIGURE 7.16 Example usage of `<video>` and `<source>` elements.

that, although the codecs parameters help the browser decide whether or not it can play a video file without having to load it first, the downside is that if it is not correctly specified, the browser will generate an error, even if it can play the file. On the other hand, if the parameters are not specified, the browser will load the file anyway and discover that it supports the file and play it. The message "Your Web browser does not support HTML video element" is displayed only if a browser does not support the `<video>` element. The formats and codecs that the major browsers support are listed in Table 7.9. Although H.264 and VP8 now have successors H.265 and VP9, respectively, they are yet to be as widely supported by browsers as of time of writing.

This means that to ensure your video works with the `<video>` element, it must be encoded in the codecs and saved in the file formats. There are several free and cheap **video file format converters** available on the Web, including on-line converters,

TABLE 7.9

File Formats and Codecs and Browser Support

Format	Supported Codecs	Browser Support
MP4	H.264 video + AAC audio	Internet Explorer, Firefox, Chrome, Opera, Safari
OGG/OGV	Theora video + Vorbis audio	Chrome, Firefox, Opera
WebM	VP8 video + Vorbis audio	Chrome, Opera

which can be used to convert existing media files to these formats. A commonly used one designed specifically for converting to HTML5 media formats is Miro Video Converter.

CHALLENGE 7.12

Cite some possible problems that embedding a video in a page might cause but linking to it might not.

7.5.2.2.1.1 Adding Captions and Subtitles The addition of subtitles and captions to videos is worth mentioning, not least because of its importance to accessibility. The element used to achieve it is the <track> element. It allows you to specify a **timed text track** (a file) that is played along a video delivered using the <video> element. The element is incidentally also used with the <audio> element. The format of the timed text track supported is WebVTT (Web Video Text Tracks), which carries a .vtt extension. Figure 7.17 shows an example of the content of a WebVTT file. It says to display the caption "First caption" at timecode 00:00.000 of the video and remove it at 00.01.980 and so on for the remaining captions.

Essentially, the browser plays a video and overlays the caption on it but only if the caption or subtitle function is enabled. This is typically done via the **captioning (CC) menu** of the media player, which is usually displayed at the bottom of the window. A WebVTT file can be created using one of the various tools, including free ones on the Web. An example is **HTML5 Video Caption Maker**, which allows a video to be opened in it and automatically inserts start and end time codes for every caption added (either via typing or via pasting). Before creating a caption file, naturally, a video first needs to be transcribed, which involves writing down the dialog and commentary in the video and the time codes of where they start and end.

Table 7.10 lists the attributes supported by the <track> element, and Figure 7.18 shows an example of how it is used.

```
WEBVTT
00:00.000 --> 00:01.980
First caption

00:01.980 --> 00:07.980
Second caption

00:07.980 --> 00:14.510
Third caption
```

FIGURE 7.17 Example of a WebVTT caption file.

TABLE 7.10

Attributes Supported by the `<track>` Element

Attribute	Function
default	Enables track if user's preferences do not indicate to use another track or if no other track is more suitable.
kind	Specifies the type of text track. The values supported are keywords: `subtitles` (which provides translation of content, such as dialogue and text, and is the **default**), `captions` (which provides transcription of audio, including non-verbal sounds), `descriptions` (which provides text description of video content), `chapters` (which provides chapter titles), and `metadata` (which provides information that is only visible to scripts).
src	Specifies address of WebVTT (.vtt) file and is mandatory.
srclang	Specifies the language of text track.
label	Specifies title of track and is used by the browser to show available text tracks.

```
HTML
<video src="jumper.mp4">
 <track kind="subtitles" srclang="en"
  label="English subtitles"src="jumper_en.vtt"default>
 <track kind="subtitles" srclang="de"
  label="Deutsch Untertitel"src="jumper_de.vtt">>
</video>
```

FIGURE 7.18   Example usage of the `<track>` element.

7.5.2.2.2 `<embed>` *and* `<object>...</object>`

Since the `<embed>` and `<object>` elements are designed to be used for dynamic media, they can also be used to embed video in a Web page; however, it is most commonly used to embed Flash video and animation (discussed later in the chapter). The attributes supported by the `<embed>` element were listed earlier in Table 7.4, and those supported by the `<object>` element in were listed in

```
HTML
<object data="video/video.mp4" type="video/mp4" width="320"
 height="240">
  <param name="autoplay" value="false">
  <!-- The embed element is used as fallback -->
  <embed src="video/video.mp4" type="video/mp4" width="320"
   height="240">
</object>
```

FIGURE 7.19   Example usage of `<object>` and `<embed>` elements.

Table 7.5. Figure 7.19 shows both elements used together. The `<embed>` element is used as fallback, so that if the browser does not support one element, for example, it can try the other.

CHALLENGE 7.13

In the code example, what would happen if the `<embed>` element is placed outside the `<object>` element?

7.5.3 Video in Design

Various factors need to be considered when incorporating videos in Web design, in order to ensure that they are used effectively. Some relate to technical aspects of video, such as quality, file size, file formats, and compatibility, while others relate to appropriateness of use.

7.5.3.1 Video File Size

Video is made up of series of consecutive bitmapped images displayed per second. These images are referred to as **frames,** and their dimension (i.e., pixel dimension) are referred to as **frame size**. The number of bits used to represent each pixel of each frame is known as **color depth**, and the number of frames displayed per second is known as **frame rate**. Figure 7.20 shows a broad illustration of the anatomy of a video, including an audio accompaniment.

When shooting and editing a video, frame size, color depth, and frame rate are some of the properties that need to be specified. In principle, the higher the values of these properties, the better the quality of video. The size of the file produced, of course, is also larger. As you might recollect from Chapter 6, a high-quality bitmapped image produces a relatively large file. Imagine many of this per second, and you might get a general idea of the file size generated by high-quality digital video. Where there is an audio accompaniment, this naturally adds to the size.

As an example, a 1-second **standard definition** (SD) resolution (720 × 576) video digitized at 16-bit color depth and 25 frames per second, with CD-quality audio accompaniment, can generate as much as 20.91 MB of data. Standard definition resolution is the traditional resolution used in television. More current definitions

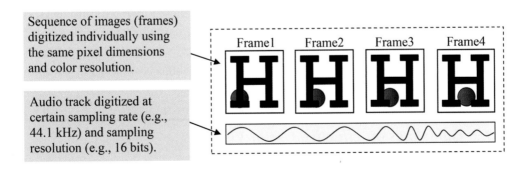

Sequence of images (frames) digitized individually using the same pixel dimensions and color resolution.

Audio track digitized at certain sampling rate (e.g., 44.1 kHz) and sampling resolution (e.g., 16 bits).

Frame1 Frame2 Frame3 Frame4

FIGURE 7.20 An illustration of the components of a digital video track.

include **high definition** (HD) and **ultra-high definition** (UHD), which support resolutions up to 8192 × 4320, both of which support higher resolutions. Whichever standard is used to encode a video, the amount of data generated is simply more than what Internet connections or systems can handle speedily. This is why compression is needed even more for the delivery of video than for other media object types.

Like with audio, the amount of bits generated per second in video is known as **bitrate**, and the quality of video is generally defined in these terms. The formula to calculate it is:

$$\text{Video bitrate} = \textbf{frame size} \times \textbf{color depth} \times \textbf{frame rate}$$

This means that the bitrate of the example cited earlier is 167 Mbps. To minimize bitrate without significantly compromising video quality, video compression standards use various techniques, including reducing the number of bits used to represent the color of the pixels of a frame and using various other techniques.

CHALLENGE 7.14

Video file size can be calculated by multiplying its bitrate by its duration in seconds. Given this, how long will it take to download a 1.15 MB video file over a connection that offers an average speed of 2 Mbps?

7.5.3.2 Video File Formats and Codecs

There are numerous video file formats, each of which supports different frame sizes, color depths, and frame rates. Where they support compression, they offer these parameters at different bitrates. A video file format can support only its native codecs, or, if it is a **container format**, it can support many types of codecs. When preparing a video for a Web page, the video editing program that you use would typically offer the opportunity to choose various combinations of formats and codecs. Standalone video encoders, such as free Mediacoder, also allow you to do this. The recommended formats and codecs when using HTML5 have been presented earlier in Table 7.9. Video encoded with **H.264** codec and placed in **MP4** file container format is by far the most commonly used video on the Web. The full name for MP4 is **MPEG-4 Part 14**, and H.264 is also known as **MPEG-4 Part 10** or **MPEG-4 AVC** (Advanced Video Coding). As of time of writing, the successor to H.264, **H.265**, is yet to be as widely adopted. H.265 is also known as **MPEG-H Part 2 HEVC** (High-Efficiency Video Coding) or **H.265/ HEVC**. It is designed to provide higher resolutions at the same bitrates as H.264. It has been said, for example, to be capable of twice the compression produced by H.264 at the same level of video quality and better quality at the same bitrate. Other commonly used formats that you might come across include AVI, WMV, and FLV (which is used for Flash videos).

7.5.3.3 Guidelines on Effective Use of Video

The use of video on the Web has gone up tremendously over the last decade or more, owing to the advent of video-sharing websites, such as YouTube, and the migration of news media to the Web. However, delivering videos on video-sharing websites is different from delivering them on your own site. While capturing and uploading video to a video website may only require the knowledge of how to shoot a good video at best, incorporating video in Web page design requires more than the basic desire to do so or indeed personal preferences; it requires the knowledge of issues such as when it is appropriate to use it, what to use it for, its effects when combined with other media object types in a design, the relationship between quality and the effectiveness of the message being communicated, and the frame size that is appropriate.

7.5.3.3.1 Appropriateness of Video in Design

Video in Web design should be used only if it is essential to the understanding of the message being communicated. Content should take advantage of the dynamic nature of video for the use of video to be justified; that is, if there are no significant movements, static images combined with text are adequate. Even when it may be useful to use video, if the quality is lacking (e.g., in terms of clarity, size, and speed), then using it is pointless and it seldom adds any value. Even more, this often projects lack of professionalism. Also, rather than using video, animation may be considered if it can communicate the same message effectively. Of course, there are the production advantages and disadvantages. For example, creating a video can be as easy as pointing a camcorder and shooting, while creating an animation typically requires more skill, time, and effort; however, it produces a smaller file and offers more control over the details of the content.

CHALLENGE 7.15

For which of the following would you use video and for which you would not?

- Showing dance moves.
- Illustrating how a bicycle pump works.
- Sports training.

7.5.3.3.2 Video Quality in Design

As mentioned earlier, **video quality revolves around bitrate**. It determines the frame size and frame rate that produce acceptable quality. Essentially, the higher the bitrate, the bigger the frame size and frame rate that you can use and still maintain good picture and motion quality. For example, a bitrate of 1.5 Mbits/sec will not produce good-quality video with a 720 × 576 frame size, let alone HD resolutions such as 1280 × 720 and 1920 × 1080. This means that it is important to choose a format and a codec that offer the bitrate that supports the frame size and frame rate needed for a design. A codec that is capable of producing high quality at low bitrate, such as H.264, and the successor, H.265, is ideal. However, low bitrates typically do not cope very well with high levels of movements in a video. Among the factors considered when balancing quality against bitrate are the level of clearness and detail required for a video, which in turn depend on other factors, such as **video content** and the **screen size of the target device**. For example, in terms of video content, a low bitrate and frame size would probably suffice for a talking-head video that is unlikely to be viewed full screen, while high bitrate and large frame size are required for a video with a scene that contains a lot of things that need to be seen clearly.

Obviously, given the direct relationship between bitrate and frame rate, the higher the bitrate, the higher the frame rate that can be used. However, not all types of videos require high frame rate. The summary of the relationship between frame rate and quality is that high bitrate and low frame rate would produce clear images, but motion can be choppy, while a video stream with low bitrate and high frame rate will likely produce blurry images and "trailing" effects (particularly if frame size is large) but smooth motion. Generally, the more the movements in a video, the higher the frame rate required to make it appear smooth. Above all, when video is intended for the Web, the consideration of the target audience's connection speed is paramount, particularly when delivery is live, as in a broadcast.

To help balance the quality against bitrate, most modern codecs, such as H.264 and H.265, offer different bitrates that are optimized for specific frame sizes and frame rates, making them best suited for different applications. H.264 offers these properties in the form of **profiles and levels**, examples of which are shown in Table 7.11, and H.265 offers them in the form of **profiles, tiers, and levels**, examples of which are

TABLE 7.11

Example of the Profile-Level Concept in H.264

Level	Max. Resolution@ Frame rate	Profile			
		Baseline, Main, Extended	High	High 10	. . .
1	128 × 96@30.9 176 × 144@15.0	64 kbps	80 kbps	192 kbps	. . .
1b	128 × 96@30.9 176 × 144@15.0	128 kbps	160 kbps	384 kbps	. . .
1.1	176 × 144@30.3 320 × 240@10.0 352 × 288@7.5	192 kbps	240 kbps	576 kbps	. . .
1.2	320 × 240@20.0 352 × 288@15.2	384 kbps	480 kbps	1152 kbps	. . .
1.3	320 × 240@36.0 352 × 288@30.0	768 kbps	960 kbps	2304 kbps	. . .
. . .	. . .	. . .	. . .	. . .	. . .
5.2	1920 × 1080@172.0 2560 × 1920@108.0 3840 × 2160@66.8 4096 × 2048@63.3 4096 × 2160@60.0 4096 × 2304@56.3	240 Mbps	300 Mbps	720 Mbps	. . .

TABLE 7.12

Example of the Profile-Level-Tier Concept in H.265

Level	Max. Resolution@ Frame Rate	Main and Main 10 Profiles		Main 12 Profiles		. . .
		Main Tier	**High Tier**	**Main Tier**	**High Tier**	. . .
1	128 × 96@33.7	128 kbps	–	192 kbps	–	. . .
	176 × 144@15.0					
2	176 × 144@100.0	1500 kbps	–	2250 kbps	–	. . .
	320 × 240@45.0					
	352 × 240@37.5					
	352 × 288@30.0					
2.1	320 × 240@90.0	3000 kbps	–	4500 kbps	–	. . .
	352 × 240@75.0					
	352 × 288@60.0					
	352 × 480@37.5					
	352 × 576@33.3					
	640 × 360@30.0					
3	352 × 480@84.3	6000 kbps	–	9000 kbps	–	. . .
	352 × 576@75.0					
	640 × 360@67.5					
	720 × 480@42.1					
	720 × 576@37.5					
	960 × 540@30.0					
3.1	720 × 480@84.3	10 Mbps	–	150 Mbps	–	. . .
	720 × 576@75.0					
	960 × 540@60.0					
	1280 × 720@33.7					
. . .	. . .	. . .	. . .	. . .	. . .	. . .
6.2	3840 × 2160@300.0	240 Mbps	800 Mbps	360 Mbps	1200 Mbps	. . .
	4096 × 2048@300.0					
	4096 × 2160@300.0					
	4096 × 2304@300.0					
	7680 × 4320@128.0					
	8192 × 4320@120.0					

shown in Table 7.12. Main profiles are suitable for most applications, and high profiles are suitable for applications that are more demanding. Notice that you have a choice of different bitrates (quality) for the same frame rates and frame sizes. Also, notice that the same frame sizes and rates can be achieved with less bitrates in H.265 than in H.264. You should know that the lists are not comprehensive; more comprehensive ones can be found on the Web for different codecs. There are also various on-line **bitrate calculators** designed to help calculate the optimal bitrate at which to encode a video file to achieve what is considered good quality.

CHALLENGE 7.16

For which of the following videos would you use high or low frame rates, and why?

- Racing
- A lecture
- A church service

7.5.3.3.3 Video Content in Design

Videos are used in various ways online as well as are delivered on various types of devices. They are used to deliver entertainment as well as information, in which they are combined with other types of contents, such as text and images, and it is within this latter context that more design issues arise and the guidelines given here apply.

7.5.3.3.3.1 Using Only Video to Provide Information   Avoid relying solely on video to provide information. This is because users may not be able to access it, or the video may not play properly. Also, users may not be able to see or hear it. Instead, also provide content via other communication channels, such as text, which can be read or read out by the screen reader. Captions and a full transcript should be provided to comply with accessibility guideline.

7.5.3.3.3.2 Starting Video Automatically   Like with audio, **videos should not start automatically**, either as users arrive at a page or while they are browsing it. Asking users to stop a video if they do not want it, rather than letting them start it if they want it, amounts to giving them an unnecessary task to do, and this can be irritating. Not only this, it can make a page inaccessible to people using screen readers, because the sound from the video can interfere with the output of the screen reader and it can be difficult for them to know what to do to turn off the video.

Videos that start automatically in the middle of browsing can be especially irritating, because it is not always obvious where on the page the video is or which out of the many videos is playing. Even with the sound turned off, a video that starts without user's content can be distracting to the user, as moving objects consistently attract attention.

Even when users click a link text to arrive at a page for a story, video should not start automatically. Users may not want to see the video and may instead only want to read the text equivalent of the story. This means that starting video automatically gives them the extra task of having to turn it off. Not only that, it can cause download-speed problem, which can result in a page to freeze up for a considerable amount of time, during which period you can neither watch the video nor scroll down to read the text.

In all cases, users should be provided with controls to start, stop, restart, or mute a video, as well as to adjust its volume. If relevant, provide information to users about how they can find out more about a video after they have finished viewing it. This may, for example, be in the form of related links and/or thumbnails. A thumbnail should be of good quality and be able to scale well, so that it can still be clear when bigger. It should also be representative of a video's content. Ideally, it should be taken from the middle of the video, where content is better represented, rather than from the beginning.

7.5.3.3.3.3 Information about Video Content Provide information about the content of the video in order to help users know what they are viewing or help them decide whether or not they want to view it. This can ensure that those interested in the content of a video do not skip it. Information provided should include a descriptive but concise name or title of the video, the topic covered, information about content (e.g., presenter and/or people), and duration, as users usually like to know how long they are going to spend to download and view a video. If video is long, to make it possible for users to skim through its content, a list of content or topics, or transcript, should be provided to help them navigate to the desired parts of the video.

For people who cannot see or hear or those who cannot hear or read rapidly, provide text or audio alternative, as appropriate, that conveys the same information as in the video, so that they can have access to the video's content. The link to the text or audio file for the alternative should be placed near the video. Link text should always describe video content accurately.

7.5.3.3.3.4 Conciseness of Video Videos that provide information should be straight to the point. Introduction should be short, ideally 5 s or less, and the goal should be to identify source of information and the video's content. Users generally need to know what a video is about and determine whether or not they want to see it. **Long introductions or slow and weak start to a video are a put-off** and can cause users to lose interest quickly and leave, even if they might have stayed if the true content had been revealed sooner. This is one of the reasons why well-planned and thoughtful editing is crucial. Where there are many videos to watch, providing introduction with each can quickly become annoying. It may be best to provide an introduction clip and skip any detailed introduction in the rest of the videos.

CHALLENGE 7.17

Assume that you are browsing a news website (e.g., CNN) and you click a link because you are interested in knowing more about the link text. However, when you arrive at the relevant page, a video is presented that has no direct relevance to the link text and it also starts playing automatically. Below it is the text form of the actual story described in the link text. What is wrong with this practice, and how would you fix it?

CHALLENGE 7.18

Again, assume that you are browsing a news website and a video is presented to you, together with its text equivalent under it. Then, after the video has finished, another video starts, but the article underneath does not change accordingly, so that the video content no longer matches the article under it. Say why this is good or bad for user experience, and if you think it is bad, suggest a better design approach.

7.5.4 Acquiring Video for Design

Video can be acquired in a number of ways, including via stock videos, ripping from optical discs, digitization of analog videos, from scratch, and via screen capture. Which one is used depends on various factors, such as type and quality requirements of project and the availability of skills, equipment, and time.

7.5.4.1 Stock Videos

For short generic or even subject-specific videos, such as those used in adverts or public information, it is often worth considering the free and stock videos available on the Web, instead of choosing to produce a video purposely. Although free videos might be adequate for some personal projects, for professional projects, stock videos are typically the best choice, because they are professionally produced and of high quality. Many websites that offer images and audio also offer videos, usually for a fee. A license may be for **unlimited use** (as is the case with royalty-free stock videos) or for just **one-time use** (as is the case with rights-managed stock videos), or there might be other terms involved. They are available in various resolutions, including SD, HD, and UHD resolutions, and in compressed or uncompressed file formats, typically MOV, MJPEG, Photo-JPEG, and MP4. Where videos are going to be edited before use, it is best to get them in uncompressed formats or formats that use **intra-frame-only compression** (i.e., the compression of only individual frames), as they support editing better than those that **use inter-frame compression** (i.e., compressing frames relative to one another). Essentially, intra-frame-only compression allows easier access to individual frames and easier editing.

7.5.4.2 Ripping Video from DVD Video/Blu-Ray Disc

If the video to be used is in DVD-video or Blu-ray format, then it needs to be ripped (i.e., extracted) from the disc. **Ripping a video from a DVD-video disc** generally involves little more than opening the DVD in the relevant ripping program and then following the procedure supported by the program to extract the video files, which are typically **MPEG-2 files** encoded in **H.262/MPEG-2 Part 2** video compression standard in the **VOB** (Video Object) container files, which are normally in the **VTS sub-folder** of the **Video_TS folder**. It is usually possible to specify that files should be ripped in a different file format from MPEG-2. If not, then the resulting MPEG-2 files can be transcoded (converted) into the desired format, such as MP4. There are various programs available on the Web for ripping and transcoding, including free ones.

   Ripping from Blu-ray discs follows the same general principle as ripping from DVD. Some programs even support both tasks. The complexity of workflow depends on program and whether or not a disc is right-protected to prevent copying, but again, the procedure requires little more than opening the disc in the ripping program and initiating the ripping process, which, in time, rips the video files to the specified location on the hard disk. Where a disc is locked and the ripping program cannot unlock it, a separate program is needed to do this. The video on Blu-ray is typically encoded in

H.264/MPEG-4 AVC in **M2TS files** but can also be encoded in any of the two other video compression formats supported by Blu-ray (i.e., H.262 and VC-1). Whatever the case, the format ripped can be transcoded into the desired format. Like with DVD ripping, there are various programs available on the Web for Blu-ray disc ripping, some of which are free. Some names are provided at the end of the chapter. One of the easiest workflows is to rip by using the free program called MakeMKV (which rips video into an MKV format) and then transcode the MKV files with HandBrake, another free program. Naturally, it is important to note that ripping videos from someone else's disc is illegal, as is ripping from your own disc and using videos in a design without permission. Indeed, some countries do not permit ripping from DVD or Blu-ray discs at all.

7.5.4.3 *Video from Video Devices*

Video sources can either be analog or digital. Although analog video devices are all but extinct, sometimes, it may be necessary to use them in the process of digitizing analog videos. Obtaining video from an analog source, typically a tape, involves connecting the analog device, such as VCR and analog camcorder, to the analog input of a video capture card inside or outside the computer. A capture program provided with the card or a video-editing program is then used to perform and manage the capture by responding to dialog boxes, as they appear. This setup is illustrated in Figure 7.21. Communication between the card and the device is usually via a serial connector, such as **RS-232** and **RS-422**, that is separate from the cables that carry the actual video signals. Once the process is initiated from the program, the card essentially digitizes the video and makes it available in the program, where it can be edited, if necessary, and saved.

If a video capture card is not available but a digital camcorder is available, an analog video can still be converted. Assuming that the analog video is on a VHS tape, one way in which this is done is to play the tape in a VCR or an analog camcorder, whose output is connected to the analog input of a digital camcorder that is set to playback mode, whose digital output is connected to any of the digital ports of a computer, through where the video is recorded using a video editing program.

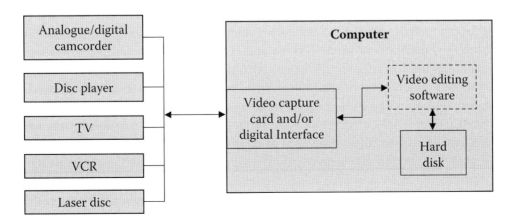

FIGURE 7.21 Inputting from various video devices.

When video is being acquired from a digital video device, it is usually only a matter of connecting the device to the computer via a digital interface, such as **IEEE 1394** (Firewire), **USB** (Universal Serial Bus), and **HDMI** (High-Definition Multimedia Interface), and uploading the video to the computer's hard disk for editing. Every digital device has at least one of these interfaces and so do most modern computers or capture cards. Some high-end professional digital camcorders and devices also have **SDI** (Serial Digital Interface), a high-capacity connection for exporting uncompressed **SD** and **HD** digital videos in real time, typically in TV broadcasting. Where a digital device uses a removable storage medium, such as disc or memory card, for which a computer has a drive installed, files can be transferred directly from it onto the computer's hard disk.

7.5.4.4 *Producing Video from Scratch*

Producing a high-quality video is increasingly easily achievable, given that many devices today are capable of producing high-resolution video. However, where the creation of an elaborate video in which there is a large cast or shooting is at locations is required, then the knowledge of videography and of what is required for a professional shoot is useful, such as the knowledge of the right lighting to use and the meaning of various types of framing and composition. Obviously, all modern video-capture devices are digital, so the video captured is automatically digitized and saved on some sort of medium, such as tape, disc, and flash memory.

A digital camcorder can also be used to capture and transmit video directly onto the computer's hard disk in real time, using a video editing program to initiate and stop the process. Where this is the case, the speed of connection is important, but more modern connection speeds are often adequate. For example, as of time of writing, USB 2.0 supports up to 60 Mbps and USB 3.1 supports up to 10 Gbps; Firewire supports 400 Mbps, 800 Mbps, 1.6 Gbps, and 3.2 Gbps; and HDMI supports speeds of up to about 18 Gbps.

7.5.4.5 *Video Screen Capture*

Video screen capture, also known as **screencast**, is a technique of recording the computer screen output, typically with audio narration. The video produced is different from the conventional kind of video and is used to demonstrate how a computer application is used to accomplish a task or to demonstrate new application software. It is a more efficient way of recording screen activities than pointing a camcorder at the screen and videoing it. Screencasting does not require the use of a video-capture device. It requires only a screen-capture program. In principle, to record the screen, the program is opened, the screen area to capture is defined, and the capture process is initiated, after which any screen activity is recorded along with any sound (such as narration) captured by any active microphone. On completion, the captured video is saved. Most screencast programs allow the video to be edited and annotated with text or graphics. The final video can be integrated into a Web page like any video produced through the conventional method.

7.6 Animation

The file format of an animation piece largely determines the types of HTML elements that can be used to add it to a Web page. The most commonly used file formats include animated GIF, SVG, SWF, and any of the video file formats previously introduced under video, and these formats are all used to store 2D animation. A **2D animation** is so called because it has only two dimensions (width and height). The other kind of animation is **three-dimensional** (3D) animation, which has a third dimension, depth. The use of 3D animation for delivering information is yet to be common on the Web and implemented primarily using CSS and scripting. The use of CSS for creating 2D and 3D animation is discussed in Chapter 18 and how HTML and CSS are combined with scripts in Chapter 22.

Animated **GIF** format is a very old format but still commonly used on the Web for very short repetitive animations. It is a series of bitmapped images saved in animated GIF file format. Since it is basically an image file, it is added to a Web page using the `<img>` element, the element used for adding static images. Refer to Chapter 6 on how to use the element to add image. Adding animation created using **SVG** (or even SVG combined with JavaScript) is done the same way as adding SVG images using the `<svg>` element, also introduced in Chapter 6. The **SWF** format is a Flash file format that is still commonly used for delivering animation on the Web, although its use is not recommended because the trend is toward making it obsolete in the future. This is because Flash technology is still a popular tool for creating vector-based animation. However, using the tool does not mean that what is produced must be saved in SWF. It can be exported in one of various formats supported by HTML5, such as MP4, WebM, or OGG. Or an SWF file can be converted to these formats using a free on-line converter. Once in any of these formats, an animation can be delivered in the same way as a video, using `<video>`, `<object>`, or `<embed>` to embed it, or `<a>` to link to it. Figure 7.22 shows how the `<object>` element is used to embed an animation in a Web page and Figure 7.23 the result. The animation was created in an old Flash program and converted to MP4.

In the example, the `data` attribute specifies the animation to embed and its location (which is the same as that of the source code), the `type` attribute specifies the MIME type, and `width` and `height` the size. The `name` attribute in the `<param>` element says to loop the animation infinitely.

```
HTML
<h3>Embedding animation</h3>
<object data="walk_motion.mp4" type="video/mp4" width="320"
 height="240">
   <param name="loop" value="true">
</object>
```

FIGURE 7.22 Using the `<object>` element to embed animation.

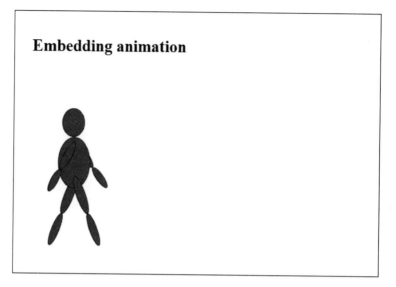

Embedding animation

FIGURE 7.23   Rendered result of Figure 7.22.

CHALLENGE 7.19

Implement Figure 7.22 with your own animation, using the `<video>` and `<embed>` elements and experiment with the `width` and `height` attributes.

CHALLENGE 7.20

Given that the animation in the example starts automatically and loops forever, modify the code to make its presentation more user-friendly and say why it is? You can use the `<video>` element instead of the `<object>` element.

7.6.1 Animation in Design

Animation is similar in anatomy to video in that it is made up of a series of images, except that animation is not a capture of the real life. While animation can be bitmapped- or vector-based, it is vector-based animation, which has made animation widespread on the Web, because it produces much smaller files. This means that the need for compression is not as much a major issue in the preparation and delivery of animation as it is in video.

7.6.1.1 Guidelines on Effective Use of Animation

The popularity of 2D animation had been largely due to the advent of Flash technology, and now, the advent of HTML5 and CSS3 is set to take this to a higher level, with functionalities such as transform, transition, and animation. These functionalities allow for a whole new range of animations to be seamlessly and easily incorporated into a Web page, such as moving objects around, changing their color and shape, making messages appear to notify users and then disappearing, and so on.

Unfortunately, the problem with the abundance of such functionalities is that attention often seems to be paid more to using as much of them as possible to showcase what can be done than to using them selectively and purposefully to ensure that usage helps user experience. Even large corporations that presumably employ professionals to build their websites still seem to end up with designs that are frustrating to use because of too many movements going in them. For example, there might be videos starting automatically, animations going on at the peripheral of vision, and texts expanding and collapsing, because it is updating in real time, causing the position of the content to shift without warning. All this leads to bad user experience. Moving objects are especially powerful things, because they attract our attention, whether we like it or not. However, this same property can also cause distraction and annoyance. This is why thoughtfulness is essential when using animation. Some guidelines based on results from studies, for example, from Nielsen Norman Group, a group specializing in interaction design, are presented here.

7.6.1.1.1 Common Uses of Animation

Animations are used for many purposes. Knowing what animations are commonly used for and determining whether or not they match your reasons for using animations can help in using them appropriately. Some of the ways in which they are used include:

- **Attracting user's attention**, for example, to a notification that the user is required to respond to or notice immediately.
- **Illustrating change over time**, such as how something or an area has changed over time.
- **Showing transition**, such as between states, as animation enables users to follow and understand the change from one state to another better than if the change is abrupt.
- **Showing relationship between objects** on which the user is already focused, such as showing how the parts of a machine work.
- **Providing feedback** to inform users that an action has been successful or that something is going on. Examples include rollover effect, depicting progress, such as when a file is being downloaded.
- **Setting mood**. For example, it can be used to create a sense of liveliness on a page that is providing information about a party. Party balloons, for instance, can be animated to float down the screen on entry or to float in the background. Similarly, falling snow can be simulated to set a Christmas mood. Naturally, when these are done, care should be taken not to compromise legibility. One way of achieving this is by placing text in a plain-color box, as illustrated in Figure 6.32 in Chapter 6.

- **Adding entertainment or fun value**, which includes elements changing color or moving, especially in designs targeted at children.
- **Showcasing new technologies and techniques**; however, this is not usually appreciated if it compromises user experience, as is sometimes the case.

7.6.1.1.2 Using Animation Effectively

While using animations appropriately ensures that your desired goals are achieved, it does not address the matter of how they affect user experience. In order for the use of animation to be considered completely effective, it should cause users little or no inconvenience.

- Notifications that appear near the edge of the screen should be made to appear slowly, either by slowly sliding in or by gradually fading into place. This is because we instinctively direct our attention to movement, especially fast, abrupt, or large movement, at the periphery (i.e., corners of the eyes). The periphery of a Web page includes areas outside the central area and is where animation adverts are typically placed.
- Animation is best used based on the user's action, rather than on indirect actions, such as on the loading of a page, when the user is scrolling, or on some other events; otherwise, it might confuse users. For example, when text is collapsed or expanded, it should be as a response to the user's action, such as when user checks a checkbox in a form or clicks some other element on a page.
- The user should not be made to encounter an animation too frequently in a session. Once, it might be tolerable, but when it happens repeatedly, it can be irritating. An example is using unnecessary animation for the start of every page, such as objects zooming into place. Another example is hiding and revealing the main menu of a page, either from the top or from the side, compelling users to go through the animation each time they want to access the menu. If space permits, main menu should be permanently displayed. Users will not miss the animation.

7.6.2 Acquiring 2D Animation for Design

The ways in which 2D animations can be obtained for use in a design are via stock 2D animations, 2D animation programs, and Web coding languages.

7.6.2.1 Stock 2D Animation

Like images, audio, and video, royalty-free 2D animations abound on the Web in various categories and at various prices and can be with or without audio. The animations are typically in HD 1080 and uncompressed video file formats or in formats that use **intra-frame-only** codecs. A common practice is to provide them in Photo JPEG wrapped in QuickTime MOV or AVI containers. They may also be provided compressed, for example, in MP4. Naturally, this format is appropriate only when no editing is intended; otherwise, an uncompressed format is better, which is then converted to a compressed format after editing. Where audio accompaniments are involved, they too are in uncompressed formats such as PCM and AIFF-C/SOWT. Character packs are also available for cartoons characters. These packs, which are typically in Flash file format, usually contain parts to use to build a character in different poses. For example, there are different hand positions; front, side, and back views; facial expressions; and backgrounds.

7.6.2.2 2D Animation Programs

Most programs designed for 2D animation production are frame-based in one sense or another, in that they use the concept of frames. Consequently, what typically distinguishes them is whether or not they incorporate a timeline, along which the frames of an animation are aligned. Programs for creating animated GIF, known as **GIF Animators**, generally do not incorporate a timeline; rather, they involve importing or drawing of images in each of the defined frames of an animation. Image qualities can be manipulated and effects and audio added, and speed is usually specified in terms of the display time for each frame. Programs for creating other types of 2D animations are typically timeline-based, some of the most popular being Adobe Flash and After Effects. These programs also use layers, which allow several images to be overlaid on each other in a frame. Most of them also have a native scripting language that can be used to produce advanced functions.

7.6.2.3 Coding

It should not be surprising that coding (i.e., computer programming) is another method of creating animation, since this is what is used to create animation software in the first place. Indeed, most, if not all, of the advanced animations on the Web and elsewhere, especially fast-action computer games, involve coding. Naturally, there are different types of coding languages, each suitable for different types and levels of animation. For the purpose of explanation, they are grouped as general-purpose and Web coding languages. **General-purpose coding languages** are powerful and can be used to develop virtually any type of computer application. A general-purpose language, for example, C++, can be used for any type of animation. Where advanced animations with a lot of media, fast-moving actions, and high level of interactivity are involved, it would certainly be one of the main choices.

In contrast, **Web coding languages** used for animation, which are commonly SVG, CSS, and JavaScript, are not as powerful as general-purpose coding languages. However, they are increasingly capable of producing relatively advanced interactive animations. While SVG and CSS can be used only for relatively basic animations, JavaScript extends the capability, making advanced interactivity possible. Examples of the types of animation for which SVG and CSS are best-suited include animating the drawing of objects (including text), interactive maps, morphing of SVG vector objects, and roll-over effect. More specifically, they are used for the types of animation that seldom perform specific tasks but can enhance user experience if used appropriately.

7.7 Useful Info

7.7.1 Web Links

HTML specifications: w3.org/TR/html51, w3.org/standards
Web development documents: docs.webplatform.org
Accessibility: w3.org/WAI/tutorials, webaim.org
HTML5 support testing: html5test.com
HTML tutorials (*Here are just a few free tutorial sites on HTML and other Web languages*): w3.org/wiki, html5rocks.com, sitepoint.com, w3schools.com, codecademy.com, quackit.com, developer.mozilla.org/en-US/docs/Web tutorialspoint.com, whatwg.org, htmlgoodies.com, htmldog.com, htmlcodetutorial.com, echoecho.com, learn.shayhowe.com, html.net, tizag.com, html-5-tutorial.com, docs.webplatform.org, developers.google.com, webdesignermag.co.uk
Design guidelines: nngroup.com
Online animation: www.animatron.com.

7.7.2 Free Software

Multiple download sites can be found for the following software by doing a search:

2D Animation: Unity (*Cross Platform*), Synfig (*Cross Platform*), KToon (*Unix only*), Pencil (*Win, Mac*), Lightspark (*Linux*), Stykz (*Cross Platform*), Pivot (*Win*), Tisfat (*Win*), Animationonline (*online*)
On-line 2D animator: Ajax Animator, Doink, Fluxtime, Scratch
On-line GIF Animator: GIF creator, GifPal, GifNinja, MakeGif
For 2D Games: Stencyl (*Win, Mac*), Gamesalad (*for mobile devices*), Construct 2 (*Cross Platform*)
Online game authoring: Gamefroot, AgentCubes
Morphing: WinMorph (*Win, Mac*), xmorph (*Win*), Norrkross MorphX (*MacOS*)
On-line morphing: Morphthing

Part II

CSS

8

Introduction to CSS

8.1 Introduction

Cascading Style Sheets (CSS) is a style sheet language that allows rules to be created that are used to determine how documents written in a markup language should appear when rendered. In this case, it allows the properties of the content of HTML elements, such as color, size, and position, to be controlled, as appropriate. This chapter introduces the fundamental principles of how it works.

8.2 Learning Outcomes

After studying this chapter, you should:

- Understand the concept of box model used by CSS.
- Know the structure of various types of CSS rules.
- Understand how precedence is determined when there are multiple CSS rules.
- Know the methods used for specifying CSS rules.

8.3 Introduction to CSS

CSS uses a **box model**, in which a marked up document is viewed as a hierarchy of rectangular boxes, with each box representing an element in the document. The size of the box depends on the size of the element's rendered content, and it is by controlling both the properties and the contents of the boxes of a document that the appearance of a Web page is controlled. The content of a box is the content between the two tags of an element. The properties of a box are shown in Figure 8.1. Of the properties, the ones that can be controlled with CSS are border, padding, and margin. **Border** (which is invisible by default) separates the edge of one box from the next box; **padding** is the space between the border of a box and the content of the box; and **margin** is the space outside the border.

Although there are many types of boxes, the main ones are **block-level type** (e.g., a paragraph containing lines of text and a section containing paragraphs) and **inline-level type** (e.g., words in a line of text; however, an inline-level box may contain a block-level

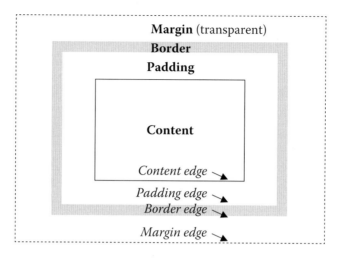

FIGURE 8.1   An illustration of CSS box model for an element.

box). The block-level boxes represent block-level elements, and the inline-level boxes represent inline-level elements. As mentioned in Chapter 2, block-level elements always start on the next line, while inline elements start on the same line. Apart from the box that represents the topmost element (i.e., the `<html>` element), every other box is inside another box, which could be inside another, and so on. An element that is inside another element is a **child element** of that element, and the element containing it is referred to as the **containing** or **parent element**. This means that an element that is a parent of one element can be a child element of another, and so on. Figure 8.2 shows a rendered

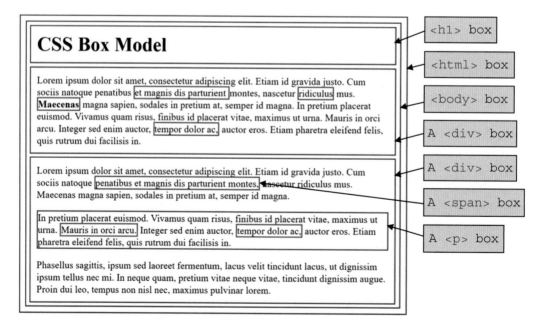

FIGURE 8.2   An illustration of the boxes that enclose HTML elements, using a rendered document.

Web document with a hierarchy of block boxes (in blue) and inline ones (in red). The outmost is the <html> element, the next is the <body> element, and the rest are the <h1> and two <div> elements; in the <div> elements are inline elements, such as <span> and <b>, and the <p> element. The leftover text at the bottom that is not enclosed in its own box is known as an **anonymous block box**. It cannot be styled by its own and is influenced only by the styling properties of its parent, which in this case is the bottom <div> element.

8.3.1 Anatomy of CSS Rules

A CSS rule determines how the content of the element or elements that it is associated with should be displayed. It comprises two parts: a **selector** and a **declaration block**. The selector selects the element or elements to which the instructions specified in the declaration block are to be applied. A declaration block may contain one or more declarations and is enclosed in curly brackets, with the declarations separated by semicolons. Although it is not mandatory to place a semicolon after the last declaration, it is generally considered a good practice. For example, it can help avoid omitting one when hurriedly adding a declaration to the end of a block. Each declaration comprises **a property** and **a value**, separated by a colon. Property specifies the aspects of the selected element to change, such as font, color, width, height, and border, and value specifies the setting for the property. Figure 8.3 illustrates the format. The example in Figure 8.3 specifies that the content of all occurrences of the <h1> element should be given a foreground color of yellow and a font in the family of Arial. The CSS properties are dealt with more fully later.

The example in Figure 8.4 shows more than one element specified in a selector and specifies to apply the same color and font family to the contents of the <h1>, <h2>, and

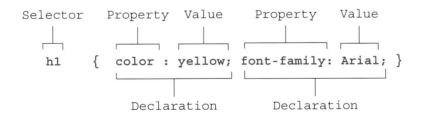

FIGURE 8.3 The structure of a CSS rule.

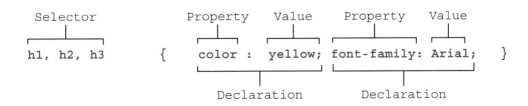

FIGURE 8.4 Structure of the rule for applying the same style to multiple elements.

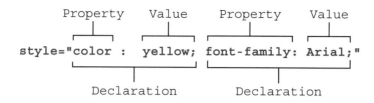

FIGURE 8.5   Using the `style` attribute to specify a declaration.

`<h3>` elements, so that they look the same, except for their size (recall from Chapter 3 that different heading elements have different sizes).

CSS rules can be declared in a separate document, to which the HTML document to be styled is then linked, or they can be declared in an HTML document, using the `<style>` element or the `style` attribute. When declared in a `<style>` element, they are simply placed between the element's opening and closing tags. When declared using the `style` attribute, the declaration block is made the value of the attribute and placed in quotes, as shown in Figure 8.5.

The declarations in the example say to display the text content of the element on which the `style` attribute is in yellow and has Arial family of font. The value of the `style` attribute is a rule, too, except that there is no selector, which it does not need, since it is inside an element and applies only to the element. More about how CSS rules are kept in a separate document or defined within an HTML document is discussed later in the chapter.

NOTE: Vendor prefixes

Because CSS is implemented differently by different browser vendors, particularly in older browsers, it is sometimes necessary to add prefixes to CSS rules to ensure that they are recognized by as many browsers as possible. The common prefixes used with major browsers are `-webkit-` (Chrome, Android, Safari, and iOS), `-moz-` (Firefox), `-ms-` (Internet Explorer), and `-o-` (Opera). To ensure that a property called `border-radius` is recognized by as many versions of major browsers as possible, for example, the declarations in your rule might look like the following:

```
.round-edge {
     -webkit-border-radius: 12px;
     -moz-border-radius: 12px;
     -ms-border-radius: 12px;
     -o-border-radius: 12px;
     border-radius: 12px;
}
```

There are some free scripts on the Web that free you from the use of these prefixes and typically only require including them on your page. An example is **prefixfree.js**.

CHALLENGE 8.1

In the .round-edge{} rule in the example in the NOTE box, which is the selector and which are the declarations and values?

8.3.1.1 *CSS Selector Types*

CSS provides many different selector types that enable rules to be crafted to style various complex combinations of elements in an HTML document. Table 8.1 lists the main ones. They will be referenced from other chapters, as they are used in more practical design situations.

Elements can also be selected for styling, based on attributes or their values. Table 8.2 lists common attribute selectors and how values are matched.

TABLE 8.1

Common CSS Selectors

Selector	Function	Example Usage
Universal selector	Selects all the elements in a document.	`* { }` for example, `*{ color=red; }` Applies to all elements.
Type selector	Selects all elements that match selector.	`ul { }` for example, `ul { color=red; }` Applies to all unordered list elements.
ID selector	Selects elements whose id attribute's value matches the selector.	`#intro { }` for example, `#intro { color=red; }` Applies to the element identified as "intro."

Class selector	Selects elements whose class attribute's value matches the selector.	`.side { }`
		for example, `.side { color=red; }`
		Applies to all elements whose class attribute's value is "side"
		`p.side { }`
		Applies to all `<p>` elements whose class attribute's value is "side."

Multiple class selector	Selects elements whose class attribute's values match the selector.	`.side.front.back { }` Applies to all elements whose class attribute values are "side front back."
Descendant selector	Selects an element that is a descendant of another specified element.	`div p { }` for example, `div p { color=red; }` Applies to all `<p>` elements in a `<div>` element.

(Continued)

TABLE 8.1 (*Continued*)

Common CSS Selectors

Selector	Function	Example Usage
Child selector	Selects an element that is a direct child of another specified element.	`div>p { }` for example, `div>p { color=red; }` Applies to only `<p>` elements that are direct children of a `<div>` element.
Adjacent sibling selector	Selects an element that is the next sibling of another element.	`h3+p { }` for example, `h3+p { color=red; }` Applies to only the first `<p>` element after an `<h3>` element.
General sibling selector	Selects an element that is a sibling of another element.	`h3~p { }` for example, `h3~p { color=red; }` Applies to all `<p>` elements that are siblings of an `<h3>` element.
Attribute selector	Selects an element that has a specified attribute or an attribute-value pair.	`em[lang] { }` for example, `em[lang] { color=red; }` Applies to all `<em>` elements with a "lang" attribute.

TABLE 8.2

How Attribute Selectors Match Attributes and Their Values

Attribute Selector Expression	Function	Example Usage
`[attribute]` (Existence)	Selects any element that has a specified attribute.	`p[id]` Applies to all `<p>` elements with an `id` attribute.
`attribute = value` (Equality)	Selects an element with an attribute whose name matches the specified attribute name and value matches the specified value.	`em[lang="zh"] { }` Applies to all `<em>` elements with a `lang` attribute whose value is "zh."
`attribute~ = value` (White space)	Selects an element with an attribute whose name matches a specified attribute name and whose value is a white-space-separated list of words (e.g., "en-us en-gb en-au en-nz"), one of which is a match.	`em[lang~="en-gb en-us"] { }` Applies to all `<em>` elements with a `lang` attribute whose value is a white-space-separated list that contains "en-gb en-us."

(Continued)

TABLE 8.2 (*Continued*)

How Attribute Selectors Match Attributes and Their Values

Attribute Selector Expression	Function	Example Usage
`attribute|` = `value` (Hypen-Minus)	Selects an element with an attribute whose name matches a specified attribute name and value matches the specified value or begins with it, immediately followed by "-" (hyphen-minus sign).	`em[lang|="zh"] { }` Applies to all `<em>` elements with a `lang` attribute whose value is "zh," or "zh-," as in "zh-CN" or "zh-TW," which represent simplified and traditional Chinese, respectively.
`attribute^` = `value` (Prefix)	Selects an element with an attribute whose name matches a specified attribute name and the value starts with the specified value.	`a[href^="#"] { }` Applies to all `<a>` elements with an `href` attribute whose value starts with "#."
`attribute$` = `value` (Suffix)	Selects an element with an attribute whose name matches a specified attribute name and the value is suffixed by the specified value.	`a[href$=".org"] { }` Applies to all `<a>` elements with an `href` attribute whose value is suffixed by ".org."
`attribute*` = `value` (Substring)	Selects an element with an attribute whose name matches a specified attribute name and the value contains one or more instances of the specified string value.	`a[href*="America"] { }` Applies to all `<a>` elements with an `href` attribute whose value contains one or more instances of "America."

8.3.1.2 Pseudo-Elements

CSS defines pseudo-elements to allow the selection and styling of specific parts of elements, such as the first letter of the first line of a paragraph, that are not accessible by using normal CSS selectors, because they are not defined in the HTML document tree model, since the model sees a document only as a hierarchical tree of elements whose properties can be controlled by CSS. Essentially, pseudo-elements behave like elements, even though they are not real elements, since they are not part of the HTML document tree. Table 8.3 lists the elements.

Although one colon, instead of double colon, may also be used with pseudo-elements, CSS3 uses double colon to distinguish pseudo-elements from pseudo-classes. Figure 8.6 shows the format for using a pseudo-element. It says to make the first letter of the content of every `<p>` element yellow. More examples of usage can be found in Chapter 14.

TABLE 8.3

Common Pseudo-Elements

Pseudo-Element	Function
::first-letter	Selects the first letter of the first line of the text content of an element.
::first-line	Selects the first line of the rendered text content of an element. This means the first line in the browser.
::before	Creates a pseudo-element and places it immediately before an element and is used with the content property, which is used to insert an object. Usage is discussed more fully in Chapter 14, where it is more relevant.
::after	Creates a pseudo-element and places it immediately after an element and is used with the content property, which is used to insert an object. Usage is discussed more fully in Chapter 14, where it is more relevant.
::selection	Applies styling to text that is selected or highlighted, for example with mouse. Only some properties can be used with it, such as color, background, text-decoration, text-shadow, outline, and cursor. These properties are also discussed more fully in Chapter 14.

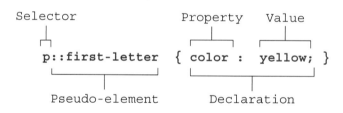

FIGURE 8.6   Syntax for using a pseudo-element.

8.3.1.3 Pseudo-Classes

Pseudo-classes are designed to allow elements to be classified on characteristics that are broader than those possible, for example, with the class attribute. Figure 8.7 shows the format for specifying them, and Table 8.4 lists them. Note that only a few of them are commonly used. Examples are provided in Chapters 14 and 17.

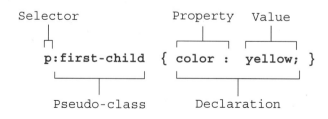

FIGURE 8.7   Syntax for using pseudo-classes.

TABLE 8.4

Pseudo-Classes and Examples of Usage

Selector	Function	Example
The Link History Pseudo-Classes		
:link	Selects all unvisited links.	a:link{} Applies to all unvisited <a> elements.
:visited	Selects all visited links.	a:visited{} Applies to all visited <a> elements.
The Dynamic Pseudo-Classes		
:active	Selects an element, such as a button, that is being activated by the user.	a:active{} Applies to an <a> element being activated.
:focus	Selects the <input> element that has focus.	input:focus{} Applies to <input> element that has focus.
:hover	Selects link when the mouse is over it.	a:hover{} Applies to all <a> elements.
The User Interface Element States Pseudo-Classes		
:checked	Selects a checked checkbox or radio button <input> element.	input:checked{} Applies to checked <input> elements.
:disabled	Selects disabled <input> elements.	input:disabled{} Applies to all disabled elements.
:enabled	Selects every enabled <input> element.	input:enabled{} Applies to all enabled <input> elements.
:required	Selects <input> elements that have the required attribute specified.	input:required{} Applies to all <input> elements that have the required attribute set.
:optional	Selects <input> elements that do not have the required attribute specified.	input:optional{} Applies to all <input> elements that do not have the required attribute set.
The Range Pseudo-Classes		
:in-range	Selects an element whose attribute's value is within the range of values specified for the element. Used to provide feedback to user input.	input:in-range{} Applies to an <input> element whose inputted value is out of specified range.

(Continued)

TABLE 8.4 (*Continued*)

Pseudo-Classes and Examples of Usage

Selector	Function	Example
:out-of-range	Selects an element whose attribute's value is outside the range of values specified for the element. Used to provide feedback to user input.	input:out-of-range{} Applies to an <input> element whose inputted value is outside specified range.
The Validity Pseudo-Classes		
:valid	Selects an <input> element whose content is correct, based on its type. Used to provide feedback to user input.	input:valid{} Applies to any <input> element whose input is valid.
:invalid	Selects an <input> element whose content is incorrect, based on its type. Used to provide feedback to user input.	input:invalid{} Applies to any <input> element whose input is not valid.
The Default-Option Pseudo-Class		
:default	Selects the default user interface element, such as the default button among a group of buttons.	:default{} Applies to the default element.
The Structural Pseudo-Classes		
:root	Selects a document's root element, which is the <html> element. It is the same as using html selector, except that is has higher **specificity** (i.e., precedence). Specificity is discussed later in the chapter.	:root{} Applies to the <html> element.
:nth-child(n)	Selects every element that is the nth child of its parent, where n is an integer. See Chapter 17 for more details.	tr:nth-child(2){} Applies to every <tr> element that is a second child.
:nth-last-child(n)	Selects the nth child of its parent, starting from the last child. See Chapter 17 for more details.	tr:nth-last-child(2){} Applies to every <tr> element that is a second to the last child.

(Continued)

TABLE 8.4 (*Continued*)

Pseudo-Classes and Examples of Usage

Selector	Function	Example
:nth-of-type(n)	Selects the nth sibling of its type. See Chapter 17 for more details.	p:nth-of-type(2){} Applies to every <p> element that is a second sibling.
:nth-last-of-type(n)	Selects the nth sibling of its type, starting from the last sibling. See Chapter 17 for more details.	p:nth-last-of-type(2){} Applies to every <p> element that is a second sibling from last.
:first-child	Selects an element that is the first child of its parent, same as :nth-child(1).	p:first-child{} Applies to first child <p> elements.
:last-child	Selects an element that is the last child of its parent, same as :nth-last-child(1).	p:last-child{} Applies to last child <p> elements.
:first-of-type	Selects the first sibling of its type. See Chapter 17 for more details.	p:first-of-type{} Applies to first child <p> elements.
:last-of-type	Selects the first sibling of its type. See Chapter 17 for more details.	p:last-of-type{} Applies to last child <p> elements.
:only-child	Selects an element that is the only child of its parent. See Chapter 17 for more details.	p:only-child{} Applies to <p> elements that are the only children.
:only-of-type	Selects an element that is the only sibling of its type. See Chapter 17 for more details.	p:only-of-type{} Applies to <p> elements that are the only sibling.
:empty	Selects elements that have no children. See Chapter 14 for more details.	p:empty{} Applies to empty <p> elements.

The Target Pseudo-Class

:target	Selects the element that is the target element of the referring URI. See Chapter 14 for more details.	:target{} Applies to the element that is being referred to by a URI.

(Continued)

TABLE 8.4 (*Continued*)

Pseudo-Classes and Examples of Usage

Selector	Function	Example
The Language Pseudo-Class		
`:lang (identifier)`	Selects every element that has its `lang` attribute's value equal to the identifier. See Chapter 14 for more details.	`p:lang(fr){}` Applies to all `<p>` elements that have `lang` attribute whose value is "fr."
The Directionality Pseudo-Class		
`:dir (identifier)`	Selects every element that has its `dir` attribute's value equal to the identifier. See Chapter 14 for more details.	`p:dir(rtl){}` Applies to any `<p>` element that has the `dir` attribute and whose value is "rtl."
The Negation Pseudo-Class		
`:not (selector)`	Selects an element that is not represented by the selector. See Chapter 14 for more details.	`p:not(#pro){}` Applies to any element that does not have "pro" as its id attribute value.

8.3.1.4 :nth *Selectors*

Instead of the :nth-based selectors listed in Table 8.4 taking just n (i.e., a number), they can also take a mathematical expression. This enables them to be used to specify multiple child selections, such as every second or third child element in a list of children of the same parent. The expression's syntax is **an+b**, and it represents an element that has **an+b–1** siblings before it in a list of children that share the same parent with it. For example, if an element has three siblings before it, then its position is 4th and can also be said to have an index of 4. The index numbering of the children of an element starts at 1 (i.e., the first child has an index of 1).

Another way to think of the an+b expression is that it selects child elements whose index matches the value to which the expression evaluates. The value of n can be a positive integer or zero, and the value of a or b must be a positive or negative integer or zero. Basically, the way it works is that n is progressively assigned the values of 0,1,2,3, and so on and the expression evaluated each time for each value. In the end, the element selected is the one with the index that matches the result of the evaluation. So, for the expression 2n + 1, for example, n is first given the value of 0, which makes the expression evaluate to 1 (i.e., [2 × 0] + 1). So, the first child is selected. Next, n is given the value of 1, which makes the expression evaluate to 3 (i.e., [2 × 1] + 1). So, the third child element is also selected. In the same way, the values of 2,3,4, and so on evaluate to 5,7,9, and so on, and the corresponding child elements are selected, if available. If the expression evaluates to zero or a negative number, no element is selected, since no child element has a zero or negative index.

To show an example of the application of nth selectors, `li:nth-child(4n-7)` `{color: brown; }` says to make text brown for all `<li>` child elements that have the index of 1,5,9, and so on. This is done by giving n the value of 0, which makes the expression evaluate to –7 (i.e., [4 × 0] – 7), for which there is no matching element index. Next, n is given 1, which evaluates to –3, for which there is also no matching index. Next, n is 2, which evaluates to 1, which matches the first child element, and so on.

Instead of using n or an expression, the `odd` or `even` keywords could also be used. The `odd` keyword selects child elements 1,3,5,7, and so on, and the `even` keyword selects child elements 2,4,6,8, and so on. The `odd` keyword, for example, can be specified as `tr:nth-child(odd) {}`. It is useful to know that there are :nth checkers on the Web for trying out outputs of expressions.

CHALLENGE 8.2

Given the following expressions, state the positions of the child elements selected:

- 1n + 0 (or simply n).
- 2n + 0 (or simply 2n).
- 2n + 1.
- 3n – 4.
- n + 5.
- –2n + 3.

8.3.2 CSS Cascading Properties

The cascading properties of CSS refer to the principles that govern how CSS rules take precedence over each other when multiple rules are targeting the same element. Understanding them is important when creating style sheets, as this can help minimize possible problems, as well as lead to the creation of cleaner, more efficient style sheets. Three main principles used are **last rule**, **specificity**, and **inheritance**.

8.3.2.1 Last Rule Principle

This principle says that if two rules have identical selectors, then the last one takes precedence. For example, in the example in Figure 8.8, the second selector takes precedence.

```
CSS
p { color: red; }
p { color: blue; }

HTML
<p>This text is styled by the last CSS rule.</p>
```

FIGURE 8.8 Illustration of the last rule principle.

CHALLENGE 8.3

Which of the following rules has precedence, and what does it do?

```
p#intro { color=red; }
p#intro { color=blue; }
```

8.3.2.2 Specificity Principle

The principle of specificity states that where more than one rule apply to an element, the more specific rule takes precedence over the more general ones. In the example in Figure 8.9, the most specific is `div#larger p{}` (because it identifies the element specifically), followed by `p.largest{}` (because a class selector is more general than an `id` selector) and then `p{}` (because a type selector is more general than either).

Note that using the `!important` **exception** with any rule gives the rule precedence over all other rules. For instance, using it with the least specific rule in the previous example, as shown in Figure 8.10, gives the rule precedence over the most specific rule.

However, using this exception is **not considered a good practice**, as it makes debugging (i.e., resolving errors in code) difficult, since it disrupts the natural cascading flow of style sheets. Where it must be used, the advice is to use it only on page-specific CSS designed to override some site-wide or global styles. When used in this way, its effect is more localized and therefore more traceable and manageable.

```
CSS
p { color: red; }
p.largest { color: green; }
div#larger p { color: blue; }

HTML
<div id="larger">
  <p class="largest">Example</p>
</div>
```

FIGURE 8.9 Illustration of the specificity rule principle.

```
CSS
p { color: red !important }
p.largest { color: green; }
div#larger p { color: blue; }

HTML
<div id="larger">
  <p class="largest">Example</p>
</div>
```

FIGURE 8.10 Illustration of the `!important` exception rule.

A more accurate way of determining which CSS rule has precedence is to calculate the specificity of each selector and compare it with the others. This calculation is based on a set of four criteria, designated as **a, b, c,** and **d.** Each occurrence of a criterion in a selector counts as 1 for the criterion. So, if only one occurrence is found of the "d" criterion in a selector and nothing else, then the selector's specificity is 0,0,0,1; if one occurrence of the criterion "d," two occurrences of the criterion "c," and nothing else are found, the specificity is 0,0,2,1. Criterion "a" has the most importance, while "d" has the least importance. In theory, one criterion "a" carries more weight than any number of "b," "c," or "d." The four criteria and how they are scored are described as follows:

- If declarations are made via a `style` attribute, rather than via a selector, this represents one count for "a," so that, the score is a = 1, b = 0, c = 0, d = 0 (or 1,0,0,0).

- If declarations are made via `id` attributes in a selector, the number of such declarations represents the count for "b."

- If declarations are made via non-id attributes and pseudo-classes in a selector, the number of such declarations represents the count for "c."

- If declarations are made via element names and pseudo-elements, the number of such declarations represents the count for "d."

According to the criteria, the `style` attribute has the highest specificity, and this is so because its declarations apply specifically to the element in which it is and to no other. This is followed by the selector with the highest number of `id` attributes (because an `id` attribute is specific to only one element), then the selector with the highest number of non-id attributes and pseudo-classes, then the selector with the highest number of element names and pseudo-elements, and then everything else. By applying these criteria to Figure 8.11, the color of the content of the `<p>` element will be purple. Table 8.5 shows the specificity of each selector, which involves examining each selector and counting the number of occurrences of each of the four criteria.

```
CSS
* { color: red; }
p { color: blue; }
div p { color: orange; }
div p.yellow { color: yellow; }
#green { color: green; }

HTML
<div>
  <p id="green" class="yellow" style="color: purple">CSS
    Specificity Hierarchy</p>
</div>
```

FIGURE 8.11 Example showing different levels of specificity.

TABLE 8.5

Explanation of How Specificity Level Is Determined

Selector	Criteria Occurrences	Specificity
`*{color:red}`	a = 0 b = 0 c = 0 d = 0 (general)	0,0,0,0
`p { color: blue }`	a = 0 b = 0 c = 0 d = 1 (has one element)	0,0,0,1
`div p { color: orange }`	a = 0 b = 0 c = 0 d = 2 (has two elements)	0,0,0,2
`div p.yellow { color: yellow }`	a = 0 b = 0 c = 1 d = 2 (has two elements and a non-id attribute; i.e., class attribute)	0,0,1,2
`#green { color: green }`	a = 0 b = 1 c = 0 d = 0 (has one id attribute)	0,1,0,0
`style="color: purple"`	a = 1 b = 0 c = 0 d = 0 (has a style attribute, which overrides all other selectors)	1,0,0,0

CHALLENGE 8.4

Using the four criteria presented earlier and Table 8.3 as a guide, determine which of the following rules has the highest specificity level.

```
div p { color: red; }
p { color: grey; }
p#blue { color: blue; }
div p.green { color: green; }
```

8.3.2.3 Inheritance

The inheritance principle relates to whether or not child elements get properties passed on to them by the parent elements. Basically, some properties are inherited by default, while others are not. Inheritance determines what happens when no value is specified for a property of an element. When no value is specified for an inherited property of an element, the element uses the value of the parent element. When no value is specified for a non-inherited property of an element, the element uses the default value of the property. The `inherit` keyword can be used with any property to specify to inherit its value from the parent element. Figures 8.12 and 8.13 show how this works. The content of the `<em>` element is blue, like that of the `<p>` element, because the `color` property is an inherited property, which means that its value is inherited from the parent `<p>` element. In contrast, the `<em>` element shows no border even though the parent `<p>` element does. This is because the `border-style` property is a non-inherited property, and the default value for it on the `<em>` element is none (i.e., no border). The `color` property is discussed more fully in Chapter 9, and the `border-style` property is discussed in Chapter 10.

```
CSS
p { color: blue; }
p { border-style: dotted; }

HTML
<h3>Property inheritance</h3>
<p>The color property is an inherited property, so<em>the
    content of the em element</em> is blue just like that of
    the parent p element...</p>
```

FIGURE 8.12   A demonstration of property inheritance.

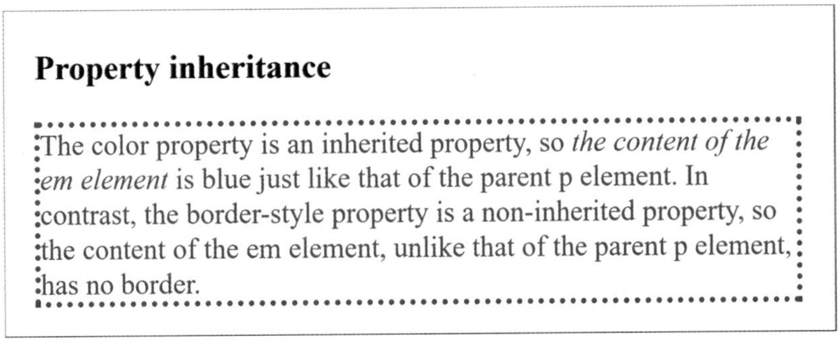

Property inheritance

The color property is an inherited property, so *the content of the em element* is blue just like that of the parent p element. In contrast, the border-style property is a non-inherited property, so the content of the em element, unlike that of the parent p element, has no border.

FIGURE 8.13   The rendered result of Figure 8.12.

CHALLENGE 8.5

Given the HTML and CSS codes below, in which color will the content of the <em> element be rendered?

CSS

```
span {color: red; }
p { color: blue }
p { border-style: dotted }
```

HTML

```
<h3>Property inheritance</h3>
<p>The color property is an inherited property, so <span><em>the
    content of the em element</em></span> is blue just like
    that of the parent p...</p>
```

The principle of inheritance can save a lot of time, as it prevents having to repeatedly write the same set of rules for child elements that share the same properties. Many properties that are not inherited by default can be forced to inherit values from their parent elements by using `inherit` as the value for the relevant properties. Figures 8.14–8.16 illustrate this with two <div> elements, which are children of the <body> element.

In the example, the properties specified in the body{ } rule (i.e., font-family, color, padding, and margin) are inherited by the two <div> elements, except padding and margin, which are non-inherited by default. The properties specified in the div.part1{ } rule (i.e., border and background-color) apply to only the first <div> element, and those specified in the div.part2{ } rule apply to only the second <div> element. The second <div> element also inherits the non-inherited padding and margin properties of the <body> element, because it is forced to do so with the use of the inherit keyword as value. Again, all the various properties are used here only to explain inheritance and are discussed

```
HTML
<body>
  <h2>CSS Inheritance</h2>
  <div class="part1">
    <p>This element has been forced to inherit the padding
       and margin properties of the body element</p>
  </div>
  <div class="part2">
    <p>This element has not inherited the padding and margin
       properties of the body element</p>
  </div>
</body>
```

FIGURE 8.14   HTML for demonstrating CSS inheritance principle.

```
CSS
body {
  font-family: Arial;
  color: brown;
  padding: 20px;
  margin: 20px;
}
div.part1 {
  border: 2px solid; orange
  background-color: white;
}
div.part2 {
  border: 2px solid; orange
  background-color: white;
  padding: inherit;
  margin: inherit;
}
```

FIGURE 8.15   CSS used with Figure 8.14 for demonstrating inheritance principle.

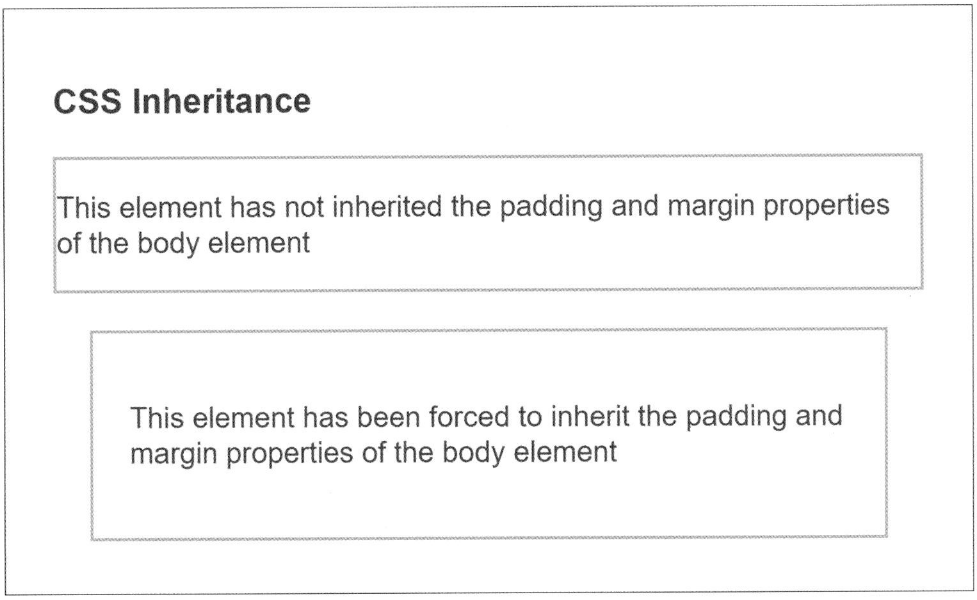

> ## CSS Inheritance
>
> > This element has not inherited the padding and margin properties of the body element
>
> > This element has been forced to inherit the padding and margin properties of the body element

FIGURE 8.16   The result of Figures 8.14 and 8.15.

more fully in later chapters. The `font-family` is discussed in Chapter 13; `color` and `background-color` are discussed in Chapter 9; and `border`, `padding`, and `margin` are discussed in Chapter 10.

CHALLENGE 8.6

Rewrite the CSS code in Figure 8.15 to make it more efficient.

8.3.3 Methods of Specifying CSS Rules

As mentioned earlier, CSS can be specified in an HTML document or in a separate document. When it is specified within an HTML document, it is known as **inline CSS**, and when it is specified in a separate document, it is known as **external CSS**.

8.3.3.1 Inline CSS

There are two ways in which inline CSS can be implemented; one way is to use the `style` attribute on the element to be styled, and the other way is to use the `<style>` element, which is usually placed in the `<head>` element but can also be used in the body of a document. When placed in the body of a document, the `scoped` attribute can be used on it to target a specific element and its children.

8.3.3.1.1 Using the `style` *Attribute*

Figure 8.17 shows how the `style` attribute is used, and Figure 8.18 the result. The same result can also be achieved with the `<style>` element, and how is shown in the next sub-section.

```
HTML and CSS
<h3>Inline style attribute</h3>
<p style="color: red">This paragraph element is styled with
 inline CSS, using the style attribute.</p>
<p>This paragraph element is not styled.</p>
```

FIGURE 8.17   Example usage of the `style` attribute for styling.

Inline style attribute

This paragraph element is stlyed with inline CSS, using the style attribute.

This paragraph element is not styled.

FIGURE 8.18   The result of Figure 8.17.

CHALLENGE 8.7

Implement the example, but also use one of the inline elements discussed under HTML in Part 1 to isolate a few words for styling that are different from that of the rest of the text.

8.3.3.1.2 *Using the* <style> *Element*

Figure 8.19 shows how the <style> element is used in the <head> element to achieve the same result as Figure 8.18. The type attribute specifies that the content of the <style> element is CSS, and the p.first_para{ } rule specifies to make the text contained in the element belonging to class="first_para" red.

```
HTML and CSS
<!DOCTYPE html>
<html>
  <head>
    <style type="text/css">
      p.first_para { color:red; }
    </style>
  </head>
  <body>
    <h3>Inline style element</h3>
    <p class="first_para">This paragraph element is styled
      with inline CSS, using the style attribute.</p>
    <p>This paragraph element is not styled.</p>
  </body>
</html>
```

FIGURE 8.19 Example usage of the <style> element.

CHALLENGE 8.8

Write the code to display the content between the quotes below, using the <style> element in the <head> element.

"This text is in a paragraph, this is in a span element, and this is also in the same paragraph element."

The inline CSS method is **not recommended for any serious use**. This is because it is limiting and inefficient, in that it can only be used by one document. For example, if another document requires exactly the same CSS styling as the one used in one document, the same CSS has to be repeated for it. This can be especially time-consuming and costly if a number of rules are involved. Not only that, maintenance can be unnecessarily unwieldy. So, in essence, inline should really only be used for the purpose of quick styling, such as for prototyping purposes, and, like with !important exception, for page-specific CSS designed to override some site-wide or global styles.

8.3.3.1.2.1 Using the scoped *Attribute*   The scoped attribute, when used on the <style> element, allows styles to be applied to only an element and its children and overrides previously set styles. The <style> element is placed inside the target element. Figure 8.20 shows how the attribute is used, and Figure 8.21 depicts the result.

```
HTML and CSS
<!DOCTYPE html>
<html>
  <head>
    <style type="text/css">
      p{ color:blue; }
    </style>
  </head>
  <body>
    <h3>The scoped attribute</h3>
    <div>
      <p>This text is blue because it is styled by the CSS rule
        in the head element.</p>
      <div>
        <style scoped>
          p{color: red; }
        </style>
        <p>This text is red because it is styled by the CSS
          rule in the direct parent div element of this
          paragraph element.</p>
      </div>
      <div>
        <p>This text is blue because it is also styled by the
          CSS rule in the head element.</p>
      </div>
    </div>
  </body>
</html>
```

FIGURE 8.20   Example usage of the scoped attribute.

The scoped attribute

This text is blue because it is styled by the CSS rule in the head element.

This text is red because it is styled by the CSS rule in the direct parent div element of this paragraph element

This text is blue because it is also styled by the CSS rule in the head element.

FIGURE 8.21   The result of Figure 8.20.

CHALLENGE 8.9

Can you think of why the use of the `scoped` attribute is necessary when you can use the `class` or `id` attribute to target an element?

8.3.3.2 External CSS

No doubt, the best document-styling practice for a website is to use external CSS, and the bigger a site, the more mandatory this, almost, becomes. To link an HTML document to an external CSS document, the `<link>` element, discussed in Chapter 2, is used in the `<head>` element. Figures 8.22 and 8.23 show how this is done and Figure 8.24 shows the rendered result.

```
HTML
<!DOCTYPE html>
  <head>
    <link href="styles.css" rel="stylesheet" type="text/css">
  </head>
  <body>
    <h3>External CSS</h3>
    <p>Using external CSS is the <em>recommended practice</em>
       for adding stylesto a website.</p>
  </body>
</html>
```

FIGURE 8.22   HTML document linked to the external CSS in Figure 8.21.

```
CSS
body { font-family: Arial; background-color: lightgrey;}
h3 { color: blue;}
em { color: red; }
```

FIGURE 8.23   External CSS used with HTML in Figure 8.22.

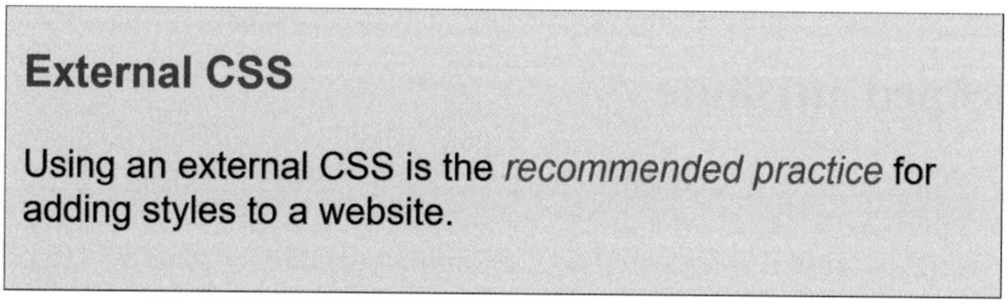

External CSS

Using an external CSS is the *recommended practice* for adding styles to a website.

FIGURE 8.24   The result of Figures 8.22 and 8.23.

In the `<link>` element in the example, the `href` attribute specifies the URL for the style sheet (i.e., style.css), `rel` specifies its relationship with the HTML document, and `type` says that the content of style.css is CSS text.

CHALLENGE 8.10

In the example in Figures 8.22 and 8.23, what is the location of the style sheet in relation to the HTML document that references it?

8.3.3.2.1 Multiple Style Sheets

It is also possible to offer multiple external style sheets, using multiple `<link>` elements. This is usually done to offer **alternative style sheets** and so to provide multiple ways of presenting the same document. This is so that users have a choice of multiple styles. Figure 8.25 shows an example of how this is done.

```
HTML
<!DOCTYPE html>
 <head>
   <link href="default.css" rel="stylesheet" type="text/css"
   title="Default Style">
   <link href="basic.css" rel="alternate stylesheet"
   type="text/css" title="Basic">
   <link href="classy.css" rel="alternate stylesheet"
   title="Classy">
 </head>
 <body>
   <h3>Alternative stylesheets</h3>
   <p>You have a choice of multiple styles to view this page via the
      View menu.</p>
 </body>
</html>
```

FIGURE 8.25   Linking to multiple (alternative) style sheets.

The example provides three style sheets (default.css, basic.css, and classy.css). Notice that in the `<link>` elements for the alternative style sheets, the `rel` attributes each has a space-separated list of values: "`alternative stylesheet`." It must be in this way in order for an alternative style sheet to be specified. Also, the `title` attribute must be used, and it must not be empty. Its value is what is listed as a style option for users to choose under the style sub-menu of the **View** menu of some browsers. When a user chooses an alternative style sheet, the page is immediately rendered using the style. Style sheets that have the same value for the `title` attribute are treated as part of the same style option.

NOTE: Commenting CSS codes

Adding comments in CSS is done using /*....*/, so in the code below, only `em { color: red; }` is interpreted as code and applied by the browser.

```
em { color: red; } /* Makes text red */
```

CHALLENGE 8.11

Implement the example in Figure 8.25, using different style sheets, to see how the concept of alternative style sheets works.

8.4 Useful Info

8.4.1 Web Links

CSS specifications: w3.org/standards

Web development documents: docs.webplatform.org

Accessibility: w3.org/WAI/tutorials, webaim.org

CSS tutorials (*Here are just a few free tutorial sites on CSS and other Web languages*): w3.org/wiki, html5rocks.com, sitepoint.com, w3schools.com, codecademy.com, quackit.com, developer.mozilla.org/en-US/docs/Web tutorialspoint.com, htmldog.com, htmlcodetutorial.com, echoecho.com, learn.shayhowe.com, html.net, tizag.com, cssbasics.com, cordova.apache. org, developers.google.com, csszengarden.com, webdesignermag.co.uk, css. maxdesign.com.au

9

Color

9.1 Introduction

Color is an essential element of Web design, in that it is capable of communicating the emotions of users. As a result, it is one of the design tools available to Web authors for creating the intended first impression for a website. This chapter introduces the CSS properties used to specify color and also discusses design guidelines and practices for the effective use of CSS.

9.2 Learning Outcomes

After studying this chapter, you should:

- Know the methods used to specify colors with CSS.
- Understand the color representations or models supported by CSS.
- Be aware of the various considerations necessary for the effective use of color in Web design.

9.3 Specifying Color in CSS

In CSS, color is specified in a number of ways. One is by **color name**, as you have already seen in the examples in Chapter 8, used for the purpose of explaining other CSS properties. About 140 predefined color names are recognized by major browsers. The other ways of specifying color are via RGB or HSL values. How to specify these values in CSS is shown first, and how they come to be specified in these ways is explained afterward.

9.3.1 RGB Values

These values represent the amount of **red** (R), **green** (G), and **blue** (B) required to produce a color. The syntax used in CSS to specify them is `rgb(r,g,b)`, and the range of each value is 0–255. For example, red is specified using `rgb(255,0,0)`. The values can also be specified in **hex codes** (i.e., hexadecimal numbers, which are numbers derived from counting in 16s). The format for specifying them is **#xxxxxx**, where the first **xx** pair represents red, the second pair represents green, and the third pair represents blue. The hex code for red, for example, is `#ff0000`. When **alpha** (i.e., transparency or opacity) level is specified for a color that is specified in RGB values, the color is represented as RGBA and the syntax used to specify it is `rgba(r,g,b,a)`. The value range for alpha is 0–1.0. For example, red with 50% transparency is `rgba(255,0,0,0.5)`. To specify transparency, when hex codes are used to specify a color, the `opacity` property, which is **non-inherited**, has to be used. Its value range is also 0–1.0. For example, specifying 50% opacity is written as `opacity: 0.5`.

9.3.2 HSL Values

In contrast to RGB values, HSL values represent the amount of **hue** (H), **saturation** (S), and **lightness** (L) required to produce a color, and the syntax used to specify them is `hsl(h,s,l)`. **H** is expressed in terms of an angle between 0° and 360°; **S** is expressed in terms of percentage between 0% (minimum hue saturation) and 100% (maximum hue saturation); and **L**, too, is expressed in terms of percentage between 0% (minimum light, which is black) and 100% (maximum light, which is white). For example, red is `hsl(0, 100%, 50%)`. HSL values cannot be specified in hex codes. Like RGB, when alpha (transparency or opacity) is specified for a color that is specified in HSL values, it is represented as **HSLA,** and the syntax is `hsla(h,s,l,a)`, with its value ranging between 0 and 1.0. Red with 50% alpha, for example, is `hsla(0,100%,50%,0.5)`.

9.3.3 Foreground and Background Color

Foreground color in CSS refers to the color of the text content of an element and its decorations, such as underline, over-line, line-through, and blink; so, foreground color is probably more aptly thought of as text color. Background color refers to the color of the box that represents an HTML element. The **box is transparent by default**, which means that the background shows through it. The color of most browser windows is white, but to ensure that the background color of an element's box is white, it is a good practice to specifically specify it. As examples have shown in Chapter 8, the CSS property for specifying foreground color is `color`, and it is **inherited**. The property for specifying background color is `background-color`, and it is **non-inherited**. Figure 9.1 shows various ways of using them to specify color and transparency, and Figure 9.2 shows the result.

In the example, notice that some texts are black and others white. This is just to ensure legibility. Good contrast is necessary for text to be comfortably legible. So, it is important to bear this in mind when choosing foreground and background colors. **Low contrast makes characters and words difficult to recognize**, especially for the visually impaired users. High contrast makes text easy to read, but **too much contrast can cause eyestrain** when there is a lot to read. Medium contrast usually offers a good compromise, because it can be gentler on the eyes, and it is typically achieved by adjusting the brightness or darkness of the text. For example, instead of using white text on a dark background, off-white text could be better, and instead of black text on white background, dark-gray text may be more suitable. Figure 9.3 demonstrates this. See which one you find more legible and which ones are likely to strain your eyes after a while of reading the text.

Generally, all colors, except yellow, contrast well with a white background, and all colors, except blue and brown, contrast well with a black background. The effect of

```
CSS
/*Solid colors */
p.one { color: rgb(255,255,255); background-color:
  rgb(255,0,0); }
p.two { background-color: hsl(120,100%,50%); }
p.three { color: rgb(255,255,255); background-color:
  rgb(0,0,255); }

/*Colors plus opacity */
p.four { color: rgb(255,255,255); background-color:rgba
  255,0,0,0.5); }
p.five { background-color: hsla(120,100%,50%,0.5); }
p.six { color: #ffffff; background-color:#0000ff;
  opacity: 0.5; }
```

HTML
```
<h3>Foreground and background color:</h3>
<p class="one">{ color: rgb(255,255,255); background-color:
   rgb(255,0,0); }</p>
<p class="two">{ background-color: hsl(120, 100%, 50%); }</p>
<p class="three">{ color: rgb(255,255,255); background-color:
   rgb(0,0,255); }</p>
<br>
<p class="four">{ color: rgb(255,255,255); background-color:rgba
   (255,0,0,0.5); }</p>
<p class="five">{ background-color: hsla(120,100%,50%,0.5); }</p>
<p class="six">{ color: #ffffff; background-color:#0000ff;
   opacity: 0.5; }</p>
```

FIGURE 9.1 Different methods of specifying color.

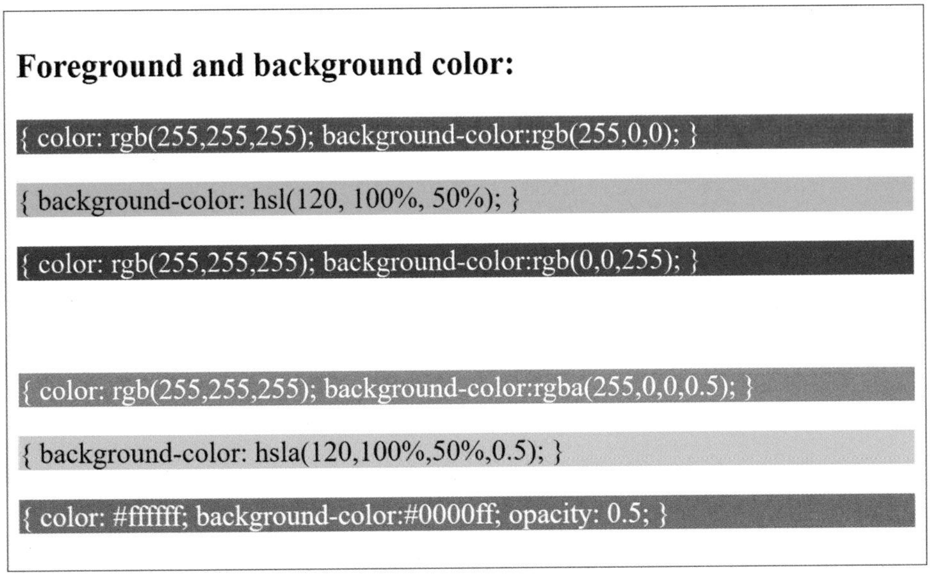

FIGURE 9.2 Rendered result of Figure 9.1.

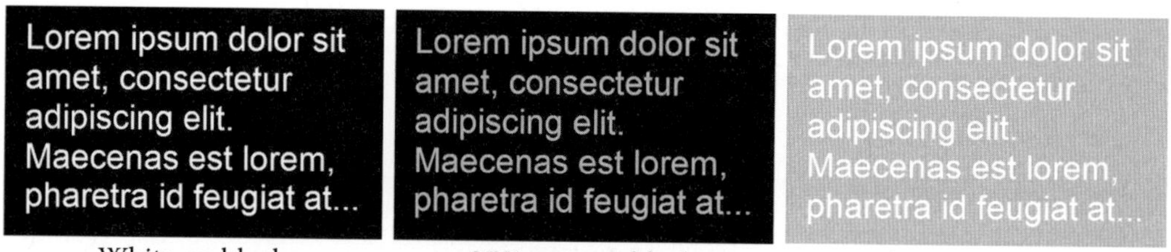

Lorem ipsum dolor sit amet, consectetur adipiscing elit. Maecenas est lorem, pharetra id feugiat at...	Lorem ipsum dolor sit amet, consectetur adipiscing elit. Maecenas est lorem, pharetra id feugiat at...	Lorem ipsum dolor sit amet, consectetur adipiscing elit. Maecenas est lorem, pharetra id feugiat at...
White on black	25% gray on black	White on 25% gray

FIGURE 9.3 Color combinations and legibility.

color combinations and contrast on legibility is just one of the considerations when choosing colors. There are others that are due to the physiology of the eyes. They are discussed later in this chapter under "Color and physiological considerations."

NOTE: Contrast and accessibility

The recommendation is that text and graphic text that are not large-scale texts should have at least **4.5:1** contrast ratio. **Color contrast checkers** are available on the Web for checking contrast for foreground-background combinations.

CHALLENGE 9.1

The default color for a Web page is white. How do you specify a different color?

CHALLENGE 9.2

What do the codes below produce, and why?

CSS

```
#square1 { background-color:rgb(255,0,0); }
#square2 { background-color:rgba(0,255,0,0.75); }
#square3 { background-color:rgba(0,0,255,0.25); }
```

HTML

```
<div id="square1"></div>
<div id="square2"></div>
<div id="square3"></div>
```

9.3.3.1 Color Transparency

When transparency (opacity or alpha) is specified for a color, apart from the color looking faded, as shown earlier in Figure 9.2, it lets the content underneath show. How much is shown depends on the level of transparency. Figure 9.4 shows an example of

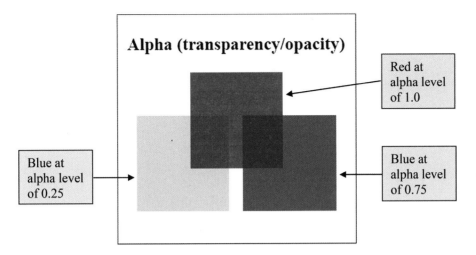

FIGURE 9.4 A demonstration of the effects of the use of transparency with a color.

the effects of transparency. The squares were created using <div> elements that were given specific widths and heights and were positioned as required. How widths and heights are specified is explained in Chapter 10, and how elements are positioned at specific points on a page is explained in Chapter 12.

NOTE: Image opacity

The opacity property can also be used to specify the transparency of an image, so that the item under it shows through. For example, img{ opacity: 0.25; } specifies to make the image displayed using the <img> element 25% transparent.

CHALLENGE 9.3

What are the ways to add transparency to the following CSS rule: p{ background-color: hsl(240,100%,50%); }?

9.4 Anatomy of Color and Color Models

The color is specified in CSS in the ways just demonstrated because of both how display technologies produce color and how humans perceive it. In display screen technologies, such as computer, mobile, tablet, and TV screens, color is produced by mixing differently colored lights. As first mentioned in Chapter 6 in relation to the color of images,

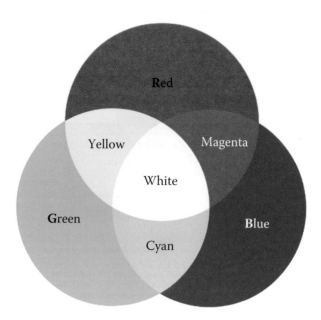

FIGURE 9.5   An illustration of the RGB color method.

the display area of a screen is essentially made up of thousands of tiny **pixels**. Each of these pixels contains red, green, and blue components, sometimes called **sub-pixels**. By illuminating specific pixels, it is possible to produce a pattern on the screen that we see as text or image. The color of each pixel at any point in time is determined by the mixture of the lights from its red, green, and blue components, whose light intensity can vary, as specified. This method of producing color is known as an **additive color method**, since it involves adding different colors together to produce the required one. The red, green, and blue colors are known as **additive primary colors,** and the colors produced in this way are known as **RGB colors**. The concept of mixing red, green, and blue colors is known as **RGB color model**. Figure 9.5 illustrates the concept.

The RGB model is capable of producing most of the colors visible to humans, and when each color is represented with 8 bits (i.e., 24 bits for all red, green, and blue together), up to 16,777,216 (i.e., 2^{24}) different colors can be produced. Representing red, green, and blue, each with 8 bits, means that 256 (i.e., 2^8) different shades of each can be produced and specified on a 0–255 scale. Recall from Chapter 6 that the number of bits used to represent a color is bit depth or color depth.

There are also other color models, such as YUV used by camcorders for encoding video and CMYK used by printers, but RGB is the only one relevant to CSS. The RGB model is the most important color model in computer application development, since most of the interaction with an application happens on the screen. Although it is suitable for describing color in terms of primaries and human perception of colors, it is not suitable for describing how humans describe color. Indeed, it is seldom obvious to most people that a color contains red, green, or blue, and we hardly know what proportions of these colors make up a color when we look at it; rather, we see a color in terms of a variation of a hue and describe it in the same way. For example, we might say "a shade of red," "deep green," and "light blue." In other words, we tend to describe colors in terms of the hue, intensity of the hue, and its lightness or darkness. The aim of the alternatives to the RGB color model is to model color in terms of these properties. The most common of these alternatives are HSL and HSV.

You have already encountered **HSL** earlier. **HSV** stands for hue, saturation, and value (lightness), which is also described in some visual-media-editing applications as **HSB** (hue, saturation, and brightness) or **HSI** (hue, saturation, and intensity). Only HSL is supported by CSS. Figure 9.6 shows a representation of the model. 0°/360° hue is red; 120° hue is green; and 240° hue is blue. In loose terms, **hue** is the same as pure color. **Saturation** is the amount of gray in a color. At 0%, the amount of gray is at maximum (100%), while the amount of hue is 0%, making the color to be displayed as gray. **Lightness** (or **value**) is the amount of white or black in a color. At 0%, the amount of black is at maximum (100%), resulting in a black color, and at 100%, the amount of white is maximum, resulting in white. At 50%, the amounts of white and black are normal, which means that saturation is also at 100%, meaning that a pure color is displayed.

The colors resulting from adding white to a color are usually referred to as **tints**; the colors resulting from adding gray to a color are referred to as **tones**; and the colors resulting from adding black to a color are referred to as **shades**. Figure 9.7 illustrates this.

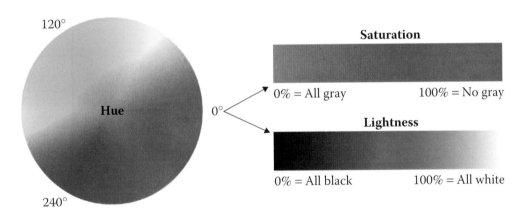

FIGURE 9.6 An illustration of the HSL color model.

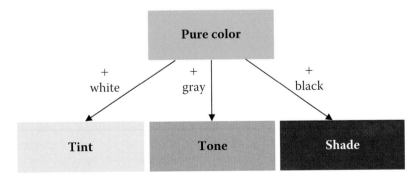

FIGURE 9.7 Example of a tint, tone, and shade of a color.

9.4.1 Determining Color Values

Most programs used for producing visual media provide a tool, typically a **color picker**, which allows color to be chosen based on more than one color model and in a number of ways. These tools can be considered in the first instance to find the RGB or HSL color component values for your desired color. Figure 9.8 shows an example. The desired color can be produced using the **spectrum slider** in conjunction with clicking on the **Color Field**. The equivalent color values are displayed in the various color model sections. Notice that it is HSB, not HSL, that is offered. The difference between the two is that lightness adds white and black, whereas brightness adds only black. Some pickers also include sliders for the alpha channel.

If these color pickers are not of adequate use, there are many free online color converters that allow the conversion of a color value from one model to another. They also allow color names to be specified, and they work on a similar principle as the one in Figure 9.8.

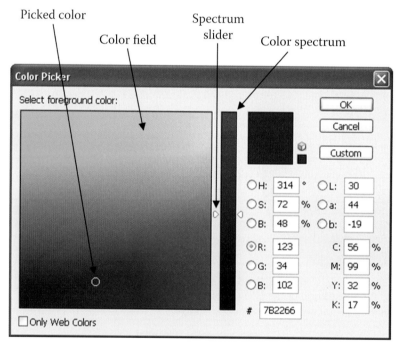

FIGURE 9.8 An examples of a color picker.

CHALLENGE 9.4

To better understand the HSL or HSB color model, create a shape in your Microsoft Word, or any other application that allows you to do this, and fill the shape with a primary color, such as red. Then, open the color picker and manipulate the values for saturation and lightness (or brightness).

9.5 Color in Design

How humans perceive color and the effects of colors on us play a big role in the effective use of color in Web design. These factors affect which colors we combine, how we combine them, how many are used, and for what purpose each color is used. The success of a design depends on making the right choices for the right situations, in particular because color combination contributes to the aesthetics of a website, which users usually partly use to judge its credibility and therefore whether or not to use it. More on the role of aesthetics in Web design is discussed in Chapters 23 and 24.

9.5.1 Choosing Color Combinations

There are various methods for choosing a color combination for a website. One is through instinct or trial and error. However, this can be limiting in that instinct can only take you so far; the knowledge of color research is necessary. Another approach is to use the goal of a website as a guide, based on past practices. For example, certain colors are more commonly used for some types of businesses than others. However, this, too, is subjective and can be unreliable. A more systematic approach tends to be more reliable, and it is because of this that the use of **color schemes** should always be considered in the decision of choosing the color combination to use for a website.

Color schemes are derived from a **color wheel** (also known as **color circle**) but can also be derived from the colors of an image. A color wheel shows the relationships between colors and provides guides on which colors can be mixed to produce which color. In visual design, it is especially useful for determining which colors can be used together effectively to create specific styles and moods. There are different variations, and the variations are also represented in a variety of ways. Two examples are shown in Figure 9.9.

A typical color wheel contains colors known as **primary colors** and colors that are produced from mixing primary colors, known as **secondary colors** and **intermediate** (or **tertiary**) **colors**. Which colors are primary colors depends on various factors such as area of application and tradition. In screen display technologies, they are red, green,

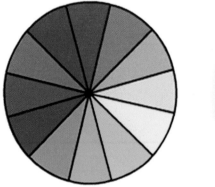

FIGURE 9.9   Examples of a color wheel.

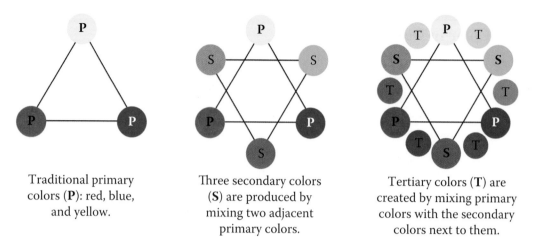

Traditional primary colors (**P**): red, blue, and yellow.

Three secondary colors (**S**) are produced by mixing two adjacent primary colors.

Tertiary colors (**T**) are created by mixing primary colors with the secondary colors next to them.

FIGURE 9.10   Illustration of the stages of a color wheel production.

and blue. In printing, they are cyan, magenta, and yellow. Artists usually use red, yellow, and blue; for little more than traditional reasons, these colors are the ones on which most color wheels are based. Because mixing them cannot produce all colors, green is often added, and together, the four colors (red, green, blue, and yellow) are sometimes referred to as the **psychological primary colors**, and they are the colors that are commonly researched in studies regarding the psychological effects of color. Figure 9.10 illustrates the production principle behind a color wheel.

The colors of a color wheel are generally grouped into cool, warm, and cool and warm, as illustrated in Figure 9.11. **Cool colors** include greens, blue-greens, and blues; **warm colors** include yellows, oranges, and reds; and purples are either cool or warm. Black is considered warm, because it absorbs all colors and reflects none, while white

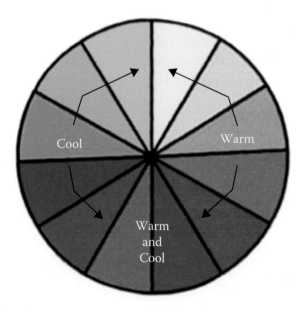

FIGURE 9.11   Cool and warm colors on the color wheel.

is considered cool, because it absorbs no colors and reflects everything. Warm colors are used to project warmth in a design, while cool colors are used to project coolness.

By combining the colors in a color wheel, using various configurations, it is possible to produce different types of **color schemes**, both basic and complex, each of which is best suited for different situations. The color schemes presented here include monochromatic, analogous, complementary, split complementary, double contrast, and triadic. However, there are others. One is the **neutral scheme**, which includes neutral colors, such as white, black, gray, beige, and brown, which are colors not found on the color wheel. Another is **accented neutral scheme**, which includes neutral colors and small amounts of one or more colors from the color wheel; for example, black and gray may be used with red.

Some websites provide dynamic **color scheme generators** with which to experiment, as a quick search should reveal. Some popular ones include **paletton.com** and **color.adobe.com**. The latter website also supports the use of images for generating a color scheme. Basically, it allows an image to be uploaded and uses the colors in it to compose a color scheme with which you can then experiment. Being able to generate a color scheme from an image is particularly useful when a design is being created around a central image, such as a logo and the image of nature.

9.5.1.1 Monochromatic

This is a relatively basic scheme that uses only one color, as implied in the name ("mono" meaning one and "chroma" meaning color). Although only one hue is used, the use of tints and shades of the same color makes it possible to produce interesting designs. The scheme is easy to work with and usually produces designs that look balanced and appealing. What constitutes balance in design is discussed in Chapter 23. The main downside of the scheme is that it is difficult to achieve strong contrast or vibrant designs with it. Figure 9.12 shows an example of a design that uses green and its tints and shades. The color palette shows the main colors used in the design, but they are only some of the colors that can be derived from green via the scheme.

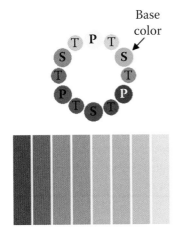
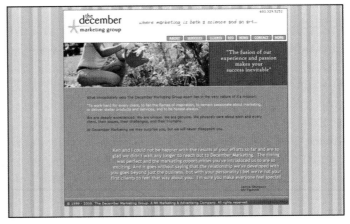

FIGURE 9.12 A screenshot of a design that uses monochromatic color scheme, the palette of the colors used, and the configuration on the wheel (decembermarketing.com).

NOTE: More about monochromatic scheme

- Used for designs where focus is meant to be on content, for example, when a color photograph needs to be dominant.
- Works quite well for designs intended for serious purposes, such as serious political and business applications (such as bank websites).
- Well suited when branding is required.

CHALLENGE 9.5

For which of the following types of websites would you use the monochromatic color scheme? Also, how would you use the scheme? For example, what color would you use for background, header, footer, text, aside, and so on?

- A kids' website.
- A marketing company.
- A stock market website.
- An e-commerce website.
- A university website.

CHALLENGE 9.6

Picking a base color other than the one used in the example, choose two types of websites from the list above and create a design for each by using the color and the monochromatic color scheme.

9.5.1.2 Analogous

The analogous scheme, too, is a basic scheme, and it uses colors that are next to each other on the color wheel. Typically, three to five colors are used, but more colors may also be used. Designs produced using the scheme are richer than those produced with monochromatic scheme. However, the scheme, too, lacks contrast because of the relatively close similarities between adjacent colors on the wheel. Variation of the scheme are the **warm scheme**, which uses only warm colors, such as reds, yellows, and oranges, and the **cool scheme**, which uses only cool colors, such as blues, greens, and purples. Figure 9.13 shows an example of a design that uses the analogous scheme of warm colors. The circular **"Award" image at bottom right is not part of the design**, so its colors are not part of the scheme; however, the blue provides a good accent. When using this scheme, attention needs to be paid to the contrast between text and background colors to ensure good level of legibility. If the colors are too close, tints and shades are usually used to improve contrast.

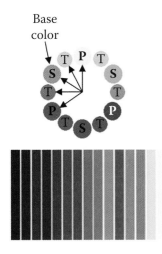

Base color

FIGURE 9.13 A screenshot of a design that uses analogous color scheme, the palette of the colors used, and the configuration on the wheel (www.itcatmedia.com/school).

NOTE: More about analogous scheme

- One color is used as the dominant color, the second to support, and the third, along with neutral colors, to accentuate. If more than three colors are used, the same principle is followed.
- Using too many colors, or combining warm and cool colors, can cause disharmony.

CHALLENGE 9.7

For which of the following types of websites would you use the analogous color scheme? Also, how would you use the scheme? For example, what color would you use for background, header, footer, text, aside, and so on?

- A kids' website.
- A marketing company.
- A stock market website.
- An e-commerce website.
- A university website.

CHALLENGE 9.8

Picking a base color other than the one used in the example, choose two types of websites from the list above and create a design for each by using the color and the analogous color scheme.

9.5.1.3 Complementary

The complementary scheme uses colors that are opposite to each other on the color wheel, such as red and green. The high contrast that results from combining complementary colors typically creates a vibrant look, particularly when the colors are highly saturated. However, combining highly saturated colors can also produce unwanted optical effects, such as vibrations, shadows, and afterimages (ghost images), particularly when they touch. Figure 9.14 shows an example of a design in complementary colors.

To avoid unwanted optical effects when using complementary colors, neutral colors may be added, particularly as background colors, such as the ones shown in Figure 9.15. Notice how the text in the left illustration is difficult to read, while it is not so in the right illustration, because white background is used.

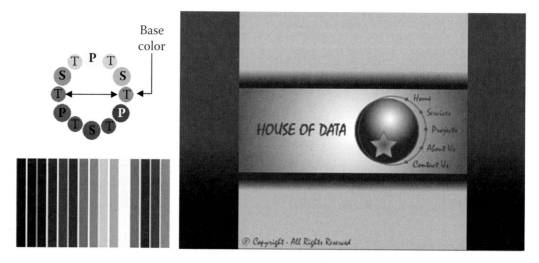

FIGURE 9.14 A screenshot of a design that uses complementary color, the palette of the colors used, and the configuration on the wheel.

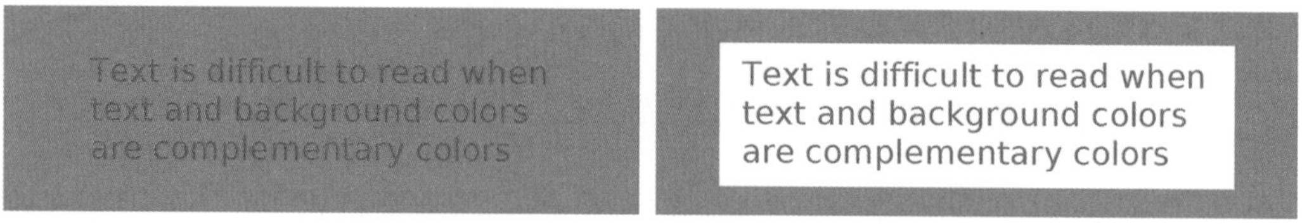

Text is difficult to read when text and background colors are complementary colors

Text is difficult to read when text and background colors are complementary colors

FIGURE 9.15 Complementary colors (left), and with a neutral color as background (right).

NOTE: More about complementary scheme

- Used when things are required to stand out and draw maximum attention.
- When a warm color is used as accent, any complementary cool color can be desaturated to give more emphasis to the warm color.

CHALLENGE 9.9

For which of the following types of websites would you use the complementary color scheme? Also, how would you use the scheme? For example, what color would you use for background, header, footer, text, aside, and so on?

- A kids' website.
- A marketing company.
- A stock market website.
- An e-commerce website.
- A university website.

CHALLENGE 9.10

Picking a base color other than the one used in the example, choose two types of websites from the list above and create a design for each by using the color and the complementary color scheme.

9.5.1.4 Split Complementary

The split complementary color scheme is a variation of the complementary scheme and includes a base color and the colors on either sides of the complementary color on the color wheel. For example, choosing purple color will give orange-yellow and yellow-green as split complementary colors. The scheme produces the same strong visual contrast as the complementary scheme but with less tension. Also, it produces more subtle variations than complementary scheme. Figure 9.16 shows a design that uses these colors and their tints and shades.

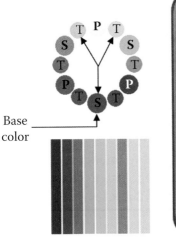
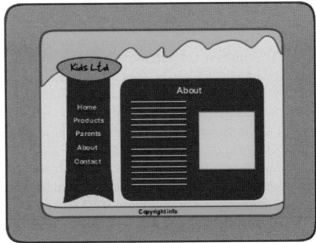

FIGURE 9.16 A screenshot of a design that uses split complementary color, the palette of the colors used, and the configuration on the wheel.

> **NOTE: More on split complementary scheme**
>
> - Split complementary scheme is friendlier than complementary scheme.
> - Split complementary is generally not as jarring as complementary scheme.
> - A warm color can be combined with cool colors to give emphasis to the warm color.

CHALLENGE 9.11

For which of the following types of websites would you use the split complementary color scheme? Also, how would you use the scheme? For example, what color would you use for background, header, footer, text, aside, and so on?

- A kids' website.
- A marketing company.
- A stock market website.
- An e-commerce website.
- A university website.

CHALLENGE 9.12

Picking a base color other than the one used in the example, choose two types of websites from the list above and create a design for each by using the color and the split complementary color scheme.

9.5.1.5 Double Contrast

The double-contrast (or **tetradic**) scheme, too, is based on the complementary scheme technique and uses four colors (i.e., two complementary color pairs). Basically, it is a double application of the complementary scheme technique, in that the colors on either sides of each of the two complementary colors are chosen. For example, if the complementary colors are blue and orange, then the colors chosen are blue-purple and blue-green on the blue side and red-orange and orange-yellow on the orange side. Because it uses four colors, the scheme offers more variety of colors than other schemes and produces bold-contrasting designs. However, it is also the hardest to balance. Figure 9.17 shows a design that uses double-contrast colors and their tints and shades.

A variation of the double-contrast scheme is the **square scheme**, in which the four colors are evenly spaced on the wheel. The scheme's characteristics are similar to those of double contrast. Figure 9.18 shows as illustration.

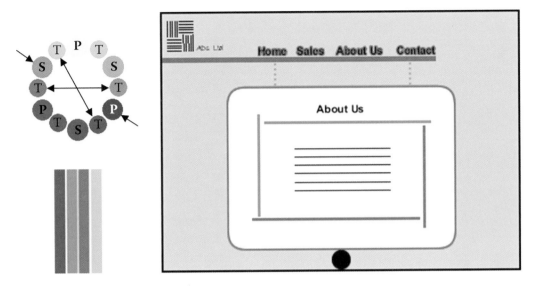

FIGURE 9.17 A screenshot of a design that uses double-contrast colors, the palette of the colors used, and the configuration on the wheel.

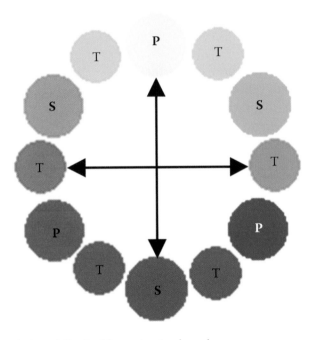

FIGURE 9.18 A variation of the double-contrast color scheme.

NOTE: More on double-contrast scheme

Using all four colors in equal amount may produce an unbalanced design, but this may be avoided by making one color dominant and subduing the rest.

CHALLENGE 9.13

For which of the following types of websites would you use the double-contrast color scheme? Also, how would you use the scheme? For example, what color would you use for background, header, footer, text, aside, and so on?

- A kids' website.
- A marketing company.
- A stock market website.
- An e-commerce website.
- A university website.

CHALLENGE 9.14

Picking a base color other than the one used in the example, choose two types of websites from the list above and create a design for each by using the color and the double-contrast color scheme.

9.5.1.6 Triadic

The triadic scheme involves three colors that are equidistant from each other on the color wheel, such as red, yellow, and blue. Although it is not as contrasting as the complementary scheme, it, too, produces strong vibrant designs, and it is relatively easy to achieve balance and harmony with it. Figure 9.19 shows a design that uses triadic colors and their tints and shades.

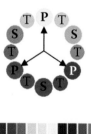
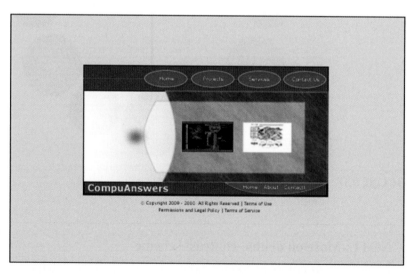
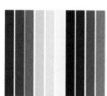

FIGURE 9.19 A screenshot of a design that uses triadic colors, the palette of the colors used, and the configuration on the wheel

> **NOTE: More on triadic scheme**
>
> - To ensure a harmonious design, one color can be made dominant and others can be used for accent.
> - If colors are too showy, they can be subdued to achieve a more harmonious design.

CHALLENGE 9.15

For which of the following types of websites would you use the triadic color scheme? Also, how would you use the scheme? For example, what color would you use for background, header, footer, text, aside, and so on?

- A kids' website.
- A marketing company.
- A stock market website.
- An e-commerce website.
- A university website.

CHALLENGE 9.16

Picking a base color other than the one used in the example, choose two types of websites from the list above and create a design for each by using the color and the triadic color scheme.

CHALLENGE 9.17

Visit `color.adobe.com`, if you have not already done so, and experiment with the color schemes that it offers. Also, create a color scheme by uploading an image, and experiment on the color scheme generated.

9.5.2 Color Proportions

While color schemes provide guidelines on the colors to combine, they do not provide information on how much to use. Although there are no steadfast rules regarding this, there are common practices. A basic rule of thumb is the **60-30-10 rule**, which is traditionally applied in interior design to produce professional quality color decoration for a space. In Web design, the space is the screen or page. The rule recommends that it should be filled in the following proportions:

- **60%** in the **dominant color**. This is the background, and typically used colors are light neutral colors (e.g., gray, black, and brown) or tints of a hue.

- **30%** in the **subdominant** (or secondary) color, which is typically a stronger color than the background.
- **10%** in the **accent color**, which is typically a vivid color and is commonly used to direct users' attention to an important feature, such as a call-to-action button, for example, a "Register" button.

You may also encounter these three components being referred to by different names in Web design. For example, dominant color may be described as base or subdominant color, secondary color as dominant, and accent color as highlight, but the general concept of 60-30-10 still applies. However, the 60-30-10 proportion is not cast in stones; it can be varied slightly, as long as the 100% total is maintained. Examples include 65-25-10 and 60-29-11. More than three colors can also be used, again, as long as the 100% total is maintained. When more than three colors are used, it is usually by adding more secondary colors, in which case, the total space occupied should not be more than the 30% proportion for the secondary color. The tints, tones, or shades of the secondary color or other colors may be used, based on the relevant color scheme. The total number of colors is normally best kept at **five plus/minus two colors**, as too many colors can make it difficult for the user to build a mental picture of a page and understand how to interact with it. **Consistency in the use of colors** across pages, naturally, contributes to the building of a mental picture of a website.

CHALLENGE 9.18

What should be the proportion of the color used for accenting? Also, which of the following colors would you use for accenting, and why?

9.5.3 Color in Content Organization

Where a website is used to present a lot of data, especially numerical data, colors can be almost indispensable in the organization. When colors are used in this way, rather than picking them randomly, a set of colors should be chosen, then a purpose or meaning should be assigned to each color, and the principle of usage should be maintained across pages for **consistency**. Color can also be used to label or group related items to help remember more items than usual or to create a **hierarchy according to the order of importance**; for example, the darkest and brightest colors can be used for the most important information in order to draw attention to them and soft natural colors can be used for most other information.

When color is used to separate items into groups, although the colors used should be distinctly different from one another, they should not vary in perceived intensity, as this can cause one color to stand out more than the others, falsely giving the impression that it is more important. For example, if red is used for one group, then green, and not bright green, should be used for another group; otherwise, the bright green group will appear more important.

Where a sequence of values is color-coded, a single hue is best used, with the intensity varying from pale colors to darker and brighter colors for low to higher values, respectively. However, this technique should be avoided where different concepts are being given colors, as shades of the same color can be difficult to distinguish. Different concepts should be assigned different hues. Also, because visual perception is relative and not absolute, the perception of the same color can change with different color background or surrounding, giving the impression that the same color represents different concepts. To avoid this (e.g., across pages), background or surrounding color must be consistent. To further ensure color consistency in the colors that different users see, it is a good practice to check a color scheme across various devices, since the appearance of colors often changes across devices.

CHALLENGE 9.19

For which of the following would you use variations of the same color and for which would you use different colors to aid organization?

- Categories of news items.
- Columns of a table.
- Series of recorded weights, with each weight indicating whether it is up or down compared with the previous and next ones.

9.5.4 Color and Aesthetics

As mentioned earlier, colors and their combinations are capable of projecting aesthetics and are a universally recognized measure of visual aesthetics. Numerous studies suggest that colors play important role in users' appraisal of the aesthetics of user interfaces, including websites' user interfaces. Studies also suggest that when users prefer the colors or color combinations of a website and judge them to have high aesthetic quality, they end up making positive decisions about the website. For example, they are highly likely to predict that the site will be easy to use as well as to decide, for example, to purchase from it if it is selling something. Users typically describe color as a factor in how they judge the aesthetic appeal of websites and how easy they feel the sites will be to use. Also, designs judged to be aesthetically pleasing are typically characterized by the harmonious use of colors. Factors that contribute to this judgment have been suggested to include preference for a color combination, perception of harmony between the colors, and preference for a color in relation to its background. For example, the more the hue's contrast is between an object's color and the background, the more the color of the object is preferred. However, while color obviously plays a significant role in the aesthetics of a website, there are also other important components of design that contribute to the aesthetics of a website as a whole. Again, the role of aesthetics in Web design is discussed in Chapters 23 and 24.

CHALLENGE 9.20

What in how colors are used contribute to a website's aesthetics? Also, is just using the right color scheme enough to achieve aesthetics? If no, say what else should be done. If yes, give reasons for your answer.

9.5.5 Color and Physiological Considerations

On the physiological level, it is the incompatibility between the way the eyes work and some color combinations that requires consideration. For example, the eyes normally cannot focus on certain shades of certain colors simultaneously when they are adjacent to each other. This means that when objects or texts are in these colors, they seem to vibrate, making the eyes to constantly refocus, which causes eye muscles to tense up and relax constantly, resulting in eye fatigue or eyestrain. Various color combinations can cause this problem. Having large areas of red and blue next to each other or red text on a blue background, or vice versa, for example, can cause it. Such color combinations can not only cause eyestrain but also **poor visibility of shapes**. For example, very bright, fluorescent, or vibrant colors can produce edges that appear to blur and/or after-image (ghost-image) effect, both of which make it difficult to make out shapes easily or correctly. An example is when yellow text is used on a white background.

Of course, colors do not have to be adjacent to each other for them to be incompatible with normal vision. The use of multiple pure or highly saturated colors, too, can cause the eyes to constantly refocus, because each color constantly attracts attention, again resulting in eyestrain. Like with legibility, these problems can largely be avoided by combining colors that produce **good contrast**, which itself is controlled primarily by **luminance** (lightness). Controlling **saturation** can also help; for example, combining colors that are widely different in saturation, such as dark (rich) colors with light (pale) ones, can produce good contrast.

Color combinations can also have more dire implications than simply compromising visibility, legibility, and so on. Research has shown, for example, that response to **photic stimulation** (caused, e.g., by the flashing of lights or patterns), which is a potential health risk, because it causes seizure in some people, happens more quickly and with more intensity with red color than with blue and green colors. This means that flashing colors at the red/yellow end of the color spectrum are more likely to cause seizure than flashing colors at the blue/green end. Also, flashing a darker color on a brighter one tends to reduce the possibility of a **seizure trigger**.

CHALLENGE 9.21

Which elements of a website are likely to have properties and behavior that can cause photic stimulation?

9.5.6 Color and Psychological Considerations

Different colors evoke different emotions in different people. This means that colors can be used to put users in the right state of mind to help in the success of a website. Similarly, the **language of color** (or **color symbolism**), which is what we have learnt colors to mean, based on natural, psychological, and cultural associations, can be used to better communicate content to users. Basically, everyone in the course of their lifetime invariably develops these associations in varying degrees. **Natural association** happens as a result of the color that we have observed a natural object to have. This type of association is universal and timeless. For example, vegetation is green and so everywhere on earth and will probably always be so. **Psychological association** develops as a result of the psychological state that we have commonly known a color to evoke. For example, deep colors are said to generally convey a sense of mystery, while bright colors are linked with liveliness and light colors are linked with coolness. This type of association is neither universal nor timeless, since it is subjective and can change. **Cultural association** arises out of cultural or common usage, and it, too, is not universal or timeless, as a color that means something in one culture or context may mean something different in another culture, today or in the future. For example, in some countries, when looking for a post box, one looks instinctively for a red box, because that is the color that symbolizes the post office in those countries, whereas in some countries, it is yellow, and this may change in the future.

Colors (typically, color schemes) can also be used to create association. For example, using the color scheme of a country's flag for a website of national relevance, such as the website of the government of a country, enhances the perception of the design. Similarly, colors can be combined to create branding, such as for a company's identity. Many organizations have brand colors that people automatically associate with them. For example, for Coca-Cola, it is a particular shade of red and white; for Starbucks, it is green and white; and for T-Mobile, it is hot pink, white, and black.

As subjective and non-standard as color symbolism is, its use should not be dismissed, especially because it can help reinforce the message or the theme that a design is meant to communicate. Table 9.1 presents a list of common colors and their associations compiled by Jill Morton, a color consultant in the use and meaning of colors, who has written many books on the subject and the use of color in Web design. The list was compiled based on research and common color usage. Although it is not necessarily a product of empirical science, it provides possible starting points that may otherwise not be considered when choosing colors to use for different Web design situations. It can save time, while also leaving ample room for experimentation. For example, it suggests that using a color such as purple for an application that relates to spirituality,

TABLE 9.1

Common Colors and Their Associations

Color	Category	Symbolisms
Red	Psychological	Energy, warmth, strength, impulse, dynamism, activity, courage, excitement, love, passion, dominance, rebellion, aggression, war and combat, violence, sexuality.
	Natural	Fire, blood, raw meat, flesh, flowers (roses, carnations, and so on), fruits, gemstones (rubies, and so on).
	Cultural	Traffic stop light and signs, post office (UK, US, and so on).
	Misc	Yellow-based reds, such as tomato color, appeal to males; and blue-based reds, such as raspberry color, appeal to females. Red is also used for attention-getting, danger, and fire equipment, is an important color in China and Japan.
Purple	Psychological	Spirituality, mysticism, magic, faith, the unconscious, dignity, mystery, creativity, awareness, inspiration, passion, imagination, sensitivity, mourning, death, aristocracy, opulence and richness (dark purple).
	Natural	Rare in nature; grapes, plums.
	Cultural	Bravery (as in purple heart in US).
	Misc	Hazardous nuclear energy (US).
Blue	Psychological	Spirituality, trust, peace, order, loyalty, truth, cleanliness, tranquillity, contentment, passivity, conservatism, masculinity, coolness and coldness, melancholy.
	Natural	Not common in nature; sky, oceans, lakes, blueberries.
	Cultural	Blue jeans, police force.
Green	Psychological	Nature, growth, fruitfulness, renewal, freshness, tranquility, hope, youth, health, peace, good luck, coolness.
	Natural	Vegetation, gemstones (emeralds, jade, and so on).
	Cultural	Ecology, conservation, traffic go light and sign, Christmas.
	Misc	Color of Islam, first aid.
Yellow	Psychological	Hope, vitality, mental and spiritual enlightenment, optimism.
	Natural	Sunlight, sand, autumn leaves, corn, squash, lemons, bananas, flowers (sunflower, daffodils, etc), gemstones (gold).
	Cultural	Traffic warning light and sign, butter, mustard, spices, caution, quarantine information.
Orange	Psychological	Energy, cheer, fun, activity, excitement, warmth.
	Natural	Fire, sunset, fruits (oranges, apricots, and so on), flowers and autumn leaves.
	Cultural	Copper.
Brown	Psychological	Nature, durability, reliability, realism, warmth, comfort.
	Natural	Earth, tree trunks, rocks, autumn leaves.
	Cultural	Beverages, chocolate, grains, tobacco, sugar.
Black	Psychological	Power, sophistication, sense of luxury and value, sexuality, ominous forces, death, corruption.

(Continued)

TABLE 9.1 (*Continued*)

Common Colors and Their Associations

Color	Category	Symbolisms
	Natural	Night, rocks, hair, birds (crow, and so on).
	Cultural	Ink, metals, mourning (in many Western cultures).
White	Psychological	Purity, sense of freedom, cleanliness, truth, innocence, chastity, spirituality, sophistication, refinement, newness, blandness, sterility, death.
	Natural	Clouds, snow, flowers, birds.
	Cultural	Peace, mourning (in many Eastern and some Western cultures), processed food.
	Misc	Holiness, purity, surrender, wedding.

Source: Adapted from Jill Morton.

faith, mourning, or death (such as a website for a funeral home) is more appropriate than using, for example, red color. On the other hand, red can be the main color used when a website is required to project energy, dynamism, speed, or passion, while blue is unlikely to be the best for projecting passion. Naturally, the same color can be suitable for multiple design situations, just like the same situation may be well-served by different colors. Furthermore, color symbolism can change or become obsolete over time. So, it is better to use timeless symbolisms than timely ones. For example, colors should not be used because they are fashionable, as fashion is transitory.

CHALLENGE 9.22

Using the information in Table 9.1 as a guide, state which colors you would use for the following types of websites and also justify your choices.

- A bank
- Luxury products
- Sports
- Hospital
- Church

9.5.7 Color Preferences

Personal preference should not be the deciding factor when choosing colors; rather, factors relating to the **target audience** and the **purpose of website** should be the deciding factors. This is because studies generally show that different sexes prefer different colors. For example, women tend to like blue, pink, purple, and green better than gray, orange, and brown, while men tend to like blue, green, and black better than purple, orange, or brown. Similarly, adults prefer different colors and color combinations compared with children. Children tend to like vibrant colors, while adults tend to like more subdued colors.

CHALLENGE 9.23

Perform a Web search for "kids websites" to see examples of the use of colors when children are the target. Also, see if you can recognize any color schemes.

9.5.8 Color and Accessibility

The main accessibility consideration when using color is **color blindness.** Color blindness is quite complex because there are different types of color blindness, and it can vary from person to person. However, its detailed understanding is not essential to be able to create content that is accessible to the color-blind people. The key point to know is that color-blind people cannot differentiate between certain color combinations, because they perceive colors differently. The recommendation for Web design is that visual information, messages, or instructions should not be conveyed via color only. This is achieved by providing information through multiple forms. For example, you can:

- **Provide text explanation**, such as "red dots on white background." Note, however, that using the technique of displaying text explanation on cursor hovering over an item will not work on a touch-screen device. Also, you should use actual color names rather than aliases, wherever possible. For example, purple should be used instead of grape, as not all grapes are purple. Incidentally, the technique of providing text explanation also benefits blind users, since screen readers can read out the text.
- **Annotate color use** to provide more information. For example, apply labels that show category name and, possibly, values or percentages. Such labels can be inside or outside the relevant elements.
- **Use different text styles** for different colors (e.g., italic, bold, underline), if possible and they are compatible with overall design goal.
- **Use shades of the same color**, since color-blind people can differentiate between lightness.
- **Use texture, pattern, shape, size, or data table** in addition to color, where possible, to make information more accessible to color-blind people. Typical candidates are pie and bar charts, as well as maps. The illustration in Figure 9.20, for example, uses different patterns. A data table should provide exactly the same information and in the same order.

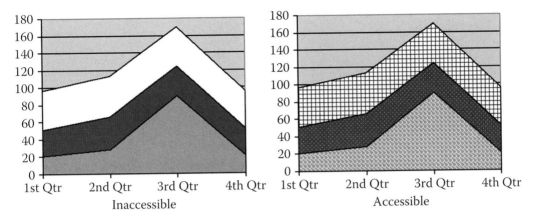

FIGURE 9.20 Using pattern to convey color information.

NOTE: Other uses of color

Color is also commonly used to:

- Identify different types of elements or contents for easy search and recognition.
- Attract attention to important information.
- Give structure to content.
- Differentiate between different types of information.
- Create mood.
- Communicate association between objects (e.g., by using the same color for different objects).
- Communicate identity (as in branding).

CHALLENGE 9.24

In which of the following cases is it necessary to provide a text explanation of the use of color or an annotation for the benefit of color-blind or blind users? Also, give reasons for your answer.

- The color scheme used on a page.
- The image of a T-shirt on sale.
- The color of call-to-action buttons.
- A color railway network map.
- A color swatch used to pick a color for the required item on a site.
- A pie or bar chart.

9.6 Useful Info

9.6.1 Web Links

CSS specifications: w3.org/standards

Web development documents: docs.webplatform.org

Accessibility: w3.org/WAI/tutorials, webaim.org

CSS tutorials (*Here are just a few free tutorial sites on CSS and other Web languages*): w3.org/wiki, html5rocks.com, sitepoint.com, w3schools.com, codecademy.com, quackit.com, developer.mozilla.org/en-US/docs/Web tutorialspoint.com, htmldog.com, htmlcodetutorial.com, echoecho.com, learn.shayhowe.com, html.net, tizag.com, cssbasics.com, cordova.apache.org, developers.google.com, csszengarden.com, webdesignermag.co.uk, css.maxdesign.com.au

Color scheme tools: colorzilla.com, web.colorotate.org, colorlovers.com

Color wheel: colorschemedesigner.com, color.adobe.com, colorsontheweb.com

Color usage: colorusage.arc.nasa.gov

Color contrast and accessibility checker: wave.webaim.org

Color corrector for color blindness: vischeck.com

Color contrast checker: checkmycolors.com

10

Boxes: Size and Border

10.1 Introduction

The concept of CSS box model was introduced in Chapter 8. The concept says that every element in an HTML document is represented with a rectangular box, whose properties, such as width, height, border, padding, and margin, can be controlled to help determine the design of a Web page. This chapter presents the CSS properties used to achieve this.

10.2 Learning Outcomes

After studying this chapter, you should:

- Know how to specify the dimensions of an element's box and how to control content overflow.
- Be able to control an element's border, padding, and margin.
- Be able to control an element's box sizes, including making boxes user-resizable.
- Be able to add shadows to an element's box.
- Know how to add outline to an element.
- Know how to convert between inline and block elements and why this can be necessary.
- Know how to hide elements and when this is necessary.

10.3 Box Dimensions

The dimensions of a CSS box are defined mainly by `width` and `height`, `min-width` and `max-width`, and `min-height` and `max-height`, all of which can take any of a number of value types. The commonly used ones as of time of writing are `auto` (which is a keyword that lets the browser determine value), `inherit` (which is a keyword that says to inherit value from the parent), `initial` (which sets value to default value), **length values** (which are any measure of distance, such as `px` and `em`), and **percentage values** (which define value as a percentage of the size of the containing block). Box dimensions can also be specified using **CSS logical properties**. These properties define logical border edges based on flow direction of text within a line (e.g., left to right) and the flow direction of lines of text (e.g., top to bottom). The property used to define this direction is `writing-mode` and is introduced more fully later in Chapter 14. As of time of writing, the CSS logical properties are still in the draft stage. This means that some of the things presented here may be a little different in the finalized specification. Also, only Firefox supports the properties as of time of writing.

10.3.1 `width` **and** `height`

The `width` and `height` properties, both of which are **non-inherited**, specify the width and height, respectively, of an element's box, which by default is just high enough for the element's content but occupies the full width of the page. Figure 10.1 shows how these properties are used with both absolute and relative units, and Figure 10.2 depicts the result. In the example, 400px width and 200px height are specified for the

```
CSS
div { width: 400px; height: 200px; background-color: lightgrey; }
p { width: 90%; height: 50%; background-color: lightpink; }

HTML
<h3>Box width and Height</h3>
<div>
  <h4>About Couscous</h4>
  <p>Steamed couscous is much lighter and fluffier than the one
     simply soaked in hot water. Steamed with lemon and thyme,
     it can be used as a tasty lunch dish or a side dish with
     other salads.</p>
</div>
```

FIGURE 10.1   Example usage of the `width` and `height` properties.

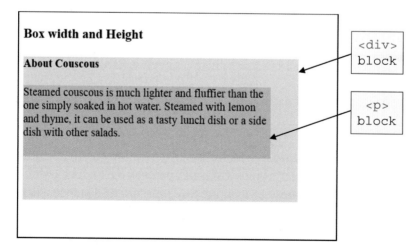

FIGURE 10.2   The rendered result of Figure 10.1.

`<div>` element, and the width and height of the `<p>` element are specified as 90% and 50% of these, respectively.

CHALLENGE 10.1

Modify the code in Figure 10.1, as necessary, to produce the output below:

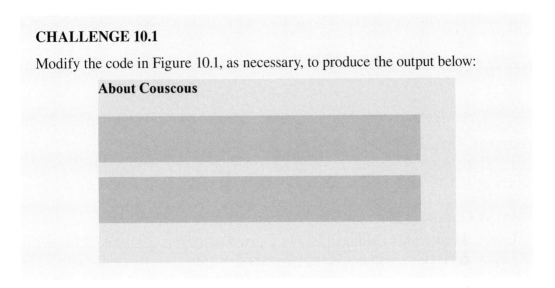

10.3.1.1 Specifying Logical Width and Height

The properties used to specify the logical width and height of an element are `block-size` and `inline-size`, and whether each defines width or height depends on the value of the `writing-mode` property (discussed in Chapter 14). Both of them are **non-inherited** and take the same values as the `width` and `height` properties; however, **keyword values**, such as `border-box`, `content-box`, `min-content`, `max-content`, `available`, `fit-content`, and `auto`, may also be supported. Figures 10.3 and 10.4 show how the properties are used and depict the result.

```
CSS
.size {
  background-color: pink;
  text-align: center;
  font-size: 24px;
  writing-mode: horizontal-tb;
  block-size: 300px;
  inline-size:600px;
}

HTML
<div>
  <p class="size">In right-to-left top-to-bottom text-flow
  direction, block-size specifies height and inline-size
  width</p>
</div>
```

FIGURE 10.3 Example usage of the `block-size` and `inline-size` properties.

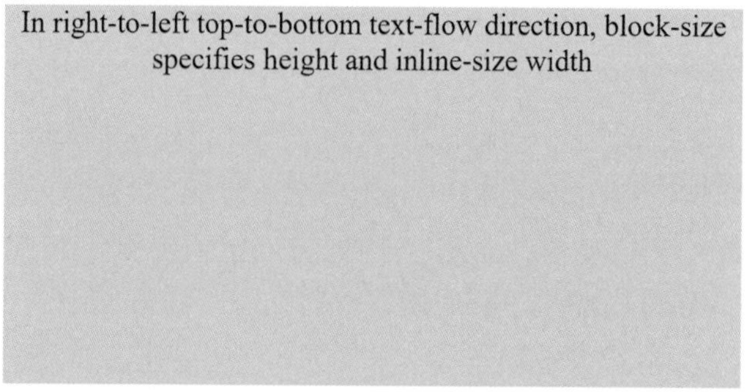

In right-to-left top-to-bottom text-flow direction, block-size
specifies height and inline-size width

FIGURE 10.4   The result of Figure 10.3.

CHALLENGE 10.2

In the example, what would `block-size` and `inline-size` define if writing
mode is from top to bottom and right to left?

10.3.2 `min-width` **and** `min-height` **and** `max-width` **and** `max-height`

The `min-width` and `min-height` and `max-width` and `max-height` properties,
all of which are **non-inherited**, are used to control the lower and upper limits of the
size of a box, that is, the smallest size and the largest size at which a box can be displayed, irrespective of the size of browser window. Limiting dimensions in this way is
necessary for various reasons. With respect to width, it is to ensure that pages are not
displayed so small on small screens that their contents are not legible or so wide on
large screens that they require extreme movements of the eyes and head on the part of
the user to view or read them. With respect to height, although setting `min-height`
may seldom be necessary, setting `max-height` can be important, because if, during
display, the depth of the content of a box is greater than the height of the box, the content will likely overrun the content of the box below, creating an unsightly presentation
and text that is not possible to read. Figure 10.5 shows how the four properties are used,
and Figure 10.6 depicts the result.

The rules in the example basically specify that the content of each `<div>` element box should not be displayed beyond the width of 630px, even if the width of the
browser is greater than this. Similarly, it specifies that the content should not shrink
beyond 400px, which means that if the browser window becomes narrower than this,
the content will be cropped off. It also specifies a `max-height` of 120px, which
means that if the content is more in height than this, it overflows into the content of
the box below, displaying over it, as evident in Figure 10.6. Fortunately, CSS provides
means of addressing this overflow problem.

```
CSS
div.courg { min-width: 400px; max-width: 630px;
           max-height: 120px; }
div.salmon { min-width: 400px; max-width: 630px;
            max-height: 120px; }
HTML
<h3>Width and height limiting</h3>
<h4>Steaming Courgette</h4>
<div class="courg">Lorem ipsum dolor sit amet, consectetur
 adipiscing elit. Integer aliquet facilisis dui, non... </div>
<h4>Salmon and Vegetables</h4>
<div class="salmon">Donec a mauris sapien. Suspendisse mollis
 feugiat sem, eget porta...</div>
```

FIGURE 10.5 Example usage of min- and max-dimension properties.

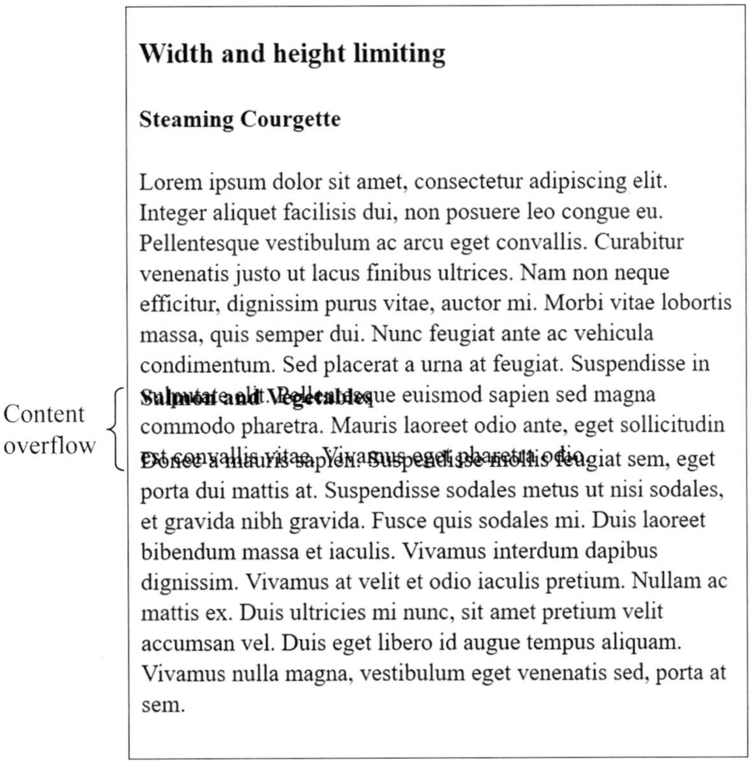

FIGURE 10.6 The rendered result of Figure 10.5.

10.3.2.1 Handling Content Overflow

Content overflows, both the one that overflows the bottom of a box and the one that overflows the side, are mainly handled using the combination of the `over-flow`, `white-space`, and `text-overflow` properties, as necessary. Some of them hide or show overflow, while some can be used to specify to wrap content to the next line. When content wrapping is determined on the fly by the browser based on various current conditions, it is generally known as a **soft wrap**, while a deliberate wrap, such as the one created by a `<p>` element, is known as a **hard wrap**. The properties introduced here for managing content overflow in an element's box can also be used for the content of a table. The styling of tables is discussed in Chapter 17.

10.3.2.1.1 `overflow`

The `overflow` property, which is **non-inherited**, specifies what to do with the content that overflows the borders of a box container or table cells. The common keyword values that it takes and their functions are listed in Table 10.1.

Figure 10.7 shows the addition of the `overflow` property to the rules shown earlier in Figure 10.5, and Figure 10.8 shows the effects. Notice that the browser sees it fit to add scrollbars.

TABLE 10.1

The Values Supported by the `overflow` Property

Value	Function
visible	Does not clip overflow, and the rendered content overflows the element's box if too large for the box.
hidden	Clips overflow and makes the rest of content invisible or unavailable.
scroll	Clips overflow and provides a scrollbar to scroll to the rest of the content.
auto	Lets the user agent (e.g., browser) to decide on the best solution.

```
div.courg { min-width: 400px; max-width: 630px; max-height:
          120px; overflow: auto; }
div.salmon { min-width: 400px; max-width: 630px; max-height:
          120px; overflow: auto; }
```

FIGURE 10.7   How the overflow property is used.

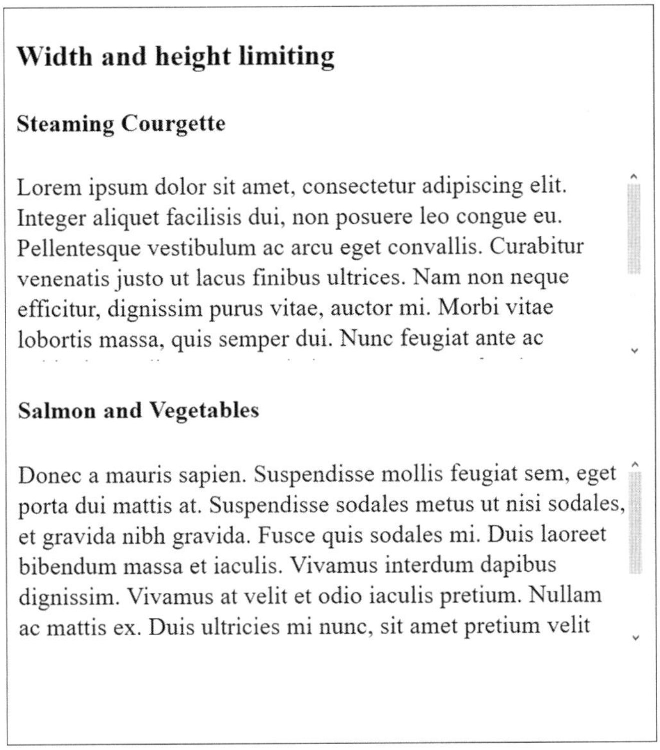

Width and height limiting

Steaming Courgette

Lorem ipsum dolor sit amet, consectetur adipiscing elit.
Integer aliquet facilisis dui, non posuere leo congue eu.
Pellentesque vestibulum ac arcu eget convallis. Curabitur
venenatis justo ut lacus finibus ultrices. Nam non neque
efficitur, dignissim purus vitae, auctor mi. Morbi vitae
lobortis massa, quis semper dui. Nunc feugiat ante ac

Salmon and Vegetables

Donec a mauris sapien. Suspendisse mollis feugiat sem, eget
porta dui mattis at. Suspendisse sodales metus ut nisi sodales,
et gravida nibh gravida. Fusce quis sodales mi. Duis laoreet
bibendum massa et iaculis. Vivamus interdum dapibus
dignissim. Vivamus at velit et odio iaculis pretium. Nullam
ac mattis ex. Duis ultricies mi nunc, sit amet pretium velit

FIGURE 10.8   The result of Figure 10.5, with the `overflow` property added to the rules, as shown in Figure 10.7.

CHALLENGE 10.3

Use the `visible`, `hidden`, and `scroll` values with the `overflow` property to see their effects. Notice especially the difference between scroll and auto by resizing the width of the browser.

CHALLENGE 10.4

The two rules in Figure 10.7 are identical. Implement Figure 10.5, substituting the rules, and then modify the whole code to remove repetitions and to make it more efficient.

10.3.2.1.2 white-space

The white-space property is **inherited** and allows you to control how white space inside an element is handled. The values that it supports are listed in Table 10.2.

Figure 10.9 shows how the property is used, and Figure 10.10 depicts the result. Notice in the code that there is white space between the starting <p> tags and where the content starts. Then, notice how the value used with each white-space property determines how the space is handled when the contents are displayed.

TABLE 10.2

The Value Supported by the white-space Property

Value	Function
normal	Specifies to collapse sequences of white space. Wraps text.
nowrap	Specifies to collapse white space as normal but ignores line breaks. Does not wrap.
pre	Specifies to preserve sequences of white space and break lines at new-line characters or elements. Does not wrap.
pre-wrap	Specifies to preserve sequences of white space and break lines at new-line characters or elements and, as necessary, to fill box. Wraps text.
pre-line	Specifies to collapse sequences of white space and break lines at new-line characters or elements and, as necessary, to fill box. Wraps text.

```
CSS
p { width: 250px; border: 2px solid red; }
.normal { white-space: normal; }
.nowrap { white-space: nowrap; }
.pre { white-space: pre; }
.pre-wrap { white-space: pre-wrap; }
.pre-line { white-space: pre-line; }

HTML
<h2>White space</h2>
<p class="normal">Phasellus sagittis, ipsum sed laoreet
  fermentum, lacus ...</p>
<p class="nowrap">Phasellus sagittis, ipsum sed laoreet
  fermentum, lacus ...</p>
<p class="pre">Phasellus sagittis, ipsum sed laoreet fermentum,
  lacus ...</p>
<p class="pre-wrap">Phasellus sagittis, ipsum sed laoreet
  fermentum, lacus ...</p>
<p class="pre-line">Phasellus sagittis, ipsum sed laoreet
  fermentum, lacus ...</p>
```

FIGURE 10.9   Example usage of the white-space property.

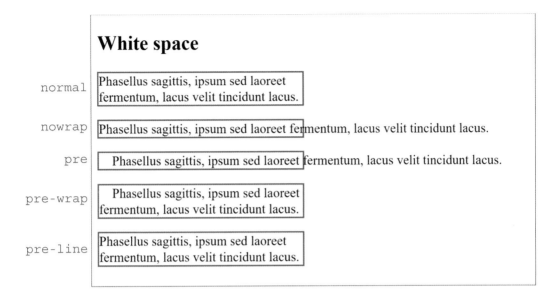

FIGURE 10.10   The result of Figure 10.9.

CHALLENGE 10.5

Given the CSS rule, `.normal { white-space: normal; }`, what is the rendered output for the following?

```
<p class="normal">
    Phasellus sagittis, ipsum sed laoreet fermentum,
    lacus ...
</p>
```

10.3.2.1.3 `text-overflow`

The `text-overflow` property is **non-inherited** and is used to specify how the browser should communicate to the user that there is content overflow that is not displayed. It applies to content that is overflowing only the side of a container box, not the bottom. Text can overflow when it is stopped from wrapping, for example, due to the use of `white-space: nowrap` declaration or a word being too long. The property does not make overflow to occur by itself. So, for it to have an effect, properties that cause overflow, such as the `overflow` property, must first be applied to an element. The typical values used with the property are described in Table 10.3. Figures 10.11 and 10.12 show how it is used and depict the effect.

In the rule, the `white-space: nowrap;` declaration says not to wrap the text. This means that when the text reaches the border, it is clipped. The `overflow: hidden;` declaration hides the overflow, and `text-overflow: ellipsis;` adds ellipsis, as shown in Figure 10.12, to show that the text is clipped.

TABLE 10.3

Values Supported by the `text-overflow` Property

Value	Function
clip	Specifies to clip text at the border of the box. The clipping can occur in the middle of a character but can be made to occur between characters if the **empty string value** ' ' is used. It is the default.
ellipsis	Specifies to display an ellipsis ('...') to indicate that text has been clipped. If there is not enough space, the ellipsis is clipped.
\<string\>	Specifies a custom string (e.g., '***' and '-') to use to indicated that text is clipped.

```
CSS
.overflow { min-width: 400px; max-width: 630px; max-height:
          120px; min-height:5px;
  white-space: nowrap;
  overflow: hidden;
  text-overflow: ellipsis;
}

HTML
<h3>Horizontal overflow</h3>
<h4>Steaming Courgette</h4>
<div>Lorem ipsum dolor sit amet, consectetur adipiscing elit.
 Integer aliquet...</div>
<h4>Salmon and Vegetables</h4>
<div class="overflow">Donec a mauris sapien. Suspendisse mollis
 feugiat se...</div>
```

FIGURE 10.11   Handling horizontal overflow.

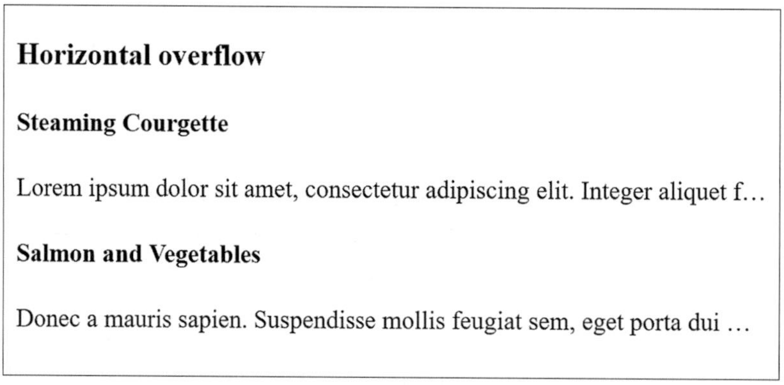

Horizontal overflow

Steaming Courgette

Lorem ipsum dolor sit amet, consectetur adipiscing elit. Integer aliquet f...

Salmon and Vegetables

Donec a mauris sapien. Suspendisse mollis feugiat sem, eget porta dui ...

FIGURE 10.12   The result of Figure 10.11.

CHALLENGE 10.6

Implement the example and experiment with the values of the properties to see their effects.

10.3.2.1.4 `overflow-wrap`

The `overflow-wrap` allows you to specify whether or not the browser should break text lines in the middle of words to prevent them from overflowing the right or left edge of an element's box. The element was originally known as `word-wrap` and is **inherited**. As of time of writing, only Chrome and Opera support the new name. The values that the property takes are `normal` (which means to break lines at normal word breakpoints) and `break-word` (which means that lines may be broken in the middle of words). Figures 10.13 and 10.14 shows how the property is used and depict the result.

CHALLENGE 10.7

In the example, why is it necessary to specify width for the elements to demonstrate the `overflow-wrap` property?

```
CSS
p { border: 2px solid red; }
p.nobreak { width: 15em; overflow-wrap: normal; }
p.break { width: 15em; overflow-wrap: break-word; }

HTML
<h2>Overflow wrap</h2>
<p class="nobreak">Lorem ipsum dolor sit amet, consectetur
adipiscing elit. Aenean rhoncus ipsum sem, nec euismod libero
porttitor eu. Nulla ut
urnaaligulatinciduntcondimentumquissitametdiam. Morbi sed magna
odio. Nam non ultricies eros.</p>
<p class="break">Lorem ipsum dolor sit amet, consectetur
adipiscing elit. Aenean rhoncus ipsum sem, nec euismod libero
porttitor eu. Nulla ut
urnaaligulatinciduntcondimentumquissitametdiam. Morbi sed
magna odio. Nam non ultricies eros.</p>
```

FIGURE 10.13 Example usage of the `overflow-wrap` property.

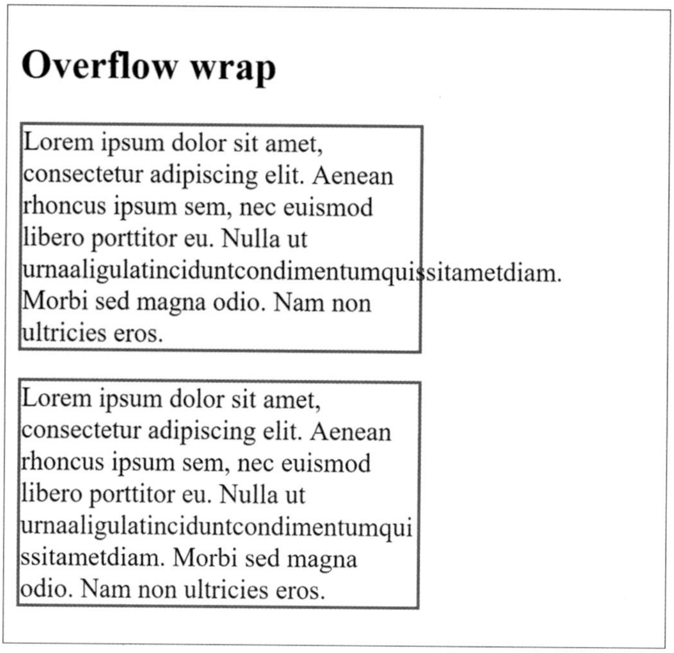

Overflow wrap

> Lorem ipsum dolor sit amet, consectetur adipiscing elit. Aenean rhoncus ipsum sem, nec euismod libero porttitor eu. Nulla ut urnaaligulatinciduntcondimentumquissitametdiam. Morbi sed magna odio. Nam non ultricies eros.

> Lorem ipsum dolor sit amet, consectetur adipiscing elit. Aenean rhoncus ipsum sem, nec euismod libero porttitor eu. Nulla ut urnaaligulatinciduntcondimentumqui ssitametdiam. Morbi sed magna odio. Nam non ultricies eros.

FIGURE 10.14   The result of Figure 10.13.

The `word-break` property, which is also **inherited**, performs similar functions as `overflow-wrap`, except that it is more suitable for where text contains multiple languages, especially **CJK** (Chinese, Japanese, and Korean). The values supported are `normal` (which means to use default line break rule), `break-all` (which means to allow word breaks for non-CJK text), and `keep-all` (which disallows word breaks for CJK text and behaves as `normal` for non-CJK text).

CHALLENGE 10.8

Implement the example in Figure 10.13 by using `word-break` and its values, instead of `overflow-wrap`, to see the difference between the two.

10.3.2.1.5 `hyphens`

The `hyphens` property allows you to specify how to hyphenate words when text is wrapped. It is **inherited**, and Table 10.4 lists the values that are supported. Figures 10.15 and 10.16 show how it is used and depict the result.

In the example, the `p.none{}` rule says to wrap text, based on white space. The `p.manual{}` rule says to break the word "demonstrates" where the soft (invisible) hyphen character is inserted. Note that the soft hyphen can also be specified using its Unicode (thus: `&#x00AD;`). The `p.auto{}` rule says that the browser should decide.

TABLE 10.4

Values Supported by the hyphens Property

Value	Function
none	Wraps text only at white space.
manual	Wraps only where the characters in a word suggest it. You can suggest breakpoints by inserting in a word one of the two Unicode characters, **U+2010** (hard hyphen) and **U+00AD** (soft hyphen), which can be specified in HTML as ‐ and ­, respectively. How to specify special characters is explained in Chapter 3. The hard hyphen is rendered even if word is not broken, while the soft hyphen is rendered only if break is broken.
auto	Browser determines where to break words.

```
CSS
p { width: 175px; border: 2px solid red; }
p.none { hyphens: none; }
p.manual { hyphens: manual; }
p.auto { hyphens: auto; }

HTML
<h3>Hyphens</h3>
<p class="none">This example demonstrates the use of the
 hyphens property</p>
<p class="manual">This example demonstra&shy;tes the use of
 the hyphens property</p>
<p class="auto">This example demonstrates the use of the
 hyphens property</p>
```

FIGURE 10.15   Example usage of the hyphens property.

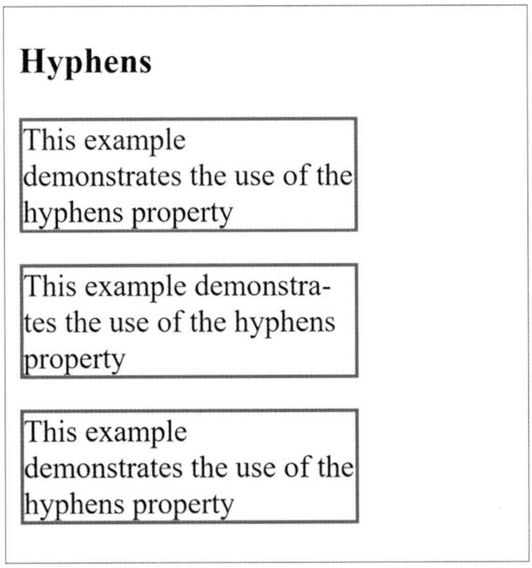

FIGURE 10.16   The result of Figure 10.15.

CHALLENGE 10.9

Implement the example in Figure 10.15 separately for each value, using a lot of text and a wider width, to get a good sense of how the property works. Also, use the hard hyphen (i.e., ‐) where wrapping is not necessary, in order to see the effect. If the property does not work well in a browser, try using the vendor prefixes, as shown in Chapter 8.

10.3.2.2 Specifying Minimum and Maximum Logical Width and Height

The properties used to specify the logical minimum and maximum width and height of an element are `min-block-size`, `min-inline-size`, `max-block-size`, and `max-inline-size`, and whether each defines minimum or maximum width or height depends on the value of the `writing-mode` property (discussed in Chapter 14). They are **non-inherited** and take the same values as the `min-width`, `min-height`, `max-width`, and `max-height` properties introduced earlier; however, **keyword values**, such as `none`, `min-content`, `max-content`, `fit-content`, and `fill-content`, may also be supported in the finalized specification. Figure 10.17 shows how the properties are used.

```
CSS
.size {
  text-align: center;
  font-size: 24px;
  background-color: pink;
  writing-mode: horizontal-tb;
  min-block-size: 300px;
  max-block-size: 900px;
  min-inline-size: 400px;
  max-inline-size: 1200px;
}

HTML
<div>
  <p class="size">In right-to-left top-to-bottom text-flow
  direction, min-block-size specifies minimum height,
  max-block-size maximum height, min-inline-size minimum width,
  and max-inline-size maximum width</p>
</div>
```

FIGURE 10.17 Example usage of properties for specifying the minimum and maximum logical width and height of an element.

In the example, given the value of `writing-mode` (which is in right-to-left, top-to-bottom text-flow direction), `min-block-size` defines minimum height, `max-block-size` defined maximum height, `min-inline-size` defined minimum width, and `max-inline-size` defined maximum width. The example produces the same result as specifying `min-height: 300px; max-height: 900px; min-width: 400px; max-width: 1200px;`, but if writing mode is changed, a different result is produced.

CHALLENGE 10.10

In the example, what would `min-block-size`, `max-block-size`, `min-inline-size`, and `max-inline-size` define if writing mode is from top to bottom and left to right?

10.3.3 `calc()`

As mentioned in Chapter 6, the `calc()` function allows you to tell the browser to calculate values dynamically and can be used with any CSS numeric values, such as length, angle, time, and integer. It especially makes it easy to position elements symmetrically in a container, such as in the middle. It takes a mathematical expression that evaluates to the value used for a property. The expression combines operators such as +, −, *, and /, which specify addition, subtraction, multiplication, and division, respectively. Figure 10.18 shows how the function is used, and Figure 10.19 depicts the result.

```
CSS
div {
  border: solid black 1px;
  background-color: lightpink;
  padding: 6px;
  text-align: center;
}
.one { width: calc(100% - 90px); }
.two { width: calc(100% - 200px); }

HTML
<h2>cal() function</h2>
<div class="one">One</div>
<div class="two">Two</div>
```

FIGURE 10.18 Example usage of the `calc()` function.

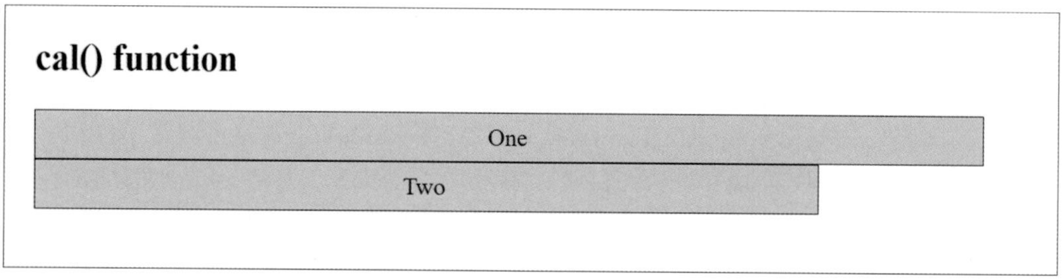

---

cal() function

One

Two

FIGURE 10.19   The result of Figure 10.18.

In the example, the rules say to make the widths of the `<div>` elements as the width of the browser minus 90px and 200px, respectively. The browser-width percentages can also be specified using the `vw` (viewport width) unit, introduced in Chapter 6, under responsive images. So, for example, the CSS declaration `min-width: calc(50vw-100px)` specifies that whatever be the width of the viewport, the minimum width (`min-width`) of the element to which the declaration is applied should be 50% of it minus 100px. Using it in center-aligning an element requires the use of other CSS properties, especially `margin`, which is discussed in the next section.

CHALLENGE 10.11

Place a `<div>` element inside another `<div>` element and use the `calc()` function to make the width of the inner `<div>` element half of the outer one and the width of the outer one-three quarters that of the viewport.

10.4 Border, Padding, and Margin

The border, padding, and margin of an element's box can be manipulated independently, and all the CSS properties used to do this have both **longhand** and **shorthand** formats to make working with elements' boxes more flexible and more efficient. In principle, the longhand properties allow you to specify the value for only one edge of a box at a time, while a shorthand property allows this to be done for more than one edge at a time, using either one value that applies to all four edges or a list of space-separated values that may contain two, three, or four values. How these values are assigned depends on whether one, two, three, or four values are specified; this is explained later in this section under the individual properties.

Like with properties for defining box dimensions, discussed earlier in the chapter, border, padding, and margin can also be specified using **CSS logical properties**. Again, their effects depend on the set value for the `writing-mode` property, discussed more fully in Chapter 14.

> **NOTE: About padding, border, and the size of element's box**
>
> It is useful to know that, by default, the specified values for the padding and border of an element are added to the specified width and height. However, there is a property, `box-sizing`, that allows this to be changed, so that the values do not affect an element's width or height. This property is discussed more fully later in this chapter.

10.4.1 Border

The appearance of an element's border, which is described mainly in terms of **line style**, **color**, and **line width**, can be specified in different ways by using longhand and shorthand properties. There are:

- Longhand properties for specifying line style, color, or line width for a specific border edge, for example, `border-top-style`.
- Shorthand properties for specifying line style, color, or line width for all or a combination of border simultaneously, for example, `border-style`.
- Shorthand properties for specifying line style, color, and line width for a specific border edge simultaneously, for example, `border-top`.
- Shorthand property, `border`, for specifying line style, color, and line width simultaneously.

In addition to properties for setting line style, color, and line width, there are those for specifying images and radius to use for a border, all of which are available in longhand and shorthand. It is worth knowing that **for the border of a box and the changes made to it to be visible, the line style must be specified**. This is because the browser displays no border for an element by default. Note that border properties, in general, can also be used for table's `<th>` and `<td>` elements. How this is done is shown under the styling of tables in Chapter 17.

10.4.1.1 `border-style`

The `border-style` property is a **shorthand property** for specifying the line style for all the four edges of an element's border. It is **non-inherited,** and the values that it supports are listed in Table 10.5. Figures 10.20 and 10.21 show how the property is used and depict the result.

TABLE 10.5

The Values Supported by the `border-style` Property

Border-Style Value	Description
none	Displays no border, and it is the browser's default.
hidden	Displays no border.
solid	Displays a single straight line.
dotted	Displays a series of rounded dots.
dashed	Displays a series of short lines.
double	Displays two solid lines that are apart by the amount of border-width property specified.
ridge	Displays a raised (3D-looking) border.
groove	Displays a border that looks as if it is carved in the page.
inset	Displays a border that makes the box appear embedded in the page.
outset	Displays a border that makes the box appear pushed out of the page.

```
CSS
p.solid { border-style: solid; }
p.dashed { border-style: dashed; }
p.dotted { border-style: dotted; }
p.double { border-style: double;}
p.groove { border-style: groove; }
p.ridge { border-style: ridge; }
p.inset { border-style: inset; }
p.outset { border-style: outset; }

HTML
<h3>Shorthand border-style</h3>
<p class="solid">{ border-style: solid; }</p>
<p class="dashed">{ border-style: dashed; }</p>
<p class="dotted">{ border-style: dotted; }</p>
<p class="double">{ border-style: double; }</p>
<p class="groove">{ border-style: groove; }</p>
<p class="ridge">{ border-style: ridge; }</p>
<p class="inset">{ border-style: inset; }</p>
<p class="outset">{ border-style: outset; }</p>
```

FIGURE 10.20   Example usage of the `border-style` property.

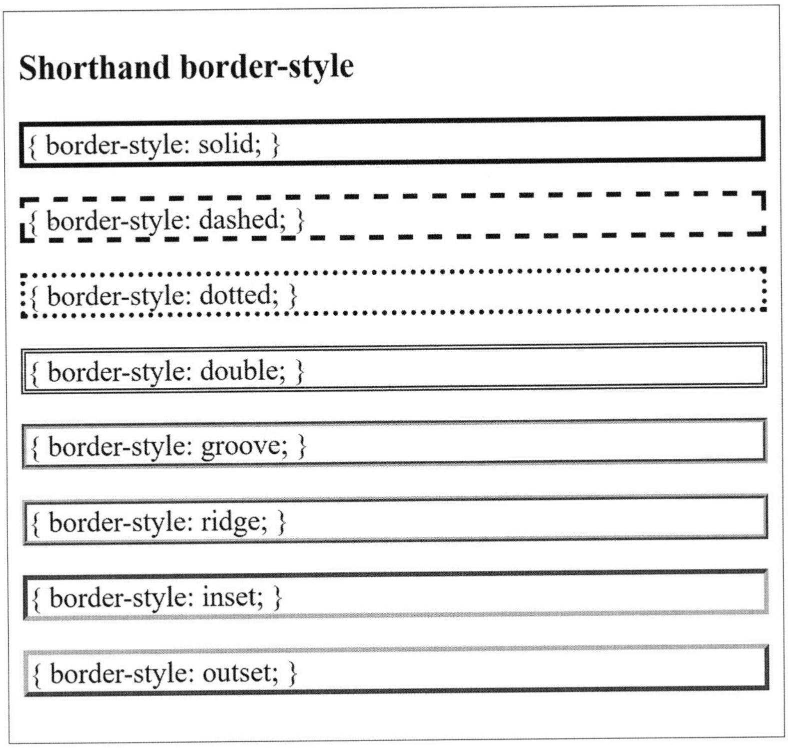

Shorthand border-style

{ border-style: solid; }

{ border-style: dashed; }

{ border-style: dotted; }

{ border-style: double; }

{ border-style: groove; }

{ border-style: ridge; }

{ border-style: inset; }

{ border-style: outset; }

FIGURE 10.21 The rendered result of Figure 10.20.

Figure 10.22 shows how a **list of space-separated values** may be specified, so that different edges are given different styles, without using the longhand `border-style` properties. Figure 10.23 shows the rendered result. How the values are assigned to the edges is listed in Table 10.6.

```
CSS
p.all { border-style: solid; }
p.top_hori_vert { border-style: dotted solid; }
p.top_vert_bot { border-style: hidden double dashed; }
p.top_right_bot_left { border-style: none dashed dotted solid; }

HTML
<h3>Space-separated values</h3>
<p class="all">{ border-style: solid; }</p>
<p class="top_hori_vert">{ border-style: dotted solid; }</p>
<p class="top_vert_bot">{ border-style: hidden double
 dashed; }</p>
<p class="top_right_bot_left">{ border-style: none dashed
 dotted solid; }</p>
```

FIGURE 10.22 Using `border-style` property to specify multiple values.

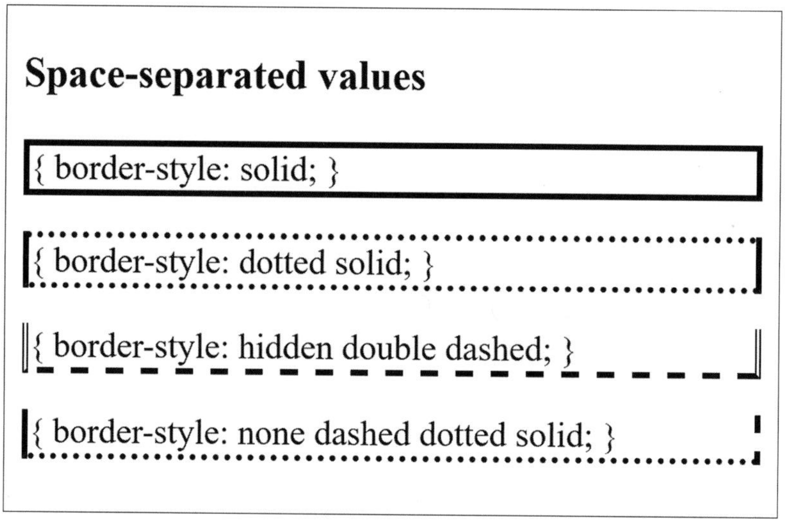

Space-separated values

{ border-style: solid; }

{ border-style: dotted solid; }

{ border-style: hidden double dashed; }

{ border-style: none dashed dotted solid; }

FIGURE 10.23   The result of Figure 10.22.

TABLE 10.6

How the Values of the Shorthand `border-style` Property Are Assigned

Number of Values	Application of Values
One	Value is assigned to all four edges.
Two	First value is assigned to top and bottom, and second value is assigned to right and left.
Three	First value is assigned to top, second to right and left, and third to bottom.
Four	First value is assigned to top, second to right, third to bottom, and fourth to left.

CHALLENGE 10.12

Write the code to produce something similar to the following:

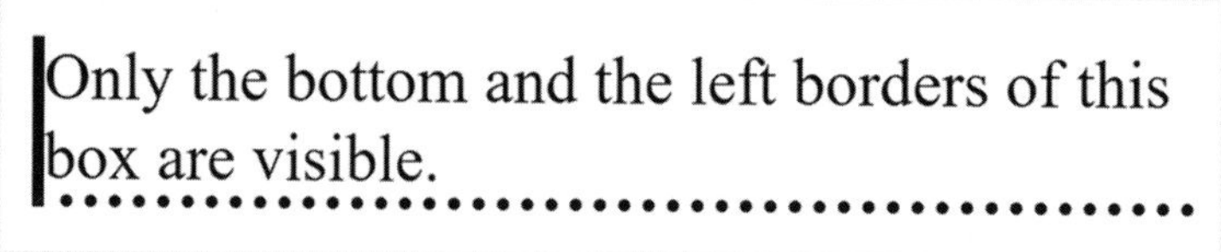

Only the bottom and the left borders of this box are visible.

10.4.1.1.1 Longhand `border-style`

The longhand versions of the `border-style` property are `border-top-style`, `border-right-style`, `border-bottom-style`, and `border-left-style`; these are used to apply style to the top, right, bottom, and left edges, respectively. Like the shorthand, they are **non-inherited**. Figure 10.24 shows how they are used, and Figure 10.25 shows the result.

```
CSS
p { border-top-style: double; }
p { border-right-style: solid; }
p { border-bottom-style: dashed; }
p { border-left-style: solid; }

HTML
<h3>Longhand border-style</h3>
<p>border-top-style: double; border-right-style: solid;
    border-bottom-style: dashed; border-left-style: solid;</p>
```

FIGURE 10.24   Example usage of longhand `border-style` property.

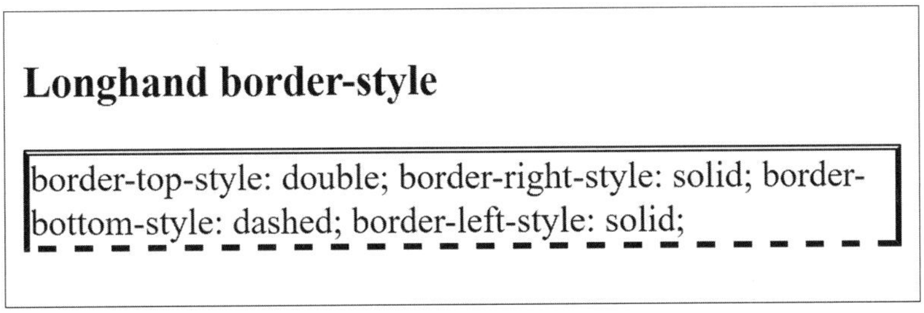

Longhand border-style

border-top-style: double; border-right-style: solid; border-bottom-style: dashed; border-left-style: solid;

FIGURE 10.25   The result of Figure 10.24.

CHALLENGE 10.13

In the code in Figure 10.24, what would happen if the `<p>` element contains no content, and what is the reason for this?

CHALLENGE 10.14

Again, in relation to Figure 10.24, if you do not want any content in the `<p>` element but want it to be as if it has content by putting space in it, how would you do this?

10.4.1.1.2 Specifying Style for Logical Border Edges

The properties used to specify the line style for the logical border edge of an element are `border-block-end-style`, `border-block-start-style`, `border-inline-end-style`, and `border-inline-start-style`. Whether each defines the style for the top, bottom, left, or right border edge of the element depends on the value of the `writing-mode` property (discussed in Chapter 14). The properties are **non-inherited** and take the same values as the `border-top-style`, `border-right-style`, `border-bottom-style`, or `border-left-style` property. Figures 10.26 and 10.27 show the usage and result.

```
CSS
.style {
  writing-mode: horizontal-tb;
  border: 5px solid blue;
  border-block-start-style: dashed;
}

HTML
<div>
  <p class="style">In right-to-left top-to-bottom text-flow
  direction, border-block-start-style targets border top edge
  and styles it</p>
</div>
```

FIGURE 10.26   Example usage of properties for specifying line style for logical border.

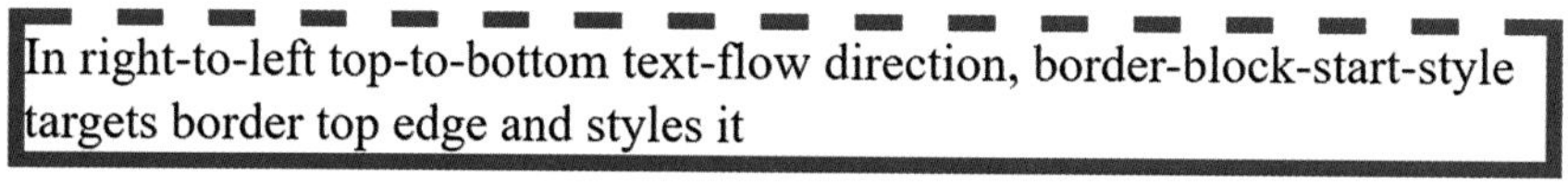

In right-to-left top-to-bottom text-flow direction, border-block-start-style targets border top edge and styles it

FIGURE 10.27   The result of Figure 10.26.

CHALLENGE 10.15

Implement the example and experiment with the value of the `border-block-start-style` attribute.

10.4.1.2 `border-width`

The `border-width` property is a shorthand property for specifying the thickness of the border of an element's box. The longhand properties are `border-top-width`, `border-right-width`, `border-bottom-width`, and `border-left-width`, and the values supported by the properties are non-negative **length values** (e.g., `pixels`, `em`, `rem`, and `cm`) and **keywords** (e.g., `thin`, `medium`, and `thick`). The properties are **non-inherited**. Figures 10.28 and 10.29 show how they are used with various combinations of values and depict the rendered result. Table 10.7 shows how the values are assigned to produce the result.

```
CSS
p.one { border-style: solid; border-width: 2px; }
p.two { border-style: solid; border-width: 2px 10px; }
p.three { border-style: dashed; border-width: 0.3em thin 4px; }
p.four { border-style: ridge; border-width: thin medium thick
        0.2em; }
```

HTML
```
<h3>Border width</h3>
<p class="one">{ border-style: solid; border-width: 2px; }</p>
<p class="two">{ border-style: solid; border-width: 2px
 1em; }</p>
<p class="three">{ border-style: dashed; border-width:
 0.2em thin 6px; }</p>
<p class="four">{ border-style: ridge; border-width:
 thin medium thick 0.2em; }</p>
```

FIGURE 10.28 Different ways of using the `border-width` property.

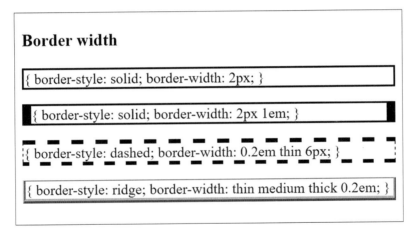

FIGURE 10.29 The rendered result of Figure 10.28.

TABLE 10.7

How the Values of the Shorthand `border-width` Property Are Assigned

Number of Values	Application of Values
One	Value is assigned to all four edges.
Two	First value is assigned to top and bottom, and second value is assigned to right and left.
Three	First value is assigned to top, second to right and left, and third to bottom.
Four	First value is assigned to top, second to right, third to bottom, and fourth to left.

CHALLENGE 10.16

Using the example in Figure 10.24 as guide, write a code by using longhand properties to specify the width for each of the four edges of a `<div>` element separately.

CHALLENGE 10.17

Using the example in Figure 10.28, write a code by using the shorthand `border-width` property to specify the width for the four edges of a `<div>` element, making the right and left edges the same and the top and bottom edges different.

CHALLENGE 10.18

In the example in Figure 10.28, why is it necessary to specify the `border-style` property?

10.4.1.2.1 Specifying Width for Logical Border Edges

The properties used to specify the logical border width of an element are `border-block-end-width`, `border-block-start-width`, `border-inline-end-width`, and `border-inline-start-width`. Whether each defines the thickness of the top, bottom, left, or right border edge of an element depends on the value of the `writing-mode` property (discussed in Chapter 14). The properties are **non-inherited** and take the same values as the `border-top-width`, `border-right-width`, `border-bottom-width`, or `border-left-width` property. Figures 10.30 and 10.31 show the usage and the result.

```
CSS
.width {
  writing-mode: horizontal-tb;
  border: 1px solid darkorange;
  border-block-start-width: 5px;
}

HTML
<div>
  <p class="width">In right-to-left top-to-bottom text-flow
  direction, border-block-start-width targets border top edge
  and sets the border thickness</p>
</div>
```

FIGURE 10.30 Example usage of properties for specifying width for logical border.

In right-to-left top-to-bottom text-flow direction, border-block-start-width targets border top edge and sets the border thickness

FIGURE 10.31 The result of Figure 10.30.

CHALLENGE 10.19

Implement the example and experiment with the value of the `border-block-start-width` attribute.

10.4.1.3 `border-color`

The `border-color` property is a shorthand property used to specify the color of the four edges of an element's border. Like other border properties, it has longhand versions for specifying colors of individual edges, which are `border-top-color`, `border-right-color`, `border-bottom-color`, and `border-left-color`, all of which are **non-inherited**. The values that they support are **color names** and **color values** in decimal and hexadecimal numbers, and the **alpha channel** (i.e., rgba and hsla) is supported. See Chapter 9 for more on the syntax used for specifying color. Figure 10.32 shows how the property is used with various types of values, and Figure 10.33 shows the rendered result. Table 10.8 again lists how the `border-color` property values are assigned.

```
CSS
p.one { border-style: solid; border-color: red; }
p.two { border-style: solid; border-color: red green; }
p.three { border-style: dashed; border-color: hsl(0,100%,50%)
        green rgb(0,0,255); }
p.four { border-style: ridge; border-color: hsla(0,100%,50%,0.3)
        green rgba(0,0,255,0.3) #36d6ff; }

HTML
<h3>Border color</h3>
<p class="one">{ border-style: solid; border-color: red; }</p>
<p class="two">{ border-style: solid; border-color:
 red green; }</p>
<p class="three">{ border-style: dashed; border-color:
 hsl(0,100%,50%) green rgb(0,0,255); }</p>
<p class="four">{ border-style: ridge; border-color:
 hsla(0,100%,50%,0.3) green  rgba(0,0,255,0.3) #36d6ff; }</p>
```

FIGURE 10.32 Example usage of the `border-color` property.

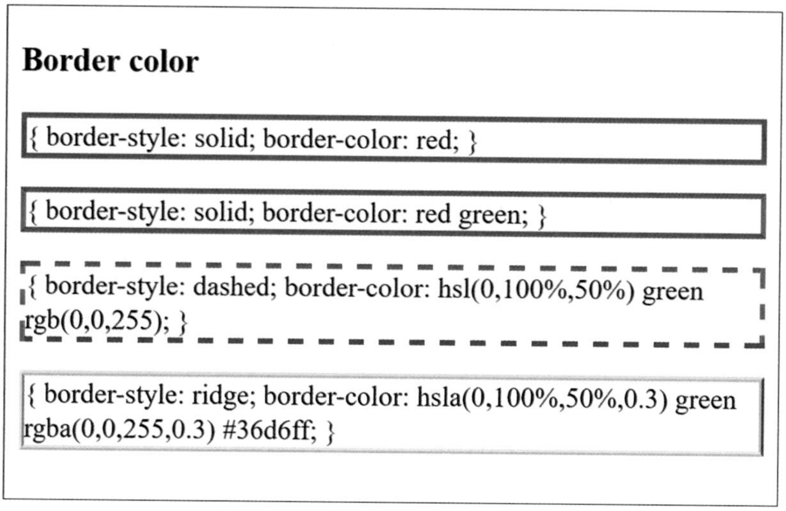

Border color

{ border-style: solid; border-color: red; }

{ border-style: solid; border-color: red green; }

{ border-style: dashed; border-color: hsl(0,100%,50%) green rgb(0,0,255); }

{ border-style: ridge; border-color: hsla(0,100%,50%,0.3) green rgba(0,0,255,0.3) #36d6ff; }

FIGURE 10.33   The rendered result of Figure 10.32.

TABLE 10.8

How the Values of the Shorthand `border-color` Property Are Assigned

Number of Values	Application of Values
One	Value is assigned to all four edges.
Two	First value is assigned to top and bottom, and second value is assigned to right and left.
Three	First value is assigned to top, second to right and left, and third to bottom.
Four	First value is assigned to top, second to right, third to bottom, and fourth to left.

CHALLENGE 10.20

Implement the code in Figure 10.32 by using the `<div>` element and also apply background color. How to apply color has been dealt with in Chapter 9.

10.4.1.3.1 Specifying Color for Logical Border Edges

The properties used to specify the color of the logical border edge of an element are `border-block-end-color`, `border-block-start-color`, `border-inline-end-color`, and `border-inline-start-color`. Whether each defines the color for the top, bottom, left, or right border edge of an element depends on the value of the `writing-mode` property (discussed in Chapter 14). The properties are

```
CSS
.color {
  writing-mode: horizontal-tb;
  border: 5px solid black;
  border-block-start-color: red;
}

HTML
<div>
  <p class="color">In right-to-left top-to-bottom text-flow
    direction, border-block- start-color targets border top edge
    and sets the border color</p>
</div>
```

FIGURE 10.34   Example usage of properties for specifying color for logical border.

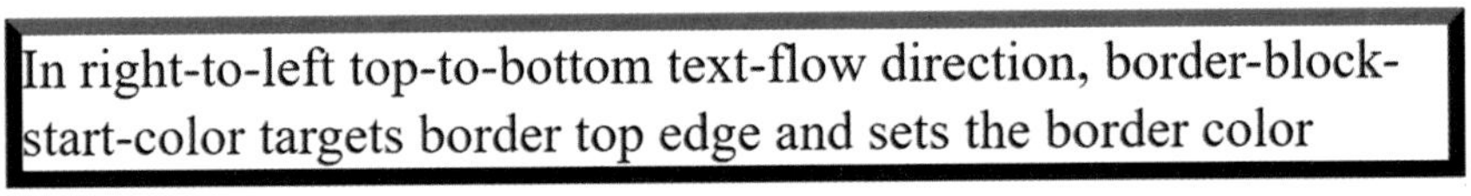

In right-to-left top-to-bottom text-flow direction, border-block-start-color targets border top edge and sets the border color

FIGURE 10.35   The result of Figure 10.34.

non-inherited and take the same values as the `border-top-color`, `border-right-color`, `border-bottom-color`, or `border-left-color` property. Figures 10.34 and 10.35 show the usage and the result.

CHALLENGE 10.21

Implement the example and try the rest of the properties for applying color to logical border edges.

10.4.1.4 `border-top` *and* `border-bottom` *and* `border-right` *and* `border-left`

The `border-top` and `border-bottom` and `border-right` and `border-left` shorthand properties allow you to specify the values for the color, style, and width of a specific border edge at once and in any order. Also, any of the values can be omitted; the browser will understand. All these properties are **non-inherited**. Table 10.9 lists the values that each is used to set. Figure 10.36 shows how the properties are used and Figure 10.37 the result.

TABLE 10.9

Values Allowed for border-top, border-bottom, border-right, border-left

Shorthand	Longhand Properties Set
border-top	Specifies border-top-color, border-top-style, and border-top-width.
border-bottom	Specifies border-bottom-color, border-bottom-style, and border-bottom-width.
border-right	Specifies border-right-color, border-right-style, and border-right-width.
border-left	Specifies border-left-color, border-left-style, and border-left-width.

```
CSS
.one { border-top: dashed red 2px; }
.two { border-top: solid 2px; }
.three { border-bottom: red 2px; }

HTML
<h3>border-top, border-bottom, border-right, border-left</h3>
<p class="one">{ border-top: dashed red 2px; }</p>
<p class="two">{ border-top: solid 2px;}</p>
<p class="three">{ border-bottom: red 2px; }</p>
```

FIGURE 10.36 Example usage of shorthand properties for defining border edge.

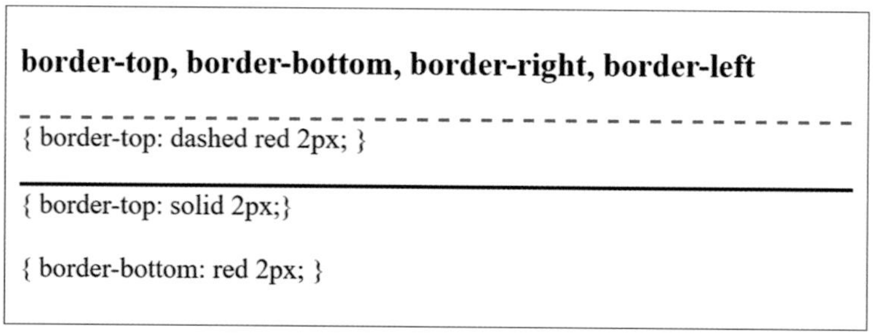

border-top, border-bottom, border-right, border-left

- -
{ border-top: dashed red 2px; }
_____
{ border-top: solid 2px;}

{ border-bottom: red 2px; }

FIGURE 10.37 The result of Figure 10.36.

In the example, the .one{} rule makes the top border edge 2px thick, dashed, and red. In the .two{} rule, the color value is omitted, so the default, black, is used. In the .three{} rule, no style is specified, so the border is not displayed.

CHALLENGE 10.22

What will the rule .three { border-bottom: red; } produce with the HTML code in Figure 10.36? Also, what will the rule .one { border-top: dashed red 2px; } in the example produce if 2px comes before red?

10.4.1.4.1 Specifying Logical Border Edges

The properties used to specify the logical border edge for an element are `border-block-end`, `border-block-start`, `border-inline-end`, and `border-inline-start`. Whether each defines the top, bottom, left, or right border edge of an element depends on the value of the `writing-mode` property (discussed in Chapter 14). The properties are **non-inherited** and take the same values as the `border-top`, `border-right`, `border-bottom`, or `border-left` property. Figures 10.38 and 10.39 show the usage and the result.

```
CSS
.edge {
  writing-mode: horizontal-tb;
  border: 1px solid black;
  border-block-end: 5px dashed blue;
}

HTML
<div>
  <p class="edge">In right-to-left top-to-bottom text-flow
  direction, border-block-end targets border bottom edge and
  applies thespecified values</p>
</div>
```

FIGURE 10.38 Example usage of properties for specifying logical border edges.

In right-to-left top-to-bottom text-flow direction, border-block-end targets border bottom edge and applies the specified values

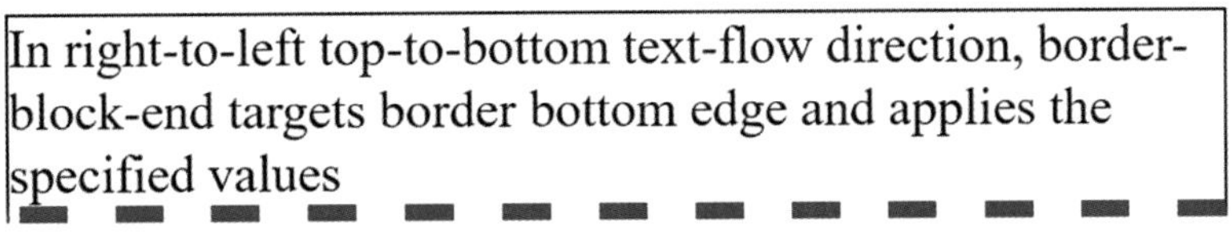

FIGURE 10.39 The result of Figure 10.38.

CHALLENGE 10.23

Implement the example in Figure 10.38 and try the rest of the properties for specifying logical border edges to see the effects. Also, what line style will be displayed if the "dashed" value is omitted in the example, and why? Also, what will happen if the order of the values is changed?

10.4.1.5 `border`

The `border` property is a **non-inherited** shorthand property that allows you to specify `border-width`, `border-style`, and `border-color` properties in one go with one rule. However, only one value is allowed for each of these properties, meaning that the same value is applied to all four edges of a box. Figure 10.40 shows examples of how it is used, and Figure 10.41 depicts the rendered result.

The values must be specified in the specific order shown in the example (i.e., `border-width`, `border-style`, and `border-color`). If one value is missing, the `initial` (default) value for the property is used. For example, the border for the first `<p>` element is not shown because no `border-style` is specified in the corresponding rule (i.e., `p.one { border: thick; }`) and `initial` value is none. The `border-color` property is also not specified. Although the `initial` value is black, it does not show, because the value of `border-style` is none. In the second `<p>` element, `border-color` is not specified, so the `initial` value, black, is used.

```
CSS
p.one { border: thick; }
p.two { border: thick dotted; }
p.three { border: 10px ridge green; }

HTML
<h3>Border property</h3>
<p class="one">{ border: thick; }</p>
<p class="two">{ border: thick dotted; }</p>
<p class="three">{ border: 10px ridge green; }</p>
```

FIGURE 10.40   Example usage of `border` property.

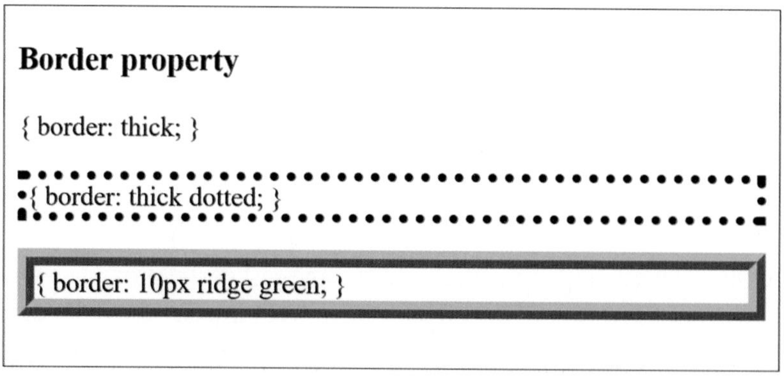

FIGURE 10.41   The rendered result of Figure 10.40.

CHALLENGE 10.24

In the example, the reason why the border is not shown for the first `<p>` element in Figure 10.41 is because the `p.one{}` rule in Figure 10.40 is not written properly. True or false? Give reasons for your answer.

10.4.1.6 `border-image`

The `border-image` property is **non-inherited** and is a shorthand property for specifying the image to be used to style the border of a box, instead of the line styles provided by the CSS `border-style` property. The values supported by the property specify the image to use, where to place the slice lines to divide up the image, and how to display the sliced pieces. Figure 10.42 shows the image used here to demonstrate how the property works. It is 90px × 90px in dimension and is designed so that it is straightforward to determine the location of the slicing lines. The lines are specified in terms of how far in from the top, right, bottom, and left edges of the image to place them (i.e., where to slice the image). The image was created in Photoshop but can be created in any graphics program and should be in a standard image file format (e.g., jpeg, png, and gif).

Figure 10.43 shows how Figure 10.42 is used with the `border-image` property, and Figure 10.44 depicts the result. In the example, the `border-style` property is set to a visible style to allow the image to show, and the `border-width` property **is set** to a value that is large enough to let it show at the required size. The `p{}` rule specifies the properties common to the two `<p>` elements. The `border-image` property values in the `p.round{}` rule say to use the image in

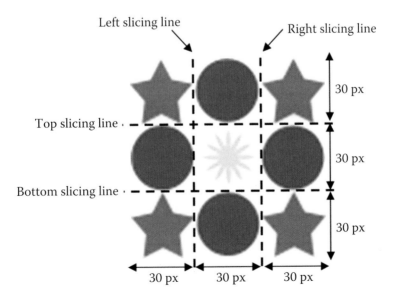

FIGURE 10.42 Image used with `border-image` property.

```
CSS
p { width: 400px;
    border-style: solid;
    border-width: 20px;
}
p.round {
    border-image: url(star_oval.png) 30 30 30 30 round;
}
p.stretch {
    border-image: url(star_oval.png) 30 30 30 30 stretch;
}

HTML
<h3>Border image</h3>
<p class="round">Lorem ipsum dolor sit amet, consectetur ...</p>
<p class="stretch">Lorem ipsum dolor sit amet,
  consectetur ...</p>
```

FIGURE 10.43 Example usage of the `border-image` property.

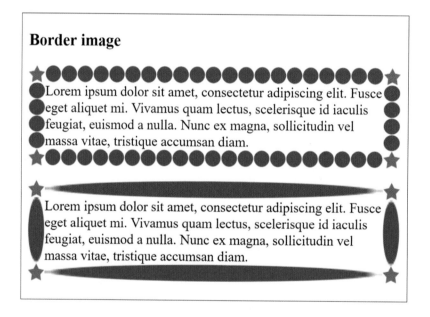

FIGURE 10.44 The rendered result of Figure 10.43.

Figure 10.42 (called "**star_oval.png**") for the border of the first `<p>` element. It says to slice it at 30px in from the top, right, bottom, and left edges, respectively, and repeat and scale the edge pieces (i.e., the ovals) as necessary. The corner pieces are always placed at the corners, as they are. The values of `border-image` property in the `p.stretch{}` rule say the same thing for the border of the second `<p>` element, except to stretch the edge pieces. Note that the `border-image` property may need to be repeated with vendor prefixes for older browsers. This is because the property is one of those implemented differently in browsers, especially in older ones. You will find more on vendor prefixes in Chapter 8.

You would have noticed that the middle piece of the image in Figure 10.42 is not used.

CHALLENGE 10.25

Create an image in a graphics program of your choice, following the guidelines already given, and then use the image to implement the example in Figure 10.43. Also, experiment with the slice values to see the effects.

In order to use it, the longhand versions of the `border-image` property usually need to be used. Note that these longhand properties can also be used to achieve the same goal as Figure 10.44. Table 10.10 lists them and their functions.

TABLE 10.10

Longhand `border-image` Properties

Border-Image Values	Function
`border-image-` `source`	Specifies the image to use for border style and takes the **URL of the image** as value. If no value is specified or the image specified cannot be found or displayed, the `border-style` specified will be used.
`border-image-` `slice`	Specifies how to divide the specified image into nine pieces (i.e., four corners, four edges, and the middle). It takes one, two, three, or four values, and these values can be space-separated **number values** or **percentage values**. When the number of values specified is **one**, it is used for all four edges; when it is **two**, the first is for top and bottom and the second is for right and left; when it is **three**, the first is for top, second is for right and left, and third is for bottom; when it is **four**, the first is for top, the second is for right, third is for bottom, and fourth is for left. Also, the fill keyword can be used to force the middle piece of the image to be displayed as background. When used, it is used in place of the top or left value.

(Continued)

TABLE 10.10 (*Continued*)

Longhand border-image Properties

border-image Values	Function
border-image-repeat	Specifies how to treat the four edge pieces and the middle piece of the sliced image. It takes one or two space-separated **keyword values**, each of which can be stretch (which stretches the piece), repeat (which repeats the piece), and round (which repeats and scales the pieces, so that they fit exactly). If **one** value is used, it is applied to all four edges and the middle piece. If **two** are used, the first is applied to horizontal (top and bottom) edges and the width of the middle piece and the second is applied to the vertical (right and left) edges and the height of the middle piece.
border-image-width	Specifies the width of the border and affects the size of the image-slice pieces. If specified, it supersedes the value of the border-width property. The values taken can be **length values** (e.g., px), **percentage values**, **number values**, or auto. Like the border-width property, it takes one to four values, and the values are assigned in the same way as described earlier in Tables 10.4 and 10.5.
border-image-outset	Specifies the amount by which the border image area extends beyond the border box. It takes one to four space-separated values, which can be **length values** or **number values**. The values are assigned in the same way as for border-image-width.

CHALLENGE 10.26

How would you rewrite the code in Figure 10.43, using the longhand border-image properties described in Table 10.10?

Figure 10.45 shows how the middle piece of a sliced image is used, and Figure 10.46 shows the result. The p{} rule specifies the properties that are common to the two <p> elements. The border-image-source and border-image-slice properties work as described earlier in Table 10.6, and the fill value says to use the middle image piece as background. Notice that it is specified in place of the value for the top edge of the box. The p.round{} rule says to repeat the edge-image pieces for all the edges of the border and the middle piece for the background. The p.stretch{} rule says not to repeat but stretch them.

```
CSS
p { width: 400px;
    border-style: solid;
    border-width: 20px;
    border-image-source: url(star_oval.png);
    border-image-slice: fill 30 30 30;
}
p.round { border-image-repeat: round; }
p.stretch { border-image-repeat: stretch; }

HTML
<h3>Border image fill</h3>
<p class="round">Lorem ipsum dolor sit amet,
 consectetur ...</p>
<p class="stretch">Lorem ipsum dolor sit amet,
 consectetur ...</p>
```

FIGURE 10.45   How border-image-slice property is used to apply the middle image piece.

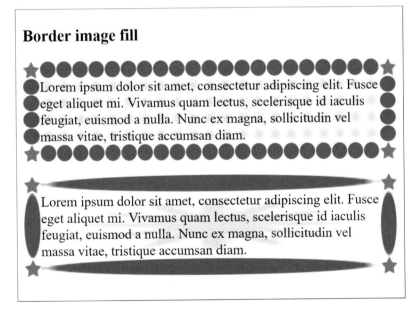

FIGURE 10.46   The result of Figure 10.45.

CHALLENGE 10.27

What is the obvious problem posed to the user by the rendered result in Figure 10.46 in relation to the use of image as background, and how can you address it?

CHALLENGE 10.28

Using the image that you created in the previous challenge to implement Figure 10.43, implement the code in Figure 10.45 and experiment with the values of the `border-image-slice` and `border-image-repeat` properties. For example, move the `fill` around for the former and use two different values for the latter.

CHALLENGE 10.29

Given your knowledge from Chapter 6 of the use of images and accessibility, what accessibility considerations, if any, are necessary when using an image for an element's border (i.e., for decoration), and why?

10.4.1.7 `border-radius`

The `border-radius` property is a shorthand property used to make the corners of a box round. It is **non-inherited** and takes one or two sets of values, each comprising one to four space-separated values, which can be in **length values** (e.g., `px` and `em`) or **percentage values**. When one set of values is specified, the corners drawn are **circle-based**, with each value representing the radius for each corner. When two sets of values are specified, the corners drawn are **ellipse-based**, with the first set representing the **horizontal radii** and the second set representing the **vertical radii**. The two sets of values are separated by a forward slash (/), as in 12px/5px. Table 10.11 describes how a set of values is interpreted.

Longhand `border-radius` properties are also used for specifying radius or radii for individual corners. They are `border-top-right-radius`, `border-bottom-right-radius`, `border-bottom-left-radius`, and `border-top-left-radius`, all of which are also non-inherited. Figures 10.47 and 10.48 show how the shorthand property is used with one value and depict the result.

TABLE 10.11

How the Values of the `border-radius` Property Are Assigned

Number of Values	Application of Values
One	Value is assigned to all four corners.
Two	First value is assigned to top-left and bottom-right corners, and second value is assigned to top-right and bottom-left corners.
Three	First value is assigned to top-left corner, second to top-right and bottom-left corners, and third to bottom-right corner.
Four	Values are assigned to top-left, top-right, bottom-right, and bottom-left corners, respectively.

```
CSS
p {
   border: 5px solid orange;
   width: 300px;
   border-radius: 20px;
}
HTML
<h3>Border radius</h3>
<p>Lorem ipsum dolor sit amet, consectetur adipiscing elit.
  Fusce eget...</p>
```

FIGURE 10.47 Example usage of the `border-radius` property with a single value.

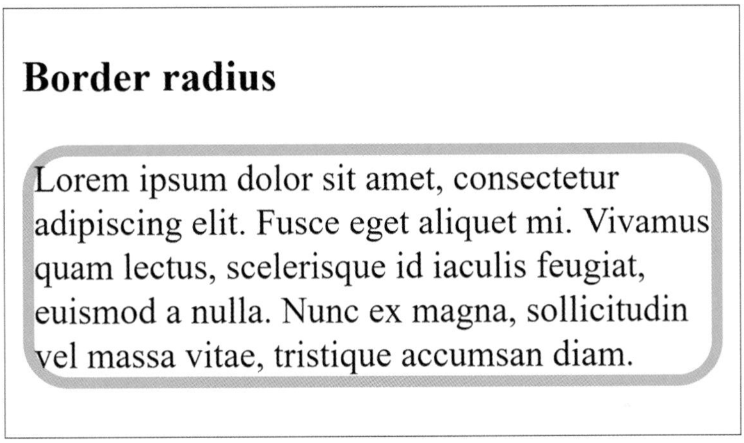

Border radius

Lorem ipsum dolor sit amet, consectetur adipiscing elit. Fusce eget aliquet mi. Vivamus quam lectus, scelerisque id iaculis feugiat, euismod a nulla. Nunc ex magna, sollicitudin vel massa vitae, tristique accumsan diam.

FIGURE 10.48 The rendered result of Figure 10.47.

Each corner is drawn with a radius of 20px. The declaration could also have been written as `border-radius: 20px 20px 20px 20px;`. Notice that the content of the box is too close to the border. This is not aesthetically pleasing. However, it can be rectified by using the `padding` property, which is discussed shortly.

CHALLENGE 10.30

Implement the example in Figure 10.47 and experiment with the value of the radius to see how the shape of the corners changes and the limit.

CHALLENGE 10.31

Using longhand `border-radius` properties, write the code to implement the same output as the declaration: `border-radius: border-radius: 25px 25px 25px`.

Figures 10.49 and 10.50 show how horizontal and vertical values are used with the `border-radius` property and depict the rendered result. The `border-radius` in the p.one{} rule says to use a horizontal radius of 25 em and a vertical radius of 1.5 em to draw all four corners. The `border-radius` in the p.two{} rule specifies a set of four horizontal radii, followed after the slash by a set of four vertical radii.

Using horizontal and vertical radii allows you to create non-symmetric and interesting shapes and even a circle, which is achieved, for example, by using the same width and

```
CSS
p.one {
   border: 5px solid orange;
   width: 300px;
   border-radius: 25em/1.5em;
}
p.two {
   border: 5px solid orange;
   width: 300px;
   border-radius: 20px 15em 30px 1em / 20px 15em 30px 35em;
}

HTML
<h3>Border two radii</h3>
<p class="one"> { border: 5px solid orange; width: 300px;
 border-radius:... }</p>
<p class="two"> { border: 5px solid orange; width: 300px;
 border-radius:... }</p>
```

FIGURE 10.49   Example usage of the border-radius property with two radii.

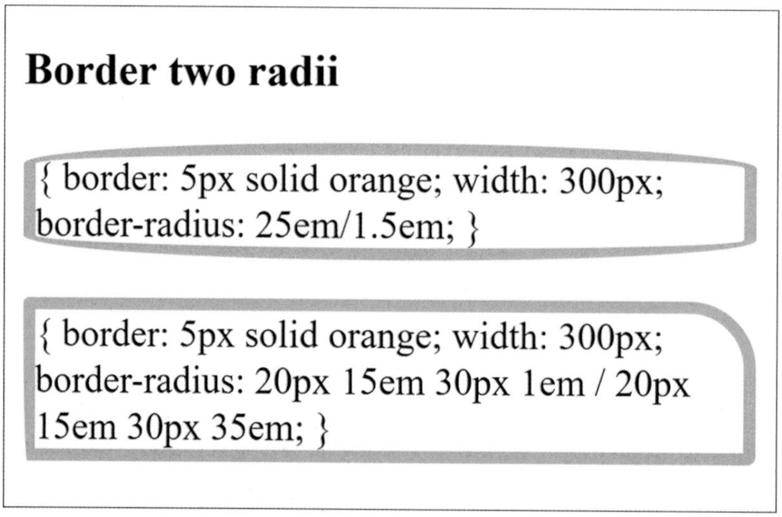

Border two radii

{ border: 5px solid orange; width: 300px; border-radius: 25em/1.5em; }

{ border: 5px solid orange; width: 300px; border-radius: 20px 15em 30px 1em / 20px 15em 30px 35em; }

FIGURE 10.50   The rendered result of Figure 10.49.

height for the box and any radius more than half their size (e.g., `{ width: 100px; height: 100px; border-radius: 50%; }`). Unfortunately, it is not always easy to produce the required shape with the `border-radius` property. To help out, there are free online **border-radius generators**, such as cssmatic.com, that allow you to design boxes with different combinations of radii and generate the corresponding code.

CHALLENGE 10.32

Using the `<div>` element, create an empty box with fixed width and height, and with the top-left and bottom-right corners having the same radius and the top-right and bottom-left corners having same radius that is different from the one used for top-left and bottom-right corners. Also, give the border one color and the background a different one.

10.4.2 `padding`

The `padding` property is a shorthand property for specifying the amount of space between the content of an element and the element's border. It is the space that surrounds the content. It is **non-inherited** and has the initial value of 0. It takes one to four space-separated values, which can be in **length values** (e.g., px and em) or **percentage values**. If percentage is used, then padding is a percentage of the width of the parent element. For example, if it is directly in a browser window, then it is a percentage of the window's width, and if it is in another box, then it is a percentage of the width of the box. How values are assigned is explained in Table 10.12.

The longhand properties for specifying different padding values for each edge of a box are `padding-top`, `padding-right`, `padding-bottom`, and `padding-left`, all of which are also **non-inherited**. Figures 10.51 and 10.52 show how the shorthand property is used and depict its effects.

Notice how the bottom box is bigger than the top one, even though they are set to the same width. This, as mentioned earlier, is because padding value is automatically added to the width and height of a box. Also, note that you can achieve the same padding as shown with the declaration `padding: 12px 12px 12px 12px;`.

TABLE 10.12

How the Values of the `padding` Property Are assigned

Number of Values	Application of Values
One	Value is assigned to all four edges.
Two	First value is assigned to top and bottom, and second value is assigned to right and left.
Three	First value is assigned to top, second to right and left, and third to bottom.
Four	First value is assigned to top, second to right, third to bottom, and fourth to left.

```
CSS
p.nopad { width: 260px; border: medium ridge green; }
p.haspad { width: 260px; border: medium solid green;
          padding: 12px; }
HTML
<h3>Padding</h3>
<p class="nopad">This paragraph element has no padding...</p>
<p class="haspad">This paragraph element has padding on all
 sides...</p>
```

FIGURE 10.51   Example usage of the padding property.

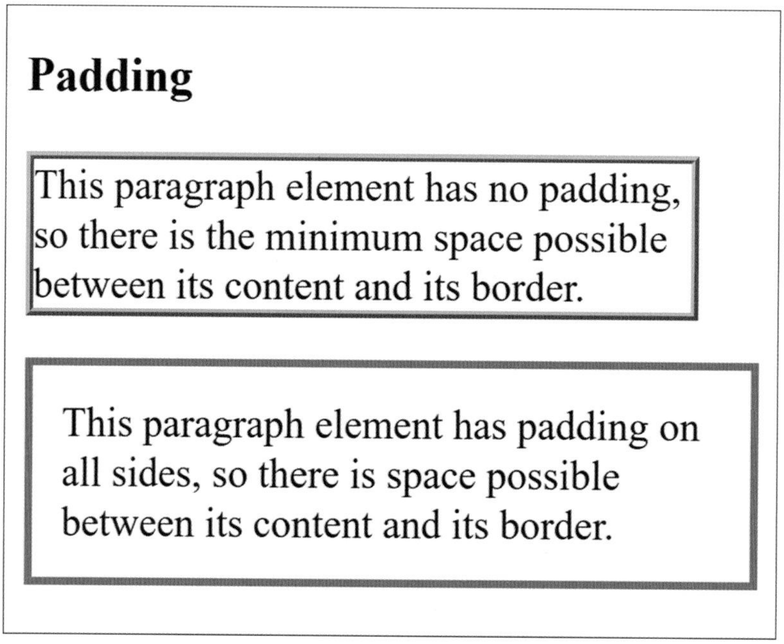

FIGURE 10.52   The rendered result of Figure 10.51.

CHALLENGE 10.33

Write a code that applies padding to the example in Figures 10.47 and 10.48. How do you think this contributes to the quality of the presentation of the content?

10.4.2.1 *Specifying Padding for Logical Edges*

The properties used to specify padding for the logical edges of an element are `padding-block-end`, `padding-block-end`, `padding-block-end`, and `padding-block-end`. Whether each targets the top, bottom, left, or right edge of an element depends on the value of the `writing-mode` property (discussed in Chapter 14).

```
CSS
p { width: 260px; border: medium} ridge green;
p.haspad {
    writing-mode: horizontal-tb;
    padding-block-start:12px;
    padding-block-end: 12px;
    padding-inline-start: 12px;
    padding-inline-end: 12px;
}
HTML
<h3>Padding</h3>
<p>This paragraph element has no padding...</p>
<p class="haspad">This paragraph element has padding on
all sides...</p>
```

FIGURE 10.53   Example usage of properties for specifying padding for logical edges.

The properties are **non-inherited** and take the same values as the `padding-top`, `padding-right`, `padding-bottom`, or `padding-left` property. Figure 10.53 shows the usage of the properties and produces the same result as shown earlier in Figure 10.38. Given the writing mode, `padding-block-start` specifies left edge, `padding-block-end` specifies right edge, `padding-inline-start` specifies top edge, and `padding-inline-end` specifies bottom edge.

CHALLENGE 10.34

Go to the "Specifying Content Directionality" section of Chapter 14, make note of other values for the `writing-mode` property, and try them in the example to see the effects.

10.4.3 `margin`

The `margin` property is a shorthand property for specifying the amount of space around the outer edge of an element's box and serves to separate one box from another. Like the `padding` property, it is **non-inherited** and has the initial value of 0. It also takes one to four space-separated values, which can be in **length values** (e.g., `px` and `em`), **percentage values**, or `auto` keyword. If percentage is used, the value is relative to the width of the containing element's box. The `auto` keyword leaves it to the browser to determine margin values as it sees fit. How values are assigned is explained in Table 10.13.

The longhand properties of the `margin` property are `margin-top`, `margin-right`, `margin-bottom`, and `margin-left`. Figures 10.54 and 10.55 show how the shorthand property is used and depict the effects.

TABLE 10.13

How the Values of the `padding` Property Are Assigned

Number of Values	Application of Values
One	Value is assigned to all four edges.
Two	First value is assigned to top and bottom, and second value is assigned to right and left.
Three	First value is assigned to top, second to right and left, and third to bottom.
Four	First value is assigned to top, second to right, third to bottom, and fourth to left.

```
CSS
p { border: 2px solid blue; width: 250px; padding: 5px; }
p.one { margin: auto; }
p.two { margin: 20px 0px 0 0px; }
p.three { margin: 20px 0px 0 -20px; }
p.four { margin: 20px 0px 0 20px; }

HTML
<h3>Margin</h3>
<p class="one">margin: auto;</p>
<p class="two">margin: 20px 0 0 0px;</p>
<p class="three">margin: 20px 0 0 -20px;</p>
<p class="four">margin: 20px 0 0 20px;</p>
```

FIGURE 10.54   Example usage of the `margin` property.

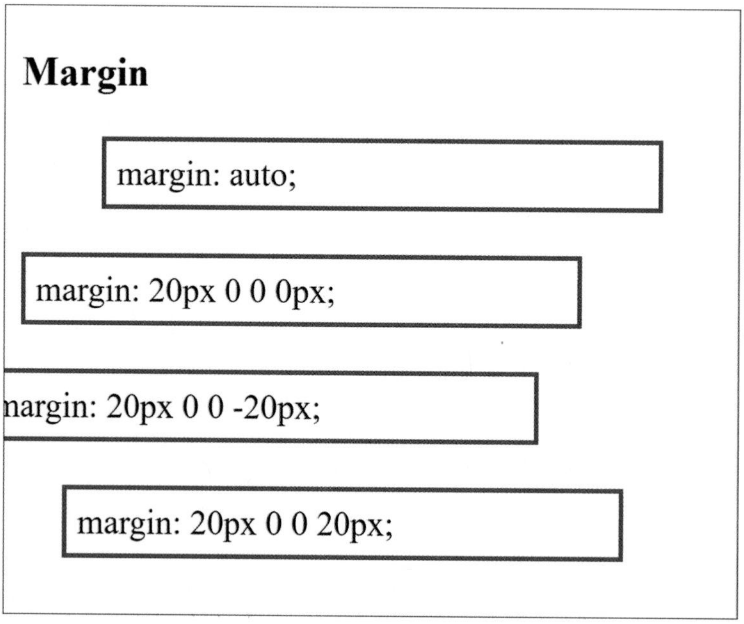

FIGURE 10.55   The rendered result of Figure 10.54.

In the example, the first rule applies to all <p> elements, while each of the remaining rules applies to individual <p> elements of matching class. Note that setting margin to `auto`, as done in the example, horizontally centers a box in the browser window or inside the element's box that it is in. As mentioned earlier, if width is not specified, a box occupies the full width of the page, making it impossible to center it. Notice in the example that the text is not centered in the box. To do this, you need to use the `text-align` property, discussed in Chapter 14.

NOTE: Vertical distance between boxes

The vertical distance between two adjacent boxes (blocks) is determined by the greater of the values of the `margin-bottom` and `margin-top` properties. For example, if `margin-bottom` is 20px and the `margin-top` is 10px, 20px is used.

CHALLENGE 10.35

Which is outside an element's box, padding or margin? Also, what is the longhand of `margin: 15px 5px`?

CHALLENGE 10.36

What is the difference between margin and padding? Which would you use to change the space between elements, and which would you use to change the space between an element's border and its content?

10.4.3.1 Specifying Margin for Logical Edges

The properties used to specify margin for the logical edges of an element are `margin-block-end`, `margin-block-end`, `margin-block-end`, and `margin-block-end`. Whether each defines the top, bottom, left, or right edge of an element depends on the value of the `writing-mode` property (discussed in Chapter 14). The properties are **non-inherited** and take the same values as the `margin-top`, `margin-right`, `margin-bottom`, or `margin-left` property. Figure 10.56 shows example of how the properties are used, and Figure 10.57 depicts the result. Given the writing mode, `margin-inline-start` defines the left edge.

```
CSS
p { border: 2px solid blue; width: 250px; padding: 5px; }
p.margin {
  writing-mode: horizontal-tb;
  margin-inline-start: 30px;
}

HTML
<h3>Margin via logical property</h3>
<p>No margin</p>
<p class="margin">margin-inline-start: 30px;</p>
```

FIGURE 10.56 Example usage of properties for specifying margin for logical edges.

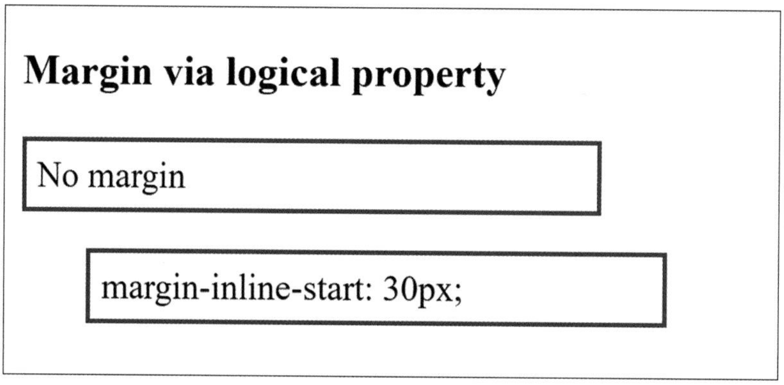

Margin via logical property

> No margin

> margin-inline-start: 30px;

FIGURE 10.57 The result of Figure 10.56.

CHALLENGE 10.37

Again, go to the "Specifying Content Directionality" section of Chapter 14, make note of other values for the `writing-mode` property, and try them in the example to see the effects.

10.4.3.2 Margins in Design

Margins essentially help provide contrast and visual interest, because they form a frame of negative space around the content of a page. This can add to the aesthetics of a layout and also makes text easy to read, since it reduces, for example, the width of text (i.e., number of characters per line). Figure 10.58 shows some illustrations. Notice the differences in the "airiness" of the pages. Most would say that the ones on the right are more aesthetically pleasing.

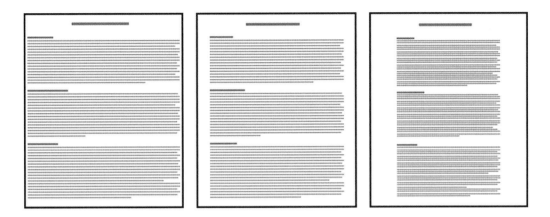

FIGURE 10.58 Effects of different amounts of margins.

10.5 Controlling Box Sizes

This involves specifying how the browser should adjust elements' box sizes in relation to each other when rendering them and whether or not boxes should be resizable, once rendered.

10.5.1 Specifying How Boxes Are Rendered

The default way in which the browser calculates the rendered size of an element is by adding the values specified for the `border`, `padding`, and `margin` properties to those specified for the `width` and `height` properties. The `box-sizing` property allows this relationship to be changed and is used to specify how the browser should calculate the rendered widths and heights of elements. Being able to do this can make creating layouts easier and more intuitive, in that it allows you to prevent a change in the size of an element's box when border, margin, or padding is added. It is **non-inherited,** and the two values it takes are described in Table 10.14.

TABLE 10.14

Values Supported by the `box-sizing` Property

Value	Function
content-box	Specifies to add padding and border to width and height to determine the actual width and height of an element. For example, if the specified width is 300px and padding is 20px, then an element's actual width is 320px (i.e., 300 + 20). It is the **default**.
border-box	Specifies that padding or border should not affect the actual width or height of an element's box (i.e., width and height should include padding and border). For example, if specified width is 300px and padding is 20px, then the actual width is 300px; the content is simply adjusted accordingly to accommodate the padding.

Figure 10.59 shows how the `box-sizing` property is used, and Figure 10.60 depicts the result. The example uses only the `border-box` value, but the result of using the `content-box` value (the default) is also shown on the left of Figure 10.60.

In the example, the `*{}` rule says to apply the specified `box-sizing` to all elements. As introduced in Chapter 8, `*` is a universal selector. The `body{}` rule makes the width of the page 50% that of the browser window, plus 20px padding. The `div{}` rule centers the text for all the `<div>` elements (`text-align` is discussed fully in Chapter 14). The `parent{}` rule makes the width of the `<div>` element of class "parent" 50% that of the page. The `child1{}` rule makes the width of the child1 `<div>` element 90% that of the parent `<div>` element, plus a padding of 20% of its width and a border of 2px on all four edges. This is why the child1 box extends beyond the width of the parent box with the default box-sizing setting. Lastly, `child2{}` makes the width of the child2 `<div>` element 50% that of the parent `<div>` element, plus 20px padding and 2px border.

```
CSS
* { box-sizing: border-box; }
body { width: 50%; padding: 20px; }
div { text-align: center; }
.parent { width: 50%; border: 2px solid black; }
.child1 { width: 90%; padding: 20%; border: 2px solid red; }
.child2 { width: 50%; padding: 20px; border: 2px solid gold; }

HTML
<body>
  <div class="parent">Parent
    <div class="child1">Child 1</div>
    <div class="child2">Child 2</div>
  </div>
</body>
```

FIGURE 10.59 Example usage of the `box-sizing` property.

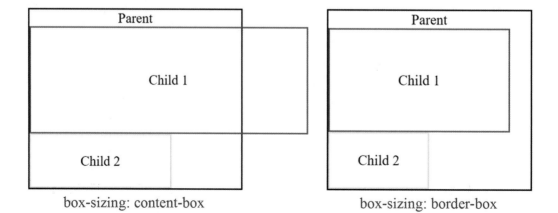

FIGURE 10.60 The result of default (left), and the result of Figure 10.59 (right).

CHALLENGE 10.38

Implement the example in Figures 10.59 and 10.60, populate the boxes, and then manipulate the size of the browser's window to see the effect.

CHALLENGE 10.39

In the example, if the width of the document is 960px (a standard width for layouts), what will be the rendered widths of the `<div>` elements with default box-sizing setting?

10.5.2 Making Boxes Resizable

By default, once an element is rendered, its size cannot be altered by the user. This behavior can be changed by using the `resize` property. It is **non-inherited,** and when specified, it displays a control mechanism at the bottom-right corner of an element's box; when the cursor is over it, the cursor changes shape to indicate the direction in which the user is allowed to resize the box. However, in order for the property to work, the `overflow` property, introduced earlier in this chapter, must be used and the value must be `hidden`, `scroll`, or `auto`. The standard values supported by the property as of time of writing are listed in Table 10.15. Figures 10.61 and 10.62 show how the property is used and depict the result.

In the example, notice that the shorthand `border` property is used to create the solid-line border around the element. This is not mandatory but helps to better visualize the border of the element and the resizing control mechanism at the bottom-right corner.

TABLE 10.15

Values Supported by the `resize` Property

Value	Function
none	Specifies to allow no resizing.
horizontal	Specifies to allow resizing in only horizontal direction and displays the mechanism for doing it.
vertical	Specifies to allow resizing in only vertical direction and displays the mechanism for doing it.
both	Specifies to allow resizing in both horizontal and vertical directions and displays the mechanism for doing it.

```
CSS
div {
  height: 350px;
  width: 350px;
  border: 1px solid black;
  overflow: auto;
  resize: both;
}

HTML
<h3>Box Resizing</h3>
<div>
  Lorem ipsum dolor sit amet, consectetur adipiscing elit.
  Quisque mollis dolor eu...
</div>
```

FIGURE 10.61   Example usage of the `resize` property.

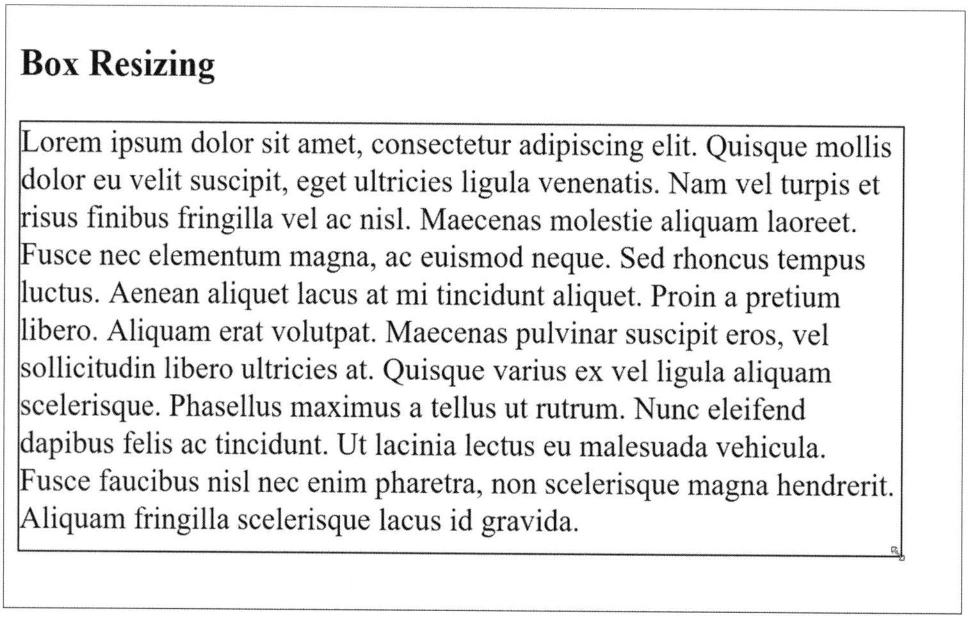

Box Resizing

Lorem ipsum dolor sit amet, consectetur adipiscing elit. Quisque mollis dolor eu velit suscipit, eget ultricies ligula venenatis. Nam vel turpis et risus finibus fringilla vel ac nisl. Maecenas molestie aliquam laoreet. Fusce nec elementum magna, ac euismod neque. Sed rhoncus tempus luctus. Aenean aliquet lacus at mi tincidunt aliquet. Proin a pretium libero. Aliquam erat volutpat. Maecenas pulvinar suscipit eros, vel sollicitudin libero ultricies at. Quisque varius ex vel ligula aliquam scelerisque. Phasellus maximus a tellus ut rutrum. Nunc eleifend dapibus felis ac tincidunt. Ut lacinia lectus eu malesuada vehicula. Fusce faucibus nisl nec enim pharetra, non scelerisque magna hendrerit. Aliquam fringilla scelerisque lacus id gravida.

FIGURE 10.62   The result of Figure 10.61.

CHALLENGE 10.40

Using the example in Figure 10.61 as guide, create a `<div>` element, populate it, then create a smaller size `<div>` element or `<p>` element inside it, and populate it too. Then, specify the `resize` property for both elements and see the effects when the boxes are resized. Also, can you think of any applications for such a design?

10.6 Adding Shadows to a Box

Shadows are added to a box by using the `box-shadow` property. It is **non-inherited** and allows one or more shadows to be applied to the edges of an element's box. If `border-radius` is also specified, the corners of the shadows are rounded. Table 10.16 lists the value types that are supported.

The values are specified in the following order:

<offset-x> <offset-y> <blur-radius> <spread-radius> <color>

The set of values can be specified multiple times, separated with commas. Each set specifies the settings for a shadow, and the first two values must be the x- and y-offset. The `inset` keyword may be added to the front of a rule to specify shadow type. Where there is more than one shadow, the shadow specified first is placed on top. Figure 10.63 shows how the `box-shadow` property is used, using different values, and Figure 10.64 shows the rendered results.

TABLE 10.16

Values Supported by the `box-shadow` Property

Values	Function
inset	This is a keyword. It is placed at the beginning of a rule to create **inner-shadows**. If absent, **drop shadows** (those that seem outside and behind a box) are created. The default is not to use it.
<x-offset>	This value moves a shadow **right** (when positive) or **left** (when negative), relative to the box. It is also known as **horizontal offset** and takes **length values** (e.g., px and em).
<y-offset>	This value moves a shadow **up** (when positive) or **down** (when positive). It is also known as **vertical offset** and takes **length values** (e.g., px and em).
<blur-radius>	Specifies the amount by which the edges of a shadow are blurred. It takes **length values** (e.g., px and em) and can only be positive. The default is 0.
<spread-radius>	Specifies the amount by which a shadow is expanded or contracted. It takes **length values** (e.g., px and em) and can be **positive** (to expand) or **negative** (to contract). The default is 0.
<color>	Specifies color of shadow and supports transparency.

```
CSS
p { border: 1px solid black; padding: 20px; width: 150px; }
p.one { box-shadow: 5px 5px 2px 0px #4d4d4d; }
p.one_up { box-shadow: -5px -5px 2px 0px #4d4d4d; }
p.one_blur { box-shadow: 10px 10px 10px 5px #4d4d4d; }
p.one_center{ box-shadow: inset 0px 0px 10px 5px #4d4d4d; }
p.one_center_no_blur { box-shadow: 0px 0px 0px 5px #4d4d4d; }
p.multi { box-shadow: inset 0 0 1em 0.5em orange,

            0 0 1em 0.5em blue; }

HTML
<p class="one">{ 5px 5px 2px 0px #4d4d4d; }</p>
<p class="one_inset">{ -5px -5px 2px 0px #4d4d4d; }</p>
<p class="one_blur">{ 10px 10px 10px 5px #4d4d4d; }</p>
<p class="one_center">{ inset 0px 0px 10px 5px
 #4d4d4d; }</p>
<p class="one_center_no_blur">{ 0px 0px 0px 5px
 #4d4d4d; }</p>
<p class="multi">{ inset 0 0 1em 0.5em orange, 0 0 1em
 0.5em blue; }</p>
```

FIGURE 10.63 Example usage of the box-shadow property.

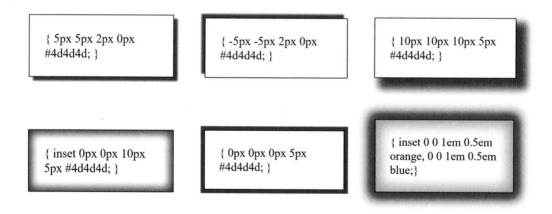

FIGURE 10.64 The result of Figure 10.63.

In the example, the p.one{} rule specifies the x-y offsets as 5px 5px, a blur-radius of 5px, spread radius of 0px, and a shadow color of #4d4d4d. Rules p.one_up{}, p.one_blur {}, and p.one_center_no_blur {} follow the same pattern. The p.one_center{} and p.multi{} rules have the inset keyword to specify an inner shadow. The p.multi{} rule also shows how multiple shadows are specified, as well as uses em unit instead of px. Notice that they are separated by a comma and that the inset keyword is only at the start of the rule, not at the start of every shadow setting.

CHALLENGE 10.41

Thinking of the various features of a Web page, list some possible useful applications of the `box-shadow` property in Web design.

10.7 Applying Outline to an Element

The property used to add outline is the `outline` property. It is a shorthand property that allows you to set the style, width, and color of the outline of an element and is **non-inherited**. The longhand properties are `outline-style`, `outline-width`, and `outline-color`. The property is similar to the `border` property, introduced earlier, in that its size can be affected by padding, but it is also different in a number of ways, for example:

- Unlike border, it does not take up space. Rather, it is placed, like a layer, on top of an element's box, which means that, ordinarily, if it has the same styling as a border, it is indistinguishable.
- Unlike border, the edges of outline cannot be styled individually.
- Unlike border, it may be non-rectangular.

The values supported by the `outline` property are listed in Table 10.17. The values can be specified in any order. Where one is missing, its initial value is used.

Figure 10.65 shows how the property is used, and Figure 10.66 depicts the result. The `border` property is also used for comparison. The outline is dashed, and the border is solid line. Notice the identical positioning of the two properties.

TABLE 10.17

The Values Allowed for the `outline` Property

Values	Function
`<outline-width>`	Can be keywords `thin`, `medium`, or `thick`, or **length values** (e.g., `px` and `em`).
`<outline-style>`	Can be `auto`, or any of the values given earlier for the `border` property (e.g., `none`, `dotted`, `dashed`, `solid`, `double`, `ridge`, `groove`, `inset`, and `outset`).
`<outline-color>`	Can be any color supported by CSS and the various keywords and notations used to specify them. The keyword `invert` may also be used, which inverts the color of the background to make the outline more visible.

```
CSS
p.one { outline: 1px dashed black; }
p.two { outline: 1px dashed black; border: 1px solid red; }

HTML
<h3>Outline</h3>
<p class="one">Lorem ipsum dolor sit amet, consectetur adipiscing
  elit. Viv...</p>
<p class="two">Lorem ipsum dolor sit amet, consectetur adipiscing
  elit. Viv...</p>
```

FIGURE 10.65   Example usage of the `outline` property.

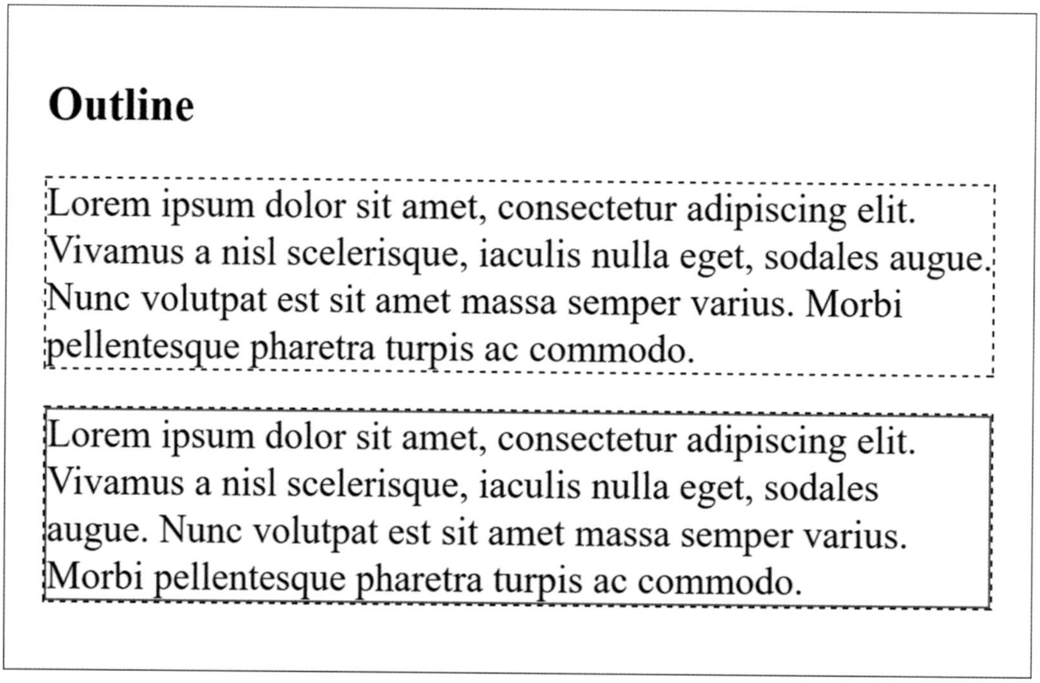

FIGURE 10.66   The result of Figure 10.65.

CHALLENGE 10.42

Implement the example, using your own content, and then experiment with the width to see how this affects the content.

CHALLENGE 10.43

A common application of the `outline` property is its use for creating the roll-over effect, in which an element changes appearance when the cursor is over it. In the example, replace the `p.one` selector with `p.one:hover` to see how outline behaves when the cursor is over the first `<p>` element. Then, do the same thing with the `p.two` selector. Explain why the second `<p>` element moves when the cursor is over it and the first one does not. The `:hover` pseudo-class selector was first briefly introduced in Chapter 8. More example applications are shown in Chapters 12–18.

10.7.1 `outline-offset`

The `outline-offset` property is **non-inherited.** It allows you to specify a transparent space between an outline and the border of an element. The only value that it takes is a **length value**, such as `px` and `em`. A negative value draws outline inside border and the element. Figures 10.67 and 10.68 show how it is used and the result.

```
CSS
p.one {
    outline: dashed thin;
    outline-offset: 5px;
    border:1px solid red;
}

HTML
<h3>Outline offset</h3>
<p class="one">Lorem ipsum dolor sit amet, consectetur
 adipiscing elit. Viv...</p>
```

FIGURE 10.67   Example usage of the `outline-offset` property.

Outline offset

Lorem ipsum dolor sit amet, consectetur adipiscing elit. Vivamus a nisl scelerisque, iaculis nulla eget, sodales augue. Nunc volutpat est sit amet massa semper varius. Morbi pellentesque pharetra turpis ac commodo.

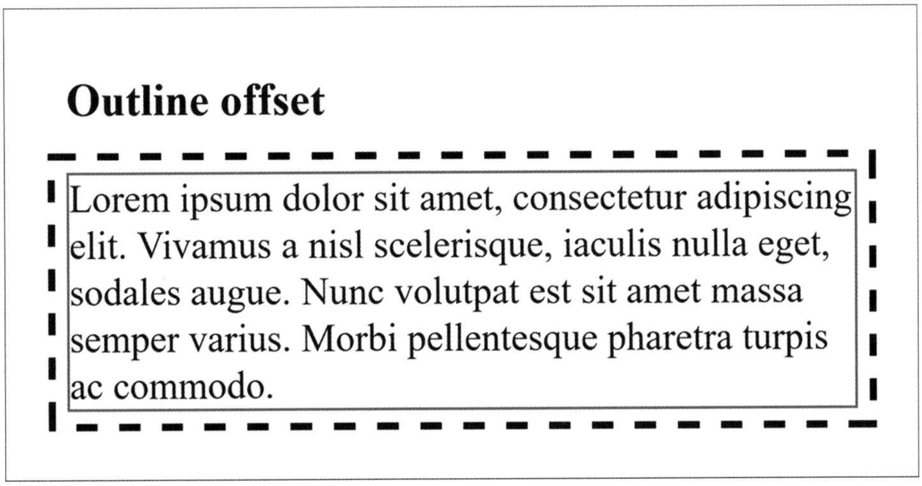

FIGURE 10.68   The result of Figure 10.67.

CHALLENGE 10.44

Given that outlines take no space and are placed over elements, what happens when an outline has a negative value and is thick?

10.8 Changing between Inline and Block Elements

Sometimes, it is necessary to make an inline element display like a block element, and vice versa. A good example is when list elements, which are block elements by default, are made to display as inline elements, so that they are displayed on the same line, as is sometimes done when designing global navigation. The CSS property used for doing this is the `display` property. It is **non-inherited** and takes one of several values. Table 10.18 lists some of the commonly used standard ones. Figures 10.69 and 10.70 show how the property is used and depict its effect.

In the example, both the `ul{}` and `ul li a{}` rules specify properties used to style text and are included here to only complement the example. The `ul{}` rule uses the `font-family` and `text-align` properties to specify to use Arial font and align the text to the center of each `<a>` element's box, and the `ul li a{}` uses the `text-decoration` property to specify not to underline the text. More about these text properties is discussed in Chapters 13 and 14. The `ul li{}` uses the `display:inline` declaration to force the `<li>` elements to be displayed as inline elements.

TABLE 10.18

Some of the Common Values Supported by the `display` Property

Value	Function
inline	Displays a block-level element as an inline-level element, so that it flows with text.
block	Displays an inline-level element as a block-level element.
inline-block	Makes a block-level element behave like an inline-level element (i.e., flow with text), while the content can be treated as in a block-level element.
none	Removes and hides an element from a page and collapses the space that the element occupies.

CSS
```
ul { font-family: Arial; text-align: center; }
ul li {
        display: inline;
        background-color: yellow;
        box-shadow: 2px 2px 2px #4d4d4d;
        padding: 8px;
}
ul li a { text-decoration: none; }
```

HTML
```
<ul>
    <li><a href="home.html">Home</a></li>
    <li><a href="about_us.html">About us</a></li>
    <li><a href="products.html">Products</a></li>
    <li><a href="downloads.html">Downloads</a></li>
    <li><a href="contact_us.html">Contact us</a></li>
</ul>
```

FIGURE 10.69 Example usage of the `display` property.

FIGURE 10.70 The result of Figure 10.69.

NOTE: Space between the menu buttons

Notice the space between the buttons (i.e., the `<li>` elements). This is generally considered a bug, because it is not supposed to be there; the elements should simply merge into each other if they have no margin, as it is the case here. Although the space is desirable in this case, sometimes, it is not, such as when you want a continuous menu bar. There are various workarounds to remove the space, but one of the most straightforward is to omit the end tags for the `<li>` elements.

NOTE: Drop-down menus

As mentioned in Chapter 3, drop-down menus are common features in Web design, and the `<menu>` and `<menuitem>` elements designed to implement them are not yet properly supported by major browsers as of time of writing. How the menus in Figure 10.70 can be transformed into drop-down menus by using combinations of other elements is explained in Chapter 12.

NOTE: Other uses of the `display` **property**

In addition to its use to make inline elements behave like block elements, and vice versa, the `display` property can be used to make an element behave like various other types of elements, such as ruby elements (see Chapter 14), table and list elements (see Chapter 17), and layout elements (see Chapters 19–21).

CHALLENGE 10.45

Implement the code presented in Figure 10.69 and experiment with the values of various properties to see their effects, especially the padding and the box-shadow; then, create your own design, putting more space between the buttons. (*Hint*: Consider character entity references discussed in Chapter 3).

CHALLENGE 10.46

In the example code, remove the end tags from the `<li>` elements to remove the gaps between the buttons.

CHALLENGE 10.47

Write a CSS code to render the HTML code below to produce the output that follows.

```
<h3>Inline-block</h3>
<div>This text is in a block element displayed as a block element, <p>while this
text is in a block element displayed as an inline element</p>, and this also is text
in a block element displayed as a block element.</div>
```

Inline-block

This text is in a block element displayed as a block element, while this text is in a block element displayed as an inline element, and this also is text in a block element displayed as a block element.

10.9 Hiding Content

Content hiding refers to the hiding of elements from view. Although it is a viable technique in Web design and development, it can also be used to try to manipulate search engines to get higher rankings, and for this reason, it is frowned up and considered deceptive by search engine companies and can result in your site being blacklisted and not included in search results. An example of usages that are considered deceptive is "**keyword stuffing**," which specifying many keywords as the value of the `alt` attribute and hiding them.

One of the most important uses of content hiding is to improve accessibility of users to screen readers. In essence, textual cues or indicators are added and then hidden for content that is apparent to sighted users but not to screen reader users. For example, hidden text could be used to inform the screen reader about breadcrumbs (i.e., "You are here" indicators) or a form control, such as a search box, that has no visual label, because its function is apparent to sighted users.

As mentioned Chapter 4, hiding content also has application in the technique of **skipping unimportant content at the start of a page** and jumping to the main content, which is especially beneficial to screen reader and keyboard-only users. It is usually necessary when style sheet is disabled (i.e., when CSS styles are not applied) and navigation menu turns into a long vertical list of items. In such a case, to spare users from having to go through the long list before getting to the main content, a hidden link is provided at the very top of the page that is accessible to the screen reader and appears when tab action by sighted keyboard users gives it focus. Normal users also benefit from the technique, because the link becomes visible when CSS is disabled, since all hidden content implemented with CSS becomes visible when CSS is disabled. An example of how to implement the technique is shown in Chapter 12 under "Absolute position."

There are various ways of hiding an element. Common ones are via using the `display` or `visibility` properties. The `opacity` property of an element (discussed in Chapter 9) can also be set to 0, or it can be hidden behind another, using the `z-index` property, which is discussed in Chapter 12, or the element can be pushed off screen to the left, using, for example, a large **negative margin value** (you saw this in the third `<p>` element in the example in Figure 10.55) or **element positioning**. Here, only how to use the `display` and `visibility` properties is shown. How elements are positioned is discussed in Chapter 12.

10.9.1 Hiding Content by Using the `display` Property

The code in Figure 10.69 showed an example of how the `display` property can be used. The addition of "omit" class to the fourth `<li>` element and the addition of the `il.omit{ display:none; }` rule to the code, as shown in Figure 10.71, remove the element from the normal flow of content and also collapse the space that it has been occupying. Figure 10.72 shows the result.

CSS
```
ul{ font-family: Arial; text-align: center; }
ul li {
  display: inline;
  background-color: yellow;
  box-shadow: 2px 2px 2px #4d4d4d;
  padding: 8px;
}
ul li a { text-decoration: none; }
li.omit { display: none; }
```

HTML
```
<ul class="nav">
  <li><a href="home.html">Home</a></li>
  <li><a href="about_us.html">About us</a></li>
  <li><a href="products.html">Products</a></li>
  <li class="omit"><a href="downloads.html">Downloads</a></li>
  <li><a href="contact_us.html">Contact us</a></li>
</ul>
```

FIGURE 10.71   Using the none value with the `display` property to hide an element.

FIGURE 10.72   The rendered result of Figure 10.71.

CHALLENGE 10.48

Describe a situation in which removing a button or link dynamically might be applicable.

10.9.2 Hiding Content by Using the `visibility` Property

In contrast to the `display` property, the `visibility` property hides an element's box without collapsing the space that it occupies, thereby leaving a blank space. The values that it takes are `hidden` (which hides an element) and `visible` (which shows the element). To show how it is used, the `display: none` declaration in Figure 10.71 is replaced with `visibility: hidden`. The effect is shown in Figure 10.73. The property can also be used to hide table rows or columns. When used with tables, it also takes `collapse` as value, which hides a row or column and removes the space that a hidden row or column leaves.

FIGURE 10.73   The effect of the `visibility` property.

NOTE: Accessibility and `display` and `visibility` properties

It is worth noting that the content that is hidden by using the `display` or `visibility` property is also invisible to screen readers and is therefore not useful for accessibility purposes.

CHALLENGE 10.49

Write a CSS code to make the content of the second `<p>` element in the code below invisible:

```
<body>
     <p>This paragraph is visible.</p>
     <p>This paragraph should not be visible.</p>
</body>
```

CHALLENGE 10.50

What creative and accessible uses can you find for the `visibility` property, bearing in mind that it hides content from all users, including screen reader users?

10.10   Useful Info

10.10.1   Web Links

CSS specifications: w3.org/standards

Web development documents: docs.webplatform.org

Accessibility: w3.org/WAI/tutorials, webaim.org

CSS tutorials (*Here are just a few free tutorial sites on CSS and other Web languages*): w3.org/wiki, html5rocks.com, sitepoint.com, w3schools.com, codecademy.com, quackit.com, developer.mozilla.org/en-US/docs/Web tutorialspoint.com, htmldog.com, htmlcodetutorial.com, echoecho.com, learn.shayhowe.com, html.net, tizag.com, cssbasics.com, cordova.apache. org, developers.google.com, csszengarden.com, webdesignermag.co.uk, css. maxdesign.com.au

Border radius generator: cssmatic.com, css3maker.com, css3gen.com

Browser compatibility info: caniuse.com

11

Boxes: Transform and 3D

11.1 Introduction

Being able to orientate an element's box or change its shape is useful for many creative and interesting concepts in Web design, both static and dynamic. The provision of various transform properties in CSS allows this to be done relatively easily and the use of element transformation is becoming increasingly common, especially its animation, which is discussed in Chapter 18. This chapter presents these properties, how to use them, and their effects.

11.2 Learning Outcomes

After studying this chapter, you should:

- Know how to use transform properties to create both two-dimensional (2D) and three-dimensional (3D) design elements.

11.3 Transforming Elements

Transforming elements in CSS refers to the modification of their coordinates, in order to **translate** (move), **rotate**, **scale** (size), or **skew** (distort) them. Transformation can be in a 2D or 3D space. The 2D space is described in terms of two dimensions: **horizontal** (the *x*-axis) and **vertical** (the *y*-axis); while the 3D space in three dimensions: **horizontal** (the *x*-axis), **vertical** (the *y*-axis), and **depth** (the *z*-axis). The *z*-axis can be seen as an imaginary line that comes out of the screen that is perpendicular (at 90°) to it. The two main properties used to achieve transformation are `transform-origin` and `transform`. The properties used to enhance the perception of 3D include `transform-style` and `backface-visibility`.

11.3.1 `transform-origin`

The `transform-origin` property is a **non-inherited** property that allows you to specify the origin for the transformation of an element and used with the `transform` property. The position of the origin has an effect on the result of a transform operation. By default, the origin of an element is at its center. Table 11.1 lists the values the property supports.

TABLE 11.1

Values for the `transform-origin` Property

Value	Function
`<x-offset>`	Specifies how far from the left edge of the box to set the transform-origin and takes **length values** (e.g., px and em) or **percentage values**. For example, transform-origin: 3px;.
`<x-offset-keyword>`	Specifies left, right, or center keyword to describe how far from the left edge of box to set origin (e.g., transform-origin: left;).
`<y-offset>`	Specifies how far the top edge of the box to set the transform-origin and takes **length values** (e.g., px and em) or **percentage values**. For example, transform-origin: 3px;.
`<y-offset-keyword>`	Specifies top, bottom, or center keyword to describe how far from the left edge of box to set transform-origin (e.g., transform-origin: bottom;).
`<z-offset>`	Specifies how far from the user to set the z = 0 origin and takes only **length values** (e.g., px and em). For example, transform-origin: 3px;.
`<offset-keyword>`	A shorthand for specifying multiple values (e.g., transform-origin: left bottom 3px;)

11.3.2 `transform`

The `transform` property allows you to specify how the coordinates of an element should be modified. It is **non-inherited** and the values it supports are the none keyword and **transform-functions**, which allow various types of transformations to be specified. Table 11.2 lists the functions supported. Multiple functions can be specified in a list of space-separated values.

TABLE 11.2

Values for the `transform` Property

Value	Function
`translate()`	Specifies by how much to move an element from its current position along the x- and y-axis. For example, translate(5, 10) moves an element 5px right and 10px down. If the y-axis value is missing, it is assumed to be the same as for the x-axis.
`translateX()`	Specifies by how much to move an element horizontally (e.g., translateX(5) moves an element 5px right).
`translateY()`	Specifies by how much to move an element vertically (e.g., translateY(5) moves an element 5px down).

(Continued)

TABLE 11.2 (*Continued*)

Values for the `transform` Property

Value	Function
`translateZ()`	Moves an element toward or away from the viewer (e.g., `translateZ(-5)` moves an element away from the viewer, making it smaller).
`translate3d()`	Specifies by how much to move an element in a 3D space. This involves specifying movement along the *z*-axis, which is along the depth (e.g., `translate3d(5, 10, 5)` moves an element 5px right, 10px down, and 5px toward the viewer).
`scale()`	Specifies the amount by which to increase or decrease the size of an element along the *x*- and *y*-axis. (e.g., `scale(3,5)` increases an element 3px right and 5px down).
`scaleX()`	Specifies the amount by which to increase or decrease the size of an element along the *x*-axis (e.g., `scaleX(3)` increases the size of an element 3px right).
`scaleY()`	Specifies the amount by which to increase or decrease the size of an element along the *y*-axis (e.g., `scaleY(-3)` decreases the size of an element 3px up).
`scaleZ()`	Specifies the amount by which to increase or decrease the size of an element along the *z*-axis (e.g., `scaleZ(9)` increases the size of an element 9px along the *z*-axis).
`scale3d()`	Specifies the amount by which to increase or decrease the size of an element along the *x*-, *y*-, and *z*-axis (e.g., `scale3d(5, 5, 5)` increases the size of an element by 5px along the *x*-, *y*-, and *z*-axis, respectively).
`rotate()`	Specifies by how much angle to rotate an element clockwise or anti-clockwise around a fixed point, which can be specified by the `transform-origin` property. The angle is in **degrees** (deg), for example, `rotate(45deg)` rotates an element 45° clockwise.
`rotateX()`	Specifies by how much to rotate an element around the *x*-axis (e.g., `rotateX(-45%)` rotates an element 45° anti-clockwise around the *x*-axis).
`rotateY()`	Specifies by how much to rotate an element around the *y*-axis (e.g., `rotateY(45%)` rotates an element 45° clockwise around the *y*-axis.)
`rotateZ()`	Specifies by how much to rotate an element around the *z*-axis (e.g., `rotateZ(45%)` rotates an element 45° clockwise around the *z*-axis).

(Continued)

TABLE 11.2 (*Continued*)

Values for the `transform` Property

Value	Function
rotate3d()	Specifies by how much angle to rotate an element around a fixed axis. The values for the x-, y-, and z-axis determine a point in a 3D space, and a line from 0,0,0 origin (i.e., where the axes meet) through the point is the fixed axis (i.e., axis of rotation). For example, rotate3d(5,5,5,45deg) rotates an element 45° clockwise around an axis through 0 origin and a point that is at 5px along the x-, y-, and z-axis, respectively.
skew()	Specifies by how much angle to distort an element along the x- and y-axis (e.g., skew(45deg, 45deg) distorts an element by 45° along the x- and y-axis, respectively).
skewX()	Specifies by how much angle to distort an element along the x-axis (e.g., skewX(45deg) distorts an element by 45° along the x-axis).
skewY()	Specifies by how much angle to distort an element along the y-axis (e.g., skewY(45deg) distorts an element by 45° along the y-axis).
perspective()	Specifies the distance between the $z = 0$ plane (basically the screen) and the user, so as to give perspective to an element positioned in a 3D space and create the illusion of depth. The smaller the distance, the greater the perspective produced.
matrix()	Combines all the 2D transform functions into one and requires the knowledge of mathematics to use effectively.
matrix3d()	Like matrix(), combines all the 3D transform functions into one and requires the knowledge of mathematics to use effectively.

11.3.2.1 Applying Rotation and Skewing

Figure 11.1 shows how the `rotate()` and `skew()` functions are used and Figure 11.2 the result. The `div{}` rule styles all the boxes in the same way (using properties already discussed in the chapter) and uses the `display:inline-block` declaration to place them on the same line. The `text-align:center` declaration centers the text in the boxes and, again, is discussed more fully in Chapter 14. The `#box2{}` rule rotates the second `<div>` element clockwise around the z-axis by 45°. The `#box3{}` rule skews the third `<div>` element along the x-axis by 30° by moving its points by amounts equivalent to the angle.

```
CSS
div {
  height: 75px;
  width: 150px;
  padding: 10px;
  display: inline-block;
  border: 1px solid black;
  background-color: pink;
  text-align: center;
}
#box2{ transform: rotateZ(45deg);}
#box3{ transform: skewX(30deg); }

HTML
<h3>Transform</h3>
<div id="box1">Normal shape</div>
<div id="box2">Clockwise Rotation</div>
<div id="box3">Skewing along x-axis</div>
```

FIGURE 11.1   Rotating and skewing an element.

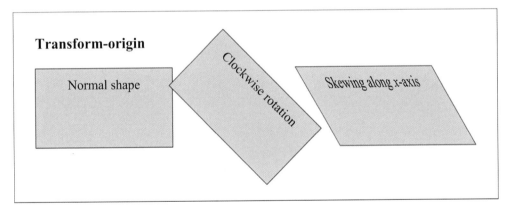

FIGURE 11.2   The result of Figure 11.1.

CHALLENGE 11.1

Implement the code in Figure 11.1 and experiment with the parameters of the functions, including negative values, to know how they work and better use them.

CHALLENGE 11.2

In the example, where do you understand the transform-origin and the axis of rotation of the rotated box to be?

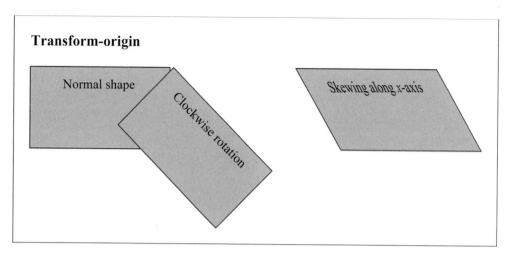

FIGURE 11.3   The effect of changing default `transform-origin`.

Figure 11.3 shows the effect of setting the `transform-origin` property to 0px 0px (i.e., top left corner of an element). This is done by adding `transform-origin: 0px 0px;` to the #box2{} rule in Figure 11.1.

CHALLENGE 11.3

Implement the example by adding `transform-origin: 0px 0px;` to #box2{} rule in Figure 11.1. In reference to what is the 0px 0px, is it #box2 or the browser window? Also, what would be the effect if the same declaration is added to the #box3{} rule? Lastly, experiment with different values.

11.3.2.2 Applying Perspective

Figure 11.4 shows how the `perspective()` function is used to create perspective and Figure 11.5 the effect. In the example, the #box1{} rule styles the outer <div> element. The #box2{} rule specifies the `width` and `height` of the inner <div> element as 50% of that of the outer one and the `padding` extends the size. The `perspective()` gives the element depth and `rotateY()` rotates it around the y-axis by 50° to make the perspective show.

CHALLENGE 11.4

Write a code to create something similar to Figure 11.5 but with rotation around the x-axis.

```
CSS
#box1 {
  height: 200px;
  width: 200px;
  padding: 10px;
  border: 1px solid black;
}
#box2 {
  width: 50%; height: 50%;
  padding: 50px;
  background-color: orange;
  border: 1px solid black;
  transform: perspective(400px) rotateY(50deg);
}

HTML
<div id="box1">
  <div id="box2">PERSPECTIVE</div>
</div>
```

FIGURE 11.4 Example usage of the `perspective()` function.

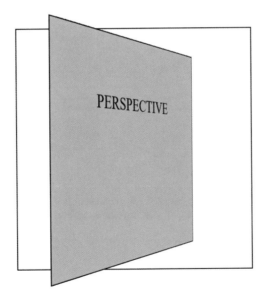

FIGURE 11.5 The result of Figure 11.4.

11.3.3 `perspective`

The `perspective` property is a **non-inherited** property and used to specify the distance between the user and the $z = 0$ **plane** (i.e., vertical plane through the origin) so as to give perspective to a 3D-positioned element and create the sense of depth. The smaller the distance, the greater the perspective produced. Note that the property performs a different function from the `transform` property's `perspective()`

function described in Table 11.2 and does not give perspective to individual elements, but to the children of an element as a single unit. This means that it is **applied to a parent element not the child elements**. The **vanishing point**, which is the point at which parallel lines meet, is by default at the center of the parent element, but can be changed using the `perspective-origin` property. Figures 11.6 and 11.7 show an example of usage and Figure 11.8 the result.

The example uses both the `perspective` property and the `perspective()` function for comparison. The `.parent{}` rule styles the two parent `<div>` elements. The `.parent.perspective{}` rule gives perspective to the element whose `class`

```
HTML
<body>
   <div class="parent perspective">
      <h2>perspective property</h2>
      <div class="child"></div>
      <div class="child"></div>
      <div class="child"></div>
   </div>
<div class="parent transform">
      <h2>perspective() function</h2>
      <div class="child"></div>
      <div class="child"></div>
      <div class="child"></div>
   </div>
</body>
```

FIGURE 11.6   HTML for comparing `perspective` property and `perspective()` function.

```
CSS
.parent { width: 50%; padding: .5em; }
.parent.perspective { perspective-origin: 100px; perspective: 50px;
}
.parent.perspective .child {
  transform: rotateX(30deg);
  background-color: orange;
}
.child {
  margin: .5em;
  width: 3em;
  height: 3em;
  display: inline-block;
  border: 1px solid black;
}
.parent.transform .child {
  transform: perspective(50px) rotateX(30deg);
  background-color: grey;
}
```

FIGURE 11.7   CSS used with Figure 11.6.

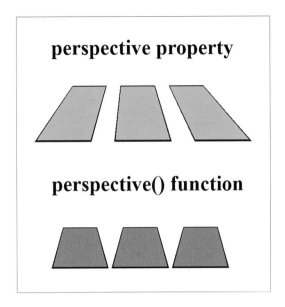

FIGURE 11.8 The result of Figures 11.6 and 11.7.

attribute is equal to a list of space-separate values that includes "parent" and "perspective." Notice that there is no white space between `.parent` and `.perspective` selectors, since they are part of a list of space-separate class values. The `.parent.perspective .child{}` rule rotates all elements of "child" class around the x-axis by 30°. Notice that there is a space between `.parent.perspective` and `.child`. This is because "child" is not part of a list of space-separated class values. The `.child{}` rule styles each element of "child" class and changes them to inline-block elements to display them on the same line. The `.parent.transform .child{}` rule specifies perspective and rotation values for each element that is of "parent transform" class and also of "child" class.

CHALLENGE 11.5

Implement the example in Figures 11.6 and 11.7 and experiment with the values for the `perspective` and `perspective-origin` properties and rotation. Also, see if you can make the code more efficient by reducing the number of values for the classes.

11.3.3.1 *Example Application of the* `perspective` *Property*

Figures 11.9 through 11.11 show a basic but practical application of the `perspective` property, in which images are displayed, usually for the user to click and be linked to another page.

In the example, the `* { }` rule says not to let any specified value of `padding` or `border` affect the size of any element. This ensures that the sizes of the elements are adjusted to fit inside the specified size for their container element and not wrapped to the next line.

The `.wrapper{}` rule specifies the `width`, `margin`, and `perspective` of the `<div>` element of "wrapper" class, and the `.inner{}` rule rotates the `<div>` element of "inner" class around the *y*-axis by 40°, thereby rotating the `<figure>` elements and their contents. The `.inner figure{}` rule specifies the width of each `<figure>` element, the padding between them and the edges of the `<figure>` elements, the margin between the images, the gold background, and displays the images as if they are both inline and block elements. The `.inner img{}` rule specifies that the width of each image must not exceed the one specified for the parent element (i.e., the `<figure>` element). The `.inner figcaption{}` rule styles the image captions. The `src` attributes specify the names and locations of the images.

```html
HTML
<div class="wrapper">
  <div class="inner">
    <figure><img src="images/fractal_pink_spiral.jpg"
    alt="Abstract">
      <figcaption>Abstract</figcaption>
    </figure>
    <figure><img src="images/pine_forest.jpg" alt="Nature">
      <figcaption>Nature</figcaption>
    </figure>
    <figure><img src="images/surfer.jpg" alt="Sports">
      <figcaption>Sports</figcaption>
    </figure>
  </div>
</div>
```

FIGURE 11.9 HTML code for 3D display of images.

```css
CSS
* { box-sizing: border-box; }
.wrapper {
  perspective: 1200px; margin: 64px auto; width: 800px;
}
.inner { transform: rotateY(40deg); }
.inner figure {
  width: 176px;
  padding: 16px;
  margin-right: 16px;
  background-color: rgb(250, 200, 0);
  display: inline-block;
}
.inner img { max-width: 100%; }
.inner figcaption {
  text-align: center;
  margin: 8px 0;
  font-family: Arial, sans-serif;
  font-weight: bold;
  color: #000000;
}
```

FIGURE 11.10 CSS code for Figure 11.9.

FIGURE 11.11   The result of Figures 11.9 and 11.10. (Image from www.freeimages.co.uk.)

CHALLENGE 11.6

Implement Figures 11.9 and 11.10 using your own images and experiment with various properties, including `padding`, `margin`, and `max-width`, to see the effect.

CHALLENGE 11.7

Implement Figures 11.9 and 11.10 again, but instead of specifying images that are stored locally on your computer for the `src` attribute, link to images online. For example, you could link to free placeholder images at www.lorempixel.com that randomly selects images from the categories specified in the URL. More instructions on how to use them can be found at the site.

CHALLENGE 11.8

The border shown around the rendered output in Figure 11.11 is not the one created with CSS. Add an actual `border` to the example and style it with inset shadows. Also, try adding the border property to the rules to see the sizes and boundaries of the elements.

11.3.4 `transform-style`

The `transform-style` property allows you to specify whether the children of an element should be displayed in 3D or in the same plane as the element (i.e., flat). It is **non-inherited** and supports two values: `preserve-3d` (which displays

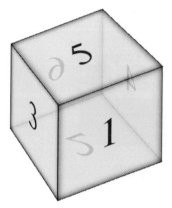

transform-style: preserve-3d;   transform-style: flat;

FIGURE 11.12   The effects of the values of `transform-style` property.

children in the 3D space) and `flat`, the default (which displays children in the same plane as the parent). Figure 11.12 shows their effects. A more detailed demonstration of how the property is used is shown later in Figures 11.15 and 11.16, along with related properties.

CHALLENGE 11.9

For which of the following situations would you need to use the `transform-style` property: a `<div>` element containing other `<div>` elements, or individual `<div>` elements?

11.3.5 `backface-visibility`

The `backface-visibility` property is **non-inherited** and used to specify whether or not the backface of an element should be visible, making it look as if it is being reflected in a mirror. The values supported are `visible` (which makes the backface of an element visible) and `hidden` (which makes the backface of an element invisible). Figure 11.13 shows an illustration of the effects of these values and Figure 11.14 their effect with a 3D shape.

CHALLENGE 11.10

Write a code to produce something similar to the middle example in Figure 11.13.

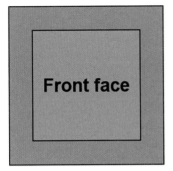

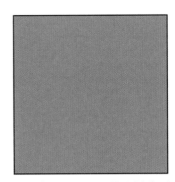

No rotation | transform: rotateY(180deg); backface-visibility: visible; | transform: rotateY(180deg); backface-visibility: hidden;

FIGURE 11.13 The effects of the `backface-visibility` property.

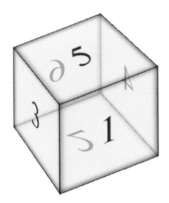
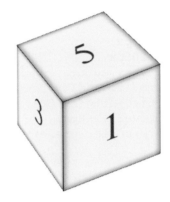

backface-visibility: visible;   backface-visibility: hidden;

FIGURE 11.14 The effects of the `backface-visibility` values on a 3D object.

11.3.5.1 *Full Explanation of the Cube Example*

Figures 11.15 and 11.16 show the codes for the cube, and Figure 11.17 shows the cube again. The `.cube{}` rule builds the container for the faces of the cube. It specifies the size (`width` and `height`), centers it (with `margin`), rotates it to show its 3D features properly (using **transform rotate functions**), gives it perspective (with `perspective-origin` and `perspective`), and makes it display as 3D (with `transform-style`). The `.face{}` rule styles the `<div>` elements that represent the faces. It gives them absolute positions to ensure that all have the same top-left position, specifies the size of the faces, the font size, leading, alignment, and color of the text, and also styles the border of the faces and specifies the backface visibility. The `.one{}`, `.two{}`, `.three{}`, `.four{}`, `.five{}`, and `.six{}` rules rotate and move the faces to the respective positions. Notice that the widths and heights of the faces are twice the amount by which they are translated.

```
HTML
<div class="cube">
   <div class="face one">1</div>
   <div class="face six">6</div>
   <div class="face four">4</div>
   <div class="face three">3</div>
   <div class="face five">5</div>
   <div class="face two">2</div>
</div>
```

FIGURE 11.15   HTML for the cube.

```
CSS
.cube {
 width: 200px;
 height: 200px;
 margin: 75px auto;
 transform: rotateX(-40deg) rotateY(30deg);
 perspective-origin: 50% 50%;
 perspective: 1200px;
 transform-style: preserve-3d;
}
.face {
 position: absolute;
 width: 144px;
 height: 144px;
 line-height: 140px;
 font-size: 60px;
 text-align: center;
 color: black;
 background-color: rgba(235, 230, 0, 0.8);
 border: 1px solid black;
 box-shadow: inset 0 0 10px black; opacity: 0.8;
 backface-visibility: visible
}
.one { transform: translateZ(72px); }
.six { transform: rotateY(180deg) translateZ(72px); }
.four { transform: rotateY(90deg) translateZ(72px); }
.three { transform: rotateY(-90deg) translateZ(72px); }
.five { transform: rotateX(90deg) translateZ(72px); }
.two { transform: rotateX(-90deg) translateZ(72px); }
```

FIGURE 11.16   CSS used with the HTML in Figure 11.15.

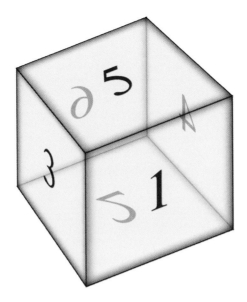

FIGURE 11.17   The result of Figures 11.15 and 11.16.

CHALLENGE 11.11

In the HTML code in Figure 11.15, what would happen if the `<div>` elements that represent the cube's faces are ordered numerically in ascending or descending order?

11.4 Useful Info

11.4.1 Web Links

CSS specifications: w3.org/standards

Web development documents: docs.webplatform.org

Accessibility: w3.org/WAI/tutorials, webaim.org

CSS tutorials (*Here are just a few free tutorial sites on CSS and other Web languages*): w3.org/wiki, html5rocks.com, sitepoint.com, w3schools.com, codecademy.com, quackit.com, developer.mozilla.org/en-US/docs/Web tutorialspoint.com, htmldog.com, htmlcodetutorial.com, echoecho.com, learn.shayhowe.com, html.net, tizag.com, cssbasics.com, cordova.apache.org, developers.google.com, csszengarden.com, webdesignermag.co.uk, css.maxdesign.com.au

3D transform examples: desandro.github.io/ 3dtransforms

CSS transform generator: css3maker.com

Browser compatibility info: caniuse.com

12

Positioning Elements

12.1 Introduction

The positioning of elements at the desired points on a page is crucial in achieving the intended design. Since HTML elements are typically displayed by default to the left of the page and design layouts require more than this, the need for positioning them in Web design is a foregone conclusion. This chapter presents the CSS properties used for positioning elements.

12.2 Learning Outcomes

After studying this chapter, you should:

- Be aware of the various methods of positioning elements to achieve various design goals, including layouts and drop-down menu.
- Know how to create multi-column layouts.

12.3 CSS Positioning Methods

CSS allows you to position an element anywhere on a page as well as specify its relationship with the normal flow of elements on the page. It provides a variety of methods for achieving these goals. They include **static, relative, absolute, fixed,** and **sticky** positioning, and **element floating**. The property used to position elements is the `position` property. It is **non-inherited** and the values it supports are `static`, `relative`, `absolute`, `fixed`, or `sticky`. The **box offset properties** (i.e., `top`, `right`, `bottom`, and `left`), which are also **non-inherited**, are used with it to specify where to position the elements, and how the browser interprets them depends on the value specified for the `position` property. The values they support are **length values** (e.g., `px` and `em`), **percentage values** (`%`), and `auto`.

The box offset properties can also be specified using **CSS logical properties,** which are used to define logical border edges based on text-flow direction within a line (e.g., left to right) and the direction lines of text flow (e.g., top to bottom).

The property used to define this direction is `writing-mode` and introduced more fully in Chapter 14. As of time of writing, these logical properties are still in the draft stage and supported only by Firefox. Being able to specify where to position elements on a page is useful in many ways. For example, it is useful in implementing page layout and also drop-down menus. Where elements overlap, CSS also allows you to specify which should be on top of the other, using the `z-index` property. To make elements not follow the normal flow of content, it provides the `float` property. These two properties are discussed more fully after element positioning.

12.3.1 Static Positioning

This is the default method used by browsers for positioning HTML elements and represents the normal flow of elements on a page, where the elements are displayed in the order as they appear in an HTML document. **Starting at the top-left corner of the containing block**, block-level elements are positioned one on top of the next, and inline elements are positioned one after another horizontally, wrapping to the next line when space runs out on the current line. The value used with the `position` property to achieve the method is `static` and the syntax is `position: static`. However, since it is the default positioning method, it is normally not necessary to specify it, except when changing to it from another positioning type. Note also that static positioning is not affected by the box offset properties, since specifying static is essentially specifying default positioning. Figures 12.1 and 12.2 show how specifying static positioning does not affect the normal flow of the elements on a page.

```
CSS
p { width: 600px; }
p.noMove { position: static; }

HTML
<h2>Static positioning</h2>
<p>In quis nibh eget nisl pharetra varius. Mauris eget
   velit turpis. Vivamus erat mauris,...</p>
<p class="noMove">Nulla eget varius tortor, a egestas risus.
   Nunc interdum commodo...</p>
<p>Fusce dictum nisl ipsum, at dictum elit efficitur ut.
   Suspendisse cursus lorem et...</p>
```

FIGURE 12.1   Example of static positioning.

Static positioning

In quis nibh eget nisl pharetra varius. Mauris eget velit turpis. Vivamus erat mauris, pretium pharetra risus eget, ornare rutrum tortor. In sollicitudin congue porttitor. Nunc ante sem, vehicula sit amet feugiat nec, pharetra vitae velit. Suspendisse nec ipsum congue, fermentum dolor elementum, volutpat dolor. Vivamus lobortis id erat ac scelerisque.

Nulla eget varius tortor, a egestas risus. Nunc interdum commodo hendrerit. Aliquam rutrum ligula elit, vitae efficitur dolor ultrices sollicitudin. Duis leo neque, porttitor id laoreet ac, imperdiet vel leo. Vivamus mollis ac purus non fermentum. Fusce mattis sagittis enim, tincidunt pretium enim rutrum ac. Donec maximus accumsan augue non efficitur. Class aptent taciti sociosqu ad litora torquent per conubia nostra, per inceptos himenaeos. Fusce sed nunc non ante viverra eleifend. Maecenas egestas magna sit amet varius dictum.

Fusce dictum nisl ipsum, at dictum elit efficitur ut. Suspendisse cursus lorem et maximus placerat. Donec lectus magna, fringilla vel orci a, condimentum mattis tellus. Maecenas a sodales orci, vel iaculis nisi. Proin sagittis auctor sagittis. Vestibulum id interdum urna. Praesent metus enim, euismod at dui eget, varius sagittis risus. Interdum et malesuada fames ac ante ipsum primis in faucibus.

FIGURE 12.2   The rendered result of Figure 12.1.

CHALLENGE 12.1

Rewrite the example without explicitly specifying static positioning.

12.3.2 Relative Positioning

Relative positioning places an element in relation to where it would have been placed in a normal flow. To specify that an element should be relatively positioned, the value of `relative` is used with the `position` property and the `top` or `bottom` and the `left` or `right` properties are then used to specify the distance to place the element from where it would have been in a normal flow. Figures 12.3 and 12.4 show how these properties are used and the effect.

In the example, the `p.moveRight{}` rule moves the top edge and left edge of the second `<p>` element's box 10px down and 50px right, respectively, from where they would have been in a normal flow. If only the `top` or `left` offset is specified, the position for the normal flow is used for the other.

```
CSS
p { width: 600px; }
p.moveRight {
  position: relative;
  top: 10px;
  left: 50px;
}

HTML
<h2>Relative positioning</h2>
<p>In quis nibh eget nisl pharetra varius. Mauris eget velit
   turpis. Vivamus erat...</p>
<p class="moveRight">Nulla eget varius tortor, a egestas risus.
   Nunc interdum hendrerit. Aliquam...</p>
<p>Fusce dictum nisl ipsum, at dictum elit efficitur ut.
   Suspendisse cursus lorem et maximus placerat. Donec...</p>
```

FIGURE 12.3   Example of relative positioning.

Relative positioning

In quis nibh eget nisl pharetra varius. Mauris eget velit turpis. Vivamus erat mauris, pretium
pharetra risus eget, ornare rutrum tortor. In sollicitudin congue porttitor. Nunc ante sem,
vehicula sit amet feugiat nec, pharetra vitae velit. Suspendisse nec ipsum congue, fermentum
dolor elementum, volutpat dolor. Vivamus lobortis id erat ac scelerisque.

> Nulla eget varius tortor, a egestas risus. Nunc interdum commodo hendrerit. Aliquam rutrum
> ligula elit, vitae efficitur dolor ultrices sollicitudin. Duis leo neque, porttitor id laoreet ac,
> imperdiet vel leo. Vivamus mollis ac purus non fermentum. Fusce mattis sagittis enim,
> tincidunt pretium enim rutrum ac. Donec maximus accumsan augue non efficitur. Class
> aptent taciti sociosqu ad litora torquent per conubia nostra, per inceptos himenaeos. Fusce
> sed nunc non ante viverra eleifend. Maecenas egestas magna sit amet varius dictum.

Fusce dictum nisl ipsum, at dictum elit efficitur ut. Suspendisse cursus lorem et maximus
placerat. Donec lectus magna, fringilla vel orci a, condimentum mattis tellus. Maecenas a
sodales orci, vel iaculis nisi. Proin sagittis auctor sagittis. Vestibulum id interdum urna.
Praesent metus enim, euismod at dui eget, varius sagittis risus. Interdum et malesuada fames
ac ante ipsum primis in faucibus.

FIGURE 12.4   The rendered result of Figure 12.3.

CHALLENGE 12.2

Use the following to see the effect of positioning a paragraph relatively to the right and bottom edges of the box:

```
body {margin-left: 60px;}
p { width: 600px;}
p.moveLeft{
position: relative;
bottom: 10px;
right: 50px;}
```

12.3.2.1 Specifying Offset for Logical Edges

The properties used to specify the logical offset of an element are `offset-block-end`, `offset-block-start`, `offset-inline-end`, and `offset-inline-start` and whether each defines top, bottom, left, or right offset depends on the value of the `writing-mode` property (discussed later in Chapter 14). They are **non-inherited** and take the same values as the `top`, `bottom`, `left`, or `right` properties already introduced earlier, which are **length values** (e.g., px and em), **percentage values** (%), and `auto`. Figure 12.5 shows how the properties are used. The code produces the same result as Figure 12.4. Given the set writing mode, `offset-block-start` means top and `offset-inline-start` means left.

```
CSS
p { width: 600px; }
p.moveRight {
  writing-mode: horizontal-tb;
  position: relative;
  offset-block-start: 10px;
  offset-inline-start: 50px;
}

HTML
<h2>Relativepositioningwith logical offset</h2>
<p>In quis nibh eget nisl pharetra varius. Mauris eget velit
   turpis. Vivamus erat...</p>
<p class="moveRight">Nulla eget varius tortor, a egestas risus.
   Nunc interdum commodo...</p>
<p>Fusce dictum nisl ipsum, at dictum elit efficitur ut.
   Suspendisse cursus lorem et...</p>
```

FIGURE 12.5   Example usage of logical box offset properties.

CHALLENGE 12.3

Go to the "Specifying Content Directionality" section in Chapter 14, make note of other values for the `writing-mode` property and try them in the example to see the effects.

12.3.3 Absolute Positioning

Absolute positioning removes an element from the normal flow of elements without leaving behind the space it had occupied, so that it no longer influences the positions of other elements. The other elements simply flow normally underneath as if it is not there. To specify that an element should be absolutely positioned, the value of `absolute` is used with the `position` property and the `top` or `bottom` and the `left` or `right` properties are then used to specify where to place the element relative to the border of the containing element's box (i.e., the next parent element's box). In the absence of a containing element, the element is placed relative to the `<html>` element. Figures 12.6 and 12.7 show how the properties are used and the effect.

In the example, the h{ } rule absolutely positions the `<h2>` element 10px from the top and 50px from the left edges of the `<html>` element, since there is no next parent element. The background color has been added to make it easier to see the layering of the elements. Note that the reason the absolutely positioned element is so far from the top, even though only a value of 10px is specified, is because browsers usually add margin to the top of the heading element. To remove the margin for the `<h2>` element in the example, zero-margin declaration can be added to its rule.

```
CSS
p { width: 600px; }
h2 {
 background-color: pink;
 position: absolute;
 top: 10px;
 left: 50px;
}

HTML
<h2>Absolute positioning</h2>
<p>In quis nibh eget nisl pharetra varius. Mauris eget velit
   turpis. Vivamus erat mauris, pretium pharetra...</p>
<p>Nulla eget varius tortor, a egestas risus. Nunc interdum
   commodo hendrerit. Aliquam rutrum ligula elit...</p>
<p>Fusce dictum nisl ipsum, at dictum elit efficitur ut.
   Suspendisse cursus lorem et maximus placerat...</p>
```

FIGURE 12.6   Example of absolute positioning.

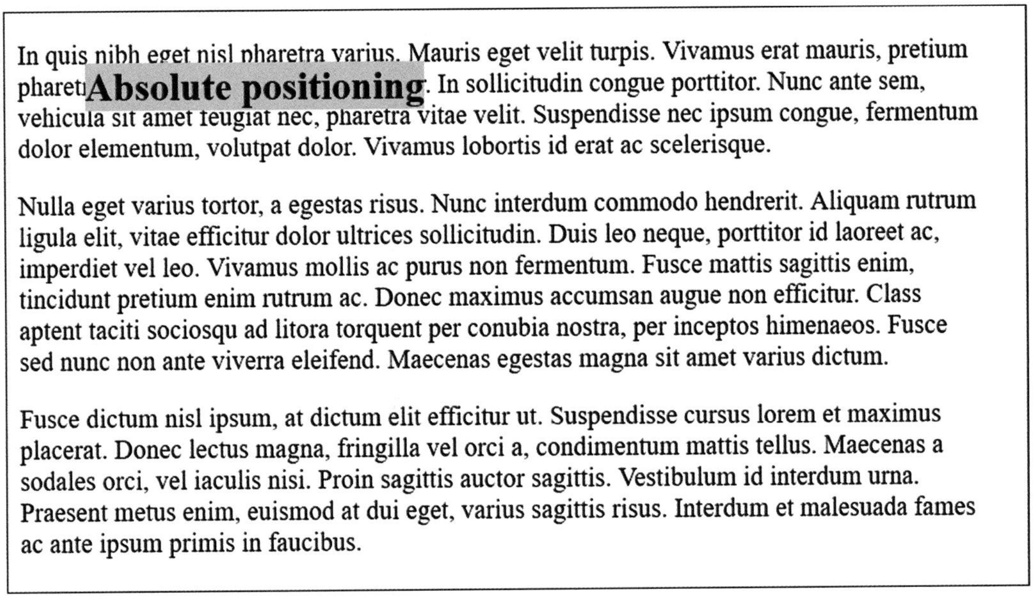

In quis nibh eget nisl pharetra varius. Mauris eget velit turpis. Vivamus erat mauris, pretium pharetr**Absolute positioning**. In sollicitudin congue porttitor. Nunc ante sem, vehicula sit amet feugiat nec, pharetra vitae velit. Suspendisse nec ipsum congue, fermentum dolor elementum, volutpat dolor. Vivamus lobortis id erat ac scelerisque.

Nulla eget varius tortor, a egestas risus. Nunc interdum commodo hendrerit. Aliquam rutrum ligula elit, vitae efficitur dolor ultrices sollicitudin. Duis leo neque, porttitor id laoreet ac, imperdiet vel leo. Vivamus mollis ac purus non fermentum. Fusce mattis sagittis enim, tincidunt pretium enim rutrum ac. Donec maximus accumsan augue non efficitur. Class aptent taciti sociosqu ad litora torquent per conubia nostra, per inceptos himenaeos. Fusce sed nunc non ante viverra eleifend. Maecenas egestas magna sit amet varius dictum.

Fusce dictum nisl ipsum, at dictum elit efficitur ut. Suspendisse cursus lorem et maximus placerat. Donec lectus magna, fringilla vel orci a, condimentum mattis tellus. Maecenas a sodales orci, vel iaculis nisi. Proin sagittis auctor sagittis. Vestibulum id interdum urna. Praesent metus enim, euismod at dui eget, varius sagittis risus. Interdum et malesuada fames ac ante ipsum primis in faucibus.

FIGURE 12.7 The rendered result of Figure 12.6.

CHALLENGE 12.4

To see how an absolutely positioned element behaves, implement the example and then resize the browser until the scroll panel appears and then scroll the page up and down.

NOTE: Content positioning and accessibility

As mentioned in Chapter 4, under within-page linking, element positioning can be used to hide the content for the purpose of accessibility. This is typically done by positioning an element off-screen to the left so that it is not visible on the screen but visible to the screen reader. For the benefit of sighted keyboard users, the element can also be made to come on-screen when it receives focus. The property used to achieve these goals is the `position` property with the `static` and `absolute` values. An example of how to implement them is shown below.

CSS

```
#jump a { position:absolute; left:-9999px; top:auto; }
#jump a:focus { position:static; }
```

(Continued)

NOTE (*Continued*): **Content positioning and accessibility**

HTML

```
<div id="jump"><a href="#main">Jump to Main Content</a></div>
```

The `#jump a{}` rule positions the "Jump to Main Content" link off-screen at a point `-9999px` to the left and anywhere between the top and the bottom as determined by the browser. When the keyboard tab action gives focus to the link, the `#jump a:focus{}` rule moves it to the default position (i.e., where it would have been if it was not absolutely positioned), making it visible. Once it loses focus, it goes back to the off-screen position. The `:focus` is one of the many **pseudo-class selectors** introduced in Chapter 8.

12.3.4 Fixed Positioning

Fixed positioning is like absolute positioning, except that it positions an element relative to the browser window. Like absolute positioning, it removes an element from the normal flow of elements without leaving behind the space for it, so that it no longer influences the positions of other elements, which simply flow normally underneath as if it is not there. Unlike in absolute positioning, when a page is scrolled up and down, the fixed position element remains in the same place. To specify that an element should be fixed positioned, `fixed` is used as the value of the `position` property and the `top` or `bottom` and the `left` or `right` properties are used to specify where to place the element relative to the edges of the browser window. Figure 12.8 and 12.9 show how the properties are used and the effect.

Notice that the result is similar to Figure 12.7. The `h{}` rule fixed positions the `<h2>` element 10px from the top and 50px from the left edges of the `<html>` element. Again, the background color has been added to make it easier to see the layering of the elements.

```
CSS
p { width: 600px; }
h2 {
 background-color: pink;
 position: fixed;
 top: 10px;
 left: 50px;
}

HTML
<h2>Fixed positioning</h2>
<p>In quis nibh eget nisl pharetra varius. Mauris eget
    velit turpis. Vivamus erat mauris, pretium...</p>
<p>Nulla eget varius tortor, a egestas risus. Nunc
    interdum commodo hendrerit. Aliquam rutrum...</p>
<p>Fusce dictum nisl ipsum, at dictum elit efficitur ut.
    Suspendisse cursus lorem et maximus placerat...</p>
```

FIGURE 12.8   Example of fixed positioning.

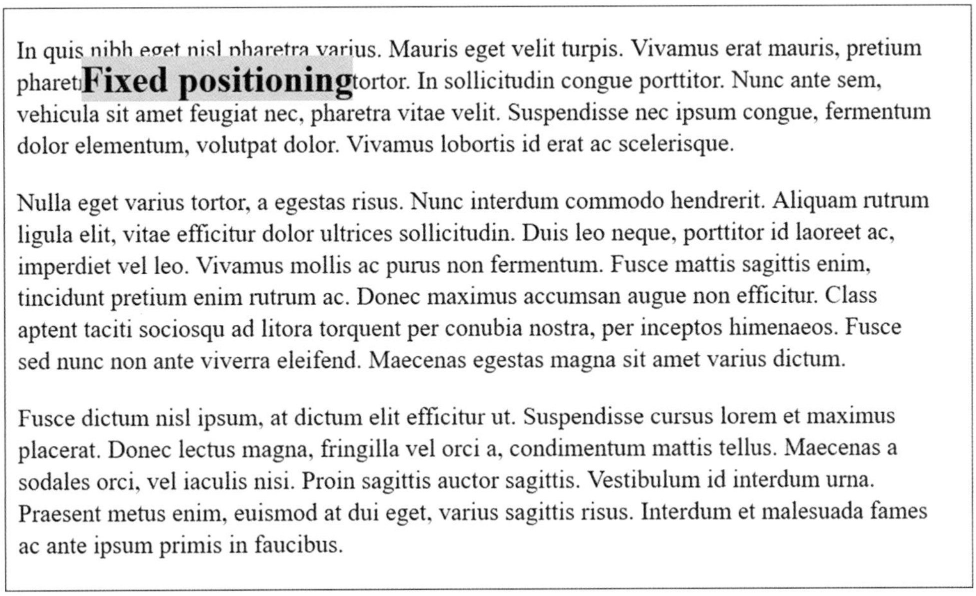

In quis nibh eget nisl pharetra varius. Mauris eget velit turpis. Vivamus erat mauris, pretium
pharet**Fixed positioning**tortor. In sollicitudin congue porttitor. Nunc ante sem,
vehicula sit amet feugiat nec, pharetra vitae velit. Suspendisse nec ipsum congue, fermentum
dolor elementum, volutpat dolor. Vivamus lobortis id erat ac scelerisque.

Nulla eget varius tortor, a egestas risus. Nunc interdum commodo hendrerit. Aliquam rutrum
ligula elit, vitae efficitur dolor ultrices sollicitudin. Duis leo neque, porttitor id laoreet ac,
imperdiet vel leo. Vivamus mollis ac purus non fermentum. Fusce mattis sagittis enim,
tincidunt pretium enim rutrum ac. Donec maximus accumsan augue non efficitur. Class
aptent taciti sociosqu ad litora torquent per conubia nostra, per inceptos himenaeos. Fusce
sed nunc non ante viverra eleifend. Maecenas egestas magna sit amet varius dictum.

Fusce dictum nisl ipsum, at dictum elit efficitur ut. Suspendisse cursus lorem et maximus
placerat. Donec lectus magna, fringilla vel orci a, condimentum mattis tellus. Maecenas a
sodales orci, vel iaculis nisi. Proin sagittis auctor sagittis. Vestibulum id interdum urna.
Praesent metus enim, euismod at dui eget, varius sagittis risus. Interdum et malesuada fames
ac ante ipsum primis in faucibus.

FIGURE 12.9   The rendered result of Figure 12.8.

CHALLENGE 12.5

Like in the previous challenge, resize the browser until the scroll panel appears and
then scroll the page up and down to see how a fixed positioned element behaves.

CHALLENGE 12.6

Implement the example in Figures 12.8 and 12.9, using the logical offset properties
introduced earlier in Figure 12.5 under Relative Positioning.

12.3.4.1 An Application of Fixed Positioning

This fixed method of element positioning is sometimes used for the header or left
sidebar to present permanently visible navigation. However, if not used properly, this
can create side-effects which make a design difficult to use. For example, a design
that looks fine on a standard screen may, on a smaller screen, have the sidebar cut
off or footer content obscured when the page is scrolled that far down. Figures 12.10
and 12.11 demonstrate an application of fixed positioning that fixes the sidebar. The
`.sidebar{}` rule specifies the dimensions, color, and position of the sidebar, as

```
CSS
.sidebar {
    width: 100px;
    height: 300px;
    margin: 10px;
    background: pink;
    position: fixed;
    top: 55px;
    left: 0px;
}
.content {
    width: 500px;
    height: 300px;
    padding-left: 130px;
    overflow: auto;
}

HTML
<h2>Fixed Company</h2>
<div class="content">
  <div class="sidebar">Side Menu</div>
  <p><h3>About us</h3>Lorem ipsum dolor sit amet...</p>
  <p>Lorem ipsum dolor sit amet, consectetur adipiscing...</p>
</div>
```

FIGURE 12.10   An application of fixed positioning.

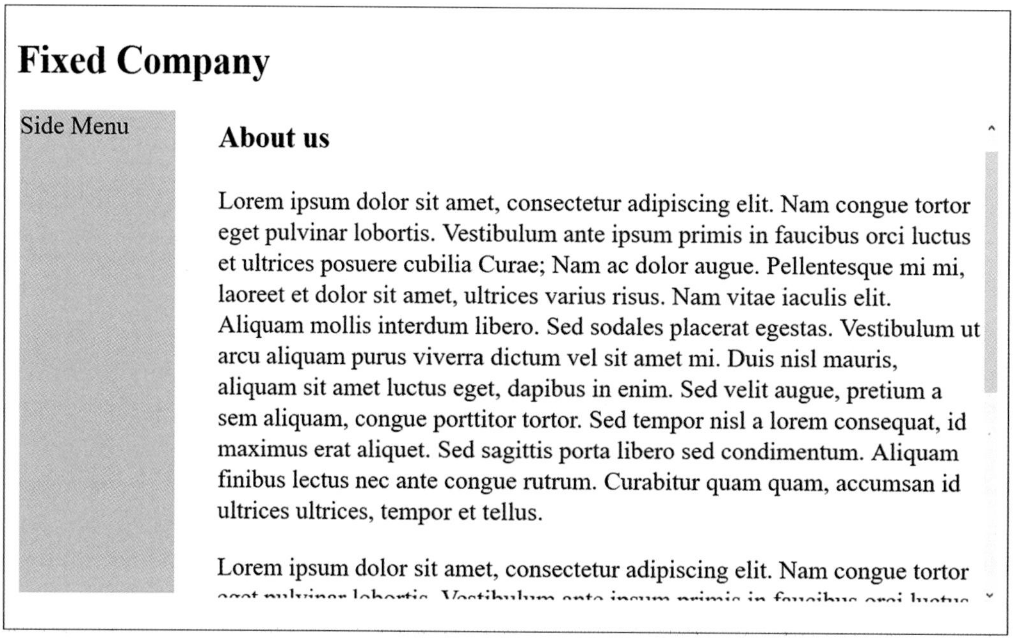

Fixed Company

Side Menu

About us

Lorem ipsum dolor sit amet, consectetur adipiscing elit. Nam congue tortor eget pulvinar lobortis. Vestibulum ante ipsum primis in faucibus orci luctus et ultrices posuere cubilia Curae; Nam ac dolor augue. Pellentesque mi mi, laoreet et dolor sit amet, ultrices varius risus. Nam vitae iaculis elit. Aliquam mollis interdum libero. Sed sodales placerat egestas. Vestibulum ut arcu aliquam purus viverra dictum vel sit amet mi. Duis nisl mauris, aliquam sit amet luctus eget, dapibus in enim. Sed velit augue, pretium a sem aliquam, congue porttitor tortor. Sed tempor nisl a lorem consequat, id maximus erat aliquet. Sed sagittis porta libero sed condimentum. Aliquam finibus lectus nec ante congue rutrum. Curabitur quam quam, accumsan id ultrices ultrices, tempor et tellus.

Lorem ipsum dolor sit amet, consectetur adipiscing elit. Nam congue tortor

FIGURE 12.11   The rendered result of Figure 12.10.

well as margin. The `.content{}` rule specifies the dimensions of the container for the sidebar and the paragraphs of text, as well as the space between the sidebar and the paragraphs and how to handle overflow.

CHALLENGE 12.7

In the example, the scrollbar affects only the text content of the `<div>` element of "content." What does the scrollbars of the browser window affect when the window gets too small for the content?

CHALLENGE 12.8

Implement the example in Figure 12.10, using the logical offset properties introduced earlier in Figure 12.5 under Relative Positioning.

CHALLENGE 12.9

Modify the code in Figure 12.10 to add menu links to the sidebar.

12.3.5 Sticky Positioning

Sticky positioning is a combination of relative and fixed positioning. Basically, during scrolling, a sticky positioned element behaves as if it is relatively positioned until it goes beyond a specified point. If there is another sticky positioned element at that point, it is replaced. To specify `sticky` positioning for an element, sticky is used as the value of the `position` property and a box offset property is used to specify the "sticky point." Figures 12.12 and 12.13 show how this is done and the effect.

In the example, as the user scrolls down, the "Article One" heading moves up, and when it gets to the top edge of the browser window it stops there and remains there as the user continues to scroll down until the "Article Two" heading gets there to replace it. The `.art1{}` and `.art2{}` rules specify the styles for the two `<div>` elements. The `auto` values specified for the right and left margin ensure that the elements are horizontally centered in the browser window. In the `h2{}` rule, the `position:sticky` and `top:0px` declarations say to apply sticky positioning at 0px from the top of the browser window.

```
CSS
.art1, .art2 { width: 600px; margin: 0px auto 20px auto;
               background-color: lightgrey; padding: 15px;
}
h2 { background-color: lightblue;
     border: 1px outset lightblue;
     position: sticky;
     top: 0px;
     margin: 0px 0px 10px 0px;
     padding: 10px;
}

HTML
<div class="art1">
  <h2>Article One</h2>
  Lorem ipsum dolor sit amet, consectetur adipiscing elit...
</div>
<div class="art2">
  <h2>Article Two</h2>
  Nisi est sit amet facilisis magna etiam tempor orci. Sapien...
</div>
```

FIGURE 12.12   Example of sticky positioning.

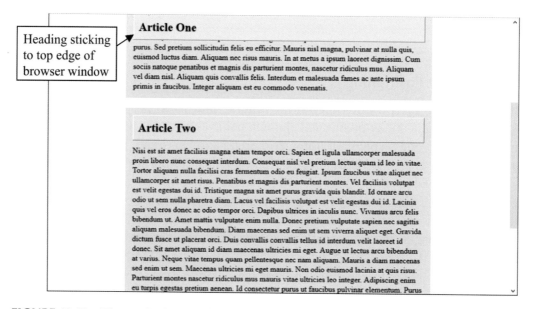

FIGURE 12.13   The result of Figure 12.12.

CHALLENGE 12.10

Implement the example, ensuring you have enough text in each paragraph so that the scroll bar can be activated. Then use it to see how sticky positioning works. Also, experiment with the offset property to see how it affects the positioning of the headings.

CHALLENGE 12.11

Again, implement the example in Figure 12.12, using the logical offset properties introduced earlier in Figure 12.5 under Relative Positioning.

12.3.5.1 Sticky Global Navigation

Another common application of sticky positioning is its use to make global navigation remain in view while a page is being scrolled up and down. Figures 12.14 and 12.15 show the codes for demonstrating the application and Figure 12.16 the result.

In the example, the body{} sets the width of the page to be 90% of the browser window and centers it horizontally with the margin property. The header{} rule sticky positions the banner and the menu 0px from the top edge of the page.

```
HTML
<body>
  <header>
    <div class="logo">
      <h1>The Web Company</h1>
    </div>
    <nav>
      <ul>
        <li><a href="#">Home</a>
        <li><a href="#">About us</a>
        <li><a href="#">Services</a>
        <li><a href="#">Contact us</a>
      </ul>
    </nav>
  </header>
  <div class="container">
    <p>Lorem ipsum dolor sit amet, consectetur...</p>
    ...
  </div>
</body>
```

FIGURE 12.14 HTML code for an example of sticky global navigation.

```
CSS
body {
  width: 90%;
  margin: 0 auto 0 auto;
}
header {
  position: sticky;
  top: 0px;
}
.logo {
  height: 100px;
  background-color: lightgrey;
  text-align: center;
}
.logo h1 {
  margin-top: 0;
  padding-top: 30px;
}
nav ul {
  margin: 0px;
  padding: 0;
  background-color: pink;
  width: 100%
}
nav ul li {
  display: inline-block;
  text-align: center;
  width: 25%;
}
nav ul li  a {
  display: block;
  padding: 10px 0;
  text-decoration: none;
  font-weight: bold;
}
nav ul li a:hover {
  background-color: violet;
  color: white;
}
```

FIGURE 12.15   CSS code for Figure 12.14.

The .logo{} rule specifies the height and background color for the banner and centers the <h1> element inside it. To align the <h1> element properly, the .logo h1{} rule sets its top margin to 0px to remove it and adds padding at the top. The nav li{} specifies 0px margin and padding and a pink background for the <ul> element and also makes its width 100% that of the containing element (i.e., <nav> element), which is the same width as the <header> element. The nav ul li{} rule displays the <li> elements as inline-block elements (i.e., horizontally), centers

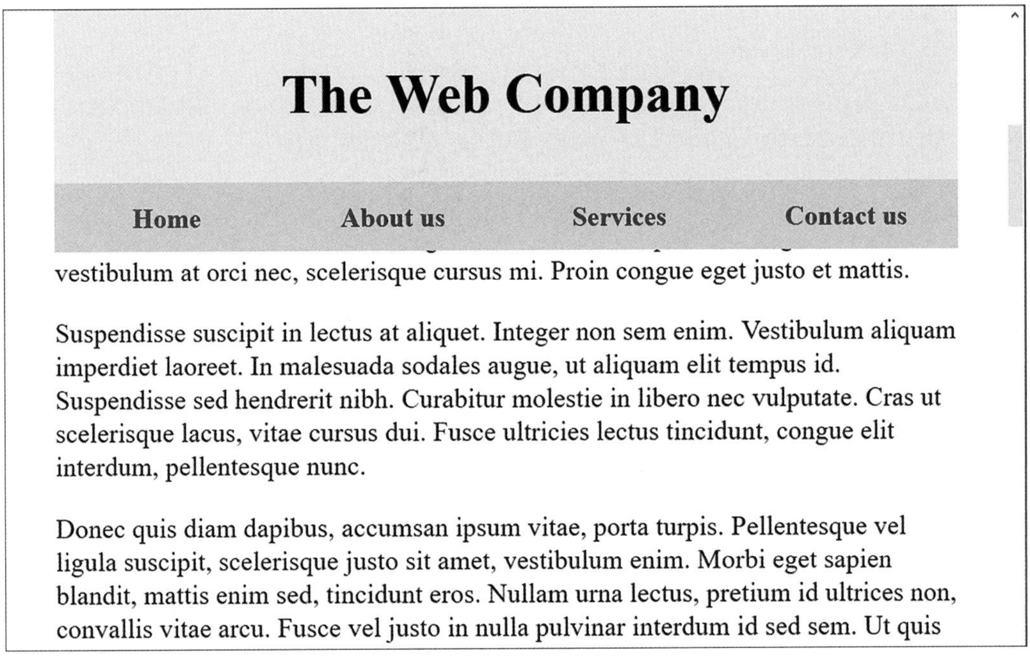

The Web Company

| Home | About us | Services | Contact us |

vestibulum at orci nec, scelerisque cursus mi. Proin congue eget justo et mattis.

Suspendisse suscipit in lectus at aliquet. Integer non sem enim. Vestibulum aliquam imperdiet laoreet. In malesuada sodales augue, ut aliquam elit tempus id. Suspendisse sed hendrerit nibh. Curabitur molestie in libero nec vulputate. Cras ut scelerisque lacus, vitae cursus dui. Fusce ultricies lectus tincidunt, congue elit interdum, pellentesque nunc.

Donec quis diam dapibus, accumsan ipsum vitae, porta turpis. Pellentesque vel ligula suscipit, scelerisque justo sit amet, vestibulum enim. Morbi eget sapien blandit, mattis enim sed, tincidunt eros. Nullam urna lectus, pretium id ultrices non, convallis vitae arcu. Fusce vel justo in nulla pulvinar interdum id sed sem. Ut quis

FIGURE 12.16 The result of Figures 12.14 and 12.15.

the text inside them, and makes each 25% of the `<ul>` element. The `nav ul li a{ }` rule changes the `<a>` elements to block elements so that padding can be added to them. It also removes the underlining (with `text-decoration: none` declaration) and makes the text bold. The `nav ul li a:hover{ }` rule says to change the background color of the `<a>` elements to violet and the text color to white when the cursor is over them.

CHALLENGE 12.12

To help the understanding of the layout in the example, add border to `header{ }`, `.logo{ }`, `.logo h1{ }`, and `nav ul li{ }` rules to see the relationship between the elements. Also, experiment with the values of the `display` property to see how they affect the menu.

CHALLENGE 12.13

In the example, make only the menu sticky, so that it is the only feature that sticks to the top during scrolling.

CHALLENGE 12.14

Again, implement the example in Figure 12.16, using the logical offset properties introduced earlier in Figure 12.5 under Relative Positioning.

12.3.6 Using Element Positioning in Drop-Down Menus

As mentioned earlier, element positioning has application in drop-down menus and as of time of writing is still one of the commonly used approaches. Again, this is mainly because the `<menu>` and `<menuitem>` elements (introduced in Chapter 3), which are designed specifically for this purpose, are still waiting to be supported by major browsers. The common principle is to use the `<ul>` or `<button>` element to display the menu, the `display` property to hide and show the drop-down menu as necessary when the cursor is on a menu, and positioning properties to position the drop-down menu relatively to the menu.

12.3.6.1 Drop-Down Menu Using List Elements

Figures 12.17 and 12.18 show an example of how list elements are used with positioning properties for creating the drop-down menu. Figure 12.19 shows the result.

In the example, the `body{}` rule sets the font for all text to Arial and aligns all elements to the center of the page. In the `.menubar li{}` rule, `display`:

```
HTML
<body>
  <ul class="menubar">
    <li><a href="home.html">Home</a></li>
    <li><a href="about_us.html">About us</a></li>
    <li><a href="products.html">Products</a>
      <ul class="dropdown_menu">
        <li><a href="audio_software.html">Audio software</a></li>
        <li><a href="virtual_instruments.html">
          Virtual instruments</a></li>
        <li><a href="effect_modules.html">Effect modules</a></li>
      </ul>
    </li>
    <li><a href="downloads.html">Downloads</a></li>
    <li><a href="contact.html">Contact us</a></li>
  </ul>
</body>
```

FIGURE 12.17 HTML for drop-down menu using list elements.

```
CSS
body { font-family: Arial; text-align: center; }
.menubar li {
 display: inline-block;
 background: yellow;
 padding: 10px 20px;
 cursor: pointer;
 position: relative;
}
.menubar li a { color: black; text-decoration: none; }
.menubar li:hover { background: orange; }
.menubar li ul {
 display: none;
 padding: 0;
 box-shadow: 2px 2px 2px #4d4d4d;
 position: absolute;
 top: 39px;
 left: 0;
 text-align: left;
}
.menubar li ul li { background: orange; color: white; display:
 block; }
.menubar li ul li a { color: white; white-space: nowrap; }
.menubar li:hover ul { display: block; }
.menubar li ul li:hover { background: grey; }
```

FIGURE 12.18   CSS for HTML in Figure 12.17.

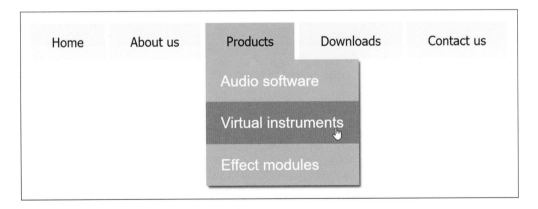

FIGURE 12.19   The result of Figures 12.17 and 12.18.

inline-block changes the alignment of the <li> elements of the <ul> of class="menubar" from default vertical to horizontal and removes the bullet points; background:yellow makes the background of each <li> element yellow; padding gives the elements more width and height; cursor:pointer changes the cursor type to a finger when the cursor is on an `<li>` element; and `position:` `relative` positions the content of each `<li>` element relative to the position of the element. This ensures that each drop-down menu is aligned under its menu, as shown in Figure 12.19.

In the `.menubar li a{}` rule, `color:black` makes the color of all the text in the `<a>` elements and the `<li>` elements black and `text-decoration:none` removes the default underline decoration. The `.menubar li:hover{}` rule changes the background color of any `<li>` element to orange when the cursor hovers over it. The `.menubar li ul {}` rule styles the drop-down menu (i.e., `<ul>` of `class="dropdown_menu"`). In it, `padding` removes the padding for all edges so that the left edge is aligned with that of the menu; `box-shadow` adds shadow to it; `text-align:left` aligns its content to the left; `position:absolute` absolutely positions it; `top:39px` positions it so that its top edge is flush with the bottom edge of the menu; and `left:0` positions it so that the left edge is aligned with that of the menu. This is necessary because `<li>` elements are right-indented by default. In this case, they need to be moved left to 0, which is the position of the left edge of the containing `<ul>` element.

In the `.menubar li ul li{}` rule, `background: orange` makes the `<li>` elements in the drop-down orange; `color:white` makes the text white; and `display:block` makes the `<li>` elements behave like a block element again. Recall that all `<li>` elements were made to behave like inline-block elements before.

In the `.menubar li ul li a{}` rule, `color:white` makes the color of the text in the `<a>` elements in the drop-down menu white; and `white-space:` `nowrap` ensures that the text does not wrap to the next line. This means that the longest text length determines the width of the drop-down menu. Alternatively, you could specify a fixed width. The `.menubar li:hover ul{}` rule displays the drop-down menu when the cursor hovers over the menu (i.e., `<li>` element in the `<ul>` element of `class="menubar"`). The `.menubar li ul li:hover{}` rule changes the background color of any menu item in the drop-down menu to grey when the cursor hovers over it. This is any `<li>` element in the `<ul>` element of `class="dropdown_menu"`.

NOTE: Why use `class="dropdown _ menu"`**?**

Notice that the `class="dropdown _ menu"` used on the `<ul>` element was not referenced in the CSS. This is because it was not necessary and was only used to make the explanation of the code easier.

CHALLENGE 12.15

Implement the example in Figures 12.17 through 12.19, using the logical offset properties introduced earlier in Figure 12.5 under Relative Positioning.

12.3.6.2 *Drop-Down Menu Using the* <button> *Element*

Figures 12.20 and 12.21 show an example of how the <button> element is used with positioning properties for creating the drop-down menu. It produces the same result as Figure 12.19.

```
HTML
<body>
 <div class="menubar">
   <div class="menu">
     <button><a href="home.html">Home</a></button>
   </div>
   <div class="menu">
     <button><a href="about_us.html">About us</a></button>
   </div>
   <div class="menu">
     <button><a href="products.html">Products</a></button>
     <div>
       <a href="audio_software.html">Audio software</a>
       <a href="virtual_instruments.html">Virtual instruments</a>
       <a href="effect_modules.html">Effect modules</a>
     </div>
   </div>
   <div class="menu">
     <button><a href="downloads.html">Downloads</a></button>
   </div>
   <div class="menu">
     <button><a href="contact.html">Contact us</a></button>
   </div>
 </div>
</body>
```

FIGURE 12.20   HTML for drop-down menu using the <button> element.

```
CSS
body { font-family: Arial; text-align: center; padding: 20px; }
.menu { display: inline-block; position: relative; }
.menubar .menu a { text-decoration: none; color: black; }
button {
  padding: 10px 20px;
  margin-right: 1px;
  border: none;
  background: yellow;
  cursor: pointer;
}
.menubar .menu div {
  display: none;
  box-shadow: 2px 2px 2px #4d4d4d;
  position: absolute;
  text-align: left;
  background: orange;
}
.menubar .menu div a {
  display: block;
  white-space: nowrap;
  padding: 12px 16px;
  color: white;
}
.menubar .menu:hover button { background: orange; }
.menubar .menu:hover  div { display: block; }
.menubar .menu div a:hover { background: grey; }
```

FIGURE 12.21 CSS for Figure 12.20.

CHALLENGE 12.16

What does `padding:12px 16px` in the `.menubar .menu div a{}` rule
in the example in Figure 12.21 do? Also, in the `.menubar .menu div{}` rule,
why is it not necessary to specify offset positions with `position:absolute`
to align the drop-down menu vertically with the menu?

12.3.7 Ordering Overlapping Elements

As mentioned earlier, when elements overlap, the property used to specify which
one is on top of which is the `z-index` property. More specifically, `z-index`
controls the vertical stacking order of overlapping elements; and it only affects

elements that are relatively, absolutely, or fixed positioned. Elements positioned using these methods always appear on top of those with default static positioning. Normally, elements are stacked in the order that they appear in an HTML document, with the last one rendered topmost. The property is **non-inherited** and its value is a number. An element with a higher z-index is generally placed on top of that with a lower one. For example, an element with a z-index of 2 appears on top of one with 1. Figure 12.22 shows how the property is used and Figure 12.23 shows the rendered result. Each rule specifies the size, background color, absolute position, and z-index of each of the four elements.

```
CSS
.bar {
  width: 550px;
  height: 120px;
  background: grey;
  opacity: 0.9;
  position: absolute;
  left: 10px;
  top: 110px;
  z-index: 2;
}
.peg1 { width: 120px;  height: 200px; background: gold;
  opacity: 0.9; position: absolute; left: 65px; top: 70px;
  z-index: 1;
}
.peg2 { width: 120px;  height: 200px; background: gold;
  opacity: 0.9;position: absolute; left: 225px; top:70px;
  z-index: 3;
}
.peg3 { width: 120px;  height: 200px; background: gold;
  opacity: 0.9; position: absolute; left: 385px; top: 70px;
  z-index: 1;
}
```

```
HTML
<h2>z-index</h2>
<div class="bar">z-index: 2;</div>
<span class="peg1">z-index: 1;</span>
<span class="peg2">z-index: 3;</span>
<span class="peg3">z-index: 1;</span>
```

FIGURE 12.22 Example usage of the z-index property.

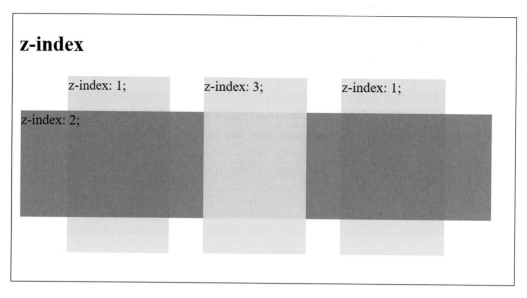

FIGURE 12.23   The rendered result of Figure 12.22.

CHALLENGE 12.17

In the example in Figure 12.22, what will happen if the `<div>` element is used instead of the `<span>` element, and why?

CHALLENGE 12.18

In the CSS code in Figure 12.22, some properties are repeated for `.peg1{}`, `.peg2{}`, and `.peg3{}` rules. Rewrite the code without the repetitions to make it more efficient. Also, state what you think the pros and cons are of writing codes in this way.

12.3.8 Floating Elements

The property used to float elements is the `float` property and the way it works is that it removes an element from the normal flow and positions of it as far as possible toward the left or right edge of the containing element. If there are no elements in its path, it is placed at the left or right edge, and if there are, it is placed next to the last floated one. For this reason, the property is commonly used to place elements next to each other. When an element is floated, everything else in the containing element it is in is wrapped around it. The property is **non-inherited** and the values it takes are `left`, `right`, or `none` (which says not to float an element). Figure 12.24 shows how the property is used and Figure 12.25 its effect.

NOTE: The use of float in layout

Although a very common application of element floating is for implementing the layout of elements on a page, the **flexbox properties**, which are newer properties and discussed in Chapter 19, are the future and recommended for implementing layout.

CSS
```css
blockquote {
  width: 200px;
  border-top: 1px solid #000000;
  border-bottom: 1px solid #000000
  margin: 10px 10px 10px 10px;
  padding: 10px;
  background-color: #ffc0cb;
  font-style: italic;
  float: right;
}
figure {
  margin: 0px 10px 0px 0px;
  font-style: italic;
  float: left;
}
```

HTML
```html
<h2>Contents floated right and left</h2>
<blockquote>"Suspendisse cursus lorem et maximus
            placerat."</blockquote>
<p>In quis nibh eget nisl pharetra varius. Mauris eget velit
   turpis. Vivamus erat...</p>
<figure>
  <img src="rabbit.png" alt="The rabbit" width="80" height="80">
  <figcaption>The rabbit</figcaption>
</figure>
<p>Nulla eget varius tortor, a egestas risus. Nunc...</p>
<p>Morbi eget sem feugiat, pretium velit in, vehicula...</p>
```

FIGURE 12.24 Example usage of the `float` property.

Contents floated right and left

In quis nibh eget nisl pharetra varius. Mauris eget velit turpis.
Vivamus erat mauris, pretium pharetra risus eget, ornare rutrum
tortor. In sollicitudin congue porttitor. Nunc ante sem, vehicula sit
amet feugiat nec, pharetra vitae velit. Suspendisse nec ipsum
congue, fermentum dolor elementum, volutpat dolor. Vivamus
lobortis id erat ac scelerisque.

"Suspendisse cursus lorem et maximus placerat."

The rabbit

Nulla eget varius tortor, a egestas risus. Nunc interdum commodo hendrerit. Aliquam
rutrum ligula elit, vitae efficitur dolor ultrices sollicitudin. Duis leo neque, porttitor id
laoreet ac, imperdiet vel leo. Vivamus mollis ac purus non fermentum. Fusce mattis sagittis
enim, tincidunt pretium enim rutrum ac. Donec maximus accumsan augue non efficitur.
Class aptent taciti sociosqu ad litora torquent per conubia nostra, per inceptos himenaeos.
Fusce sed nunc non ante viverra eleifend. Maecenas egestas magna sit amet varius dictum.

Morbi eget sem feugiat, pretium velit in, vehicula elit. Sed suscipit mi eu lorem ultrices fringilla. Integer
tempus dapibus dui, a pharetra eros aliquet sed. Phasellus elementum neque enim, et sagittis mauris
posuere a. Curabitur non purus ut orci facilisis facilisis nec id ligula. Mauris quis ipsum sit amet ligula
congue gravida. Donec porta dui erat, non tristique nibh lobortis ut.

FIGURE 12.25   The rendered result of Figure 12.24.

In the `blockquote{}` rule in the example, `width` specifies the `width` of the `<blockquote>` element to ensure that it does not occupy the entire width of the containing element (i.e., `<body>` element), `border` gives the element black top and bottom line-style borders, `margin` specifies the amount of surrounding space, `padding` specifies the amount of surrounding space for its content, `background-color` specifies its background color, `font-style` italicizes the text content, and `float` says to float it right. The `font-style` property is discussed fully in Chapter 13 and only used here for the purpose of demonstration. The `figure{}` rule specifies `margin` for the `<figure>` element and `font-style` for its text content (i.e., the caption) and also says to float the element left. Using the `<figure>` element rather than just the `<img>` element makes it easier to include a caption with the image.

CHALLENGE 12.19

Can you think of any advantages to having a separate rule for the `<figcaption>` element to style its content, rather than using the rule for the containing element (the `<figure>` element)?

CHALLENGE 12.20

Write a code to float three differently colored `<div>` elements so that they are aligned as shown below:

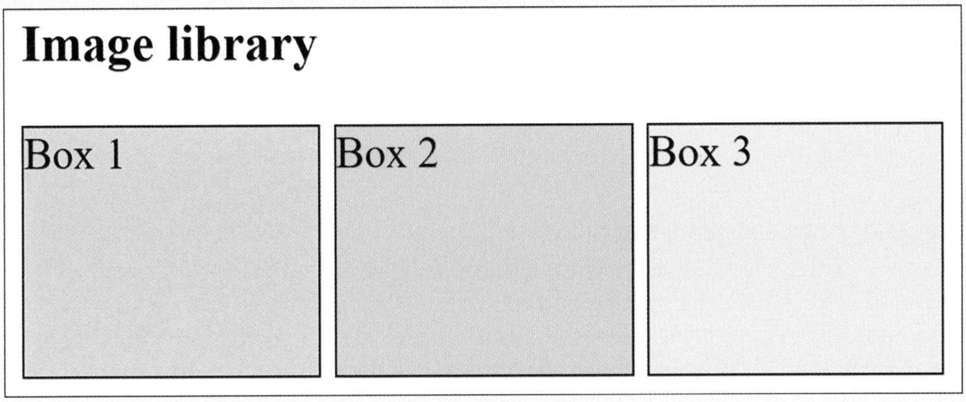

Image library

| Box 1 | Box 2 | Box 3 |

12.3.9 Clearing Obstructed Floated Elements

The `clear` property lets you specify whether a floated element should be moved down to prevent its positioning from being obstructed by other floated elements in its path. The property is typically used to solve the problem caused when the height of a floated element that is before another floated element prevents it from being placed as far as possible toward the left or right edge of the containing element. Figures 12.26 and 12.27 show an example of this problem, in which the fourth box is being blocked by the first from going all the way to the left, because its height makes it get in the way. The `body{}` rule specifies the width of the page and the properties in the `p{}` rule play the same functions as described in the previous example. The `font:size` in the `b{}` rule makes the size of the numbers larger and only used here to make the numbering of the boxes more discernible to aid the demonstration. The property is discussed more fully in Chapter 13.

To address the problem in the example, the `clear` property is used to move the fourth block down so that it can clear the obstruction. It is **non-inherited** and the values it commonly takes are listed in Table 12.1. Figure 12.28 shows how the property is used and Figure 12.29 the effect.

In the example, the fourth box is moved down so that its path is no longer obstructed and can be moved left as far as possible. To do this, the fourth `<p>` element is assigned to the "clearfix" class and the `.clearfix { clear: left; }` rule says to move the element. Using `both` as value would achieve the same result.

CSS
```css
body { width: 800px; }
b { font-size: 24px; }
p {
  width: 220px;
  margin: 5px;
  padding: 5px;
  background-color: #ffc0cb;
  float: left;
}
```

HTML
```html
<h2>Floating element obstruction</h2>
<p><b>1.</b><br>Lorem ipsum dolor sit amet, consectetur...</p>
<p><b>2.</b><br>Pellentesque dictum elementum augue sit...</p>
<p><b>3.</b><br>Cras mauris lacus, pulvinar non...</p>
<p><b>4.</b><br>Integer at dignissim quam, non fringilla...</p>
<p><b>5.</b><br>Nunc non finibus ipsum, eu blandit odio...</p>
<p><b>6.</b><br>Vivamus non nisi nec orci cursus...</p>
```

FIGURE 12.26 Demonstration of when a floated element's path is obstructed.

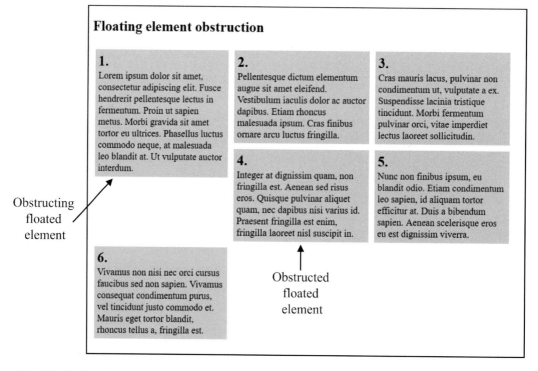

FIGURE 12.27 The rendered result of Figure 12.26.

TABLE 12.1

The Values Taken by the `clear` Property

Value	Function
left	Moves element down to clear the elements on the left that are blocking it.
right	Moves element down to clear the elements on the right that are blocking it.
both	Moves element down to clear the elements on both left and right blocking it.
none	Element is not moved.

```
CSS
body { width: 800px; }
b { font-size: 24px; }
p {
  width: 220px;
  margin: 5px;
  padding: 5px;
  background-color: #ffc0cb;
  float: left;
}
.clearfix { clear: left; }

HTML
<h2>Floating element obstruction solved</h2>
<p><b>1.</b><br>Lorem ipsum dolor sit amet, consectetur...</p>
<p><b>2.</b><br>Pellentesque dictum elementum augue sit...</p>
<p><b>3.</b><br>Cras mauris lacus, pulvinar non....</p>
<p class="clearfix"><b>4.</b><br>Integer at dignissim...</p>
<p><b>5.</b><br>Nunc non finibus ipsum, eu blandit odio...</p>
<p><b>6.</b><br>Vivamus non nisi nec orci cursus faucibus...</p>
```

FIGURE 12.28 Example usage of the `clear` property.

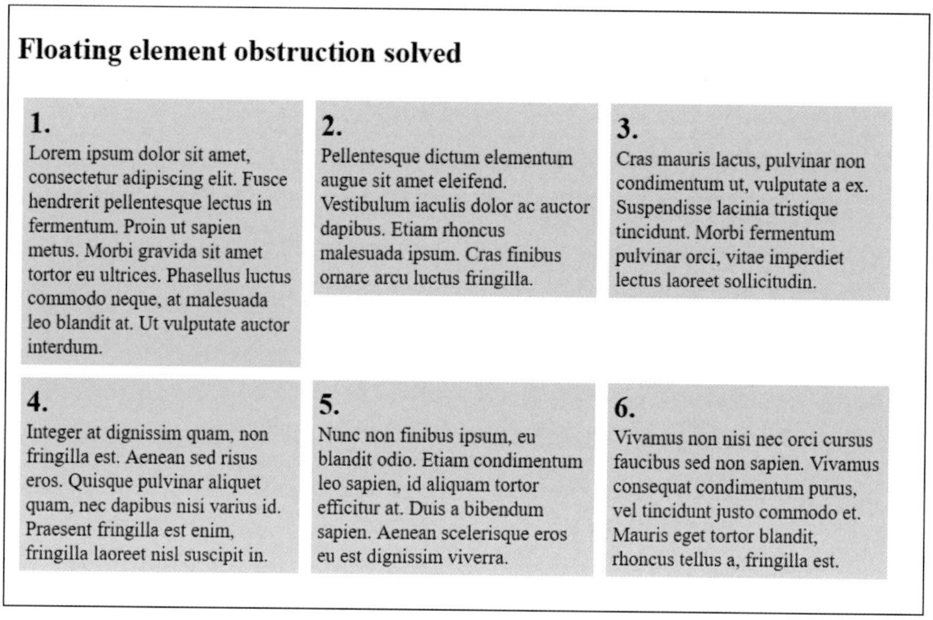

Floating element obstruction solved

1.
Lorem ipsum dolor sit amet, consectetur adipiscing elit. Fusce hendrerit pellentesque lectus in fermentum. Proin ut sapien metus. Morbi gravida sit amet tortor eu ultrices. Phasellus luctus commodo neque, at malesuada leo blandit at. Ut vulputate auctor interdum.

2.
Pellentesque dictum elementum augue sit amet eleifend. Vestibulum iaculis dolor ac auctor dapibus. Etiam rhoncus malesuada ipsum. Cras finibus ornare arcu luctus fringilla.

3.
Cras mauris lacus, pulvinar non condimentum ut, vulputate a ex. Suspendisse lacinia tristique tincidunt. Morbi fermentum pulvinar orci, vitae imperdiet lectus laoreet sollicitudin.

4.
Integer at dignissim quam, non fringilla est. Aenean sed risus eros. Quisque pulvinar aliquet quam, nec dapibus nisi varius id. Praesent fringilla est enim, fringilla laoreet nisl suscipit in.

5.
Nunc non finibus ipsum, eu blandit odio. Etiam condimentum leo sapien, id aliquam tortor efficitur at. Duis a bibendum sapien. Aenean scelerisque eros eu est dignissim viverra.

6.
Vivamus non nisi nec orci cursus faucibus sed non sapien. Vivamus consequat condimentum purus, vel tincidunt justo commodo et. Mauris eget tortor blandit, rhoncus tellus a, fringilla est.

FIGURE 12.29   The rendered result of Figure 12.28.

CHALLENGE 12.21

Write a code to position `<div>` elements as shown below, using the float property:

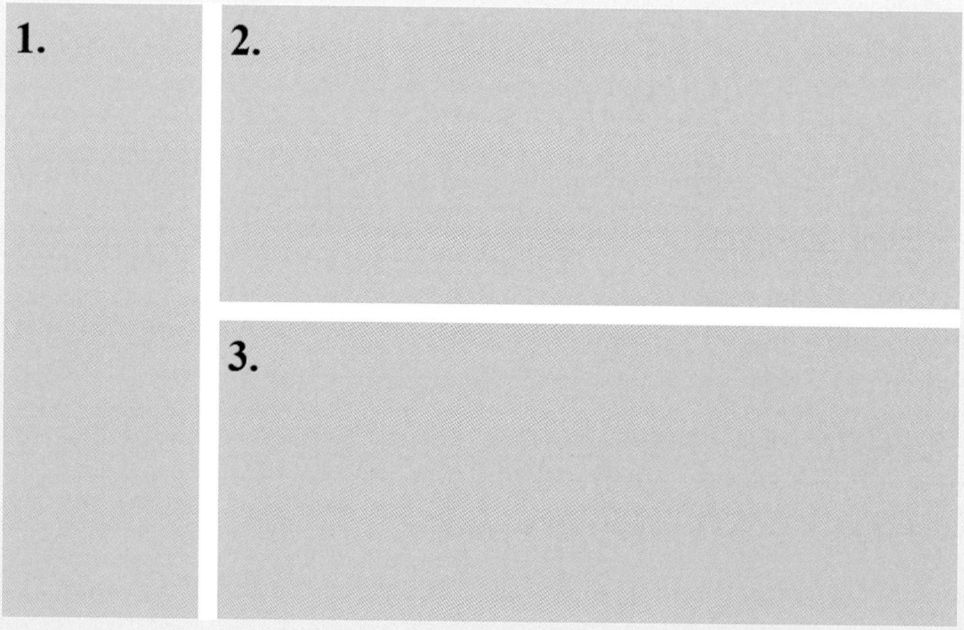

1.

2.

3.

12.3.9.1 A Common Problem with Non-Floated Parent Elements

It is sometimes desired to add a border around floated elements. In order to achieve this, it is necessary to place the floated elements in a containing element that is not floated. However, when a non-floated containing element contains only floated elements, browsers may display it as if it has a height of 0px. This means that if the `border` property is specified for it, the border is collapsed and displayed as a line above the floated elements, instead of around them. Figures 12.30 and 12.31 demonstrate this problem using a code similar to that in Figure 12.28. Notice how the border of the `<div>` element is collapsed into a top edge.

```
CSS
body { width: 750px; }
b { font-size: 24px; }
div { border: 1px solid black; }
p {
  width: 220px;
  margin: 5px;
  padding: 5px;
  background-color: #ffc0cb;
  float: left;
}

HTML
<h2>Collapsed parent-element problem</h2>
<div>
  <p><b>1.</b><br>Integer at dignissim quam, non fringilla...</p>
  <p><b>2.</b><br>Nunc non finibus ipsum, eu blandit odio...</p>
  <p><b>3.</b><br>Vivamus non nisi nec orci cursus...</p>
</div>
```

FIGURE 12.30   Demonstration of collapsed non-floated parent element.

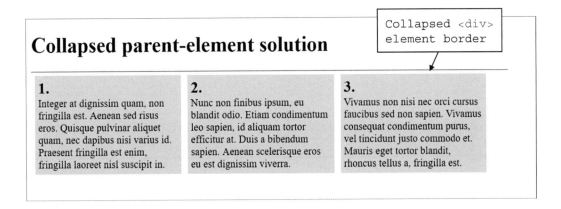

FIGURE 12.31   The rendered result of Figure 12.30.

Collapsed parent-element solution

1.	2.	3.
Integer at dignissim quam, non fringilla est. Aenean sed risus eros. Quisque pulvinar aliquet quam, nec dapibus nisi varius id. Praesent fringilla est enim, fringilla laoreet nisl suscipit in.	Nunc non finibus ipsum, eu blandit odio. Etiam condimentum leo sapien, id aliquam tortor efficitur at. Duis a bibendum sapien. Aenean scelerisque eros eu est dignissim viverra.	Vivamus non nisi nec orci cursus faucibus sed non sapien. Vivamus consequat condimentum purus, vel tincidunt justo commodo et. Mauris eget tortor blandit, rhoncus tellus a, fringilla est.

FIGURE 12.32 The rendered result of Figure 12.30 after adding `overflow`.

The problem demonstrated in the example can be solved in a number of ways, each of which has pros and cons and therefore suitable for different design situations. The following are some of the commonly used:

- Giving the containing element **specific height**.
- Floating the containing element.
- Specifying the `overflow` property on the containing element and giving it the value of `auto` or `hidden`. The property was introduced in Chapter 10 and is actually designed to handle the content overflow but works for this problem. To resolve the problem in Figure 12.31, `overflow:auto;` is simply added to the `div{}` rule in Figure 12.32. Figure 12.33 shows the result.

CHALLENGE 12.22

Write a code to display images in the same way as in Figure 12.32 instead of the text.

CHALLENGE 12.23

In what sort of situation do you think adding a border around floating elements as in Figure 12.32 would be desirable?

12.3.9.2 Multi-Column Content with Floats

Although CSS provides properties that are designed specifically for creating multi-column layouts, the `float` property can be used to produce a version of this. Note that a multi-column layout is different from what you have seen so far (e.g., in Figure 12.32). This is because whereas columns are clipped in the examples when the browser is reduced beyond the width of the content, in a float-based multi-column layout, the rightmost column moves to the left edge of the containing element as soon as there is not enough width-space for it, and this continues until all columns are in a single column at the left edge. Figures 12.33 and 12.34 show an example implementation.

CSS
```
.one, .two, .three {
  width: 250px;
  float: left;
  margin: 0px 10px 0px 5px;
}
```

HTML
```
<h2>Multi-column layout with float</h2>
<div class="one">In quis nibh eget nisl pharetra...</div>
<div class="two">Nulla eget varius tortor, a egestas...</div>
<div class="three">Morbi eget sem feugiat, pretium...</div>
```

FIGURE 12.33   Example of the use of float for multiple columns.

Multi-column layout with float

In quis nibh eget nisl pharetra varius. Mauris eget velit turpis. Vivamus erat mauris, pretium pharetra risus eget, ornare rutrum tortor. In sollicitudin congue porttitor. Nunc ante sem, vehicula sit amet feugiat nec, pharetra vitae velit. Suspendisse nec ipsum congue, fermentum dolor elementum, volutpat dolor. Vivamus lobortis id erat ac scelerisque.

Nulla eget varius tortor, a egestas risus. Nunc interdum commodo hendrerit. Aliquam rutrum ligula elit, vitae efficitur dolor ultrices sollicitudin. Duis leo neque, porttitor id laoreet ac, imperdiet vel leo. Vivamus mollis ac purus non fermentum. Fusce mattis sagittis enim, tincidunt pretium enim rutrum ac. Donec maximus accumsan augue non efficitur. Class aptent taciti sociosqu ad litora torquent per conubia nostra, per inceptos himenaeos.

Morbi eget sem feugiat, pretium velit in, vehicula elit. Sed suscipit mi eu lorem ultrices fringilla. Integer tempus dapibus dui, a pharetra eros aliquet sed. Phasellus elementum neque enim, et sagittis mauris posuere a. Curabitur non purus ut orci facilisis facilisis nec id ligula. Mauris quis ipsum sit amet ligula congue gravida. Donec porta dui erat, non tristique nibh lobortis ut.

FIGURE 12.34   The rendered result of Figure 12.33.

CHALLENGE 12.24

Create a three-column layout with each column having its heading.

12.4 Multi-Column Layout

Multi-column layouts produced using CSS multi-column properties behave differently from float-based ones. More specifically, they behave more typically, in that the columns resize and text wraps accordingly as the browser window is resized. Multi-column layouts are invaluable in content design because they help achieve various goals. The primary one is to vertically divide the content on a wide screen into smaller chunks, so that the text is easier to read, since text lines that are too long can make reading difficult. As well as making the text easier to be read, columns improve the look and feel of the content presentation, because they increase the amount of white space in a presentation. The amount of space between columns, known as **gutter**, also plays a role in this. Columns can also be used to separate topics. For example, main text can be separated from excerpts or a list of links. You should know too that columns that are too narrow can make the text difficult to be read. Table 12.2 lists the CSS properties used to create and style columns. They are all **non-inherited**.

TABLE 12.2

Multi-Column Properties

Property	Function
column-count	Specifies the number of columns into which to divide an element's content. The values taken are number or the keyword auto (which means the number is determined by other properties, such as column-width).
column-width	Suggests a column width around which the browser can work to create scalable layouts to fit different screen sizes. The values taken include **length values** (e.g., px and em) and auto.
columns	Shorthand property for specifying column-width and column-count together, which can be in any order. It takes the values of these properties and auto.
column-span	Specifies how an element should span columns. The values allowed include all (which says to span all columns) and none (which says to span only one column).
column-fill	Specifies how contents are divided into columns. The values allowed are balance (which makes the contents in all columns the same height) and auto (which makes content fill all the space available in one column before going to the next).
column-gap	Specifies the size of the space between columns (i.e., gutter). The values allowed include the keyword normal (which says to use the browser's default setting) and **length values** (e.g., px and em).
column-rule-width	Specifies the width of the line drawn between columns. The values allowed include **keywords** (e.g., thin, medium, or thick) and **length values** (e.g., px and em).
column-rule-color	Specifies the color of the line drawn between columns. Color value can be in name, rgb, rgba, hsl, and hsla.
column-rule-style	Specifies the type of the line drawn between columns. It takes the same values as the border-style property (i.e., none, hidden, dotted, dashed, solid, double, groove, ridge, inset, and outset), discussed in Chapter 10.
column-rule	Shorthand property for specifying column-rule-width, column-rule-color, and column-rule-style, in any order.

> **NOTE: Multi-column properties and vendor prefixes**
>
> The multi-column properties are some of the CSS properties that are implemented differently by browsers and require the use of vendor prefixes to ensure that they are rendered correctly in as many browsers as possible. You will notice them in the examples and can find more about them in Chapter 8.

12.4.1 `columns` and `column-span`

Figures 12.35 and 12.36 show how the `columns` and `column-span` properties are used and the result.

In the example, the `div{}` rule specifies to create three 100px columns. The `.article1{}` rule says to make the `<h2>` element of `class="article1"` span only the first column (i.e., the default) and the `.article2{}` rule says to make the `<h2>` element of `class="article2"` span all the three columns. Note that even with the use of vendor prefixes, as of time of writing, Firefox does not support the `column-span` property and span is always one column.

```
CSS
div {
  columns: 3 100px;
  -webkit-columns: 3 100px; /* Chrome, Safari, Opera */
  -moz-columns: 3 100px; /* Firefox */
}
.article1 {
  column-span: none;
  -webkit-column-span: none;/* Chrome, Safari, Opera */
  -moz-column-span: none;/* Firefox */
}
.article2 {
  column-span: all;
  -webkit-column-span: all; /* Chrome, Safari, Opera */
  -moz-column-span: all;/* Firefox */
}

HTML
<div>
  <h2 class="article1">This heading uses default setting...</h2>
  Lorem ipsum dolor sit amet, consectetur adipiscing elit...
</div>
<br>
<div>
  <h2 class="article2">This heading uses a setting of...</h2>
  Aenean suscipit accumsan elit, non bibendum magna fringilla...
</div>
```

FIGURE 12.35 Example usage of `columns` and `column-span` properties.

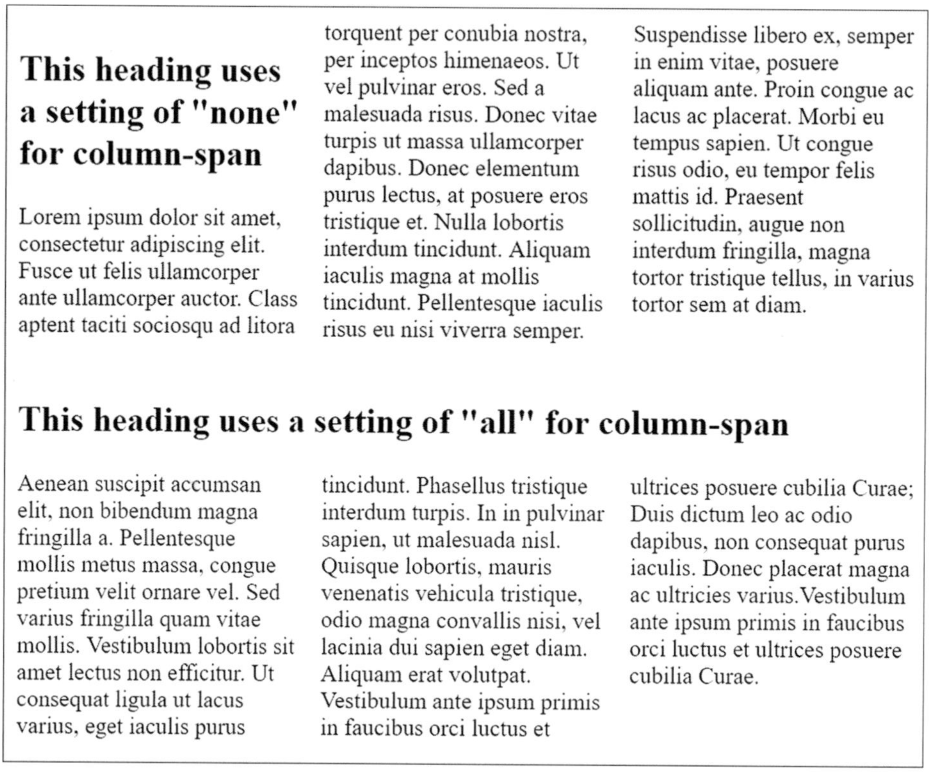

This heading uses a setting of "none" for column-span

Lorem ipsum dolor sit amet, consectetur adipiscing elit. Fusce ut felis ullamcorper ante ullamcorper auctor. Class aptent taciti sociosqu ad litora torquent per conubia nostra, per inceptos himenaeos. Ut vel pulvinar eros. Sed a malesuada risus. Donec vitae turpis ut massa ullamcorper dapibus. Donec elementum purus lectus, at posuere eros tristique et. Nulla lobortis interdum tincidunt. Aliquam iaculis magna at mollis tincidunt. Pellentesque iaculis risus eu nisi viverra semper. Suspendisse libero ex, semper in enim vitae, posuere aliquam ante. Proin congue ac lacus ac placerat. Morbi eu tempus sapien. Ut congue risus odio, eu tempor felis mattis id. Praesent sollicitudin, augue non interdum fringilla, magna tortor tristique tellus, in varius tortor sem at diam.

This heading uses a setting of "all" for column-span

Aenean suscipit accumsan elit, non bibendum magna fringilla a. Pellentesque mollis metus massa, congue pretium velit ornare vel. Sed varius fringilla quam vitae mollis. Vestibulum lobortis sit amet lectus non efficitur. Ut consequat ligula ut lacus varius, eget iaculis purus tincidunt. Phasellus tristique interdum turpis. In in pulvinar sapien, ut malesuada nisl. Quisque lobortis, mauris venenatis vehicula tristique, odio magna convallis nisi, vel lacinia dui sapien eget diam. Aliquam erat volutpat. Vestibulum ante ipsum primis in faucibus orci luctus et ultrices posuere cubilia Curae; Duis dictum leo ac odio dapibus, non consequat purus iaculis. Donec placerat magna ac ultricies varius.Vestibulum ante ipsum primis in faucibus orci luctus et ultrices posuere cubilia Curae.

FIGURE 12.36   The rendered result of Figure 12.35.

CHALLENGE 12.25

Write a code that displays something similar to the following, using your own content for the text:

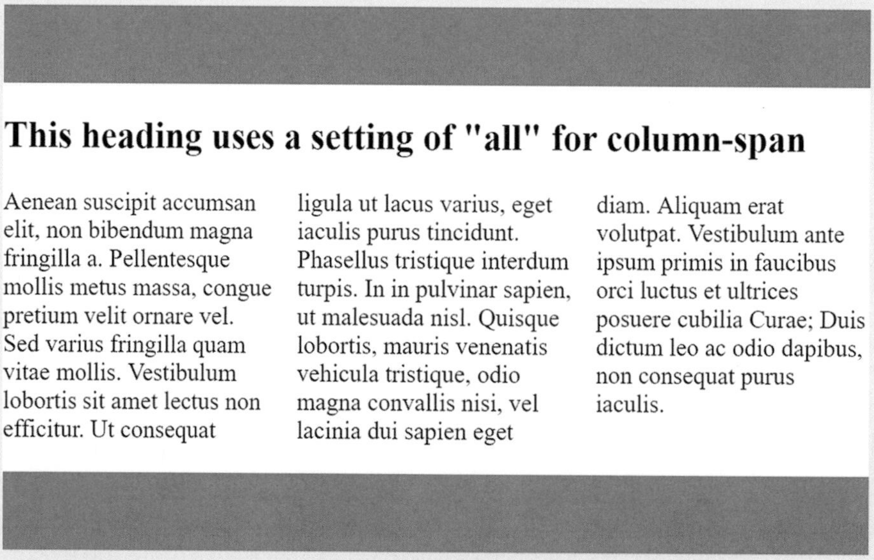

This heading uses a setting of "all" for column-span

Aenean suscipit accumsan elit, non bibendum magna fringilla a. Pellentesque mollis metus massa, congue pretium velit ornare vel. Sed varius fringilla quam vitae mollis. Vestibulum lobortis sit amet lectus non efficitur. Ut consequat ligula ut lacus varius, eget iaculis purus tincidunt. Phasellus tristique interdum turpis. In in pulvinar sapien, ut malesuada nisl. Quisque lobortis, mauris venenatis vehicula tristique, odio magna convallis nisi, vel lacinia dui sapien eget diam. Aliquam erat volutpat. Vestibulum ante ipsum primis in faucibus orci luctus et ultrices posuere cubilia Curae; Duis dictum leo ac odio dapibus, non consequat purus iaculis.

12.4.2 `column-count`, `column-rule`, and `column-gap`

Figures 12.37 and 12.38 show how the `column-count`, `column-gap`, and `column-rule` properties are used and the result. The properties have the effects described earlier in Table 12.2. The rule specifies to three columns, with 25px gutters between them as well as blue lines.

```
CSS
div {
  column-count: 3;
  -webkit-column-count: 3;
  -moz-column-count: 3;

  column-gap: 25px;
  -webkit-column-gap: 25px;
  -moz-column-gap: 25px;

  column-rule: 2px solid #0000ff;
  -webkit-column-rule: 2px solid #0000ff;
  -moz-column-rule: 2px solid #0000ff;
}

HTML
<div>
  <h2>Investigationes demonstraverunt lectores</h2>
  Lorem ipsum dolor sit amet, consectetuer adipiscing elit,...
</div>
```

FIGURE 12.37 Using `column-count`, `column-gap`, and `column-rule` properties.

Investigationes demonstraverunt lectores

Lorem ipsum dolor sit amet, consectetuer adipiscing elit, sed diam nonummy nibh euismod tincidunt ut laoreet dolore magna aliquam erat volutpat. Ut wisi enim ad minim veniam, quis nostrud exerci tation ullamcorper suscipit lobortis nisl ut aliquip ex ea commodo consequat. Duis autem vel eum iriure dolor in hendrerit in vulputate velit esse molestie consequat, vel illum dolore eu feugiat nulla facilisis at vero eros et accumsan et iusto odio dignissim qui blandit praesent luptatum zzril delenit augue duis dolore te feugait nulla facilisi. Nam liber tempor cum soluta nobis eleifend option congue nihil imperdiet doming id quod mazim placerat facer possim assum. Typi non habent claritatem insitam; est usus legentis in iis qui facit eorum claritatem. Investigationes demonstraverunt lectores legere me lius quod ii legunt saepius.

FIGURE 12.38 The rendered result of Figure 12.37.

CHALLENGE 12.26

Modify the code in Figure 12.37 to make the heading span all columns.

12.4.3 `column-fill`

As of time of writing, the `column-fill` property is only supported by Firefox and the `-moz-` prefix must be used for it to recognize it. Figure 12.39 shows how it is used and Figure 12.40 the result. The `div{}` rule specifies the number of columns and the rule. The `.article1{}` and `.article2{}` rules specify different values for the `column-fill` property. Notice that the `div{}` rule only takes effect when the value for `column-fill` is `balance`.

```
CSS
div {
  column-count: 3;
  -moz-column-count: 3;
  -webkit-column-count: 3;

  column-rule: 2px solid #0000ff;
  -moz-column-rule: 2px solid #0000ff;
  -webkit-column-rule: 2px solid #0000ff;
}
.article1 {
  column-fill: auto;
  -moz-column-fill:auto;
}
.article2 {
  column-fill: balance;
  -moz-column-fill: balance;
}

HTML
<h2>Investigationes demonstraverunt lectores</h2>
<div class="article1">
   Lorem ipsum dolor sit amet, consectetuer...
</div>
<br>
<h2>Investigationes demonstraverunt lectores</h2>
<div class="article2">
   Lorem ipsum dolor sit amet, consectetuer...
</div>
```

FIGURE 12.39   Example usage of the `column-fill` property.

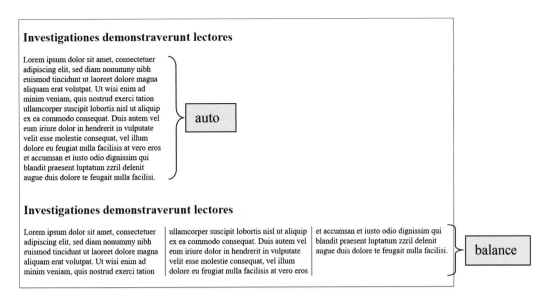

FIGURE 12.40   The rendered result of Figure 12.39.

CHALLENGE 12.27

Write a code that displays something similar to the one below. Please note that the column dividers are double lines.

Investigationes demonstraverunt lectores

| Lorem ipsum dolor sit amet, consectetuer adipiscing elit, sed diam nonummy nibh euismod tincidunt ut laoreet dolore magna aliquam erat volutpat. | Ut wisi enim ad minim veniam, quis nostrud exerci tation ullamcorper suscipit lobortis nisl ut aliquip ex ea commodo consequat. Duis autem | vel eum iriure dolor in hendrerit in vulputate velit esse molestie consequat, vel illum dolore eu feugait nulla facilisis at vero eros et accumsan et iusto odio | dignissim qui blandit praesent luptatum zzril delenit augue duis dolore te feugait nulla facilisi. |

12.5 Useful Info

12.5.1 Web Links

CSS specifications: w3.org/standards

Web development documents: docs.webplatform.org

Accessibility: w3.org/WAI/tutorials, webaim.org

CSS tutorials (*Here are just a few free tutorial sites on CSS and other Web languages*): w3.org/wiki, html5rocks.com, sitepoint.com, w3schools.com, codecademy.com, quackit.com, developer.mozilla.org/en-US/docs/Web tutorialspoint.com, htmldog.com, htmlcodetutorial.com, echoecho.com, learn.shayhowe.com, html.net, tizag.com, cssbasics.com, cordova.apache. org, developers.google.com, csszengarden.com, webdesignermag.co.uk, css. maxdesign.com.au

Browser compatibility info: caniuse.com

13

Text: Typefaces and Fonts

13.1 Introduction

In Chapter 3, how HTML elements are used to add and structure text was discussed. CSS allows you to control the appearance of such text in various ways. Some of these include specifying typefaces, fonts, size, and style. These text characteristics play many important roles in Web design, including influencing how users perceive a page. In this chapter, the CSS properties used to specify these text characteristics and the guidelines on how best to use the characteristics are discussed.

13.2 Learning Outcomes

After studying this chapter, you should:

- Be aware of the anatomy of a typeface.
- Be able to specify fonts, font size, style, and weight and know how to best use them.

13.3 Anatomy of Type

The properties CSS provides for styling text are derived largely from the characteristics of letterforms and characters, that is, the shapes of the letters and characters that constitute text. The characteristics of letterforms, illustrated in Figure 13.1, determine the way different types of letterform fit together, the appearances of text, and the design situations for which they are suitable. The art and techniques of designing letterforms, which is usually described as **typography** or **type design**, is typically out of the scope of Web design, but there are enough types available to suit almost any design situation.

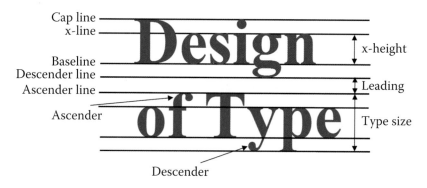

FIGURE 13.1   The main characteristics of a type.

13.4 Typefaces and Fonts

A typeface (or type) is a unique set of letterforms and characters (or glyphs or symbols) with common visual design features. A collection of related typefaces that share common design features and name is referred to as a **type family**. A common type family is the Arial family, which includes Arial, Arial Black, Arial Narrow, and Arial Rounded MT Bold. A **font**, on the other hand, is a specific combination of size, style, and weight of a typeface; for example, "Times New Roman 12pt bold" is a font, and so is "Times New Roman 14pt bold," both of which are derived from the Times New Roman typeface. The fonts of a typeface are altogether known as a **family of fonts** or a **font family**. The two terms, typeface and font, are commonly used interchangeably. In CSS, it is the font that is favored and the two primary CSS components used for specifying it are the `font-family` property and the `@font-face` at-rule.

13.4.1 `font-family`

The `font-family` property allows a typeface or a list of typefaces to be specified for the text inside selected element or elements. It is **inherited** and the two types of values it takes are described in Table 13.1.

A font family name or a generic font family name can be specified alone, or the two can be specified together. When the two are used together, the generic family name is placed last. It is good practice to specify a generic family name, as this ensures that the essence of a design is largely maintained even when the specified font is not available. How it works is that when the browser displays a document, it uses the first font from the list that it can find. Figures 13.2 and 13.3 show an example of how the property is used and the result.

In the example, the `body{}` rule tells the browser to use Times, but if this is not available to use "Times New Roman," and if this is not found to use Georgia, and if this is not available use any *serif* font. The `h3{}` and `p.author{}` rules are interpreted similarly. A prioritized list of fonts specified in the `font-family` property is known as a **font stack** and various suggestions can be found on the Web.

TABLE 13.1

The Values Supported by the `font-family` Property

Value	Function
`<family-name>`	This is the name of a font family, such as "Times" and "Helvetica." **Font-family names containing whitespace are enclosed in quotes**. If a list is specified (which is good practice because there is usually no guarantee that the only font specified will be available on the user's system), the **names on the list are comma-separated and prioritized** according to suitability or preference.
`<generic-name>`	Generic font family names are keywords and those supported are serif, sans serif, monospace, cursive, and fantasy. They **must not be in quotes**. Generic font families are used as fallback to enable the browser to use the closest alternative when the specified font is not found. When a list of names is specified, the names must be comma-separated.

CSS
```
body { font-family: Times, "Times New Roman", Georgia, serif; }
h3 { font-family: Verdana, Arial, Helvetica, sans-serif; }
p.author { font-family: "Courier New", Courier, monospace; }
```

HTML
```
<h3>Origin of All</h3>
<p class="author">by Wu Knows</p>
<p>Lorem ipsum dolor sit amet, consectetur adipiscing elit.
   Etiam id gravida...</p>
```

FIGURE 13.2   Example usage of the `font-family` property.

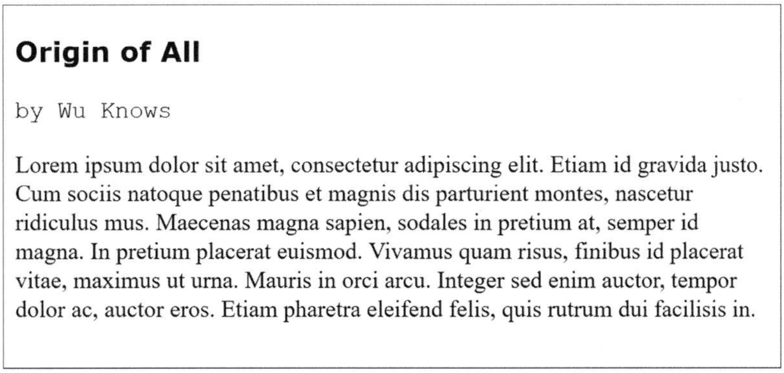

FIGURE 13.3   The result of Figure 13.2.

CHALLENGE 13.1

Why is the `font-family` declaration in the rule below invalid?

```
body { font-family: Gill Sans Extrabold, Helvetica, sans-
serif; }
```

CHALLENGE 13.2

When you change the order of the rules in Figure 13.2, the fonts applied to the elements do not change. Can you explain why? *Hint*: Refer to specificity principle in Chapter 8.

13.4.2 `@font-face`

The `@font-face` at-rule allows online fonts and their URLs to be specified, so that copies can be downloaded for use within a page. Fonts that are downloaded from the Web for use in a page are known as **Web fonts**. They are very important in Web design, as they remove the restriction that specified fonts must be installed on the user's system. An additional advantage of the approach is that it allows the use of custom fonts. Table 13.2 lists the descriptors that the at-rule takes and their functions, and Figures 13.4 and 13.5 show the basic use of the at-rule and the result.

In the `@font-face{}` rule in the example, the `font-family` specifies a made-up name "My Serif Bold" to describe the font to be specified. This name could be anything, but **must be in quotes if it contains white space**. The `src` property uses the `url()` function to specify the name and location of the font. In this case, it says the font file is in the **fonts** folder/directory inside the folder in which the stylesheet referencing it is located. The `.one{}` rule uses the `font-family` property as normal to specify to use the font declared in the `@font-face{}` rule for the `<p>` element of `class="one"`, quoting the made-up name and a generic font to use if the specified one is not available.

In the example, all the glyphs in the specified font family are downloaded, even if only a small part of them will be used. To minimize the amount of font data downloaded, just the set of glyphs required can be specified using other descriptors listed in Table 13.2. For example, to limit the number of glyphs downloaded to include only those that represent the **normal** font-style, you would include the `font-style` descriptor and set its value to `normal`. Similarly, the `unicode-range` descriptor can be used to limit the set of glyphs downloaded. Figure 13.6 shows an example of how this is done. It says to download from the specified font family only the glyphs that represent normal characters in Latin and Japanese. The `font-style` descriptor, and others in the table (i.e., `font-stretch`, `font-weight`, and `font-variant`), are fully discussed later in this chapter as CSS properties.

TABLE 13.2

Descriptors Used in the `@font-face` at-rule

Descriptor	Function
font-family	Specifies a name (which can be any name) that will be used as the value of the font-family property in the CSS rule.
src	Specifies from where to get the font to be used. It takes a list of comma-separated local() and/or url() functions, each containing different addresses of the font.
font-stretch	Specifies normal, condensed (semi-, extra-, ultra-), or expanded (semi-, extra-, ultra-) form of a font.
font-weight	Specifies the weight or boldness of the specified font (values include normal, bold, lighter, bolder, and numbers between 100 and 900 for bold).
font-style	Specifies italic or oblique of the specified font. Values include normal, italic, and oblique.
font-variant	Shorthand for longhand properties used for specifying font variations for a specified font.
unicode-range	Specifies the range of Unicode code-points to which the @font-face rule applies. Value is a comma-separated list Unicode range values, each of which can be **single code-point** (e.g., U+0025), **interval range**, which specifies the start and end of the range (e.g., U+0025-00FF, i.e., U+0025–U+00FF), and **wildcard range** (e.g., U+5??, i.e., U+500–U+5FF). "?" stands for any hexadecimal number.

```
CSS
@font-face {
  font-family: "My Serif Bold";
  src: url("fonts/VeraSeBd.ttf");
}
p.one { font-family: "My Serif Bold", serif; }
h3 { font-family: Verdana, Arial, Helvetica, sans-serif; }

HTML
<h3>Font-face at-rule</h3>
<p class="one">This text is styled using the downloaded...</p>
<p class="two">This text is styled using the default...</p>
```

FIGURE 13.4 A basic use of the `@font-face` at rule.

Font-face at-rule

This text is styled using the downloaded VeraSeBd font.

This text is styled using the default local font.

FIGURE 13.5   The result of Figure 13.4.

```
CSS
@font-face {
  font-family: "My Serif Bold";
  font-style: normal;
  src: url("fonts/VeraSeBd.ttf");
  unicode-range: U+000-5FF, U+3000-9FFF;
}
p.one { font-family: "My Serif Bold", serif; }
h3 { font-family: Verdana, Arial, Helvetica, sans-serif; }

HTML
<h3>Font-face at-rule</h3>
<p class="one">This text is styled using the downloaded...</p>
<p class="two">This text is styled using the default...</p>
```

FIGURE 13.6   Limiting the amount of font data downloaded with the @font-face at rule.

CHALLENGE 13.3

Implement the example in Figure 13.4 and then misspell the family name in the font-family declaration to see if the generic alternative used by the browser resembles the specified font.

13.4.2.1 Providing Broad Browser Support

Different Web browsers support different font file formats, therefore in order to ensure that as many users as possible get to see a design as intended, it is important to provide a font in all the commonly used formats. One of the benefits of the @font-face rule is that it allows multiple sources to be specified with the src descriptor. How this is done is shown in Figure 13.7.

In the example, the local() tells the browser to check for the font specified on the user's system before attempting to download it. More than one local location is specified to account for the possibility of different file-naming conventions. The url() values specify the name and location for different font formats on the Web server. The format() values are used to specify the format of a font file. The formats specified are as of time of writing the five main formats, although the trend is more toward WOFF and WOFF2, because they are compressed and therefore load faster. They are also widely supported by browsers and

```
CSS
@font-face {
  font-family: "MyPreferredSerif";
  src: local("Afta Serif"),
    local("Afta-Serif"),
    url("fonts/AlfaSerif.eot"),
    url("fonts/AftaSerif.eot?#iefix")format("embedded-opentype"),
    url("fonts/AftaSerif.woff2") format("woff2"),
    url("fonts/AftaSerif.woff") format("woff"),
    url("fonts/AftaSerif.ttf") format("truetype"),
    url("fonts/AftaSerif.svg#AftaSerif") format("svg");
}
body { font-family: MyPreferredSerif, serif }

HTML
<p>This is Afta Serif.</p>
```

FIGURE 13.7   Providing multiple font format options.

with minimal licensing restrictions. With multiple font declarations, the browser basically goes through each in turn, using the first one it can successfully use. The order in which the formats appear in the example (i.e., **eot**, **woff2**, **woff**, **ttf/otf**, and **svg**) is arbitrary but the typically recommended. The order is generally based on various factors, such as the fonts that are most likely to be available and the fastest to load on most systems. This means that it can change according to the prevailing situations.

The `?#iefix` used with the `eot` value is to address font-loading problems with Internet Explorer 8 and below, although just a question mark is usually enough. The # in the **svg** value points to the ID of the `<font>` element that defines the **svg font** in the SVG file, so that only the font definition is loaded. Not including the hash will cause the entire SVG file to be loaded, including headers that may prevent the defined font from being recognized. The name after the # is the name given to the **svg font** when it was created. If not known, it can be found by opening the SVG font file in a text editor and looking at the beginning inside the opening tag of the `<font>` element. If all necessary formats for a font are not available for the font you want to use, the font can be converted to different formats, using, for example, online services, such as **fontsquirrel.com**, that provide format conversion. These websites convert fonts to just the specified format or provide a folder containing all the common font formats. Either way, they also typically generate the necessary CSS code for the `@font-face` rule. In all cases, once the `@font-rule` is set, the relevant font is specified in the `body{}` rule, using the `font-family` property as normal.

CHALLENGE 13.4

Download a font into a folder called "fonts," and then write a `@font-face{}` rule to use it.

In the examples in Figures 13.4, 13.6, and 13.7, the online font file, VeraSeBd.ttf, is downloaded from the same Web server that serves the HTML document and the corresponding stylesheet. However, an online font does not have to be located on the same server that serves the HTML document and the corresponding stylesheet. It can be downloaded from another server, in which case, the absolute URL for the location must be specified. Typically, you will get an online font from a **Web font** or **font-hosting service**, such as Google Fonts, Typekit, FontSquirrel, Fonts.com, Font Deck, and Cloud Typography. Using Web fonts from these services can typically be achieved through using the CSS @import rule, which is used to import rules from other stylesheets. Font-hosting services would typically generate the necessary @import rule for adding a font, which can then be copied and pasted. At Google Fonts, for example, all that was required to obtain the @import rule used in Figure 13.8 to get the result in Figure 13.9 was to choose the required font and character set and the rule was automatically generated.

GoogleFonts also generates a link that can be used in the <link> element to link to a font file on its server, much like when you link to an external stylesheet. For example, the following line links to the same font file used in Figure 13.8.

```
<link href="//fonts.googleapis.com/css?family=Indie+
  Flower" rel="stylesheet" type="text/css">
```

```
CSS
@import url(http://fonts.googleapis.com/css?family=Indie+Flower);
  .one { font-family: "Indie Flower", cursive; }
```

```
HTML
<h3>Import rule</h3>
<p class="one">This text is styled Google font.</p>
<p>This text is styled using the default local font.</p>
```

FIGURE 13.8   Using the @import rule to specify font.

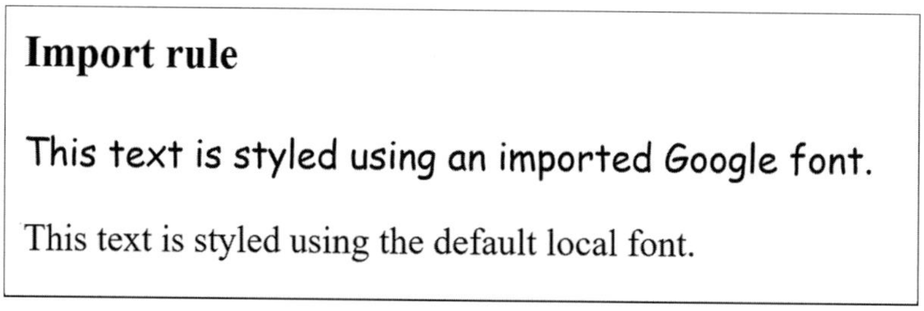

Import rule

This text is styled using an imported Google font.

This text is styled using the default local font.

FIGURE 13.9   The result of Figure 13.8.

CHALLENGE 13.5

Write a code that uses the <link> element to link to a font at www.google.com/fonts and then write a CSS to use it.

13.4.3 Fonts in Design

There are numerous typefaces, the result of a collection that has built up over centuries and still being added to today. This means that there is an incredibly wide variety of typefaces to choose from that both compare and contrast in characteristics, such as shown in Figure 13.10. The result of this is that identifying the most appropriate fonts for a design is seldom straightforward, if common fonts are not used. It often requires the consideration of various factors, such as similarities and differences typefaces, design situation, how well different typefaces combine, and availability.

13.4.3.1 Typeface Classifications

In order to make navigating and working with typefaces easy, people have tried to classify them. The most commonly known classification standard is the **Vox-ATypI classification**, which attempts to put typefaces into classes based on similarities and differences in their characteristics. However, the Vox-ATypI classification and indeed many classifications are seldom of much use to a beginner. A detailed understanding and interpretation is normally necessary to be able to make use of them productively. This is why they are mostly used by professional designers. Indeed, most text design programs, such as Word, simply list typefaces in alphabetical order. Only professional design programs, such as some of those by Adobe, offer them within classifications.

FIGURE 13.10   An illustration of variation in typefaces (all in 12pt).

Other ways of grouping typefaces often prove to be easier to use and more useful than classifications, including grouping them under:

- Those that have *serifs*, known as *serif* typefaces.
- Those that do not have *serifs*, known as *sans serif* typefaces.
- Those that simulate handwriting, known as script or cursive typefaces.
- Those that simulate fifteenth century Northern European manuscript decorative handwriting, known as decorative or fantasy typefaces.
- Whether they are suitable for body-text or display.
- Whether they are monospaced or proportionally spaced.

13.4.3.1.1 Serif and Sans Serif Typefaces

A *serif* is the extra detail, typically a line, at the end of the stroke of a letter, as illustrated in Figure 13.11. The origin of the word "*serif*" is said to be probably Dutch, German, and Latin, while that of "*sans*" is French. The "*sans*" means "without", and "*serif*" means "stroke." So, "*sans serif*" itself translates into "without stroke."

Traditionally, it is believed that **serif typefaces are easier to read in print**. Their strokes are supposed to guide the eyes along from one character to the next, making it easy to follow text. This is one reason *serif* typefaces are often **used for body of text in print**. Some also find them easier to read on screen, but others consider **sans serif typefaces to be more legible on screen** and think that the strokes in *serif* can create cluttering, interference, and lack of clarity, particularly when the text is small in size. In all cases, **sans serif typefaces are typically used for headings, labels, and titles**, as they tend to stand out when mixed with *serif*, thereby creating separation and attracting attention.

Whether *serif* or *sans serif* is used depends largely on the tone a design is intended to project. For example, for serious and conservative applications, *serif* typefaces are a good choice, whereas *sans serif* is more appropriate for projecting a more modern or contemporary feel and the more commonly used on the Web for the body of text. As to legibility, the difference between the two is unlikely to be significant, as long as other factors that affect legibility, such as text size and color, are addressed properly.

FIGURE 13.11   The difference between *serif* and *sans serif* typeface.

CHALLENGE 13.6

Compare and contrast *serif* and *sans serif* typefaces and then say which you would use for the following, giving your reasons:

- Headings
- Subheadings
- Body of text
- Emphasized words

13.4.3.1.2 Script and Decorative Typefaces

Examples of these typefaces are shown in Figure 13.12. **Script typefaces** are designed to look like handwriting. This means that they are mostly used to create the impression that a text has been created using pen, marker, or engraving. There are two kinds: those with joined-up lowercases (known as **scripts**), and those with all-separate letters (known as **cursive**). **Decorative typefaces** (sometimes called **fantasy typefaces**), on the other hand, are designed for visual impact, so they tend to be bold, have character, and can even be three dimensional. They can be *serif, sans serif*, or script, but are not as legible as plain *serif* or *sans serif* typefaces. Because they can be fashion-driven, they can, like any fashion, quickly go out of date and can also easily become boring after their initial impact, so overuse is not recommended. Also, as with most things that are decorative, they are more prone to provoke stronger reactions, which can be positive or negative, than typefaces that project neutral moods.

13.4.3.1.3 Body-Text and Display Typefaces

Body-text typefaces are those used in order to ensure text is easy to read. They are usually used for the body of text and small prints. Therefore, if there is a lot of text to deliver on a Web page, for example, these should be considered. **Display typefaces** are

Script typefaces

Decorative typefaces

FIGURE 13.12 Examples of script and decorative typefaces.

Body-text typefaces   Display typefaces

FIGURE 13.13   Examples of body-text and display typefaces.

generally those considered most useful at large sizes. For this reason, some are only available in uppercases. Some are also considered best suited for decorative purposes. They are usually used for situations where there is not a lot of text to read, such as in logos and for headlines and short text. Because some have different characteristics that project different looks, they are suitable for expressing specific moods. While body-text typefaces can be used successfully for display purposes, using display typefaces for reading purposes is likely to make text difficult to read. Compared to display typefaces, body-text typefaces are usually simpler, tidier, and more serious-looking, while display typefaces are relatively complex, less tidy, have character, and are more expressive; or perhaps more fun, even if some of them can also look weird and crazy. Figure 13.13 presents some common examples of each type.

13.4.3.1.4 Monospaced and Proportional Typefaces

The words "monospaced" and "proportional" refer to the amount of space used by each character of a typeface, which means that legibility, and indeed aesthetics, can be affected by whether a typeface is monospaced or proportional. In **mono-spaced typefaces**, every character uses the same (i.e., fixed) amount of space. Although they were typically designed for typewriters, and so possibly old-fashioned, monospaced typefaces are still used, but not widely. The most common use is for displaying computer source codes. Examples include Courier and Monaco. You may remember from Chapter 3 that the `<code>`, `<samp>`, and `<kbd>` elements display their content in monospaced fonts and are used to display computer code and outputs.

In **proportional typefaces**, different characters take up variable amounts of space. They are usually easier to read and more visually appealing than monospaced, because the space between words are relatively uniform. They are also more commonly used. Figure 13.14 shows an example of each type. Note the differences in the spaces between the words.

In monospaced typefaces, every character uses the same, or fixed, amount of space. They tend to be more difficult to read than proportional typefaces.	In proportional typefaces, different characters take up different amounts of space. They are usually easier to read and more visually appealing than monospaced typefaces and more commonly used.
Monospaced	Proportional

FIGURE 13.14 Example of monospaced and proportional typeface.

13.4.3.2 Choosing a Typeface

A number of factors influence the choice of the right typeface, some of which have already been implied earlier under typeface classification. More guidelines worth knowing about are discussed here.

13.4.3.2.1 About the Rules

You should know the rules that guide how to use typefaces and fonts effectively, but not be afraid to break them. Most of the rules are only there to inform about what has been tried and tested, but not cast in stones. As well as being seen as providing a safe way of working, they should be seen to serve as a comfortable starting point that gives the confidence to experiment with new things where possible. Essentially, knowing and understanding rules provides the knowledge necessary to make intelligent decisions about what rules to break and how to break them, and how to evaluate a design effectively. In many cases nothing different from what is tried and test is required, even if they are familiar and unexciting. There is a reason that some typefaces have been used in certain ways and for certain purposes for ages—they work well.

13.4.3.2.2 Legibility

Legibility is whether people are able to see, distinguish, and recognize the characters and words of a text. This should not be confused with **readability**, which more describes how easy the words and sentence structure of a text are to understand. A typeface should be used that has letters and characters that have good level of legibility. Typefaces that enable this include:

- Typefaces with conventional letterforms, that is, without novel shapes or characteristics, as these make it difficult for readers to quickly recognize letters.
- Typefaces with ample spacing, as very tight spacing can, again, make it difficult to recognize letters and words. Note, of course, that it is possible to increase letter-spacing for any typeface in most text production programs. Letter-spacing is discussed later in the chapter.
- Typefaces with x-height that is not too small, as a small x-height can make some letters less legible; for example, the smaller the x-height, the less distinguishable some lowercase letters, such as "c" and "e," become.

- Typefaces designed to enhance legibility, such as body-text typefaces discussed earlier. If numbers are involved, whether or not a typeface has numbers that are as legible as the letters should be checked.
- Typefaces which look similar across different operating systems and devices. For example, text that renders smoothly on a Mac may render less smoothly on a PC and be less legible.

13.4.3.2.3 Fitness for Purpose

Some typefaces are more suitable for certain audience and for projecting certain images or moods than others. An important aspect of choosing the right typeface for a design is to find which best fits the defined goals. Whether a typeface is fit for purpose is determined by multiple factors, ranging from its appearance to its history, including its original intent. Appearance contributes to the image or mood projected, while history contributes to appropriateness. For example, if a typeface is associated with the oppression of a people, it would be insensitive and inappropriate to use it in a design intended to celebrate the freedom of those people. Likewise, a typeface designed for a purpose is likely to be best used for that purpose.

Typeface should **match the image being projected**. For example, it would be inappropriate to use a playful-looking or fancy typeface for a business website, unless, of course, the business is about fun, as might be in the case of travel, holiday, or music websites. By the same logic, a playful-looking or casual typeface may be more appropriate for a celebration website than a formal, traditional, no-frills one like Garamond.

Typeface should **match the sense of aesthetics of the target audience**. For example, a typeface that works well with an adult audience might not be the most effective for children. The typeface on the left in Figure 13.15, for example, is more formal than the one on the right and more likely to be acceptable for adults, while the one on the right is more casual and more playful and more likely to be appreciated by children. Naturally, cheerful **text color** can also add to the fun for children.

Typefaces can also be used to **communicate sensory information**. To consciously experience the effects of different typefaces, **try a little experiment**: Study a collection of different typefaces, and you would soon find that it is possible to roughly

WEB DESIGN	**WEB DESIGN**
Web design requires a range of skills because it covers many different areas, such as graphic design, interfaces design, and user experience design.	Web design requires a range of skills because it covers many different areas, such as graphic design, interfaces design, and user experience design.

FIGURE 13.15   Formal (left) and less formal (right) typeface.

group them according to the character, personality, mood, or attitude they project. You probably would find that they project various senses, such as fun, seriousness, weirdness, time period, childlikeness, masculinity, femininity, and so on. You might even be able to sense that some actually suit some human personalities more than others; or one gender more than the other. In text design, the expressive properties of typefaces should not be overlooked and should be put to good use in evoking the desired mood. To choose the right typeface to communicate a particular type of sensory information, a good practice is to actually study a typeface and write down words that it "communicates" to you and compare these with the design goal.

CHALLENGE 13.7

State whether or not you think the sensory information communicated by the fonts in the example below matches or complements the words for which they are used? Also, give your reasons.

13.4.3.2.4 Typeface Range

Choose a typeface that has all the characters as well as enough variations to cover all the fonts, such as sizes, weights, italics, and mall caps, needed in a design. For example, some typefaces, such as display typefaces, only have uppercases; and while the letters of some may be all right, their numbers may not be very legible, or they may not have numbers at all, which means that if the use of numbers is required in a design they will not be the best choice to make. Likewise, if a typeface does not have a lot of fonts, then it would not be the best choice for a design that has an **extended hierarchy of text**. To have enough fonts for big and diverse projects, an extended type family, such as Arial or Helvetica, is usually the best, as extended families usually have a wide range of elements, including multiple weights, as well as full sets of characters and even *serif* and *sans serif* versions. The goal of choosing a typeface that adequately serves all the typographical needs of a design is best achieved by analyzing situations right at the beginning of a Web design project and mapping out the level of hierarchy required.

CHALLENGE 13.8

Why is a typeface that has a lot of fonts required for extended hierarchy of importance? Also, is using an extended type family for a personal website appropriate and why?

13.4.3.2.5 Combining Typefaces

The use of more than one typeface on a page is an acceptable and common practice, but it is not necessarily considered good practice to use too many. One school of thought is that no more than two should be used, but this is really just an arbitrary rule, although still a good recommendation. To some extent, whether or not to use more than one typeface depends on the quantity of text and the complexity. If there is very little text, using more than one typeface is hardly necessary. On the other hand, if there is a lot of text and/or the need to project different feels and purposes, then the use of more than one may be justified. By far the most common practice is to use two typefaces; one for the headings and subheadings, and the other for the body of text.

If more than one typeface is used, there should be enough difference between them to easily tell them apart, otherwise the exercise may be pointless. Also, it is likely to make people think an error has been made, thereby diminishing the quality of a design. Ways to ensure there is enough difference or contrast include using size, weight, structure (i.e., shape, e.g., *serif* or *sans serif*), and color (e.g., black and white), as well as choosing from different typeface classes. The general rule is to combine a neutral *serif* (i.e., an ordinary one) with a *sans serif*. Even though this may not create excitement, it is widely acceptable and unlikely to damage your reputation as a designer. When there are enough differences, some rather simple but elegant designs can result; for example, a *serif* and a *sans serif*, or *sans serif* typefaces from different classes, or two different fonts of the same typeface, can be combined. Figure 13.16 shows examples of typefaces with different characteristics combined.

Typefaces can also be mixed in various other creative ways. For example, different typefaces can be mixed in different cases. Figure 13.17 shows variations of the phrase "black magic," using only Times New Roman, Bradley Hand ITC, Century Gothic, and Monotype Corsiva typefaces.

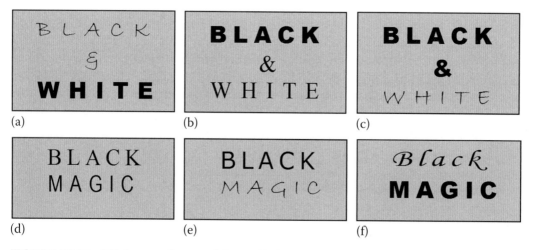

FIGURE 13.16   Mixing typefaces and fonts: (a) Bradley Hand ITC and Arial Black, (b) Arial Black and Times New Roman, (c) Arial Black and Bradley Hand ITC, (d) Times New Roman and Arial Narrow, (e) Verdana and Bradley Hand ITC, and (f) Monotype Corsiva and Arial Black.

BLACK magic (Times, Bradley H.)	BlacK magic (Times, Bradley H.)	blackMAGIC (Times, Bradley H.)
BlAcK MaGiC (Times, Bradley H.)	Black magic (Times, Bradley H.)	blackMAGIC (M. Corsiva, Bradley H.)
BlAcK MaGiC (Times, Bradley H.)	bLACK mAGIC (Times, Bradley H.)	BLAckmaGIC (Times, Bradley H., C. Gothic)

FIGURE 13.17 Mixing lower- and uppercase and typeface in text design.

CHALLENGE 13.9

In what types of situations might you combine fonts in the way shown in the box? Also, write a code to display one of the combinations or one of your own, also in mixed colors.

13.4.3.2.6 Typeface Availability

The typefaces used in an application will only be displayed correctly if they are installed in users' computers. If they are not installed, the browser uses default or substitute typefaces instead. This means that it is important to use only typefaces supported by type standards, such as PostScript, TrueType, OpenType, or FreeType, if the correct display of typefaces is essential to the integrity of a design. These standards provide similar typefaces, and at least one comes preinstalled with most operating systems. Common typefaces include Times New Roman (Microsoft)—Times on Apple, Arial (Microsoft & Apple), Courier, Georgia (Microsoft), Helvetica (Apple), Verdana (Microsoft), and Geneva (Apple). Commonly installed typefaces are known as **Web-safe fonts**, because most users are likely to have them on their systems. Web browsers are expected to support them, or at least one from each of the groups discussed earlier (i.e., *serif*, *sans serif*, script, decorative, and monospaced). If non-standard typefaces are used in a design, then access to them should be provided one way or another, using the methods shown earlier, such as the `@font-face` rule, `@import rule`, or the `<link>` element.

NOTE: Other Designers' Works

Paying attention to other designers' work can be a good source of knowledge and ideas, so the habit is worth cultivating. Some websites, such as `fontsinuse.com` provide collections of various examples.

> **NOTE: Personal preference in design**
>
> It is often difficult to separate subjectivity from objectivity in many aspects of design. Where typeface choice is through personal preference and it works, then this is fine. However, just because a typeface looks good to you does not mean that it will to most, so seeking a second or third opinion is useful. Also, just because a typeface looks good does not mean that it is appropriate, so it is useful to read up on the typeface, just in case there are things that disqualify its use for the intended purpose.

13.5 Size of Text

Like typefaces and fonts, the size of text plays multiple roles in textual content design. The two properties used for controlling it are `font-size` and `font-size-adjust`.

13.5.1 `font-size`

The `font-size` property is used to specify the size of font for selected HTML elements, pseudo-element, or pseudo-classes, and whatever value is set may change the size of other items, if they are in relative lengths like `em`, `percentage`, and `ex`. The property is **inherited** and Table 13.3 lists the types of values the property takes.

Each of the value-types or their combination is suitable for different Web design situations. For example, keywords make it easy to scale size up or down relative to the font size of body element, length-based types like `px` are good for accuracy, and relative types like `%` and `em` in combination with `px`, for example, are good for scalable and dynamic designs. Table 13.4 further defines standard length units.

TABLE 13.3

Types of Values Supported by the `font-size` Property

Type	Description
Absolute size	Comprises the absolute-size keywords, `xx-small`, `x-small`, `small`, `medium`, `large`, `x-large`, and `xx-large`, which are relative to the default size set by the user, which is regarded as medium.
Relative size	Comprises the keywords, `larger` and `smaller`, which are relative to the parent element's font size. The amount of increment or decrement is roughly the same as that between neighboring absolute-size keywords.
Percentage	Refers to a percentage of the font size of the parent element. The current size is 100%. For example, the default size of text in a browser is 16px, so, 16px is 100%., and a size of 32px is 200%.
Length	Refers to distance measurements, which can be **absolute units** (e.g., `px`, `pt`, `in`, `cm`, `mm`, `pc`) or **relative units** (e.g., `em`, `ex`, `ch`, `rem`, `vh`, `vw`, `vmin`, `vmax`)

TABLE 13.4

The Length Units Supported by the `font-size` Property

Length Units	Description
px	The actual size of a pixel (px) is relative to device and may represent one or more dots on the screen, depending on screen resolution. So, the same size will look different on different-resolution screens. The following are its relation to other absolute units: 1in (or 2.54 cm or 25.4 mm) is equivalent to 96px. 1px = 3/4pt; 1pt = 4/3px.
em	This represents the size of the text in the parent element and allows you to change the size of text for any child element relative to this. For example, if the size of text in the parent element is 12px, then 1em is 12px, and 1.5em is 18px. Em is also usually the width of the letter "m" of the relevant font.
rem	This unit (**root em**) represents the font size of the document's root element (i.e., `<html>` element). It is used mainly for scalable layouts.
ex	This represents the **x-height** of a font and is rarely used.
vh, vw, vmin, vmax	These are viewport-percentage units and specify lengths relative to the size of the viewport, thus, vh specifies 1/100th of height, vw 1/100th of the width, vmin 1/100th of the minimum value between the height and width, and vmax 1/100th of the maximum value between height and width.

Figures 13.18 and 13.19 show an example of how to use the `font-size` property with various types of values, and Figure 13.20 shows the result.

In the example, the `body{}` rule specifies a font and makes all text 12px. The `.xxsmall{}` and `.small{}` rules display the text in the elements of `class="xxsmall"` and `class="small"` in reduced absolute sizes that are based on the browser's default font size (i.e., 16px). The `.larger{}` rule displays text in enlarged relative size based on the font size specified for the parent element (`<body>`,

```
HTML
<body>
  <h1 class="xxsmall">xxSmall H1</h1>
  <h1 class="small">Small H1</h1>
  <h1 class="larger">Larger H1</h1>
  <h1 class="percent">200% H1</h1>
  <h1 class="em">1.5em H1</h1>
  <p>Lorem ipsum dolor sit amet, consectetur adipiscing elit.
     Etiam id gravida...</p>
</body>
```

FIGURE 13.18 HTML for demonstrating the use of font-size values.

```
CSS
body {
    font-family: Arial, Verdana, sans-serif;
    font-size: 12px;
}
.xxsmall { font-size: xx-small; }
.small { font-size: small; }
.larger { font-size: larger; }
.percent { font-size: 200%; }
.em { font-size: 1.5em; }
```

FIGURE 13.19   CSS for HTML in Figure 13.18.

xxSmall H1

Small H1

Larger H1

200% H1

1.5em H1

Lorem ipsum dolor sit amet, consectetur adipiscing elit. Etiam id gravida justo. Cum sociis natoque penatibus et magnis dis parturient montes, nascetur ridiculus mus. Maecenas magna sapien, sodales in pretium at, semper id magna. In pretium placerat euismod. Vivamus quam risus, finibus id placerat vitae, maximus ut urna. Mauris in orci arcu. Integer sed enim auctor, tempor dolor ac, auctor eros. Etiam pharetra eleifend felis, quis rutrum dui facilisis in.

FIGURE 13.20   The result of Figures 13.18 and 13.19.

in this case). The .percent{} rule displays text at 200% (twice) larger than the font size of the parent element and, likewise, the .em{} rule displays text at 1.5 times larger than the font size of the parent element. Note that if no font size is specified for the body element, the size of the element usually defaults to default browser size.

CHALLENGE 13.10

In the example in Figure 13.19, if no font size is specified for the <body> element, what font size applies?

13.5.2 font-size-adjust

The font-size-adjust property is sometimes used with the font-size property to ensure the legibility of lowercase letters when a font is substituted. This is useful because sometimes when the specified first-choice font is unavailable and an alternative

```
p {
  font-family: Verdana, "Times New Roman", serif;
  font-size: 12px;
  font-size-adjust: 0.5;
}
```

FIGURE 13.21 Using the `font-size-adjust` property.

is used by the browser, lowercase letters in the alternative font might not be legible. The property is **inherited** and allows you to specify that the font size should be chosen based on the height of the lowercase letters (i.e., x-height) instead of the height of the upper-case letters. The values it supports are `none` and **number values**. The number is usually **set to the aspect ratio of the first-choice font**. The aspect ratio of a font is the **ratio of its x-height to its height** (i.e., x-height divided by the font size). See Figure 13.1 earlier for more on these properties. When the aspect ratio is specified, the browser basically adjusts the size of the available alternative font so that its aspect ratio matches the one specified. For example, in the example in Figure 13.21, the browser adjusts the aspect ratio of the alternative font to 0.58. More specifically, it multiplies the specified number by the font size of the first-choice font and adjusts the x-height of the lowercase letters of the alternative font to match the result. In the example, this x-height would be roughly 6 (i.e., 0.5 × 12px). You can find the aspect ratios for common fonts on the Web.

13.5.3 Font Size in Design

Font size is one of the elements of design that contribute to legibility and structuring of con-tent. A design would most certainly contain more than one font size. At the minimum, the heading would be of one size and the body of text, a much smaller size. While the structure created using different font sizes may remain relatively stable across different systems configurations, the same font size can produce varying levels of legibility, depending on various factors, such as typeface, screen resolution, operating system, delivery device, and target audience. Some of these factors and how to deal with them are discussed here.

13.5.3.1 Font Size and Typeface

A font size that is legible in one typeface may not be in another. For example, text that is in **10pt Arial** is legible, but the same text in **10pt Times New Roman** is smaller and less legible. This is why the choice of the font size is not usually made until typeface has been determined. **Most typefaces are legible at a size of 10–12pt** and suitable for body of text displayed on a standard computer screen.

13.5.3.2 Font Size, Operating Systems, Resolution, and Screen Size

Like with typefaces, the same font size can produce varying levels of legibility across operating systems. For example, a font size tends to be larger on a PC than on a Mac. Similarly, the same font size will appear smaller on a higher-resolution screen than on a lower-resolution screen. For example, the same text will be larger on 1024 × 768 than on 1920 × 1080. Also, differences in screen size such as exist between a standard screen and mobile devices' screen can cause a font size that is legible on one to be illegible in the other. This problem is commonly tackled in a number of ways. One is to create a different version of a design for each screen, using the best font size. Another is to use the **Responsive Web Design** (RWD) technique, which adapts font size (as well as other screen contents) to screen size. RWD is discussed more fully in Chapter 21. In all cases, it is good practice to try out a design on as many different system configurations as possible.

13.5.3.3 Type Size and Target Audience

The choice of font size can also depend on target audience, since age can influence how people perceive text. For example, children tend to prefer larger font sizes than adults. This is why children' books are typically in larger prints. Even some adults, specifically older adults, due to the effects of aging, prefer larger font sizes than younger adults. Ideally, **users should be allowed to change font size to suit their preference**. A table of comparison is given in Chapter 24 that includes other design elements worth knowing about.

13.5.3.4 Type Size and Visual Hierarchy

Another important role of font size in design is in creating **visual hierarchy of importance**, which is the use of progressively smaller sizes to attach varying levels of importance to different parts of content. Figure 13.22 shows an illustration that uses 18, 16, 14, and 12 pt.

Structuring text in this way (along with the application of other types of styling) guides the reader's eyes easily through the content of a design. There is no one correct set of sizes for achieving a good visual hierarchy, since what is suitable and acceptable depends on various factors, including typeface and screen size. However, the size used for the body of text should be the smallest in all cases, or at least not larger than those

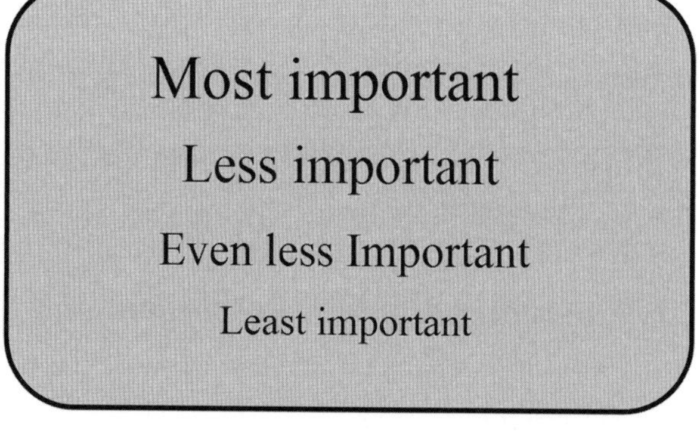

FIGURE 13.22   Visual hierarchy of important using font size.

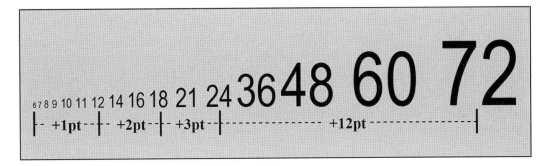

FIGURE 13.23 A typographic scale.

of headings or subheadings. One general guideline is that whatever the sizes used, they should be from the sizes in the **typographic scale**, shown in Figure 13.23.

The scale was developed in the sixteenth century by European typographers and it was believed that using only sizes from it can more easily produce an aesthetically pleasing design than selecting outside it. The scale has carried through till today and its variants are what are offered today in virtually any application that allows the font size to be specified. So, although other sizes can be used in Web design, it is good practice to consider the sizes from the scale or its variants in the first place. While the scale is in points (pt), the size ratios can be achieved using the units more commonly used in Web design, such as pixels (px), percentages (%), or EMs (em).

13.6 Weight of Text

The weight of text is its degree of boldness or thickness. The property used to control it is the font-weight property.

13.6.1 font-weight

The font-weight property is an **inherited** property that is used to specify the weight or boldness for the textual content of an element. While some fonts are only available in normal and bold, others are in various **weight levels**. This means that a variety of values are supported by the property, including normal, bold, lighter, and bolder keywords, and numeric weight values, which include 100 (thin), 200 (extra light), 300 (light), 400 (normal), 500 (medium), 600 (semi bold), 700 (bold), 800 (extra bold), and 900 (heavy). In order for these values to have an effect, the relevant typeface must have them. If the specified value is not available, the browser uses various schemes to determine an alternative. Note that weights hold no semantic meaning to the browser. If you want to assign importance to a text, you should use the <strong> element introduced in Chapter 3. Figure 13.24 shows how the font-weight property is used and Figure 13.25 the result.

```
CSS
body { font-family: Arial, Verdana, sans-serif;}
p.normal { font-weight: normal; }
p.bolder { font-weight: bolder; }
p.lighter { font-weight: lighter; }
p.bold { font-weight: bold; }
p.weight700 { font-weight: 700; }
p.weight900 { font-weight: 900; }

HTML
<body>
 <h3>Text Weight</h3>
 <p class="normal">This is normal.</p>
 <p class="bolder">This is bolder.</p>
 <p class="lighter">This is lighter.</p>
 <p class="bold">This is bold.</p>
 <p class="weight700">This is 700 weight.</p>
 <p class="weight900">This is 900 weight.</p>
</body>
```

FIGURE 13.24 Example usage of `font-weight`.

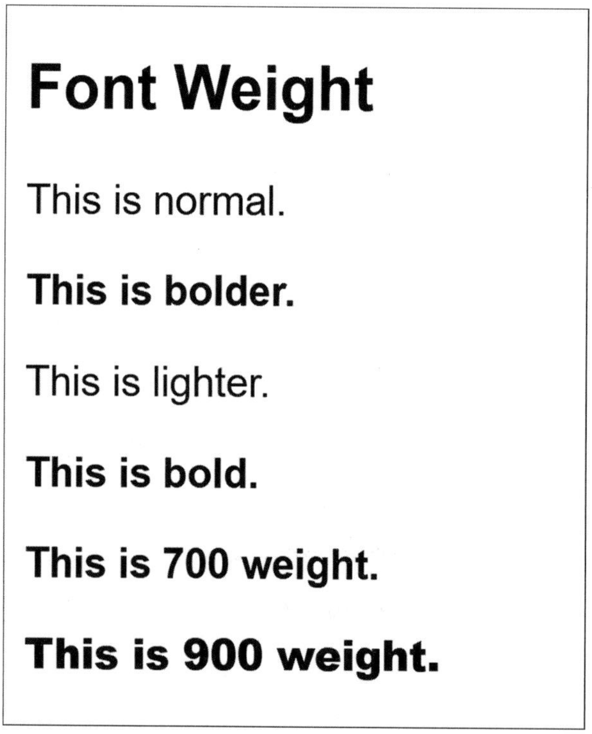

Font Weight

This is normal.

This is bolder.

This is lighter.

This is bold.

This is 700 weight.

This is 900 weight.

FIGURE 13.25 The result of Figure 13.24.

CHALLENGE 13.11

Use the `@import` rule to import a font from Google Fonts, as shown earlier, and then use the `font-weight` property to display all its weights to get a feel of the differences between the values.

13.6.2 Font Weight in Design

Font weight is used to achieve various goals. When combined with the font size it can help to enhance the effects of visual hierarchy of importance. It can be used to direct attention to a word or short texts, or give text a specific feeling. Used properly, different levels of weights can help the reader navigate a long complex document with little difficulty. However, the use of weights on too many texts can be confusing and disruptive, making the eyes jump about. Furthermore, saying too many words are important defeats the purpose of saying any is important. A balance is therefore necessary. The standard use of weights involves applying them to headings, subheadings, short messages, and page numbers (where applicable). Here are some guidelines to bear in mind.

- When selecting a typeface, an important consideration is whether or not it has a bold weight. The more weights it has the better, as this provides more options and opportunities to experiment.
- Bold texts should be bold enough to stand out from surrounding text, but not so bold that it is overpowering, as this can cause visual interference, which, for example, can be in the form of the eyes being continually drawn to back them.
- Weight level should not make text illegible at the intended size. Typically, lighter weights are better for smaller text sizes and while darker ones are more appropriate for larger text sizes.
- Using a single typeface with a variety of weights is always safe, but can be a bit too conservative in some contexts, while using more than one typeface can provide more variety and more visual contrast and interest.

CHALLENGE 13.12

Which of the two paragraphs below demonstrates a better use of weight and why?

Lorem ipsum dolor sit amet, **consectetur** adipiscing elit. **Vestibulum** vulputate rhoncus consequat. Sed dui sem, varius congue est non, placerat tempor metus.

Lorem ipsum dolor sit amet, **consectetur** adipiscing elit. **Vestibulum** vulputate rhoncus consequat. Sed dui sem, varius congue est non, placerat tempor metus.

13.7 Text Style

Text style refers to whether a font is displayed in upright or slanted form. The property used to specify it is `font-style`. It is **inherited** and the values it takes are `normal`, `italic`, and `oblique`. Normal is normal or regular font, `italic` fonts are generally cursive in appearance, while `oblique` fonts are the slanting versions of normal fonts. It is often hard to differentiate between italic and oblique, so they are interchangeable and it is not unusual where neither is unavailable in a font family for the browser to simulate them by sloping a normal font to achieve it. It is worth noting that using the property to make a text italic is not the same as using the `<em>` element introduced in Chapter 3, which gives text emphasis and also typically makes it italic. Figure 13.26 shows how the property is used and Figure 13.27 the result. Notice that the same font is used for italic and oblique.

```
CSS
p.normal { font-style: normal; }
p.italic { font-style: italic; }
p.oblique { font-style: oblique; }

HTML
<h3>Font style</h3>
<p class="normal">This paragraph is in normal font</p>
<p class="italic">This paragraph is in italic font</p>
<p class="oblique">This paragraph is in oblique font</p>
```

FIGURE 13.26   Example usage of `font-style` property.

Font style

This paragraph is in normal font

This paragraph is in italic font

This paragraph is in oblique font

FIGURE 13.27   The rendered result of Figure 13.26.

> **NOTE: Italics in design**
>
> Italicized text is harder to read than normal-styled text and so should be avoided for large amount of text. However, because italicized words are difficult to read and requires extra effort and concentration, it has been suggested that they tend to be more remembered than normal text. The implication of this is that words intended to be remembered may benefit from being italicized.

CHALLENGE 13.13

For which of the following would you use italic and why?

- An emphasized word.
- Body of text.
- Important words.
- A word to register in user's mind.

13.8 Useful Specialized Font Properties

Some font properties are for performing specialized functions and typically used by advanced CSS users for fine-tuning text presentation. Some of them and their functions are presented here, namely `font-feature-settings`, `font-synthesis`, `font-variant`, `font-stretch`, and `font`. More detailed discussion of them is beyond the scope of this book.

13.8.1 `font-feature-settings`

The `font-feature-settings` property is **inherited** and allows you to control over the advanced typographical features of OpenType fonts, which are **scalable fonts**. The values it supports are `normal` keyword (which specifies to use default settings) and **feature-tag-value** (which specifies the list of comma-separated OpenType feature tag-values to use). A tag value indicates which feature to turn on or off. The `on` and `off` keywords can be used. For example, `p { font-feature-settings: "smcp"; }` specifies to turn on the small-caps feature, and `p { font-feature-settings: "smcp" off; }` says to turn it off.

13.8.2 `font-synthesis`

The `font-synthesis` property is used to specify which missing typefaces, italic or bold, can be synthesized by the browser if needed. It is **inherited** and the keyword values it takes are `none` (says nothing should be synthesized), `weight` (says to synthesize bold), and `style` (says to synthesize italic). The following rule, p { `font-synthesis: bold;` }, for example, says to synthesize bold typeface for the content of the `<p>` element.

13.8.3 `font-variant`

The `font-variant` property is **inherited** and shorthand for all `font-variant` subproperties, such as `font-variant-caps`, `font-variant-numeric`, `font-variant-alternatives`, `font-variant-ligatures`, `font-variant-position`, and `font-variant-east-asian`. Table 13.5 lists the

TABLE 13.5

Longhand `font-variant` Properties

Property	Function
`font-variant-caps`	Specifies various sizes of capital letters, such as `small-caps` and `petite-caps`.
`font-variant-numeric`	Specifies alternatives for numbers, fraction, and ordinal markers, as in 1st, 2nd, and so on.
`font-variant-alternates`	Allows alternative names defined for fonts using `@font-feature-values`, which allows friendly or useful names to be given to fonts.
`font-variant-ligatures`	Specifies the type of ligature to use. A ligature is when two or more letters are combined into a single one to make text more legible. An example is combining f and i into fi. Many typefaces contain ligatures. This property is simply used to activate them.
`font-variant-position`	Specifies whether to activate the use of alternative small-size glyphs (characters) positioned as subscript or superscript, such as used in `<sup>` and `<sub>` elements. The values taken are normal, sub, and super.
`font-variant-east-asian`	Specifies the type of Asian characters to use.

functions of these properties. The rule, p {font-variant: small-caps; }, specifies to display the content of <p> element in small capital letters. The longhand would be p {font-variant-caps: small-caps; }.

13.8.4 `font-stretch`

The `font-stretch` property is used to select the most appropriate face (design), if more than one is provided for a font. Unlike the name might suggest, the property does not stretch a font, but simply selects a face. It is inherited and the values it takes are `normal` (which specifies a normal font face), `semi-condensed`, `condensed`, `extra-condensed`, and `ultra-condensed` (all of which specify a face more condensed than normal), and `semi-expanded`, `expanded`, `extra-expanded`, `ultra-expanded` (all of which specify a face more expanded than normal). Naturally, these values only take effect if a font provides the faces. Example usage: h1 {font-stretch: extra-expanded; }.

13.9 Specifying Multiple Font Properties

Many of the font properties introduced so far can be specified together with a single declaration. The property used to do this is the `font` property. It is **inherited** and the shorthand for setting `font-style`, `font-variant`, `font-weight`, `font-stretch`, `font-size`, `line-height`, and `font-family` properties. The `line-height` property specifies line spacing and discussed shortly in the chapter. The `font` property is also used to set the font of an element to a system default font, using specific keywords. The things to bear in mind are:

- Specifying the `font-size` and `font-family` properties is mandatory, except when using a keyword.
- Only `normal` and `small-caps` are allowed as values for `font-variant`.
- The values of `font-stretch`, `font-size-adjust`, and `font-kerning` are reset to initial values.
- The order is that if `font-style`, `font-variant`, and `font-weight` are specified, they must be before the `font-size` value. The `line-height` value must be immediately after `font-size` and preceded by a mandatory "/" (e.g., 12px/1.5em).
- The `font-family` property must be the last value specified.

The example, p{font: bold small-caps bolder 18px/3em "Open Sans" sans-serif;}, says to assign to the content of the <p> element bold `font-style`, small-caps `font-variant`, bolder `font-weight`, 18px `font-size`, and 3em `line-height`, and "Open Sans" *sans-serif* `font-family`.

CHALLENGE 13.14

One of the more commonly used of the more advanced properties just presented is the `font` property, as it can be efficient. Use the rule, `p { font: bold small-caps bolder 18px/3em "Open Sans" sans-serif; }` for a paragraph and experiment with the values to see how the property works.

13.10 Useful Info

13.10.1 Web Links

CSS specifications: w3.org/standards
Web development documents: docs.webplatform.org
Accessibility: w3.org/WAI/tutorials, webaim.org
CSS tutorials (*Here are just a few free tutorial sites on CSS and other Web languages*): w3.org/wiki, html5rocks.com, sitepoint.com, w3schools.com, codecademy.com, quackit.com, developer.mozilla.org/en-US/docs/Web tutorialspoint.com, htmldog.com, htmlcodetutorial.com, echoecho.com, learn.shayhowe.com, html.net, tizag.com, cssbasics.com, cordova.apache.org, developers.google.com, csszengarden.com, webdesignermag.co.uk, css.maxdesign.com.au
Fonts: http://www.fontspace.com/, http://www.dafont.com/
Testing codes: jsfiddle.net, codepad.org, jsbin.com, cssdesk.com
Browser compatibility info: caniuse.com

14

Text: Formatting and Decoration

14.1 Introduction

In addition to typefaces and fonts, various other factors play a role in shaping the look of text in design. These include alignment, indentation, spacing, capitalization, directionality, and decoration. This chapter presents the CSS properties used to control these factors.

14.2 Learning Outcomes

After studying this chapter, you should:

- Know how to align the content of an element as well as the element itself.
- Know how to create text indents and hanging indents.
- Be able to specify the text and line spacing and be aware of their role in design.
- Be able to specify letter cases and know how best to use them.
- Know the properties used to control text directionality and the importance.
- Know how to apply decoration, such as lines, emphasis marks, and shadows, to the text.
- Be able to style parts of an element using pseudo-elements,
- Be able to style text using pseudo-classes.
- Know how to style ruby text.

14.3 Content Alignment

Content alignment covers many goals in design, ranging from the alignment of each line of text in an element with the left, right, or both left and right edges of the element's box to the alignment of an entire block element within the browser window. These types of alignments are presented here.

14.3.1 `text-align`

The `text-align` property is **inherited** and allows you to specify the alignment of inline content in its parent block element's box. The commonly supported values are listed in Table 14.1.

Figures 14.1 and 14.2 show how the property is used and the result. The heading is aligned to the center and the paragraph justified.

TABLE 14.1

Commonly Used Values for `text-align`

Value	Function
left	Aligns text to the left edge of an element's box.
right	Aligns text to the right edge of an element's box.
center	Aligns text to the center of an element's box.
justify	Aligns text with both the left and right edges of an element's box.
justify-all	Same as justify, except that the last line is also justified.

```
CSS
h1, .author {text-align: center; }
p { text-align: justify; }

HTML
<h1>Text alignment</h1>
<p class="author">by James Hart</p>
<p>Lorem ipsum dolor sit amet, consectetur adipiscing...</p>
```

FIGURE 14.1   Example usage of the `text-align` property.

Text alignment

by James Hart

Lorem ipsum dolor sit amet, consectetur adipiscing elit. Aenean rhoncus ipsum sem, nec euismod libero porttitor eu. Nulla ut urna a ligula tincidunt condimentum quis sit amet diam. Morbi sed magna odio. Nam non ultricies eros. Cras vehicula lobortis justo. Ut congue dapibus odio, in cursus nisl consectetur quis. Aenean volutpat volutpat vehicula. Phasellus tempor purus sed commodo posuere.

FIGURE 14.2   The result of Figure 14.1.

CHALLENGE 14.1

Write a code that displays blocks of text with right, left, and center values. The border of each of the elements containing the texts must be shown and the boxes must be positioned at the center of the browser window. *Hint*: See Chapters 10, 11, and 12 about how to show borders and position boxes, respectively.

14.3.1.1 Text Alignment in Design

There are four types of text alignment: left, right, center, and justification. Because people read from left to right in Western culture, **left alignment** makes text easier to read than right or center alignment. It is, therefore, the *de facto* alignment for the Western audience. The reverse is the case with **right alignment**, which is used where people read from right to left, such as the Middle East, although it is also used simply to express style in design. In contrast, **center alignment** is not commonly used, mainly because it makes the text difficult to read, due to each line starting and ending at different points, giving the eyes and the brain extra work. Unless it is being used for artistic expression, it should be avoided, particularly for a lot of text. It is quite suitable, however, for short texts like headings, titles, boxed text, and callouts. **Justification** (forced-justified) is like a combination of left and right alignment. Because both sides have to be aligned, the result is that all text lines are stretched to the same length, whether or not there are enough words to fill the length, resulting in uneven word-spacing and gaps (known as **rivers**) running down the text that make the text difficult to read. It is not commonly used.

CHALLENGE 14.2

In the previous challenge, see if you agree that some types of text alignment make the text more difficult to read than others and give your reasons for not agreeing.

14.3.2 `vertical-align`

The `vertical-align` property is used to specify the vertical alignment of inline box, or table-cell content, rather than the text inside the block-level elements. It is **inherited** and common to use it with the `<img>` element to align images within the text. The values it takes are shown in Table 14.2 and Figures 14.3 and 14.4 show examples of how some of them are used and how they render.

TABLE 14.2

The Values for `vertical-align` Property

Value Type	Function
text-top	Aligns the top of an element with that of the font of the parent element.
text-bottom	Aligns the bottom of an element with that of the font of the parent element.
middle	Aligns the middle of an element with that of the parent element. In tables, it aligns the padding box within a row.
baseline	Aligns the baseline of an element with that of the parent element. This is usually the default in browsers.
sub	Aligns the baseline of an element with that of the subscript of its parent element.
super	Aligns the baseline of an element with that of the superscript of the parent element.
length value	Aligns the baseline of an element above the baseline of its parent at a distance specified by a length value (such as px and em). Negative values are allowed.
percentage value	Aligns the baseline of an element above the baseline of its parent at a distance specified as a percentage of the line-height property. Negative values are allowed.
top	Aligns the top of an element and its child elements with the top of the line to which they belong, rather than that of its parent.
bottom	Aligns the bottom of an element and its child elements with the bottom of the line to which they belong, rather than that of its parent.

CSS

```
body { background-color: lightgrey; }
img.baseline { vertical-align: baseline; }
img.bottom { vertical-align: text-bottom; }
img.top { vertical-align: text-top; }
img.middle { vertical-align: middle; }
```

HTML

```
<h3>Vertical Align</h3>
<p><img class="baseline" src="rabbit.png" alt="Rabbit" width="50" height="50">
   This image is aligned using the baseline value.</p>
<p><img class="bottom" src="rabbit.png" alt="Rabbit" width="50" height="50">
   This image is aligned using the text-bottom value.</p>
<p><img class="top" src="rabbit.png" alt="Rabbit" width="50" height="50">
   This image is aligned using the text-top value.</p>
<p><img class="middle" src="rabbit.png" alt="Rabbit" width="50" height="50">
   This image is aligned using the middle value.</p>
```

FIGURE 14.3 The values for vertical-align property.

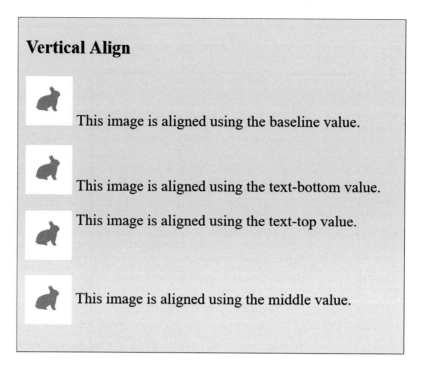

FIGURE 14.4   The rendered result of Figure 14.3.

CHALLENGE 14.3

Implement the code in the example, using an image of your choice, and modify the code so that a border shows around each image and the `<p>` element and each paragraph has a background color. Do you think this is an improvement aesthetically? Also, what would happen if the container elements are `<div>` elements?

14.3.3   Centering Blocks of Text

The centering of a block of text can be horizontal or vertical, or both, so that the block is in the middle of the browser window or another container. However, as of time of writing, there is no single CSS property designed specifically for any of these goals. They can only be accomplished through combining properties. Although they can be accomplished using more recently introduced **flexbox** properties, which are discussed later in Chapter 19, it is how general-purpose properties can be used that is presented here.

14.3.3.1   Horizontal Centering

The most common way of achieving the horizontal centering of a block of text is to add equal margin on either side, and this can be done by giving the `margin-left` and `margin-right` properties the value of `auto`, as shown in Figures 14.5 and 14.6. Note that the two margin declarations can be replaced with the `margin` shorthand property, thus: `margin: 0 auto;`.

```
CSS
h2 { text-align: center; }
p.blocktext {
  margin-left: auto;
  margin-right: auto;
  width: 480px;
}

HTML
<h2>Text horizontal centering</h2>
<p class="blocktext">Lorem ipsum dolor sit amet, consectetur
  adipiscing elit. Aen....</p>
```

FIGURE 14.5 Centering a block of text horizontally.

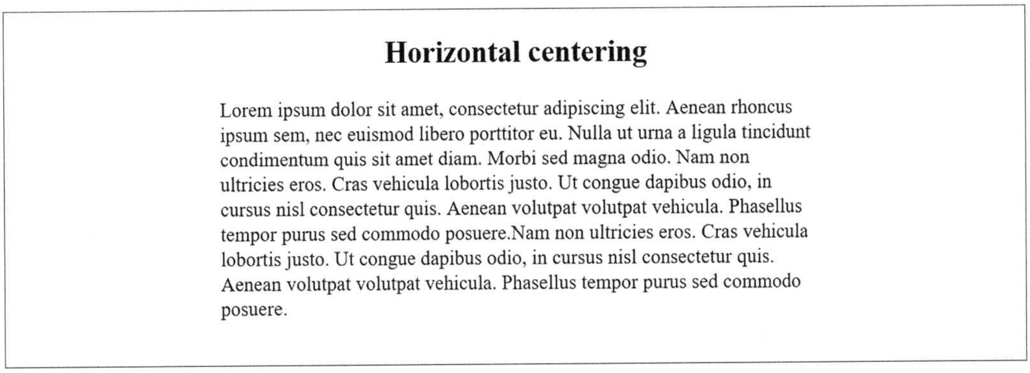

Horizontal centering

Lorem ipsum dolor sit amet, consectetur adipiscing elit. Aenean rhoncus ipsum sem, nec euismod libero porttitor eu. Nulla ut urna a ligula tincidunt condimentum quis sit amet diam. Morbi sed magna odio. Nam non ultricies eros. Cras vehicula lobortis justo. Ut congue dapibus odio, in cursus nisl consectetur quis. Aenean volutpat volutpat vehicula. Phasellus tempor purus sed commodo posuere.Nam non ultricies eros. Cras vehicula lobortis justo. Ut congue dapibus odio, in cursus nisl consectetur quis. Aenean volutpat volutpat vehicula. Phasellus tempor purus sed commodo posuere.

FIGURE 14.6 The result of Figure 14.5.

CHALLENGE 14.4

In the `p.blocktext{}` rule, in the example in Figure 14.5, use the shorthand margin property to achieve the same goal achieved by the two longhand properties.

14.3.3.2 *Vertical Centering*

Centering a block of text vertically is less straightforward than centering it horizontally. This is because the situation in which it is required determines how it is done and situations vary widely. This means that there are many methods of vertically centering a block of text. Figure 14.7 shows a moderately generic method and Figure 14.8 the rendered result.

The example essentially uses the `position` property to position the `<div>` element at a fixed point 50% (halfway) down the window's height. The `transform`

```
CSS
h2 { text-align: center; }
div {
  position: absolute;
  top: 50%;
  padding: 20px;
  transform: translateY(-50%);
}

HTML
<h2>Vertical centering</h2>
<div>Lorem ipsum dolor sit amet, consectetur adipiscing elit.
 Aenean rhoncus...</div>
```

FIGURE 14.7 Centering a block of text vertically.

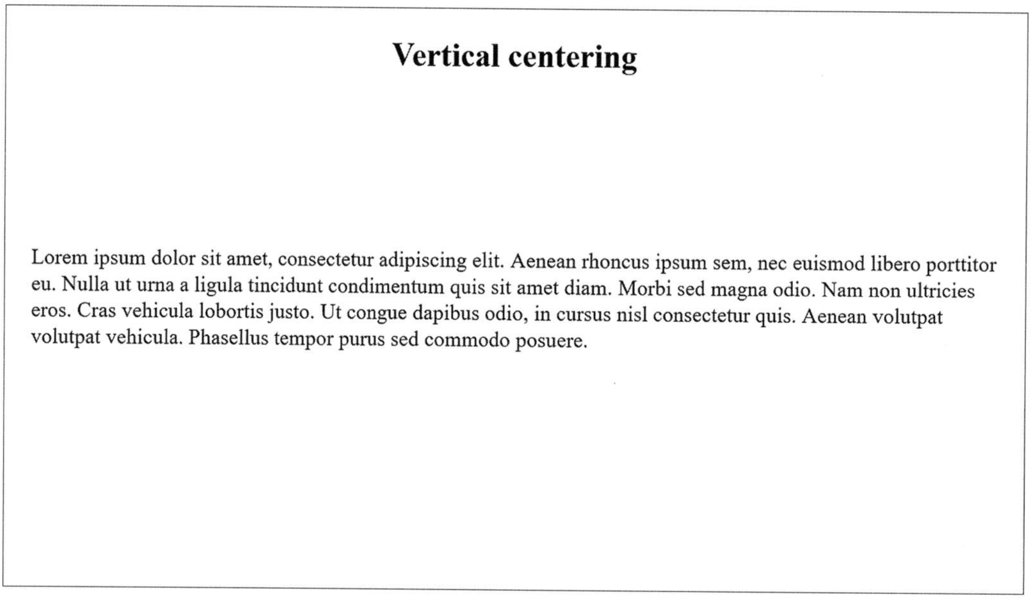

Vertical centering

Lorem ipsum dolor sit amet, consectetur adipiscing elit. Aenean rhoncus ipsum sem, nec euismod libero porttitor eu. Nulla ut urna a ligula tincidunt condimentum quis sit amet diam. Morbi sed magna odio. Nam non ultricies eros. Cras vehicula lobortis justo. Ut congue dapibus odio, in cursus nisl consectetur quis. Aenean volutpat volutpat vehicula. Phasellus tempor purus sed commodo posuere.

FIGURE 14.8 The result of Figure 14.7.

property takes the `translateY(-50%)` as value, which moves the `<div>` element up the *y*-axis (vertical axis) by half its own height to properly align the middle of the element's box with the vertical middle of the window. This is because the `position` property positions an element using the top-left corner and not the center.

CHALLENGE 14.5

In the example in Figure 14.7, why would you not use "relative" for the value of the `position` property?

14.3.3.3 *Vertical and Horizontal Centering*

Centering a block of text horizontally and vertically can be as simple as combining the CSS rules for achieving each. Figure 14.9 shows how to do this and Figure 14.10 the rendered result.

```
CSS
h2 { text-align: center; }
div {
  position: absolute;
  top: 50%;
  margin-left: 300px;
  margin-right: 300px;
  transform: translateY(-50%);
}

HTML
<h2>Vertical and horizontal centering</h2>
<div>Lorem ipsum dolor sit amet, consectetur adipiscing elit.
  Aenean rhoncus ips...</div>
```

FIGURE 14.9 Centering a block of text horizontally and vertically.

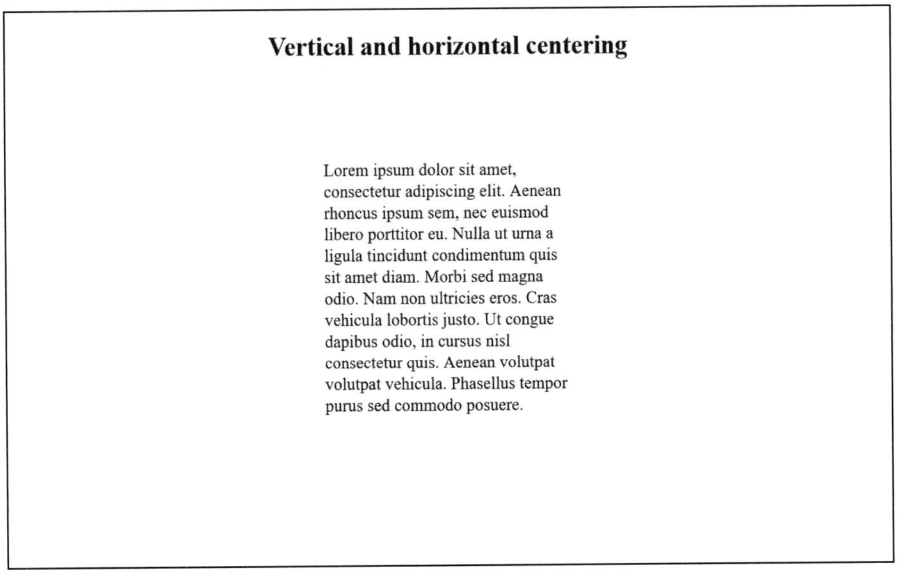

FIGURE 14.10 The result of Figure 14.9.

CHALLENGE 14.6

Implement the example in Figure 14.9 and experiment with the value of the `transform` property, including the sign. Also say why it is more effective to use % instead of px or em.

14.4 Text Indenting and Outdenting

Indenting and outdenting text are done using the `text-indent` property. It is **inherited** and allows you to specify by how much to move, horizontally (left or right), the beginning of the first line of text content of an element. When the first line is pushed in to the right, it is known as an **indent**. When it is pushed out to the left, it is an **outdent** (or a **hanging indent**). The types of values the property takes are **length values** (such as `px` and `em`), which may be negative values, and **percentage values**, which specifies distance as a percentage of the block containing the text. How the property is used and its effects are shown Figures 14.11 and 14.12.

In the example, the `p.indent{}` rule moves the first line of the `<p>` element of `class="indent"` right by 3em. The `p.outdent{}` rule moves the first line of the `<p>` element of `class="outdent"` left by -3em, but also specifies 3em `margin-left` for the element to move all the paragraph right by the same amount.

```
CSS
p.indent { text-indent: 3em; }
p.outdent { text-indent: -3em; margin-left: 3em; }

HTML
<p>Phasellus sagittis, ipsum sed laoreet fermentum, lacus velit
   tincidunt...</p>
<p class="indent">Phasellus sagittis, ipsum sed laoreet
   fermentum, lacus...</p>
<p class="outdent">Phasellus sagittis, ipsum sed laoreet
   fermentum, lacus...</p>
```

FIGURE 14.11   Example usage of `text-indent`.

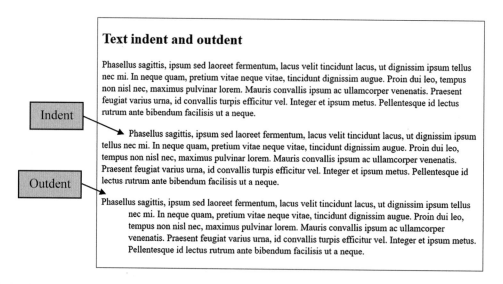

FIGURE 14.12   The result of Figure 14.11.

CHALLENGE 14.7

Implement the example, making the `margin-left` larger than the `text-indent` value to see the effect and why the paragraph has to be moved right by the same amount of indent.

14.5 Text Spacing

Text spacing refers to the amount of space between the letters of a word or between the words of a text. The CSS properties typically used for controlling it are `letter-spacing`, `font-kerning`, and `word-spacing`.

14.5.1 `letter-spacing`, `font-kerning`, **and** `word-spacing`

The `letter-spacing`, `font-kerning`, and `word-spacing` properties are all **inherited**. Table 14.3 lists their functions and Figures 14.13 and 14.14 show how they are used and their effects.

The rules in the example and their effects are self-explanatory. In the rendered outputs of the `.kerningnormal{}` and `.kerningnone{}` rules, notice the differences in spacing between some letters (i.e., "A," "W," "A," "V," "L," and "Y"). Notice also that the text looks better when the kerning information is applied.

TABLE 14.3

Text Spacing Properties

Property	Function
`letter-spacing`	Specifies the amount space between characters. The values taken are the normal (which is the default) and **length values** (e.g., px and em), which can be positive or negative.
`font-kerning`	Allows the control of whether or not the spacing information (kerning information) stored in a font should be used. If a font is well-kerned, using the information makes the spacing between characters similar. Not using it can make the spacing uneven. The values it takes are normal (which uses the information), none (which does not use information), and auto (the default, which lets the browser decide).
`word-spacing`	Specifies the amount space between words. The values it supports are the normal (which is the default) and **length values** (e.g., px and em), which can be positive or negative.

```
CSS
.letter04em { letter-spacing: 0.4em; }
.letter-05em { letter-spacing: -0.05em; }
.word15px { word-spacing: 15px;}
.word3em { word-spacing: 3em; }
.kerningnormal { font-kerning: normal; }
.kerningnone { font-kerning: none; }

HTML
<h3>Text Spacing</h3>
<p>This paragraph has default spacing</p>
<p class="letter04em">This paragraph has 0.4em
 letter-spacing</p>
<p class="letter-05em">This paragraph has -0.05em
 letter-spacing</p>
<p class="word15px">This paragraph has 15px word-spacing</p>
<p class="word5em">This paragraph has 5em word-spacing</p>
<p class="kerningnone">AWFULLY AVANT GARDE - normal</p>
<p class="kerningnormal">AWFULLY AVANT GARDE - none</p>
```

FIGURE 14.13   Example usage of text spacing properties.

Text Spacing

This paragraph has default spacing

T h i s   p a r a g r a p h   h a s   0 . 4 e m   l e t t e r - s p a c i n g

This paragraph has -0.05em letter-spacing

This   paragraph   has   15px   word-spacing

This   paragraph   has   5em   word-spacing

AWFULLY AVANT GARDE - normal

AWFULLY AVANT GARDE - none

FIGURE 14.14   The rendered result of Figure 14.13.

CHALLENGE 14.8

What is the possible implication of using the em unit to specify text spacing?

NOTE: Word wrapping

It is worth noting that text spacing can affect text wrapping, with the effects depending on the values set for various content overflow-related properties discussed in Chapter 10, such as `overflow`, `white-space`, `text-overflow`, `overflow-wrap`, and `hyphens`.

14.5.2 `text-rendering`

The `text-rendering` property is actually not a CSS-defined property as of time of writing but supported by most browsers. It is **inherited** and used to optimize text spacing and balance quality against rendering speed. The values supported include `auto` (which lets browser decide), `optimizeSpeed` (which prioritizes speed over legibility and geometric precision), `optimizedLegibility` (which optimizes legibility over speed and precision), and `geometricPrecision` (which optimizes geometric precision). A rule, for example, could be `p  {  text-rendering: optimizeReadability;  }`.

14.5.3 Text Spacing in Design

Text spacing, whether it is achieved via `letter-spacing`, `font-kerning`, or `word-spacing`, can influence legibility when used in an informed way. Generally, the characteristics of a font and the spacing between letters and words interact to optimize legibility level. This means that adjusting one might require adjusting others. For example, the larger the space between letters, the larger should be the space required between words. Also, the bigger the font sizes are, the more legible the text is likely to be with bigger spacing between letters and words. For example, when an all-uppercase text is used, increasing the space between the letters a little can improve the speed at which the characters can be distinguished. Headings are especially likely to benefit from kerning, because their larger size makes the uneven spacing between letters more noticeable, particularly when in all-uppercase, although the problem also occurs when uppercase and lowercases are mixed. Not all letters cause this problem, and the magnitude also depends on typeface.

CHALLENGE 14.9

Write a code to display the words "LAWFULLY" and "Lawfully" in Times New Roman and Arial, without using the kerning information, to see the differences in the spacing between the letters.

14.6 Line Spacing

Line spacing is also known as **leading**, which, as previously illustrated in Figure 13.1 in Chapter 13, is the spacing between the descender on one line and the ascender on the next line down. The property used to specify it is the `line-height`.

14.6.1 `line-height`

The `line-height` property is **inherited** and used to specify the spacing between one line of text and the next. The values it supports are listed in Table 14.4 and Figures 14.15 and 14.16 show how the `line-height` property is used and the result.

TABLE 14.4

Values Taken by the `line-height` Property

Value	Function
normal	Specifies to use the browser's default. Value depends on font-family, but is commonly between 1.2 and 1.4.
<number>	Any unit-less integer or fraction. However, it does not specify the actual spacing directly. **The value used is the number specified multiplied by the element's** font-size. It is the most preferred, because it does not produce unexpected results.
<length>	Distance measurement (e.g., px and em). May produce unexpected results.
<percentage>	Percentage relative to the element's font size. May produce unexpected results.

```
CSS
div.unit-less { line-height: 1.2; }
div.unit {  line-height: 1.2em; }

HTML
<div class="unit-less">
  <h2>Line-height is applied to the text in this element using
      unit-less values (i.e., just numbers)</h2>
  <p>Lorem ipsum dolor sit amet, consec...</p>
</div>
<div class="unit">
  <h2>Line-height is applied to the text in his element using
      em unit, which is a relative unit</h2>
  <p>Lorem ipsum dolor sit amet, consec...</p>
</div>
```

FIGURE 14.15 Example usage of `line-height`.

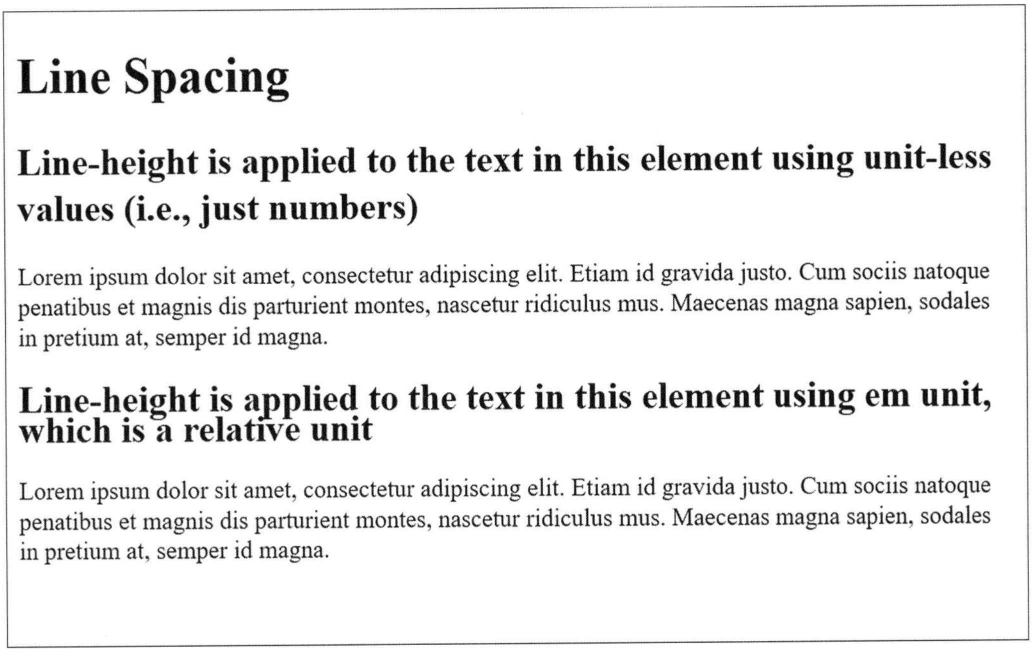

Line Spacing

Line-height is applied to the text in this element using unit-less values (i.e., just numbers)

Lorem ipsum dolor sit amet, consectetur adipiscing elit. Etiam id gravida justo. Cum sociis natoque penatibus et magnis dis parturient montes, nascetur ridiculus mus. Maecenas magna sapien, sodales in pretium at, semper id magna.

Line-height is applied to the text in this element using em unit, which is a relative unit

Lorem ipsum dolor sit amet, consectetur adipiscing elit. Etiam id gravida justo. Cum sociis natoque penatibus et magnis dis parturient montes, nascetur ridiculus mus. Maecenas magna sapien, sodales in pretium at, semper id magna.

FIGURE 14.16   The rendered result of Figure 14.15.

Notice in the example the unexpected result produced by the `em` unit with a larger font size, even though the text in smaller font size looks all right. This problem can also happen with other measurement units like `px`.

CHALLENGE 14.10

Implement the example in Figure 14.15, using a text of your choice, but express the `line-height` in the `div.unit{}` rule in percentage.

CHALLENGE 14.11

What is the actual value used for the line spacing in the example, given the 1.2 value specified in the `div.unit-less{}` rule?

14.6.2 Line Height in Design

Having lines too closely or too widely spaced can cause legibility problems. If lines are too closely spaced, the eyes can continually stray into the line below instead of moving along the current one; if they are too widely space, the eyes are forced to make extreme unnatural jumps from one line to the next. Spacing of between 1.5 and 2 is recommended for Web accessibility, especially for users with cognitive disabilities who can have problems tracking lines of text that are too close. However, other text properties, such as font size and font weight, might warrant using spacing outside of this recommendation. One rule of thumb is to try to make `line-spacing` bigger than the spacing between words. Additionally, where the `<sub>` or `<sup>` elements are used, in order to ensure leading is not disrupted, `line-height` may also be set for the elements.

CHALLENGE 14.12

Mark up some words in the previous example with the `<sup>` and `<sub>` elements and apply `line-height` to the elements to see the effects.

14.7 Specifying Lowercase or Uppercase

It is sometimes necessary to specify whether to make text lowercase or uppercase, such as when you want to convert the case of a user's text input. The property used to achieve this is the `text-transform` property. It is **inherited** and used to specify to capitalize all text, make all text lowercase, or capitalize just the first letter of each word. The values it takes are listed in Table 14.5. Figure 14.17 shows how the property is used and Figure 14.18 the result.

TABLE 14.5

Values Supported by the `text-transform` Property

Value	Function
uppercase	Capitalizes all the text.
lowercase	Makes all the text lowercase.
capitalize	Capitalizes the first letter of every word in a text.

```
CSS
h1 { text-transform: uppercase; }
h2 { text-transform: capitalize; }
p.paragraph { text-transform: lowercase; }

HTML
<h1>text heading</h1>
<h2>text subheading</h2>
<p class="paragraph">THIS.IS ALL-UPPERCASE TEXT THAT IS CONVERTED
    TO ALL-LOWERCASE.</p>
```

FIGURE 14.17   Example usage of `text-transform` property.

> # TEXT HEADING
>
> ## Text Subheading
>
> this is all-uppercase text that is converted to all-lowercase.

FIGURE 14.18 The result of Figure 14.17.

CHALLENGE 14.13

Write a code to produce the following:

> **PLEASE DO NOT IGNORE WARNINGS, AS THIS CAN LEAD TO FATAL ACCIDENTS!**

14.7.1 Text Capitalization in Design

Traditionally, lowercase is used for the body of text, with a few exceptions, such as the first letter of a sentence and proper nouns (i.e., names of particular things). This is because text written in lowercase is easier to read. While lowercase letters generally have enough visible differences to make people quickly and easily distinguish between them, uppercase letters have similar rectangular forms that tend to not make text easily legible, thereby forcing people to read words letter by letter. On the other hand, **all-uppercase can be effective for attracting attention** and well-suited for short texts, such as headings. This is why it is used for warnings, as in, for example, WARNING! It is essentially synonymous with shouting. This is another reason it should be used with caution and purpose.

CHALLENGE 14.14

For which of the following would you use or not use all-uppercase, and why?

- Subheading
- Advice
- Welcome greeting
- Body of text
- Small text
- Quotation

14.8 Specifying Content Directionality

In Chapter 3, the `dir` attribute and `<bdo>` and `<bdi>` elements were introduced that are used in specifying text direction and ordering. Ideally, these should always be used instead of CSS properties, such as those introduced here, because some user agents may not support CSS. In CSS, the properties used to specify the direction flow of content are addressed under the general banner of **writing modes**. These properties are intended to provide support for various international writing modes, such as **left-to-right** (used, for example, in Latin and Indic languages), **right-to-left** (used, for example, in Arabic and Hebrew), **bidirectional** (used, for example, in mixed Latin and Arabic), and **vertical** (used, for example, in some Asian languages).

Writing mode is determined in terms of the **inline base direction** of text and the **direction of block flow**. For example, the inline base direction of text in English writing is left-to-right and the direction of block flow is top-to-bottom. The main properties used in writing modes are `direction`, `writing-mode`, `text-orientation`, and `text-combine-upright`. Another, the `unicode-bidi` property, which is used to override the **Unicode bidi algorithm**, is not recommended for Web designers. See Section 3.16 in Chapter 3 for more on the Unicode bidi algorithm.

14.8.1 `direction`

The `direction` property is generally equivalent to the HTML `dir` attribute introduced in Chapter 3. It is used to specify the inline base direction of the content of an element, but can also be used with the `unicode-bidi` property to override the ordering of the characters of text, as can be done using the `<bdo>` element discussed in Chapter 3. It is **inherited** and the values it takes are `ltr` (which displays content left to right and is **default**) and `rtl` (which displays content right to left). When used on a `<table>` element, it contributes to how the contents of table columns are ordered. It can also be used on specific `<tr>`, `<td>`, and `<th>` elements. Figure 14.19 shows example of how it is used and Figure 14.20 the effect.

```
CSS
.first { direction: ltr; }
.second { direction: rtl; }
.third { direction: rtl; }
.fourth{ direction: rtl; unicode-bidi: bidi-override; }

HTML
<h2>Text directionality</h2>
<p>This text uses the default direction value of ltr.</p>
<p class="first">This text uses specified direction...</p>
<p class="second">This text uses specified direction...</p>
<p> الحياة هي سر W3C!</p>
<p class="third"> الحياة هي سر W3C!</p>
<p class="fourth">This text uses specified direction...</p>
```

FIGURE 14.19   Example usage of the `direction` property.

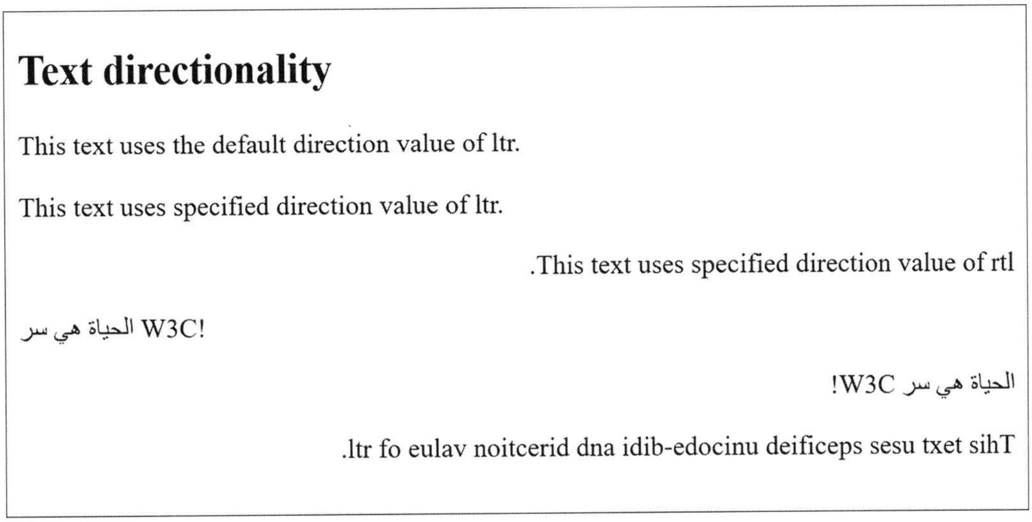

Text directionality

This text uses the default direction value of ltr.

This text uses specified direction value of ltr.

.This text uses specified direction value of rtl

‫الحياة هي سر‬ W3C!

‫الحياة هي سر‬ W3C!

.ltr fo eulav noitcerid dna idib-edocinu deificeps sesu txet sihT

FIGURE 14.20   The result of Figure 14.19.

In the example, the content of the first `<p>` element is displayed using the default `ltr` base direction. In the `<p>` element of `class="first"`, specifying `ltr` does not make a difference. In the `<p>` element of `class="second"`, `rtl` makes the text start from the right. In the fourth `<p>` element, the Arabic text is not displayed from the right as it should be, because the default `ltr` base direction is used. In the `<p>` element of `class="third"`, specifying `rtl` makes the text display correctly from the right. In the `<p>` element of `class="fourth"`, the `unicode-bidi` property is used to override the bidi algorithm and set the base direction to `rtl`, even though the correct direction for displaying the text is left to right. Notice that the result is similar to when the `dir` attribute and `<bdo>` element were used in Chapter 3.

CHALLENGE 14.15

Why should you use HTML to specify text directionality instead of CSS?

14.8.2 `writing-mode`

The `writing-mode` property allows you to specify whether the inline content should be laid out horizontally or vertically, and the direction of block flow (i.e., direction in which new lines are stacked). It is **inherited** and the values supported are listed in Table 14.6. Figures 14.21 and 14.22 show how the property is used, using English and Japanese, and Figure 14.23 the effects.

In the example, `horizontal-tb` was used for the content of each cell in the first row; `vertical-lr` for those in the second, and `vertical-lr` for those is the third. The horizontal and vertical scripts say "Introduction to Writing Modes," while the mixed script says "Introduction to Writing Modes 2016."

TABLE 14.6

Values Taken by the `writing-mode` Property

Value	Function
horizontal-tb	Makes the content flow horizontally from left to right and top to bottom.
vertical-rl	Makes the content flow vertically from top to bottom and horizontally from right to left.
vertical-lr	Makes the content flow vertically from top to bottom and horizontally from left to right.
sideways-lr	Makes the content flow vertically from top to bottom and left to right, with glyphs set on their side to the right. May not be used in the future.
sideways-rl	Makes the content flow vertically from top to bottom and right to left, with glyphs set on their side to the left. May not be used in the future.

```
HTML
<body>
  <h2>Writing Modes</h2>
  <table>
    <tr class="dkgrey">
      <th>Value</th>
      <th>Horizontal script</th>
      <th>Vertical script</th>
      <th>Mixed script</th>
    </tr>
    <tr>
      <td>horizontal-tb</td>
      <td class="horizontal-tb">Introduction to Writing Modes</td>
      <td class="horizontal-tb">書き込みモードの概要</td>
      <td class="horizontal-tb">書き込みモード2016の概要</td>
    </tr>
    <tr>
      <td>vertical-lr</td>
      <td class="vertical-lr">Introduction to Writing Modes</td>
      <td class="vertical-lr">書き込みモードの概要</td>
      <td class="vertical-lr">書き込みモード2016の概要</td>
    </tr>
    <tr>
      <td>vertical-rl</td>
      <td class="vertical-rl">Introduction to Writing Modes</td>
      <td class="vertical-rl">書き込みモードの概要</td>
      <td class="vertical-rl">書き込みモード2016の概要</td>
    </tr>
  </table>
</body>
```

FIGURE 14.21   HTML for example usage of `writing-mode`.

CSS
```
body{ margin-left: 20px; }
table { border-collapse: collapse; }
td, th { padding: 5px; border: 1px solid black; }
td { width: 70px; height: 120px; vertical-align: top; }
th { text-align: left; border-bottom: 2px solid black; }
tr.dkgrey { background-color: darkgrey; }
.horizontal-tb { writing-mode: horizontal-tb; }
.vertical-lr { writing-mode: vertical-lr; }
.vertical-rl { writing-mode: vertical-rl; }
```

FIGURE 14.22   CSS for Figure 14.21.

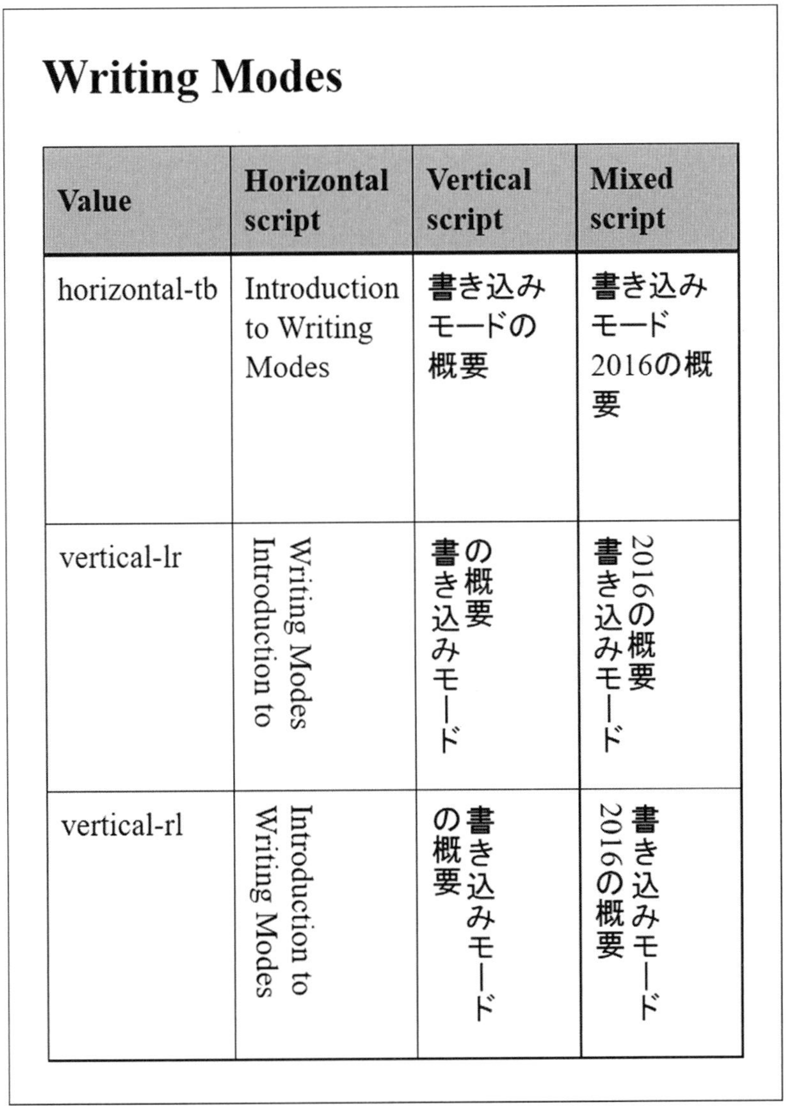

Writing Modes

Value	Horizontal script	Vertical script	Mixed script
horizontal-tb	Introduction to Writing Modes	書き込みモードの概要	書き込みモード2016の概要
vertical-lr	Writing Modes Introduction to	の概要書き込みモード	2016の概要書き込みモード
vertical-rl	Introduction to Writing Modes	書き込みモードの概要	書き込みモード2016の概要

FIGURE 14.23   The result of Figures 14.21 and 14.22.

CHALLENGE 14.16

Which `writing-mode` value would you use for text that is written from right to left and top to bottom?

14.8.3 `text-orientation`

The `text-orientation` property allows you to specify the orientation of text within a line. It is useful for controlling how vertical scripts are displayed and also for presenting table headers. As of time of writing, it only has an effect on vertical writing mode. It is **inherited** and the values it supports are listed in Table 14.7. Figure 14.24 shows their effects using English and Chinese text.

TABLE 14.7

Values Taken by the `text-orientation` Property

Value	Function
mixed	Turns horizontal-script characters 90° clockwise and leaves the vertical-script glyphs upright, unchanged.
upright	Leaves both horizontal-script characters and vertical-script glyphs upright, unchanged.
sideways	Turns both horizontal-script characters and vertical-script glyphs 90° clockwise, as if the whole line has been displayed horizontally and then rotated 90° clockwise. It is the same as sideways-right, which is used for backward compatibility.

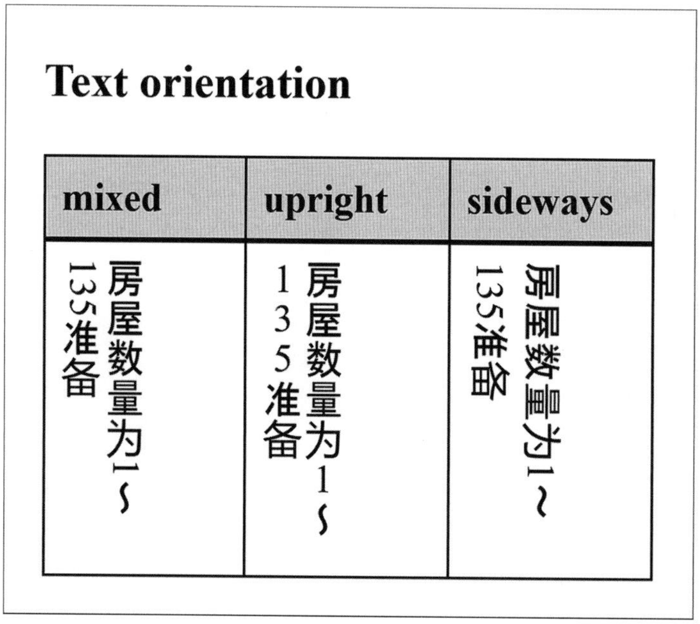

FIGURE 14.24   The effect of the `text-orientation`.

To achieve the example, each of the three rules used to specify the `text-orientation` property also specifies the `writing-mode` property with the value of `vertical-rl`.

CHALLENGE 14.17

Using the table-based method used in the previous example, see if you can create Figure 14.24. You can get the Chinese script from Google Translate. *Hint*: The syntax for the `text-orientation` property is `text-orientation: <value>`, for example `text-orientation: upright`.

14.8.4 `text-combine-upright`

The `text-combine-upright` property is used to combine and place multiple characters in the space of a single character in vertical writing mode. The combined text must not be displayed wider than 1em and is displayed as a single upright glyph. If there are too many characters in a sequence to fit into 1em (e.g., 2016), the characters are not combined; rather, each character is displayed vertically and upright. The property is often used to display horizontal text (e.g., Latin-based dates and initials) in East Asian documents. The property is **inherited** and only has effect in vertical writing mode. Table 14.8 list the values it supports and Figures 14.25 and 14.26 show its usage and the illustration of the effect.

In the example, the `.date{}` rule says to fit two characters into the space for one. Note that Figure 14.26 does not show the actual output of the code, only a rough illustration of what should be produced, as the property is not yet supported by major browsers as of time of writing.

TABLE 14.8

Values Taken by the `text-combine-upright` Property

Value	Function
none	Applies no special processing. It is the **default**.
all	Tries to fit all consecutive characters in an element horizontally into the space of a single character within a vertical line box.
digits <integer>	Tries to fit into the space of a single character in a vertical line box a sequence of consecutive ASCII digits (1–9) that contains as many digits as, or fewer digits than, the specified integer. If the integer is missing, the value of 2 is used. Only an integer range of 2–4 is supported.

```
CSS
.date { writing-mode: vertical-lr; text-combine- upright:
        digits 2; }

HTML
<h3>Text combine upright</h3>
<p class="date">日付は12月31日です</p>
```

FIGURE 14.25   Example usage of `text-combine-upright` property.

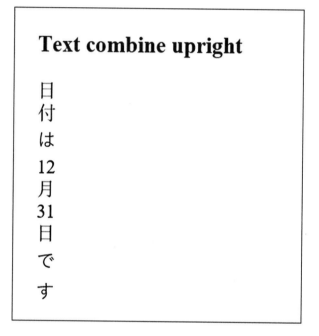

FIGURE 14.26   Illustration of the effect of Figure 14.25.

CHALLENGE 14.18

The date in the example can also be marked up with the `<date>` element discussed in Chapter 5. How would you do this and which of the two approaches is more appropriate for the example, and why?

14.9 Text Decoration

Text decoration refers to the various treatments given to text to decorate it, such as underlining, giving the line style and colors, giving text shadows, and adding emphasis mark to characters. The properties used for these treatments are discussed here.

14.9.1 `text-decoration`

The `text-decoration` property is a **non-inherited** shorthand property used to specify the text formatting or the decoration to apply to a text. It allows you to specify lines, how to use them, the style and the color, all at once, in any order. Its effects always extend to all child elements of the element to which it is applied. For example, if it is applied to a `<p>` element that contains a `<span>` element, the `<span>` element is also affected and the effects cannot be disabled. The longhand properties are `text-decoration-line`, `text-decoration-style`, and `text-decoration-color`. Table 14.9 lists the values supported by the `text-decoration-line` and Table 14.10 lists those supported by the `text-decoration-style`. Color value is specified for `text-decoration-color` in the same ways as described earlier in Chapter 9.

Figure 14.27 shows various ways the property is used and Figure 14.28 shows the result. The `p.under{}` rule specifies only type of line. The `p.through{}` rule specifies the line type, style, and color. Notice that the `p.over{}` rule specifies the same things, but in a different order. Notice also in `p.overunder{}` that more than one type of line can be specified at once, along with style and color. As of time of writing, most browsers support only `underline`. Firefox supports all values except `blink`.

TABLE 14.9

The Values for `text-decoration-line` Property

Value	Function
underline	Draws a line under text.
overline	Draws a line over text.
line-through	Draws a line through text.
blink	Makes text flash. However, it can be annoying, because it continually attracts the user's attention.
none	Removes the currently applied decoration from a text, including the underline from a hyperlink.

TABLE 14.10

The Values for `text-decoration-style` Property

Value	Function
solid	Draws a single line.
double	Draws a double line.
dotted	Draws a dotted line.
dashed	Draws a dashed line.
wavy	Draws a wavy line.

CSS

```
p.under { text-decoration: underline; }
p.through { text-decoration: line-through solid red; }
p.over { text-decoration: overline blue wavy; }
p.blink { text-decoration: blink; }
p.overunder{ text-decoration: overline underline double red; }
a.none { text-decoration: none; }
```

HTML

```
<h3>Text decoration</h3>
<p>This pararaph has no decoration</p>
<p class="under">This paragraph has underline decoration</p>
<p class="through">This paragraph line-through decoration</p>
<p class="over">This paragraph has overline decoration</p>
<p class="blink">This paragraph has blink decoration</p>
<p class="overunder">This paragraph has overline and underline
 decoration</p>
<p><a href="bbc.co.uk" class="none">This link has no underline
 decoration</a></p>
```

FIGURE 14.27 Example usage of `text-decoration` property.

Text decoration

This pararaph has no decoration

This paragraph has underline decoration

~~This paragraph has line-through decoration~~

This paragraph has overline decoration

This paragraph has blink decoration

This paragraph has overline and underline decoration

This link has no underline decoration

FIGURE 14.28 The rendered result of Figure 14.27.

NOTE: Text decorations carry no semantics

The styles produced by the `text-decoration` properties carry no semantics and are therefore not recognized by the browser. This means that they should not be used in place of the HTML elements introduced in Chapter 3 that produce the same effects and carry semantics. For example, `underline` should not be used instead of the `<ins>` element (which also underlines), nor should the `line-through` be used instead of the `<del>` or `<s>` elements, both of which draws a line through the text.

CHALLENGE 14.19

Write the following rule using the longhand `text-decoration` properties.

```
p.overunder{ text-decoration: overline underline
double red; }
```

14.9.2 `text-decoration-skip`

The `text-decoration-skip` property is **inherited** and used to specify which parts of an element's content the text decoration line affecting it must skip. It affects both the text decoration lines drawn by the element to which it is applied and those by the parents. So, for example, if `text-decoration-line` is applied to a `<p>` element that contains a `<span>` element to which `text-decoration-line` is also applied, then, if `text-decoration-skip` is applied to the `<span>` element, both lines are affected. However, as of time of writing, most browsers do not yet support the property, so its effect cannot be demonstrated here, only illustrated. Table 14.11 lists the values supported, Figure 14.29 shows how the property is used, and Figure 14.30 illustrates the expected result. In the example, the rule says to underline the content of the `<p>` element and `text-decoration-skip` says that the decoration line must skip all descenders. See Figure 13.1 in Chapter 13 for the meaning of a descender.

TABLE 14.11

The Values for `text-decoration-skip` Property

Value	Function
none	No skipping is done.
objects	Decoration line skips inline objects (e.g., images) and inline-block objects.
spaces	Decoration line skips spaces and word-separator characters, including adjacent letter-spacing or word-spacing.
ink	Decoration line skips where it crosses glyphs and descenders.
edges	Decoration line is made slightly shorter than the content's length at either ends to prevent the lines applied to adjacent elements from meeting.
box-decoration	Decoration line skips the margin, border, and padding areas. Affects only the decoration imposed by a parent.
trailing-spaces	Decoration skips trailing spaces preserved with the white-space property. See Chapter 10.

```
CSS
p{
 text-decoration-line: underline;
 text-decoration-skip: ink;
}

HTML
<h3>Text decoration skip</h3>
<p>In this text, the underline skips all descenders.</p>
```

FIGURE 14.29   Example usage of the `text-decoration-skip` property.

Underlying psychology

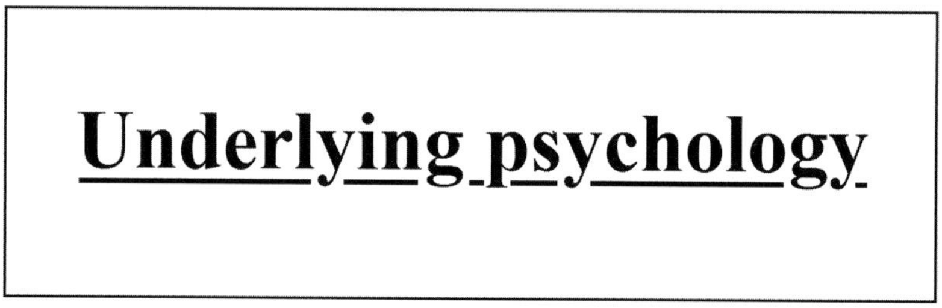

FIGURE 14.30   Illustration of the effects the Figure 14.29.

CHALLENGE 14.20

In what ways do you think the `text-decoration-skip` property can improve the content of a design?

14.9.3 `text-underline-position`

The `text-underline-position` property is used to specify the position of an underline specified on the same element using the `text-decoration` property. It does not affect the underline specified by parent elements. It is **inherited** and takes the values in Table 14.12. As of time of writing, it is still unsupported by most browsers. Figure 14.31 shows how it is used and Figure 14.32 shows an illustration (not actual output) of what the property is intended to do.

TABLE 14.12

The Values for `text-underline-position` Property

Value	Function
auto	The browser decides between using alphabetic or under.
alphabetic	Positions underline relative to the text baseline. This means that the underline is likely to cross descenders. See Figure 14.1 earlier to see what baseline is.
under	Positions underline relative to the bottom edge of the content box. This means that it does not cross descenders. It is the type of underline typically used in accounting documents.
left	In vertical writing mode, such as in Eastern Asian text, positions underline to the left. Equivalent to under in horizontal writing mode.
right	In vertical writing mode, such as in Eastern Asian text, positions underline to the right. Also equivalent to under in horizontal writing mode.

```
CSS
h1{ text-decoration: underline; text-underline-position:
    under; }

HTML
<h1>Underlying Psychology</h1>
<p>Phasellus sagittis, ipsum sed laoreet fermentum...</p>
```

FIGURE 14.31   Example usage of the `text-underline-position` property.

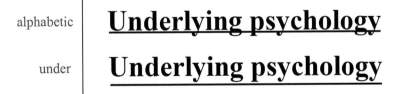

FIGURE 14.32   Illustration of the effects the `alphabetic` and `under` values.

CHALLENGE 14.21

Given that underline is by default used to represent hyperlinks on Web pages, what are the implications of using underline for other purposes, and in which situations do you think it might be more acceptable to do so?

14.9.4 `text-emphasis`

The `text-emphasis` property is a shorthand property that allows you to specify emphasis mark for each character of an element's text content, except separators and control characters. The size of the mark is about 50% of the font-size of the text and may affect line spacing, depending on whether or not the current line spacing is enough for it. The property is especially useful when the text is in languages that use accent marks, such as Eastern Asian languages. The longhand properties are `text-emphasis-style` and `text-emphasis-color`. The `text-emphasis` property can be used to specify both. If one is missing, the initial value is used for it, which is no style for `text-emphasis-style` and current color for `text-emphasis-color`. All the properties are **inherited**. The value supported by `text-emphasis-color` is color, which can be specified in **name**, **rgb()**, **rgba()**, **hsl()**, **hsla()**, or **hex codes**, all of which were discussed in Chapter 9. The values supported by `text-emphasis-style` are listed in Table 14.13.

TABLE 14.13

The Values for `text-emphasis-style` Property

Value	Function
none	No emphasis mark is applied.
filled	Fills the shape applied.
open	Specifies hollow shape.
dot	Displays small circles as marks, which can be **filled** (U+2022) or **open** (U+25E6).
circle	Displays large circle marks, which can be **filled** (U+25CF) or **open** (U+25CB).
double-circle	Displays double circles as marks, which can be **filled** (U+25C9) or **open** (U+25CE).
triangle	Displays triangles as marks, which can be **filled** (U+25B2) or **open** (U+25B3).
sesame	Displays sesame as marks, which can be **filled** (U+FE45) or **open** (U+FE46).
<string>	Displays specified single character as marks. Character must be in quotes.

NOTE: Availability of emphasis marks

Note that not all fonts have the characters in the table. Where one is not available on the user's system, a "**tofu**" (a little open box) is displayed. One of the fonts that users could install in their system to prevent "tofu" is free Google's **Noto** family of fonts that is intended to support all languages and multiple styles and weights. For CJK fonts, the **Noto Sans CJK** may also need to be installed.

The third longhand property used in relation to emphasis marks is the `text-emphasis-position`, which cannot be specified with the shorthand `text-emphasis` property. It is **inherited** and used to specify where to draw emphasis marks. The values supported are `over` (which positions the mark over text), `under` (which positions it under text), `right` (which positions it to the right of text in vertical writing mode), and `left` (which positions it to the left). As of time of writing, only Chrome, Opera, and Safari support the `text-emphasis` properties with `-webkit-`. Figures 14.33 and 14.34 show how the properties are used and the result in the Chrome browser.

```
CSS
em:lang(zh) {
  font-style: normal;
  -webkit-text-emphasis: dot red;
  -webkit-text-emphasis-position: over;
}

HTML
<h3>Text emphasis</h3>
<p>"The Red Dragon again!" in <em>Traditional Chinese</em> is:
    <span lang="zh">红龙 <em>是活 </em>过来了！</span></p>
```

FIGURE 14.33 Example usage of text emphasis properties.

Text emphasis

"The Red Dragon is alive again!" in *Traditional Chinese* is: 红龙是活过来了！

FIGURE 14.34 The result of Figure 14.33 in Chrome browser.

In the example, the `<span>` element is used to isolate the Chinese text so that necessary language information can be provided about it. The `<em>` element is used to isolate two of the Chinese glyphs for emphasis styling. The `em:lang(zh){}` rule applies to the content of the `<em>` element that has a `lang` attribute of "zh" that affects it. These are the two Chinese glyphs. The rule says to make their font style normal (this removes any style applied by the `<em>` element, which is typically italic), use a red dot for emphasis, and place it above each of them. Note that instead of using the `dot` keyword, the mark can also be specified using a backward slash and its **Unicode** as the `<string>` value, thus: '\2022', so that the declaration becomes: `-webkit-text-emphasis: '\2022' red;`. How to use Unicode codes to display characters with HTML can be found in Chapter 3. Note that the Chinese text was generated using **Google Translate**, and then copied and pasted into the code.

NOTE: `:dir`(**identifier**)

The `:dir`(identifier) pseudo-class selector can be used in a similar way as the `:lang()` selector. For example, if the `dir` attribute in an element is set to "ltr" value, the selector can be used to select the element for styling.

CHALLENGE 14.22

Implement the example, using the filled `circle` value in Unicode. Also, specify your own single character, using the `<string>` value. Furthermore, try enclosing more than one character within the quotes and see what happens.

CHALLENGE 14.23

One of the main benefits of using the `lang` attribute is that it lets you style the content by language. Write the HTML and CSS code to present the content in single quotes below, inserting the `lang` attribute as appropriate and using the `:lang()` pseudo-class selector introduced in Chapter 8 to style the French text differently from the rest of the text.

"The French phrase for 'good afternoon' is 'bon après-midi', don't you know?"

14.9.5 `text-shadow`

The `text-shadow` property is **inherited** and used to add shadows to the text. It takes comma-separated sets of values, each of which specifies the settings for a shadow. A set comprises four values: the first two specify the *x* **and** *y* **coordinates of the shadow offset**, the third the **radius of the blur effect** (which is optional and 0 by default), and the fourth the **color of the shadow**, which also supports transparency (RGBA). Positive *x–y* coordinates values move the shadow right and downward. Figure 14.35 shows how the property is used and Figure 14.36 the effect.

In the example, the p{ } rule makes the paragraphs 24px to make them more legible. The .shadow{ } rule specifies two sets of values. The first one says to position the shadow at 1px down and 1px right from the top-left corner of the box of the <p> element of class="shadow", make the radius of the blur effect 2px, and the color gray.

```
CSS
p { font-size: 24px; }
.shadow {
  text-shadow: 1px 1px 2px black, 0 0 1em grey;
  color: black;
}

HTML
<h1>Text shadow</h1>
<p>Lorem ipsum dolor sit amet, consectetur adipiscing elit.
 Donec in ipsum at...</p>
<p class="shadow">Lorem ipsum dolor sit amet, consectetur
 adipiscing elit...</p>
```

FIGURE 14.35 Example usage of text-shadow.

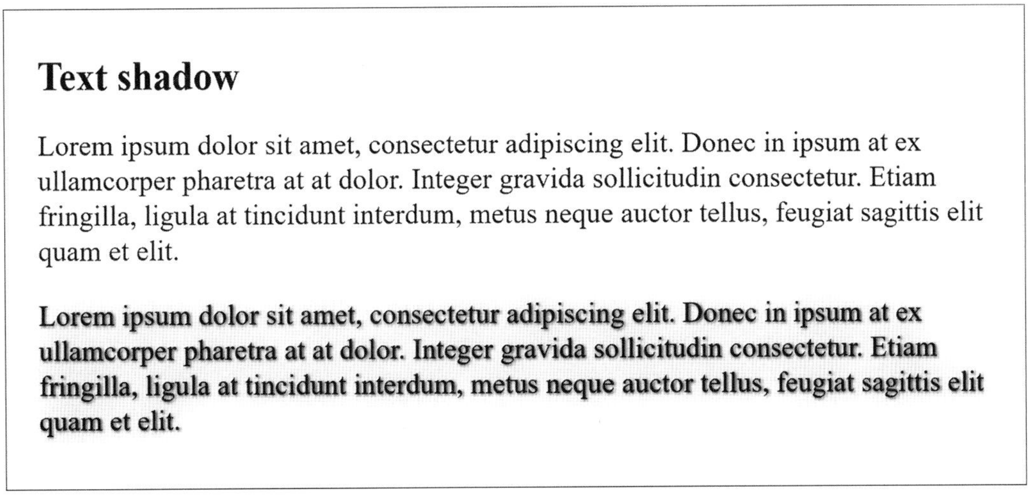

Text shadow

Lorem ipsum dolor sit amet, consectetur adipiscing elit. Donec in ipsum at ex ullamcorper pharetra at at dolor. Integer gravida sollicitudin consectetur. Etiam fringilla, ligula at tincidunt interdum, metus neque auctor tellus, feugiat sagittis elit quam et elit.

Lorem ipsum dolor sit amet, consectetur adipiscing elit. Donec in ipsum at ex ullamcorper pharetra at at dolor. Integer gravida sollicitudin consectetur. Etiam fringilla, ligula at tincidunt interdum, metus neque auctor tellus, feugiat sagittis elit quam et elit.

FIGURE 14.36 The result of Figure 14.35.

CHALLENGE 14.24

Implement the example and experiment with the values of the shadows to see how legibility is affected.

```
CSS
p.button {
  font-family: Arial;
  font-size: 30px;
  font-weight: bold;
  width: 67px;
  padding: 5px 40px 5px 40px;
  border: none;
  border-radius: 4px;
  background-color: green;
  color: black;
  text-shadow: 2px 2px 5px red;
}

HTML
<p class="button">Start</p>
```

FIGURE 14.37 Using `text-shadow` for a button.

FIGURE 14.38 The rendered result of Figure 14.37.

You should notice from the challenge that shadows tend to compromise legibility. For this reason, adding shadows to the text should be avoided for a lot of text content. On the other hand, adding shadows to a very short text, such as to the label of a button or icon, can help produce interesting visual effects, such as embossed effect, that would otherwise require lengthy processes to produce with graphics tools, which also produce larger image files that can compromise page download and rendering speed. Figure 14.37 shows an example of how the `text-shadow` property is used in creating button effects and Figure 14.38 shows the result. Notice that various other properties that have already been introduced in this chapter and previous ones are also used to give the text and its box character.

CHALLENGE 14.25

Create a button design of your own using the `text-shadow` property.

14.10 Styling with Pseudo-Elements

Pseudo-elements, as mentioned in Chapter 8, allow parts of the content of an element to be treated as an element, making it possible to style just part of an element or add objects, such as images, to an element. Table 14.14 lists, again, standard pseudo-elements.

Table 14.15 lists the values supported by the content property mentioned in Table 14.14. With the exception of normal and none, most of the values can be specified together.

TABLE 14.14

Common Pseudo-Elements

Pseudo-Element	Function
::first-letter	Selects the first letter of the first line of the text content of an element.
::first-line	Selects the first line of the rendered text content of an element. This means the first line in the browser.
::before	Creates a pseudo-element and places it immediately before an element and used with the content property, which is used to insert a specified object.
::after	Creates a pseudo-element and places it immediately after an element, and used with the content property, which is used to insert a specified object.
::selection	Applies styling to the text that is selected/highlighted, for example with the mouse. Only some properties can be used with it, such as color, background, text-decoration, text-shadow, outline, and cursor.

TABLE 14.15

Values Supported by the content Property

Value	Function
none	Keyword that generates no pseudo-element.
normal	Keyword that means none for the ::before and ::after pseudo-elements.
<string>	Stands for characters in quotes (e.g., "<<"). The characters are inserted as content.
<url>	Stands for the URL for the object to insert as content.
attr(X)	Returns the value of an element's attribute X as a string. For example, content: attr(id) returns the value of the id attribute of an element (i.e., displays it).
open-quote, close-quote	Keywords insert the quote characters, as defined by the quotes property, which takes two types of values: none and [<string> <string>...], for example quotes: "«" "«"; "<" ">" defines two levels of quotation marks.
no-open-quote, no-close-quote	Keywords insert no content, but makes it seem one is inserted.
<counter>	Stands for counter that is generated by the counter-reset and counter-increment properties. Used for automatic numbering.

14.10.1 `::first-letter, ::first-line,`
       `::before, ::after, ::selection`

Figure 14.39 shows various ways that the pseudo-elements are used to add styling to part of an element and Figure 14.40 shows the result.

In the example, the `p.author::before{}` rule says to place the value of the `content` property before the `<p>` element of `class="author"`, give it red color, and make it bold. The `p.author::after{}` rule says to do a similar thing with the value of the `content` property but after the element. The `p.cap::first-line{}` rule makes the words of the `<p>` element of `class="cap"` all-uppercase. The `p.first::first-letter{}` makes the first letter of the `<p>` element of `class="first"` red and 150% of the default `font-size` (i.e., 16px), making

```
CSS
body { font-family: Times, "Times New Roman";}
h3 { font-family: Verdana, Arial, Helvetica, sans-serif; }
p.author { font-family: "Courier New", Courier, monospace; }
p.author::before { content: "<<"; color: red; font-weight: bold }
p.author::after { content: ">>"; color: red; font-weight: bold }
p.cap::first-line { text-transform: uppercase }
p.first::first-letter { color: red; font-size: 150%; }
p.first::-moz-selection { color: gold; background-color: red; }
p.first::selection { color: gold; background-color: red; }

HTML
<h3>Pseudo-elements World</h3>
<p class="author">by Wu Knows</p>
<p class="cap">Lorem ipsum dolor sit amet, consectetur...</p>
<p class="first">Cum sociis natoque penatibus et magnis...</p>
```

FIGURE 14.39   Example usage of common pseudo-elements.

Pseudo-elements World

`<<by Wu Knows>>`

LOREM IPSUM DOLOR SIT AMET, CONSECTETUR ADIPISCING ELIT.

Cum sociis natoque penatibus et magnis dis parturient montes, nascetur ridiculus mus.Maecenas magna sapien, sodales in pretium at, semper id magna. In pretium placerat euismod. Vivamus quam risus, finibus id placerat vitae, maximus ut urna. Mauris in orci arcu. Integer sed enim auctor, tempor dolor ac, auctor eros. Etiam pharetra eleifend felis, quis rutrum dui facilisis in.

FIGURE 14.40   The rendered result of Figure 14.39.

the size 24px. The `p.first::selection{}` rule says to make the selected text gold and its background red.

CHALLENGE 14.26

Implement the example in Figure 14.39 using your own content. Also, what is the `-moz-` prefix for in the `p.first::-moz-selection` rule?

14.10.2 Using `content` **Property Values**

Figure 14.41 shows more about how the values of the `content` property are used and Figure 14.42 the result. The `body{}` rule resets the count of the counter named "section" to 0, which is the default. The `h3::before{}` rule increments the section counter by 1 and uses the `content` property to insert the string "Section," the section counter, and ":" before the `<h3>` element. The `.intro{}` rule says to use "^" and "^" as open and close quotation marks for the element of class "intro." The `.intro::before{}` and `.intro::after{}` rules insert the quotation marks defined in the `.intro{}` rule before and after the element of class "intro," respectively. The `a::before{}` rule uses the `content` property to insert a favicon and the string "TEDCO" before the content of the `<a>` element, makes the text small, Arial, and brown. A **favicon** is a small icon (e.g., 16 × 16 and 32 × 32)

```
CSS
body { counter-reset: section; }
h3::before { counter-increment: section;  content: "Section"
counter(section) ": ";  }
.intro { quotes: "^" "^"; }
.intro::before { content: open-quote; }
.intro::after { content: close-quote; }
a::before {
  content: url(images/favicon.ico) " TEDCO: ";
  font: x-small Arial, sans-serif;
  color: brown;
}
a::after { content: " (" attr(id) ")"; }

HTML
<h2>The content property</h2>
<p class="quote">There is nothing fundamentally wrong...</p>
<h3>Introduction</h3>
<h3>Discussion</h3>
<h3>Conclusion</h3>
<a id="That's it folks!" href="http://www.example.com">
   More information</a>
```

FIGURE 14.41 Example usage of the `content` property values.

The content property

^There is nothing fundamentally wrong with building on the contributions of others.^

Section 1: Introduction

Lorem ipsum dolor sit amet, consectetur adipiscing elit. Integer quam sapien, bibendum in enim quis, iaculis vehicula tortor. Proin luctus dapibus eleifend. Donec sed mollis erat, at elementum libero.

Section 2: Discussion

Duis eget magna ut nisi sollicitudin blandit. Cras nec arcu ipsum. Curabitur placerat nec ex vel posuere. Vivamus lacus mi, lacinia sed metus et, auctor egestas dui. Lorem ipsum dolor sit amet, consectetur adipiscing elit.

Section 3: Conclusion

Cras purus libero, feugiat ut luctus sed, aliquam in libero. Sed non aliquet mauris. Donec pretium, mi et euismod fermentum, sem ex pharetra metus, in suscipit massa erat at odio.

 TEDCO: More information (That's it folks!)

FIGURE 14.42   The result of Figure 14.41.

associated with a website, typically displayed next to the URL. A favicon format (.ico) can be created from many image formats and there are free online generators. The `a::after{}` rule inserts after the content of the `<a>` element: "(," followed by the value of the `id` attribute of the element, "That's it folks!", followed by ")."

NOTE: `::marker`

It is worth noting that there is also a newer pseudo-element, `::marker`, that allows you to specify custom list-item markers and used with `<li>` elements. For example, the following rule:

```
li::marker { content: "(" counter(counter) ")"; }
```

...should produce list items that start with (1), (2), (3), and so on. However, the pseudo-element is not yet supported by any major browser as of time of writing.

CHALLENGE 14.27

Write the `a::before{}` rule in the example in Figure 14.41 using longhand properties.

14.11 Styling Text with Pseudo-Classes

As seen in Chapter 8, pseudo-classes can be used to select the elements of a document based on their characteristics, such as their status, relationship between them and other elements, and value of their attributes. This makes it possible to apply styling to elements based on these characteristics and so extending the capability of HTML. For example, changes in the appearance and behavior of HTML elements can be specified based on the interaction of the cursor with an element to produce **interactivity**. Pseudo-classes used for styling the contents of links, the targets of links, and the contents of generic elements (e.g., `<p>` and `<div>`) and their effects are presented here. Others, which are typically used for styling list, table, and form elements, are discussed in Chapter 17.

14.11.1 Styling Links

The pseudo-classes commonly used for styling link text are listed in Table 14.16. Figure 14.43 shows how the pseudo-classes listed in the table are used and Figure 14.44 the result.

In the example, all the rules refer to any `<a>` element in the `<body>` element. The `a.link{}` rule says to display an unvisited link in blue; `a.visited{}` says to display a visited link in purple; `a:hover{}` says to display the link text in bold and red when the cursor hovers over it; and `a:active{}` says to make the link text green when being activated (i.e., being clicked or pressed). The order of the pseudo-classes should be like in the example for them to work together properly.

TABLE 14.16

Common Pseudo-Classes for Styling Link Text

Pseudo-Class	Function
`:active`	Selects an element, such as a button, when it is being activated by the user.
`:hover`	Selects an element, such as a hyperlink, when cursor is on it.
`:link`	Selects hyperlinks that have not yet been visited.
`:visited`	Selects hyperlinks that have been visited (clicked or pressed).

```
CSS
a:link { color: blue }
a:visited { color: purple }
a:hover { font-weight: bold; color: red; }
a:active { color: green }

HTML
<h3>News Outlets</h3>
<div>
  <p><a href="">BBC</a></p>
  <p><a href="">ITV</a></p>
  <p><a href="">Channel 4</a></p>
  <p><a href="">Channel 5</a></p>
  <p><a href="">ABC</a></p>
  <p><a href="">CBS</a></p>
  <p><a href="">CNN</a></p>
</div>
```

FIGURE 14.43   How pseudo-classes are used on link text.

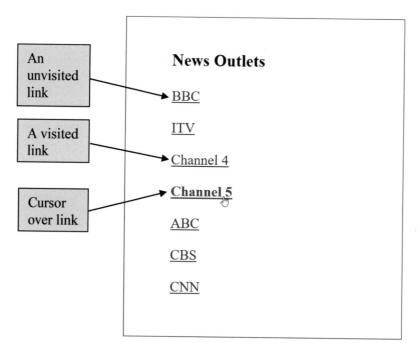

FIGURE 14.44   The rendered result of Figure 14.43.

CHALLENGE 14.28

Implement the example in Figure 14.44 but without the line decoration under the link text. *Hint*: Refer to text decoration.

14.11.2 :target

The :target pseudo-class allows you to style the element to which a URL points. You might recall from Section 4.5 in Chapter 4 that it is possible to link to a specific element on the same page using the # symbol with the href attribute's value. The :target pseudo-class basically says to select the element whose id attribute's value matches the part preceded by the # symbol in the href attribute's value. For example, if an href value contains #orange, :target selects the element of id="orange". One of the common applications of the pseudo-class is for making a hidden element appear when a link is clicked. Figure 14.45 shows how it is used and Figure 14.46 shows the result after the link has been clicked.

```
CSS
#extrainfo {
  display: none;
}
#extrainfo: target {
  display: block;
}

HTML
<h2>:target</h2>
<p><a href="#extrainfo">Extra Information</a></p>
<div id="extrainfo">
  <form>
    <p>Please provide additional information:<br>
    <textarea rows="4" cols="35" name="info"
     id="info"></textarea></p>
  </form>
</div>
```

FIGURE 14.45 Example usage of the :target pseudo-class.

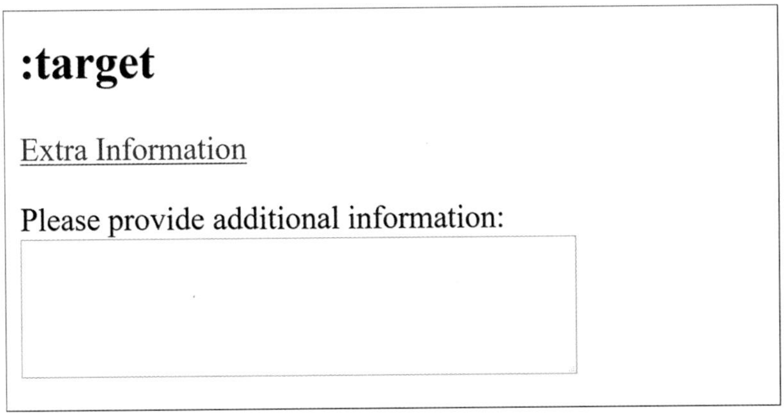

FIGURE 14.46 The rendered result of Figure 14.45.

In the example, the `#extrainfo{}` rule hides the `<div>` element of `id="extrainfo"` (which contains the `<form>` element) when the link is clicked, and the `#extrainfo:target{}` rule shows the element. Note that once the link is clicked and the target element displayed, the page has to be reopened afresh (not reloaded/refreshed) for it to work as intended again.

14.11.2.1 *Lightbox Display and the* `:target` *Pseudo-Class*

A common application of the `:target` pseudo-class is the lightbox display, in which a **modal window** is displayed on top of the current page and the page dimmed; a modal window being a window or dialog box that requires user interaction in order to close it and return to the page that opened it. The window can contain any media object type (e.g., text. image, or video) and the closing mechanism is typically an interactive X positioned at its right-hand corner. A lightbox display is usually implemented using scripting, but can also be implemented using `:target` and various other CSS properties already introduced in this chapter and previous ones. Figures 14.47 and 14.48 show a basic implementation and Figures 14.49 and 14.50 the result.

Although the code for the example is long and might look complex, the principle used is rather basic in which a page-size semi-transparent element containing a smaller element placed in its center is first hidden and then shown and overlaid on the current page when a link on the page is clicked. In the example, the `h2, .link{}` rule centers the heading for the current page and the link that activates the lightbox display. The

```
HTML
<h2>Lightbox with :target</h2>
<p>Lorem ipsum dolor sit amet, consectetur adipiscing elit.
   Sed id arcu ut nunc... </p>
<p class="link"><a href="#window">Click to see a
 lightbox</a></p>
<p>Ut non risus vel ex tincidunt lobortis ut auctor diam.
   Vestibulum id leo venen...</p>
<p>Sed at enim erat. Nulla placerat odio vel finibus pulvinar.
   In varius, nulla.... </p>
<p>Morbi eget dapibus erat, id pharetra purus. Quisque cursus
   sed metus ac hend... </p>
<div id="window">
  <div class="box">
    <a href="#" class="close">X</a>
    <p>This is a basic example a lightbox or modal window.</p>
    <p>This box can contain any media object type, such as
       image or video.</p>
    <p>(Clicking the X closes it.)</p>
  </div>
</div>
```

FIGURE 14.47   HTML for a basic lightbox display.

```
CSS
h2, .link { text-align: center; }
#window {
  width: 100%;
  height: 100%;
  background-color: rgba(0, 0, 0, 0.7);
  position: fixed;
  left: 0;
  top: 0;
  display: none;
}
.box {
  width: 300px;
  height: 300px;
  padding: 15px 20px 0 20px ;
  position: relative;
  top: 50%;
  transform: translateY(-50%);
  margin: 0 auto;
  font-size: 24px;
  font-weight: bold;
  background-color: white;
  text-align: center;
  border: 1px solid black;
  box-shadow: inset 0 0 1em 0.5em blue, 0 0 1em 0.5em orange;
}
.close {
  text-decoration: none;
  font-size: 22px;
  font-weight: bold;
  color: white;
  background-color: orange;
  border: 1px solid black;
  border-radius: 50%;
  width: 36px; height: 2px;
  padding: 7px 1px 30px 2px;
  position: absolute;
  top: -16px;
  left: 317px;
}
.close:hover {  color: black; cursor: pointer; }
#window:target { display: block; }
```

FIGURE 14.48   CSS for Figure 14.47.

`#window{}` rule styles the `<div>` element of `id="window"`, which is the element that is used to cover the current page and make it look dimmed. The rule makes the size of the element the same as that of the page; makes its background color black and slightly transparent (so that the page underneath looks dimmed); positions its top-left corner at the top-left corner of the page, and hides it.

Lightbox with :target

Lorem ipsum dolor sit amet, consectetur adipiscing elit. Sed id arcu ut nunc cursus rutrum sit amet id eros. Nunc iaculis risus lacus, nec malesuada sapien placerat sed. Maecenas elit urna, euismod at ipsum ut, sagittis fermentum elit. Donec blandit mi mauris, at iaculis diam gravida sit amet. Nulla vestibulum pulvinar arcu hendrerit molestie. Interdum et malesuada fames ac ante ipsum primis in faucibus. Ut sit amet magna consectetur, sagittis purus id, tincidunt velit. Donec sed nunc vel metus consectetur vulputate. Duis semper lacinia posuere. Ut vel tristique mi. Nullam tempor erat ac vulputate sagittis. Etiam in libero vehicula, venenatis mauris non, faucibus enim.

Click to see a lightbox

Ut non risus vel ex tincidunt lobortis ut auctor diam. Vestibulum id leo venenatis nisi posuere bibendum. Nulla tempor eget erat a volutpat. Maecenas at mollis neque, et ornare risus. Nam sed orci rhoncus, posuere erat in, venenatis nibh. Sed rhoncus elit et imperdiet semper. Integer massa eros, scelerisque ac arcu et, rhoncus blandit metus. Nam sit amet dignissim magna. Suspendisse rhoncus porttitor erat in efficitur. Vestibulum eget ligula sodales eros porta euismod. Curabitur suscipit nulla vitae nisi volutpat, non sagittis justo sagittis. Nullam et accumsan enim, at aliquet massa. In nec porttitor massa.

Sed at enim erat. Nulla placerat odio vel finibus pulvinar. In varius, nulla vitae euismod pharetra, justo ipsum mattis felis, cursus imperdiet dolor quam a arcu. Ut feugiat varius nunc, nec aliquet nunc porta id. Curabitur id rhoncus lectus, viverra auctor tellus. In hac habitasse platea dictumst. Aenean sollicitudin augue sed aliquam feugiat. In dolor justo, blandit id ultricies ac, finibus a diam.

Morbi eget dapibus erat, id pharetra purus. Quisque cursus sed metus ac hendrerit. Cum sociis natoque penatibus et magnis dis parturient montes, nascetur ridiculus mus. Phasellus vitae pretium urna, nec rutrum nulla. Phasellus non sollicitudin elit. Curabitur id varius felis, vitae vulputate justo. Praesent eget ex non lacus vulputate sollicitudin. Curabitur quis orci tincidunt, mollis diam et, ullamcorper nisl. Ut dictum magna at sapien gravida, id egestas est bibendum.

FIGURE 14.49   The result of Figures 14.47 and 14.48 before link is clicked.

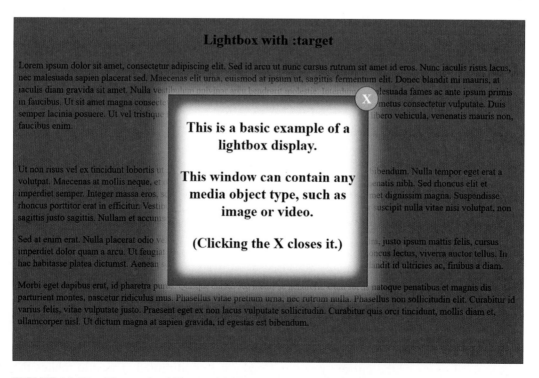

FIGURE 14.50   The result of Figures 14.47 and 14.48 after link is clicked.

The .box{} rule styles the `<div>` element of `class="box"`, which is the element used for the smaller window that displays the intended content. The rule specifies the size of the element (using `width`, `height`, and `padding`), positions it at the center of the `<div>` element of `id="window"` (using `position`, `top`, `transform`, and `margin`), styles the content (using `font-size`, `font-weight`, `background-color`, and `text-align`), and specifies the border and shadow (using `border` and `box-shadow`). Note that positioning the smaller window inside the larger one can be more straightforward by making the elements behave like a table, using the `table` and `table-cell` values with the `display` property. These values are introduced more fully in Chapter 17.

The .close{} rule styles the `<a>` element of `class="close"`, which is the control for closing the lightbox display. Essentially, when the link is clicked, the user is returned to the start of the page underneath. The rule removes the underline from the element's content, X (using `text-decoration`), specifies the size, weight, and color of X and the background-color and border of the element (using `font-size`, `font-weight`, `color`, `background-color`, and `border`), specifies the shape of the element (using `width`, `height`, `border-radius`, and `padding`), and positions the element (using `position`, `top`, and `left`). It is worth noting that the sizing and positioning of the element is largely through trial and error rather than calculations.

The .close:hover{} rule makes the X black and cursor-shape a pointer when the cursor is over it. The #window:target{} rule displays the `<div>` element of `id="window"` (hidden in the #window{} rule) as well as its children (i.e., the smaller window and its content).

CHALLENGE 14.29

A common way lightbox displays are used is to display images. Implement the example, but, instead of text, display an image.

CHALLENGE 14.30

Implement the example, but without the element that is used to make the current page look dimmed.

CHALLENGE 14.31

If you use the lightbox display to display a form, how would you let the user close the form and at the same time submit it for processing? *Hint*: Consider elements and attributes introduced in Chapter 5.

CHALLENGE 14.32

In the .box{} rule in the example, change the value of the position property from relative to absolute, fixed, and static, respectively, and explain the effects on the positioning of the box and the close button, based on your understanding of the values from Chapter 12.

CHALLENGE 14.33

Do a search on the Web, using, for example, "css lightbox" as a search term, and study the codes used for different types of lightboxes.

NOTE: Animated lightbox displays

Sometimes a lightbox display is animated, such as in the form of the content box zooming in from outside the page or starting from being small and growing to full size. Animation is discussed later in Chapter 18.

14.11.3 :not(X)

The :not(X) pseudo-class, known as **negation CSS pseudo-class**, is a function that allows you to specify elements that you do not want to be selected for styling. Essentially, it selects elements that do not match the selector represented by the X (which is known as the argument of the function). Figure 14.51 shows how the pseudo-class is used and Figure 14.52 the result.

In the example, the p{}rule applies padding to all edges of all <p> elements and the p:not(.middle){} rule applies a pink background color to the <p> elements that are not of class="middle".

```
CSS
p { padding: 5px; }
p:not(.middle) { background-color: pink; }

HTML
<h2>:not(X)</h2>
<p>Lorem ipsum dolor sit amet, consectetur adipiscing elit.
 Donec in ipsum at ex...</p>
<p class="middle">Integer suscipit justo fermentum, elementum
 purus id, tempus...</p>
<p>Donec et porta dolor, in sollicitudin nisi. Morbi vulputate
 augue ac maximus...</p>
```

FIGURE 14.51 Example usage of the :not(X) pseudo-class.

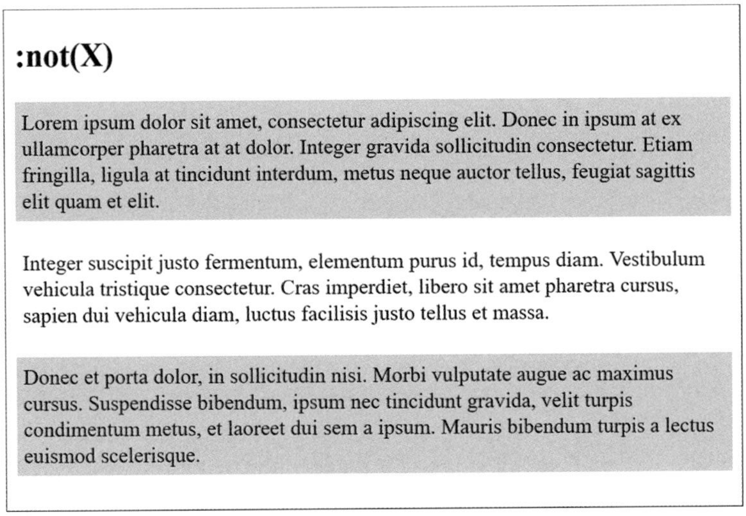

:not(X)

Lorem ipsum dolor sit amet, consectetur adipiscing elit. Donec in ipsum at ex ullamcorper pharetra at at dolor. Integer gravida sollicitudin consectetur. Etiam fringilla, ligula at tincidunt interdum, metus neque auctor tellus, feugiat sagittis elit quam et elit.

Integer suscipit justo fermentum, elementum purus id, tempus diam. Vestibulum vehicula tristique consectetur. Cras imperdiet, libero sit amet pharetra cursus, sapien dui vehicula diam, luctus facilisis justo tellus et massa.

Donec et porta dolor, in sollicitudin nisi. Morbi vulputate augue ac maximus cursus. Suspendisse bibendum, ipsum nec tincidunt gravida, velit turpis condimentum metus, et laoreet dui sem a ipsum. Mauris bibendum turpis a lectus euismod scelerisque.

FIGURE 14.52 The result of Figure 14.51.

CHALLENGE 14.34

In the example, what would the selector :not(.middle) select?

14.11.4 :empty

The :empty pseudo-class allows you to select elements that have no child elements or white space. Comments or scripts are irrelevant and ignored. Figure 14.53 shows an example of the pseudo-class in use and Figure 14.54 the result.

```
CSS
p {
  height: 75px;
  padding: 5px;
  background-color: pink;
}
p:empty { background-color: grey; }

HTML
<h2>:empty</h2>
<p>Integer suscipit justo fermentum, elementum purus id, tempus
  diam. Vestibu...</p>
<p><!--This element is empty because comment is not
    considered content--></p>
<p> <!--This element is not empty because it contains
    white space --></p>
```

FIGURE 14.53 Example usage of the :empty pseudo-class.

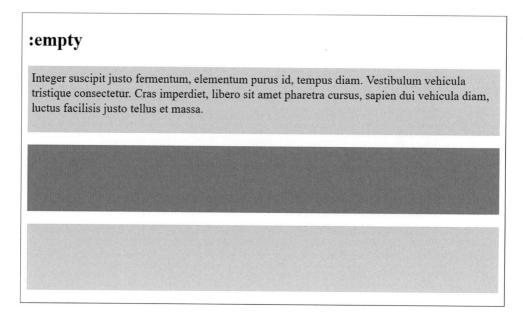

FIGURE 14.54   The result of Figure 14.53.

In the example, the p{ } rule specifies the height, padding, and background color for all <p> elements, and the p:empty{ } rule specifies the background color for empty elements. Notice the white space between the start tag of the last <p> element and the comment tag. This is why it is not considered empty. The same result will occur if the white space is between the comment tag and closing tag of the element, or if there is a carriage return between an element's tag and the comment tag.

CHALLENGE 14.35

In the example, why is it necessary to specify the height for the <p> elements?

14.12 Ruby Properties

Ruby-specific properties fall into two main categories. There are those for styling and formatting ruby elements, which were first introduced in Chapter 3, and there are those for making other elements behave like ruby elements. These properties are introduced here.

14.12.1 Ruby Properties for Styling and Formatting

Ruby elements and their contents can be styled and controlled by many of the generic CSS properties discussed so far. However, there are also properties that are unique to ruby elements. Those defined as of time of writing are `ruby-position`, `ruby-align`, and `ruby-merge`, all of which are not yet widely supported by major browsers. The examples presented here were rendered in Firefox.

14.12.1.1 `ruby-position`

The `ruby-position` property specifies the position of the ruby text (i.e., `<rt>` element) relative to the corresponding ruby base (i.e., `<rb>` element) and is **inherited**. Table 14.17 lists the values it takes.

Figure 14.55 shows how the `ruby-position` property is used and Figure 14.56 the result. The example uses the `under` value. Notice that the HTML code is the same as the one used in Figure 3.46 in Chapter 3.

TABLE 14.17

The Values for the `ruby-position` Property

Value	Function
over	Places the ruby text above the base text for horizontal script and to the right for vertical and is the **default**.
under	Places the ruby text below the base text for horizontal script and to the left for vertical.
inter-character	Places the ruby text between the base text characters.

```
CSS
ruby { ruby-position: under; }

HTML
<h3>Ruby text position</h3>
<ruby>
   <rb>红</rb><rb>龙</rb><rb>是</rb><rb>活</rb><rb>过</rb>
       <rb>来</rb><rb>了</rb><rb>!</rb>
   <rt>紅</rt><rt>龍</rt><rt>是</rt><rt>活</rt><rt>過</rt><rt>
       來</rt><rt>了</rt>
       <rt>!</rt>
</ruby>
```

FIGURE 14.55 Example usage of the `ruby-position` property.

Ruby text position

红龙是活过来 了！
紅 龍   過 來

FIGURE 14.56   The result of Figure 14.55.

CHALLENGE 14.36

Implement the example and also make the base text and ruby text of different colors using appropriate CSS properties from the ones introduced in previous chapters.

14.12.1.2 `ruby-align`

The `ruby-align` property allows you to specify how the ruby text in a `<rt>` element should be distributed across the base text in the corresponding `<rb>` element and is **inherited**. Table 14.18 lists the values for the property.

Figure 14.57 shows how the property is used and Figure 14.58 the result. Note that there must be a space between the characters of a ruby text in order for some values to have the desired effect.

TABLE 14.18

The Values for the `ruby-align` Property

Value	Function
start	Aligns the ruby text with the start of the base text.
center	Aligns the ruby text in the middle of the base text.
space-between	Distributes extra space between ruby text characters.
space-around	Distributes extra space between and around ruby text characters and is the default.

```
CSS
.start { ruby-align: start; }
.center { ruby-align: center; }
.around { ruby-align: space-around; }
.between { ruby-align: space-between; }
```

```
HTML
<h3>Ruby text alignment</h3>
<ruby class="start"><rb>World Wide Web</rb><rt>W W W</rt></ruby><br>
<ruby class="center"><rb>World Wide Web</rb><rt>W W W</rt></ruby><br>
<ruby class="around"><rb>World Wide Web</rb><rt>W W W</rt></ruby><br>
<ruby class="between"><rb>World Wide Web</rb><rt>W W W</rt></ruby>
```

FIGURE 14.57 Example usage of the `ruby-align` property.

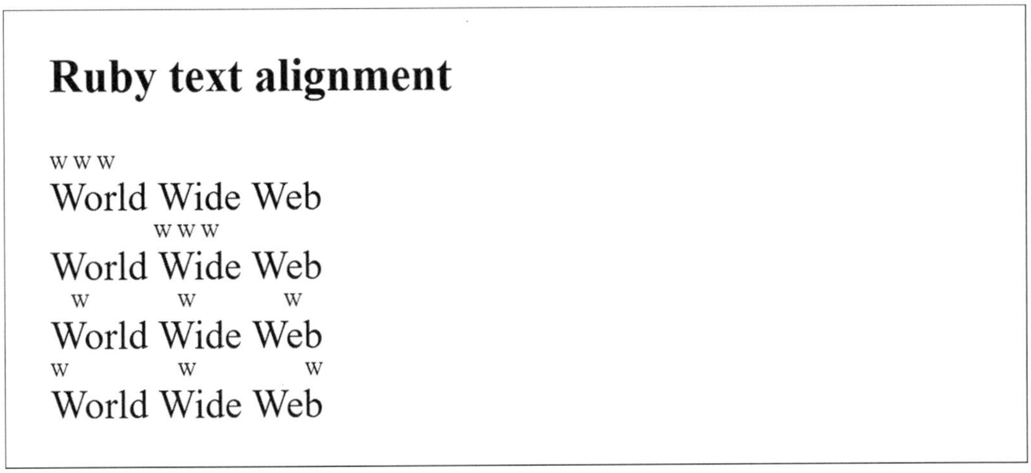

FIGURE 14.58 The result of Figure 14.57.

CHALLENGE 14.37

Implement the example but without any space between the characters in the `<rt>` elements to see the effects. Also, give reasons for why having no space between the characters makes some values not produce the desired alignment.

14.12.1.3 `ruby-merge`

The `ruby-merge` property allows you to specify how `<rt>` elements are rendered when there is more than one in a `<ruby>` element and is **inherited**. Table 14.19 lists the values it takes.

TABLE 14.19

The Values for the `ruby-merge` Property

Value	Function
separate	Renders `<rt>` elements in the same column as the corresponding `<rb>` element and is the **default**.
collapse	Joins together all `<rt>` elements and makes them span the corresponding `<rb>` element.
auto	Makes the browser decide how each `<rt>` element is rendered relative to the corresponding `<rb>` element.

The property is not yet implemented in any major browser as of time of writing, so, a demonstration is not possible here, but it is specified in a similar way as the other two.

14.12.2 Converting Elements to Ruby Elements

It is possible to make other elements behave like ruby elements, using the `display` property first introduced in Chapter 10. However, it is usually best to use the dedicated elements, as this ensures that screen readers and browsers that do not support CSS or have it turned off can recognize them. The ruby-specific `display` values are listed in Table 14.20 and Figures 14.59 and 14.60 show how they are used and the effect.

In the example, the first `<div>` element and the `<span>` elements inside it are not converted and so behave as normal. In contrast, the `.ruby{}` rule makes the `<div>` element of `class="ruby"` behave like a `<ruby>` element.; the `.rb{}` rule makes the `<span>` element of `class="rb"` behave like an `<rb>` element; the `.rbc{}` rule makes the `<span>` element of `class="rbc"` behave like an `<rbc>` element, and so on for the rest of the rules.

TABLE 14.20

The Ruby `display` Values

Value	Function
ruby	Makes an element behave like the `<ruby>` element.
ruby-base	Makes an element behave like the `<rb>` element.
ruby-text	Makes an element behave like the `<rt>` element.
ruby-base-container	Makes an element behave like the `<rbc>` element.
ruby-text-container	Makes an element behave like the `<rtc>` element.

```
CSS
.ruby { display: ruby; }
.rb { display: ruby-base; }
.rt { display: ruby-text; }
.rtb{ display: ruby-base-container; }
.rtc{ display: ruby-text-container; }

HTML
<h3>Ruby display values</h3>
<div>
  <span><span>World Wide Web</span></span>
  <span><span>W W W</span></span>
</div>
<br>
<div class="ruby">
  <span class="rbc"><span class="rb">World Wide Web</span></span>
  <span class="rtc"><span class="rt">W W W</span></span>
</div>
```

FIGURE 14.59 Example usage of ruby `display` values.

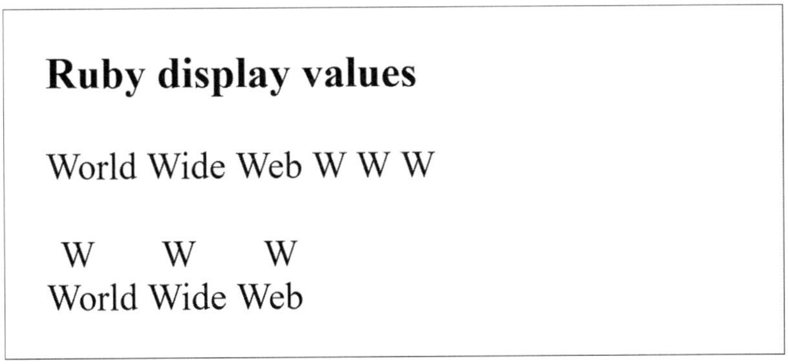

FIGURE 14.60 The result of Figure 14.59.

CHALLENGE 14.38

Implement Figure 14.59 using the dedicated ruby elements introduced in Chapter 3.

14.13 Useful Info

14.13.1 Web Links

CSS specifications: w3.org/standards

Web development documents: docs.webplatform.org

Accessibility: w3.org/WAI/tutorials, webaim.org

CSS tutorials (*Here are just a few free tutorial sites on CSS and other Web languages*): w3.org/wiki, html5rocks.com, sitepoint.com, w3schools.com, codecademy.com, quackit.com, developer.mozilla.org/en-US/docs/Web tutorialspoint.com, htmldog.com, htmlcodetutorial.com, echoecho.com, learn.shayhowe.com, html.net, tizag.com, cssbasics.com, cordova.apache. org, developers.google.com, csszengarden.com, webdesignermag.co.uk, css. maxdesign.com.au

Testing codes: jsfiddle.net, codepad.org, jsbin.com, cssdesk.com

Browser compatibility info: caniuse.com

15

Images: Content and Background Images

15.1 Introduction

The ability to control the use of images and tailor them to specification is very important in Web design in order to achieve the desired design goal. CSS provides numerous properties that enable this, including those for sizing, positioning, and clipping. This chapter introduces the common ones of these properties.

15.2 Learning Outcomes

After studying this chapter, you should:

- Know how to size images.
- Be able to align images on a page.
- Know how to clip an image into the desired shape.
- Be able to place an image in the desired box in CSS box model.
- Know how to add, size, and clip background images.
- Know how to keep an image fixed on a page.

15.3 Sizing Images

While the sizes of images can be specified using HTML `width` and `height` attributes on the `<img>` element, only the size of one image can be controlled at a time. In contrast, CSS allows you to control the size of multiple images simultaneously, the same way that the size of other elements can be controlled, using the `width` and `height` properties, which are **non-inherited.** Using CSS to control image size is especially useful because images on Web pages are often organized in groups in which all images in a group are the same size. For example, the images in the same row, column, or area are typically made the same size. This projects the sense of organization within a page and consistency across pages, all of which contribute to the extent to which users judge website pages to be aesthetically pleasing.

Furthermore, specifying image sizes, rather than leaving it for the browser to determine them in relation to the rest of the content of a page, can make the loading of a page go faster, as the browser can go ahead and load the rest of the page, leaving the space to fit in the images, which usually take longer than text to download. One of the most efficient ways of controlling the sizes of multiple images is to assign the respective `<img>` elements to the same class, for which a CSS rule is then defined that specifies the required width and height. Figure 15.1 shows how this is done, and Figure 15.2 the rendered result. Each `<img>` element is assigned to a class and `width` and `height` properties specified for that class.

```
CSS
.large { width: 480px; height: 480px; }
.medium { width: 240px; height: 240px; }
.small { width: 120px; height: 120px; }

HTML
<h1>Image sizing</h1>
<figure>
  <img class="small" src="images/beach.jpg" alt="a clean_beach">
  <img class="medium" src="images/beach.jpg" alt="a clean_beach">
  <img class="large" src="images/beach.jpg" alt="a clean_beach">
</figure>
```

FIGURE 15.1   Example usage of the `width` and `height` property.

FIGURE 15.2   The result of Figure 15.1. (Image from www.freeimages.co.uk.)

CHALLENGE 15.1

What is the difference between using % and em unit to size an image?

15.3.1 Specifying the Quality of Resized Images

When an image is scaled up or down, its quality may also be altered. By default, the browser decides on how to manage this process, determining, for example, which images to degrade more than others, if at all, and by what degree, all of which may or may not produce the desired results for specific contexts. For example, the browser may decide to smooth a pixelated image even though you want to display the image with the pixelation preserved. The CSS image-rendering property is provided to address this problem and allows you to specify how the browser should manage quality of scaled images. It is **inherited** and the values it takes are listed in Table 15.1. As of time of writing, the property is supported by only Opera and Chrome browsers.

Figure 15.3 shows how the property is used and Figure 15.4 the effects of all the values as rendered in the Chrome browser. The original image before scaling up is 25 × 25 pixels, which upon scaling up 3× (i.e., to 75 × 75, as shown in the code) got visibly degraded and pixelated.

TABLE 15.1

The Values Taken by the image-rendering Property

Value	Function
auto	The browser decides, using an image resampling technique that maximizes the appearance of an image, typically by smoothing the colors of an image. It is **default** and recommended for photographs.
crisp-edges	Preserves the contrast, colors, and edges of an image without any color smoothing or image blurring. Recommended for pixel-art images, which are raster images created through editing individual pixels.
pixelated	Preserves pixelated appearance of an image.
high-quality	The same as auto, except that images with the value are given priority over those with auto when there are limited system resources (i.e., images with auto may be degraded first or by greater amount). Note that the value is new as of time of writing and may still have its name changed.

```
CSS
img { image-rendering: auto; }

HTML
<h2>Image-rendering</h3>
<img src="images/pixel_stars.png" width="75" height="75">
```

FIGURE 15.3 Example usage of the image-rendering property.

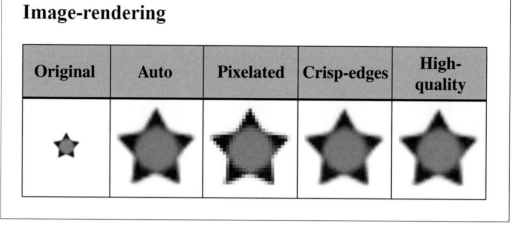

Image-rendering

Original	Auto	Pixelated	Crisp-edges	High-quality
☆				

FIGURE 15.4   The effects of the values of the image-rendering property.

CHALLENGE 15.2

Apart from specifying the image-rendering property because you have scaled images with your code, for what other reasons would specifying the property be useful? *Hint*: Consider, for example, user interaction.

15.3.2 Specifying Size for Responsive Images

In Chapter 6, how to specify responsive images was explained. As mentioned there, although the dimensions of an image are best specified using the HTML width and height attributes because this ensures faster and cleaner rendering of pages, these dimensions can also be specified using CSS. This is done using the width and height properties and the @media rule CSS at-rule, which allows these properties to be set for the image source specified in a <source> element. The at-rule takes a **media condition** and the CSS rule for specifying the width and height properties. As it will be shown in Chapter 21, the rule is also used in creating responsive layouts. Figure 15.5 shows an example of how the dimensions of responsive images are specified.

In the example, the #size{} rule specifies the dimensions for the image specified in the <img> element, the @media(min-width: 960px){} rule specifies a different #size{} rule for the specified media condition, and the @media(min-width: 1200px){} does similar. This means that when a condition is true, the srcset attribute provides the corresponding image source to the <img> element to embed and the #size{} rule provides the dimensions of the image. If none of the conditions are true, the image in the <img> element's src attribute is embedded and its dimensions are provided by the #size{}. To ensure that browsers that do not support CSS and the <picture> element have access to the image in the <img> element, the width and height attributes can be used on the element and CSS used for other browsers. Figure 15.6 shows how to do this, using the scoped attribute on the <style> element.

```
CSS
#size { width: 400px; height: 268px; }
@media (min-width: 960px) { #size { width: 800px;
       height: 536px; } }
@media (min-width: 1200px) { #size { width: 1024px;
       height: 686px; } }
HTML
<picture>
  <source media="(min-width: 1200px)" srcset="images/
  speech-fullshot.jpg">
  <source media="(min-width: 960px)" srcset="images/
  speech-midshot.jpg">
  <img src="images/speech-closeshot.jpg" alt="The president's
  speech" id="size">
</picture>
```

FIGURE 15.5   Specifying the dimensions for responsive images using CSS.

```
<picture>
  <style scoped media="(min-width: 960px)">
    #size { width: 800px; height: 536px; }
  </style>
  <style scoped media="(min-width: 1200px)">
    #size { width: 1024px; height: 686px; }
  </style>
  <source media="(min-width: 1200px)" srcset="images/
  speech-fullshot.jpg">
  <source media="(min-width: 960px)" srcset="images/
  speech-midshot.jpg">
  <img src="images/speech-closeshot.jpg" width="400"
  height="268" id="size" alt="The president's speech">
</picture>
```

FIGURE 15.6   Specifying the dimensions using both HTML and CSS.

In the example, when a condition is true, the `srcset` provides the corresponding image source for the `<img>` element to embed and the `#size{}` in the `<style>` element that matches the condition specifies the dimensions of the image. If no condition is true, the image source and the dimensions specified in the `<img>` element are used.

CHALLENGE 15.3

Implement the examples in Figures 15.5 and 15.6 with your own images and experiment the order of the `<source>` elements and see if there are any changes in behavior when the width of the browser is varied.

NOTE: Specifying responsive image resolutions

As mentioned in Section 6.3 of Chapter 6, the same image can be delivered in different resolutions to cater for different device resolutions by combining the `srcset` attribute with other attributes. It is useful to note that the CSS function, `image-set()`, being proposed as of time of writing may make it possible to achieve this goal much more easily. For example, the declaration below specifies three versions of the same image in different resolutions: the first is for normal-resolution devices, the second for high-resolution (e.g., retina display), and the third for extra-high-resolution (e.g., as needed by printers).

```
background-image: image-set("example.png" 1x,
                            "example-2x.png" 2x,
                            "example-print.png" 300dpi);
```

15.4 Clipping Images

The `clip-path` property allows you to specify which portions of an element to crop off to prevent them from being displayed, so that only a part of an image is shown. This is done through specifying a path, which can be specified as a URL referencing an inline or external SVG file, or a shape method, such as `circle()`. It is **non-inherited** and the values it supports are listed in Table 15.2. It is worth noting that it is supported only by Chrome and Opera with the `-webkit-` prefix as of time of writing.

TABLE 15.2

Values Supported by the `clip-path` Property

Values	Function
none	Specifies no clipping path.
clip-source	Specifies the URL to a clip path element.
basic-shape	Specifies a basic shape function, such as `inset()` (which defines an inset rectangle), `polygon()`, `circle()`, and `ellipse()`. The parameters specified and the syntax depends on the shape. For the circle and ellipse, the radius and the x-y coordinate of the center are specified. For the angular shapes, the coordinates of the corners are specified.
geometry-box	If specified with a basic-shape function, provides reference box for the shape. If specified alone, uses the edges of specified box as clipping path.
fill-box	Uses object's bounding box as reference box.
stroke-box	Uses the stroke of bounding box as reference box.
view-box	Uses the nearest SVG viewport as reference box.

```
CSS
.clipped {
  -webkit-clip-path: circle(30% at 50% 50%);
  clip-path: circle(30% at 50% 50%);
}

HTML
<h2>Image clipping</h2>
<img class="clipped" src="images/yacht.jpg">
```

FIGURE 15.7 Example usage of the `clip-path` property.

FIGURE 15.8 The result of Figure 15.7. (Image from www.freeimages.co.uk.)

See Chapter 8 on more on vendor prefixes. Figures 15.7 and 15.8 show how the property is used and the effect.

In the example, notice how the parameters for the `circle()` method are specified. The first specifies the radius as 30% of the width of the `<img>` element (i.e., reference box), and the last two specify the x-y coordinate for the center as 50% of the width from left and 50% of the height from the top. The browser essentially resolves these percentages from the reference box width and height using a formula. Note that textual contents too can be clipped.

CHALLENGE 15.4

Implement the example using a paragraph of text instead of image and experiment with the parameters of the `circle()` method.

CHALLENGE 15.5

Creating polygon clip paths can be difficult. Search the Web for a clip-path generator or maker and use it to create a polygon clip path (e.g., a star) and then use the
code generated with your own image, using Figure 15.7 as guide.

15.5 Aligning Images

Aligning images usually refers to aligning them horizontally along the width of the
browser window, since the height of a page is very arbitrary. Although this used to be
done using the HTML `align` attribute on the `<img>` element, this is no longer recommended and not supported in HTML5. Instead, this goal is accomplished using CSS
properties. What is required to center an image depends on whether or not the `<img>`
element that contains the image is inside the `<figure>` element. If it is, then the
`<figure>` element needs only be centered like any block level element, since it is one.
If it is not, then the `<img>` element first needs to be turned into a block level element,
using the `display` property. This is because the `<img>` element is an inline element
and therefore flows with text as if it is just another word. Centering a block basically
involves making the margin on either side of it equal, and the most efficient way to do
this is to set `margin-left` and `margin-right` to `auto`, so that the browser determines the values to use. Figure 15.9 shows how to do this and Figure 15.10 the result.

The `img{}` rule in the example sets the width and height of the image, changes the
`<img>` element to a block-level element, and sets the right and left margins. Note that
a declaration using the `margin` shorthand property (thus: `margin:  0  auto;`) will
produce the same result.

```
CSS
img {
  width: 240px;
  height: 240px;
  display: block;
  margin-left: auto;
  margin-right: auto;
}

HTML
<h3>Horizontal image centering</h3>
<p>Lorem ipsum dolor sit amet, consectetur adipiscing elit.
   Aenean rhoncus...</p>
<img src="beach.jpg" alt="A clean beach">
<p>Nulla tincidunt ornare nisl. Morbi hendrerit magna libero,
   ac tempus risus...</p>
```

FIGURE 15.9   Aligning images horizontally.

Horizontal image centering

Lorem ipsum dolor sit amet, consectetur adipiscing elit. Aenean rhoncus ipsum sem, nec euismod libero porttitor eu. Nulla ut urna a ligula tincidunt condimentum quis sit amet diam. Morbi sed magna odio. Nam non ultricies eros. Cras vehicula lobortis justo. Ut congue dapibus odio, in cursus nisl consectetur quis. Aenean volutpat volutpat vehicula. Phasellus tempor purus sed commodo posuere.

Nulla tincidunt ornare nisl. Morbi hendrerit magna libero, ac tempus risus dapibus pretium. Suspendisse venenatis scelerisque nibh sed gravida. Quisque aliquet mauris neque, vel sollicitudin nulla bibendum non.

FIGURE 15.10   The result of Figure 15.9. (Image from www.freeimages.co.uk.)

CHALLENGE 15.6

The declaration `margin: 0 auto;` will produce the same result as using the longhand properties used in Figure 15.9. How?

CHALLENGE 15.7

Implement the example in Figure 15.9, but with your image contained in a `<figure>` element, bearing in mind that the element is a block-level element.

15.6 Positioning and Fitting Images in Element's Box

It is also possible to align an image within an element's box as well as specify how to fit it in the box. The property for aligning is `object-position` and the one for fitting is `object-fit`.

15.6.1 `object-position`

The `object-position` property lets you specify the position of an image (or any object, including video) relative to the edges of the element's box. It is **inherited** and the values it takes are x-y coordinates of where to position an image. The values are expressed in **length values** and can be in absolute length units (e.g., px), box-relative lengths (i.e., %), font-relative lengths (e.g., em), or viewport-percentage lengths (e.g., vh and vw). Positive values move image toward the right or bottom, and negative toward the left or top. Figure 15.11 shows how the property is used and Figure 15.12 the result.

In the example, the `img{}` rule specifies the size of the `<img>` element, the border width, style and color, the background color, and right margin to put some space between the images. The `.object-position{}` rule positions the `<img>` element of

```
CSS
img {
 width: 200px;
 height: 136px;
 border: 1px solid #000;
 background-color: grey;
 margin-right: 5px;
}
.object-position {
 object-position: 60px 30px;
}

HTML
<h3>Object positioning</h3>
<img src="images/buttercup.png" alt="buttercup flower ">
<img class="object-position" src="images/buttercup.png"
 alt="buttercup flower">
```

FIGURE 15.11 Example usage of the `object-position` property.

FIGURE 15.12 The result of Figure 15.11. (Image from www.freeimages.co.uk.)

`class="object-position"` 60px from the left edge of the element's box and 30px from the top edge. Notice that the background of the image is transparent and that is why the element's background color is visible.

CHALLENGE 15.8

Implement the example, but with an image that has a non-transparent background in order to see the relationship between the background of the element and boundaries of the image.

15.6.2 `object-fit`

The `object-fit` property allows you to specify in a number of ways how the content of an element should be made to fill the element's content box. Its effect depends on the difference between the **aspect ratio** of the content and the aspect ratio produced by the specified dimensions for the element's content box. Aspect ratio is the ratio of width to height (i.e., width:height). The property is **non-inherited** and the values it takes are listed in Table 15.3. Figure 15.13 shows how the property is used and Figure 15.14 the effects of the values (not the output of Figure 15.13).

Notice in the example the large differences between the outputs of the values. This is because the aspect ratio of the image (content) is significantly different from that of the element's content box. The actual size of the image is 800 × 536 pixels, making its aspect ratio 1.49:1 (i.e., 800:536), while the size of the element's content box is 200 × 70 pixels, making its aspect ratio 2.86:1 (i.e., 200:70). The reference image represents the image displayed without `object-fit`.

TABLE 15.3

The Values of the `object-fit` Property

Value	Function
`fill`	Makes content fill the element's content box and may stretch content.
`contain`	Makes content retain aspect ratio as well as fit it within the element's content box, which means content may not fill element's content box.
`cover`	Makes content retain aspect ratio as well as fill the element's content box, which means content may be clipped at the edge.
`none`	Content is not resized to fit in the element's content box. The box simply shows the area of the image its size spans.
`scale-down`	Sizes content as if `none` or `contain` is specified, depending on which value makes the content smaller.

```
CSS
img {
  width: 200px;
  height: 70px;
  object-fit: contain;
}

HTML
<img src="images/yacht.jpg">
```

FIGURE 15.13   Example usage of the `object-fit` property.

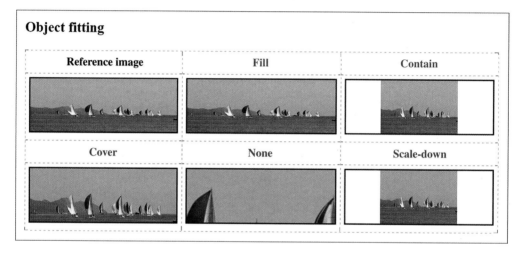

FIGURE 15.14   The effects of the values of the `object-fit` property. (Image from www.freeimages.co.uk.)

CHALLENGE 15.9

Implement the example, using your own image, and then experiment with the aspect ratio of the box to see the effects to better understand how to use the property.

15.7 Background Images

CSS allows you to add images to the background of an HTML element and also provides properties for controlling them in various ways.

15.7.1 Adding Background Images

The property used to add background images is the `background-image` property. It is **non-inherited** and can be used to place one or more images behind an element and use them as background. When multiple images are used, the one specified first is placed on top and the border of the element's box is drawn on top and the background color beneath everything. This means that when an element has an image as background, its background color is obscured. By default, an image is positioned at top-left corner of an element's box and then repeated to cover the area of the box. This means that the same image in different sizes will produce different visual effects. Figure 15.15 shows the image used here to demonstrate the use of the `background-image` property. It is called "wood.png" and is 512 × 512 in size.

Figure 15.16 shows how the `background-image` property is used and Figure 15.17 the result. In the `body{}` rule, `background-image` says to use the

FIGURE 15.15 The 512 × 512 image used for background. (Image from www.subtlepatterns. com.)

```
CSS
body {
  background-image: url("image/wood.png");
  padding: 15px;
}

HTML
<h2>Background image</h2>
<p>Lorem ipsum dolor sit amet, consectetur adipiscing elit.
   Aenean rhoncus ...</p>
```

FIGURE 15.16 Example usage of the `background-image` property.

Background image

Lorem ipsum dolor sit amet, consectetur adipiscing elit. Aenean rhoncus ipsum sem, nec euismod libero porttitor eu. Nulla ut urna a ligula tincidunt condimentum quis sit amet diam. Morbi sed magna odio. Nam non ultricies eros. Cras vehicula lobortis justo. Ut congue dapibus odio, in cursus nisl consectetur quis. Aenean volutpat volutpat vehicula. Phasellus tempor purus sed commodo posuere.

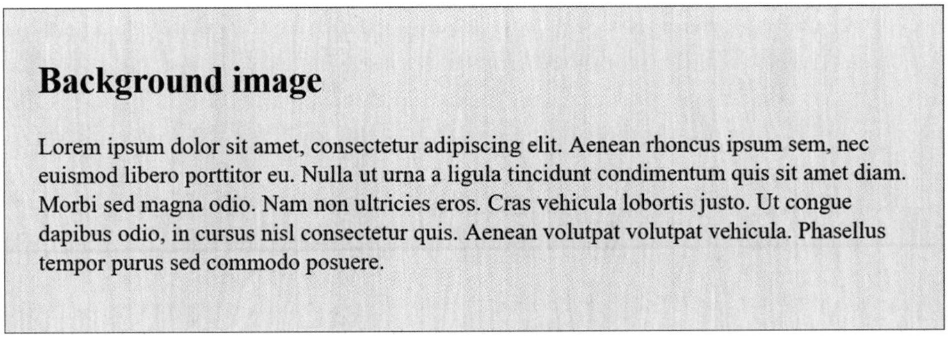

FIGURE 15.17 The result of Figure 15.16.

image, "wood.png," found at the location specified by the `url()` method for the background of the `<body>` element and `padding` specifies the space between the content of the element and its border.

Figures 15.18 and 15.19 show the same image used in the previous example in the `<p>` element instead of in the `<body>` element. A similar effect will be obtained with the `<div>` element.

```
CSS
p {
    background-image:
     url("data:image/png;base64,iVBORw0KGgoAAAANSUh...");
    padding: 15px;
}

HTML
<h2>Background image</h2>
<p>Lorem ipsum dolor sit amet, consectetur adipiscing elit.
   Aenean rhoncus ...</p>
```

FIGURE 15.18   Another example usage of the `background-image` property.

Background image

Lorem ipsum dolor sit amet, consectetur adipiscing elit. Aenean rhoncus ipsum sem, nec euismod libero porttitor eu. Nulla ut urna a ligula tincidunt condimentum quis sit amet diam. Morbi sed magna odio. Nam non ultricies eros. Cras vehicula lobortis justo. Ut congue dapibus odio, in cursus nisl consectetur quis. Aenean volutpat volutpat vehicula. Phasellus tempor purus sed commodo posuere.

FIGURE 15.19   The result of Figure 15.18.

NOTE: Another way to add background image

In Chapter 6, Section 6.3, you saw how **base64 encoding and data URI scheme** can be used with HTML to embed images in a page. This is possible too when using CSS to add image. The p{} rule below shows the same one in Figure 15.18, specifying the image in base64 data form. See Chapter 6 for the main advantage and disadvantage of the method.

```
p {
    background-image: url("data:image/png;base
            64,iVBORw0KGgoAAAANSUh...");
    padding: 15px;
}
```

CHALLENGE 15.10

What effect would different values of the `width` and `height` properties have on the size of the background image and the content of a page and why?

CHALLENGE 15.11

As noted in Chapter 6, the most common use of images for backgrounds is for decoration. What are the useful considerations you need to make when using background images, especially in terms of contrast, legibility, aesthetics, performance, etc.?

15.7.2 Repeating Background Images

As just mentioned, the image specified for background is by default repeated to make it fill the background of an element. One of the consequences of this is that the last image can sometimes get clipped if it does not fit precisely. The property that controls whether or not this repetition should happen and if it does how an image should be repeated is the `background-repeat` property. It is **non-inherited** and the values it takes are listed in Table 15.4.

The effects of the values listed in the table are demonstrated in Figures 15.21 through 15.28, using the image in Figure 15.20. Note that it is the 32x32 version of the image that is used in Figure 15.28.

15.7.2.1 `repeat-x` *and* `repeat-y`

Figure 15.21 shows how to use the `repeat-x` value and Figure 15.22 shows the result. Notice that the last image on the right is clipped.

TABLE 15.4

Values Used with the `background-repeat` Property

Value	Function
repeat	Repeats image horizontally and vertically (i.e., along x- and y-axis). As mentioned earlier, it is the default when background-image is specified.
repeat-x	Repeats image horizontally.
repeat-y	Repeats image vertically.
space	Repeats image horizontally and vertically without clipping any image at the edges. To achieve this, the images are evenly spaced.
round	Repeats image horizontally and vertically and scales it up or down so that it can be repeated without any images getting clipped at the edges.
no-repeat	Displays image only once and does not repeat it.

FIGURE 15.20   The 64 × 64 image used in Figures 15.20 through 15.28.

```
CSS
body {
  background-image: url("images/club_64.jpg");
  background-repeat: repeat-x;
  padding: 15px;
}

HTML
<body>
  <br>
  <h1>Background-repeat (repeat-x)</h1>
  <p>Lorem ipsum dolor sit amet, consectetur adipiscing elit.
     Aenean rhoncus,..</p>
</body>
```

FIGURE 15.21   Example usage of `repeat-x` value.

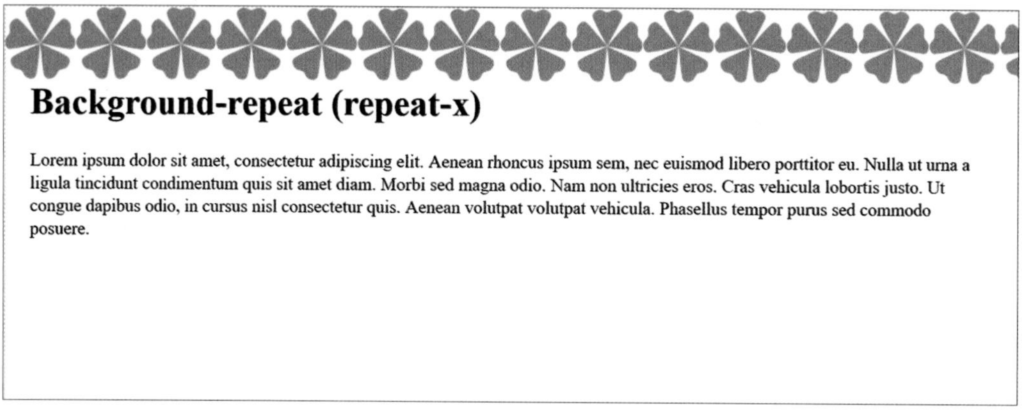

Background-repeat (repeat-x)

Lorem ipsum dolor sit amet, consectetur adipiscing elit. Aenean rhoncus ipsum sem, nec euismod libero porttitor eu. Nulla ut urna a ligula tincidunt condimentum quis sit amet diam. Morbi sed magna odio. Nam non ultricies eros. Cras vehicula lobortis justo. Ut congue dapibus odio, in cursus nisl consectetur quis. Aenean volutpat volutpat vehicula. Phasellus tempor purus sed commodo posuere.

FIGURE 15.22   The result of Figure 15.21.

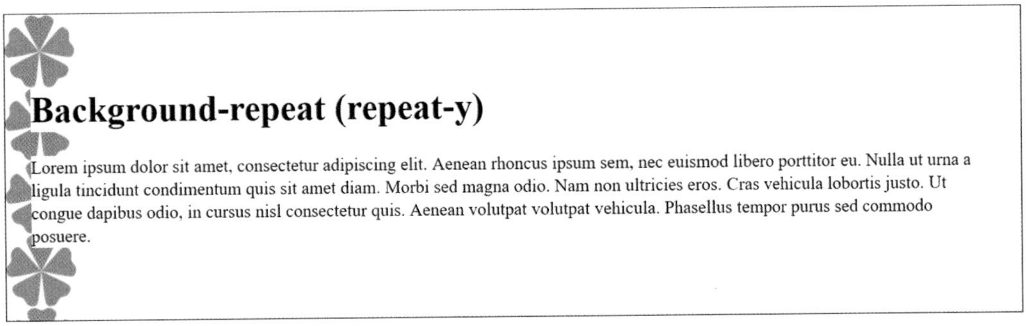

Background-repeat (repeat-y)

Lorem ipsum dolor sit amet, consectetur adipiscing elit. Aenean rhoncus ipsum sem, nec euismod libero porttitor eu. Nulla ut urna a ligula tincidunt condimentum quis sit amet diam. Morbi sed magna odio. Nam non ultricies eros. Cras vehicula lobortis justo. Ut congue dapibus odio, in cursus nisl consectetur quis. Aenean volutpat volutpat vehicula. Phasellus tempor purus sed commodo posuere.

FIGURE 15.23   The result of Figure 15.21 with `repeat-y` value.

Figure 15.23 shows the result of the code in Figure 15.21 when `repeat-y` is used instead of `repeat-x`, so that the declaration becomes `background-repeat: repeat-y;`.

CHALLENGE 15.12

To produce the example in Figure 15.23, an extra rule was added to the code in Figure 15.21 to make the background of the `<h1>` and `<p>` elements white so that their contents are legible on the image. Rewrite the example to reflect this.

15.7.2.2 `space` *and* `round`

Figure 15.24 shows an example of how the `space` value is used and Figure 15.25 the result in Opera. Figure 15.26 shows the effect of using `round`.

```
CSS
body {
  background-image: url("images/club_64.jpg");
  background-repeat: space;
  padding: 15px;
}
h1, p { background-color: #988670; color: #fff; padding: 10px; }

HTML
<body>
  <br>
  <h1>Background-repeat (space)</h1>
  <p>Lorem ipsum dolor sit amet, consectetur adipiscing elit.
     Aenean rhoncus...</p>
</body>
```

FIGURE 15.24   Example usage of the `space` value.

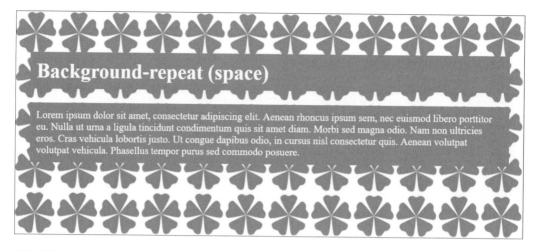

FIGURE 15.25   The result of Figure 15.24.

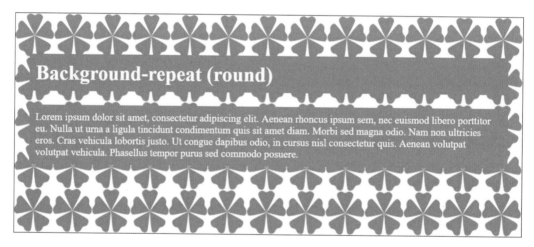

FIGURE 15.26   The result of Figure 15.24 using the `round` value.

Notice that there are 12 images in the first example, while there are 13 in the second, yet the width of the browser is the same in both cases. In the first, the images are equally spaced to cover the browser's width to avoid clipping the last one, while in the second the images are scaled down and another added to prevent it.

CHALLENGE 15.13

In what categories of websites might you use background images that are shown in the example and why?

15.8 Specifying Background Image Position Area

A background image may be positioned with reference to the border box, padding box, or content box, which are based on the CSS box model explained in Chapter 8. The property used to specify background image position area is the `background-origin` property. It is **non-inherited**, and the values it supports are listed in Table 15.5. Figures 15.27 and 15.28 show how the property is used and the effects of the values.

TABLE 15.5

Values Used with the `background-origin` Property

Value	Function
border-box	Places background image at the top-left corner of the border box.
padding box	Places background image at the top-left corner of the padding box.
content-box	Places background image at the top-left corner of the content box.

```
CSS
div {
  border: 10px solid gray;
  padding: 20px;
  background-image: url("images/club_32.jpg");
  background-repeat: repeat-x;
}
#border { background-origin: border-box;}
#padding { background-origin: padding-box;}
#content { background-origin: content-box;}

HTML
<div id="border">
 <h1>Background-origin (border-box)</h1>
 <p>Lorem ipsum dolor sit amet, consectetur adipiscing elit.
    Donec in ipsum at ex...</p>
</div>
<div id="padding">
 <h1>Background-origin (padding-box)</h1>
 <p>Lorem ipsum dolor sit amet, consectetur adipiscing elit.
    Donec in ipsum at ex...</p>
</div>
<div id="content">
 <h1>Background-origin (content-box)</h1>
 <p>Lorem ipsum dolor sit amet, consectetur adipiscing elit.
    Donec in ipsum at ex...</p>
</div>
```

FIGURE 15.27   Example usage of the `background-origin` property.

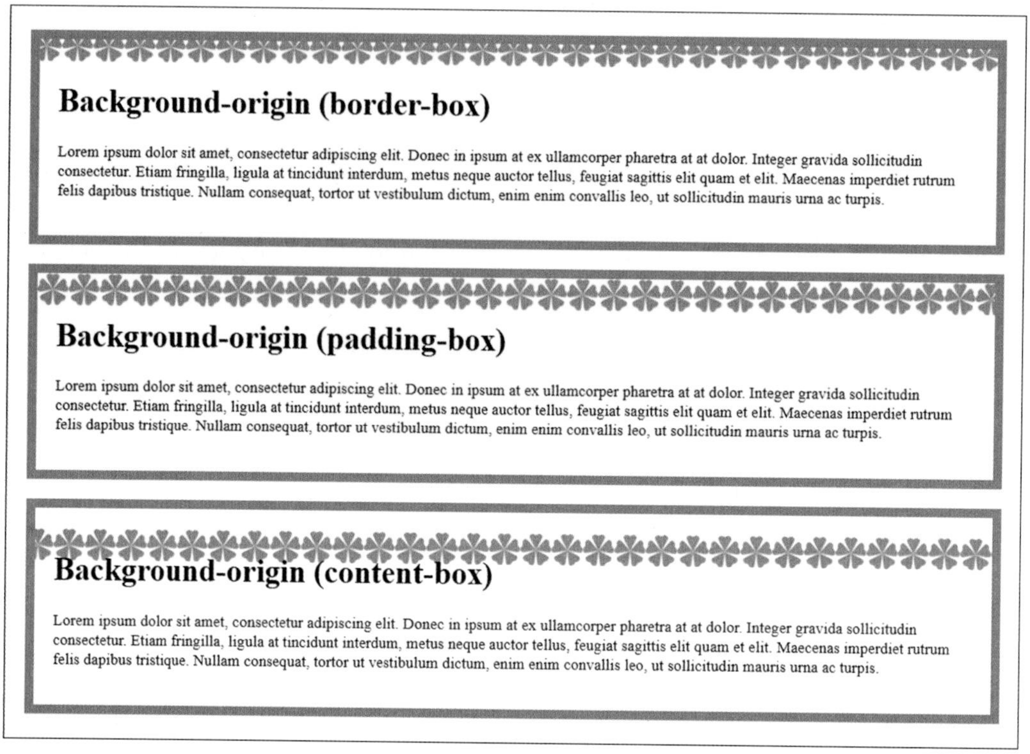

FIGURE 15.28 The result of Figure 15.27.

In the example, the div{} rule applies to all the <div> elements. The border property makes the borders 10px-thick solid line and grey; padding specifies the space between their content and their border; background-image specifies the image to use for their background (i.e., club.jpg); and background-repeat says to repeat the image only along the x-axis. The #border{}, #padding{}, and #content{} rules say to place the specified image at the top-left corner of the border box, padding box, and content box of the elements, respectively, from where it is then repeated.

CHALLENGE 15.14

Implement Figure 15.28 with the images aligned vertically.

15.9 Clipping Background Images

CSS allows you to crop the edges of a background image (or plain background) so that they do not extend to the outer edges of an element's border, padding, or content box. The property used to specify whether or not this should be done is the background-clip property. It is a **non-inherited** property and takes one of a number of values.

The standard ones are listed in Table 15.6. Figure 15.29 shows how the values are used and Figure 15.30 the effects.

In the example, the div{} rule says to make the border of the <div> elements 10px-thick dotted line and black; make the space between their content and their border 10px, and the background color lightpink. The div#one{}, div#two{}, and

TABLE 15.6

Values for the background-clip Property

Value	Function
border-box	Extends the background to the outer edge of the border box and is the default.
padding-box	Extends the background to the outer edge of the padding box.
content-box	Extends the background to the outer edge of the content box.

```
CSS
div {
  border: 10px dotted black;
  padding: 10px;
  background: light pink;
}
div#one { background-clip: border-box; }
div#two { background-clip: padding-box; }
div#three { background-clip: content-box; }

HTML
<h1>Background-clip</h1>
<div id="one">
 <h2>border-box</h2>
 <p>Lorem ipsum dolor sit amet, consectetur adipiscing elit.
    Aenean rhoncus ...</p>
</div>
<br>
<div id="two">
 <h2>padding-box</h2>
 <p>Lorem ipsum dolor sit amet, consectetur adipiscing elit.
    Aenean rhoncus ...</p>
</div>
<br>
<div id="three">
 <h2>content-box</h2>
 <p>Lorem ipsum dolor sit amet, consectetur adipiscing elit.
    Aenean rhoncus ...</p>
</div>
```

FIGURE 15.29 Example of how the background-clip property is used.

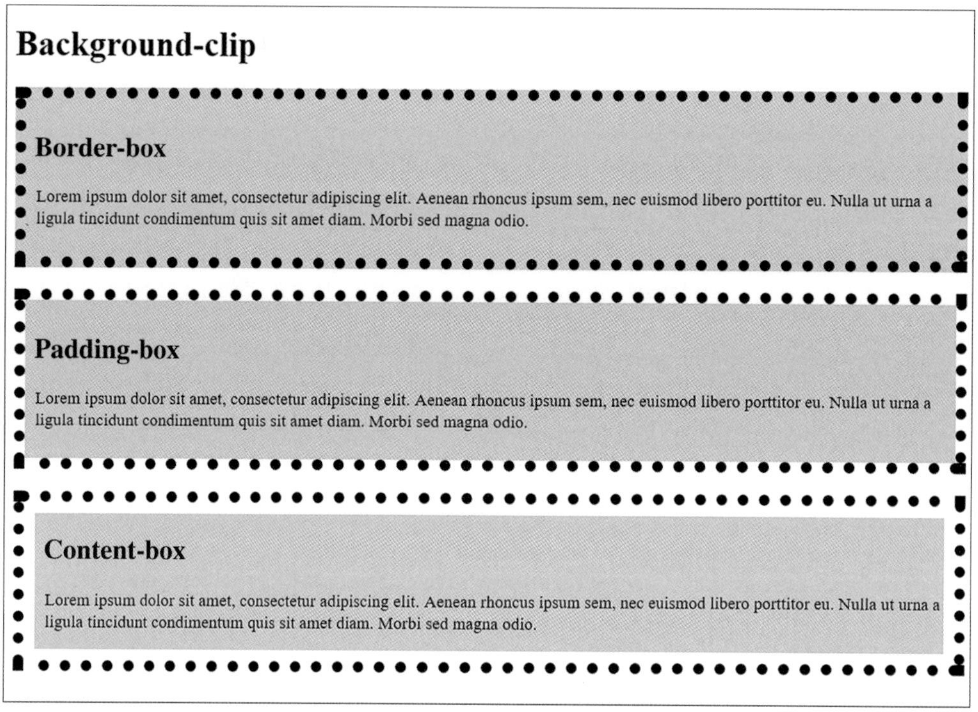

Background-clip

Border-box

Lorem ipsum dolor sit amet, consectetur adipiscing elit. Aenean rhoncus ipsum sem, nec euismod libero porttitor eu. Nulla ut urna a ligula tincidunt condimentum quis sit amet diam. Morbi sed magna odio.

Padding-box

Lorem ipsum dolor sit amet, consectetur adipiscing elit. Aenean rhoncus ipsum sem, nec euismod libero porttitor eu. Nulla ut urna a ligula tincidunt condimentum quis sit amet diam. Morbi sed magna odio.

Content-box

Lorem ipsum dolor sit amet, consectetur adipiscing elit. Aenean rhoncus ipsum sem, nec euismod libero porttitor eu. Nulla ut urna a ligula tincidunt condimentum quis sit amet diam. Morbi sed magna odio.

FIGURE 15.30   The result of Figure 15.29.

`div#three{}` rules say the background color must not extend to the outer edges of the `<div>` elements' border-box, padding-box, and content-box, respectively.

CHALLENGE 15.15

In the first two `<div>` elements, there seems enough space between the content and the left and right edges of the background color. How would you create the same thing in the third `<div>` element?

CHALLENGE 15.16

In the example, replace the plain background with an actual image.

15.10 Sizing Background Images

The size of background images is controlled with the `background-size` property. It is **non-inherited** and the standard values it supports are listed in Table 15.7. Figure 15.31 shows a two-value example and Figure 15.32 the rendered result.

TABLE 15.7

Values for the `background-size` Property

Value	Function
`auto`	Keyword that tells the browser to determine size based on the actual width and height of image and the aspect ratio. It is the default value.
`<length>`	Specifies image's width and height in **length values** (e.g., px and em). The first value represents the width and the second height. If only one value is specified, the second defaults to `auto`.
`<percentage>`	Specifies image's width and height as percentage of the containing element. The first value represents the width and the second height. If only one value is specified, the second defaults to `auto`.
`cover`	Keyword that specifies to uniformly scale image so that it covers the whole of the background positioning area, even if one of the edges extends beyond the background positioning area and is clipped.
`Contain`	Keyword that specifies to uniformly scale image to be as large as possible, but not larger than the background positioning area, so that no edge is clipped, even if this means that the image ends up not covering the entire background positioning area.

```
CSS
body {
  background-image: url("images/rose_transparent.png");
  background-repeat: repeat-x;
  background-size: 80px 80px;
}
h1, h2, p { text-align: center; }

HTML
<h1>Background-size (80x80px)</h1>
<p>Background image size is resized to 80x80px</p>
<br>
<h2>Actual size of image</h2>
<p>Below is the actual size of the image, which is 300x265px</p>
<p><img src="images/rose_transparent.png" alt="peach roses"></p>
```

FIGURE 15.31 Example usage of the `background-size` property.

FIGURE 15.32   The result of Figure 15.31. (Image from www.freeimages.co.uk.)

In the body{} rule in the example, background-image specifies the image to use for background, background-repeat says to repeat the image across the x-axis, and background-size says to resize it to 80 × 80. The h1, h2, p{} rule horizontally centers the content of the <h1>, <h2>, and <p> elements. Note that the auto and percentage values can be specified the same way as px. The example also displays the image in its actual size using the <img> element.

CHALLENGE 15.17

Rewrite the code in Figure 15.32 using your own image so that the heading is not on the repeated image but under it and the positions of other texts are adjusted accordingly. Also, what do you think the design benefits are of this modification?

15.10.1 background-size **with Keywords**

When using keywords to size an image, only one value (i.e., cover or contain) can be specified. Figures 15.33 and 15.34 show the usage and the different results they produce. In the div{} rule in the example, the width and height properties specify the size of the <div> element, border makes the element's border 1px-thick solid line and black, background-image specifies the image to use as

```
CSS
div {
 width: 800px;
 height: 350px;
 border: 1px solid #000;
 background-image: url("images/yacht.jpg");
 background-repeat: no-repeat;
}
.cover { background-size: cover; }

HTML
<h2>Background-size (cover)</h2>
<div class="cover"></div>
```

FIGURE 15.33 Using keywords with the `background-size` property.

FIGURE 15.34 The result of Figure 15.33. (Image from www.freeimages.co.uk.)

background (i.e., yacht.jpg), and `background-repeat` says not to repeat it. The `#cover{}` rule says to scale the image so that it covers the entire background position area (i.e., containing `<div>` element), which means that some part of the bottom has to be cut off.

Figure 15.35 shows the result of Figure 15.33 with the value of the `background-size` property changed to `contain` in the `.cover{}` rule. The resulting rule therefore says to scale the background image so that it is contained in the element, which means part of the container is left unfilled.

Background-size (contain)

FIGURE 15.35   The result of Figure 15.33 using the `contain` value. (Image from www.freeimages.co.uk.)

CHALLENGE 15.18

Rewrite the code in Figure 15.33 to make it more efficient and say why it is more efficient.

CHALLENGE 15.19

Rewrite the code in Figure 15.33 so that the effects of `cover` and `contain` are shown together on the same page.

15.11 Multiple Background Images

Some design goals involve the use of multiple background images. Figure 15.36 shows the code for creating multiple background images and Figure 15.37 shows the result.

In the `div#multi{}` rule, the `width` and `height` properties specify the size of the `<div>` element of `id="multi"`, the `background-image` property specifies the two images ("rose_transparent.png" and "grey_wall.png") to use for its background (the first image occupies the top-most position and the last the bottom-most), the `background-repeat` property says the first image should be repeated across the x-axis and the second not repeated, and the `background-size` property says to make the size of the first image 60 × 60px and use the `cover` value for the second. Note that the **image specified first is displayed on top**. Also, the **images on top must have transparent background** in order for those underneath to be visible. This means that they must be saved in a file format that supports transparency (e.g., png).

In the `div#inner{}` rule, the `width` property specifies the width of the `<div>` element of `id="inner"`, the `padding` property centers the element, both horizontally

CSS
```
div#multi {
  width: 800px;
  height: 400px;
  background-image: url("images/rose_transparent.png"),
  url("images/grey_wall.png");
  background-repeat: repeat-x, no-repeat;
  background-size: 60px 60px, cover;
}
div#inner {
  width: 500px;
  padding: 100px 150px;
  color: #F9F0B5;
}
h2 { text-align: center; }
```
HTML
```
<h1>Multiple background images</h1>
<div id="multi">
  <div id="inner">
   <h2>Peach Roses</h2>
   Lorem ipsum dolor sit amet, consectetur adipiscing elit.
   Aenean rhoncus ipsum...
  </div>
</div>
```

FIGURE 15.36 Specifying multiple background images.

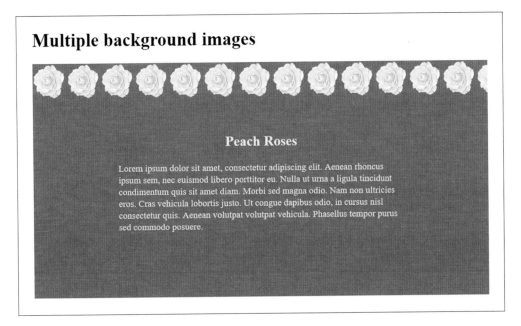

FIGURE 15.37 The result of Figure 15.36. (Image from www.freeimages.co.uk.)

and vertically, inside the `<div>` element of `id="multi"`, and `color` says to give the text content #F9F0B5 color. The `h2{}` rule centers the content of the `<h2>` element horizontally.

CHALLENGE 15.20

Implement the example using your own images and modify the code so that it also has the smaller image repeated vertically. Also, state for what types of websites such design would be acceptable and why.

15.12 Fixing the Position of Background Images

A background image can be made to remain in one position or move when a page is scrolled up or down. The `background-attachment` property is the property that is used to do this. It is **non-inherited** and the standard values it supports are `fixed` (which makes the image remain in one position) and `scroll` (the default value, which makes the image move up and down as the page is scrolled up and down). Figure 15.38 shows how the property is used and Figure 15.39 the effect during scrolling.

```
CSS
body {
  background-image: url("images/club_64.jpg");
  background-repeat: no-repeat;
  background-attachment: fixed;
  padding: 15px;
}

HTML
<h1>Background-attachment</h1>
<p>Lorem ipsum dolor sit amet, consectetur adipiscing elit.
   Aenean rhoncus ipsum...</p>
```

FIGURE 15.38   Example usage of the `background-attachment` property.

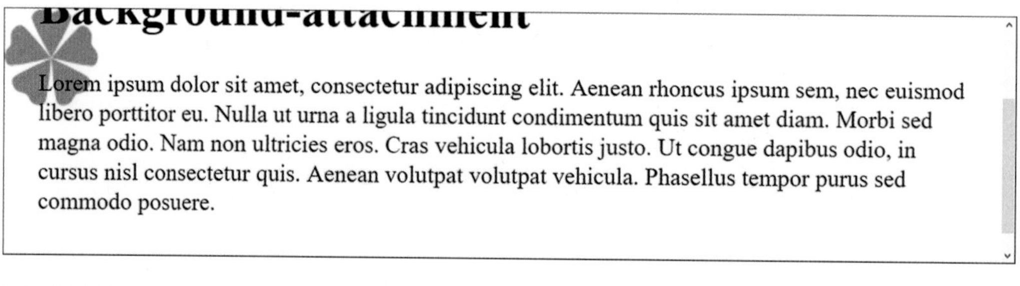

FIGURE 15.39   The result of Figure 15.38.

In the example, the `background-image` property specifies the image to use for the `<body>` element's background, the `background-repeat` property says not to repeat it, the `background-attachment` property says to make its position fixed, and `padding` specifies the space between all the contents of the `<body>` element and the border of the element's box. In Figure 15.39, notice that the heading is scrolling off screen while the background image remains at the top-left corner of the window.

CHALLENGE 15.21

What types of images usually benefit best from being fixed as shown in the example? Give reasons for your answer.

15.13 Positioning Background Images

A background image can be positioned in a number of places within an element's box. The property used to do this is the `background-position` property and it allows you to specify where in the browser window to place a background image that is not repeated. It is **non-inherited** and typically takes a pair of values. The first value specifies the horizontal position and the second the vertical. Each pair can be a pair of **keywords, length values** (such as `px` and `em`), or **percentage values**. The allowed keyword pairs and the demonstration of how they position a background image are shown in Figure 15.40. One way to look at it is that you can only specify `left`, `center`, and `right` for the first value, and `top`, `center`, and `bottom` for the second. If only one value is specified, a default of `center` is used for the other.

Figure 15.41 shows how keyword values are used with the `background-position` property and Figure 15.42 the result. In the example, the `background-image` property specifies the URL of the image to use for the `<body>` element's background, the `background-repeat` property says not to repeat the image, the `background-attachment` property specifies to make the position fixed, the `background-position` property says to position it at the horizontal and vertical center of the page (i.e., the `<body>` element), and `padding` specifies the space

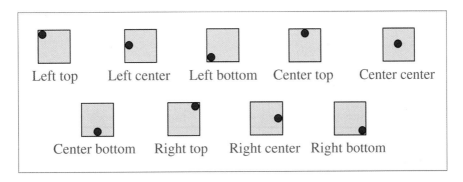

FIGURE 15.40 Illustration of the values for the `background-position` property.

```
CSS
body {
    background-image: url("images/rose_transparent.png");
    background-repeat: no-repeat;
    background-attachment: fixed;
    background-position: center center;
    padding: 0 15px;
}

HTML
<h1>Background-position</h1>
<p>Lorem ipsum dolor sit amet, consectetur adipiscing elit.
    Donec in ipsum at...</p>
```

FIGURE 15.41   Example usage of the `background-position` property.

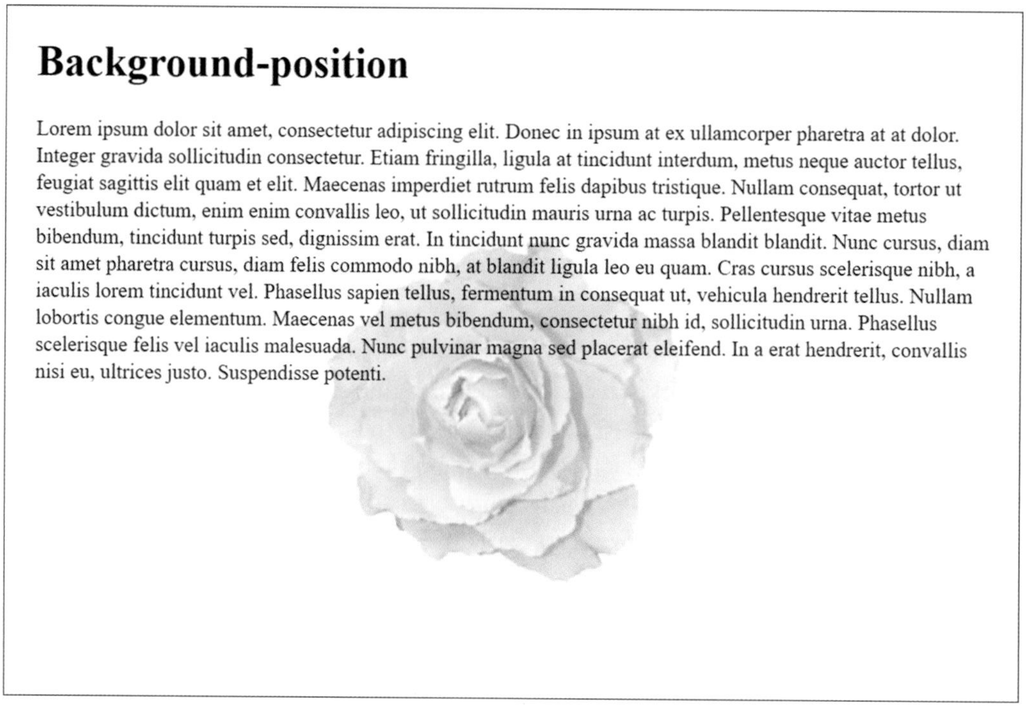

Background-position

Lorem ipsum dolor sit amet, consectetur adipiscing elit. Donec in ipsum at ex ullamcorper pharetra at at dolor.
Integer gravida sollicitudin consectetur. Etiam fringilla, ligula at tincidunt interdum, metus neque auctor tellus,
feugiat sagittis elit quam et elit. Maecenas imperdiet rutrum felis dapibus tristique. Nullam consequat, tortor ut
vestibulum dictum, enim enim convallis leo, ut sollicitudin mauris urna ac turpis. Pellentesque vitae metus
bibendum, tincidunt turpis sed, dignissim erat. In tincidunt nunc gravida massa blandit blandit. Nunc cursus, diam
sit amet pharetra cursus, diam felis commodo nibh, at blandit ligula leo eu quam. Cras cursus scelerisque nibh, a
iaculis lorem tincidunt vel. Phasellus sapien tellus, fermentum in consequat ut, vehicula hendrerit tellus. Nullam
lobortis congue elementum. Maecenas vel metus bibendum, consectetur nibh id, sollicitudin urna. Phasellus
scelerisque felis vel iaculis malesuada. Nunc pulvinar magna sed placerat eleifend. In a erat hendrerit, convallis
nisi eu, ultrices justo. Suspendisse potenti.

FIGURE 15.42   The result of Figure 15.41.

between all the contents of the `<body>` element and the edges of the element's box.
Note that if the height for the element containing the image is not specified, the vertical positioning may not work properly, unless the `background-attachment: fixed` declaration is also included to fix the image, as used in the example.

Figure 15.43 shows how the same example in Figure 15.41 and Figure 15.42 can be achieved with percentage values. The values represent, respectively, the horizontal and

```
CSS
body {
  background-image: url("images/rose_transparent.png");
  background-repeat: no-repeat;
  background-attachment: fixed;
  background-position: 50% 50%;
  padding: 0 15px;
}

HTML
<h1>Background-position</h1>
<p>Lorem ipsum dolor sit amet, consectetur adipiscing elit.
  Donec in ipsum at...</p>
```

FIGURE 15.43   Using % values in Figure 15.41 to achieve Figure 15.42.

vertical distances from the top-left corner of the browser window, which is 0% 0%. So, 50% 50% specifies a position that is 50% of the browser's width and 50% of the height from the top-left corner.

CHALLENGE 15.22

From design principles point of view, say why using an image as in the example may not be good practice and also say how to minimize any adverse effects of using images in this way. *Hint*: See Decorative images in Chapter 6.

15.14 Shorthand Background Property

The `background` property is shorthand for specifying the various longhand background sub-properties just introduced (i.e., `background-clip`, `background-color`, `background-image`, `background-origin`, `background-position`, `background-repeat`, `background-size`, and `background-attachment`). One or more of these sub-properties can be specified in any order in a space-separated list. The only exception is that the value for `background-size` must be specified after that for `background-position`, separated with a forward slash (/). The property can also be used to specify multiple images. Figure 15.44 shows how it is used for a single background image and Figure 15.45 the result.

In the example, the `background` property specifies the `background-color`, `background-image`, `background-position/background-size`, `background-repeat`, and `background-clip properties` for the `<p>` element, the `border` property says to make its border 10px-thick dotted line and black, and the `padding` property specifies the space between the content of the element and the border.

```
CSS
p {
  background: lightgrey url("images/rose_transparent_full.png")
   right bottom/80px no-repeat padding-box;
  border: 10px dotted black;
  padding: 20px;
}

HTML
<h2>Background shorthand</h2>
<p>Lorem ipsum dolor sit amet, consectetur adipiscing elit.
   Donec in ipsum at...</p>
```

FIGURE 15.44   Example usage of the background property.

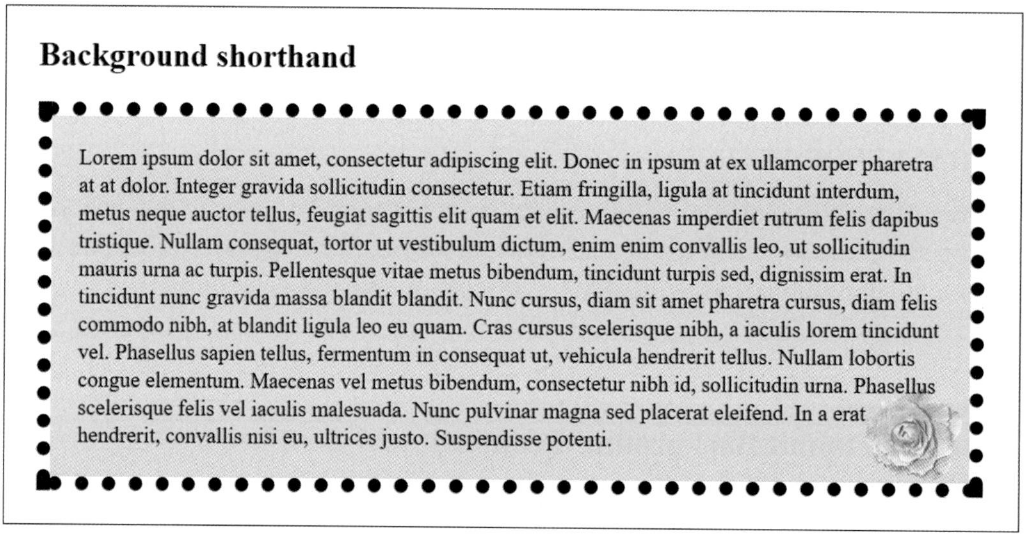

FIGURE 15.45   The result of Figure 15.44.

CHALLENGE 15.23

Implement the example in Figure 15.45, using your own content, but with the image positioned center-bottom in a <div> element and the text in a <p> element. What do you think are the pros and cons of both design approach? *Hint:* Varying the browser width for both approaches may give you some additional ideas.

15.14.1 Multiple Background Images with background Property

Figure 15.46 shows how the background property can be used to specify multiple background images and implements the example presented earlier in Figures 15.36 and 15.37.

In the div#multi{} rule in the example, the width and height properties specify the size of the <div> element of id="multi", the first set of values of the background property says to use the image "peach_rose.png" for background, repeat it across the x-axis, position it at top-left corner of the element, and size it to 60 × 60px. The second set of values says to also use the image "grey_wall.png" for the same background, not repeat it, position it at top-left corner, and make it cover the element's box. Essentially, all the values relating to one image are specified, followed by those of another, separated by comma. The first image specified occupies the topmost position.

In the div#inner{} rule, the width property makes the width of the <div> element of id="inner" 500px, the margin property centers the element horizontally and vertically inside the <div> element of id="multi", and the color property says to give the text content #F9F0B5 color. The h2{} rule centers the content of the <h2> element horizontally.

```
CSS
div#multi {
   width: 800px;
   height: 400px;
   background: url("images/rose_transparent.png") repeat-x
      top left/60px 60px, url("images/gray_wall.png"),
      no-repeat, top left/cover;
}
div#inner {
   width: 500px;
   margin: 100px auto;
   color: #F9F0B5;
}
h2 { text-align: center; }

HTML
<h1>Multiple background images</h1>
 <div id="multi">
 <div id="inner">
   <h2>Peach Roses</h2>
   Lorem ipsum dolor sit amet, consectetur adipiscing elit.
   Aenean rhoncus ipsum...
 </div>
</div>
```

FIGURE 15.46 Specifying multiple background images with the background property.

CHALLENGE 15.24

Would using the `background` property twice produce the same result as in the example? If not, why?

15.15 Useful Info

15.15.1 Web Links

CSS specifications: w3.org/standards

Web development documents: docs.webplatform.org

Accessibility: w3.org/WAI/tutorials, webaim.org

CSS tutorials (*Here are just a few free tutorial sites on CSS and other Web languages*): w3.org/wiki, html5rocks.com, sitepoint.com, w3schools. com, codecademy.com, quackit.com, developer.mozilla.org/en-US/docs/ Web tutorialspoint.com, htmldog.com, htmlcodetutorial.com, echoecho.com, learn.shayhowe.com, html.net, tizag.com, cssbasics.com, cordova.apache. org, developers.google.com, csszengarden.com, webdesignermag.co.uk, css.maxdesign.com.au

Testing codes: jsfiddle.net, codepad.org, jsbin.com, cssdesk.com

CSS generators for various features: enjoycss.com, bennettfeely.com, cssplant.com

Placeholder images: lorempixel.com

Browser compatibility info: caniuse.com

16

Images: Effects

16.1 Introduction

The use of images to create visual effects is standard practice in Web design. Image effects are essential in creating interactivity, such as in rollover effect, and some, such as gradients, filters, and image blending, can be useful for adding aesthetics to a page. In this chapter, some of the CSS properties used in creating image effects are introduced.

16.2 Learning Outcomes

After studying this chapter, you should:

- Understand how to create and use image sprites for buttons.
- Know how to create gradients and more complex visual effects with them.
- Know how to blend images.

16.3 Image Sprites

An **image sprite** is an image that is one of multiple smaller images contained in a single larger image that is isolated for use as necessary. For example, a single larger image might contain all the icons or buttons used for a page, each of which is then displayed only when needed. The main advantage of the method is that it helps Web pages load faster. It is able to do this because it saves creating separate image files for each image, which requires multiple downloads that can be demanding on the Web server and also cause long download times. This problem is especially exaggerated when each icon or button has multiple versions for use for their states. The typically defined states for an interactive icon or button are **normal** (the normal appearance), **hover** (appearance when cursor is over it), and **active** (appearance when it is being pressed). A fourth one, known as **disabled** (appearance when not available), is seldom relevant in most Web applications. The term used to describe the changes that occur when the cursor moves over an interactive object is sometimes known as **rollover**.

Naturally, before sprites can be used they have to be created or obtained in some other ways. Whatever the case, it is important to know the positions of the smaller images in the larger image so that they can be specified accurately to display them properly. Figure 16.1 shows, on a transparent background in Photoshop, the image sprites for the three states of a button. The grid is displayed to help illustrate the dimensions. It is these dimensions that are used to specify which sprite to display. The more consistent the dimensions of images and the distances between them, the easier they are to work with and the more professional the changes from one state to another will be. The pixels-grid helps tremendously in achieving this goal. This consistency guideline, of course, goes with the standard design guideline that graphics items to be used on the same row should have the same height and those in the same column should have the same width. Figure 16.2 shows how to use CSS to implement sprites from the above image, and Figure 16.3 shows the results.

To understand how the use of image sprites works, imagine that the `<a>` element's box is a window or cutting in a card and in order to display a sprite, the image is moved to align it with the window accordingly. In the `a.button{}` rule in the example, the `background-image` property specifies the image "buttons" containing the sprites, and `display:inline-block` changes the `<a>` element from an inline element (which it is by default) to an inline-block element. This enables the width and height of the element to be specified to match the size of the sprites. The `width` property specifies the width of the `<a>` element. The width of 220px (200+10+10) is specified so that it is wide enough to allow each sprite and its shadow to show. To display the **normal-state** sprite, the `a#register{}` rule moves the image to 0px 0px with the `background-position` property and specifies the height of the sprite as 60px (50+10) so as to include the shadow. This positions the top-left corner of the image at the top-left corner of the `<a>` element's box and the sprite inside the box.

To display the **hover-state** sprite when the cursor is inside the `<a>` element's box, the `a#register: hover{}` moves the image up 60px (i.e., –60px) so that coordinate point 0px 60px on it (which is where the hover-state sprite starts) is at the top-left corner of the element's box. This moves the hover-state sprite into the box. The rule also specifies a height of 60px for the box to show the sprite.

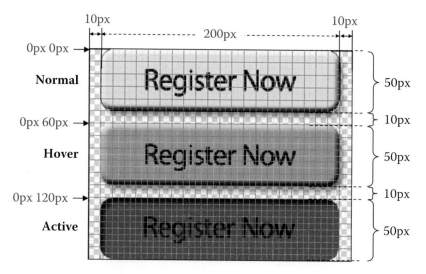

FIGURE 16.1 An image comprising button sprites.

```
CSS
a.button {
  background-image: url("images/buttons.png");
  display: inline-block;
  width: 220px;
}
a#register {
  background-position: 0px 0px;
  height: 60px;
}
a#register:hover {
  background-position: 0px -60px;
  height: 60px;
}
a#register:active {
  background-position: 0px -120px;
  height: 50px;
}

HTML
<a class="button" id="register"></a>
```

FIGURE 16.2 Code for displaying the button sprites in Figure 16.1.

Normal state   Hover state   Active state

FIGURE 16.3 The results of Figure 16.2.

To display the **active-state sprite** when the inside of the `<a>` element is clicked, the `a#register: active{}` rule moves the image up 120px (i.e., −120px) so that coordinate 0px 120px on it (where the active-state sprite starts) aligns with the top-left corner of the box and also specifies a height of 50px. Note that moving an image up or left requires a **negative value**, while moving it down or right requires a **positive value**.

CHALLENGE 16.1

Use a graphics editor, such as Photoshop or GIMP, to create your own icon or button sprites and use them to create an interactive icon or button, using the code in Figure 16.2. Alternatively, or in addition, you could search the Web for "CSS sprites generators" and use one to create the sprites.

CHALLENGE 16.2

Add a border declaration to the `a.button{}` rule in your implementation from the previous challenge to show the border so that you can see the relationship between the placement of the sprite and the `<a>` element's box. Also, try reducing the width and height of the element to see how much of the image is shown.

CHALLENGE 16.3

The code in Figure 16.2, or your implementation, can be made more compact by combining some rules. Which and how?

16.3.1 Using Image Sprites with the `<input>` Element

Image sprites can also be used with the `<input>` element. Indeed, if you are dealing with forms and want to use image sprites, then you are most likely to use them with the `<input>` element (typically **image-input type**), rather than the `<a>` element. Figure 16.4 shows the same code in Figure 16.2 with a few modifications to deal with an `<input>` element of the image-button type first introduced in Chapter 5. The code produces the same output as Figure 16.3.

As mentioned in Chapter 5, the **image-input type** is the type of `<input>` element that allows an image to be specified for use as a submit button. The function of the button is predetermined, in that when it is pressed, it initiates form submission. In the example, the CSS rules do the same thing as those in Figure 16.2, except that there is no need for the `display: inline-block;` declaration, since although the `<input>` element, like the `<a>` element, is an inline element, it allows its size to be specified, which is necessary to specify a big enough size to let the element's background image sprite show.

```
CSS
#register {
  background-image: url("images/buttons.png");
  width: 220px;
  height: 60px;
  background-position: 0 0;
}
#register:hover { background-position: 0 -60px; height: 60px; }
#register:active { background-position: 0 -120px; height: 50px; }

HTML
<form>
  <input type="image" name="regButton" id="register" alt="submit
  form" src="images/transparent_image.png">
</form>
```

FIGURE 16.4 Code for using the image sprites in Figure 16.1 with image-input type.

So, in the `#register{}` rule, the `background-image` property specifies the image to use for the background of the `<input>` element, the `width` and `height` properties specify the element's size, and the `background-position` property positions the image at the top-left corner of the element's box. The `#register:hover{}` and `#register:active{}` rules perform exactly the same functions as described for Figure 16.2. It is in the HTML code that the most important change is made. Notice there that another image is specified for the `<input>` element. This is because the element requires that an image is specified, otherwise a default label or the alternative text is displayed, depending on browser. This means that if no image is specified, the text is displayed on the specified background image, and if an image is specified, it is similarly displayed on the background image. To work around this, a transparent image is specified. This is an image that contains nothing and has a transparent background. The image can be any size, since it is only symbolic, but should be as small as possible for obvious download performance reasons. The one used in the example is 5 × 5px. Common image formats that allow a transparent background include PNG and GIF.

CHALLENGE 16.4

In the example, why does the amount of space occupied by the transparent image on the rendered page not depend on the size of the image? Also, specify the same image for the `src` attribute as specified with the `background-image` property to better understand why the transparent image workaround is necessary.

NOTE: Sprite accessibility

HTML does not provide a method for adding text alternative to sprites as it does for normal images. This raises accessibility issues. One of the easiest ways this is fixed is by including alternative text inside the element to which the CSS background image is attached; in the case of the examples, the `<a>` and `<input>` elements.

16.4 Gradients

Gradients work on the general basis of an imaginary line that has a start and an ending. Each point on the line has a different color and defines the color of the gradient that runs through it. A specified color starts at a specified point on the line, known as a **color stop**, and gradually changes to another that is specified at another stop. In theory, there can be as many stops as possible and the shape of a gradient can be **linear** or **radial**. Figure 16.5, which is the type of graphical interface used in graphics programs to create a gradient, illustrates this basic principle. The image shows both the stops, for colors and the opacity (i.e., transparency). The stops at the bottom are for the colors,

FIGURE 16.5   A typical graphical gradient tool.

and those at the top are for the opacity for each stop. The gradient starts with orange, gradually changes to black, then to orange, and then black. CSS can be used to specify the various parameters for creating gradients in this way.

Gradients are seldom used in the design of a Web page. This is because they are mostly suitable for adding visual effects, and adding visual effects to a whole page is not usually desirable, especially because gradients can compromise legibility. However, gradients are commonly used in buttons and icons to help add the illusion of depth to them. CSS supports both linear and radial gradients, and the properties used to create them are the `background-image` property or the shorthand `background` property.

16.4.1 Linear Gradients

Linear gradients are gradients that follow a specific direction. The imaginary line that defines this direction is known as the **gradient line** and the lines of colors that constitute the gradient are drawn perpendicular to it. To create a linear gradient, the `background-image` or `background` property is used with the CSS `linear-gradient()` function and it is this function that takes the values used to create the gradient. These values are listed in Table 16.1.

The syntax for specifying these values in the table to create a linear gradient is:

```
background: linear-gradient(<angle> or to <side or corner>,
   color-stop1, color-stop2, ...);
```

Figures 16.6 and 16.7 show how the `linear-gradient()` function is used with the `background` property to create a gradient and Figure 16.8 shows the result.

In the example, the `div{}` rule defines the size of all the `<div>` elements, the color and size of their text content, and the space between their border and the content. The rest of the rules show different ways the parameters for the `linear-gradient()` function can be specified. The first four are relatively basic. The `#grad1{}` rule creates gradient that starts from top with orange and ends at bottom with black. When no direction is specified, gradient goes from top to bottom. The `#grad2{}` rule creates gradient that goes from right to left, starting with #ffa500 and ending with black. The `#grad3{}` rule creates gradient that goes from left to right, starting with rgb(255,165,0) and ending with rgba(0,0,0,0.1). Similarly, the `#grad4{}` rule creates gradient that goes from left to right, but specifies color in a different format. For more on different methods of specifying color, refer to Chapter 9.

In the `#grad5{}` rule, the direction of the gradient line is specified as `45deg` and the gradients are drawn along and perpendicular to it, starting from orange. Where to

TABLE 16.1

Values Supported by the `linear-gradient` Function

Value Type	Function
`<side or corner>`	Specifies the direction of the gradient line and takes **one value** or a **space-separated pair of values**, which can be left or right and top or bottom (e.g., `left`, `right`, `left top`, or `right top`). The default direction is top to bottom. In standard syntax, the "to" keyword is placed before specified value or values.
`<angle>`	Specifies angle of direction for the gradient line and is typically in "deg" (i.e., degrees). Degrees are measured from top (0deg) to bottom (180deg). Positive angles represent angles that go right and negative those that go left. 0deg (or 360deg) means gradient goes from bottom to top, 180deg means top to bottom, 90deg means left to right, and -90deg (270deg) right to left. Basically, the direction of gradient is toward the angle specified.
`<color-stop>`	Specifies the color to apply to a gradient and may be followed by the position of the stop (in px or %) along the gradient line (e.g., `red 30%`). For a gradient to be produced, the value of the previous stop must be less than that of the next. If the first position is not specified, it is set to 0 (i.e., the starting point of the gradient line) and if none is specified for the last, it is set to 100% (i.e., the end point). When no positions are specified, the colors of the gradient are evenly spaced. Color can be specified in name, hex, RGB, RGBA, HSL, or HSLA.

```
HTML
<h1>Linear Gradient</h1>
<div id="grad1">(orange, black)</div><br>
<div id="grad2">(to left, orange, black)</div><br>
<div id="grad3">(to right, #ffa500, rgb(0,0,0))</div><br>
<div id="grad4">(to right, orange, rgba(0,0,0,0.1))</div><br>
<div id="grad5">(45deg, orange 50%, black)</div><br>
<div id="grad6">(to right, red, transparent 70%, blue)</div><br>
<div id="grad7">(to right, gray 15%, orange 15%, orange 85%,
   gray 85%)</div><br>
<div id="grad8">(to top right, red, orange, yellow, green,
   blue, indigo, violet)</div>
```

FIGURE 16.6 HTML for demonstrating how `linear-gradient()` is used.

```
CSS
div { height: 50px; width: 600px; color: white; font-size: 24px;
   padding: 10px; }
#grad1 { background: linear-gradient(orange, black); }
#grad2 { background: linear-gradient(to left, #ffa500, black); }
#grad3 { background: linear-gradient(to right, rgb(255,165,0),
   rgba(0,0,0,0.1)); }
#grad4 { background: linear-gradient(to right, hsl(39,100%,50%),
   hsla(0,0%,0%,0.1)); }
#grad5 { background: linear-gradient(45deg, orange 50%, black); }
#grad6 { background: linear-gradient(to right, red,
   transparent 70%, blue)}
#grad7 { background: linear-gradient(to right, gray 15%,
   orange 15%, orange 85%, gray 85%); }
#grad8 { background: linear-gradient(to top right, red, orange,
   yellow,green, blue, indigo, violet); }
```

FIGURE 16.7 CSS for the HTML in Figure 16.6.

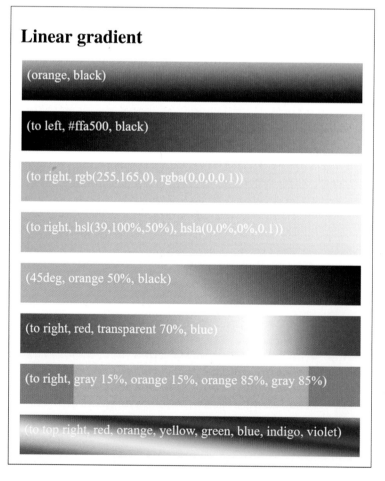

FIGURE 16.8 The result of Figures 16.6 and 16.7.

start changing to black is specified as 50% along the gradient line. The #grad6{} rule creates gradient that goes from left to right, starting with red, turning completely transparent at 70%, and ending with blue. The transparent keyword is a short-hand for transparent black (i.e., rgba(0,0,0,0)), which also has the same effect as white. Similarly, the #grad7{} rule creates gradient that goes from left to right, but one with solid-color stripes, which are produced by making the position of a stop less than or equal to that of the one before it. Notice in the example that the first gray stops at the same point the orange starts (i.e., at 15%) and, similarly, the orange stops where the second gray starts (i.e., at 85%). The #grad8{} rule creates gradient that goes from bottom-left to top-right and gives equal percentage to each color specified, since no positions are specified.

CHALLENGE 16.5

Implement the example in Figures 16.6 and 16.7 and experiment with the values to better understand how linear gradient works.

16.4.1.1 Repeating Linear Gradients

Gradients can be repeated to create a uniform pattern. You can achieve this using the repeating-linear-gradient() function and the same value-types as a linear gradient. Figures 16.9 and 16.10 show how this is done and the result.

```
CSS
div { height: 50px; width: 600px; padding: 10px;
    font-size: 24px; }
span { background-color: gray; color: white; }
#grad1 { background: repeating-linear-gradient(180deg, gray,
    gray 7%, black 15%); }
#grad2 { background: repeating-linear-gradient(45deg,
    black 20px, white 50px); }
#grad3 { background: repeating-linear-gradient(-45deg,
    transparent,black 20px, white 50px); }

HTML
<h1>Repeating linear gradient</h1>
<div id="grad1"><span>(180deg, gray, gray 7%,
    black 15%)</span></div><br>
<div id="grad2"><span>(45deg, black 20px,
    white 50px)</span></div><br>
<div id="grad3"><span>(-45deg, transparent, black 20px,
    white 50px)</span></div>
```

FIGURE 16.9 Using the repeating-linear-gradient() function.

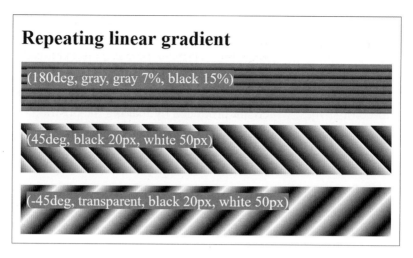

FIGURE 16.10   The result of Figure 16.9.

The values used in the rules are mostly similar to those you already saw in the previous examples. The `div{}` rule specifies the size of box and the `span{}` rule the color of the text and its background to ensure good enough legibility. The `#grad1{}` rule creates a gradient that goes in 180° direction (i.e., top to bottom), starting with gray, then gray again for 7% and black for 15%. This sequence is then repeated for the height of the box. The `#grad2{}` rule specifies gradient that goes in 45° direction (i.e., bottom-left to top-right), starting with black, changing to white after 20px, and going on for 50px. This sequence is repeated for the width of the box. The `#grad3{}` rule specifies −45° direction (i.e., bottom-right to top-left), starting with the `transparent` keyword (i.e., rgba(0,0,0,0)), changing to black after 20px, and white after 50px. Various patterns can be created by adjusting the value of the stops, number of transparent keyword, and the transparency of colors, using RGBA or HSLA.

CHALLENGE 16.6

Why is it necessary in the example to use the `<span>` element for the purpose described, instead of just including the declarations in the `span{}` rule in the `div{}` rule?

CHALLENGE 16.7

Implement the example with various other colors and experiment with the positions to see the obscure effects of the `repeating-linear-gradient()` function.

CHALLENGE 16.8

The screenshot below is an example application of repeating linear gradient and the gradient pattern is created using the `#grad1{}` rule in Figure 16.9. The challenge is to write a code to create the design (using different colors, if you like). Also, in what other ways might you use repeating linear gradient in a design and what are the important considerations with using it or other types of patterns?

16.4.2 Radial Gradients

Radial gradients can be either circular or elliptical in shape. A radial gradient starts in the center and spreads outward like ripples in concentric circles or ellipses. The color and radius of each circle or ellipse are defined by points on an imaginary line (the **gradient ray**) that starts from the center and extends outward horizontally. A radial gradient is therefore defined in terms of its center, the ending shape contour and position, and color stops along the gradient ray. Radial gradients are created in CSS by using the CSS `radial-gradient()` function with the `background-image` or `background` property. The parameters taken by function are listed in Table 16.2.

The syntax for specifying these values to create a gradient is:

```
background: radial-gradient(<shape> <size> at <position>,
    color-stop1, color-stop2, ...);
```

Figures 16.11 and 16.12 show the codes for how the radial- gradient function is used and Figure 16.13 the result.

The declarations in the rules work in similar ways as explained under linear gradients. The `#gradient1{}` rule specifies a circular-shaped gradient that touches the farthest corner of the `<div>` element's box, has its center at the top-right corner of the box, starts with yellow, and changes to dark orange at 50% along the gradient ray. The `#gradient2{}` rule specifies the same, except that the gradient's center is positioned differently. Similarly, gradients defined in the `#gradient3{}` and

TABLE 16.2

Values Supported by the `radial-gradient()` Function

Value Type	Function
`<shape>`	Specifies the end shape of gradient, which can be `circle` or `ellipse` keyword. The horizontal and vertical radius of the shape can also be specified in **length values** (e.g., thus, 50px 50px).
`<position>`	Specifies the x-y coordinate for the center of the gradient and can be in **length values** (e.g., px and em) or %. Coordinate 0 0 is top-left corner of the box.
`<color-stop>`	Specifies the color to apply to a stop. The value comprises a **color value** and an **optional stop position** along the gradient ray (e.g., red 30%). A length of 0 or a percentage of 0% represents the center of the gradient and 100% represents where the gradient ray meets the ending shape contour. If the position for the first color-stop is not specified, it is set to 0 (i.e., the starting point of the gradient ray) and if none is specified for the last color-stop, it is set to 100% (i.e., where gradient ray meets the ending shape). When no positions are specified for any color stops, the colors of the gradient are evenly spaced. Color can be specified in name, hex, RGB, RGBA, HSL, or HSLA.
`<size>`	Specifies size of the radial gradient and is specified using 1 of 4 keywords: `closest-side` (end shape touches all sides of the box or the side closest to the gradient's center), `farthest-side` (touches the side of the box farthest from the gradient's center), `closest-corner` (touches all corners or the corner closest to gradient's center), and `farthest-corner` (touches the farthest corner from gradient's center). Generally, closet-corner and farthest-corner make a gradient bigger, and the other two make it smaller.

`#gradient4{}` rules are the same, except that they have different sizes. In the `#gradient5{}` rule, the distinct boundary between the colors was created by specifying the same color stops for the colors. In the `#gradient6{}` and `#gradient7{}` rules, no color stops are specified, so the colors are evenly spaced out. The `#gradient8{}` rule shows how the shape of a gradient can be specified with length values instead of keywords. The first value specifies the horizontal radius, and the second vertical. Equal values specify a circle and non-equal ones create an ellipse.

HTML
```
<h1>Radial Gradients</h1>
<div id="gradient1">(circle farthest-corner at 100% 0%, yellow,
 dark orange 20%)</div><br>
<div id="gradient2">(circle farthest-side at 50% 50%, yellow,
 dark orange 20%)</div><br>
<div id="gradient3">(circle closest-side at 50% 50%, yellow,
 dark orange 20%)</div><br>
<div id="gradient4">(ellipse farthest-corner at 50% 50%, yellow,
 dark orange 20%)</div><br>
<div id="gradient5">(circle farthest-side at top right,
 yellow 20%, dark orange 20%)</div><br>
<div id="gradient6">(circle farthest-side at 50% 50%, yellow,
 dark orange, blue, gray)</div><br>
<div id="gradient7">(circle closest-side at 50% 50%, yellow,
 dark orange, blue, gray)</div><br>
<div id="gradient8">(35px 35px at 50% 50%, yellow, dark orange,
 blue, violet)</div>
```

FIGURE 16.11   HTML for demonstrating how `radial-gradient()` is used.

CSS
```
div { height: 70px; width: 650px; color: black; text-align:
  center; font-size: 24px; }
#gradient1 { background: radial-gradient(circle farthest-corner
  at 100% 0%, yellow, dark orange 20%); }
#gradient2 { background: radial-gradient(circle farthest-side
  at 50% 50%, yellow, dark orange 20%); }
#gradient3 { background: radial-gradient(circle closest-side
  at 50% 50%, yellow, dark orange 20%); }
#gradient4 { background: radial-gradient(ellipse farthest-corner
  at 50% 50%, yellow, dark orange 20%); }
#gradient5 { background: radial-gradient(circle farthest-side
  at top right, yellow 20%, dark orange 20%); }
#gradient6 { background: radial-gradient(circle farthest-side
  at 50% 50%, yellow, dark orange, blue, gray); }
#gradient7 { background: radial-gradient(circle closest-side
  at 50% 50%, yellow, dark orange, blue, gray); }
#gradient8 { background: radial-gradient(35px 35px
  at 50% 50%, yellow, dark orange, blue, violet); }
```

FIGURE 16.12   CSS for the HTML in Figure 16.11.

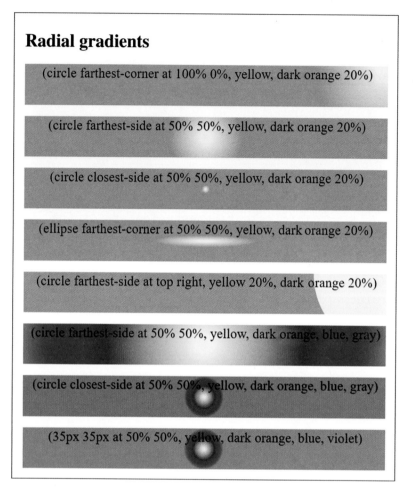

FIGURE 16.13   The result of Figures 16.11 and 16.12.

CHALLENGE 16.9

Implement some of the gradients in the example and experiment with the parameters.

16.4.2.1 Example Application of Radial Gradient

One of the common ways radial gradients are used, apart from their use in buttons, is using them for background, usually in less formal websites. Figures 16.14 and 16.15 show an example.

In the #gradient{} rule in the example, the width and height properties specify the size of the <div> element and the alignment and size of the text. The radial-gradient() function says to create an elliptical gradient that touches the farthest corner of the <div> element's box, has its center at the top-right corner of the box, and starts with yellow that begins to change to dark orange at 5% along the gradient ray.

```
CSS
#gradient {
  width: 800px; height: 400px; text-align: center;
    font-size: 24px; background: radial-gradient(ellipse
    farthest-corner at 100% 0%, yellow 5%, darkorange);
}

HTML
<h1>Radial Gradient as background</h1>
<div id="gradient">
  (ellipse farthest-corner at 100% 0%, yellow 5%, dark orange)
</div>
```

FIGURE 16.14   Example application of radial gradient.

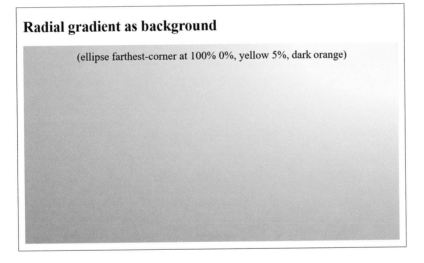

FIGURE 16.15   The result of Figure 16.14.

CHALLENGE 16.10

What are the important things to bear in mind when using gradients as background in terms of how usable a page is?

16.4.2.2 Repeating Radial Gradient

Like linear gradients, radial gradients can be repeated to create patterns. You can achieve this by using the `repeating-radial-gradient()` function and the same value types as a radial gradient. Figure 16.16 shows an example and Figure 16.17 the result.

In the `#outerbox{}` in the example, the `width` property specifies the width of the `<div>` element of `id="outerbox"` (i.e., the bigger box), the `border` property says to make the element's border 1px-thick solid line and pink, and the `background-color` property gives the background `rgba(255,192,203,0.3)` color. The `#gradient{}` rule sets the size of the `<div>` element of `id="gradient"` (i.e., the smaller box), the color and size of its text content, and the alignment of the text. The `repeating-radial-gradient()` function says to create and repeat a circular gradient that touches the farthest corner of the element's box, has its center at the top-right corner of the box, and starts with transparent, changes to `rgba(255,192,203,0.4)` after 40px, and then to `rgba(255,255,255,0.2)` after 50px. Using transparency makes the colors less imposing, making the pattern more suitable, for example, for a background.

```
CSS
#outerbox {
  width: 1000px; border: 1px solid pink; background-color:
    rgba(255,192,203,0.3);
}
#gradient {
  height: 500px;
  width: 250px;
  color: black;
  text-align: center;
  font-size: 24px;
  background: repeating-radial-gradient(circle
    farthest-corner at 100% 0%, transparent,
    rgba(255,192,203,0.4) 40px, rgba(255,255,255,0.2) 50px);
}

HTML
<h1>Repeating radial gradient</h1>
<div id="outerbox">
  <div id="gradient">(circle farthest-corner at 100% 0%,
    transparent, rgba(255,192,203,0.3) 40px,
    rgba(255,255,255,0.2) 50px)</div>
</div>
```

FIGURE 16.16 Using the `repeating-radial-gradient` property.

Repeating radial gradient

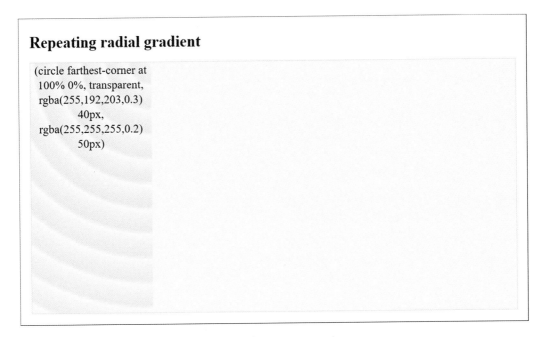

(circle farthest-corner at
100% 0%, transparent,
rgba(255,192,203,0.3)
40px,
rgba(255,255,255,0.2)
50px)

FIGURE 16.17 The result of Figure 16.16.

CHALLENGE 16.11

Create a design with the `repeating-radial-gradient()` and state for what type of site it might be suitable.

CHALLENGE 16.12

Complex gradients can be produced by using more of the background properties, especially `background-size`. For example, adding `background-size:30px 30px;` to the `#grad5` rule in Figure 16.7 or the `#grad1` rule in Figure 16.9, or the `#gradient7` rule in Figure 16.12 will change the gradient patterns produced. Give these a try and also experiment with various values to form further understanding about how CSS gradient works.

16.5 Filters

Image filters are image processors that make it possible to achieve various visual effects with an image, similar to some of those achievable in Photoshop and other graphics programs, such as blurring and color manipulation. The property used to implement these effects in CSS is the `filter` property. It can be useful for adding effects to a background or border. It is **non-inherited** and the values it takes are functions that take parameters that specify what to do to produce the desired effects. Different functions

TABLE 16.3

Values Supported by the `filter` Property

Value Type	Function
`blur()`	Makes an image look blurry. Takes **length values** (e.g., px).
`brightness()`	Controls brightness. Takes **percentage values** from 0% to 100%.
`contrast()`	Controls contrast. Takes **percentage values**. 0% makes image black, 100% produces no change, and over 100% produces less contrast.
`drop-shadow()`	Creates drop shadow. Takes **<offset-x> <offset-y>** (horizontal and vertical length values from top-left), **<blur-radius>** (makes shadow bigger and lighter), **<spread-radius>** (makes shadow expand), and **<color>**. An example: drop-shadow (16px 16px 20px red).
`grayscale()`	Converts image to grayscale. Takes **percentage values** from 0% to 100%.
`hue-rotate()`	Shifts the hue in HSL or HSV color model, thereby changing the colors for different parts of an image. Refer to Chapter 9 for more on color models. Takes **angle values** from 0° to 360°.
`invert()`	Inverts the colors of an image. Takes **percentage values** from 0% to 100%.
`opacity()`	Controls transparency of an image. Takes **percentage values** from 0% to 100%. 0% is transparent and 100% has no effect.
`saturate()`	Controls the saturation of an image. Takes **percentage values**. 0% produces unsaturated image, 100% no change, and over 100% saturation.
`sepia()`	Converts image to sepia, which makes it brownish in color. Takes **percentage values** from 0% to 100%.
`url()`	Used to specify the location of an SVG filter to use with CSS. It may also point to a specific element in a file; for example, url(effects. svg#one) points to the element of id="one".

take different parameters and the property can take multiple space-separated functions. Table 16.3 lists the functions supported and what they do.

Figures 16.18 and 16.19 show how the `filter` property is used. The `<img>` attribute specifies the target image and the `img{}` rule two filter functions: `hue-contrast()` and `saturate()`. The first says to apply hue rotation at 90° and the second 190% contrast, resulting in the color and contrast of the image being changed. The `-webkit-` declaration is for browser that only supports the property via webkit. See the note on vendor prefixes in Chapter 8 for more on the prefix.

```
CSS
img {
  -webkit-filter: hue-rotate(90deg) contrast(190%);
  filter: hue-rotate(90deg) contrast(190%);
}

HTML
<h1>Filter</h1>
<img src="images/yacht.jpg" alt="A yacht race">
```

FIGURE 16.18   Using the `filter` property.

FIGURE 16.19   The result of Figure 16.18.

CHALLENGE 16.13

Implement the example using your own image and experiment with the various functions to see how they can be useful.

16.6 Blending Images

The way images that overlap blend with each other is important in image production for creating various interesting effects. That is why most image editing programs (e.g., Photoshop) provide the command for doing this. In CSS, the properties provided to manage image blending are `background-blend-mode`, `mix-blend-mode`, and `isolation`.

16.6.1 `background-blend-mode`

The `background-blend-mode` property allows you to specify how an element's background image blends with the one below it and the element's background color, including gradient. The content behind the element is unaffected. The property is **non-inherited** and takes one value, which specifies the **blending mode** to apply. Figure 16.20 shows an image and the available CSS blending modes and their effects on a gray background color. The `normal` blending mode is the default and shows the actual appearance of the image.

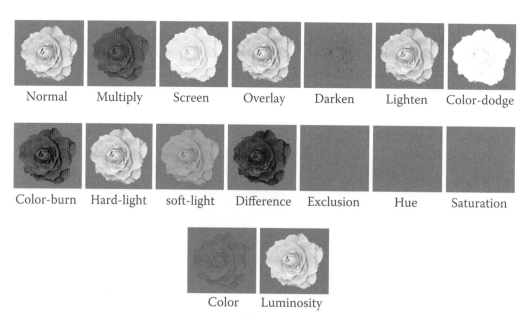

FIGURE 16.20   Blending modes and their effects for a specific image and background.

> **NOTE: Plain color effect**
>
> Notice in the example that some modes produce just a plain color. This is the result of the blending between the specific background color and image. Different background colors produce different effects with the same blending mode.

Figure 16.21 shows how the `background-blend-mode` property is used. It is the code used to produce the examples in Figure 16.20, with the value of the property changed as necessary. Note that the background of the image is transparent. In the example, the `background-image` property specifies the background image for the `<body>` element, `background-repeat` says not to repeat it, `background-color` specifies a gray background, and `background-blend-mode` specifies the `multiply` blending mode.

When multiple blending modes are specified, they are applied in the same order as the images specified by the `background-image` property. The **image specified first occupies the topmost layer**. This means that in Figure 16.22, `overlay` specifies how the first gradient blends with the second; `multiply` specifies how the second gradient blends with the third; `screen` specifies how the third gradient blends with the first image; `difference` specifies how the first image blends with the second, and because no value is specified for how to blend the second image with the third, the browser starts from the beginning of the list of values again, that is, it uses `overlay`. Figure 16.23 shows the effect of the code. Note that changing the order in which the images are specified will also change the blending result.

```
CSS
body {
  background-image: url("images/peach_rose.png");
  background-repeat: no-repeat;
  background-color: gray;
  background-blend-mode: multiply;
}

HTML
<body></body>
```

FIGURE 16.21 An example of how the `background-blend-mode` property is used.

```
CSS
div{
  width: 640px; height:640px;
  background-size: 640px 640px;
  background-repeat: no-repeat;
  background-image: linear-gradient(green, transparent),
                    linear-gradient(90deg, skyblue, transparent),
                    linear-gradient(-90deg, red, transparent),
                    url("images/peach_rose.png"),
                    url("images/gray_wall.png"),
                    url("images/flora.png");
  background-blend-mode: overlay, multiply, screen, difference;
}

HTML
<body><div></div></body>
```

FIGURE 16.22 Example of how multiple blending modes are specified.

FIGURE 16.23   The result of Figure 16.22.

CHALLENGE 16.14

In the example in Figure 16.22, if you specify a background color for the `<body>` element, how will it affect the blending of the images in the `<div>` element, and why?

16.6.2 `mix-blend-mode`

The `mix-blend-mode` property allows you to specify how an element's content should blend with the content and background of the element below it. It is **non-inherited** and, like the `background-blend-mode` property, takes one value, which is the **blending mode** to apply and can be any of those in Figure 16.20. Figure 16.24 shows how the property is used and Figure 16.25 the result.

```
CSS
div {
  background-image: url("images/yacht_400.png");
  background-repeat: no-repeat;
  text-align: center;
  width: 400px; height: 268px;
}
img { mix-blend-mode: overlay; }

HTML
<div>
  <img src="images/rose_transparent_full.png">
</div>
```

FIGURE 16.24   Example of how the `mix-blend-mode` property is used.

FIGURE 16.25   The result of Figure 16.24. (Image from www.freeimages.co.uk.)

In the example, the div{} rule specifies the background image; says not to repeat it; says to center any content of the <div> element; and specifies the size of the element to make it the same as that of the background image so that when content is centered in the element it is also centered in the background image. The img{} rule blends the image specified in the <img> element with the background image.

CHALLENGE 16.15

What will happen if the mix-blend-mode:overlay declaration is placed in the div{} rule instead of the img{} rule, and why?

16.6.3 isolation

The isolation property is usually used in conjunction with the mix-blend-mode property and allows you to isolate elements from a group of blended elements. It is **non-inherited** and the values it takes are auto (which means no isolation, and is the default) and isolate (which says to isolate element from blend group). Figure 16.26 shows how it is used and Figure 16.27 shows the result when isolation is not used and when it is used. The div{} rule positions the images at the same point to make them overlap. The img{} rule blends all the images, and the .three{} rule isolates the third (bottom) image.

```
CSS
div { position: absolute; left:0; top:0; }
img { mix-blend-mode: difference;   }
.three { isolation: isolate; }

HTML
<div class="one"><img src="images/yacht_400.png"></div>
<div class="two"><img src="images/beach.png"></div>
<div class="three"><img src="images/rose_transparent_full.png">
  </div>
```

FIGURE 16.26   Example usage of the isolation property.

Without isolation   With isolation

FIGURE 16.27   The result of Figure 16.26.

CHALLENGE 16.16

Implement Figure 16.26, using your own images, and experiment isolating different elements to see the effects and learn more about how the `isolation` property works.

CHALLENGE 16.17

Use the `:hover` pseudo-class discussed in Chapter 14 with the code in Figure 16.26, so that the image is isolated only when the cursor hovers over it. Also, can you think of situations in which you might use the `isolation` property?

16.7 Useful Info

16.7.1 Web Links

CSS specifications: w3.org/standards

Web development documents: docs.webplatform.org

Accessibility: w3.org/WAI/tutorials, webaim.org

CSS tutorials (*Here are just a few free tutorial sites on CSS and other Web languages*): w3.org/wiki, html5rocks.com, sitepoint.com, w3schools.com, codecademy.com, quackit.com, developer.mozilla.org/en-US/docs/Web tutorialspoint.com, htmldog.com, htmlcodetutorial.com, echoecho.com, learn.shayhowe.com, html.net, tizag.com, cssbasics.com, cordova.apache. org, developers.google.com, csszengarden.com, webdesignermag.co.uk, css.maxdesign.com.au

Gradient patterns: lea.verou.me/css3patterns

Testing codes: jsfiddle.net, codepad.org, jsbin.com, cssdesk.com

CSS generators for various features: enjoycss.com, bennettfeely.com, cssplant. com

Placeholder images: lorempixel.com

Browser compatibility info: caniuse.com

17

Lists, Tables, and Forms

17.1 Introduction

Lists, tables, and forms are created using special types of HTML elements introduced in Chapters 4 and 5. Although some of the CSS properties encountered in the previous chapters can be used to style the contents of these elements, CSS also provides properties that are designed specifically for controlling the formatting and styling of the elements. In this chapter, both the generic and element-specific properties are discussed.

17.2 Learning Outcomes

After studying this chapter, you should:

- Know how to apply styles to different types of lists.
- Know how to style tables and their content.
- Know how to style and format forms and the controls.

17.3 Lists

The four properties used to format and style the contents of list elements are `list-style-type`, `list-style-position`, `list-style-image`, and `list-style`.

17.3.1 `list-style-type`

The `list-style-type` property is used to specify the shape or style of bullet points (or markers) and can be used with `<ul>`, `<ol>`, or `<li>` element. The property is **inherited** and the values taken depend on whether it is used to style an unordered (`<ul>`) or ordered (`<ol>`) element. Table 17.1 lists the values and Figures 17.1 and 17.2 show how it is used and the result.

TABLE 17.1

Values Supported by the `list-style-type` Property

List Type	Marker Type	Description
Unordered	none	No bullet point
	disc	●
	circle	o
	square	■
Ordered	decimal	1 2 3...
	decimal-leading-zero	01 02 03...
	lower-alpha	a b c...
	lower-Latin	
	upper-alpha	A B C...
	upper-Latin	
	lower-roman	i ii iii...
	upper-roman	I II III...

```
CSS
ol { list-style-type: lower-latin; }

HTML
<h3>Shopping List</h3>
<ol>
  <li>Bread</li>
  <li>Milk</li>
  <li>Eggs</li>
  <li>Fruits and juices</li>
  <li>Rice and pasta</li>
  <li>Butter</li>
</ol>
```

FIGURE 17.1   Example usage of the `list-style-type` property.

Shopping list

  a. Bread
  b. Milk
  c. Eggs
  d. Fruits and juices
  e. Rice and pasta
  f. Butter

FIGURE 17.2   The rendered result of Figure 17.1.

CHALLENGE 17.1

Write a code to produce the following list:

There are three types of items:

A. Item number 1, which in turn contains 2 smaller items:
   i. Smaller item 1
   ii. Smaller item 2
B. Item number 2
C. Item number 3

17.3.2 `list-style-image`

The `list-style-image` property allows an image to be used as a bullet point. It is **inherited** and takes two values: `url()` (which specifies the location of image) and `none`. Figures 17.3 and 17.4 show how the property is used and the result. The `url()` value says that the image (oval.png) to use for the bullet point is in the "images" folder.

CHALLENGE 17.2

For which of the following types of websites do you think using `list-style-image` is likely to add to user experience and why? Also suggest the style you think would be appropriate.

- Financial
- Kids
- Fashion
- Religion

```
CSS
ul { list-style-image: url("images/oval.png"); }
li { margin: 10px; }

HTML
<h3>Shopping List</h3>
<ul>
  <li>Bread</li>
  <li>Milk</li>
  <li>Eggs</li>
  <li>Fruits and juices</li>
  <li>Rice and pasta</li>
  <li>Butter</li>
</ul>
```

FIGURE 17.3 Example usage of the `list-style-image` property.

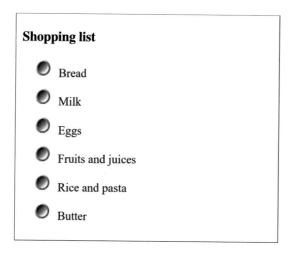

FIGURE 17.4   The rendered result of Figure 17.3.

17.3.3 `list-style-position`

The `list-style-position` allows you to specify whether markers (i.e., bullet points) should be inside or outside the box containing list-items. It is **inherited** and the values it takes are `outside` (which places marker outside the box), and `inside` (which places marker inside list-item box, after which the content follows). Figures 17.5 and 17.6 show how the property is used and the result.

```
CSS
ul { width: 475px; }
ul.one { list-style-position: outside; }
ul.two { list-style-position: inside; }

HTML
<h3>Marker outside</h3>
<ul class="one">
  <li>Lorem ipsum dolor sit amet, consectetur....</li>
  <li>Nunc accumsan euismod leo adapibus. Mauris id...</li>
</ul>
<h3>Marker inside</h3>
<ul class="two">
  <li>Lorem ipsum dolor sit amet, consectetur...</li>
  <li>Nunc accumsan euismod leo a dapibus. Mauris id ...</li>
</ul>
```

FIGURE 17.5   Example usage of the `list-style-position` property.

Marker outside

- Lorem ipsum dolor sit amet, consectetur adipiscing elit. Praesent maximus iaculis lacus a eleifend.
- Nunc accumsan euismod leo a dapibus. Mauris id condimentum velit, a lacinia nisi. Quisque varius orci accumsan nibh feugiat.

Marker inside

- Lorem ipsum dolor sit amet, consectetur adipiscing elit. Praesent maximus iaculis lacus a eleifend.
- Nunc accumsan euismod leo a dapibus. Mauris id condimentum velit, a lacinia nisi. Quisque varius orci accumsan nibh feugiat.

FIGURE 17.6 The rendered result of Figure 17.5.

CHALLENGE 17.3

Add a border to the `<li>` elements to show which side of the list-element box the marker is placed.

17.3.4 `list-style`

The `list-style` property is shorthand for specifying list styles. It is **inherited** and used to specify `list-style-type`, `list-style-image`, and `list-style-position` properties all at once in any order. In theory, `list-style-type` and `list-style-image` would not be specified together, since you cannot have two different things as a marker. Figure 17.7 shows how the property is used and says to use a square marker and place it inside the list-item box. Figure 17.8 shows the result.

CSS
```
ul { width: 475px;}
ul {list-style: square inside;}
```

HTML
```
<h3>List</h3>
<ul>
  <li>Lorem ipsum dolor sit amet, consectetur adipiscing...</li>
  <li>Nunc accumsan euismod leo a dapibus. Mauris id...</li>
</ul>
```

FIGURE 17.7 Usage of the shorthand `list-style` property.

List

- Lorem ipsum dolor sit amet, consectetur adipiscing elit. Praesent maximus iaculis lacus a eleifend.
- Nunc accumsan euismod leo a dapibus. Mauris id condimentum velit, a lacinia nisi. Quisque varius orci accumsan nibh feugiat.

FIGURE 17.8　The result of Figure 17.7.

CHALLENGE 17.4

Rewrite the code in Figure 17.7, using longhand properties. Also, state the difference between specifying `width` for the `<ul>` instead of the `<li>` element; and what would happen if `width` is not specified at all for the list.

17.3.5 Styling Lists with Generic Properties

Lists can also be styled using most of the generic properties already introduced, such as `:nth child` pseudo-classes (in Chapter 8), `background-color` and `color` (in Chapter 9), `width`, `padding`, `margin`, `border`, `border-radius`, `box-shadow` (in Chapter 10), `text-styling properties` (in Chapter 14), `linear-gradient`, `radial-gradient`, and `background-image` (in Chapter 15). Here some examples are presented.

17.3.5.1 Styling `<ol>` and `<ul>` Elements with Generic Properties

The `<ol>` and `<ul>` elements would usually be styled using similar techniques, since they are similar in structure. Figures 17.9 and 17.10 show an ordered list styled using various generic properties and Figure 17.11 the result. You will notice that **dot leaders**, such as used in table of contents, are used. CSS as of time of writing does not yet provide special properties for implementing these. The approach used in the example is simplistic but serves the purpose. It involves pushing the prices right, then a little in again, and then adding dots and spaces between them and the content on the left as appropriate. Various more sophisticated techniques can be found on the Web for doing the same thing.

In the example, the `body{}` rule says to make the text of the page Arial and bold and move it away from the left edge of the window. In the `ol{}` rule, `width` sets the width of

```
HTML
<h1>Menu List</h1>
<ol>
 <li>Full Baby Chicken Grill . . . . . . . . . . . . .
     <span>3.50</span></li>
 <li>Chicken Tikka (Boneless) . . . . . . . . . . . .
     <span>3.00</span></li>
 <li>Lamb Tikka (Boneless) . . . . . . . . . . . . .
     <span>3.00</span></li>
 <li>Sheek Kebab . . . . . . . . . . . . . . . . . .
     <span>0.60</span></li>
 <li>Quarter Tandoori Chicken . . . . . . . . . . . .
     <span>1.50</span></li></ol>
</ol>
```

FIGURE 17.9   HTML for styling an ordered list with generic properties.

```
CSS
body {
 font-family: Arial; font-weight: bold; padding-left: 30px;
}
ol {
 width: 700px;
 padding: 20px;
 list-style-position: inside;
 background-image: url("images/beach.jpg");
 border-radius: 20px;
 box-shadow: inset 0 0 1em 0.5em orange, 0 0 1em 0.5em blue;
}
span{ float: right; }
li:nth-child(2n+1) { border-style: solid; }
ol li {
 padding: 5px 100px 5px 5px;
 margin: 0 10px;
 background-color: #cce5ff;
 border-style: none solid none solid; border-color: #b3d9ff;
}
```

FIGURE 17.10   CSS for the HTML in Figure 17.9.

the list; padding sets the space between the `<li>` elements and all the four border edges of the `<ol>` element; list-style-position says to place the list items' markers inside the list-item boxes; background-image sets to use the image "beach.jpg" for `<ol>` element's background; border-radius makes the corners of the element's box round; and box-shadow creates two inner shadows (orange and blue) around the border. In the span{} rule, float pushes the `<span>` elements, which contain the prices, to the right

Menu List

1. Full Baby Chicken Grill 3.50
2. Chicken Tikka (Boneless) 3.00
3. Lamb Tikka (Boneless) 3.00
4. Sheek Kebab 0.60
5. Quarter Tandoori Chicken 1.50

FIGURE 17.11   The result of Figures 17.9 and 17.10. (Image from www.freeimages.co.uk.)

edge of the <li> elements' boxes so that they are aligned. The li:nth-child(2n+1){} rule says to give the border of alternate <li> elements solid line style. This is so that the borders of adjacent elements do not meet to form double lines. In the ol li{} rule, padding sets the space between all four edges of each <li> element's box and its content. The right padding is made bigger so that it can push in the content (i.e., the prices) and not make each line too long; the margin property horizontally centers the <li> elements inside the <ol> element; background-color gives the background of the <li> elements #cce5ff color; and border-style says to give the right and left edges of the <li> elements solid line style and #b3d9ff color. This also gives any existing visible border edges the same color (i.e., those created by the li:nth-child(2n+1) rule).

CHALLENGE 17.5

Implement the example, using your own image and content, then experiment with different values for the properties, especially padding, list-style-position, and border style.

CHALLENGE 17.6

Using the discussion of :nth child pseudo-classes in Chapter 8 as guide, explain how the li:nth-child(2n+1){} rule in the example styled only the borders of alternate <li> elements.

17.3.5.2 Styling Definition Lists

Definition lists can look very bland and without contrasts to guide the eyes easily between the terms and definitions. Styling the terms (i.e., the <dt> elements) can help enable them to stand out from the definitions. Figure 17.12 shows an example that specifies

```
CSS
dt { background-color: pink; font-weight:bold; }

HTML
<h2>Web Technologies</h2>
<dl>
<dt>Internet</dt>
 <dd>The Internet is a global network of interconnected
  computer...</dd>
<dt>Web</dt>
  <dd>The Web, also known as the World Wide Web (WWW), is
   an...</dd>
</dl>
```

FIGURE 17.12 Styling a definition list.

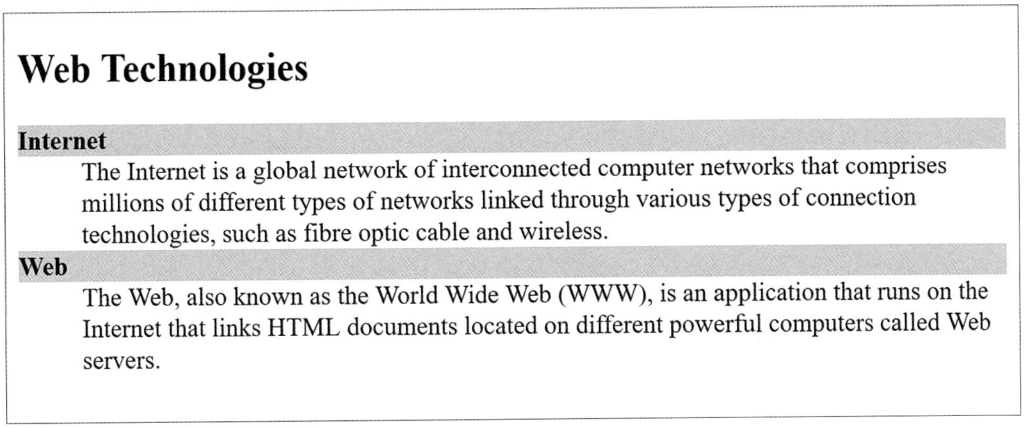

Web Technologies

Internet
The Internet is a global network of interconnected computer networks that comprises millions of different types of networks linked through various types of connection technologies, such as fibre optic cable and wireless.

Web
The Web, also known as the World Wide Web (WWW), is an application that runs on the Internet that links HTML documents located on different powerful computers called Web servers.

FIGURE 17.13 The result of Figure 17.12.

background color for the <dt> elements and bold for the text. Figure 17.13 shows the result. The indentation of the <dd> element is because it has a default margin-left (or margin-inline-start) value of 40px.

CHALLENGE 17.7

Modify the code in Figure 17.12 so that the definitions are not indented right.

17.3.6 Converting Other Elements to list-items

CSS allows you to make other elements behave like a <li> element by using the list-item value with the display property. Once an element is converted, any of the list-specific properties already introduced can be used to style it. This means, for example, that you can dynamically take the content of a <p>, <div>, or <span> element, usually using scripting, and display it as a list item. Figure 17.14 shows how this is done and Figure 17.15 shows the result.

```
CSS
body { padding:10px; }
.tolist{ display: list-item; }

HTML
<h2>List-item display value</h2>
<div>
  <span>This is the content of an inline element.</span>
  <span>This is the content of another inline element.</span>
</div>
<br>
<div>
  <span class="tolist">This is the content of an inline element
    converted to a list-item element.</span>
  <span class="tolist">This is the content of another inline
    element converted to a list-item element.</span>
</div>
```

FIGURE 17.14   Converting an element to a list-item element.

List-item display value

This is the content of an inline element. This is the content of another inline element.

• This is the content of an inline element converted to a list-item element.
• This is the content of another inline element converted to a list-item element.

FIGURE 17.15   The result of Figure 17.14.

In the example, the first `<div>` element and the contained `<span>` elements behave as normal, since they are not converted. In contrast, the `.tolist{}` rule makes the `<span>` elements of `class="tolist"` behave like a `<li>` element.

CHALLENGE 17.8

Implement the example and also use some of the list-specific properties to further format and style the list items.

17.4 Tables

Like lists, tables are styled using generic properties as well as properties designed specifically for styling the features of a table.

17.4.1 Styling Tables with Generic Properties

All the properties used for specifying fonts, text styling, text spacing, text alignment, box dimensions, border, padding, and margin can be used on table header and data cells and their content to perform the same functions they are used for with other elements and contents. Figures 17.16 through 17.18 show how some of these properties are used with a table.

In the example, the `body{ }` rule specifies the font, color, and size to use for all text in the document. The `table{ }` rule says to put space of 0.5 em between table and the edges of the window. The `td, th{ }` rule specifies 0.4 em space between the content of the table cells and their borders, and makes the borders solid and black. The `th{ }`

```
HTML
<h2>Best Sellers</h2>
<table>
   <caption>Five Top All-time Best-selling Books</caption>
   <tr class="dkgray">
      <th>Book</th>
      <th>Author(s)</th>
      ...
   </tr>
   <tr>
      <td>Don Quixote</td>
      <td>Miguel de Cervantes</td>
      ...
   </tr>
   <tr class="gray">
      <td>A Tale Of Two Cities</td>
      <td>Charles Dickens</td>
      ...
   </tr>
   <tr>
      <td>The Lord of the Rings</td>
      <td>J. R. R. Tolkien</td>
      ...
   </tr>
   <tr class="gray">
      <td>The Hobbit</td>
      <td>J. R. R. Tolkien</td>
      ...
   </tr>
   <tr>
      <td>LePetit Prince</td>
      <td>Antoine de Saint-Exupéry</td>
      ...
   </tr>
</table>
```

FIGURE 17.16 HTML for styling an ordered list with generic properties.

```
CSS
body { font-family: Arial, Verdana, sans-serif; color: black;
       font-size: 100%; }
table { margin: 0.5em; }
td, th { padding: 0.4em; border: 1px solid #000; }
th {
  text-transform: uppercase;
  letter-spacing: 0.1em;
  text-align: left;
  border-bottom: 2px solid #000;
}
tr.dkgray { background-color: #aeaeae; }
tr.gray { background-color: #f3f3f3; }
```

FIGURE 17.17   CSS for the HTML in Figure 17.16.

Best Sellers

Five Top All-time Best-selling Books

BOOK	AUTHOR(S)	FIRST PUBLISHED	APPROX. SALES
Don Quixote	Miguel de Cervantes	1605	315 million
A Tale Of Two Cities	Charles Dickens	1859	200 million
The Lord of the Rings	J. R. R. Tolkien	1954/1955	150 million
The Hobbit	J. R. R. Tolkien	1937	140.6 million
Le Petit Prince	Antoine de Saint-Exupéry	1943	140 million

FIGURE 17.18   The result of Figures 17.16 and 17.17.

rule makes the headers all-caps, spaces them a little to make them more distinguish-able, aligns them left, and makes the bottom edges of the borders thicker than those of the data cells to visually separate the headers from the data cells. The `tr.dkfrey{}` rule specifies a background color for the headers, and the `tr.grey{}` rule specifies background color for `<tr>` elements of `class="grey"` to create alternating and contrasting rows for easier reading.

CHALLENGE 17.9

In the `body{}` rule in the example, what is the font size 100% of, and what would happen if it is not specified? Also, why is the `<th>` element aligned left and the `<td>` element not?

CHALLENGE 17.10

The alternate background colors of the table rows can also be created using the
`:nth-child` expression shown earlier in Figure 17.10. Use this to implement the
same effect as in the example in Figure 17.18.

CHALLENGE 17.11

This challenge was first presented in challenge 4.5 in Chapter 4. Center the content
of the data cells.

	Introduction to Web Design Academic Session 2015/2016			
	No. of Years	Courses	Weeks	Project
Day	1	Mixed	13	Yes
Evening	2	Mixed		
Enjoy the unit!				

> **NOTE: Content wrapping in tables**
>
> The properties discussed in Chapter 10 for controlling content overflow in an
> element's box, such as `overflow`, `white-space`, `text-overflow`, and
> `hyphens`, can also be used to control overflow in table cells.

17.4.2 Styling with Table-Specific Properties

The main properties designed specially for styling tables are `border-collapse`,
`border-spacing`, `caption-side`, `empty-cells`, and `table-layout`.

17.4.2.1 `border-collapse`

The `border-collapse` property is used to specify whether the borders of adjacent
table cells should be separated or combined into one. It is **inherited** and the values it
takes are `separate` (which is the default) and `collapse`. Figure 17.19 shows the
output of Figure 17.17 after the `border-collapse: collapse;` declaration has
been added to the `table{}` rule, so that it looks like this: `table{ margin:
0.5em; border-collapse: collapse; }`. Notice that the borders of the
cells are now represented with single lines.

CHALLENGE 17.12

What is the effect of the `padding` property on the table cells, and how is this
compared with the effect on the whole table?

Best Sellers

Five Top All-time Best-selling Books

BOOK	AUTHOR(S)	FIRST PUBLISHED	APPROX. SALES
Don Quixote	Miguel de Cervantes	1605	315 million
A Tale Of Two Cities	Charles Dickens	1859	200 million
The Lord of the Rings	J. R. R. Tolkien	1954/1955	150 million
The Hobbit	J. R. R. Tolkien	1937	140.6 million
Le Petit Prince	Antoine de Saint-Exupéry	1943	140 million

FIGURE 17.19   Shows Figure 17.18 after the cell borders are collapsed.

17.4.2.2 `border-spacing`

The `border-spacing` property allows you to specify the space between table cells when the value of the `border-collapse` property is "collapse." It is **inherited** and the value it allows is the **length value** (e.g., `px` and `em`). When a **single value** is specified, it is used for both horizontal and vertical borders. When **two values** are specified, the first is used for **horizontal spacing** (which is the space between the cells of adjacent columns) and the second is used for **vertical spacing** (which is the space between the cells of adjacent rows). Figure 17.20 shows the result of the code in Figure 17.17 after the `border-spacing: 5px 20px;` declaration is added to the `table{}` rule so that it looks like this: `table{ margin: 0.5em; border-spacing: 5px 20px; }`. It says to make horizontal spacing 5px and vertical 20px.

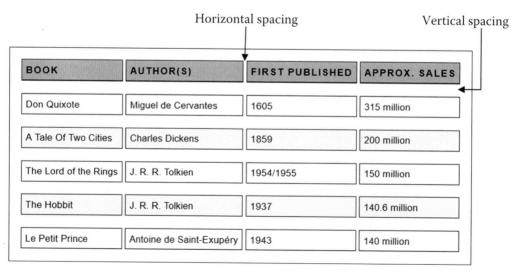

FIGURE 17.20   The result of adding `border-spacing`.

CHALLENGE 17.13

Interesting and aesthetically pleasing effects can be produced by large border width values and color transparency. Implement the example in Figures 17.16 and 17.17, using your own content if more convenient, and experiment with these properties and also 0px horizontal spacing, for example.

17.4.2.3 `empty-cells`

The `empty-cells` property is used to specify how the borders and backgrounds of cells that have no visible content should be rendered. It is **inherited** and the values it takes are `show` (which displays the borders of empty cells and is the default) and `hide` (which makes the borders of empty cells invisible). Figures 17.21 and 17.22 show how the property is used and the effects.

CSS
```
table { margin: 0.5em; border-collapse: separate; }
td, th { padding: 0.4em; border: 1px solid #000; }
table.one { empty-cells: show; }
table.two { empty-cells: hide; }
```

HTML
```
<table class="one">
  <tr><th>Fruit</th><th>Quantity</th></tr>
  <tr><td>Apples</td><td>200</td></tr>
  <tr><td>Banana</td><td></td></tr>
</table>
<table class="two">
  <tr><th>Fruit</th><th>Quantity</th></tr>
  <tr><td>Apples</td><td>200</td></tr>
  <tr><td>Banana</td><td></td></tr>
</table>
```

FIGURE 17.21 Example usage of the `empty-cells` property.

Fruit	Quantity
Apples	200
Banana	

empty-cells: show;

Fruit	Quantity
Apples	200
Banana	

empty-cells: hide;

FIGURE 17.22 The rendered result of Figure 17.21.

CHALLENGE 17.14

What would happen if all cells in a row are set to hide and have no visible content?

17.4.2.4 `table-layout`

The `table-layout` property is used to specify how the browser determines the width of the cells of a table. It is **non-inherited** and the values it takes are `auto` (which is the default) and `fixed`. When value is `auto`, the width of cells depends on their content. When it is `fixed`, the width of cells is fixed and the same for all cells. The fixed method is supposed to make tables render faster than the auto. Figure 17.23 shows how the property is used and Figure 17.24 the result. Notice the differences in the widths of the cells and how content is wrapped in the fixed layout when it is longer than the width.

```
CSS
body { font-family: Arial, Verdana, sans-serif; color: black;
       font-size: 100%; }
table { margin: 0.5em; border-collapse: collapse; width: 80%; }
td, th { padding: 0.4em; border: 1px solid #000; }
table.one { table-layout: auto; }
table.two { table-layout: fixed; }

HTML
<table class="one">
   <tr>
     <td>Le Petit Prince </td>
     <td>Antoine de Saint-Exupéry</td>
     <td>1943</td>
     <td>140 million</td>
   </tr>
</table>
<table class="two">
   <tr>
     <td>Le Petit Prince</td>
     <td>Antoine de Saint-Exupéry</td>
     <td>1943</td>
     <td>140 million</td>
   </tr>
</table>
```

FIGURE 17.23 Using the `table-layout` property.

Le Petit Prince	Antoine de Saint-Exupéry	1943	140 million	auto
Don Quixote	Miguel de Cervantes	1605	315 million	
The Lord of the Rings	J. R. R. Tolkien	1954/1955	150 million	

Le Petit Prince	Antoine de Saint-Exupéry	1943	140 million	fixed
Don Quixote	Miguel de Cervantes	1605	315 million	
The Lord of the Rings	J. R. R. Tolkien	1954/1955	150 million	

FIGURE 17.24 The result of Figure 17.23.

CHALLENGE 17.15

Using your own content, implement the example in Figure 17.23 to know more about the effects of `auto` and `fixed` values.

17.4.3 Converting Other Elements to Table Elements

Like with list and ruby elements, CSS allows you to make other elements behave like table elements by using the appropriate values with the `display` property. However, using these values effectively typically requires advanced CSS knowledge. Table 17.2 lists them and Figures 17.25 and 17.26 show how they are used in principle and the effect. Refer to Chapter 4 for table elements.

TABLE 17.2

Table-Specific `display` Values

Value	Function
table	Makes an element behave like the `<table>` element.
inline-table	This value does not have an equivalent HTML element. Like the table value, it makes an element behave like a `<table>` element, but in an inline box rather than in a block-level box.
table-caption	Makes an element behave like the `<caption>` element.
table-cell	Makes an element behave like the `<td>` element.
table-column	Makes an element behave like `<col>` element.
table-column-group	Makes an element behave like `<colgroup>` element.
table-row	Makes an element behave like `<tr>` element.
table-footer-group	Makes an element behave like `<tfoot>` element.
table-header-group	Makes an element behave like `<thead>` element.
table-row-group	Makes an element behave like `<tbody>` element.

```
CSS
<h2>Display table value</h2>
.table { display: table; border:1px solid black; }
.head { display: table-row; font-weight: bold;
       background-color: gray; }
.row { display: table-row; }
.cell { display: table-cell; width: 150px; border:1px
       solid black; }

HTML
<div class="table">
 <div class="head">
  <span class="cell">ID_No</span>
  <span class="cell">Name</span>
  <span class="cell">Age</span>
  <span class="cell">Height</span>
 </div>
 <div class="row">
  <span class="cell">10001</span>
  <span class="cell">James Normal</span>
  <span class="cell">28</span>
  <span class="cell">6ft 1in</span>
 </div>
 <div class="row">
  <span class="cell">10002</span>
  <span class="cell">Amanda Holmes</span>
  <span class="cell">24</span>
  <span class="cell">5ft 6in</span>
 </div>
</div>
```

FIGURE 17.25   Example usage of table display values.

Display table value

ID_No	Name	Age	Height
10001	James Normal	28	6ft 1in
10002	Amanda Holmes	24	5ft 6in

FIGURE 17.26   Result of Figure 17.25.

In the example, normal <div> and <span> elements are converted to table elements. The .table{} rule makes the <div> element of class="table" a <table> element; the .head{} rule makes the <div> element of class="head" a <tr> element and styles the content and background; the .row{} rule makes the <div> element of `class="row"` a `<tr>` element; and the `.cell{}` rule makes the `<div>` element of `class="cell"` a `<td>` element.

CHALLENGE 17.16

Implement the example and remove the formatting and styling to see how the content is displayed without them.

17.4.4 Guidelines for Designing Effective Tables

A table should be easy to understand and scan, and this goal is achieved through effective formatting and styling, which can be done using both generic and table-specific CSS properties. The following are some guidelines.

- **Make table aesthetically pleasing** to make it easy to read. This can be achieved through making a table as simple as possible and using ample space, such as ample padding.
- **Aid comprehension of data**: This can be done through using meaningful caption and headings and avoiding abbreviations or acronyms. If abbreviations or acronyms are used, one or two sentences of explanation should be provided, typically as footnotes.
- **Structure data to match table's purpose**: For example, if the purpose is to compare the quantity of things produced by different sources (e.g., countries), it is better to organize data by quantity, such as from smallest to largest, or vice versa, than alphabetically. On the other hand, if the purpose is to communicate changes in quantity over time, then it is better to organize data based on time than on quantity.
- **Include only important data** in order to avoid a cluttered table that has everything but is difficult to read and understand. For example, only totals might be included instead of also including all the components that make up the totals.
- **Make use of visual hierarchy** to communicate levels of importance to facilitate scanning. This can be done using font style, font size, font color, and font weight. For example, headings should be in larger font size and bolder weight and data that needs to be emphasized can be made bold or given a different color from the rest of the data.
- **Round data to integers**, unless presenting them in decimal points is important to their understanding. This is because rounded numbers are usually easier to compare. Where decimal numbers are used, it is generally recommended that no more than one decimal place is used, because the more there are, the harder it is to determine which values are lower or higher.
- **Perform necessary calculations for the user**, because it is hard to hold the result of one calculation in memory while doing another calculation for comparison. For example, if reference is made to the sum of the data in a row or column, it is helpful to provide an additional row or column for presenting it.

- **Ensure consistency**, both in appearance and in communicating data meaning. The way specific messages are communicated should be consistent. For example, if a color is used to indicate values that are above a specific level, it should be used for the same purpose throughout the table and, also, no other color should be used for the same purpose.
- **Ensure there is enough contrast** between foreground and background to aid legibility.
- **Group similar data**, where applicable, to facilitate the scanning and comparison of data. This can usually be done using background color.
- **Make use of gridlines** to structure and separate data for easier comprehension. This can be done through the use of different line thicknesses and/or shades of colors. For example, the lines enclosing a row that contains totals might be made bolder.

17.5 Forms

Forms, as mentioned in Chapter 5, are essential for collecting information from users. It is also important that they are made easy to complete and attractive. This can largely be achieved by grouping and ordering fields in a logical way and properly aligning them. You would have already seen in Chapter 5 how form elements can be grouped into sections using, for example, the <fieldset> element. Here, how to style these elements is shown. Figure 17.27 shows the HTML code for a form and Figure 17.28 shows the result without CSS styling.

Notice in Figure 17.27 that unlike the ones in Chapter 5, the <div> element is used to contain the form controls. This is to make it easy to apply styling to them, for example, as a group. Also, notice in Figure 17.28 that the controls and the labels are not aligned and slightly packed too closely together. The main goal of formatting and styling here is to improve this appearance. Figure 17.29 shows the CSS for doing this and Figure 17.30 the result.

In the example, the form{} rule sets the form's width with the width property. In the fieldset{} rule, border property sets the border of the <fieldset> element to solid line and #c6c4c4 color; the border-radius property makes the corners of the box round. In the legend{} rule, text-transform makes the content of the <legend> element all-uppercase; background-color makes its background #e4f0f6 color; border makes its border solid line and #d4d4d4 color; border-radius makes its corners round; and padding specifies the space between its content and the top and bottom edges as 5px and between the right and left edges as 15px. The div{} rule specifies 10px margin for every <div> element so as to add space between the form controls and produce a more spacious and easy-to-read form.

The .box{} rule specifies background color for the elements of class="box" (i.e., the text-input boxes) in order to make them stand out. The .field{} rule vertically aligns the text-input boxes and the labels. In it, the float property moves all elements of class="field" (i.e., the <label> elements for the text-input boxes and the radio

```
HTML
<form>
  <fieldset>
    <legend>Personal Info</legend>
    <div>
       <label class="field">First name:</label>
       <input class="box" type="text" name="fname" required>
    </div>
    <div>
       <label class="field">Last name:</label>
       <input class="box" type="text" name="lname">
    </div>
    <div>
      <label class="field">Email:</label>
      <input class="box" type="email" size="25" maxlength="35"
       name="email" placeholder="e.g., joe@example.com">
    </div>
    <div>
       <label class="field">Personal URL (if any):</label>
        <input class="box" type="url" name="website">
    </div>
    <div>
      <span class="field">Sex:</span>
      <input type="radio" name="sex" class="moveleft"
       value="male">
         <label>Male</label>
      <input type="radio" name="sex" class="moveleft"
       value="female">
         <label>Female</label>
    </div>
    <div class="buttons">
      <input type="submit" value="Submit"/>
      <input type="reset" value="Cancel"/>
    </div>
  </fieldset>
</form>
```

FIGURE 17.27   The code for the form to style.

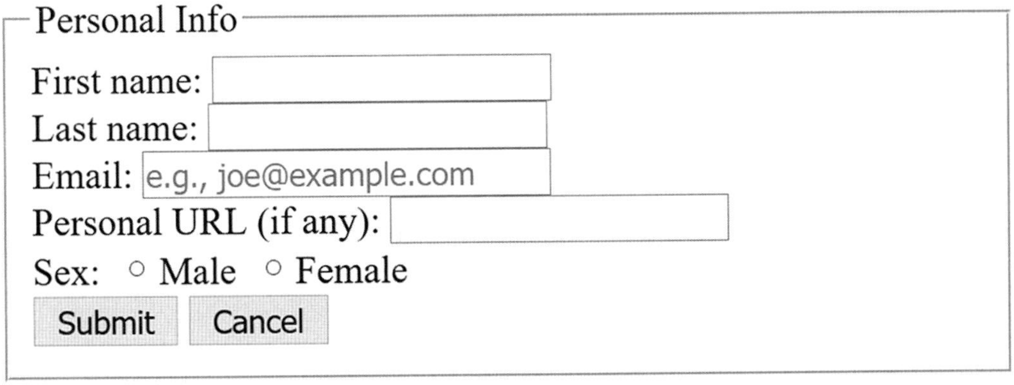

FIGURE 17.28   The result of Figure 17.27.

```
CSS
form { width: 500px; }
fieldset {
  border: 1px solid #c6c4c4;
  border-radius: 10px;
}
legend {
  text-transform: uppercase;
  background-color: #e4f0f6;
  border: 1px solid #d4d4d4;
  border-radius: 10px;
  padding: 5px 15px;
}
div { margin: 10px; }
.box { background-color: #e4f0f6; }
.field { width: 150px; float: left; text-align: right;
        padding-right: 10px; }
.moveleft { margin-left:0;}
.buttons { text-align: right; }
```

FIGURE 17.29   CSS code for styling the HTML Figure 17.27.

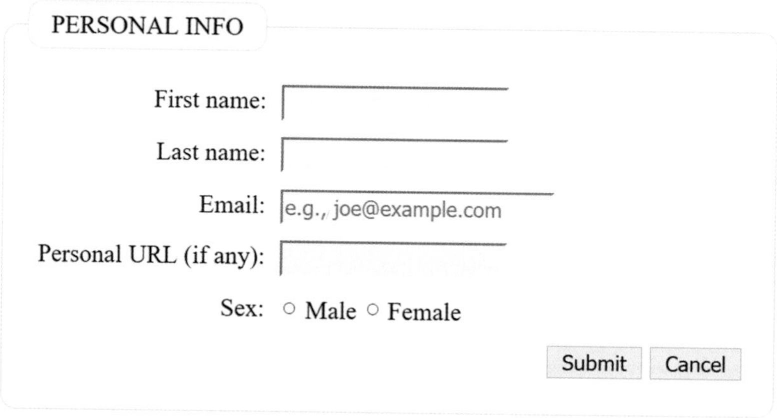

FIGURE 17.30   The result of Figures 17.27 and 17.29.

buttons) left; the `width` property makes their width the same, so that their left and right edges, and the left edges of the text boxes, are vertically aligned; the `text-align` property aligns the elements' contents to the right, so that their ends are vertically aligned; and the `padding-right` property adds padding to the right edges of the labels to put some space between them and the text-input boxes. The `.moveleft{}` rule removes the padding around elements of `class="moveleft"` (i.e., the radio buttons) so as to vertically align the first one with the left edges of the text-input boxes. The `.buttons{}` rule aligns the element of `class="buttons"` (i.e., the element containing the submit and reset buttons) to the right of the `<fieldset>` element's box.

CHALLENGE 17.17

How else would you create the space between the labels and the input boxes apart from using the `padding` property?

NOTE: Aligning form controls with CSS grid

It is worth noting that aligning form labels and controls can be more straightforwardly done using grid layout, which is discussed in Chapter 20.

17.5.1 Images in Input Fields

In addition to using labels to identify certain types of text input boxes, or instead of using them, a common practice is to place icons (i.e., small images) inside them typically to the left to indicate the types of information required from users. The types of information that images are used for include e-mail and password for popular social media websites, such as Twitter. They are also used with search text boxes. Figures 17.31 and 17.32 show how you can do this and Figure 17.33 the result.

In the example, the `form{}` rule specifies the width of the form. In the `fieldset{}` rule, `border` makes the border of the `<fieldset>` element a solid line of 1px thickness and gives it #c6c4c4 color; `border-radius` makes the corners of the element's box round; and `padding` makes space between the content of the element and the border 15px. The `div{}` rule specifies a margin of 15px to add space between the form controls so that they are not too close together. The `.field{}` rule vertically aligns the text boxes. The `width` property makes all elements of `class="field"` (i.e., `<label>` elements for the input boxes) the same width to align them vertically; the `float` property moves them to the left of the `<fieldset>` element; and

```
HTML
<form>
 <fieldset>
   <div><label class="field">Username:</label><input
     class="box username" type="text" name="username"></div>
   <div><label class="field">Email:</label><input
     class="box email" type="email" name="email"
     placeholder="e.g., joe@example.com"></div>
   <div><label class="field">Password:</label><input
     class="box password" type="password" name="password"></div>
   <div class="buttons"><input type="submit" value="Login">
             <input type="reset" value="Cancel"></div>
 </fieldset>
</form>
```

FIGURE 17.31 HTML code for a form.

```
CSS
form { width: 500px; }
fieldset {
    border: 1px solid #c6c4c4;
    border-radius: 10px;
    padding: 15px;
}
div { margin: 10px; }
.field { width: 150px; float: left; text-align: right; }
.buttons { text-align: right; }
.box { width:150px; border: 1px solid #b3b3a9; background-color:
       #e4f0f6; margin-left: 5px; padding: 3px 3px 3px 30px;}
.username { background:url(images/username.png) no-repeat
              #e4f0f6 3% 50%; }
.email { background:url(images/email.png) no-repeat
          #e4f0f6 3% 50%; }
.password { background:url(images/password.png) no-repeat
              #e4f0f6 3% 50%; }
```

FIGURE 17.32   CSS for the form in Figure 17.31.

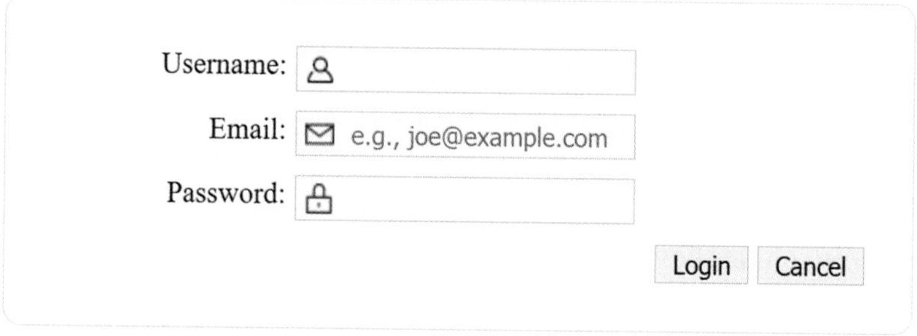

FIGURE 17.33   The result of Figures 17.31 and 17.32 (Icons by Ednes Dal [username], and Popcic [e-mail and password]).

`text-align` aligns their content right to vertically align them. The `.button{}` rule aligns elements of `class="button"` to the right.

The `.box{}` rule specifies the `width`, `border`, `background-color`, `margin-left`, and `padding` properties for the elements of `class="box"` (i.e., username, e-mail, and password input text boxes). The `margin-left` property adds space between the input boxes and their labels. The padding for the left side is set to 30px to ensure clearance in the boxes, so that when users enter data, the data does not go on top of the images.

The `.username{}` rule uses the `background` property to specify the background image to place in the box (i.e., username.png), and not to repeat it. It also specifies the background color for the box and the x-y coordinate for where to place the image. The first value specifies the horizontal position and says to place the image at 3% of the length of the element's box, starting from the left edge. The second value specifies the vertical position as 50% of the height of the element's box, starting from the top edge.

The `background` property is shorthand property for specifying various longhand background properties and was discussed in Chapter 15.

The `.email{}` and `.password{}` rules specify similar properties and values as the `.username{}` rule but use different images. The size of the images is 16 × 16 pixels. However, bigger images can be used and scaled down accordingly using the `background-size` property to specify the width and height. This property too has been introduced in Chapter 15. Note that to avoid repetition and make the code more elegant and easier to maintain, the properties and values that are common to the three rules can be placed in the `.box{}` rule, since all the text input elements belong to `class="box"`.

CHALLENGE 17.18

Implement the example in Figures 17.31 and 17.32, using your own images, and placing the properties and values common to the `.username{}`, `.email{}`, and `.password{}` rules in the `.box{}` rule to remove the repetitions.

17.5.2 Styling Form Elements

Form elements can be styled to help users quickly determine how to interact with them, and this can be done using **pseudo-classes**, which were introduced in Chapter 8 and also used in Chapter 14 for styling link text. Table 17.3 lists those used for styling form elements and Figures 17.34 and 17.35 show how they are used and the result.

In the example, the `input:required{}` rule says that all required `<input>` elements should be given a light blue background. The `input:focus{}` rule specifies to make the background color of a text-input element yellow when it receives focus (i.e., when the cursor is in the field). The `input[type=checkbox]:checked + label{}` and `input[type=radio]:checked + label{}` rules specify to make

TABLE 17.3

Example Usage of Pseudo-Classes for Styling Form Elements

Pseudo-Class	Function
`:checked`	Selects `<input>` elements, such as checkboxes, that are checked or in on state.
`:disabled`	Selects `<input>` elements that are disabled.
`:enabled`	Selects `<input>` elements that are enabled.
`:focus`	Selects an `<input>` element, such as a text input element, when it has received focus.
`:hover`	Selects an element, such as a hyperlink, when cursor is on it.
`:required`	Selects `<input>` elements that have the `required` attribute set.
`:optional`	Selects `<input>` elements that do not have the required attribute set.

```
CSS
input:required { background-color: light blue; }
input:focus { background-color: yellow; }
input[type=checkbox]:checked + label { color: red; }
input[type=radio]:checked + label { color: red; }

HTML
<h3>Registration</h3>
<form>
  <p>Please enter your details:</p>
  <label>Ref:</label><input type="ref" value="10012"
    disabled="disabled"><br>
  <label>First name: </label><input type="text"
    name="fname" required><br>
  <label>Last name: </label><input type="text"
    name="lname" required><br>
  <label>Email: </label><input type="email" required><br>
  <label>Phone: </label><input type="phone"><br>
  <input type="radio" id="male" name="sex"><label
    for="male">Male</label>
  <input type="radio" id="female" name="sex"><label
    for="female">Female</label><br>
  <input type="checkbox" id="conf"><label for="conf">Yes, send
    me confirmation</label><br>
  <input type="checkbox" id="terms"><label for="terms">Yes, I
    agree with the terms</label><br>
</form>
```

FIGURE 17.34   Example usage of pseudo-classes for styling form elements.

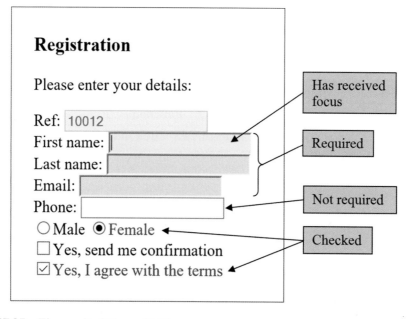

FIGURE 17.35   The result of Figure 17.34.

the label for any selected checkbox- or radio-input element red. The "+", introduced in table 8.1 of Chapter 8, specifies to select the first `<label>` element after a selected checkbox- or radio-input element. The "Ref" text field is gray because it is disabled using HTML `disabled` attribute (introduced in Chapter 5 in table 5.4) and not editable.

CHALLENGE 17.19

Implement the example in Figure 17.35 and then modify the code to align the controls, using the principles introduced in Figure 17.29.

17.5.2.1 Styling Form Buttons

Form buttons, such as submit and reset buttons, that are created using HTML, too, can be styled using many of the CSS properties already discussed in previous chapters. These properties can also be used to provide interactivity by combining them with some **pseudo-classes**, such as `:hover` and `:active`. Figures 17.36 and 17.37 show an example and the result.

In the example, the `input#button{}` rule applies to the `<input>` element of `id="button"` and determines the appearance of the button in the normal state. The `width` and the `padding` properties specify the size of the button; `background-color` specifies #ffcc66 color; `border-radius` makes the corners of the button round; `box-shadow` property specifies a dark gray shadow that has an x-y-offset of 3px 3px, a

```
CSS
input#button {
 width: 150px;
 padding: 5px 0px 5px 0px;
 background-color: #ffcc66;
 border-radius: 5px;
 box-shadow: 3px 3px 2px 0px #4d4d4d;
 font-family: Arial;
 font-size: 30px;
 font-weight: bold;
 color: black;
 text-shadow: 2px 2px 1px blue;
}
input#button:hover {
 color: blue;
 background-color: orange;
}

HTML
<form>
  <input type="submit" value="Submit" id="button">
</form>
```

FIGURE 17.36 Using CSS to style an HTML button.

Normal state   Hover state

FIGURE 17.37   The result of Figure 17.36.

blur-radius of 2px, and no spread-radius (See Chapter 10 for more on box shadow); and the rest of the properties in the rule specify the styling for the button text, including text shadow. The `input#button:hover{}` rule applies to the `<input>` element of `id="button"` that has the cursor over it and says to change text color of the element (the button) to blue and its background color to orange.

NOTE: Button states in design

Here are some design guidelines for button states:

- A button should pop up in hover state and this is usually best achieved with a brighter or more saturated color.
- Hover state can be as subtle as just changing contrast between text and background by, for example, darkening the button when the text is white or light in color or lightening the button when the text is black or dark.
- In hover state, button text should not be invisible, or illegible, because due to the limitations of short-term memory this can create a situation in which users find themselves forgetting what the text just said upon placing the cursor over it.
- Behavior should be consistent for all buttons in a design to make it easy for users to build a mental picture of how to use the design.
- Hover state does not have to be over-exaggerated, such as displacing the button significantly, as this can easily be annoying and seem unprofessional.
- Button should not look depressed on the hover state. This appearance is more appropriate for when the button is being clicked.
- Shadow should be placed under, rather than above a button, as placing it above can look unusual and even confusing.
- Gradients, discussed in Chapter 13, can be used in the design of buttons.

CHALLENGE 17.20

Using the principles in Figure 17.36, write a code to create an interactive button that has the normal, hover, and active states. The pseudo-class for the active state is :active, as shown in Table 14.16 of Chapter 14.

17.5.2.2 Styling Default Button

When the browser displays a group of associated elements, it makes one of the elements the default. In the case of a group of buttons in a form, for example, the default element is typically the first element of submit type. CSS allows you to select and style this element using the :default pseudo-class. Figure 17.38 shows how it is used and Figure 17.39 the result.

In the example, the form{} rule specifies the size of the <form> element. The div{} rule specifies the margin for all four sides of the <div> elements to put some space between the form controls and the edges of the <fieldset> element. The .box{} rule styles and formats the <input> elements of class="box" (i.e., the textboxes). The .buttons{} rule aligns the <input> elements of class="box" (i.e., the buttons) to the right. The :default{} rule makes the border of the default button 2px thick solid line and green.

```
CSS
form { width: 500px; }
div { margin: 10px; }
.box { width: 150px; margin-left: 5px; }
.buttons { text-align: right; }
:default { border: 2px solid green; }

HTML
<form>
  <fieldset>
    <div><label>Username:</label><input class="box" type=
    "text"> </div>
    <div><label>Password:</label><input class="box" type=
    "password"> </div>
    <div class="buttons">
      <input type="submit" value="Login">
      <input type="reset" value="Cancel">
    </div>
  </fieldset>
</form>
```

FIGURE 17.38   Using the :default pseudo-class.

FIGURE 17.39   The result of Figure 17.38.

CHALLENGE 17.21

In the code below, which element will the `:default` pseudo-class select and why?

```
<form>
  <p><input type="text" name="lname"></p>
  <p><button type="submit">Search</button></p>
  <p><input type="button" value="Submit"></p>
  <p><input type="reset"></p>
</form>
```

17.5.3 Specifying Cursor Shape

When rollover is implemented, it is also good practice to change the shape of the cursor during the hover. The property used for this is the `cursor` property and it is used to specify the type of cursor to display when the mouse is over an element. It is **inherited** and takes many types of values that describe a shape. Table 17.4 lists some common ones.

Figure 17.40 shows the hover state for the same button in Figure 17.37 but with the cursor shape changed to a pointer.

TABLE 17.4

Values Supported by the `cursor` Property

Value	Description
default	Shows the default cursor, which is typically an arrow.
auto	The browser determines the type of cursor according to context. For example, the I-beam is shown when cursor is on text.
text	Shows an I-beam.
pointer	Shows a hand with a pointing finger. Used for clickable items or areas, such as links, buttons, and maps.
wait	Shows a busy icon, such as an hourglass.
help	Shows an arrow and a question mark. Used to show help information is available.
move	Shows an arrowed cross. Used when an object can be moved.
crosshair	Shows a cross. Used to indicate selection in a bitmap.
zoom	Shows a magnifying glass. Used to indicate something can be zoomed in or out.
url (...)	Specifies the path to the image to use for cursor (e.g., url(oval.png;)). When used, a standard fallback cursor is also included, in case the specified one is not available, thus: url(oval.png;), auto;.

FIGURE 17.40   Using pointer value with the `cursor` property.

CHALLENGE 17.22

Implement the code in Figure 17.36, or your own design, and also add the declaration, `cursor:pointer;`, to the appropriate rule to create a button that behaves like the one in Figure 17.40 in hover state.

17.5.4 Validating Form Inputs

Many of the form data validation processes traditionally done with scripting can now be done using HTML and CSS. Already some have been introduced, such as the `required` attribute. Here, some of the CSS pseudo-classes used to perform validations are introduced, namely, `:in-range`, `:out-of-range`, `:valid`, and `:invalid`.

17.5.4.1 `:in-range` *and* `:out-of-range`

The `:in-range` pseudo-class selects the element whose `value` attribute's value is within the range specified by the `min` and `max` attributes. The `:out-of-range` pseudo-class selects the element whose `value` attribute's value is outside the range specified by the `min` and `max` attributes. Figure 17.41 shows how the two are used and Figure 17.42 the result.

In the example, the `input:in-range{}` rule says that the border of any `<input>` element whose `value` attribute's value is between 1 and 10 should be 2px solid line and green.

```
CSS
input:in-range { border: 2px solid green; }
input:out-of-range { border: 2px solid red; }

HTML
<h3>:in-range and :out-of-range</h3>
<form>
  <p>Please enter your numbers:</p>
  <p><input type="number" min="1" max="10"> (Enter between
  1 and 10)</p>
  <p><input type="number" min="1" max="10"> (Enter between
  1 and 10)</p>
</form>
```

FIGURE 17.41   Using `:in-range` and `:out-of-range` pseudo-classes.

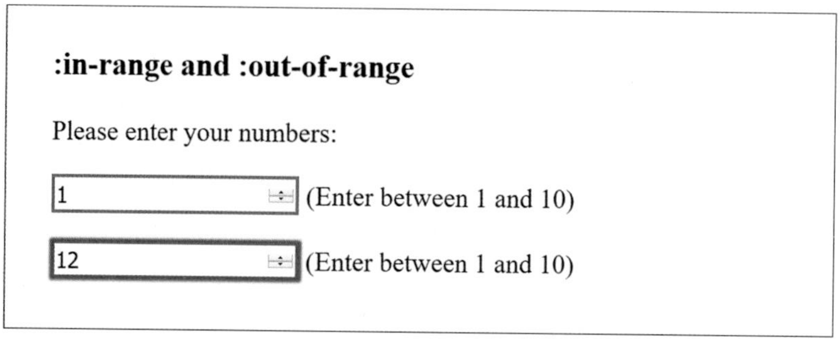

```
:in-range and :out-of-range

Please enter your numbers:

1                    ⊞  (Enter between 1 and 10)

12                   ⊞  (Enter between 1 and 10)
```

FIGURE 17.42   Result of Figure 17.41.

The `input:out-of-range{}` rule says that the border of any `<input>` element whose `value` attribute's value is outside 1–10 should be 2px solid line and red.

CHALLENGE 17.23

In the example, what would happen if "input" is not included in the selectors, so that, for example, `input:in-range{}` becomes `:in-range{}`? Also give the reason for your answer.

17.5.4.2 `:valid` *and* `:invalid`

The `:valid` pseudo-class selects `<form>` and `<input>` elements whose content is valid based on **input-type setting**. For example, an input is valid if a number is entered into a number-input type field. The `:invalid` pseudo-class, on the other hand, selects `<form>` and `<input>` elements whose content is invalid based on input-type setting. These pseudo-classes are intended to help users recognize wrong inputs they have made. Figure 17.43 shows how they are used and Figure 17.44 the result.

```
CSS
input:valid { border: 2px solid green; }
input:invalid { border: 2px solid red; }

HTML
<h3>:valid and :invalid</h3>
<form>
  Enter the first digit:<br>
  <input type="number"><br><br>
  Enter the second digit:<br>
  <input type="number">
</form>
```

FIGURE 17.43   Example usage of `:valid` and `:invalid`.

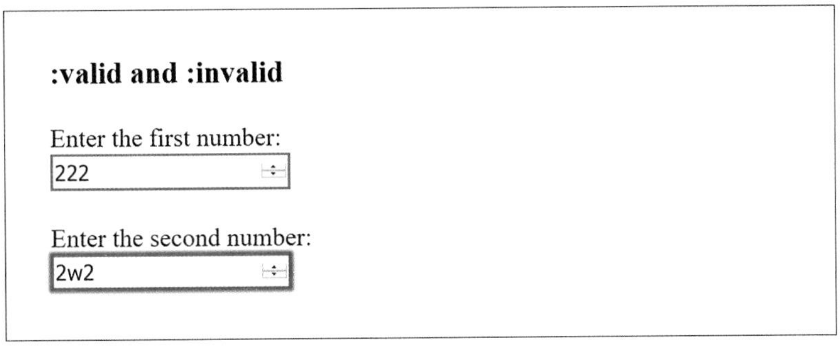

FIGURE 17.44 Result of Figure 17.43.

In the example, the `input:valid{}` rule says to make the border of `<input>` elements whose content contains only numbers 2px thick solid green line. The `:input:invalid{}` rule says to make the border of `<input>` elements whose content contains a non-digit 2px thick solid red line.

CHALLENGE 17.24

Again, in the example, what would happen if "input" is not included in the selectors, so that, for example, `input:valid{}` becomes `:valid{}`? Also, give the reason for your answer.

17.6 Useful Info

17.6.1 Web Links

CSS specifications: w3.org/standards
Web development documents: docs.webplatform.org
Accessibility: w3.org/WAI/tutorials, webaim.org
CSS tutorials (*Here are just a few free tutorial sites on CSS and other Web languages*): w3.org/wiki, html5rocks.com, sitepoint.com, w3schools.com, codecademy.com, quackit.com, developer.mozilla.org/en-US/docs/Web tutorialspoint. com, htmldog.com, htmlcodetutorial.com, echoecho.com, learn.shayhowe.com, html.net, tizag.com, cssbasics.com, cordova.apache.org, developers.google.com, csszengarden.com, webdesignermag.co.uk, css.maxdesign.com.au,
Form design: formalize.me
Button generator: button.csscook.com
Testing codes: jsfiddle.net, codepad.org, jsbin.com, cssdesk.com
CSS generators for various features: enjoycss.com, bennettfeely.com, cssplant.com
Placeholder images: lorempixel.com
Browser compatibility info: caniuse.com

18

Animation

18.1 Introduction

Animation in the serious sense is generally outside the scope of Web design. Typically, animations, such as of a story or process, would be created using other programs, after which the file is incorporated into HTML. However, basic animations, such as rollover effects used with buttons and icons to communicate a system's response to user interaction, are part of Web design and it is for these that the animation properties provided by CSS are primarily suited. Most other types of animation are difficult to put to effective use in Web design. This chapter introduces the animation properties.

18.2 Learning Outcomes

After studying this chapter, you should:

- Be aware of the nature of animation.
- Know the CSS properties used to create two-dimensional (2D) animation and how to use them.
- Know the CSS properties used to create three-dimensional (3D) animation and how to use them.
- Be aware of how animations are used in Web design.
- Be aware of other Web languages used to create animation.

18.3 About Animation

Animations are made up of individual images displayed sequentially at certain number of images per second. The images are called **frames**. Although in traditional animation production all frames needed to be created, with software-based production it is possible to create only important frames, known as **keyframes** (i.e., frames that represent significant changes in an animation sequence) and let the software calculate the in-between frames in a process known in the animation field as **in-betweening**, or **tweening**, for short. Figure 18.1 illustrates one type of tweening that is sometimes known as motion tweening, in which a filled circle is made bigger as it is moved from one location

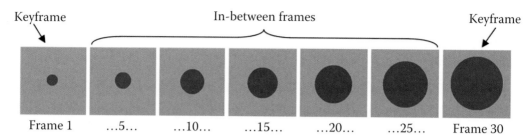

FIGURE 18.1   An illustration of location and size tweening.

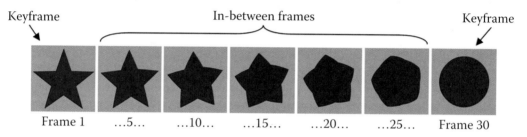

FIGURE 18.2   An example of shape tweening.

to another. Basically, to achieve this, the start and end sizes and locations are typically specified and the computer fills in the in-between frames.

Tweening can also be in the form of changing one shape into another, sometimes known as **shape tweening**. This principle is illustrated in Figure 18.2 and typically involves specifying two shapes and letting the computer fill in the in-between shapes.

CSS enables the creation of animation based on this general principle of creating frames and specifying keyframes and frames per second, except that in CSS, the frames comprise HTML elements and the contents and frame per second (or frame rate) is specified in terms of the amount of time a sequence should take to complete. The principle endures whether animation is 2D or 3D, both of which can be created either by CSS by itself or in combination with scripting. The main benefits of CSS animations are that they make it possible to create basic animations without having to learn to script, and they typically run more smoothly, even on very slow systems.

18.4 CSS 2D Animation

A 2D animation is the type of animation that has only two dimensions (i.e., x and y), although it can communicate the illusion of depth through, for example, drop shadows. A square moving from one location to another or a 2D object changing shape is an example of a basic 2D animation. Various things are animated in computing, including objects and characters, but, as of time of writing, CSS for all intent and purposes only supports the animation of objects. Many standard CSS properties can be animated. Lists of properties that can be animated can be found on the Web (e.g., at w3.org/TR/

css3-transitions). The way animations are created in CSS is through using the `@keyframes` at-rule in combination with `animation` properties, or the `transition` and `transform` properties.

18.4.1 `@keyframes`

The `@keyframes` at-rule lets you control the intermediate steps in an animation sequence by specifying the **positions of keyframes** (i.e., a list of keyframes) and the **properties to be animated**. The values it takes are listed in Table 18.1.

In order for keyframe lists to be valid, they must contain at least 0% (or `from`) and 100% (or `to`), as the two define the animation sequence. Figures 18.3 through 18.5 show examples of how the values are used with the `@keyframes` at-rule, assuming the identifier of the animation to be applied to the selected element is "shake." In Figure 18.3, the `@keyframes shake{}` rule says to make the background of the element to which the `shake` animation is applied red at 0% keyframe, blue at 50% and also scale the size of the element to 2, and green at 100% as well as scale the element back to its initial size. When a property is specified at a keyframe but not specified in the succeeding one, the property's initial value is assumed.

In Figure 18.4, the `@keyframes shake{}` rule similarly specifies to make the background of the element to which the `shake` animation is applied red at 0% keyframe, blue at 50%, and green at 100%.

In Figure 18.5, the `@keyframes shake{}` rule says to make the background of the element to which the `shake` animation is applied red at 0% keyframe and green with opacity of 0.5 at 100%.

TABLE 18.1

Values Supported by the `@keyframes` at-rule

Value	Function
`<identifier>`	Specifies a name that identifies an animation sequence (or keyframe list).
`from`	Keyword that specifies to start animation at 0%.
`to`	Keyword that specifies to end animation at 100%.
`<percentage>`	Specifies the point at which keyframes should occur. Value can be between 0% and 100%.

```
@keyframes shake {
    0% { background-color: red; }
    50% { background-color: blue; transform: scale(2);}
    100% { background-color: green; }
}
```

FIGURE 18.3 Example 1.

```
@keyframes shake {
    from { background-color: red; }
    50% { background-color: blue; }
    to { background-color: green; }
}
```

FIGURE 18.4   Example 2.

```
@keyframes shake {
    from { background-color: red; }
    to { background-color: green; opacity: 0.5; }
}
```

FIGURE 18.5   Example 3.

18.4.2 Animation Properties

CSS animation properties are used to define how an animation should progress, which involves specifying duration and timing of the animation and its other behaviors. These properties include `animation-name`, `animation-duration`, `animation-timing-function`, `animation-delay`, `animation-iteration-count`, `animation-direction`, `animation-fill-mode`, and `animation-play-state`. Table 18.2 lists their function.

TABLE 18.2

Animation Properties

Property	Function
`animation-name`	Specifies a comma-separated list of animations to be applied to the selected element. Each name specifies the @keyframes at-rule that defines the properties of an animation sequence. It is **non-inherited** and the values it takes are **names of animation** and the keyword none (used to deactivate an animation).
`animation-duration`	Specifies how long an animation sequence should take to complete. It is **non-inherited** and the value taken is a **time value**, which is specified in seconds (s) or milliseconds (ms). Larger values make animation slower. 0s specifies no animation.
`animation-timing-function`	Specifies how an animation should behave (such as how it accelerates) over its duration. It is **non-inherited** and the value it takes is one or more CSS **timing-function values**, which are specified in keywords that are linear, ease-in, ease-in-out, ease-out, step-start, and step-end. The property is **non-inherited**.

(Continued)

TABLE 18.2 (*Continued*)

Animation Properties

Property	Function
animation-delay	Specifies when animation should start after it has been triggered. It is **non-inherited** and the value it takes is a **time value** in seconds (s) or milliseconds (ms). This is usually useful for making different pieces start to move at different times.
animation-iteration-count	Specifies how many times an animation should play before it stops. It is **non-inherited** and the values it takes are infinite keyword (which specifies to play forever) and a **number value**, which is how many times to play animation. The default is 1. Iterations do not include specified delay.
animation-direction	Specifies the direction in which an animation should play. It is **non-inherited** and the values supported are the keywords: normal (which says to play forward), reverse (which says to play in reverse direction), alternate (which says play in the forward direction and then backward), and alternate-reverse (which says to play backward first and then forward).
animation-fill-mode	Specifies the styles to apply when animation is not playing. It is **non-inherited** and the values supported are none (which applies no style and is default), forward (which retains the styles applied to the last keyframe executed), backward (which retains the styles applied to the first keyframe executed and generally produces an effect similar to none), and both (which combines the rules for both forward and backward but generally produces the same effect as forward). The first keyframe (i.e., 0%, or from) or last keyframe (i.e., 100% or to) executed depends on the value of animation-direction and animation-iteration-count. The values are further explained in the NOTE box under the explanation for the example in Figures 18.6 and 18.7.
animation-play-state	Used to determine whether animation is playing or paused, or to pause or resume play from where it was paused. It is **non-inherited** and the values allowed are running (which says animation is playing) and paused (which says animation is paused).

The shorthand animation property, which is also **non-inherited**, can be used to specify the properties in the table. The properties are specified as a space-separated list that contains [animation-name] [animation-duration] [animation-timing-function] [animation-delay] [animation-iteration-count] [animation-direction] [animation-fill-mode] [animation-play-state]. The order is not mandatory, but it is useful to know that the first value encountered that has a **time value** is assigned to `animation-duration` and the second to `animation-delay`. Naturally, including `animation-name` and `animation-duration` is mandatory, since they describe the fundamental properties of an animation sequence.

18.4.3 Using `@keyframes` and Animation Properties

Figure 18.6 shows an example of how animation properties are used with the `@key-frame` at-rule and Figure 18.7 shows a snapshot of the result.

In the example, the `div{}` rule styles the content of the `<div>` element and specifies its animation properties. The `padding` property specifies the space between the element's content and its border and the `font size, text align,` and `color` properties specify

```css
CSS
div {
  padding: 50px;
  font-size: 60px;
  text-align: center;
  color: dark orange;
  animation-name: zooming;
  animation-duration: 1.5s;
  animation-delay: 1s;
  animation-fill-mode: both;
  animation-iteration-count: 3;
}
@keyframes zooming {
  0% {
     transform: scale(0.1);
  }
  50% {
     transform: scale(1.0) rotateZ(45deg);
  }
  100% {
     transform: scale(2);
  }
}
```

```html
HTML
<div>Zooming in</div>
```

FIGURE 18.6 Example usage of the animation properties and `@keyframes`.

Zooming in

FIGURE 18.7 The result of Figure 18.6.

text size, its alignment inside the element's box, and color, respectively. The `animation-name` property gives the animation a name ("zooming"), `animation-duration` specifies its duration, `animation-delay` says to wait 1 second after the animation is triggered before starting it, `animation-fill-mode` says to display, when animation completes, a combination of the styles for both first and last executed keyframes, and `animation-iteration-count` says to play the animation three times before stopping.

The `@keyframes` at-rule says to scale the content of the element to which "zooming" animation is applied to 0.1 at 0% keyframe, scale it to 1.0 and rotate it clockwise by 45% around z-axis at 50% keyframe, and scale it to 2.0 at 100% keyframe as well as rotate it back to the initial value of 0°, since the `rotateZ()` function is not specified at 100% keyframe. To make the element stay at 45°, a separate transform declaration is required to specify it. Refer to Chapter 11 for more about the `transform` property.

NOTE: The `animation-fill-mode` property

The effect of the `animation-fill-mode` property can be difficult to figure out. Below are the effects of the values on the behavior of the animation produced by Figure 18.6:

- `none`: Displays element's starting style and delays there for 1s. Actual animation sequence and the iterations do not include the delay. The final style displayed is the element's starting style.
- `forward`: Displays element's starting style and delays there for 1s. Actual animation sequence and its iterations do not include the delay. The final style displayed is the style at 100% keyframe.
- `backward`: Displays style at 0% keyframe and delays there for 1s. Actual animation sequence and its iterations do not include the delay and the final style displayed is the element's starting style.
- `both`: Displays style at 0% keyframe and delays there for 1s. Actual animation sequence and its iterations do not include the delay, and the final style displayed is the style at 100% keyframe.

CHALLENGE 18.1

Rewrite the code in Figure 18.6 using the shorthand `animation` property and make the text remain at 45% at the end of the animation instead of returning to 0° (i.e., level orientation). Also, make the text make a full rotation.

18.4.3.1 Applying Multiple Animations to an Element

More than one animation can be applied to the same element by simply specifying the animation name and properties for each and then defining the corresponding `@keyframes` at-rules. This is typically done using the shorthand `animation`

```
CSS
.ball {
  height: 200px;
  width: 200px;
  background-color: orange;
  border-radius: 100%;
  animation: move 10s ease-in infinite alternate, pulse 1s
    linear infinite alternate;
}
@keyframes move {
  0% { transform: translate(0, 0); }
  100% { transform: translate(600px, 0); }
}
@keyframes pulse {
  0% { background-color: orange; }
  100% { background-color: red; }
}

HTML
<div class="ball"></div>
```

FIGURE 18.8 Applying multiple animations to an element.

property, as it allows all the properties for an animation to be specified in one go. Each animation name and its properties are essentially specified as a comma-separated list. Figure 18.8 shows an example in which a circle is being moved slowly to and fro while its color is slowly changed as if it is pulsating.

In the .ball{} rule in the example, the width and height properties specify the size of the <div> element, background-color specifies its background color, and border-radius makes it round. The animation property specifies two animation sequences. For the first, it specifies animation-name as move, animation-duration as 10 seconds, animation-timing-function as ease-in, animation-iteration-count as infinite, and animation-direction as alternate. For the second, it specifies animation-name as pulse, animation-duration as 1 second, animation-timing-function as linear, animation-iteration-count as infinite, and animation-direction as alternate.

The @keyframes move{} at-rule says to move the element to 0 0 (top-left corner of page) at 0% keyframe and to 600px 0 (600px horizontally right) at 100%. The @keyframes pulse{} at-rule says to make the element's background color orange at 0% keyframe and red at 100%.

CHALLENGE 18.2

Using the same approach as in the example or any other, create a filled circle that changes into a square as it moves to the right of the screen and back to circle as it moves back.

18.4.3.2 Animated CSS Lightbox Display

In Figures 14.47 to 14.50 in Chapter 14, how to display a CSS lightbox was introduced. As mentioned there, a common practice is to animate it, rather than simply make it appear, so that it slides in from outside the screen into position. Figures 18.9 and 18.10 show how this is done using the same codes from Chapter 14, but with the animation instructions added to the CSS code. Essentially, the `animation: move 0.5s;` declaration was added to the .box{} rule and the following new rule was also added:

```
@keyframes move {
  0% { transform: translate(-500px, 0); }
  100% { transform: translate(0px, 0); }
}
```

The `animation` property specifies the name of the animation as "move", its duration as 0.50 seconds, and the default values of other properties, as listed in Table 18.2. The `@keyframes move{}` at-rule animates the box (i.e., the element of class="box"). It says, at 0% keyframe, to position the box, from the position specified in the .box{} rule, -500px along x-axis (which is off screen to the left) and 0px along the y-axis, and then move it to the position specified for the 100% keyframe. It is worth noting that if the `100% { transform: translate(0px, 0); }` rule is not specified, the animation will still work the same way, because the box's final position is specified in the .box{} rule, anyway. Refer to Chapter 14 for the explanation of ow the rest of the code works.

```
HTML
<h2>Lightbox with :target</h2>
<p>Lorem ipsum dolor sit amet, consectetur adipiscing elit.
 Sed id arcu utnunc...</p>
<p class="link"><a href="#window">Click to see a lightbox</a></p>
<p>Ut non risus vel ex tincidunt lobortis ut auctor diam.
 Vestibulum id leo venen...</p>
<p>Sed at enim erat. Nulla placerat odio vel finibus pulvinar.
 In varius, nulla....</p>
<p>Morbi eget dapibus erat, id pharetra purus. Quisque cursus
 sed metus ac hend...</p>
<div id="window">
  <div class="box">
    <a href="#" class="close">X</a>
    <p>This is a basic example of a lightbox or modal window.</p>
    <p>This box can contain any media object type, such as
     image or video.</p>
    <p>(Clicking the X closes it.)</p>
  </div>
</div>
```

FIGURE 18.9 HTML for a basic lightbox display.

```css
CSS
h2, .link { text-align: center; }
#window {
  width:100%;
  height:100%;
  background-color: rgba(0, 0, 0, 0.7);
  position: fixed;
  left: 0;
  top: 0;
  display: none;
}
.box {
  width: 300px;
  height: 300px;
  padding: 15px 20px 0 20px ;
  position: relative;
  top: 25%;
  margin: 0 auto;
  font-size: 24px;
  font-weight: bold;
  background-color: white;
  text-align: center;
  border: 1px solid black;
  box-shadow: inset 0 0 1em 0.5em blue, 0 0 1em 0.5em orange;
  animation: move 0.5s;
}
@keyframes move {
  0% { transform: translate(-500px, 0); }
  100% { transform: translate(0px, 0); }
}
.close {
  text-decoration: none;
  font-size: 22px;
  font-weight: bold;
  color: white;
  background-color: orange;
  border: 1px solid black;
  border-radius: 50%;
  width: 36px; height: 2px;
  padding: 7px 1px 30px 2px;
  position: absolute;
  top: -16px;
  left: 317px;
}
.close:hover {  color: black;cursor: pointer; }
#window:target { display: block; }
```

FIGURE 18.10 CSS for Figure 18.9.

CHALLENGE 18.3

Implement the example in Figures 18.9 and 18.10, but instead of the box coming from the left, make it drop down from the top.

18.4.4 CSS Transitions

Transitions in CSS define how a specified value of a property changes to another over time, including the timing of the change. By default, when change in a property is triggered, it happens instantly. With transition, the behavior of this change can be controlled. A change is triggered in various ways, such as by a page loading, using **pseudo-classes** (e.g., :hover and :active), and scripting. The properties used to create transition are transition-delay, transition-duration, transition-property, and transition-timing-function. Table 18.3 lists their functions.

The shorthand transition property can be used to specify the properties in the table and for multiple property names. There is no strict order in which the properties must be specified, except that the value for the transition-duration property

TABLE 18.3

Transition Properties

Property	Function
transition-property	Specifies the names of properties to which to apply a transition effect. It is **non-inherited** and the values taken are none (which means no transition), all (which means to apply transition to all properties that support it) and **IDENT** (which is the name of the property to which transition should apply, such as margin-left).
transition-delay	Specifies the amount of time to wait between when a change to a property is triggered and the time the change starts. It is **non-inherited** and specified in seconds (s) or milliseconds (ms). Multiple values can be specified, in which case, they are comma-separated and each value is applied to the corresponding property on the list specified by the transition-property.
transition-duration	Specifies the number of seconds (s) or milliseconds (ms) a transition takes to complete. It is **non-inherited** and its default value is 0s, which produces no transition. When multiple values are specified (which must be comma separated), each value is applied to the corresponding property on the list specified by the transition-property.

(Continued)

TABLE 18.3 (*Continued*)

Transition Properties

Property	Function
transition-timing-function	Specifies the behavior of a transition over time. In essence, it controls speed variation over time. It is **non-inherited** and the value it takes is a CSS a **timing-function value** that is specified in keywords, which are linear, ease-in, ease-in-out, ease-out, step-start, and step-end, or **function values**: cubic-bezier() and steps(). The cubic-bezier() function takes four values (x1, y1, x2, y2) that define the curve for the animation to follow. Values x1 and x2 must be between 0 and 1. Example: cubic-bezier(0.1, 0.6, 1.0, 0.2). The step() function takes one or two values that specify intervals. The first is the number of steps and the second direction, which can be start or end. Example: step(4, start). If the second value is missing, end is assumed.

must come before and that of transition-delay. Typically, the transition-property value will be first. Figures 18.11 and 18.12 show an example in which multiple transitions are applied to an element.

The div{} rule in the example specifies the initial width, height, and background-color of the <div> element. The transition property specifies two transitions. For the first, it specifies transition-property as width, transition-duration as 0.5 seconds, and transition-timing-function as ease-out. For the second, it specifies transition-property as height, transition-duration as 0.5 seconds, and transition-timing-function as ease-out. Notice that the sets of transition values are comma separated. The div:hover{} rule specifies

```
CSS
div {
  width: 50px;
  height: 50px;
  background-color: orange;
  transition: width 0.5s ease-out, height 0.5s ease-out;
}
div:hover {
  width: 150px;
  height: 150px;
  cursor: pointer;
}

HTML
<div></div>
```

FIGURE 18.11 Using the transition property.

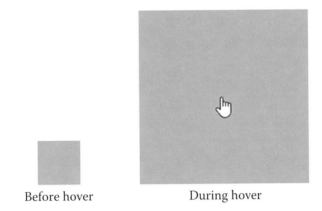

Before hover   During hover

FIGURE 18.12 The result of Figure 18.11.

the width and height to transition into when the cursor hovers over the element. Also, the `cursor` property says to change the cursor shape to a pointer.

> **NOTE: Transform versus transition**
>
> The technique used in the example is commonly used with image galleries, where an image is enlarged to show more of it when the cursor hovers over it. A similar approach can be implemented using the `transform` property with the `scale()` function, except that it provides no control over the speed of change from one size to the other.

CHALLENGE 18.4

Modify the code in Figure 18.11, combining transition with the `transform` property, so that the square rotates and changes color as it gets bigger.

CHALLENGE 18.5

Rewrite the example in Figure 18.11, using the `transform` property with the `scale(0)` function, so that when the cursor hovers over the square, it instantly becomes bigger.

CHALLENGE 18.6

Also using the `transform` property with the `scale(0)` function, implement a 3-image gallery with thumbnails, so that each thumbnail is a hyperlink to a larger version of the thumbnail and when the cursor hovers over it, it instantly becomes bigger. *Hint*: Use `<img>` element to add the images (Chapter 6) and `<a>` element to add hyperlink (Chapter 4).

18.5 3D Animation

3D animation can probably be best simplistically described as adding a third dimension (i.e., depth) to the movement of a 2D or 3D object. Movement can be along x-, y-, or z-axis and around these axes. This means 3D animation has what is described as **six degrees of freedom**, which is the ability to move forward/backward, up/down, left/right (i.e., along x-, y-, z-axis), plus yaw, pitch, and roll, as illustrated in Figure 18.13. The terms "yaw," "pitch," and "roll" essentially define the orientation of an object within a 3D space.

- **Yaw** is rotation around y-axis (i.e., left–right orientation). An example is when the head is being turned left or right.
- **Pitch** is rotation around x-axis (i.e., up or down orientation). An example is when the head is being nodded or thrown back.
- **Roll** is rotation around z-axis (i.e., side to side). An example is when the head is being cocked left or right.

18.5.1 CSS 3D Animation

The various CSS properties introduced so far, such as `transform` and `perspective`, can be animated to produce all the degrees of freedom required in 3D animation. Figures 18.14 and 18.15 show an example of how this is achieved and Figure 18.16 shows the result. The animation is basic and involves a banner rotating within the frame that holds it.

Notice that the example uses many properties already discussed in Chapter 10 to style the `<div>` elements. The `#container{}` rule styles the outer `<div>` element

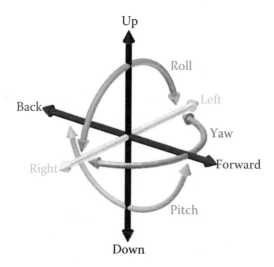

FIGURE 18.13 An illustration of the six degrees of freedom in 3D animation.

```
HTML
<body>
  <div id="container">
    <div id="banner"><p>Stop it!</p></div>
  </div>
</body>
```

FIGURE 18.14   HTML for the banner.

```
CSS
#container {
  width: 300px;
  margin: 50px;
  background-color: gray;
  border: 2px solid black;
  border-radius: 20px;
  perspective: 500px;
}
#banner {
  width: 200px;
  height: 200px;
  margin: 0 auto;
  background-color: pink;
  border: 2px solid black;
  border-radius: 20px;
  animation-name: rotation;
  animation-timing-function: linear;
  animation-duration: 6s;
  animation-iteration-count: infinite;
}
p { font: bold 32px Arial, sans-serif; text-align: center;
    margin: 75px 0px; }
@keyframes rotation {
  from { transform: rotateY(0deg); }
  to { transform: rotateY(360deg); }
}
```

FIGURE 18.15   CSS for the HTML in Figure 18.14.

of id="container". In the rule, the width property specifies the width (but the height is left to be determined by the inner <div> element), margin specifies the space between the element and the edge of the page (i.e., <body> element), background-color specifies the background color, border says to make the border 2px-thick solid line and black, border-radius makes the corners round, and perspective says to give perspective to the child elements of element (i.e., <div> element of id="banner") that are 3D-positioned, so as to create the sense of depth. An element is 3D-positioned if its positioning involves the y-axis.

FIGURE 18.16   A snapshot of the result of Figures 18.14 and 18.15.

The #banner{} rule styles the <div> element of id="banner". The width and height properties set the size, margin centers it horizontally inside the parent <div> element (i.e., id="container"), background-color sets the background color, border sets the border to black 2px-thick solid line, and border-radius makes the corners round. For the animation, the animation-name specifies the name of the animation as "rotation," animation-timing-function specifies linear motion, animation-duration sets the length of the animation sequence to 6 seconds, and animation-iteration-count says to play the animation indefinitely.

The p{} rule styles the text in the <p> element. The font property makes the text bold, 32px in size, and Arial, text-align centers it horizontally, and margin centers it vertically. The @keyframes rotation{} at-rule creates the "rotation" animation and says to rotate the element to which the rotation animation applies around the y-axis to 0° at 0% keyframe and 360° at 100%.

CHALLENGE 18.7

Implement the example and modify it to make the banner rotate in the opposite direction and also make it stop when the cursor is over it. Lastly, experiment with the value of the animation-timing-function property and also make the back-face of the banner invisible to see the effect. Refer to Chapter 11 on how to make an element's back-face invisible.

18.5.1.1 An Example Application of 3D Animation

Figures 18.17 and 18.18 show the implementation of a 3D image carousel and Figure 18.19 shows a snapshot of it in operation. The example is adapted from www.the-art-of-web.com and creates a carousel of images that goes round and round.

In the #carousel img{} rule in the example, the position property absolutely positions all <img> elements to remove them from normal flow and places

```
HTML
<div id="wrapper">
  <div id="carousel">
    <img id="image1" src="images/beach.jpg">
    <img id="image2" src="images/tunnel.jpg">
    <img id="image3" src="images/sunrise.jpg">
    <img id="image4" src="images/yacht.jpg">
    <img id="image5" src="images/south.jpg">
  </div>
</div>
```

FIGURE 18.17 HTML for carousel.

```
CSS
#carousel img { position: absolute; border: 1px solid
 light gray;
 background-color: rgba(255,255,255,0.7); width: 213px;
 height: 160px;
}
#image1 { transform: rotateY(0deg) translateX(180px);
          padding: 0 0 0 147px; }
#image2 { transform: rotateY(-72deg) translateX(180px);
          padding: 0 0 0 147px; }
#image3 { transform: rotateY(-144deg) translateX(180px);
          padding: 0 0 0 147px; }
#image4 { transform: rotateY(-216deg) translateX(180px);
          padding: 0 0 0 147px; }
#image5 { transform: rotateY(-288deg) translateX(180px);
          padding: 0 0 0 147px; }

#wrapper { perspective: 1200px; padding: 300px; height: 180px;}

#carousel {
 animation-name: carousel;
 animation-duration: 7s;
 animation-timing-function: linear;
 animation-iteration-count: infinite;
 transform-style: preserve-3d;
 transform-origin: 180px 0 0;
}

@keyframes carousel {
  0% { transform: rotateY(0deg); }
  100% { transform: rotateY(-360deg); }
}
```

FIGURE 18.18 CSS for the carousel HTML in Figure 18.17.

FIGURE 18.19   Snapshot of the result of Figures 18.17 and 18.18. (Image from freeimages.co.uk)

them at the default position at the top-left corner of the page. From there they can be rotated and moved as required to create the shape of the carousel. The `border` property makes the border of each element 1px-thick solid line and light grey, `background-color` makes the background color rgba(255,255,255,0.7), and `width` and `height` set the size.

The `#image1{}`, `#image2{}`, `#image3{}`, `#image4{}`, and `#image5{}` rules each rotates the corresponding `<img>` element around y-axis and moves it right along the x-axis to a new position as well as gives it left padding so that the contained image is at the right end of the element's box. The angles by which the elements are rotated from their initial orientation are multiple of 72 (which is derived from dividing 360° by the total numbers of images). Note that rotation must be specified before translation, because doing it the other way round will give a different result.

In the `#wrapper{}` rule, the `perspective` property gives perspective to the child elements of the `<div>` element of `id="wrapper"`, `padding` extends the left edges of the `<img>` elements by the same amount so that they meet at the central axis, and `height` produces the indirect effect of tilting the carousel up. The higher the value, the more the carousel is tilted up.

The `#carousel{}` rule sets the animation properties for the `<div>` element of `id="carousel"`. The `animation-name` property specifies the name ("carousel"), `animation-duration` sets duration of animation to 7 seconds, `animation-timing-function` sets motion type to `linear`, `transform-style` says to display the child elements of the element in 3D space, and `transform-origin` specifies the x–y–z coordinates of the point of rotation for the element, which is where the `<img>` elements meet. The `@keyframes carousel{}` at-rule creates the carousel animation and says to rotate the element to which carousel animation applies 0° around y-axis at 0% keyframe and −360° at 100%.

CHALLENGE 18.8

Implement the example in Figures 18.17 and 18.18 with your own images and experiment with the values of the transform and padding properties.

CHALLENGE 18.9

Modify the example so that when the cursor is over any of the images, the carousel stops and the cursor shape changes to a pointer. Also, when an image is clicked, link the user to another page or site. *Hint*: Try using the `:hover` pseudo-class (Chapter 8), the `animation-play-state` property, and the `<a>` element (Chapters 4 and 6).

18.6 Animation in Design

Animations are not easy to use effectively in Web design if they are not used to convey specific messages. Indeed, most uses of 2D animation on the Web are a distraction. It can often get to the point where it is difficult to concentrate on important or desired content for various things moving and flashing endlessly at the peripheral of vision. In order for the use animation to be effective, correct type of animation needs to be used, used in the right context, and with consideration. As with any other media, in order to be able to use animation effectively and in a way that does not compromise **user experience**, it is useful to know as much as possible about it, such as common uses and the shortcomings of using it. User experience refers largely to users' emotions or affective states during their interaction with your design, and many factors affect it; how animation is used is one of them. Other elements that contribute to user experience are discussed in Chapters 24 and 25.

The uses of animation vary widely, but the main ones are to attract attention, provide feedback, provide explanation, provide entertainment, and set mood. If you use it for reasons unrelated to these, then you should ask pointed questions about its appropriateness in your design.

18.6.1 Animation in Attracting Attention

On a screen with a lot of information, it can be difficult to ensure that users definitely notice a specific item. Animation can be quite useful for achieving this. This is because moving objects can often have an overwhelming effect on human peripheral vision, thereby compelling people to attend to them. However, this same property of animation can be a disadvantage if users have to constantly make conscious effort to ignore objects they do not want to see or have already seen. This can be annoying to many users and can turn them away rather than consider the message you intend to convey. This is one reason care is needed when using animation in a design. So, for example, when flashing is used to attract attention, it should not be made to go on endlessly.

A more appropriate use of flashing in attracting attention is to let any item to which you want to attract users' attention flash for only a few times, say, on entry to a page. If it is not feasible to do this, then other ways of attracting attention, such as using a different color, should be used. An option can also be provided for users to stop a flashing object, although this might be a harder option, as it might be more difficult to implement. Alternatively, a separate window could be used, so that the user can stop the animation by closing the window. Similarly, if animating a headline, for example, by moving it to and fro to draw attention to it, as done on some Web pages, it is important to remember that it can be distracting if it goes on endlessly. So, just moving the text a few times on entry to a page is usually enough to get the attention of the user.

18.6.2 Animation in Providing Feedback

The use of animation in feedback spans a variety of areas, but the most common purpose is to inform a user about what is going on in an application. Without feedback, users generally find it difficult to tell if an action has been successful, or whether or not a system is attending to a request. It is not uncommon for users to think a system has crashed when there is no feedback. The following are some of the common ways animation is used for feedbacks.

18.6.2.1 Depiction of Transition

This type of feedback involves communicating transition from one state to another, as can be achieved with the transition property. One common use of transition is when the in-between stages are shown of an opening or closing window. Using animation in this way simulates natural behavior and can help inform users about what is going on, thereby enhancing the general quality of interaction with a system. However, the image of the in-between stages of transition should not be too imposing, as this can look like a flash across the screen, which can be jarring.

18.6.2.2 Rollover Effect

Feedback can also be in the form of a direct response to an action, such as the movement of cursor or finger over a navigational aid like a button, a hyperlink, or a menu item. This is almost like a query-response situation. A user placing the cursor or finger over a button, for example, is synonymous to asking the button about itself (its state, what it does, etc.) and the button's reaction is the response. This query-response type of feedback, previously introduced as **rollover effect** or **hover effect**, can involve manipulating different elements. For example, the shape of a button can be slightly changed; the background of text may be made to change color, an active area can be made to shimmer, or display some other effects, such as surrounding marching ants or flashing background. Figure 18.20 shows an example of the use of rollover effect for giving feedback. Notice that the background of the text changes only when the cursor is in the bounding area of the text (i.e., the immediate area around the text). It is particularly common to use this form of feedback when the cursor moves over a list of menu items, whether the cursor is moved by a mouse or other types of interaction devices, such as eye-tracking devices. Notice also that the shape of the cursor is also changed. Incidentally, hover effect as of time of writing does not apply to touch screen interaction.

FIGURE 18.20 Animating background color to provide feedback.

Feedback in hover effect can also be in the form of presenting a brief description of an element's function or state. For example, placing the cursor over the icon for setting the viewing parameters for a YouTube video says "Settings." Typically, the animation used in hover effect is noncontinuous and fit for purpose. However, in some cases, it may be more useful to have continuous animation that better describes a function, particularly when icons project ambiguous messages about their functions. For example, when the cursor goes over a print-function icon, the icon can change state to one of continuous animation, in which paper seems to come out of a printer, rather than the icon or its border just changing color.

18.6.3 Animation in Providing Explanation

Content sometimes contains materials that are only best explained with motion. Using animation in this way is particularly common in Web learning applications and presentations. It is used, for example, to visualize concepts and relationships in various fields like engineering and meteorology and to show how things work, such as the movements of machine parts in engineering, how elements react in chemistry, and how animal body parts work in biology and medicine.

18.6.4 Animation in Providing Entertainment

In general, animation can provide a source of entertainment when used within the right context. Although the right contexts are not always easy to find when designing applications for adult users, they are much easier when children's applications are concerned. For example, it is almost standard to use animation in children's learning applications. It can be particularly effective in making the applications more interesting, exciting, and entertaining, and possibly more capable of retaining children's attention. Animation, along with vivid colors, is central to making children's applications entertaining. Again, even when using animation in children's applications, it still needs to be used appropriately in order for the right result to be achieved, particularly in learning applications.

18.6.5 Animation in Setting Mood

Setting mood is important to users' experience in some types of applications, and animation can play a role in doing this. For example, it can be used to create a sense of liveliness in a website that is providing information about a party. Party balloons, for instance, may be animated to float down the screen, on entry to a page; or to float in the background. Similarly, falling snow can be simulated to set a Christmas mood. Of course, it is important, again, to remember that animation that goes on all the time can be distracting, although for a party page this may be tolerable to an extent, particularly as no serious reading or comprehension is usually involved.

18.6.6 Animation in Providing a Sequence of Items

In some contexts, it is useful to inform users of available options without them having to use any navigational aids. In such contexts, animation is sometimes used to present these options in the form of a rotating sequence, as if on a revolving conveyor belt or carousel, for users to click on the item of interest and be taken to a page that provides detailed information about it. This technique is sometimes used to provide news summaries. A potential problem, though, is that the change from one summary to the next can sometimes occur before users finish reading. This can be particularly frustrating for users, which means that some sort of user control is useful in the form of an option to pause or stop the animation. One common implementation of this is to provide a set of controls at the bottom of the animation to pause, go forward or go back. Ideally, when users click any of the controls, the animation should stop, allowing users to then manually navigate the content.

> **NOTE: Appropriateness of animation use**
>
> One of the worst things to do in design is to use animation just for the sake of doing so, particularly when it is likely to compromise user experience. For example, putting animation that starts automatically on the same page as primary content is not a good idea. If animation must be used just for the fun of it, then it should be used on a home page or opening screen, where there is no content, except menu, after which the user should be left alone to concentrate on the primary content on other pages without distraction.

18.7 Beyond CSS-Only Animation

The use of CSS alone for creating animation has limitations, in that it can only produce basic level of dynamism. This means that it is not well-suited for complex animation, such as is required for Web games, be they 2D or 3D. For complex animations, other Web languages are needed and there are various. Those designed for the Web include JavaScript and WebGL. **JavaScript** is a general purpose computer programming language that can be used to manipulate HTML elements more dynamically than CSS. **WebGL** (Web Graphics Library), however, is basically a set of JavaScript routines, protocols, and tools designed for rendering (i.e., drawing) 2D and 3D graphics in Web browsers. Combining HTML, CSS, JavaScript, and WebGL, the complexity of the graphics and animation that can be achieved is possibly limited only by imagination. It makes it possible to create realistic graphics as well as interactive 2D and 3D animation, such as is required in games, using various types of materials (shaders), textures, lighting, and camera movements.

However, combining these technologies to create complex animations requires programming expertise. Fortunately, there are free JavaScript libraries that make it easier to use WebGL. One of these is **three.js**. How the libraries are used with HTML and example projects are available at the website (threejs.org). How JavaScript is used with HTML is shown in Chapter 22.

18.8 Useful Info

18.8.1 Web Links

CSS specifications: w3.org/standards

Web development documents: docs.webplatform.org

Accessibility: w3.org/WAI/tutorials, webaim.org

CSS tutorials (*Here are just a few free tutorial sites on CSS and other Web languages*): w3.org/wiki, html5rocks.com, sitepoint.com, w3schools.com, codecademy.com, quackit.com, developer.mozilla.org/en-US/docs/Web tutorialspoint.com, htmldog.com, htmlcodetutorial.com, echoecho.com, learn.shayhowe.com, html.net, tizag.com, cssbasics.com, cordova.apache. org, developers.google.com, csszengarden.com, webdesignermag.co.uk, css.maxdesign.com.au

CSS generators for various features: enjoycss.com, bennettfeely.com, cssplant. com

Examples and tools: greensock.com

Animation generator: westciv.com

HTML5-based animation: freshdesignweb.com/examples-html5-animation

Testing codes: jsfiddle.net, codepad.org, jsbin.com, cssdesk.com

Placeholder images: lorempixel.com

Browser compatibility info: caniuse.com

19

Layout with Flexible Box

19.1 Introduction

In CSS, the layout of Web pages used to be achieved through the use of various sizing and positioning of CSS properties that were not designed specifically for the purpose. This made the creation of layouts cumbersome and the results unpredictable on screens of different sizes. The introduction of the CSS flexible box and grid layout models is designed to address this problem. These models enable you to specify how a container element should control the behavior of the elements inside it, making the creation of layouts more straightforward and more intuitive. This chapter introduces the flexible box layout model, and Chapter 20 deals with grid layout.

19.2 Learning Outcomes

After studying this chapter, you should:

- Be aware of the anatomy of the flexible box layout model.
- Know how to control the flow direction of flex items.
- Be able to control the wrapping of flex lines.
- Know how to set flow direction and wrapping properties together.
- Be able to control the size of flex items.
- Know how to align flex items both as a group and individually.
- Be able to control the visual order of flex items.

19.3 Anatomy of Flexible Box Layout

The CSS flexible box, also called **flexbox**, is a layout model that is intended to allow Web authors to arrange elements on a page such that they respond predictably or as intended to changes in screen sizes. In particular, it largely eliminates the use of the `float` and `clear` properties (introduced in Chapter 12), which can be cumbersome and difficult for some to understand. In order to use flexbox effectively, it is useful to be familiar with the anatomy of the model and the terminologies used to describe its components, as this helps to better understand the functions of flexbox properties.

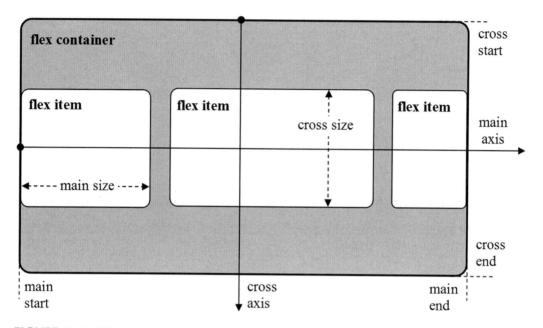

FIGURE 19.1   The anatomy of the flexbox layout model for left-to-right-top-to-bottom writing.

The central principle of the model is to give a container element (known as a **flex container**) the ability to change the size of its child elements (known as **flex items**) in a way that best fills the available space. Text that is directly contained in a flex container, known as an **anonymous flex item**, is also controlled. Figure 19.1 illustrates the anatomy of the model from the viewpoint of content that flows left to right and top to bottom.

Flex items are laid out along the **main axis** in the container starting at the **main-start** edge and going toward the **main-end** edge. The main axis goes in the same direction as the **inline axis**, which is horizontal or vertical, depending on **writing mode**, and represents the direction in which inline-level content flows. A line of flex items is contained in what is known as a **flex line**. Flex lines are laid out along the **cross axis** in the container, starting at the **cross-start** edge and going toward the **cross-end** edge. The cross axis essentially goes in the same direction as the **block axis** (which is vertical or horizontal, depending on **writing mode**) and represents the direction in which block-level content flows. The directions of the main axis (i.e., **main dimension**) and that of the cross axis (i.e., **cross dimension**) go in the same ways as the current writing mode and determine whether an edge is the main-start, main-end, cross-start, or cross-end edge. Also, whether **main size** or **cross size** represents the width or height of an item depends on these dimensions. This is because the flexbox layout model is used to represent multiple directions of content flow, such as left to right, right to left, and top to bottom.

A flex container can be single-line or multi-line, depending whether or not lines are wrapped. It is **single-line** if it has only one line of flex items that is not broken, even if the line overflows the container's edge. It is **multi-line** if the lines of items are broken into multiple lines, the same way that text is wrapped onto multiple lines in a document. With the flexbox properties, it is possible to achieve many layout goals easily, such as:

- Center an element inside a page.
- Make elements or containers flow horizontally or vertically in any order.
- Create a row of elements, such as buttons, that collapses vertically on smaller screens.

A flex container can be defined as a **block-level** or an **inline-level** container and created by assigning `flex` or `inline-flex` value to the `display` property (discussed in Chapter 10), respectively. For example, the `display: flex;` declaration says to make the element to which it is applied a block-level flex container and `display: inline-flex;` says to make it an inline-level flex container. Once created, elements inside a flex container automatically become flex items and are laid out along the direction of the main axis or the cross axis. Some flexbox properties apply only to the flex container and affect all the items inside it, while others apply only to individual flex items.

NOTE: Flexbox properties and other CSS properties

Some properties have no effect on the behavior of flex items, such as `column`, `float`, and `clear` properties (presented in Chapter 12) and `vertical-align` (introduced in Chapter 14).

19.4 Controlling Flow Direction of Flex Items

The flow direction of flex items describes the direction in which flex items are laid out within the containing flex container. The direction can be from left to right, right to left, top to bottom, or bottom to top. These directions can also be described in terms of where flow starts and ends, and how this is interpreted depends on the current writing mode, such as left-to-right-top-to-bottom. The property used to control this direction is the `flex-direction` property. It is specified in the rule for the flex container (since it applies to all its flex items) and sets the direction in which the flex items are laid out in the container. It is **non-inherited** and takes the values listed in Table 19.1. Figure 19.2 shows the effects of the values, and Figures 19.3 and 19.4 show example usage, using the `row-reverse` value.

In the `#container{}` rule in the example, the `width` and `height` properties specify the size of the `<div>` element of `id="container"`, `border` makes its border 1px-thick black solid line, `display` makes it a block-level flex container, and `flex-direction` specifies to lay out the flex items (i.e., the `<div>` elements inside it) in reverse direction. The `#container div{}` rule styles the `<div>` elements (i.e., flex items) inside the flex container, specifying the size, background color, the thickness, line-style, and color of the border, and the border radius (i.e., the roundness of the corners).

TABLE 19.1

Values Supported by the `flex-direction` Property

Value	Function
row	Lays out items in the direction of the inline axis of the current writing mode, for example, left to right. It is the **default**.
row-reverse	Lays out items in the opposite direction to the inline axis in the current writing mode.
column	Lays out items in the direction of the block axis of the current writing mode. For example, this is vertical in horizontal writing mode.
column-reverse	Lays out items in the opposite direction to the block axis in the current writing mode.

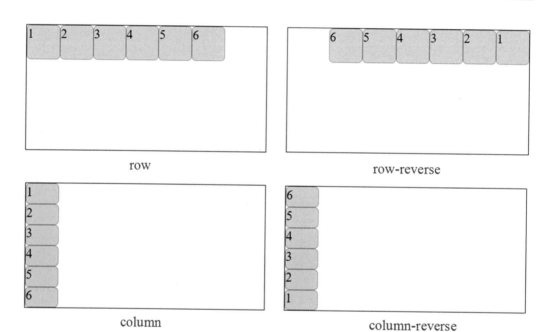

FIGURE 19.2   Effect of `flex-direction` values.

```
HTML
<div id="container">
  <div>1</div>
  <div>2</div>
  <div>3</div>
  <div>4</div>
  <div>5</div>
  <div>6</div>
</div>
```

FIGURE 19.3   HTML for example usage of `flex-direction`.

```
CSS
#container {
  width: 300px;
  height: 150px;
  border: 1px solid black;
  display: flex;
  flex-direction: row-reverse;
}
#container div {
  width: 40px;
  height: 40px;
  background-color: pink;
  border: 1px solid gray;
  border-radius: 5px;
}
```

FIGURE 19.4 CSS for HTML in Figure 19.3.

CHALLENGE 19.1

Implement the example in Figures 19.3 and 19.4, using each of the four values in Table 19.1 to see their effect. Also, vary both the size of the flex container and the flex items to better understand the behavior of the items.

19.5 Controlling the Wrapping of Flex Lines

A flex line by default overflows the edge (i.e., main-end edge) of the flex container when it is longer than the width/height of the flex container. The flex-wrap property allows you to specify whether the flex container should wrap the line onto multiple lines and is specified for the container. It is **non-inherited** and takes the values listed in Table 19.2. Figure 19.5 shows the effects of the values, and Figures 19.6 and 19.7 show example usage, using the wrap value.

TABLE 19.2

Values Supported by the flex-wrap Property

Value	Function
nowrap	Lays out items on a single line and does not wrap, squeezing the items to fit them in the container, until they can no longer be squeezed, at which point they overflow the container's main-end edge. It is the **default**.
wrap	Breaks flex lines into multiple lines when they cannot fit into the container's width/height.
wrap-reverse	Same as wrap, but with cross-start and cross-end swapped.

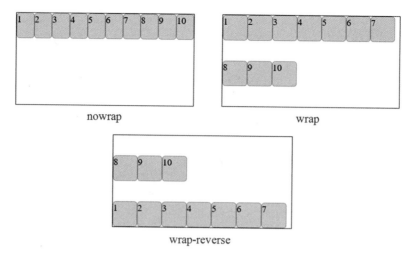

FIGURE 19.5   Effects of flex-wrap values.

HTML
```
<div id="container">
  <div>1</div>
  <div>2</div>
  <div>3</div>
      . . .
  <div>10</div>
</div>
```

FIGURE 19.6   HTML for example usage of flex-wrap.

CSS
```
#container { width: 300px; height: 150px;
   border: 1px solid black; display: flex; flex-wrap: wrap;
}
#container div { width: 40px; height: 40px;
   background-color: pink; border: 1px solid gray;
   border-radius: 5px;
}
```

FIGURE 19.7   CSS for the HTML in Figure 19.6.

In the #container{} rule in the example, the width and height properties specify the size of the <div> element of id="container", the border property makes the border 1px-thick black solid line, display makes the element a flex container, and flex-wrap says to wrap the <div> elements (i.e., flex items) inside it to the next line when necessary. The #container div{} rule styles the <div> elements (i.e., flex items) inside the flex container, specifying the size, background color, the thickness, style and color of the border, and the roundness of the corners.

CHALLENGE 19.2

Implement the example in Figures 19.6 and 19.7, using each of the three values in Table 19.2 to see their effect. Also, vary both the size of the flex container and the flex items to better understand the behavior of the items.

19.6 Specifying Flex Direction and Wrapping Together

The `flex-direction` and `flex-wrap` properties can be specified in a single declaration using the `flex-flow` shorthand property. The value of one or both of the properties can be specified in any order; the browser determines which value applies to which property.

CHALLENGE 19.3

Rewrite `flex-flow: row-reverse wrap` in longhand and explain what the declaration does.

CHALLENGE 19.4

Modify the code in Figures 19.6 and 19.7 accordingly, using the `flex-flow` property to lay out the flex items vertically and make them wrap at the top or bottom.

19.7 Controlling the Size of Flex Items

How flex items should be sized relative to other flex items in response to changes in the browser window's size is specified with three factors: the **initial size** of an item, how much it should **grow** when there is more space, and how much it should **shrink** when there is less space. These factors work together to dynamically size an item, and each can either be specified singly (using longhand properties) or together with others (using a shorthand property).

19.7.1 Specifying Flex Items Sizing Factors Individually

The properties for specifying the sizing factors for flex items individually are `flex-grow`, `flex-shrink`, and `flex-basis` longhand properties. They **apply to only individual flex items** and are, therefore, specified in rules targeting individual flex items rather than those targeting all the items within a flex container. Table 19.3 lists their function. The best way to see and understand how they work is through implementing them and varying the values and the width of the browser. So, this has been left as a challenge.

TABLE 19.3

Longhand Flex Properties

Property	Function
`flex-grow`	Specifies the flex grow factor, which is the proportion by which an item can grow (i.e., how much space it can take up) relative to other items when available space is distributed. It is **non-inherited** and takes a **number value**. Example usage: flex-grow: 2. The default is 0.
`flex-shrink`	Specifies the flew shrink factor, which is by how much an item can shrink relative to the other items when there is limited space on a line. It is **non-inherited** and a **number value**. Example usage: flex-shrink: 2. The default is 1.
`flex-basis`	Specifies the initial main size (i.e., width or height) of a flex item. It is **non-inherited** and the values it takes are auto keyword, **length values** (e.g., px, em, and %), and content keyword (which says to size item based on its content). Example usage: flex-basis: 45px and flex: content. The default is auto keyword.

CHALLENGE 19.5

Create a `<div>` flex container of `id="container"` and six `<div>` flex item inside it of `id` equal to "one," "two," "three," "four," "five," and "six," then use the CSS rules below to study how the `flex-grow`, `flex-shrink`, and `flex-basis` properties work, alternating between the properties and varying their values.

```
#container { width: 300px; height: 200px; border: 1px solid grey;
    display: flex;
}
#container div { height: 45px; background-color: orange;
    border: 1px solid black; flex-basis: 30px;
}
#container #three { flex-basis: 70px; }
```

19.7.2 Specifying All Flex Items Sizing Factors with One Property

The property for specifying `flex-grow`, `flex-shrink`, and `flex-basis` longhand properties together is the `flex` shorthand property. When used to specify the properties, values are specified in the order `flex-grow`, `flex-shrink`, and `flex-basis` (e.g., flex: 3 2 15%), but only `flex-grow` is mandatory. The property can also take `none` or `auto` keyword. When `flex-grow` is omitted, it is set to 1; when `flex-shrink` is omitted, it is set to 1; and when `flex-basis` is omitted, it is set to 0. Table 19.4 shows examples of the common ways values are specified and Figure 19.8 shows how the property is used.

In the `.flex-container{}` rule in the example, the `display` property makes the `<div>` element of `class="flex-container"` a flex container and the `border` property makes its border 2px-thick black solid line. The `.flex-container div{}` rule styles the `<div>` elements (i.e., the flex items) inside the flex container, giving them background color, padding to make them bigger, 2px-thick grey border, and horizontally center-aligning their contents. The `.one{}` and `.two{}` rules each specifies the `flex-grow`, `flex-shrink`, and `flex-basis` properties. These three properties work together to specify that the `<div>` element of `class="two"` (i.e., item 2) should take five times more space than the `<div>` element of `class="one"` (i.e., item 1) when there is enough space, and take three times less space when there is not enough space.

TABLE 19.4

Commonly Used Values for the `flex` Property

Value	Function
`flex: 0 auto`	This is the same as `flex: 0 1 auto` and sizes an item based on the specified width/height. It makes an item inflexible when there is free space left but allows it to shrink to the minimum possible when there is limited space.
`flex: auto`	This is the same as `flex: 1 1 auto`. Sizes an item based on the specified width/height and makes it fully flexible, letting it use up any available space along the main axis. If all items have `flex` set `auto`, `initial`, or `none`, then the space that remains after the items have been allocated the specified size is distributed evenly among those that have `flex` set to `auto`.
`flex: none`	This is the same as `flex: 0 0 auto`. It sizes an item based on the specified width/height, makes the item fully inflexible, and does not allow it to shrink.
`flex: 0 0 <length>`	This explicitly specifies the size of an element (e.g., `flex: 0 0 80px`).
`flex: <number>`	This is the same as `flex: <number> 1 0px`; (e.g., `flex: 5 1 0px`). It makes an item fully flexible, taking up the specified proportion of available space.

```
CSS
.flex-container { display: flex; border: 2px solid black; }
.flex-container div {
  background-color: orange;
  padding: 20px;
  border: 2px solid gray;
  text-align: center;
}
.one { flex: 1 1 10em; }
.two { flex: 5 3 10em; }

HTML
<div class="flex-container">
 <div class="one">1</div>
 <div class="two">2</div>
</div>
```

FIGURE 19.8   Example usage of the flex property.

CHALLENGE 19.6

Again, the best way to understand how the `flex` property works is to see its effect in use. Implement the code in Figure 19.8, adjusting the flex values and the width of the browser to vary the amount of available space to see the different results produced.

19.7.2.1 Vertical Space Example

Figure 19.9 shows a practical example in which elements are vertically flowed and sized with the `flex` property and Figure 19.10 the result.

In the .container{} rule in the example, the `width` and `height` properties specify the size of the <div> element of `class="container"`, the `display` property makes the element a block-level flex container, and `flex-flow` specifies to flow the children (flex items) vertically. In the .header,   .footer{} rule, the `height` property specifies the height for the <div> element of `class="header"` and <div> element of `class="footer"`, `background-color` makes their background color grey, `text-align` centers their text contents, and `flex` makes their size inflexible. In the .content{} rule, the `background-color` property makes the background color of the <div> element of `class="content"` orange, `text-align` centers its content, and `flex` makes the size fully flexible, making it fill the space in the flex container not taken by other items.

CSS
```css
.container {
  width: 500px;
  height: 400px;
  display: flex;
  flex-flow: column;
}
.header, .footer {
  height: 30px;
  background-color: gray;
  text-align: center;
  flex: none;
}
.content {
  background-color: orange;
  text-align: center;
  flex: auto;
}
```

HTML
```html
<div class="container">
  <div class="header">HEADER</div>
  <div class="content">CONTENT</div>
  <div class="footer">FOOTER</div>
</div>
```

FIGURE 19.9 Using the flex property to allocate vertical space.

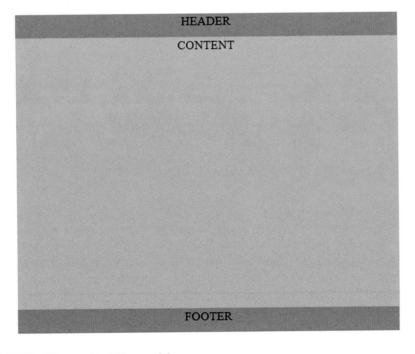

FIGURE 19.10 The result of Figure 19.9.

CHALLENGE 19.7

Implement the example in Figure 19.9 and vary the values for the flex property in the .header, .footer{}, and .content{} rules to see their effects on the layout. Also, remove the height property from the .header, .footer{} rule and explain the resulting change in the header and the footer.

NOTE: flex shorthand

It is recommended to use the flex shorthand instead of the longhand sub-properties, as it resets any specified values to accommodate common uses, such as those listed in Table 19.4.

19.8 Aligning Flex Items

Flex items can be aligned collectively as the children of the containing flex container or individually within it. Alignment can be along the inline/row and cross/column axes, and the properties used to achieve these goals are justify-content, align-content, align-items, and align-self, which are part of the set of generic alignment properties, known as **box alignment properties**, used for aligning elements' boxes.

19.8.1 Aligning All Flex Items in a Flex Container

The properties for specifying the alignment for all the flex items contained in a flex container are justify-content, align-content, and align-items, all of which are specified only in the rule for the flex container since they are designed to affect all its content.

19.8.1.1 justify-content

The justify-content property aligns flex items along the main axis of the current flex line (e.g., along the horizontal axis in a horizontal writing mode), using the space available after the space needed for flexible lengths and auto margins (margins with auto value) has been allocated. It basically controls how leftover space is distributed between flex items along the main axis. This means that if even one flex item has an indefinite need for space (e.g., flex-grow value that is greater than 0), the property will have no effect, because the item will take up all extra space and there will be no leftover. It is **non-inherited** and the values it supports are listed in Table 19.5. Figure 19.11 illustrates the effects of the values and Figure 19.12 shows example usage of the property.

TABLE 19.5

Values for the `justify-content` Property

Value	Function
flex-start	Makes flex items start from the main-start, with the margin of the first item flush with the main-start and each succeeding item flush with the end of the preceding one. It is the **default**.
flex-end	Makes items start from the main-end, with the margin edge of the item flush with the main-end and each preceding item flush with the succeeding one.
center	Places items at the center of the line, with each flush with the next and the space between the first item and the main-start and the last item and the main-end equal.
space-between	Spreads items evenly over a line, with the first item flush with main-start and the last item with the main-end.
space-around	Surrounds each item with equal space. This means that the spaces between adjacent items are equal and twice that between the first item and the main-start and the last item and the main-end.

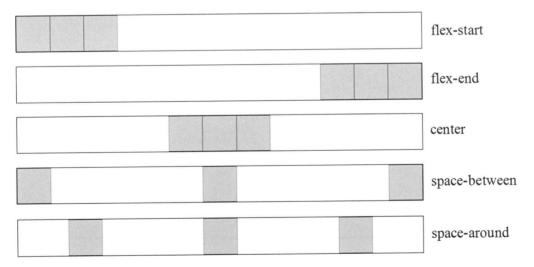

FIGURE 19.11 Effects of justify-content values.

```
CSS
#flex-container {
  border: 1px solid black; display: flex;
  justify-content: flex-start;
}
#flex-container div {
  width: 50px; height: 50px; background-color: pink;
  border: 1px solid gray;
}

HTML
<div id="flex-container">
  <div></div>
  <div></div>
  <div></div>
</div>
```

FIGURE 19.12   Example usage of justify-content.

In the `#flex-container{}` rule in the example, the `border` property makes the border of the `<div>` element of `id="flex-container"` 1px-thick black solid line, the `display` property makes the element a flex container, and `justify-content` says to lay out the elements (flex items) in the container according to the rules of the `flex-start` value described in Table 19.5. The `#flex-container div{}` rule styles the `<div>` elements (flex items) inside the flex container, specifying the size, background color, and the thickness, style, and color of the border.

CHALLENGE 19.8

Implement the example in Figure 19.12 and try out, in the `#flex-container{}` rule, the other values listed in Table 19.5 for the `justify-content` property. Also, apply `flex-grow` that is greater than 0 to any of the elements and explain what happens. Also, apply the property to all the elements and see the effect.

CHALLENGE 19.9

To better understand the behavior of the flex items, place a sizeable amount of text in them in the example you have just implemented. Also experiment with different values of width and height, and with no values specified while also varying the width of the browser window. Given your observation, how does using `justify-content` compare with using the multi-column layout properties (discussed in Chapter 12)? Is one better suited for some design requirements than the other, and which sort of requirements?

19.8.1.2 `align-content`

The `align-content` property aligns flex lines in a multi-line flex container when there is enough space in the cross axis (e.g., enough vertical space in horizontal writing mode). It does this in a similar way that the `justify-content` does it along the main axis. The property has no effect on a single-line container. This means that flex line must be longer than the flex container (and the `flex-wrap` property used to wrap the line) in order for the property to have an effect. It is **non-inherited** and the values supported are listed in Table 19.6. Figure 19.13 shows their effects.

Figure 19.14 shows an example of how the `align-content` property is used. In the `#flex-container{}` rule, the `width` and `height` properties specify the size of the `<div>` element of `id="container"`, the `border` property makes its border 1px-thick black solid line, `display` makes it a flex container, `flex-wrap` says to wrap lines of items to the next line when necessary, and `align-content` says to align lines of items according to the rules of the `flex-start` value, as described

TABLE 19.6

Values for the `align-content` Property

Value	Function
flex-start	Lays out lines of items starting from the cross-start, with the cross-start edge of the first line flush with the cross-start edge of the flex container and each line flush with the next one.
flex-end	Lays out line of items starting from the cross-end, with the cross-end edge of the last line flush with the cross-end edge of the flex container and each line flush with the next one.
center	Lays out line of items along the center of the flex container, with the lines flush with each other, and the space between the first line and the cross-start edge of the container equal to that between the last line and the cross-end edge of the container.
space-between	Lays out lines of items evenly in the flex container, with the space between adjacent items equal and the cross-start and cross-end edges of the container flush with first and last lines, respectively.
space-around	Lays out lines of items evenly in the flex container, so that the space between the first line and the cross-start edge of the container and that between the last line and the cross-end edge of the container are each half that between the lines.
stretch	Stretches lines to fill up available space, sharing the space equally between all the lines, increasing their cross size. It is the **default.**

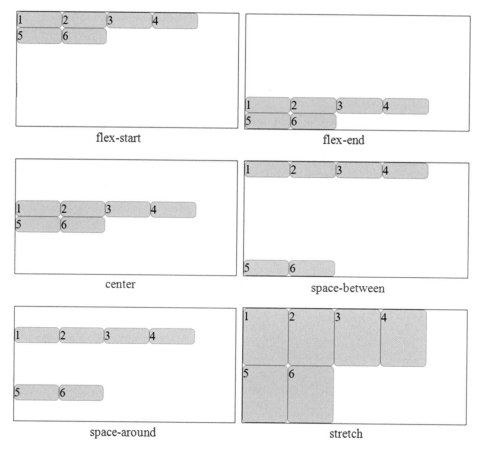

FIGURE 19.13   Effects of the values of align-content property.

```
CSS
#container {
  width: 300px; height: 150px; border: 1px solid black;
  display: flex; flex-wrap: wrap; align-content:flex-start;
}
#container div {
  width: 60px; background-color: pink;border: 1px solid gray;
  border-radius: 5px;
}
HTML
<div id="container">
  <div>1</div>
  <div>2</div>
  <div>3</div>
  <div>4</div>
  <div>5</div>
  <div>6</div>
</div>
```

FIGURE 19.14   Example usage of the align-content.

in Table 19.6. The `#container div{}` rule styles the `<div>` elements (i.e., flex items) inside the flex container, specifying the size, background color, the thickness, style, and color of the border, and the roundness of the elements' corners.

CHALLENGE 19.10

To better understand the effects of the values of the `align-content` property, implement the example in Figure 19.14 and try out the other values in Table 19.6. Also, remove the `flex-wrap` declaration to see the effect.

19.8.1.3 `align-items`

The `align-items` property aligns all items in a flex container in the cross axis of the current line of the container. This means, for example, that if the main axis is in the horizontal direction, items are vertically aligned. The property is **non-inherited** and Table 19.7 lists the values it supports. Figure 19.15 shows the effects of the values, and Figures 19.16 and 19.17 show an example of how it is used.

TABLE 19.7

Values for the `align-items` Property

Value	Function
flex-start	Places the cross-start margin-edge of items flush with the cross-start edge of the current flex line.
flex-end	Places the cross-end margin-edge of items flush with the cross-end edge of the current flex line.
center	Centers an item in the cross axis within the current flex line. If the cross size (i.e., width/height) of the item is greater than that of the flex line, the item overflows equally in both directions.
stretch	Stretches items to fill the cross size (i.e., width/height) of the current flex line, while respecting any specified min-width, min-height, max-width, or max-height. It is the **default**.
baseline	Aligns the baselines of items. Produces the same result as flex-start (as shown in Figure 19.15), if the baselines of items are the same; otherwise the item with the largest distance between its baseline and its cross-start margin edge is the one that will have its cross-start edge flush with the cross-start edge of the current flex line. The **baseline of an item** is typically the baseline of the biggest text in its first line of text. This is explained further with the example in Figure 19.16 and the subsequent CHALLENGE box.

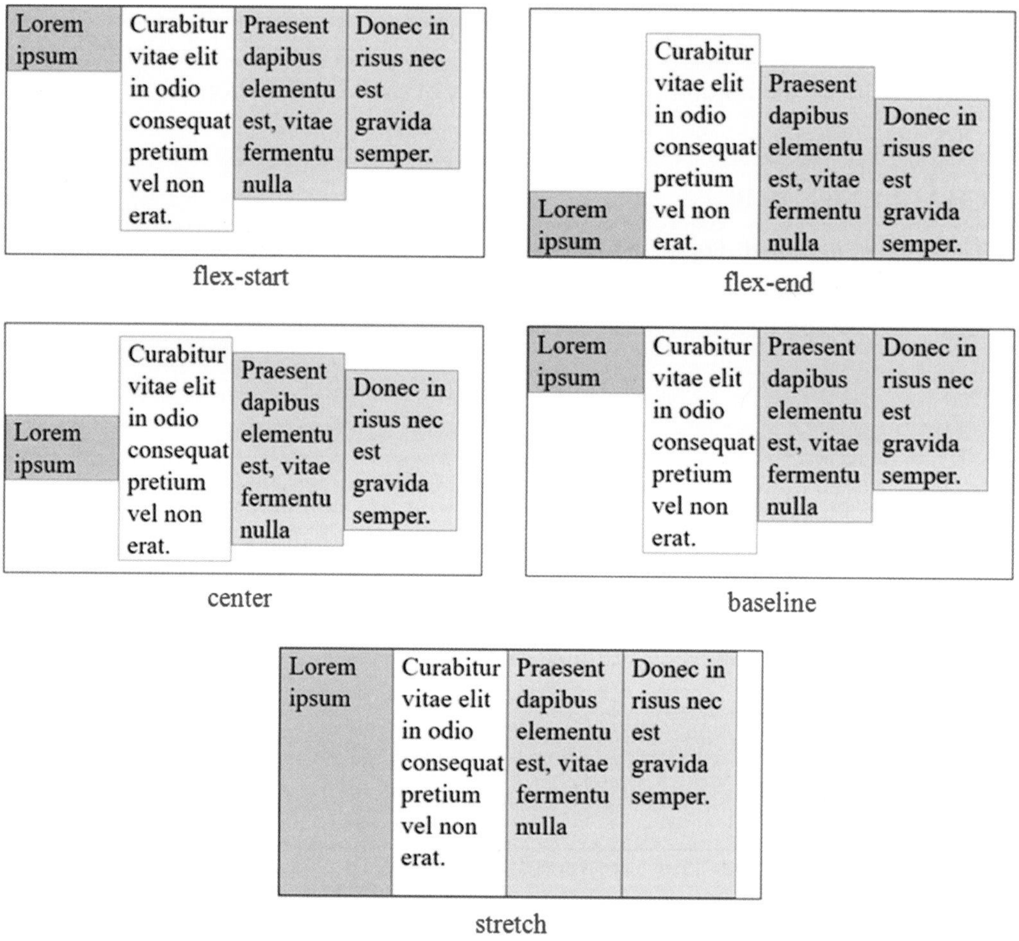

Lorem ipsum	Curabitur vitae elit in odio consequat pretium vel non erat.	Praesent dapibus elementu est, vitae fermentu nulla	Donec in risus nec est gravida semper.

flex-start

	Curabitur vitae elit in odio consequat pretium	Praesent	
Lorem ipsum	vel non erat.	dapibus elementu est, vitae fermentu nulla	Donec in risus nec est gravida semper.

flex-end

Lorem ipsum	Curabitur vitae elit in odio consequat pretium vel non erat.	Praesent dapibus elementu est, vitae fermentu nulla	Donec in risus nec est gravida semper.

center

Lorem ipsum	Curabitur vitae elit in odio consequat pretium vel non erat.	Praesent dapibus elementu est, vitae fermentu nulla	Donec in risus nec est gravida semper.

baseline

Lorem ipsum	Curabitur vitae elit in odio consequat pretium vel non erat.	Praesent dapibus elementu est, vitae fermentu nulla	Donec in risus nec est gravida semper.

stretch

FIGURE 19.15   Effects of the values of align-items property.

In the example, the `#container{}` rule specifies the size of the `<div>` element of `id="container"`, styles its border (making it 1px-thick black solid line), makes the element a flex container, and says to place the flex items vertically in the center of the container. The `#container div{}` rule specifies the width of the `<div>` elements (i.e., flex items) inside the `<div>` element of `id="container"` (i.e., flex container) and also styles their borders. The `#container .one{}`, `#container .two{}`, `#container .three{}`, and `#container .four{}` rules specify the background color and padding for each of the flex items. Notice that the content of the first and last flex items is a space (` `). This is to give them height because without content, a box collapses into a line.

CSS
```
#container {
  width: 300px; height: 150px; border: 1px solid black;
    display: flex; align-items: center;
}
#container div {
  width: 60px; border: 1px solid gray;
}
#container .one { background-color: pink; padding: 0 5px; }
#container .two { background-color: light yellow;
 padding: 0 5px; }
#container .three { background-color: light gray;
 padding: 0 5px; }
#container .four { background-color: light blue;
padding: 0 5px; }
```

HTML
```
<div id="container">
 <div class="one"> </div>
 <div class="two">Curabitur vitae elit in odio consequat pretium
  vel non erat.</div>
 <div class="three">Praesent dapibus elementu est, vitae
  fermentu nulla</div>
 <div class="four"> </div>
</div>
```

FIGURE 19.16   Example usage of the align-items property.

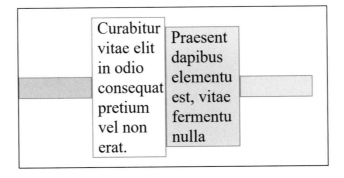

FIGURE 19.17   Result of Figure 19.16.

CHALLENGE 19.11

Using your own content, implement the example in Figure 19.16 (filling all the flex items with text), and try out the other values listed in Table 19.7. Also, to better understand the effect of the `baseline` value, increase the size of the first line of text in one of the elements to see how this affects the alignment of the top edges of the flex items against the top edge of the flex container.

CHALLENGE 19.12

Again, implement the example in Figure 19.16 but without content in items one and four, and also modify it so that all the flex items are horizontally centered in the flex container and flex items two and three are of the same size and contain an image each. Also, make the images links to other websites.

CHALLENGE 19.13

The example in Chapter 14, Section 14.3.3, in which content was both horizontally and vertically centered, can be achieved using the `justify-content` and `align-items` properties together. See if you can implement it.

19.8.2 Aligning Flex Items Individually

Individual flex items are aligned using the `align-self` property, which performs the same function as the `align-items` property, except that it applies to only an individual item rather than all the items in the flex container. It aligns an item as specified, overriding the value of the `align-items` property. If an item has its cross-axis margins (i.e., top and bottom margins in horizontal writing mode) set to `auto`, the property has no effect. The item is simply centered in the cross axis of the current flex line. The property is **non-inherited** and the values it supports are listed in Table 19.8. Figures 19.18 and 19.19 show an example of how it is used.

In the `#container{}` rule in the example, the `width` and `height` properties specify the size of the `<div>` element of `id="container"`, the `border` property makes the border 1px-thick solid line and black, the `display` property makes the element a flex container, and `align-items` vertically stretches all flex items to the full height of the container. The `#container div{}` rule specifies the width of the `<div>` elements (i.e., flex items) inside the `<div>` element of `id="container"` (i.e., flex container) and also styles their borders. The `#container .one{}` rule makes the background color of the `<div>` element of `class="one"` pink, specifies the padding for the edges, and aligns it flush with the top edge of the flex container, overriding the value specified by the `align-items` property in the `#container{}` rule. The `#container .two{}` and `#container .three{}` rules specify the background

TABLE 19.8

Values for the `align-self` Property

Value	Function
auto	Applies parent's align-items value, or stretch, if element has no parent. It is the **default**.
flex-start	Places an item's cross-start margin edge flush with the cross-start edge of the flex container.
flex-end	Places an item's cross-end margin edge flush with the cross-end edge of the flex container.
center	Centers an item vertically in the flex container. If the cross-size (height) of the item is more than that of the flex container, it overflows equally in both directions.
baseline	Aligns item such that the baselines of all items in the flex container align. The item with the largest distance between its baseline and its cross-start margin edge is placed flush with the cross-start edge of the container.
stretch	Stretches item such that its height is as close as possible to that of the flex container, while respecting any specified width or height constraints.

CSS
```
#container {
 width: 300px; height: 150px; border: 1px solid black;
   display: flex;  align-items: stretch;
}
#container div { width: 60px; border: 1px solid gray; }
#container .one { background-color: pink; padding: 0 5px;
 align-self: flex-start; }
#container .two { background-color: light yellow;
 padding: 0 5px; }
#container .three { background-color: light gray;
 padding: 0 5px; }
#container .four { background-color: light blue;padding: 0 5px;
 align-self: flex-end; }
```

HTML
```
<div id="container">
 <div class="one"> </div>
 <div class="two">Curabitur vitae elit in odio consequat pretium
  vel non erat.</div>
 <div class="three">Praesent dapibus elementu est, vitae
  fermentu nulla</div>
 <div class="four"> </div>
</div>
```

FIGURE 19.18 Example usage of the align-self property.

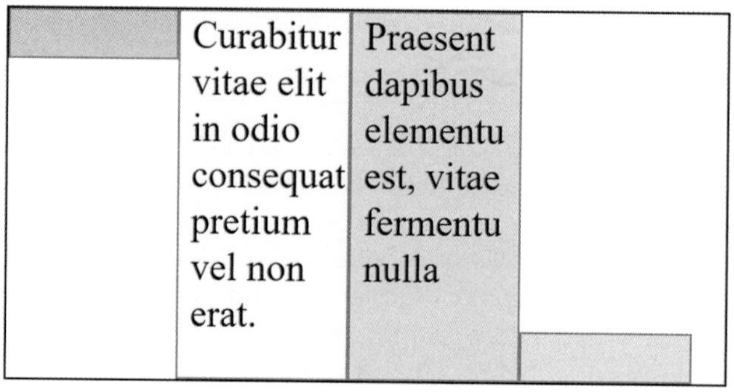

FIGURE 19.19   The result of Figure 19.18.

color and padding for the `<div>` element of `class="two"` and the `<div>` element of `class="three"`, respectively. The `#container .four{}` rule specifies the background color and padding for the `<div>` element of `class="four"` and aligns the element flush with the bottom edge of the flex container.

CHALLENGE 19.14

Implement the example in Figure 19.18 and experiment with the values of the flex properties. Also, create a full page design, using the idea in the example. For example, place headings in the items, center the flex container, and so on.

19.9 Ordering Flex Items

The default order in which flex items are displayed is according to the order they appear in the source code. However, this order can be controlled with the `order` property, which is used for specifying the position of a flex item relative to other flex items in a flex container. The property is **non-inherited** and takes an **integer value**. Elements are laid out in an ascending order using the value (i.e., an element with a value of 2 comes after one with a value of 1, and one with 3 comes after one with 2, and so on). The **default** is 0. Elements with the same value are laid out in the order in which they appear in the source code. The property only affects visual order, not logical or tab order (i.e., navigation via TAB). Figures 19.20 and 19.21 show how the property is used and the effect.

Notice in the example that the order in which the elements are displayed is different from the order they appear in the HTML code. The `body{}` rule makes text color on the page white and the `main{}` rule makes the `<main>` element a flex container. The `article{}` rule specifies the background color for the `<article>` element, says to make the element fully flexible, and sets the order. The `nav{}` and `aside{}` rules set the background color, maximum width, and order for the `<nav>` and `<aside>` elements, respectively. The `header{}` and `footer{}` rules specify the background color of the `<header>` and `<footer>` elements, and because no width is specified, they occupy the width of the browser window.

```
CSS
body{ color: white; }
main { display: flex; }
article { background: red; flex: 1 1 0px; order: 2; }
nav { background: green; width: 200px; order: 1; }
aside { background: green; width: 200px; order: 3; }
header { background: blue; }
footer { background: blue; }

HTML
<body>
  <header>HEADER</header>
  <main>
    <article>ARTICLE</article>
    <nav>NAV</nav>
    <aside>ASIDE</aside>
  </main>
  <footer>FOOTER</footer>
</body>
```

FIGURE 19.20   Example usage of the order property.

HEADER
NAV   ARTICLE   ASIDE
FOOTER

FIGURE 19.21   The result of Figure 19.20.

NOTE: Ordering items and accessibility

Because the order property only affects visual content presentation and not non-visual media (e.g., speech) or the default sequential navigation of elements, important meaning should not be communicated through its use, as the resulting order will be missed by users who use assistive technologies (e.g., screen readers) that typically present content linearly, or non-CSS user agents. To make the ordering of content accessible to these users, it should be done in the HTML source. For example, the elements in Figure 19.20 can be appropriately ordered to produce the same result as in Figure 19.21 without the use of the order property.

CHALLENGE 19.15

Modify the example so that the <nav> element is part of the header and the <aside> element is before the <article> element in the flex container. Also, center the contents of all elements.

CHALLENGE 19.16

The following layouts can be created using the flexbox properties discussed so far, and others like `margin` and `padding`. See if you can produce them.

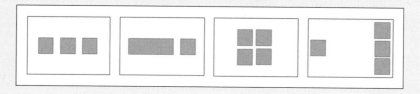

NOTE: Basic guidelines for using flexbox

For the container element:

1. Set the container element to a flex container (`display:flex`).
2. Set flow direction and wrap type for the children of the container (e.g., `flex-flow:row wrap`).

For each flex item, set the amount of space it can take up and the alignment.

19.10 Useful Info

19.10.1 Web Links

CSS specifications: w3.org/standards

Web development documents: docs.webplatform.org

Accessibility: w3.org/WAI/tutorials, webaim.org

CSS tutorials (*Here are just a few free tutorial sites on CSS and other Web languages*): w3.org/wiki, html5rocks.com, sitepoint.com, w3schools.com, codecademy.com, quackit.com, developer.mozilla.org/en-US/docs/Web, tutorialspoint.com, htmldog.com, htmlcodetutorial.com, echoecho.com, learn.shayhowe.com, html.net, tizag.com, cssbasics.com, cordova.apache. org, developers.google.com, csszengarden.com, webdesignermag.co.uk, css. maxdesign.com.au,

Testing codes: jsfiddle.net, codepad.org, jsbin.com, cssdesk.co

Flexbox generator: demo.agektmr.com/flexbox, flexboxin5.com

Browser compatibility info: caniuse.com

CSS generators for various features: enjoycss.com, bennettfeely.com, cssplant. com

Placeholder images: lorempixel.com

20

Layout with the Grid Model

20.1 Introduction

As mentioned in Chapter 19, layout was achieved in the past in CSS through the use of various sizing and positioning CSS properties that were not specifically intended for the purpose, making the creation of layouts cumbersome and their delivery unpredictable on screens of different sizes. The CSS flexible box layout model, which is one of the solutions to the problem, was fully introduced in Chapter 19. In this chapter, the grid layout model has been discussed. Like with the flexible box model, this model enables you to specify how a container element should control the behavior of the elements inside it, making it possible to create complex layouts easily. While most browsers are yet to fully implement the model as of time of writing, they are likely to soon, as it is designed to represent one of the ways forward for creating layouts in Web design.

20.2 Learning Outcomes

After studying this chapter, you should:

- Be aware of the concept of grid in visual design.
- Know the anatomy of the grid layout model.
- Know how to align a grid and the grid items.
- Be able to control the visual order of grid items.
- Be aware of the application of grid outside its use for page layout.

20.3 About Layout Grids

Layout grids are a useful tool for composition in any visual design discipline, in that they facilitate the task of organizing and accurately positioning elements both horizontally and vertically on a page. They also play a useful role in the positioning of elements in ways that make a design aesthetically more pleasing. Some of these grids, such as the **phi grid**, are covered in Chapter 23. In Web design, the effectiveness of the use of grids is no different. They help ensure consistency in the pages of a website, which makes pages easier to produce. Beyond visual grids that allow you to just sketch out design layouts on paper or screen, over the years, there have been various types of grid frameworks introduced into Web design, all of which allow the Web author to specify the number and size of columns and rows, and the gaps between them. It is on this general principle that the CSS grid layout builds.

20.4 Anatomy of the Grid Layout Model

Like the flexible box layout, the grid layout helps do away with the use of properties such as `float` and `clear`, or script that can make the creation of layouts that change according to screen size cumbersome. It essentially allows you to define the width of columns, height of rows, gutters, and other characteristics of a grid layout. Again, like with the flexible box model, in order to be able to use it effectively, it is useful to be familiar with its anatomy and the terminologies used to describe it, as this helps in the better understanding of the functions of grid properties. The basic building block of the model is the **grid container**, whose space is divided into **grid areas** (or **grid cells**) using intersecting horizontal and vertical lines, known as **grid lines**. There are two sets of grid lines: one set defines columns that run perpendicular to the writing mode axis (known as **block axis** or **column axis**) and the other set defines rows that run along the writing mode axis (known as the **inline axis** or **row axis**). This means that in horizontal writing mode, one set of grid lines define columns that run vertically and the other, rows that run horizontally. The grid areas are used to contain **grid items** (i.e., the grid container's content/children). The space contained in a grid column or grid row (i.e., the space between adjacent grid lines) is known as **grid track**. Figure 20.1 shows an illustration of a grid that has four vertical and four horizontal gridlines.

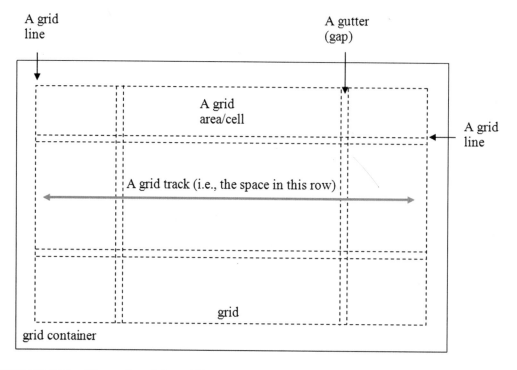

FIGURE 20.1 Illustration of the grid layout concept.

NOTE: About grid layout examples

Because the CSS grid layout is relatively new and still in development as of time of writing, and does not yet have standard support in browsers, the examples in this text were created using non-standard modes of Firefox, Chrome, and Opera. If by the time you are reading the text, these browsers are still yet to support grid layout in the standard mode, you will need to set certain flags to operate them in the experimental mode in order to try out the examples.

- In Firefox, type **about:config** in the address bar and navigate to and enable the "**layout.css.grid.enabled**" flag.
- In Chrome, type **chrome://flags** in the address bar and navigate to and enable the "**experimental web platform features**" flag.
- In Opera, type **opera://flags** in the address bar and navigate to and enable the "**experimental web platform features**" flag.

Also, some of the things introduced here may change by the time the specification is finalized, but the changes should be minimal.

20.5 Properties for Creating Grid Layout

Like with the flexible box layout, a grid layout is declared using the `display` property. A grid container can be declared as **block-level** or **inline-level**. For a block-level grid element, the property takes the `grid` keyword, thus `display: grid`, and for an inline-level grid element, it takes `inline-grid` keyword, thus, `display: inline-grid`. Essentially, this declaration makes the element to which it is applied a **grid container**, the child elements of which automatically become **grid items**. Once a grid container is declared, grid properties are used to define the structure of the grid, including its alignment within its container and the alignment of grid items within the grid areas. **Grid items are by default stretched to fit their containing grid areas**. Like many CSS properties, grid-specific properties have both longhand and shorthand versions. Figure 20.2 shows the properties for defining grid structure and the longhand-shorthand relationships. The illustration shows, for example, that `grid-template` can be used to specify `grid-template-columns`, `grid-template-rows`, and `grid-template-areas` in a single declaration, and `grid` can be used to specify all the properties.

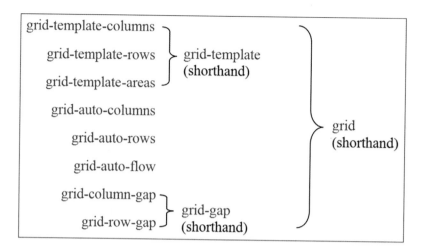

FIGURE 20.2   Grid-structure longhand-shorthand properties relationship.

20.5.1 Specifying Grid Columns, Rows, and Areas

The properties used for specifying grid columns, rows, and areas are the longhand `grid-template-columns`, `grid-template-rows`, and `grid-template-areas` properties and their shorthand, `grid-template`.

20.5.1.1 `grid-template-columns` *and* `grid-template-rows`

The `grid-template-columns` property allows you to specify the columns of a grid and their sizes, while the `grid-template-rows` property allows you to do the same for the rows. They are both **non-inherited** and take three values: `none` (a keyword that indicates that columns and rows will be generated as necessary by the browser); `subgrid` (a keyword that is used to make a grid item itself a grid container by giving it the `display:grid` declaration. The sub-grid created takes sizes of columns and rows from its parent grid and aligns to its axis). The third type of value supported is a **list of space-separated values** (known as **track list**) that specifies author-defined grid-line names and grid track sizes (i.e., column or row sizes). The **grid-line names** allow grid lines to be referred to by names, but if no names are specified, the lines can be referred to by automatically generated numerical index (i.e., 1, 2, and 3). **Track size** can be specified in a number of ways. Table 20.1 lists them. Figure 20.3 shows how some of the values are used and Figure 20.4 shows an illustration.

In the example, the `.grid{}` rule styles the `<div>` element of `class="grid"`. The `width` property makes its width 90% of that of the browser window and `height` specifies its height. The `display` property makes it a grid container and its children automatically grid items. The `grid-template-columns` property specifies "first" as the name for the first column grid line, a size of 160px for the first column, "second" as the name for the second column grid line, a size of 1fr (i.e., all free space) for the second column, and "last" as the name for the last column grid line. The `grid-template-rows` property specifies the rows in a similar manner.

Given the specified columns and rows, the browser uses the **auto-placement algorithm** to automatically place the defined grid items (i.e., <div> elements of class equal to "A," "B," "C," "D," "E," or "F") in the defined grid areas. This is how the grid items are positioned as shown in Figure 20.4 without any explicit instructions given on where to place them. Notice also that the grid items are by default stretched to fit the grid areas. The .A{}, .B{}, .C{}, .D{}, .E{}, and .F{} rules specify the background color for the respective grid item.

TABLE 20.1

The Values Used for Specifying Track Size

Track Size Value	Function
auto	A keyword that specifies that the browser should determine size relative to other specified sizes on the list of values. Typically sizes to the size of grid item's content.
<length>	Any non-negative integer, followed by a length unit (e.g., px, em, or vw)
<percentage>	A non-negative percentage value relative to the width or height of grid container, depending on writing mode. For example, in horizontal writing mode, column size is relative to width and row size to height.
<flex>	A non-negative integer followed by "fr" unit that specifies a **flexible length** (or **flex factor**) that is a fraction of the free space in the grid container after all non-flexible sizes are taken away. The space allocated to one "fr" unit is relative to the sum of all "fr" units specified in a list of values. For example, if "1fr" and "2fr" are specified, one-third (1/3) of free space is allocated to "1fr" and two-thirds (2/3) to "2fr."
min-content	A keyword that specifies that a column or row should be the minimum size it can be that will fit around its content if all possible soft wraps are implemented. It is typically used by experienced authors. For more on soft wrap, see content overflow in Chapter 10.
max-content	A keyword that specifies that a column or row should be the minimum size it can be while still fitting around its content if no soft wrap is implemented. Again, it is typically used by experienced authors. For more on soft wrap, see content overflow in Chapter 10.
minmax (min, max)	A function that defines a size range that is greater than or equal to **min** and less than or equal to **max**. Again, this is typically used by experienced authors.

```
CSS
.grid {
  display: grid;
  width: 90%;
  height: 480px;
  grid-template-columns: [first] 160px [second] 1fr [last];
  grid-template-rows: [first] 60px [second] 1fr [third]
    60px [last];
}
.A { background-color: pink; }
.B { background-color: light blue; }
.C { background-color: orange; }
.D { background-color: gray; }
.E { background-color: violet; }
.F { background-color: gold; }

HTML
<div class="grid">
  <div class="A">A</div>
  <div class="B">B</div>
  <div class="C">C</div>
  <div class="D">D</div>
  <div class="E">E</div>
  <div class="F">F</div>
</div>
```

FIGURE 20.3 Example usage of `grid-template-columns` and `grid-template-rows`.

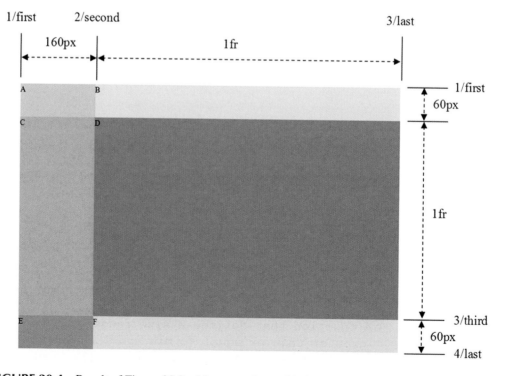

FIGURE 20.4 Result of Figure 20.3 with annotations added.

20.5.1.2 Specifying Multiple Names for a Grid Line

More than one name can be given to a grid line. This is usually done when a grid line is referred to as both the end and start of adjacent columns or rows. For example, in the declaration below:

```
grid-template-rows: [header-top] 50px [header-bottom main-top]
  1fr [main-bottom];
```

...the [header-bottom main-top] refers to the same grid line and means it represents both the bottom of a header and the top of the main row that is immediately below it.

20.5.1.3 Handling Repeating Values

If the definition for a grid contains repeating set of values, the repeat() function could be used for more coding and delivery efficiency. For example, using the function, the following declaration:

```
grid-template-columns: 10px [begin] 160px [end] 10px [begin]
  160px [end];
```

is the same as the following:

```
grid-template-columns: repeat(2, 10px [begin] 160px [end]);
```

In the declaration, the "2" specifies the number of repetitions, and the second set of values specifies the values to repeat.

CHALLENGE 20.1

Rewrite the following in full:

```
grid-template-columns: repeat(4, [column] 100px);
grid-template-rows: repeat(3, [row] auto);
```

Also, what does not make much sense about the grid produced?

CHALLENGE 20.2

Implement the example in Figure 20.3, but specify the size of the left column with the "fr" unit, using a value that produces the same result. How does this practically compare with specifying the value in absolute units in relation to screens of different sizes?

CHALLENGE 20.3

To the example in Figure 20.3, add an extra grid item and style it to make it visible, but without creating a grid area for it. Then explain what happens.

CHALLENGE 20.4

In the example in Figure 20.3, replace the track sizes with the `auto` keyword to see how the value sizes to content.

20.5.1.4 `grid-template-areas`

The `grid-template-areas` property provides another method of defining a grid. It is used to specify named grid areas that are not related to any specific grid item but can be referenced by grid properties used to specify the placement of grid items (i.e., where grid items start and end, and how many columns or rows to span). The property is **non-inherited** and takes one of two values: `none` (which defines no grid areas) or **strings of grid names**. Each string represents a row, and each name in the string a column. It is essentially like using the names to construct a grid. As well as a name, one or more full stops (".") can be used to represent **a null (empty) cell**. All cells together must form a rectangle for a grid definition to be valid. Figure 20.5 shows how the property is used and Figure 20.6 the result.

```
CSS
#grid {
  width: 90%;
  height: 480px;
  display: grid;
  grid-template-areas: "header header"
                       "nav  main"
                       "footer footer";
  grid-template-rows: 50px 1fr 50px;
  grid-template-columns: 150px 1fr;
}
#grid header { grid-area: header; background-color: light blue;}
#grid nav { grid-area: nav; background-color: orange; }
#grid main { grid-area: main; background-color: gray; }
#grid footer { grid-area: footer; background-color: light blue; }

HTML
<section id="grid">
  <header>HEADER</header>
  <nav>SIDEBAR</nav>
  <main>MAIN AREA</main>
  <footer>FOOTER</footer>
</section>
```

FIGURE 20.5 Example usage of `grid-template-areas`.

FIGURE 20.6 Result of Figure 20.5.

In the `#grid{}` rule in the example, `width` makes the width of the element of `id="grid"` 90% that of the browser window, `height` specifies its height, and `display` makes it a grid container. The `grid-template-areas` property specifies three strings with two names in each. This means that three rows and two columns are defined for the grid template. This also means that the grid has six (i.e., 3 × 2) cells. Adjacent cells that have the same name are merged and treated as one cell. When a grid item is used in the same row or column more than once, it must be used consecutively. The `grid-template-rows` property specifies the size of the three rows and `grid-template-rows` specifies the size of the two columns. In the `#grid header{}` rule, `grid-area` assigns the `<header>` element (a grid item) to each grid area named "header" and `background-color` specifies the color. The `#grid nav{}`, `#grid main{}`, and `#grid footer{}` rules perform a similar function for `<nav>`, `<main>`, and `<footer>` elements, respectively. The `grid-area` property is shorthand for specifying the start and end of columns and rows (discussed further later).

CHALLENGE 20.5

Modify the code in Figure 20.5 to include another 150px sidebar on the right.

CHALLENGE 20.6

Again, implement the code in Figure 20.5, but with "..." in place of the grid area named "main" to see the effect.

CHALLENGE 20.7

Which of these grid definitions do not form a rectangle and what does this mean?

```
grid-template-areas: "header"  "nav  main"  "footer";
grid-template-areas: "header"  "nav"  "footer footer";
grid-template-areas: "header"  "nav"  "footer";
```

20.5.1.5 `grid-template`

The `grid-template` property is the shorthand for `grid-template-columns`, `grid-template-rows`, and `grid-template-areas`, and allows you to specify columns, rows, and areas together. It is **non-inherited** and takes the values listed in Table 20.2.

TABLE 20.2

Values and Value Formats Used with `grid-template`

Value/Value Form	Function
`none`	Sets `grid-template-columns`, `grid-template-rows`, and `grid-template-areas` to none.
`subgrid`	Sets the value of `grid-template-columns` and `grid-template-rows` to subgrid, and that of `grid-template-areas` to none.
`<grid-template-columns> / <grid-template-rows>`	Sets `grid-template-columns` and `grid-template-rows` to the specified values and the value of `grid-template-areas` to none. For example: `grid-template: 160px 1fr / 60px 1fr 60px;` ...is the same as: `grid-template-columns: 160px 1fr;` `grid-template-rows: 60px 1fr 60px;` `grid-template-areas: none;` ...which produces the same layout as Figure 20.4.

(Continued)

TABLE 20.2 (*Continued*)

Values and Value Formats Used with grid-template

Value/Value Form	Function
| <track-list> /<br><line-names><br><string><br><track-size><br><line-names> | Sets grid-template-columns to the values specified in **<track-list>**; sets grid-template-rows to the values in **<line-names>** and **<track-size>**, using those in **<line-names>** for **grid-line names** and those in **<track-size>** for **track sizes**; sets grid-template-areas to the values in **<strings>**. For example:<br><br>```
grid-template: 150px 1fr /
    [header-top] "header header" 50px
    [header-bottom]
        [main-top] "nav main" 1fr [main-bottom]
        [footer-top] "footer footer" 50px
        [footer-bottom] ;
```<br><br>...is the same as:<br><br>```
grid-template-areas: "header header"
                     "nav main"
                     "footer footer";
grid-template-columns: 150px 1fr;
grid-template-rows: [header-top] 50px
    [header-bottom main-top] 1fr
        [main-bottom footer-top] 50px
        [footer-bottom] ;
```<br><br>...which produces the same result as Figure 20.5. |

CHALLENGE 20.8

Rewrite the following rule using only the grid-template property:

```
grid-template-areas: "header header header"
                     "nav main ads"
                     "footer footer footer";
grid-template-columns: 160px 1fr 160px;
grid-template-rows: [header-start] 50px
    [header-end main-start] 1fr
        [main-end footer-start] 50px [footer-end];
```

20.5.2 Controlling Implicit Tracks and Items' Auto-Placement

As you might have seen so far, grid columns and rows (i.e., grid tracks) are defined using `grid-template` and any of its longhand properties. The grid tracks created this way have fixed sizes and are known as **explicit grid tracks**, with explicit grid lines and sizes, and so on. However, grid tracks are also created in other ways, such as when a grid item is placed in a column or row that is not explicitly specified with the `grid-template` property or any of its longhand properties, or when the browser automatically generates additional columns or rows to contain grid items. Columns and rows created in these ways are known as **implicit grid tracks** and controlled with the `grid-auto-columns`, `grid-auto-rows`, and `grid-auto-flow` properties.

20.5.2.1 `grid-auto-columns` *and* `grid-auto-rows`

The `grid-auto-columns` property allows you to specify the size of an implicit grid column track, while the `grid-auto-rows` property allows you to specify the size of an implicit grid row track. Both are **non-inherited** and take a value, which can be any of the types listed earlier in Table 20.1 for `grid-template-columns` and `grid-template-rows`. Figure 20.7 shows how they are used and Figure 20.8 the result.

```
CSS
#grid {
  display: grid;
  grid-template-columns: 100px;
  grid-template-rows: 100px;
  grid-auto-columns: 100px;
  grid-auto-rows: 100px;
}
#A { grid-column: 1; grid-row: 1;background-color: pink; }
#B { grid-column: 2; grid-row: 1;background-color: light blue; }
#C { grid-column: 1; grid-row: 2;background-color: orange; }
#D { grid-column: 2; grid-row: 2;background-color: gray; }
#E { grid-column: 3; grid-row: 1;background-color: violet; }
#F { grid-column: 3; grid-row: 2;background-color: gold; }

HTML
<div id="grid">
  <div id="A">A</div>
  <div id="B">B</div>
  <div id="C">C</div>
  <div id="D">D</div>
  <div id="E">E</div>
  <div id="F">F</div>
</div>
```

FIGURE 20.7 Example usage of `grid-auto-columns` and `grid-auto-rows`.

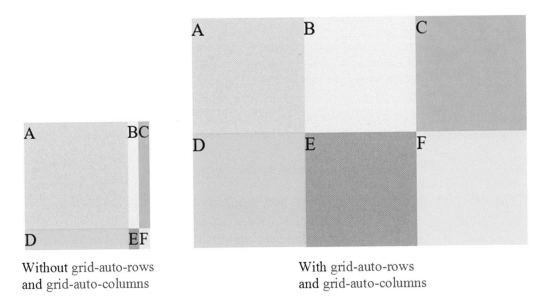

Without grid-auto-rows   With grid-auto-rows
and grid-auto-columns   and grid-auto-columns

FIGURE 20.8   Result of Figure 20.7.

In the #grid{} rule in the example, display makes the <div> element of id="grid" a grid container and its six children (i.e., <div> elements of id equal to "A," "B," "C," "D," "E," and "F") grid items, automatically. The grid-template-columns and grid-template-rows define a column and a row of 100px each, creating a grid that has only one cell and space for only one grid item. This means that given rule #A{}, which explicitly places grid item "A" in the explicitly specified column and row (using grid-column and grid-row), and rules #B{}, #C{}, #D{}, #E{}, and #F{}, which similarly explicitly place grid items "B" to "F" in the grid but in columns and rows that are not explicitly specified, the grid container automatically creates five implicit columns and rows to hold grid items "B" to "F" and sizes them to the width or height of the adjacent column or row. Notice their sizes in the output on the left in Figure 20.8 and the result on the right when the grid-auto-columns and grid-auto-rows properties are used to set their sizes to 100px. The rest of the declarations in rules #A{}, #B{}, #C{}, #D{}, #E{}, and #F{} simply specify the grid items' background color. Note that the grid-column and grid-row properties are used here only to more clearly demonstrate the functions of grid-auto-columns and grid-auto-rows, and discussed in greater detail later in this chapter with other properties used for positioning grid items in the grid.

CHALLENGE 20.9

Implement Figure 20.7 and experiment with different values for the grid-auto-columns and grid-auto-rows properties to see possible applications to page layout.

CHALLENGE 20.10

Again, implement Figure 20.7, but first without explicitly positioning any of the grid items, then without this or sizing the implicit grid columns or rows. Then explain the results in terms of how grid items are automatically placed in the grid as well as in relation to the order of the items in the HTML source.

20.5.2.2 `grid-auto-flow`

The `grid-auto-flow` property allows you to specify how the auto-placement algorithm should handle the flow of grid items that are not explicitly positioned if there are cells to contain them. It is **non-inherited** and supports the values listed in Table 20.3. Figure 20.9 shows how the property is used, and Figure 20.10 shows the effects of using different values with it.

In the `.grid{}` rule in the example, `display` makes the element of `class="grid"` a grid container and its children grid items, `grid-template-columns` specifies five columns and `grid-template-rows` three rows. The `grid-auto-flow` property specifies how the grid items whose positions are not explicitly specified should be positioned in the grid. In order to be able to demonstrate the effects of all the values for the property, the `grid-column` and `grid-row` properties are again used here, but discussed in greater detail shortly. They are used to explicitly specify the column-row positions and spans for grid items "A" and "B," and the positioning is such that a preceding cell is left empty so that the `dense` value can have an effect. Basically, "A" occupies column 2 row 1 and spans two rows,

TABLE 20.3

The Values Used for `grid-auto-flow`

Value	Function
`row`	A keyword that specifies that the flow direction of items' placement should be row by row (i.e., starting from the first column, one row is filled first, then the next, and so on).
`column`	A keyword that specifies that the flow direction of items' placement should be column by column (i.e., starting from the first row, one column is filled first, then the next, and so on).
`dense`	A keyword that represents a mode that packs the grid densely by filling in earlier holes in the grid with subsequent smaller items that fit. Using it means that items may end up appearing out of order. When not specified, the sparse mode, which is the default, is used. Because this value is a mode rather than flow direction, it can be combined with row or column, such as, thus, `row dense`; and `column dense`;.

```
CSS
.grid {
  display: grid;
  grid-template-columns: 100px 100px 100px 100px 100px;
  grid-template-rows: 50px 50px 50px;
  grid-auto-flow: row;
}
.A { background-color: gold; grid-column: 2; grid-row: span 2; }
.B { background-color: light blue; grid-column: span 2; }
.C { background-color: violet; }
.D { background-color: yellowgreen; }
.E { background-color: silver; }

HTML
<div class="grid">
  <div class="A">A</div>
  <div class="B">B</div>
  <div class="C">C</div>
  <div class="D">D</div>
  <div class="E">E</div>
</div>
```

FIGURE 20.9   Example usage of `grid-auto-flow`.

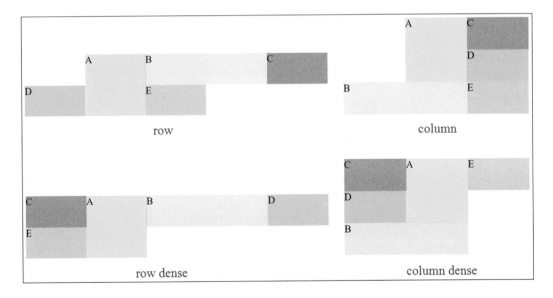

FIGURE 20.10   Result of Figure 20.9.

and "B" occupies the next column and row 1, and spans two columns. Notice in the outputs for the `row` and `column` values that the first grid cell (i.e., column 1, row 1) is empty and that it is filled with an item when the `dense` value is used and that this affects the ordering of the items. Notice also how the position of item A is always maintained because it is explicitly specified.

CHALLENGE 20.11

Implement the example but with the position of grid item "B" also explicitly specified to see how this changes the behavior of the layout with different values.

20.5.3 Specifying Gutters between Grid Columns and Rows

20.5.3.1 `grid-column-gap`, `grid-row-gap`, *and* `grid-gap`

The properties used to specify gutters (gaps) between grid columns and rows are longhand `grid-column-gap` and `grid-row-gap` properties, respectively, and the shorthand `grid-gap`, which is used to specify both together. They are all **non-inherited** and take **length values** (e.g., px and em). Figure 20.11 shows how `grid-column-gap` and `grid-row-gap` are used and Figure 20.12 the result.

The example is the same as that given earlier in Figures 20.5 and 20.6, but with `grid-column-gap: 5px;` and `grid-row-gap: 5px;` added. Notice the gaps between the columns and rows. The same values can be specified with the **grid-gap** property, thus, `grid-gap: 5px 5px;` (where the first value represents

```
CSS
#grid {
  width: 90%;
  height: 480px;
  display: grid;
  grid-template-areas: "header header"
                "nav  main"
                "footer footer";
  grid-template-rows: 50px 1fr 50px;
  grid-template-columns: 150px 1fr;
  grid-column-gap: 5px;
  grid-row-gap: 5px;
}
#grid header { grid-area: header; background-color:
 light blue;}
#grid nav { grid-area: nav; background-color: orange; }
#grid main { grid-area: main; background-color: gray; }
#grid footer { grid-area: footer; background-color:
 light blue; }

HTML
<section id="grid">
  <header>HEADER</header>
  <nav>SIDEBAR</nav>
  <main>MAIN AREA</main>
  <footer>FOOTER</footer>
</section>
```

FIGURE 20.11 Example usage of `grid-column-gap` and `grid-row-gap`.

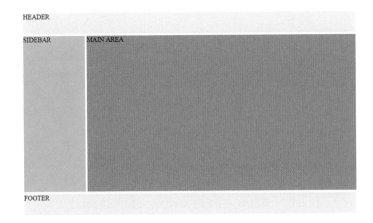

FIGURE 20.12   Result of Figure 20.11.

grid-column-gap and the second grid-row-gap) or grid-gap: 5px;, in which the single value is used as the value for both grid-column-gap and grid-row-gap.

CHALLENGE 20.12

Implement the example in Figure 20.11 and experiment with large gutters. Can you see possible design applications?

CHALLENGE 20.13

Should the sizes of gutters be specified in relative or absolute units? Give reasons for your answer? *Hint*: Think, for example, of implications in screens of different sizes.

20.5.4 Specifying All Grid Structure Properties Together

20.5.4.1 grid

All the grid properties introduced so far can be specified in a single declaration using the shorthand grid property, with the exception of grid-column, grid-row, and grid-area, which are grid item placement properties. The grid sub-properties (i.e., longhand grid properties) that can be specified with grid include **explicit grid properties** (grid-template-columns, grid-template-rows, and grid-template-areas), **implicit properties** (grid-auto-columns, grid-auto-rows, and grid-auto-flow), and **gutter properties** (grid-column-gap and grid-row-gap). The property is **non-inherited** and allows the values of the grid properties it supports to be specified in various forms. Some of these have been described in Table 20.4.

TABLE 20.4

Values and Value Formats Used with the `grid` Property

Value/Value Form	Function
`none`	Sets all sub-properties supported to none.
`subgrid`	Sets the value of grid-template-columns and grid-template-rows to subgrid, and those of sub-properties to none.

`<grid-template-columns> / <grid-template-rows>`	Sets grid-template-columns and grid-template-rows to the specified values and the values of other sub-properties to their **initial values**. For example:
	
	`grid: 160px 1fr / 60px 1fr 60px;`
	
	...is the same as:
	
	`grid-template-columns: 160px 1fr;`
	`grid-template-rows: 60px 1fr 60px;`
	`grid-template-areas: none;`
	`grid-auto-columns: auto;`
	`grid-auto-rows: auto;`
	`grid-auto-flow: row;`
	`grid-column-gap: 0;`
	`grid-row-gap: 0;`
	
	...which produces the same result as Figure 20.4 but without the names for the lines.

`<track-list> / <line-names> <string> <track-size> <line-names>`	Sets grid-template-columns to values in **<track-list>** before the slash (or to none if one is missing); after the slash, sets grid-template-areas to the values in **<strings>**; sets grid-template-rows to the values in **<track-size>** that comes after each string (or to auto if one is missing), using the grid-line names defined before and after each size; sets all other sub-properties to their **initial values**. For example:
	
	`grid: 150px 1fr /`
	    `[header-top] "header header" 50px [header-bottom]`
	      `[main-top] "nav main" 1fr [main-bottom]`
	        `[footer-top] "footer footer" 50px`
	          `[footer-bottom];`
	
	...is the same as:
	
	`grid-template-areas: "header header"`
	                     `"nav main"`
	                     `"footer footer";`
	`grid-template-rows: [header-top] 50px`
	    `[header-bottom main-top] 1fr`
	      `[main-bottom footer-top] 50px`
	        `[footer-bottom];`
	`grid-template-columns: 150px 1fr;`
	...which produces the same result as Figure 20.6.

(Continued)

TABLE 20.4 (*Continued*)

Values and Value Formats Used with the `grid` Property

Value/Value Form	Function
`<grid-auto-flow>` `<grid-auto-rows> /` `<grid-auto-columns>`	Sets `grid-auto-flow`, `grid-auto-rows`, and `grid-auto-columns` to the specified values. If `grid-auto-columns` is not specified, it is set to the value specified for `grid-auto-rows`, and if the two are not specified, they are set to `auto`. For example: `grid: column 1fr  / auto;` ...is the same as: `grid-auto-flow: column;` `grid-auto-rows: 1fr;` `grid-auto-columns: auto;`

CHALLENGE 20.14

Rewrite the following using only the `grid` property:

```
grid-template-columns: 1fr 2fr 1fr;
grid-template-rows: 60px 1fr 60px;
```

20.5.5 Specifying Grid Item Placement within the Grid

As earlier examples have repeatedly shown, it is possible to explicitly specify the position and span of a grid item in the grid. The properties used to achieve this are known as **grid-placement properties** and allow you to arrange and order grid items freely within the grid, irrespective of how the grid items are ordered in the source code. Placement is described in terms of the grid item's edge that comes first in the block-flow direction (i.e., **block-start**), the grid item's edge at the end of block-flow direction (i.e., **block-end**), the grid item's edge from which the content of a grid item starts (i.e., **inline-start**), and the grid item's edge at which the content of an item ends (i.e., **inline-end**). Which edge is which depends on the **writing mode**. For example, in the left-to-right-top-to-bottom writing mode, block-start is top, block-end is bottom, inline-start is left, and inline-end is right. The grid placement properties are `grid-column-start`, `grid-row-start`, `grid-column-end`, `grid-row-end`, `grid-column`, `grid-row`, and `grid-area`. Figure 20.13 shows the longhand-shorthand relationship between them.

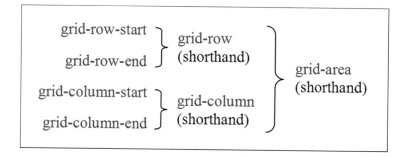

FIGURE 20.13   Grid-placement longhand-shorthand properties relationship.

20.5.5.1 *Specifying Grid-Placement Values Separately*

20.5.5.1.1 `grid-column-start`, `grid-row-start`, `grid-column-end`, *and* `grid-row-end`

The `grid-column-start`, `grid-row-start`, `grid-column-end`, and `grid-row-end` properties are longhand properties for specifying the start or end position of a grid item within a grid row or column. They are **non-inherited** and support the value forms listed in Table 20.5. Figures 20.14 and 20.15 show examples of how the properties are used and Figure 20.16 the result.

TABLE 20.5

Values and Value Forms Used with Grid-Placement Properties

Value/Value Form	Function
`auto`	A keyword that specifies that the value of the property should be determined automatically. Typically sets span to 1.
`<name>`	Specifies an author-defined case-sensitive grid-line name.
`<integer>` and `<name>`	If only an integer is specified, this indicates the position of grid line. For example, "4" means the 4th grid line. A **negative integer** means to count lines in reverse order from the end edge of the explicit grid. **If a name is specified with an integer**, grid lines of the name are counted until the count is equal to the value of the integer. For example, "4 side" specifies the fourth line of those named "side." If there are not enough lines of the name, all implicit lines are assumed to have the name.
`span` and `<integer>` or `<name>`	The `span` keyword specifies the grid lines to span. If an integer is used with it, this indicates the number of grid lines to span. For example, "span 3" means an item spans three grid lines. **Negative integers** and 0 are not allowed. **If a name is used with the keyword**, it means that an item should span grid lines up to the grid line of that name. For example, "span nav-right" means to span grid lines up to the one named "nav-right."

HTML
```
<div class="grid">
  <div class="A">A</div>
  <div class="B">B</div>
  <div class="C">C</div>
  <div class="D">D</div>
  <div class="E">E</div>
</div>
```

FIGURE 20.14   HTML for grid-placement properties usage.

CSS
```
.grid {
 display: grid;
 width: 90%;
 height: 480px;
 grid-template-columns: [first] 100px [second] 100px
   [third] 100px [fourth] 100px [last];
 grid-template-rows: [first] 100px [second] 100px [last];
}
.A { background-color: violet; }
.B {
 background-color: light blue;
 grid-column-start: 2;
 grid-column-end: span 2;
 grid-row-start: first;
 grid-row-end: span last;
}
.C { background-color: orange; }
.D { background-color: orange; }
.E { background-color: violet; }
```

FIGURE 20.15   CSS for Figure 20.14.

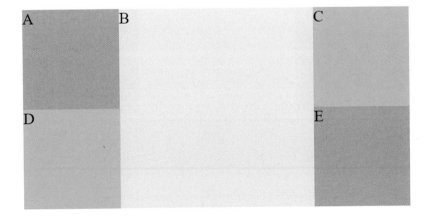

FIGURE 20.16   Result of Figures 20.14 and 20.15.

The example is again quite basic for the purpose of explanation. In the .grid{} rule, display defines a grid container (which automatically makes its children grid items), width specifies its width, height specifies the height, grid-template-columns specifies four columns and their start and end grid line names, and grid-template-rows specifies two rows in the same way, creating a total of eight grid areas (or cells). Grid items "A," "C," "D," and "E" are placed automatically by the placement algorithm and rules. A{}, .C{}, .D{}, and. E{} specify their background color. Only grid item "B" is explicitly positioned. The .B{} rule specifies its background color as well as its explicit placement thus: grid-column-start says the start position within the grid row should be grid line 2 and grid-column-end says the end position should span two grid lines (which extends the item to the "fourth" line). Similarly, grid-row-start says that the start position within the grid column should be the grid line named "first" and grid-row-end says that the end position should span grid lines up to the one named "last."

CHALLENGE 20.15

What do the following declarations say?

```
grid-column-start: -4;
grid-column-end: span 2;
```

CHALLENGE 20.16

Modify the code in Figure 20.15 to create the layout below:

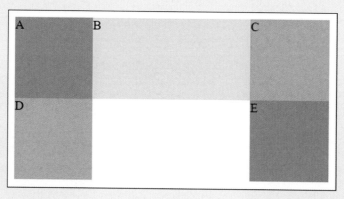

CHALLENGE 20.17

As you might have already gathered, it is possible to use most of the CSS properties introduced so far to style grids and grid items. Again, modify the code in Figure 20.15 to create the layout below, using the appropriate properties to rotate the grid items as shown. (*Hint*: See Chapter 11)

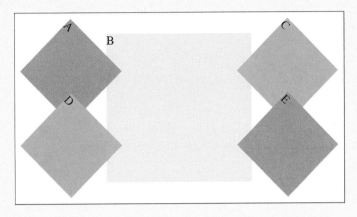

20.5.5.2 *Specifying Column and Row Grid-Placement Values Separately*

20.5.5.2.1 `grid-column` *and* `grid-row`

The `grid-column` property is shorthand for the `grid-column-start` and `grid-column-end` properties that allows you to specify them together, while `grid-row` is shorthand for `grid-row-start` and `grid-row-end` properties that allows you to do the same with them. Both are **non-inherited** and take the same types of values listed in Table 20.5 for their longhand. When either of the properties is used to specify the values of their longhand properties together, the values are separated with a slash. The value before the slash represents the value for `grid-column-start/grid-row-start`, and the one after the slash represents the value for `grid-column-end/grid-row-end`. **If the second value is omitted**, `grid-column-end/grid-row-end` is set to the same value or `auto`. Figure 20.17 shows how the properties can be used to achieve the same result as in Figure 20.16. The code works with the HTML in Figure 20.14.

The `grid-column` and `grid-row` properties in the example specify the same values specified earlier in Figure 20.15 with corresponding longhand properties thus: `grid-column` sets `grid-column-start` to "2" and `grid-column-end` to "span 2," and `grid-row` sets `grid-row-start` to "first" and `grid-row-end` to "span last."

```
CSS
.grid {
 display: grid;
 width: 90%;
 height: 480px;
 grid-template-columns: [first] 100px [second] 100px [third]
  100px [fourth] 100px [last];
 grid-template-rows: [first] 100px [second] 100px [last];
}
.A { background-color: violet; }
.B {
 background-color: light blue;
 grid-column: 2 / span 2;
 grid-row: first / span last;
}
.C { background-color: orange; }
.D { background-color: orange; }
.E { background-color: violet; }
```

FIGURE 20.17   Using grid-column and grid-row to produce Figure 20.16.

CHALLENGE 20.18

Using the HTML code in Figure 20.14, modify the values of the grid-column and grid-row properties in the .B{} rule in Figure 20.17 to achieve the structure below:

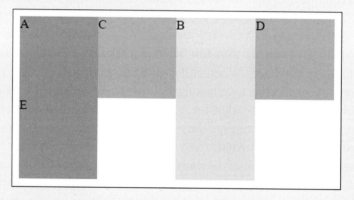

20.5.5.3 Specifying All Grid-Placement Values Together

20.5.5.3.1 grid-area

The grid-area property is a shorter shorthand property for grid-column-start, grid-column-end, grid-row-start, and grid-row-end that allows you to specify the values for these longhand properties in a single declaration in the order <grid-row-start>/<grid-column-start>/<grid-row-end>/<grid-column-end>, slashes included. Like the longhand properties, it allows you to specify the position and size of a grid item within the grid. It is **non-inherited** and supports the same types of values listed earlier in Table 20.5 for its longhand properties. The property can be used to specify single or multiple values as well as combinations of values. Table 20.6 lists some of them and how they are interpreted. Figure 20.18 shows how the property can be used to achieve, again, the same result as in Figure 20.16.

In the example, the `grid-area` property specifies the same values specified with the longhand properties in Figure 20.15. It sets `grid-row-start` to "first", `grid-column-start` to "2", `grid-row-end` to "span last", and `grid-column-end` to "span 2."

TABLE 20.6

Values Combinations for `grid-area` and Their Interpretation

Values Combination	Meaning
When four values are specified	`grid-row-start` is set to the first, `grid-column-start` to the second, `grid-row-end` to the third, and `grid-column-end` to the fourth.
When `grid-column-end` is omitted	`grid-column-end` is set to the value of `grid-column-start` or auto.
When `grid-row-end` is omitted	`grid-row-end` is set to the value of `grid-row-start` or auto.
When `grid-column-start` is omitted	All four longhand properties are set to the value of `grid-row-start` or auto.

```
CSS
.grid {
  display: grid;
  width: 90%;
  height: 480px;
  grid-template-columns: [first] 100px [second]
    100px [third] 100px [fourth] 100px [last];
  grid-template-rows: [first] 100px [second] 100px [last];
}
.A { background-color: violet; }
.B {
  background-color: light blue;
  grid-area: first / 2 / span last / span 2;
}
.C { background-color: orange; }
.D { background-color: orange; }
.E { background-color: violet; }
```

FIGURE 20.18 Using `grid-area` shorthand to produce Figure 20.16.

CHALLENGE 20.19

Using the HTML code in Figure 20.14 and modify the values of the `grid-area` property in the `.B{}` rule in Figure 20.18 to achieve the structure below:

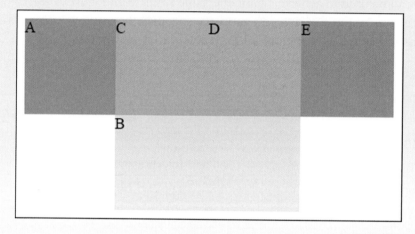

20.6 Aligning Grid and Grid Items

The alignment of grid and grid items can also be controlled, and this is achieved using the **box-alignment properties**, some of which have been introduced previously in Chapter 19. These properties allow you to control the alignment of boxes inside boxes. Essentially, they align contents within element, element within its parent, and items inside element; and alignment can be along inline/row and cross/column axes. The properties are `justify-content`, `align-content`, `justify-self`, `align-self`, `justify-items`, and `align-items`, and they take the same set of value keywords that specify the position of what is being aligned (known as **alignment subject**) relative to its containing box (known as **alignment container**). Table 20.7 lists the set of values supported in grid layout. Note that the values with "`self-`" prefix apply only to properties with "`-self`" suffix.

20.6.1 Aligning All Grid Items in a Grid Container

The properties used to align all grid items collectively inside a grid container are `justify-content` and `align-content`, and `justify-items` and `align-items`, and they are specified inside the grid container's rule.

TABLE 20.7

Values Used with Box-Alignment Properties in Grid Layout

Value	Meaning
Values for Positioning	
start	Aligns what is being aligned flush with the start edge of its container's box. The start edge in left-to-right (LTR) writing, for example, is left.
center	Centers what is being aligned within its container's box.
end	Aligns what is being aligned flush with the end edge of its container's box.
self-start	Aligns what is being aligned flush with the edge of the container's box that corresponds to the start side of what is being aligned. Applies to only justify-self and align-self.
self-end	Aligns what is being aligned flush with the edge of the container's box that corresponds to the end side of what is being aligned. Applies to only justify-self and align-self.
left	Aligns what is being aligned flush with the side of the container's box from which LTR text would start. This is left side in LTR writing.
right	Aligns what is being aligned flush with the side of the container's box from which right-to-left (RTL) text would start. This is right side in RTL writing.
Values for Distributing	
space-between	Spaces grid items evenly in the grid container, with the first item flush with the start edge and the last flush with the end edge.
space-around	Spaces grid items evenly in the grid container, with the space between the start edge and first item, and that between the end edge and the last item half that between adjacent items.
space-evenly	Spaces grid items evenly in the grid container, with the space between the start edge and first item, and that between the end edge and the last item the same as that between adjacent items.
stretch	If the combined size of all items is less than that of the container, it increases the sizes of any auto-sized items equally so that their combined size fills the container.

(Continued)

TABLE 20.7 (*Continued*)

Values Used with Box-Alignment Properties in Grid Layout

Value	Meaning
Values for Baseline Alignment	
baseline	Aligns the first baselines of the grid item with those of other grid items in the same row or column; the first baselines of a grid item are usually the baselines of the first line of text within it. See Chapter 19 for more on the behavior of baseline value.
last-baseline	Aligns the last baselines of grid item with those of other grid items in the same row or column; the last baselines of a grid item are usually the baselines of the last line of text within it. See Chapter 19 for more on the behavior of baseline value.
Values for Overflow Alignment	
safe	If what is being aligned is larger than its container, there is overflow and the possibility of content being cut off. This value aligns what is being aligned as when the start value is used to prevent this, ignoring the set alignment values.
true	Aligns what is being aligned based on the specified values, even if it is larger than the container.

20.6.1.1 justify-content *and* align-content

The justify-content and align-content properties allow you to align the contents of an element as a whole within the element itself. In the case of a grid, all the grid areas/cells, and the contained grid items, are aligned relative to the grid container. It is in a sense like using the padding property on the grid container to align the contained grid (see Chapter 10 for more on padding). The justify-content property aligns content along the row axis, while align-content aligns it along the column axis. Both are **non-inherited**. Figure 20.19 shows the effects of the values supported. The left and right values produce the same result as start and end, respectively, in left-to-right top-to-bottom writing, and stretch is not applicable. Figure 20.20 shows how the properties are used, using the center value.

In the example, the declarations in the .grid{} rule are again the same as in previous examples, except for a few differences. The rule makes the element of class="grid" a grid container and its children grid items, sets its width and height, sets three columns and two rows, sets border line-style, and centers the grid (and grid items) in the grid

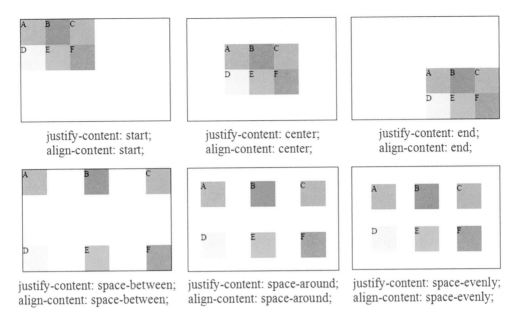

FIGURE 20.19 The effects of the main values supported by justify-content and align-content.

```
CSS
.grid {
  display: grid;
  width: 300px;
  height: 200px;
  grid-template-columns: [first] 50px [second] 50px
  [third] 50px [last];
  grid-template-rows: [first] 50px [second] 50px [last];
  border: 1px solid black;
  justify-content: center;
  align-content: center;
}
.A { background-color: dark gray; }
.B { background-color: salmon; }
.C { background-color: orange; }
.D { background-color: yellow; }
.E { background-color: MediumAquamarine; }
.F { background-color: violet; }

HTML
<div class="grid">
  <div class="A">A</div>
  <div class="B">B</div>
  <div class="C">C</div>
  <div class="D">D</div>
  <div class="E">E</div>
  <div class="F">F</div>
</div>
```

FIGURE 20.20 Example usage of justify-content and align-content.

container along both row and column axes. Notice that the `justify-content` and `align-content` properties are applied on the grid container and not on the individual grid items. This is because it is the container that is aligning the items rather than the items aligning themselves within the container. Also, as in previous examples, the .A{}, .B{}, .C{}, .D{}, .E{}, and. F{} rules simply specify the background color for the items.

CHALLENGE 20.20

If you use the `start` value with the `justify-content` property in the example, you will get the same result as using the `left` value. Why is having the two values not redundant?

CHALLENGE 20.21

A possible useful application of the layout in the example is a media gallery in which thumbnails (reduced versions of media) are displayed for users to click and be taken to the actual media objects. Implement the example, replacing the contents of the grid items with clickable image thumbnails, which when clicked take users to the actual images. You can use placeholder images from sites like http://lorempixel.com. *Hint*: See Chapter 6 for how to create clickable images.

20.6.1.2 `justify-items` *and* `align-items`

The `justify-items` and `align-items` properties are used to set the default values for the `justify-self` and `align-self` properties (which are discussed in greater detail shortly and used to control grid-item placement within its grid area). The `justify-items` property specifies default alignment along the row axis, while the `align-items` property specifies it along the column axis. Both are **non-inherited**. Figures 20.21 shows the effects of the main values supported. Notice that the grid items are auto-sized to fit their contents instead of stretched to fill their respective grid areas, which is the default behavior. This happens unless the `stretch` value is specified, or margins are set to `auto`. Using the `auto` value with the properties also computes to `stretch`. The `left`, `self-start`, `right`, and `self-end` values can also be used with the properties, with the result depending

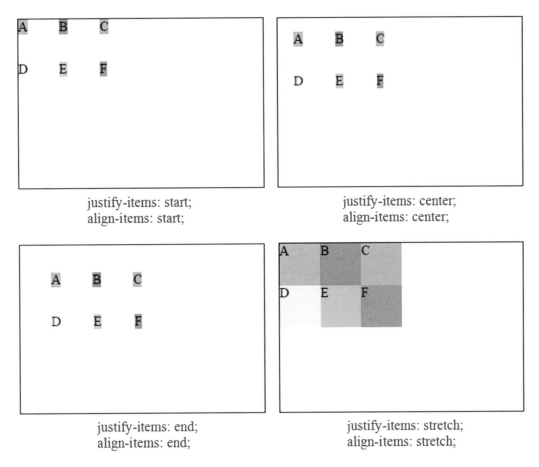

justify-items: start;
align-items: start;

justify-items: center;
align-items: center;

justify-items: end;
align-items: end;

justify-items: stretch;
align-items: stretch;

FIGURE 20.21   The effects of the main values supported by justify-items and align-items.

largely on writing mode. For example, in left-to-right top-to-bottom writing, left and self-start produce the same result as start, while right and self-end produce the same result as end. Figure 20.22 shows how the properties are used, using the center value.

In the example, the .grid{} rule again does something similar to the previous example. It makes the element of class="grid" a grid container and its children grid items, sets its width and height, sets two columns and two rows, makes its border 1px solid black line, and aligns the contained grid items. The justify-items property centers each grid item along the row axis within its containing grid area and align-items aligns each item along the column axis. The .A{}, .B{}, .C{}, .D{}, .E{}, and .F{} rules set the background color for grid items "A", "B", "C", "D", "E", and "F" (i.e., <div> elements of class equal to "A", "B", "C", "D", "E", and "F"), respectively.

```
CSS
.grid {
 display: grid;
 width: 300px;
 height: 200px;
 border: 1px solid black;
 grid-template-columns: [first] 50px [second] 50px
 [third] 50px [last];
 grid-template-rows: [first] 50px [second] 50px [last];
 border: 1px solid black;
 justify-items: center;
 align-items: center;
}
.A { background-color: dark gray; }
.B { background-color: salmon; }
.C { background-color: orange; }
.D { background-color: yellow; }
.E { background-color: MediumAquamarine; }
.F { background-color: violet; }

HTML
<div class="container">
  <div class="A">A</div>
  <div class="B">B</div>
  <div class="C">C</div>
  <div class="D">D</div>
  <div class="E">E</div>
  <div class="F">F</div>
</div>
```

FIGURE 20.22   Example usage of `justify-items` and `align-items`.

CHALLENGE 20.22

If you include the `border` property in the .A{}, .B{}, .C{}, .D{}, .E{}, and .F{} rules, what will the border be applied to the grid items or the grid areas, and why?

CHALLENGE 20.23

Implement the example, but place more content in the grid items to observe the behavior. Also, what methods would you use to make the items bigger without adding more content?

20.6.2 Aligning Grid Items Individually

20.6.2.1 `justify-self` *and* `align-self`

As you might have gathered earlier from the introduction to the `justify-items` and `align-items` properties, the properties used to align individual grid items are `justify-self` and `align-self`. They allow you to control the alignment of a box within its containing block. In the case of grid, they allow you to control the alignment of a grid item within its containing grid area. It is like setting the `margin` property on an individual grid item to align it within its containing grid area (see Chapter 10 for more on `margin`). The `justify-self` property aligns a grid item along the row axis, while `align-self` aligns it along the column axis. The properties are specified inside the rule of the grid item being aligned and both are **non-inherited**. Figures 20.23 shows the effects of the main values supported. Grid item "B" is the item that is aligned with the properties. Notice that like with the `justify-items` and `align-items` properties, the grid item is auto-sized to fit its content instead of stretched to fill its grid area like others. As mentioned before, auto-sizing a grid item to fit content happens unless the `stretch` or `auto` values are specified for the properties, or margins are set to `auto`. The `left`, `self-start`, `right`,

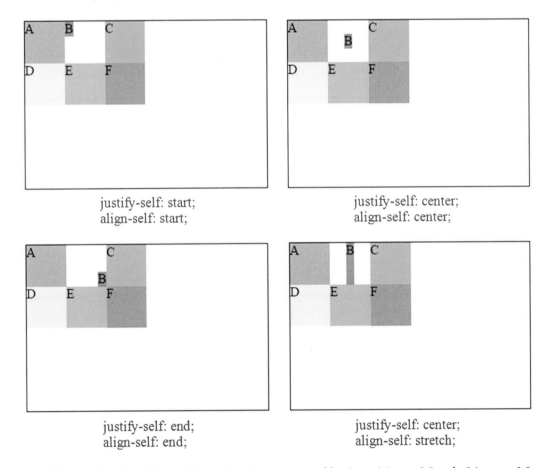

FIGURE 20.23   The effects of the main values supported by `justify-self` and `align-self`.

```
CSS
.grid {
 display: grid;
 width: 300px;
 height: 200px;
 grid-template-columns: [first] 50px [second] 50px
 [third] 50px [last];
 grid-template-rows: [first] 50px [second] 50px [last];
 border: 1px solid black;
}
.A { background-color: dark gray; }
.B { background-color: salmon; justify-self: center;
     align-self: center;}
.C { background-color: orange; }
.D { background-color: yellow; }
.E { background-color: MediumAquamarine; }
.F { background-color: violet; }

HTML
<div class="grid">
  <div class="A">A</div>
  <div class="B">B</div>
  <div class="C">C</div>
  <div class="D">D</div>
  <div class="E">E</div>
  <div class="F">F</div>
</div>
```

FIGURE 20.24   Example usage of `justify-self` and `align-self`.

and `self-end` values can also be used with the properties, with the result depending largely on direction of writing. For example, in left-to-right top-to-bottom writing, as also noted before, `left` and `self-start` produce the same result as `start`, while `right` and `self-end` produce the same result as `end`. Figure 20.24 shows how the properties are used, using the `center` value.

The `.grid{}` rule in the example, again, makes the element of `class="grid"` a grid container and its children automatically grid items; sets its width and height; sets three columns and two rows; and sets a border line-style. The `.B{}` rule sets the background color for grid item B and centers it along both row and column axes within the containing grid area with `justify-self` and `align-self`, respectively. Notice that the alignment properties are placed in the rule for the grid item and not in the rule for the grid container. This is because it is the item that aligns itself within the container rather than the container aligning the item. The `.A{}`, `.C{}`, `.D{}`, `.E{}`, and `.F{}` rules set the background color for items A, C, D, E, and F (i.e., `<div>` elements of class equal to "A", "C", "D", "E", and "F"), respectively.

CHALLENGE 20.24

In the example, why is the grid aligned flush to the top and left edges of the grid container?

CHALLENGE 20.25

Implement the example, but also center the grid in the grid container using the appropriate placement properties.

CHALLENGE 20.26

Instead of using placement properties as instructed in the previous challenge, use the `margin` property.

20.7 Ordering Grid Items

CSS allows two main types of ordering in relation to grid items: the order in which they appear in a grid container and the order in which they are stacked when they overlap. The former is achieved using the `order` property and the latter the `z-index` property.

20.7.1 Ordering Grid Items Display Sequence

20.7.1.1 `order`

Like in the flexible box layout, the `order` property allows you to specify the order in which items are laid out in the grid container, which is by default the same order they appear in the source code. The property is **non-inherited** and takes an **integer value**, which can be positive or negative. It affects only grid items that are auto-placed and not those explicitly positioned. Figures 20.25 and 20.26 show its usage and result, in which the order value of grid item "B" is changed from 0 (the default) to -1. Because it affects only the visual order, the accessibility guidelines given in Chapter 19 for the use of the property in the flexible box layout apply to its use in the grid layout too.

```
CSS
.grid {
 display: grid;
 width: 90%;
 height: 480px;
 grid-template-columns: 50px 50px 50px 50px;
 grid-template-rows: 50px;
}
.A { background-color: gold; }
.B { background-color: light blue;}
.C { background-color: pink;  order: -1;}
.D { background-color: dark gray; }

HTML
<div class="grid">
 <div class="A">A</div>
 <div class="B">B</div>
 <div class="C">C</div>
 <div class="D">D</div>
</div>
```

FIGURE 20.25 Example usage of order.

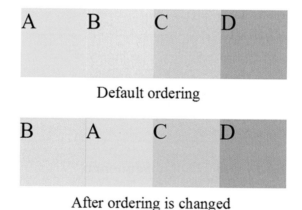

Default ordering

After ordering is changed

FIGURE 20.26 Result of Figure 20.25.

CHALLENGE 20.27

Implement the example and experiment both with the order value and the order of the elements in the HTML code to see the effects, and better understand the property and its possible applications.

20.7.2 Specifying Layer Positions for Stacked Grid Items

20.7.2.1 `z-index`

The layer ordering of elements is done with the `z-index` property, which allows you to control the **z-axis order** (i.e., vertical stacking order) of overlapping grid items. It generally works with grid in the same way as described in Chapter 12 for other elements. Grid items can be made to overlap by, for example, absolutely positioning them that way, using the `position` and **offset** properties (again, see Chapter 12), or extending the size of one grid item over another, using negative margins. The property is **non-inherited** and takes one of two values: `auto` (which is the default) or an **integer value** (positive or negative). The greater the integer is, the closer an item is to the user. Figures 20.27, 20.28, and 20.29 show the usage and the result.

```
HTML
<div class="grid">
  <div class="A">A</div>
  <div class="B">B</div>
  <div class="C">C</div>
  <div class="D">D</div>
  <div class="E">E</div>
  <div class="F">F</div>
  <div class="G">G</div>
  <div class="H">H</div>
  <div class="I">I</div>
</div>
```

FIGURE 20.27   HTML for demonstrating usage of `z-index`.

```
CSS
.grid {
 display: grid;
 width: 90%;
 height: 480px;
 grid-template-columns: 50px 50px 50px;
 grid-template-rows: 50px 50px 50px;
}
.A { background-color: gold; }
.B { background-color: light blue; }
.C { background-color: gold; }
.D { background-color: light blue; }
.E { background-color: dark gray; margin: -10px; z-index: 1; }
.F { background-color: light blue; }
.G { background-color: gold; }
.H { background-color: light blue; }
.I { background-color: gold; }
```

FIGURE 20.28   CSS for Figure 20.27.

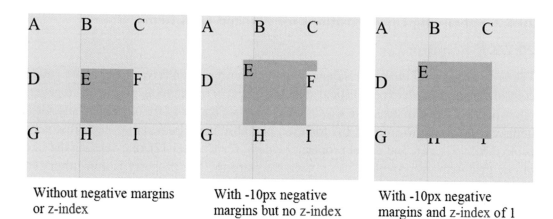

Without negative margins or z-index

With -10px negative margins but no z-index

With -10px negative margins and z-index of 1

FIGURE 20.29 Result of Figures 20.27 and 20.28.

In the example, the .grid{} rule defines the grid container and a three-column-three-row grid. In the .E{} rule, the negative margin value extends grid item "E" at all four edges and the z-index of 1 positions it on a higher layer than other items. The rules for the rest of the grid items simply specify background color. Notice in the middle image that the layer position of grid item "E" is 5th, which is its position in the HTML code.

CHALLENGE 20.28

Like in the previous challenge, implement the example and experiment both with the z-index value and the order of the elements in the HTML code to better understand how the property works.

CHALLENGE 20.29

Modify the CSS code in Figure 20.28 to produce the output below:

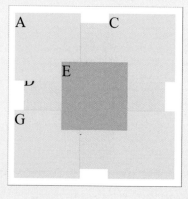

20.8 Example Application of Grid

Apart from its use for structuring layouts, grid is useful for general structuring and alignment goals. For example, as mentioned in Chapter 17, it can be used to align form controls. The example in Figures 20.30 and 20.31 shows how it can be used to achieve this, which in principle involves placing labels in one column, controls in another, and buttons at the bottom, spanning all columns.

In the example, the form{} rule defines a grid with two columns, and 5px column and row gaps. Notice that the rows are not explicitly specified. When this is done, adding rows and sizing them is done automatically for the grid items. In the form > label{} rule, grid-column places each <label> element that is a direct child of the <form> element in the column that starts at the grid line named "labels" (i.e., first column), grid-row places it automatically in the next available row, and justify-self aligns it to the end of the column. Similarly, the form > input{} rule places all <input> elements in the "controls" column. The .buttons{} rule places the element of class="buttons" (the container for the buttons) in column 1 and the next row, makes it span the two columns, and aligns it to the end. The ">" selector is one of the selectors introduced in Chapter 8.

```
CSS
form {
  display: grid;
  grid-template-columns: [labels] auto [controls] auto;
  grid-column-gap: 5px;
  grid-row-gap: 5px;
}
form > label { grid-column: labels; grid-row: auto;
               justify-self: end; }
form > input { grid-column: controls; grid-row: auto; }
.buttons {
  grid-column: 1 / span 2;
  grid-row: auto;
  justify-self: end;
}

HTML
<form>
<label>Username:</label><input type="text" name="username">
<label>Email:</label><input type="email" name="email">
<label>Password: </label><input type="password" name="password">
<div class="buttons">
  <input type="submit" value="Login">
  <input type="reset" value="Cancel">
</div>
</form>
```

FIGURE 20.30 Using grid to layout and align form labels and controls.

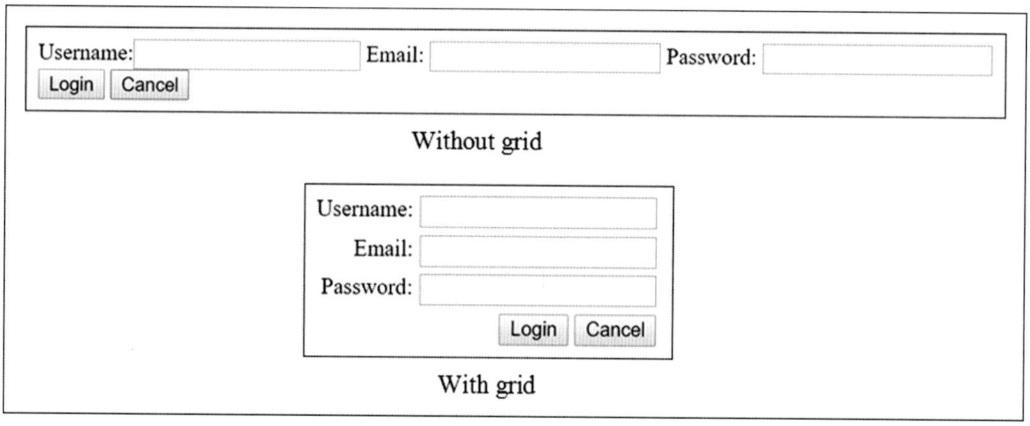

| Username: | [   ] | Email: | [   ] | Password: | [   ] |

Login Cancel

Without grid

Username:	[ ]
Email:	[ ]
Password:	[ ]

Login Cancel

With grid

FIGURE 20.31   Result of Figure 20.30.

CHALLENGE 20.30

The output below was created using the `<dl>`, `<dt>`, and `<dl>` elements and the grid. Using the principle used in Figures 20.30 and 20.31, and your own content, create it. *Hint*: Remember from Chapter 17 that the `<dd>` element has a default `margin-left` (or `margin-inline-start`) of 40px that needs to be removed.

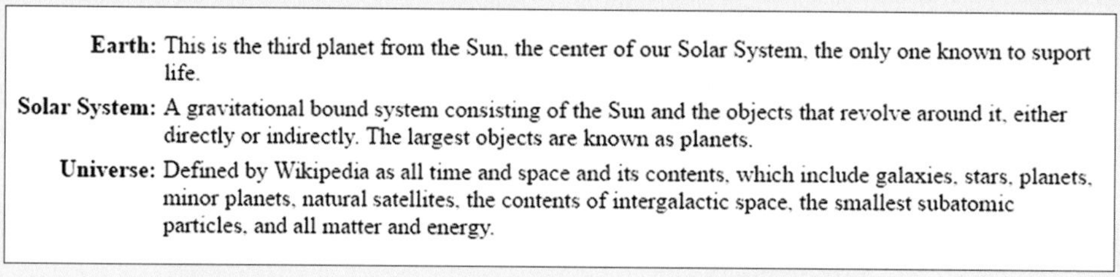

> **Earth:** This is the third planet from the Sun, the center of our Solar System, the only one known to suport life.
>
> **Solar System:** A gravitational bound system consisting of the Sun and the objects that revolve around it, either directly or indirectly. The largest objects are known as planets.
>
> **Universe:** Defined by Wikipedia as all time and space and its contents, which include galaxies, stars, planets, minor planets, natural satellites, the contents of intergalactic space, the smallest subatomic particles, and all matter and energy.

CHALLENGE 20.31

Implement the example in Figure 20.30. When you do, you should notice that the form is aligned to the right of the browser window. How would you center it?

20.9 Useful Info

20.9.1 Web Links

CSS specifications: w3.org/standards

Web development documents: docs.webplatform.org

Accessibility: w3.org/WAI/tutorials, webaim.org

CSS tutorials (*Here are just a few free tutorial sites on CSS and other Web languages*): w3.org/wiki, html5rocks.com, sitepoint.com, w3schools.com, codecademy.com, quackit.com, developer.mozilla.org/en-US/docs/Web, tutorialspoint. com, htmldog.com, htmlcodetutorial.com, echoecho.com, learn.shayhowe.com, html.net, tizag.com, cssbasics.com, cordova.apache.org, developers.google.com, csszengarden.com, webdesignermag.co.uk, css.maxdesign.com.au

CSS grid layout specification: w3.org/TR/css3-grid-layout

Responsive grid generator: gridpak.com

Testing codes: jsfiddle.net, codepad.org, jsbin.com, cssdesk.com

Browser compatibility info: caniuse.com

21

Responsive and Adaptive Web Design

21.1 Introduction

The availability of computerized devices with different screen sizes and different capabilities, and the need to deliver a website on as many of them as possible has led to the invention of various types of solutions. These solutions include designing a fixed-structure layout for a specific class of screen sizes and capability, designing a fluid layout that changes size according to screen size, and designing responsive or adaptive layouts that resize and reorganize their components to suit a user's device. This chapter discusses these layout design approaches and how they are implemented, especially through CSS flexible box and CSS grid layout properties.

21.2 Learning Outcomes

After studying this chapter, you should:

- Be aware of the role different screen sizes in the need for different layout approaches.
- Be aware of the differences between fixed and liquid layouts.
- Know the differences between responsive and adaptive layout design approaches.
- Know how to create responsive Web designs.
- Be aware of what is involved in creating adaptive Web designs.

21.3 Screen Size and Resolution Issues

The layout of Web pages is influenced by various factors. The most important of these are screen size and screen resolution. Technically, **screen size** is the diagonal length of a screen and typically measured in inches. However, in terms of Web design, it may be more practical to think of it as the width and height of a screen.

The size of a screen affects how big the browser window can be opened and, therefore, the amount of information that can be displayed in any one instance. Screen sizes vary widely both between and within different classes of devices, the most common of which are desktops, tablets (e.g., iPad), and smart phones (e.g., iPhone). Whereas the screen size of iPhone is about 3.5 inches, that of a desktop monitor can be up to 30 inches or more. Also, even users using large screens commonly feel the need to change the size of the browser for convenience, just like they might change the orientation of their phone, for example, from portrait to landscape. This means that the sizes at which users view pages vary widely.

Screen resolution commonly refers to the number of dots (called **pixels**) in each dimension of a screen and is usually quoted in terms of width and height. A resolution of 1024 × 768 pixels, for example, means that the width of a screen contains 1024 pixels and the height 768. Another screen property that influences the display of a layout is **pixels per inch** (ppi), or **pixel density**, which is the number of pixels contained in each inch of a dimension. The higher the ppi, the smaller and sharper are the text and images displayed on the screen. This is how it is possible to display a reasonable amount of content in fine details on smaller screens. Interestingly, what is referred to as screen resolution is better described as **pixel dimensions** (previously introduced in Chapter 6). Rather, it is ppi that better describes screen resolution, as it is what indicates the level of detail a screen is capable of displaying. In any case, all the above properties vary widely in value both between and within different classes of computer devices, the most common of which are desktops, tablets, and smart phones. Table 21.1 shows an example of the variation in resolution and ppi in handheld (or mobile) devices as of time of writing.

What the variation in screen size and resolution means is that a Web page is likely to be viewed on a variety of screen sizes and resolutions, making it necessary to design pages in a way that makes them look as intended on as many screens

TABLE 21.1

Example of the Variations in Device Screen Resolution and ppi as of Time of Writing

Device Type	Resolution (pixels)	Pixel/inch (PPI)
iPhone 4/4S	960 × 640	326
BlackBerry Touch	800 × 480	253
iPhone 5	1136 × 640	326
Nokia Lumia 920	1280 × 768	332
iPhone 6	1334 × 750	326
iPhone 6 plus	1920 × 1080	401
Galaxy S4	1920 × 1080	441
HTC One	1920 × 1080	468
iPad Mini	1048 × 768	163
iPad Mini 2, 3	2048 × 1536	326

as possible. In principle, a layout can be **fixed**, **liquid**, **responsive**, or **adaptive** in behavior. These descriptions essentially define how a page layout behaves when it is viewed in browser windows of different widths, and a layout can have a combination of the behaviors.

21.4 Fixed and Liquid Layouts

Although fixed layouts are still used to deliver some types of websites, for all intents and purposes, the use of liquid layouts as a single solution to the delivery of a design across screens of different sizes is outmoded. Modern websites are more likely to use a responsive or adaptive approach, both of which incorporate it.

21.4.1 Fixed Layouts

In fixed layouts (also known as fixed width or static layouts), the **sizes of elements and their position remain the same**, irrespective of screen size or change in browser width. So, for example, if the width of a page is 960px, then it will always be displayed as 960px. Sizes of elements are specified in absolute units, such as px. Using the fixed layout approach used to be the only way Web pages were built. It meant that a page that looked properly composed and professional on the screen used to create it might appear poorly designed on screen sizes that are widely different. For example:

- Content might be cropped on smaller screens.
- Horizontal scrolling might be necessary in narrower browser windows.
- There might be large gaps around the edges of pages on large screens.
- Text might look too small on higher-resolution screens.

The approach still may be suitable for when targeting specific class of devices and users who seek to perform only a specific task, such as booking of flights. It is unsuitable for when a website provides diverse types of information, which are likely to be viewed on different devices. Figure 21.1 shows how a fixed layout is cropped when displayed in a smaller window than intended.

21.4.2 Liquid Layouts

Unlike in fixed layout, the sizes of elements in liquid (or fluid) layouts do not remain the same when the size of the screen or that of the browser window changes; instead they stretch and contract accordingly. A liquid layout is typically achieved through specifying the sizes of elements in relative units, such as em and percentage. The obvious **advantage** of liquid layouts is that they adjust to screens or browser windows of different sizes, doing away with the need to create different versions of the same design

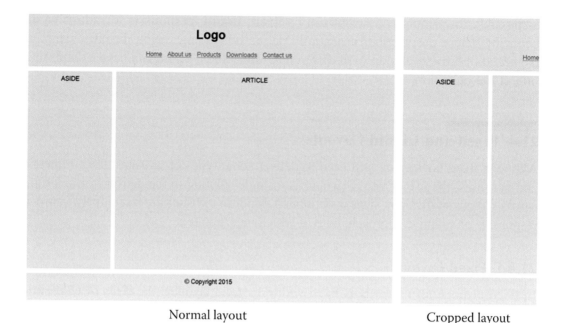

FIGURE 21.1   Fixed layout displayed in normal and reduce-width browser window.

for different devices. The **disadvantages** become apparent at very small or very large browser widths. On small screens, a multi-column layout can become too crowded when contracted too much, making content difficult to read. On large screens, the browser window can become too wide, resulting, for example, in lines of text that are much too long and again difficult to read. Figure 21.2 shows how a liquid layout is squeezed when displayed on a smaller screen.

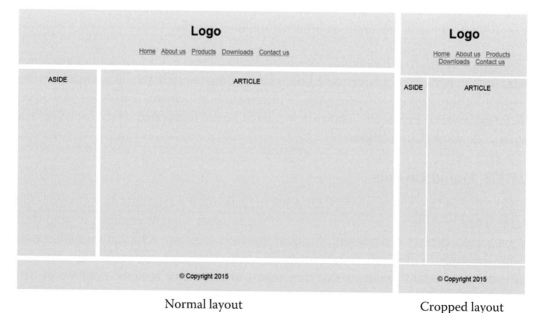

FIGURE 21.2   Liquid layout displayed in normal and reduced-width browser window.

21.5 Responsive vs. Adaptive Design

Responsive layouts are also known as **Responsive Web Design** (RWD), while adaptive layouts as **Adaptive Web Design** (AWD). The two are grouped together here because they represent a different class of approach, in that they aim to achieve the same general goals. These goals mainly are to deliver Web content across different technologies through adjusting for different factors, such as screen sizes, screen resolutions, and device capabilities, to optimize user experience. The differences between them lie mainly in the way they achieve these goals. For example, RWD enables a single design to fluidly change to fit any browser-window size. The same codes and contents are delivered to each device, where the included CSS codes determine which layout to present to a user, based on browser size.

In contrast, AWD, like the old approach of creating different versions for the same site, typically involves creating different versions of the same design and delivering the appropriate version to users, based on their devices' screen size and capabilities. It defers from the old multiple-version approach mainly in the sense that different Uniform Resource Locators (URLs) are not necessary; instead, the Web server detects the user's device type, determines what version of a design to deliver based on the device's characteristics, and even user's preferences, and delivers the most optimized design, along with the necessary components, such as media assets. This means, naturally, that different devices may receive different versions of the same site.

The term "adaptive web design" itself is another term for a design philosophy known as **progressive enhancement**, which has been around for some time and suggests the strategy of using Web technologies in a layered manner that ensures everyone can access Web content irrespective of the capabilities of their devices or Internet connections. More specifically, users whose set-up can handle only basic content and functionality should be able to have it just as those whose set-up can handle high-quality delivery should be able to have high-quality content.

Like fixed and liquid layout approaches, both RWD and AWD have advantages and disadvantages, and are best suited for different situations, which are typically determined by factors such as business goal, budget, and users' needs. The following are some points of comparison.

- **Efficiency:** On the face of it, it is more efficient to create a single design that adjusts to fit different screen sizes, as in RWD, than to create differently optimized versions for different devices, as in AWD, which can be costlier in terms of time and effort.
- **Implementation:** Typically, the implementation of RWD requires no programming, only HyperText Markup Language (HTML) and CSS, and all the decisions about what to display are made by the browser. In contrast, the implementation of AWD requires the use of programming (scripting). Using scripts is how, for example, the Web server is able to detect a user's device type to determine which optimized design version to deliver to the device and then

dynamically compose the design. For these reasons, adaptive designs are often more complicated and more expensive to implement.

- **Responsiveness:** In RWD, because all the decisions about what to display are made by the browser, a design can change dynamically according to the width of the browser window, irrespective of device. In contrast, in AWD, because the decisions about what to display are made by the Web server, once a design version is delivered to the browser, its layout or the size of its elements cannot be changed by changing the size of the browser window, unless such responsive behavior is also implemented and the codes are delivered with the design version.

- **Performance:** Because the implementation of RWD typically requires a lot of codes, and RWD delivers all the codes and content (including media assets) for a design to all devices, whether or not a device needs all of them and without consideration for a device's capabilities or connection speed, **RWD can easily overwhelm the capabilities of mobile devices**, possibly resulting in **slow download time**. In contrast, since AWD delivers to a device only what the device needs based on its capabilities, there is usually no slow download-time problem. With AWD, a server can optimize what it sends to a device, including optimizing media assets and also removing functionalities that the device does not support—all done on the fly. For example, high-resolution images can be delivered to high-resolution devices and low-resolution images to low-resolution devices. However, a **hybrid of RWD and AWD** is also possible and used. In this approach, device detection is incorporated in RWD and elements that can cause slow download time, such as large images and videos, are removed from what is delivered, especially if the server detects certain types of mobile devices, such as older mobile phones with more limited capabilities.

- **Maintenance:** If designed well, RWD should not need to be updated when new screen sizes become available, since right from the start, it is capable of delivering on virtually any screen size and can, therefore, handle future screen sizes, be they smaller, larger, or even extra large. However, if it is based only on common screen sizes, then updates are likely to be necessary in the future, just as it will be for AWD if new screen sizes and/or resolutions become available that are deemed important to serve.

- **User experience:** With RWD, because a single design is basically scaled and reorganized as necessary to fit screen size and other specific needs are not considered or catered to, usability and accessibility issues might arise. In contrast, because AWD delivers to a user specifically tailored design, these issues are less likely to arise. For example, delivering to a mobile device only information that can be handled comfortably on it, instead of information more suitable for desktop interaction, is more likely to be beneficial to the user's experience than not. This means that AWD is better suited for when what users do when they access a site via a mobile phone differs from what they do when they access via desktop, and RWD is better suited when there is little or no difference.

NOTE: Responsive website design and Google ranking

One of the factors Google uses for its ranking is how much a design satisfies user experience across devices, which means as well as other things a website needs to be **mobile friendly**. Central to this is whether a site is responsive or adaptive. This means that making a website responsive gives it a higher **search engine optimization (SEO)** ranking. SEO is the process of designing a website in ways that improve its visibility in search engines and the chances of being listed at the top of organic **search engine results pages** (SERPs). Organic search results refer to results that are not paid for or sponsored. Appearing high on SERPs generally translates into more traffic, which for e-commerce sites, for example, means more visits to convert into sales. SEO evaluation is discussed in Chapter 26.

CHALLENGE 21.1

One of the quickest ways to understand how a responsive design works, if you are not already familiar with this, is to actually see one in operation. To do this, visit a popular website, such as news websites like BBC, MSNBC, or CNN, from a desktop or laptop, then change the width of the browser window by dragging in or out the right or left side. You should notice the layout and the size of the media elements continually change to fit the current window size. This is similar to what happens when the site is displayed on different device screens. Adaptive designs can only be experienced using a mobile device to access an adaptive site. Some airline websites are adaptive.

21.6 Creating Responsive Design

A responsive design is achieved by defining layouts for different resolutions and making each layout liquid so that transition between them is fluid as screen size changes. Naturally, taken literally, there is a problem with this principle, because there are many different screen resolutions and it would be inefficient, if not impossible, to cater to all of them. So, only standard screen resolutions for classes of devices are typically considered, and these are mobile, tablet, and desktop. The primary goal is to have a design that makes the resizing and rearrangement of its elements work well on these resolutions. The most common method for achieving this is to start by creating a layout that works well with the smallest device class, which as of time writing is the mobile-phone class, and then progressively adjust the layout (e.g., by changing size and position) for larger device classes, in this case, tablet and desktop classes.

The technique of creating a design for the smallest device first is known by the term **"mobile first"** and was first coined by Luke Wrobleswki. Figure 21.3 illustrates the

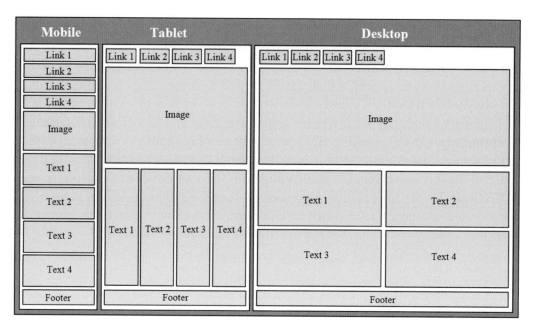

FIGURE 21.3 Illustration of the concept of responsive design.

kinds of differences in layouts that are typical between mobile, tablet, and desktop classes of devices.

Notice that all the layouts contain the same elements, which are also in the same order, and that only their sizes, shapes, and positions change. When the width of a browser displaying the desktop layout is contracted, at a specified point, the layout changes to that for the tablet, and if the contraction continues, the tablet layout changes to the mobile layout. Of course, in some cases, some elements that are present in the design for larger screens may not be in the design for smaller ones. Also, just two versions of a design may be enough: one for smaller screens and another for larger screens. Figures 21.4 and 21.5 show the wider-screen and smaller-screen versions of the same Web page. Notice the different arrangements and sizes of the design elements. Notice also that some elements are left out of the smaller version and the use of a smaller, more compact menu bar in the form of a three-line menu navigation icon (known as **navicon**). This icon is commonly used for all sizes of designs and further discussed in Chapter 25, where it is most relevant.

In the wider screen design, when the user clicks a menu, a dropdown menu is displayed, from which the user chooses a menu item and is taken to the corresponding page. In the smaller screen design, space limitation makes the process of getting to the information page a little longer. When the navicon is touched, the menus are displayed, and when the user touches a menu, a page is displayed that shows the menu items, from which the user then chooses one and is taken to the corresponding page.

FIGURE 21.4   The wider-screen version of a responsive Web page layout.

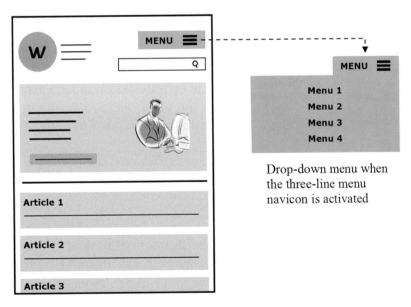

FIGURE 21.5   The smaller-screen version of the Web page layout in Figure 21.4.

21.6.1 Steps for Creating a Responsive Design

Irrespective of the number of layout versions used, the three main steps involved in producing a responsive design are:

1. Creating the layouts for different screen sizes.
2. Creating fluid media assets.
3. Creating CSS rules for changing between layouts.

21.6.1.1 Creating the Layouts for Different Screen Sizes

One way the layouts for different screen sizes are created is to first sketch out, typically on a grid paper or a grid document on the screen, the rough layouts for the device classes, starting with the mobile layout and then progressing to the tablet and desktop layouts. This would involve working out the dimensions for the page, the main containing elements, the gutters between them, margins, and so on, and creating the frameworks for the desired layouts. The use of a grid is especially important, as a grid helps in the accurate determination of dimensions of elements and their placements, thereby saving time. There are several free grid systems available on the Web that can be used for the purpose. Grid systems have been discussed later.

Once the layouts are completed, the one for the mobile class is implemented first as liquid layout, using HTML and CSS rules. The layout is created in liquid layout so that it can stretch and contract with changes in the browser window's size. At this point, although the layout stretches and contracts, any media objects it contains will usually remain fixed in size until they too are made fluid.

NOTE: Absolute units in responsive design

Note that absolute units can also be used in responsive design for some elements that are required to be fixed. For example, the size of the sidebar may be required to be constant, irrespective of screen size to maintain good usability and accessibility level.

21.6.1.2 Creating Fluid Media Assets

Whereas text is fluid by default in browsers, in that it reflows accordingly as the browser window narrows or widens, other visual media object types, such as images, videos, and animations, expect vector graphics, are not fluid and, therefore, will be cropped once the browser window becomes too small for their dimension. Making them fluid too can be done with CSS, and there are a number of ways of doing this. One of the easiest is to specify the `max-width` property on the media object's HTML element (i.e., `<img>` or `<video>`) in relative units, such as percent. For example, making the value of the property 100% will make the media object display at its full width, or the full width of its container, as well as make it scalable. However, when done in this way, the image starts resizing only when the width of the browser window becomes less than that of the image. The image will also not resize beyond its full size, even if the size of the window keeps widening.

An approach that produces a more scalable media object, which can also be used where necessary, is to express the value of the `width` property on the media object as a percentage of the width of the page layout. For example, assuming that the width of an image is 600px and that of the page is 1400px, then the relative width of the image is 42.85714285714286% (i.e., (600/1400) × 100), and this value is simply used for the `width` property. Using this approach, the image starts resizing the moment the browser window is resized and continues resizing even beyond its full width. It is usually the more preferred approach when media is within text, whereas the `max-width` approach is most typically used for header and "hero" images. In all cases, the height of the media object automatically resizes proportionately to the width, so that the aspect ratio is maintained to avoid stretchy or squashy appearance. To prevent an image from looking too small or too large relative to text in a design when screen size is too small or too large, the **minimum and maximum widths can be specified in an absolute unit**. Once all media objects have been made fluid, the next step is to define CSS rules that will resize the elements as well as rearrange them where necessary according to the screen size.

21.6.1.3 *Creating CSS Rules for Changing between Layouts*

The layouts displayed for specific screen sizes are specified using CSS **media queries**, which basically specify the points (known as **breakpoints**) at which certain style rules are to be applied.

21.6.1.3.1 *Media Queries*

A media query is created with the `@media` rule CSS at-rule, which takes a media type (i.e., a device type) and one or more expressions containing the features of the media type (e.g., width and height) that can be judged to be true or false. Figure 21.6 shows the basic structure of a media query.

The example basically says that if media type is a color computer screen and the maximum width of its viewport (display area) is equal to or less than 480px, then make the background color of the `<body>` element grey. The "and" in the query is known as a logical operator and allows for multiple expressions to be combined to form complex queries. The other operators are "not" (which specifies the negative of "and") and "only" (which restricts a query only to the media types that support it). The "max-" in the expression is a prefix that is used before media features. The other prefix is "min-," which means "equal to or greater than." Although the example has only one media query, multiple media queries can be specified with a single `@media` at-rule, in which case, they are comma separated. Also, in addition to "screen," other media types are supported by the at-rule, including several media features, although only a few are usually used in responsive Web design. Table 21.2 lists some common ones.

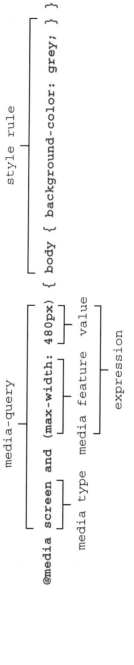

FIGURE 21.6   The structure of a CSS media query.

TABLE 21.2

Commonly Used Media Types and Features in RWD

Media Type	Description
screen	Used for color desktop, tablet, and mobile phone screens.
print	Allows contents to be styled for printing.
speech	Allows contents to be styled for screen readers.
all	Used for all media types. Assumed when no media type is specified.

Media Features	Description
width	Specifies the width of the output device's display area.
height	Specifies the height of the output device's display area.
color	Specifies the number of bits-per-color-component of the output device. The value for a non-color device is zero.
aspect-ratio	Specifies the aspect ratio of the output device's display area.
orientation	Specifies whether the device's orientation mode is portrait (i.e., display is taller than wide) or landscape (i.e., display is wider than tall).
resolution	Specifies the output device's pixel-per-inch resolution.

The style rules for a media query can be specified with it, as shown in the earlier example, or in separate stylesheets, in which case, the HTML `<link>` element is used to link to the stylesheets. Figure 21.7 shows how this is done. The first `media` attribute specifies the media query that says to link to the "mobile-phone.css" stylesheet and apply the styles in it only if `device-width` is equal to or less than 479px. The second one says to use the "tablet.css" stylesheet only if `device-width` is equal to or greater than 480px.

It is useful to note that `width` is different from `device-width`, which is the actual number of pixels that make up the width of a screen. In some devices, these properties are the same, while in others they are different. For example, some iPhone models have widths that are more than device-widths, due to the use of retina display technology, which allows

```
HTML and CSS
<link rel="stylesheet" type="text/css" media="only screen and
  (max-device-width:479px)"
 href="mobile-phone.css">
<link rel="stylesheet" type="text/css" media="only screen and
  (min-device-width:480px)"
 href="tablet.css">
```

FIGURE 21.7 Linking media queries to external stylesheets.

more pixels to be packed into the space for one pixel. In relation to responsive design, it is `width` that is usually used, because it better determines what is displayed. The `device-width` property is typically used only when specifically targeting mobile devices.

The other method of making use of CSS rules contained in separate stylesheets is through the `@import` CSS at-rule. The rule allows you to import one stylesheet into another. As mentioned in relation to typefaces and fonts in Chapter 13, the rule can be included in the `<head>` element of an HTML document. However, it can also be used in a linked stylesheet by including it at the beginning of the stylesheet, before any other rule. For example, to import a stylesheet named "menu.css" into another stylesheet, you would include the following line:

```
@import url("menu.css");
```

This is done for every stylesheet to be imported. It maybe useful to know that there is no difference between linking to a stylesheet or importing it, except that some older browsers may not support the `@import` at-rule. A common approach is to link to an external stylesheet and then use the at-rule to import stylesheets into it.

21.6.1.3.2 Breakpoints

Before media queries can be applied, decisions have to be made about points at which to apply them. These points, as mentioned earlier, are known as **breakpoints** and derived in various ways. One way is to **determine them based on the screen sizes of current device classes**, such as mobile phone (480px and below), tablet (481-768px), and desktop (769-1232px). However, using common screen sizes does not produce a versatile enough result, in that it carries with it the need for possible constant maintenance, given that new screen sizes continually emerge and there is no way of determining what will happen in the future.

A more generally preferred approach is to **determine breakpoints visually**, using the behavior of content during resizing as guide. This typically involves opening the relevant mobile fluid design in a desktop browser that is capable of displaying information about its current window size. Most browsers are able to do this once you open their development tool. In Chrome, for example, the F12 key opens the tool. Once the mobile fluid layout is opened, the browser window is narrowed as much as possible and then slowly widened. As this is done, the point is looked for at which content layout changes significantly and becomes unacceptable. This point is known as "where the content breaks." It could be, for example, the point at which whitespaces between elements become too wide, or the number of characters per line is not within 45-75 (roughly 8-10 words), or font size becomes disproportionate to the rest of content, or padding and margins of elements start to look unnatural. This point is the **first breakpoint** and two media queries are required to specify how the layout should change when browser window size reaches it. One query is for when window size is at the breakpoint or any size below it, and the other is for when it is any size above. Each query basically contains the rules that specify the required layout. Once the media queries are implemented, the browser is reset and the procedure is started again to look for the next breakpoint, and so on, until all breakpoints have been found.

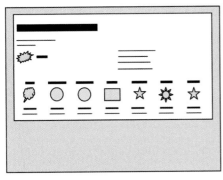
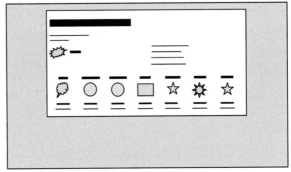

Tablet screen   Desktop screen

FIGURE 21.8   Illustration of a design displayed at the same size on a tablet and a wider desktop screen.

The number of breakpoints defined depends on the nature of content. For example, some content types may require that layouts be created only for small and large screens if the same layout looks good and the content is legible on, for example, both tablets and desktops. Indeed, a layout that suits tablet display is often adequate for most desktop screens, since both devices are viewed at similar distances from the eyes. It is important to know that a wider screen is not reason enough to make a design span the full width. Content could simply be placed in the center and white space left at both sides, as illustrated in Figure 21.8. Alternatively, if content type permits, such as if there is enough text, and the screen is wide enough, more than one column could be used, meaning, for example, that at the breakpoint defined for extra-large screens, an extra column is added via media query.

Naturally, if a design is also to be displayed on much larger screens that are viewed from much greater distances, such as TV screens, then additional breakpoints certainly need to be considered. In all cases, an important factor that should not be overlooked in a responsive design is **legibility**, given that screen size and the distance between the eyes and the screen can readily affect it. So, it is highly likely when creating a responsive design that adjusting font size will be inevitable. Generally, **the smaller the screen size, the smaller the font size** that would be most suitable, given that small screens are used close to the eyes.

Where change in font size is necessary, **size should be expressed in ems unit** rather than in an absolute unit in order to ensure both fluidity and proportionality with the font size set for the browser by the user. In all, by basing the determination of breakpoints on content behavior, the chances of incurring the fewest breakpoints are increased and future needs for maintenance are greatly minimized. To help with this approach, there are now useful tools on the Web for finding breakpoints based on content. They typically allow you to upload the relevant page, after which the sliders provided can be used to change viewport width and height while the behavior of the content is observed for possible breakpoints. One of these tools is **responsivepx**.

CHALLENGE 21.2

Why should a design not be as wide as it can be on a wide desktop screen?

21.6.2 Implementing Responsive Design via Flexbox

This example serves to demonstrate how a responsive design might be implemented following the steps just described and using the basic design used earlier to explain the fixed and liquid layouts. Starting with the mobile size, the design layout (i.e., the one in Figures 21.1 and 21.2) is repurposed into one for small screens. Figure 21.9 shows the repurposed mobile design, which is a liquid layout, and Figures 21.10 and 21.11 show the codes.

In the example, the `body{}` rule specifies the font, text color, and text alignment to use for the page; the `display` property makes the `<body>` element a flex container, and `flex-direction` says to stack its flex items (i.e., its children) vertically. The `header, aside, article, footer{}` rule specifies the background color, padding for all four edges, bottom margin, and corner roundness for the `<header>`, `<aside>`, `<article>`, and `<footer>` elements. The `ul{}` rule uses `list-style-type` to remove bullet points from the list items, `padding-left` to remove the default indentation to make the list not move off the center to the right, and `line-height` to provide enough vertical space between the items to accommodate finger-touching. The `ul li a{}` rule removes the underline decoration from the links, and the `aside{}`, `article{}`, and `footer{}` rules each specify the height of the `<aside>`, `<article>`, and `<footer>` elements, respectively. For the `auto` values, the browser uses the size of the element's content to determine height. If you specify fixed height, content

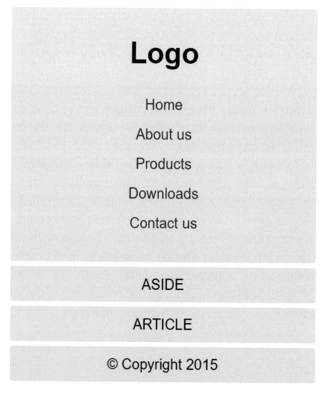

FIGURE 21.9   The fluid mobile layout created with Figures 21.10 and 21.11.

```
HTML
<body>
  <header>
    <h1>Logo</h1>
    <nav>
      <ul>
        <li><a href="">Home</a></li>
        <li><a href="">About us</a></li>
        <li><a href="">Products</a></li>
        <li><a href="">Downloads</a></li>
        <li><a href="">Contact us</a></li>
      </ul>
    </nav>
  </header>
  <main>
    <aside>ASIDE</aside>
    <article>ARTICLE</article>
  </main>
  <footer>&copy; Copyright 2015</footer>
</body>
```

FIGURE 21.10 HTML code for the fluid mobile design in Figure 21.9.

```
CSS
body {
  font-family: Helvetica;
  color: black;
  text-align: center;
  display: flex;
  flex-direction: column;
}
header, aside, article, footer {
  background-color: #d3d3d3;
  padding: 10px;
  margin-bottom: 5px;
  border-radius: 3px;
}
ul {
  list-style-type: none;
  padding-left: 0;
  line-height: 32px;
}
ul li a { text-decoration: none; }
aside {  height: auto; }
article {  height: auto; }
footer { height: 50px; }
```

FIGURE 21.11 CSS code for creating the fluid mobile layout in Figure 21.9 from Figure 21.10.

from one box may overflow into the one below. Notice that no width is specified for any element. This ensures that their widths are fluid and change with the browser's width. On the other hand, you could specify their widths in relative units (e.g., %), in which case, just specifying the width of the `<body>` element is enough.

The next step in the example implementation is to find the first breakpoint for a wider screen size. To do this, the browser window is widened until the layout no longer seems right for the browser width. This point is found to be around 600px, so, one media query is created for screen sizes that are equal to or less than 599px (1px less than the point of the break) and placed at the beginning of the CSS code for the mobile layout shown earlier in Figure 21.9. This is the query that is added: `@media all and (max-width: 599px){}`, with the rules for the mobile layout placed between the two curly brackets, as shown in Figure 21.12.

Next, a second media query is created for screen sizes that are equal to or greater than 600px and the rules for the liquid layout for a wider screen size are placed in it, as shown in Figure 21.13. Figure 21.14 shows the result, which is the same as the one shown earlier for fixed and fluid layouts in Figures 21.1 and 21.2.

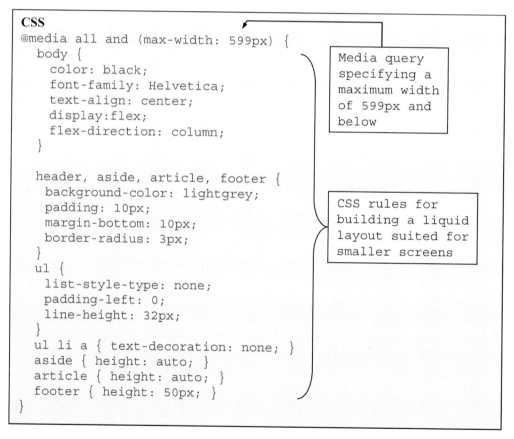

FIGURE 21.12   Specifying the breakpoint for the mobile layout.

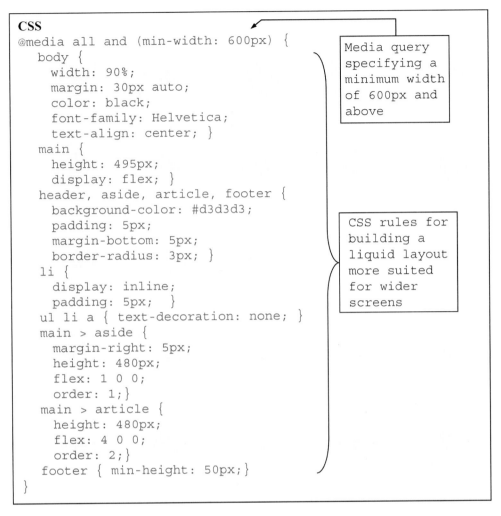

```
CSS
@media all and (min-width: 600px) {
   body {
      width: 90%;
      margin: 30px auto;
      color: black;
      font-family: Helvetica;
      text-align: center; }
   main {
      height: 495px;
      display: flex; }
   header, aside, article, footer {
      background-color: #d3d3d3;
      padding: 5px;
      margin-bottom: 5px;
      border-radius: 3px; }
   li {
      display: inline;
      padding: 5px;    }
   ul li a { text-decoration: none; }
   main > aside {
      margin-right: 5px;
      height: 480px;
      flex: 1 0 0;
      order: 1;}
   main > article {
      height: 480px;
      flex: 4 0 0;
      order: 2;}
   footer { min-height: 50px;}
}
```

Media query specifying a minimum width of 600px and above

CSS rules for building a liquid layout more suited for wider screens

FIGURE 21.13   CSS for producing a wider-screen layout with the HTML in Figure 21.10.

In the body{} rule in the media query, width makes the width of the <body> element (i.e., the page) 90% that of the browser window, margin aligns it 30px from top and bottom, and centers it horizontally, color specifies the text color, font-family specifies the font, and text-align centers the text. In the main{} rule, height sets the height of the <main> element and display makes it a flex container, making the <aside> and <article> elements flex items. The header, aside, article, footer{} rule sets the background color, padding, bottom margin, and corner roundness for the <header>, <aside>, <article>, and <footer> elements. In the li{} rule, display changes the <li> elements from block level to inline-level elements (removing the bullet points and displaying them on the same line) and padding puts some space between them. The ul li a{} rule removes the underline decoration from the links. The main > aside{} rule applies to the <aside> element that is a direct

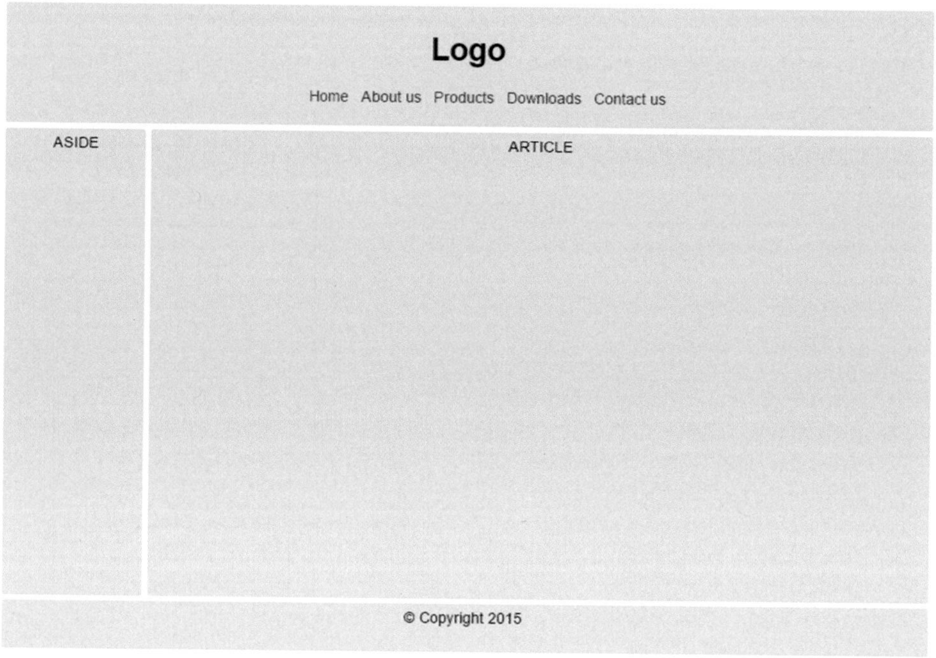

FIGURE 21.14   The result of Figure 21.13 used with Figure 21.10.

child of the `<main>` element. In it, `margin-right` puts some place between the element and the next one to the right, `height` sets its height, `flex` says to stretch it at one time the rate of the other flex items (in this case the `<article>` element), and `order` places it first. The `main > article{}` rule applies to the `<article>` element that is a direct child of the `<main>` element. It sets the height of the element, says to stretch it at four times the rate of other flex items (i.e., the `<aside>` element), and places it second. The ">" selector is one of the selectors introduced in Chapter 8.

Next, repeating the procedure for finding the next breakpoint, it is found to be around 1200px. However, because the layout created for the 600px breakpoint also looks all right for this breakpoint when stretched, no change is deemed necessary to the layout. It is also found that there is no need for the layout to stretch beyond this point, irrespective of how much wider the screen becomes, as this will only make the content difficult to read. So, to stop the layout from continuing to stretch once it gets to 1200px, a declaration is added to the `body{}` rule to specify the maximum width for the `<body>` element, using the `max-width` property, thus: `max-width: 1200px;`. The result is that a responsive design is produced in which when the browser window is 599px wide or less, the mobile liquid layout is displayed, and as the browser widens, the layout stretches until the browser window's width gets to 600px, at which point, the layout changes and then continues to stretch until the browser window's width gets to 1200px, at which point the layout no longer stretches because the `<body>` element has reached the specified maximum width.

CHALLENGE 21.3

Combine the codes in Figures 21.10, 21.12 and 21.13, and add the `max-width:1200px;` declaration appropriately to create the responsive design.

21.6.3 Implementing Responsive Design via Grid

This example serves to demonstrate how the responsive design just implemented using flexbox can be implemented using grid layout. Figures 21.15, 21.16, and 21.17 show the codes.

In Figure 21.16, the `@media` at-rule says, if the width of the viewport is 599px or less, to apply the rules within the curly brackets for all media (i.e., screen and printer). The `#grid{}` rule targets the element of `id="grid,"` sets the font and content alignment, makes it a grid container and its children grid items, and creates a 4-column-1-row grid with a row gap of 5px. The `header, aside, article, footer{}` rule specifies background color, padding, and corner radius for the `<header>`, `<aside>`, `<article>`, and `<footer>` elements; the `ul{}` rule removes the bullet points and indentation from the list items and increases the line spacing; and the `ul li a{}` rule removes the underline decoration from the menu links.

In Figure 21.17, the `@media` at-rule says, if the width of the viewport is 600px or more, to apply the rules within the curly brackets for all media (i.e., screen and printer).

```
HTML
<body id="grid">
  <header>
    <h1>Logo</h1>
    <nav>
     <ul>
       <li><a href="">Home</a></li>
       <li><a href="">About us</a></li>
       <li><a href="">Products</a></li>
       <li><a href="">Downloads</a></li>
       <li><a href="">Contactus</a></li>
     </ul>
    </nav>
  </header>
  <aside>ASIDE</aside>
  <article>ARTICLE</article>
  <footer>&copy; Copyright 2015</footer>
</body>
```

FIGURE 21.15 HTML used for grid layout.

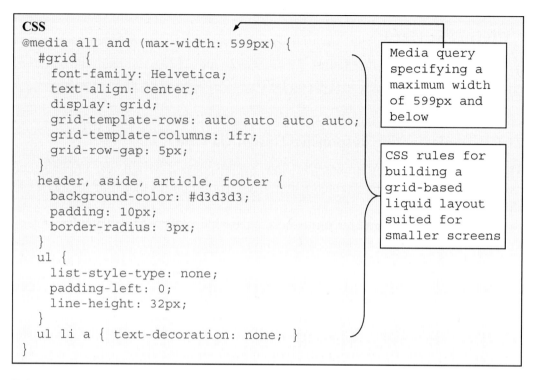

```
CSS
@media all and (max-width: 599px) {
  #grid {
    font-family: Helvetica;
    text-align: center;
    display: grid;
    grid-template-rows: auto auto auto auto;
    grid-template-columns: 1fr;
    grid-row-gap: 5px;
  }
  header, aside, article, footer {
    background-color: #d3d3d3;
    padding: 10px;
    border-radius: 3px;
  }
  ul {
    list-style-type: none;
    padding-left: 0;
    line-height: 32px;
  }
  ul li a { text-decoration: none; }
}
```

Media query specifying a maximum width of 599px and below

CSS rules for building a grid-based liquid layout suited for smaller screens

FIGURE 21.16   CSS for creating a mobile layout from the HTML in Figure 21.15 and the break-point for when to use it.

The #grid{} rule targets the element of id="grid," and sets the width, height, font to use, text color, and content alignment; display makes it a grid container and its children grid items; grid-template-areas defines six grid areas (i.e., two columns and three rows) in it; grid-template-columns defines the sizes for the columns; grid-template-rows defines the sizes for the rows; grid-column-gap defines the gaps between the columns; and grid-row-gap defines the gaps between the rows. The #grid header{}, #grid aside{}, #grid article{}, and #grid footer{} rules place the <header>, <aside>, <article>, and <footer> elements (i.e., grid items) in the specified grid areas. The header, aside, article, footer{} rule specifies background color, padding, and corner radius for the same elements; the li{} rule changes the <li> elements from block level to inline elements to align them horizontally; and the ul li a {} rule removes the underline decoration from the link text.

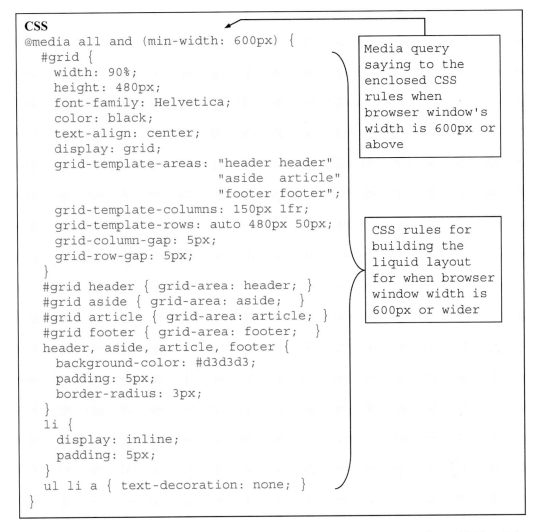

```
CSS
@media all and (min-width: 600px) {
  #grid {
    width: 90%;
    height: 480px;
    font-family: Helvetica;
    color: black;
    text-align: center;
    display: grid;
    grid-template-areas: "header header"
                         "aside  article"
                         "footer footer";
    grid-template-columns: 150px 1fr;
    grid-template-rows: auto 480px 50px;
    grid-column-gap: 5px;
    grid-row-gap: 5px;
  }
  #grid header  { grid-area: header;  }
  #grid aside   { grid-area: aside;   }
  #grid article { grid-area: article; }
  #grid footer  { grid-area: footer;  }
  header, aside, article, footer {
    background-color: #d3d3d3;
    padding: 5px;
    border-radius: 3px;
  }
  li {
    display: inline;
    padding: 5px;
  }
  ul li a { text-decoration: none; }
}
```

Media query saying to the enclosed CSS rules when browser window's width is 600px or above

CSS rules for building the liquid layout for when browser window width is 600px or wider

FIGURE 21.17 CSS for creating a widescreen layout from the HTML in Figure 21.15 and the breakpoint for when to use it.

CHALLENGE 21.4

Add an aside column on the right of the example and add images (ads) to it.

21.7 Creating Adaptive Design

In a sense, adaptive design is not as involved or tricky to figure out as RWD, because multiple goals are not being served by a single design. The complexity comes from a different direction, in that it typically involves server-side scripting. The first thing is to identify target devices and their screen sizes. A common set of these includes iPhone (320-480), tablet (760), laptop (900-1200), and desktop (1200-1600). Designing for each device is no different from when creating any fixed layout design. There is usually no need for the determination of breakpoints the same way as done in responsive design. Once all versions are built, a **device-detection** script is needed on the server side for sensing the screen size and possibly other features of the user's device. This information is then used to deliver the appropriate version to the device. Beyond this principle, how complex an adaptive design is depends on whether device-specific readymade pages are static and delivered as they are, or built and optimized dynamically to suit specific devices upon detection.

21.8 Useful Info

21.8.1 Web Links

Accessibility: w3.org/WAI/tutorials, webaim.org

Responsive Web design tutorials (search the site for "responsive Web design"): www.alistapart.com, html5rocks.com, sitepoint.com, w3schools.com, tutorialspoint.com, developer.mozilla.org/en-US/docs/Web, learn.shayhowe.com, developers.google.com, webdesignermag.co.uk, nngroup.com, udacity.com/courses, webdesign.tutsplus.com

Responsive grid generator: gridpak.com

Software for creating adaptive images: adaptive-images.com

Testing codes: jsfiddle.net, codepad.org, jsbin.com, cssdesk.com

22

Beyond HTML and CSS

22.1 Introduction

Once you are confident with using HTML and CSS, you are likely to be curious to improve your Web design and development skills so that you can produce websites that not only look professional but are also capable of providing complex functions. There are various Web languages that can be used to achieve this, including those that enable more efficient use of CSS, such as Sassy CSS (SCSS), and those that enable the dynamic manipulation of elements, such as JavaScript and PHP. To teach these languages requires a whole book for each; so, this chapter only shows how they are used with HTML and CSS. This should enable you to take free codes by others and use them with your HTML.

22.2 Learning Outcomes

After studying this chapter, you should:

- Be aware of the languages designed to extend the functionalities of CSS.
- Know how to use scripts with HTML.
- Know how to optimize content and codes for Web delivery.

22.3 Enhanced CSS

You probably have noticed in some of the examples presented so far in the CSS chapters that some declarations are repeated between rules. Figure 22.1 shows an example in which the `color:yellow` and `border: thick dotted yellow` declarations in the first rule are repeated in the second rule. This is not efficient.

Most stylesheet languages that offer ways of enhancing CSS are designed to address this issue as well as others. They are able to do this by letting you use features that are not supported yet in CSS, such as **variables, nesting**, and **mixins** (which allow the grouping of declarations for reuse). They are commonly referred to as CSS **preprocessors** and the most popular ones include **LESS, Stylus**, and **SASS** (Syntactically Awesome Style Sheets) or **SCSS**, which is version 3 of SASS. These tools are essentially scripting languages that extend CSS and allow the stylesheet that is created to be compiled into regular CSS that the browser understands. In SCSS, for example, the

```
CSS
.warning {
 color: yellow;
 border: thick dotted yellow;
}
.important-warning {
 color: yellow;
 border: thick dotted yellow;
 font-weight: bold;
}

HTML
<div class="warning">Warning!</div>
<div class="important-warning">Important Warning!</div>
```

FIGURE 22.1   Example of repetition of declarations in CSS.

```
CSS
.warning {
  color: yellow;
  border: thick dotted yellow;
}
.important-warning {
 @extend .warning;
 font-weight: bold;
}

HTML
<div class="warning">Warning!</div>
<div class="important-warning">Important Warning!</div>
```

FIGURE 22.2   Using `@extend` in SCSS to remove the repetition in Figure 22.1.

example in Figure 22.1 can be written as in Figure 22.2 in which the style defined by the `.warning{}` rule is used in the `.important-warning{}` rule, which also applies the `font-weight:bold` declaration.

The sites for CSS preprocessors, some of which are provided at the end of this chapter, usually tell you how to install and use them. A quick search should also provide tutorials. The advantages of using CSS preprocessors include:

- Producing cleaner codes because they minimize repetitions.
- Allowing the use of variables that allow long declarations to be represented with a variable that can then be used repeatedly throughout a stylesheet.
- Allowing code snippets and libraries to be shared through importing them.
- Providing functions that allow you to do things on the fly by specifying conditions, such as "if this, then do that".
- Producing CSS codes that are compatible across different browsers.

22.4 Using Scripting Languages with HTML

Scripting languages are essential to the development of Web applications. Although simple Websites that offer just links between pages can be accomplished with just HTML and CSS, complex sites that require interactivity as well as data to be processed and stored require the use of scripting languages. Scripts can be written for **client-side** or **server-side** execution. Client-side execution is done by the browser and server-side execution is done by the server. Scripting, which is programming, is much more complex than writing HTML or CSS. To learn specific scripting languages, you can use any of the many books available in the market or Web tutorial sites. Here, only how to use these scripts with HTML is discussed.

22.4.1 Client-Side Scripting

Client-side scripting was developed to prevent the Web browser from having to contact the Web server each time a user performs an action on a page. This is because such action inevitably results in the reloading of a Web page, which is inefficient. For example, it gives the server extra work and uses excessive bandwidth. It also produces poor user-experience (e.g., all page-content disappears and reappears each time). Although client-side scripting can be done in different languages, JavaScript is the most commonly used. Like CSS, scripts can be embedded in HTML code or written in a separate file to which the HTML can be linked. Embedded client-side scripts can be viewed by users the same way that ordinary HTML codes can, usually via the "View" menu in Internet Explorer and Safari, or via mouse-right-button context menu in Firefox and Chrome. Users cannot view external scripts.

22.4.1.1 Embedding Client-Side Scripts

When embedding a script in HTML, the script is placed inside the <script> element, which is placed in the <head> or <body> element. Either way, the Web browser is able to execute it. Figure 22.3 shows a JavaScript placed in the <body> element. The type attribute is used to specify in which language the script is written. This is known as the

```
<html>
 <head><title>Basic page</title></head>
 <body>
  <script type="text/javascript">
    document.write('Hello World!');
  </script>
  <noscript>
    <p>Browser does not or JavaScript has been turned off.</p>
  </noscript>
 </body>
</html>
```

FIGURE 22.3 JavaScript embedded in the <body> element.

```
<html>
  <head>
    <script type="text/javascript">
      function message() {
        document.write('Hello World!');
      }
    </script>
  </head>
  <body onload="message()">
    <noscript>
      <p>Browser does not JavaScript has been turned off.</p>
    </noscript>
  </body>
</html>
```

FIGURE 22.4 JavaScript embedded in the `<head>` and `<body>` element.

MIME type. Although it is not mandatory to include this for JavaScript, it is good practice to ensure certainty. The script in the example writes "Hello World!" when the `<body>` element loads (i.e., when the HTML document loads). The JavaScript statement more or less speaks for itself; the document is an object, whose `write` method is used to display "Hello World" on the screen. The `<noscript>` element is used to provide a message to users using browsers that do not support JavaScript or who have JavaScript turned off.

When scripts are embedded in the `<head>` element, they are usually in the form of functions (sub-routines), which are then called from within the `<body>` element. Figure 22.4 shows an example that does the same thing that the code in Figure 22.3 does. The function, `message()`, is declared when the `<head>` element is loaded and called when the `<body>` element is loaded, using `onload=message()` statement. In essence, the statement says when the `<body>` element loads, to execute the function called `message()`. The `onload` attribute is known as a **global event attribute**. As mentioned in Chapter 2, a global event attribute is generated by any element.

22.4.1.2 External Client-Side Scripts

As in external CSS, external client-side scripts are typically linked to by a single line of statement in the HTML document. Again, this line can be placed in the `<head>` or `<body>` element. The same rationale behind using external CSS instead of embedded CSS applies to using external scripts—they can be shared by more than one HTML document, making maintenance easier. Figures 22.5 and 22.6 show where the line that links to an external script is placed and how the functions in the script are called for execution. The script, in this case, "**test.js**," can be placed in the same folder as the associated HTML document in the Web server or in a sub-folder typically named "**scripts**" inside the folder containing the HTML document. When the browser sees the `src` attribute in the `<script>` element, it includes all the JavaScript in the specified file inside the element, as in Figure 22.4. Assuming the test.js script contains the same `message()` function (again shown in Figure 22.4), the function is called upon the loading of the page.

```
<html>
  <head>
    <script type="text/javascript" src="test.js"></script>
  </head>
  <body onload="message()">
  </body>
</html>
```

FIGURE 22.5 Linking to an external script via placing code in the `<head>` element.

```
<html>
  <head>
  </head>
  <body onload="message()">
    <script type="text/javascript" src="test.js"></script>
  </body>
</html>
```

FIGURE 22.6 Linking to an external script via placing code in the `<body>` element.

Instead of spending time writing JavaScript codes, a common practice is to use **JavaScript libraries**, which provide prewritten codes and are available from various sources on the Web. One of the most popular libraries is the **jQuery** library. It is a single long JavaScript file that contains codes for common functionalities and available in two versions ("**jquery. js**" and "**jquery.min.js**") at various online sites to link to or download. The two versions contain essentially the same codes. The former contains the long version of the codes and jquery.min.js the minified version. The minified version has the elements that are unnecessary for functioning (e.g., whitespace and comments), stripped out, and variable names shortened, thereby minimizing size and loading time for the file, making it more suitable for production environments where optimized performance is required. However, it is more difficult to read for the same reasons. So, jquery.js is typically used during development when it may be necessary to look in the file for helpful comments on usage.

To use the jQuery library, it is either downloaded into a folder and referenced locally, in which case "jquery.js" or "jquery.min.js" is assigned to the `src` attribute of the `<script>` element, or it may be referenced directly on any of the many Content Delivery Networks (**CDNs**), such as Google and Microsoft, that host it on their server, in which case the relevant URL is assigned to the `src` attribute. The following line, for example, links to the minified version 1.10.2 on Google's host server:

```
src="http://ajax.googleapis.com/ajax/libs/jquery/1.10.2/
  jquery.min.js"
```

Once the library is linked to, any function in it can be used, using jQuery syntax, which is much easier to use and less wordy than JavaScript. For example, the JavaScript code in Figure 22.7 produces the same result as the jQuery in Figure 22.8. Notice that what is achieved with about four lines of JavaScript code is achieved with only one line of jQuery code. The codes essentially say to make the background of the Web page gray when the button is clicked. In the jQuery, the $, which is used to select HTML elements, is used to select the <body> element, after which css is used to assign "gray" color to its background.

```
<!DOCTYPE html>
<html>
  <head>
    <script type="text/javascript">
      function changeBackground(color) {
        document.body.style.background=color;
      }
    </script>
  </head>
  <body>
   <button onclick="changeBackground('gray')">Change colour</button>
  </body>
</html>
```

FIGURE 22.7 This JavaScript does the same thing as the jQuery in Figure 22.8.

```
<!DOCTYPE html>
<html>
 <head>
 <script type="text/javascript"
             src="http://ajax.googleapis.com/ajax/libs/jquery/
             1.10.2/jquery.min.js">
 </script>
 </head>
 <body>
   <button onclick="$('body').css('background', 'gray')">
    Change colour
   </button>
 </body>
</html>
```

FIGURE 22.8 This jQuery code does the same thing as the JavaScript in Figure 22.7.

NOTE: Ready-made codes

Although it is important to know HTML and CSS as a beginner in Web design, it is not necessary to know scripting languages. It may also not be necessary to spend time writing codes if they are available on the Web to use for free. Using ready-made codes, for example, *dCodes*, from dcodes.net, can save a lot of time as well as make the creation of complex features possible for someone not very proficient in coding. All that is required is copying and pasting them as required.

CHALLENGE 22.1

Write an HTML code to create a canvas, as shown in figure 6.9 in Chapter 6. Make the border around it 1px thick, and then add the JavaScript below to the code to draw graphics on the canvas. *Hint*: Add `onload` event to the `<body>` element thus: `onload="drawSquares();"`, so that the JavaScript is executed when the page loads.

```
function drawSquares() {
    var oneCanvas = document.getElementById("oneCanvas");
    if (oneCanvas.getContext) {
        var ctx = oneCanvas.getContext("2d");
        ctx.fillStyle = "rgb(255,0,0)";
        ctx.fillRect (20, 20, 75, 70);
        ctx.fillStyle = "rgba(0, 255, 0, 0.7)";
        ctx.fillRect (50, 50, 75, 70);
    }
}
```

22.4.2 Server-Side Scripting

CHALLENGE 22.2

Trying out the examples in this section requires a client-server setup. If you want to try them out, you need to install a server on your computer. There are many free ones on the Web. A common one is WampServer. Download and install the version compatible with your system. If the installation is successful, an icon should be placed on the taskbar. Click it and then click "Put Online" on the menu, if the server is not already online. If WampServer is not running, start it (e.g., from the Desktop) and then put it online as described above. The initial aim is to ensure that the environment is correctly set up to run both HTML and server-side scripts, in this case, PHP scripts. To do this, create a **php** folder in the **www** folder that is in the **wamp** folder created during installation. Next, create the PHP script in Figure 22.9, name it "hello.php," and then place it in the PHP folder. To test if the setup is working, type the following URL in the Web browser's address window: http://localhost/hello.php. If the setup is working properly, "Hello World!" should be displayed. This means that the PHP script in the server was executed. Now you can try out the rest of the examples in this chapter, if you want to, and many others from the Web.

Like client-side scripts, server-side scripts can be written in one of various languages, including C++, PHP, Python, and Ruby. The way it works (which was generally illustrated in Figure 1.3 in Chapter 1) is that when a Web page requests a server-side script, the server fetches it, executes it, and then sends the output to the Web client, usually

```
<html>
  <head><title>PHP Test</title></head>
   <body>
      <?php echo "Hello World!"; ?>
   </body>
</html>
```

FIGURE 22.9   A PHP script embedded in HTML.

```
<html>
<head><title>PHP Test</title></head>
   <body>
      Hello World
   </body>
</html>
```

FIGURE 22.10   The output from the server after processing Figure 22.9.

in HTML. The output may also contain client-side scripts. Like client-side scripts, server-side scripts can either be embedded or be in a separate file. However, when they are embedded in HTML, the resulting document is not referred to as an HTML document and therefore does not have the **.html** extension but the extension of the language used, such as **.php** for PHP. Figure 22.9 shows PHP embedded in HTML and Figure 22.10 the HTML document outputted and sent to the browser by the server. The `<?php...?>` specifies that the line is a PHP statement and `echo` is a PHP command for outputting content; in this case it outputs "Hello World."

CHALLENGE 22.3

In the previous challenge, you tried out the script in Figure 22.9. View the source HTML source produced in the browser and see how similar it is to the one in Figure 22.10.

One of the functions that server-side scripts are used for is processing the data collected with a form. Typically, processing would involve, for example, storing the data in a database or using it to retrieve relevant data from the database and sending the retrieved data to the browser. Figures 22.11 and 22.12 show an example of how an HTML form and a server-side PHP script work together.

In the example, the form requires a user to type in their name and age. It also specifies that the script to use to process the data is "personal.php" and that it is situated in the php folder. When the submit button is pressed on the form, the data are packaged

```
personal_form.html

<html>
  <head>Form</head>
  <body>
    <form action="/php/personal.php" method="post">
      Name: <input type="text" name="name">
      Age: <input type="text" name="age">
      <input type="submit">
    </form>
  </body>
</html>
```

FIGURE 22.11   An HTML form document that is linked to a server-side script in Figure 22.12.

```
personal.php

<?php
 $name=$_POST['name'];
 $age=$_POST['age'];
 echo "Hi"." ".$name;
 echo "<p>";
 echo "You are"." ".$age." "."years old";
?>
```

FIGURE 22.12   The server-side script called by the HTML in Figure 22.11.

and sent to the Web server through the POST method where the specified server-side script is used to process the data. The script, in this case, simply extracts each of the form data, name, and age, and stores them in variables $name and $age, respectively, after which it outputs "Hi," plus a space, plus the content of $name, then a paragraph, and then "You are," plus a space, plus the content of $age, plus a space, plus "years old," after which it sends everything to the browser. So, assuming "Joe" and "35" are inputted for name and age on the form, respectively, the script returns "Hi Joe" "You are 35 years old."

If the data are to be stored in a database, then the script will open one and insert them as necessary. If the data are to be used to retrieve data from a database, then, similarly, the script opens one and uses the data to search for matches, which are then sent to the browser. Examples of the general principles that guide these operations are presented shortly. As mentioned in Chapter 5, to ensure that correct data are sent to the server in the first place, it is normal and good practice to validate them (using HTML or JavaScript) before submitting a form. All these and more are typical processes required for Web applications that collect user-data, which include e-commerce and social sites.

CHALLENGE 22.4

To try out the example in Figures 22.11 and 22.12, create the HTML file in figure 13.11 in Chapter 13 and place it in the **www** folder in the **wamp** folder. Next, create the PHP script and place it in the PHP folder. It is good practice to keep scripts separate from HTML files. Indeed, some Web host services require this. Next, ensure that WampServer is running and online, as previously described, and type the following URL in the Web browser: http://localhost/personal_form.html. A form should be displayed. Complete and submit it. If everything works, you should get a message that includes your form input.

22.4.2.1 Using Server-Side Script with AJAX

Traditionally, the way the data that are sent to the Web browser by the Web server is displayed is to replace the whole of the current page with a new one containing the sent data, even if only a small part of the current page needs to be updated with the data. This is inefficient and inconvenient. To address this issue, a more efficient technology known as Asynchronous JavaScript and XML **(AJAX)** has since been developed that allows Web applications to communicate with a server asynchronously. Basically, it allows data to be sent to and retrieved from a server in the background, without refreshing the current page or interfering with its current state in any way. The framework combines JavaScript with various Web technologies, both existing ones and new ones. Central to the asynchronous communication process is a special JavaScript object called XMLHttpRequest, which is used to send data to a server as well as receive data from it. To cater to older Internet Explorer browsers, the object may also be called ActiveXObject. A basic example of how AJAX is used with HTML is presented in Figures 22.13 and 22.14, in which a form containing a single text field and a button is displayed. Clicking the button displays the current server time both in the text field and in an alert box, just to demonstrate more than one usage.

In the example, a function, named **ajaxFunction()**, is defined that is called when the button on the form is clicked. In the function, a new instance of the XMLHttpRequest object is created and named ajaxRequest. An object is a self-contained piece of data that comprises its own set of **properties** (which can be changed or retrieved) and **methods** (which are actions it can perform, either automatically or as a result of being instructed to perform them). The open() method of the ajaxRequest object specifies via its three parameters to (1) send the form request to the server via the GET method, (2) use the specified script to process the request, and (3) handle the request asynchronously. The send() method sends the request.

When the request is sent to the server, the onreadystatechange event is triggered in the ajaxRequest object when the status of its readyState property changes. The example says when the onreadystatechange event is triggered, and if the status of the readyState property is "4" (i.e., if the server's response to request is completed), to assign the content of the responseText property of the ajaxRequest

```
serverTime.html

<html>
  <head>
    <script language="javascript" type="text/javascript">
      function ajaxFunction() {
        var ajaxRequest;
        ajaxRequest = new XMLHttpRequest();
        ajaxRequest.open("GET", "serverTime.php", true);
        ajaxRequest.send(null);
        ajaxRequest.onreadystatechange = function(){
          if(ajaxRequest.readyState == 4){
              document.dataForm.time.value = ajaxRequest.responseText;
              alert(ajaxRequest.responseText);
          }
        }
      }
    </script>
  </head>
  <body>
    <form name="dataForm">
      Current Time: <input type="text" name="time"><br>
      <input type="button" onclick="ajaxFunction()"
       value="Check Time">
    </form>
  </body>
</html>
```

FIGURE 22.13 JavaScript-AJAX used with HTML to call the server-side script in Figure 22.14 that displays current server time.

```
serverTime.php

The time is:
<?php echo date("H:i:s"); ?>
Thank you!
```

FIGURE 22.14 The server-side script called by the AJAX function in Figure 22.13.

object to the value attribute of the HTML element named "time," which is in the form named "dataForm" (which is the form that sent the request). The result is that when the form button is clicked, the ajaxFunction() is called and a request sent to the server, which executes the **serverTime.php** script in Figure 22.14, which returns the server's current time, which is sent to the browser and stored in the responseText property, which is assigned to the value attribute of the <input> element named "time" in the form named "dataForm." Assigning the returned time to the value attribute automatically displays it in the text field. Also, the alert() method displays the time (content of `responseText`) in an alert box. All this is done without reloading the page or changing anything else on it.

22.4.2.2 *Server-Side Script, AJAX, and Database*

As mentioned earlier, server-side scripting is central to storing data in or retrieving them from a database, while a database is central to any Web application that stores information. Databases come in various genre, such as relational, object-oriented, and NoSQL, just as there are many implementations of each genre. One of the most commonly used open-source software database systems is **MySQL** and it is the one used for demonstration here. It is a relational database system, which in basic terms means it is a system of databases that contain collections of tables that can be interlinked through their columns. So, a database contains many tables, each of which is used to store data in an organized way, any of which may be linked to produce a cohesive report. For example, a database called "A_Company" might contain a table called "Customer" that stores customers' details, another, "Order," that stores their current orders, and another, "Transactions," that stores the completed orders, and so on. From such a database, server-side scripting can be used to generate a report, for example, to list all customers and the outstanding and completed orders for each.

In all cases, when writing data to or reading data from a database, the typical procedure is to first connect to the database, open it, and then query the relevant tables, using statements written, for example, in a special language known as Structured Query Language (**SQL**). Again, AJAX can be used to send and receive data retrieved from a database.

22.4.2.3 *Storing Data in Database*

Figures 22.15 and 22.16 show a basic example for collecting data with an HTML form, packaging and sending it to the server using AJAX, and storing it in a MySQL database using server-side scripting.

In Figure 22.15, a form is displayed that requires the user to enter username, password, and postcode. When the submit button is clicked, the **ajaxFunction()** is called to package and send the data to the server. In the `ajaxFunction()`, as in the previous example, a new instance of the `XMLHttpRequest` is created and named `ajaxRequest`. The data entered in the input fields by the user are then stored in variables, respectively, and a string of **name-value pairs** constructed with them and placed in another variable. The `open()` method specifies via its three parameters to (1) send the form data to the server via the GET method, (2) use the specified script (**storeData.php**) to process the data, and (3) handle communication with the server asynchronously. The `send()` method submits the form data to the server.

Once the form data gets to server, the **storeData.php** script connects to the database and opens it for use, after which the code for querying it (the **SQL** statement) is built. The code is used to query a table called "**users**" in the database, which contains columns (or fields) named username, password, and postcode. Essentially, when the SQL statement is executed, the values of `$uname`, `$pword`, and `$pcode` (i.e., data from the form) are inserted in the next new row in the table.

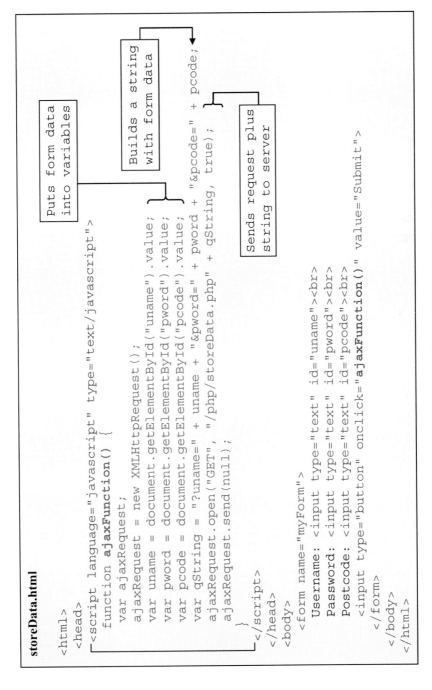

FIGURE 22.15 HTML and AJAX used to call the server-side script in Figure 22.16 to store form data.

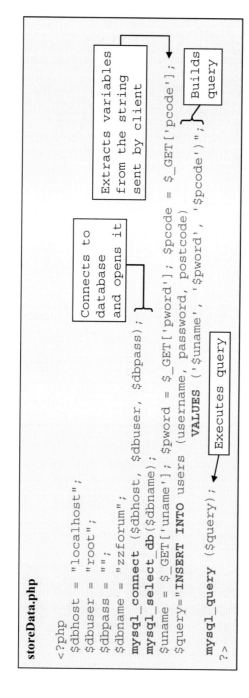

storeData.php

```php
<?php
$dbhost = "localhost";
$dbuser = "root";
$dbpass = "";
$dbname = "zzforum";
mysql_connect ($dbhost, $dbuser, $dbpass);
mysql_select_db ($dbname);
$uname = $_GET['uname']; $pword = $_GET['pword']; $pcode = $_GET['pcode'];
$query="INSERT INTO users (username, password, postcode)
          VALUES ('$uname', '$pword', '$pcode");
mysql_query ($query);
?>
```

Connects to
database
and opens it

Extracts variables
from the string
sent by client

Builds
query

Executes query

FIGURE 22.16 Server-side script called by Figure 22.15.

CHALLENGE 22.5

If you are feeling up to it, try out the example in Figures 22.15 and 22.16. To do this, you need to create the database and the table used in the example. Incidentally, you do not need to worry about installing MySQL and PHP, because these were also installed automatically when you installed WampServer in the earlier challenge. So, to create the database and the table, first, ensure that WampServer is running and online, as described in the previous challenge, and then right-click the WampServer icon on the taskbar and choose "MySQL console" on the menu. If you are asked for a password in the MySQL window that appears and you never specified one during WampServer installation and configuration, then simply press Enter to continue to the command prompt. Then, from the prompt, using the commands and examples provided at the websites listed below, or at similar MySQL tutorial sites, create a database named "**zzforum**" and "**show**" it to ensure that it is created. Next, open the database (i.e., "use it") and create a table called "**users**" that has the fields: **username** (20 characters), **password** (20 characters), and **postcode** (7 characters). The fields are all of type **varchar**. Again, "show" the table and display its structure to check that it is correctly created.

> http://www.pantz.org/software/mysql/mysqlcommands.html
> http://www.tutorialspoint.com/mysql/mysql-create-database.htm
> http://dev.mysql.com/doc/refman/5.7/en/tutorial.html

To add records to the table using the codes in the example, create **storeData. html** and place it in the **www** folder of the **wamp** folder. Then create **storeData. php** and place it in the **php** folder in the **www** folder. Next, enter http://localhost/ personal_form.html in the browser to display the form. Complete and submit it. If everything has worked properly, the record will be in the database when you query the "**users**" table, using the appropriate SQL statement (e.g., select * from users;).

22.4.2.4 Retrieving Data from Database

Figures 22.17 and 22.18 show a basic example of collecting data with an HTML form, packaging and sending it to the server with AJAX, using it to search a database, and returning the result, using server-side scripting.

Figure 22.17 displays a form that consists of a field for the user to enter a postcode, a submit button, and the text "Records are listed here" under it. Where the text is placed is where the result of the search of the database will be displayed. As in the previous example, when the submit button is clicked, the **ajaxFunction()** function is called to package and send the inputted data to the server. The `ajaxFunction()` function creates a new instance of the `XMLHttpRequest` object and names it `ajaxRequest`. It then places the postcode data from the form in a variable (`pcode`), creates a **name-value pair** with it, and stores in another variable (`qString`). The `open()` method says to send the data via

retrieveRecords.html

```html
<html>
  <head>
    <script language="javascript" type="text/javascript">
      function ajaxFunction() {
        var ajaxRequest;
        ajaxRequest = new XMLHttpRequest();
        var pcode = document.getElementById("pcode").value;
        var qString = "pcode=" + pcode;
        ajaxRequest.open("POST", "/php/retrieveRecords.php", true);
        ajaxRequest.setRequestHeader("Content-type",
                            "application/x-www-form-urlencoded");
        ajaxRequest.send(qString);
        ajaxRequest.onreadystatechange = function(){
          if(ajaxRequest.readyState == 4){
            listRecords.innerHTML = ajaxRequest.responseText;
          }
        }
      }
    </script>
  </head>
  <body>
    <form>
      Enter Postcode: <input type="text" id="pcode"></br>
      <input type="button" onclick="ajaxFunction()" value="Search">
    </form>
    <div id="listRecords">Records are listed here.</div>
  </body>
</html>
```

FIGURE 22.17 HTML and JavaScript-AJAX used to call the server-side script in Figure 22.18 for retrieving data from a database.

the POST method, process it with the script called **retrieveRecords.php**, and use asynchronous communication. The setRequestHeader() method adds an HTTP header to the request to set its content type to "application/x-www-form-urlencoded," which is the default content type for a POST request and required for a POST request via AJAX. The send() sends the data to the server.

On the server-side, the posted data are passed to **retrieved_Records.php** (the script in Figure 22.18), which opens the relevant database (**zzforum**), isolates the postcode, and uses it to search the "**users**" table in the database for record that match it, using the mysql _ query() function. If any matches are found, the records are stored in **query-result** variable. A table is then constructed with the data of the records, stored in the **record_string** variable, and outputted to the browser, where it is stored in the ajaxRequest.responseText property of the ajaxRequest object. Once the onreadystatechange event of the object is fired to indicate

```
retrieveRecords.php

<?php
$mysql_link = mysql_connect("localhost", "root", "");
mysql_select_db("zzforum") or die(mysql_error());
$pcode = $_POST["pcode"];
$query="SELECT * FROMusers WHERE postcode='$pcode'";
$query_result=mysql_query($query) or die(mysql_error());
$record_string = "<table>";
$record_string .= "<tr>";
$record_string .= "<th>Username </th>";
$record_string .= "<th>Password </th>";
$record_string .= "<th>Postcode </th>";
$record_string .= "</tr>";
while($row = mysql_fetch_array($query_result)){
    $record_string .= "<tr>";
    $record_string .= "<td>$row[username]</td>";
    $record_string .= "<td>$row[password]</td>";
    $record_string .= "<td>$row[postcode]</td>";
    $record_string .= "</tr>";
}
$record_string .= "</table>";
echo $record_string;
?>
```

> Builds a string containing the HTML code for displaying retrieved records in a table format

> The string of HTML code is outputted

FIGURE 22.18   The server-side script called by Figure 22.17.

that the status of the `readyState` property has changed and the response from the server is completed, the content of `ajaxRequest.responseText` is placed in the `<div>` element of `id="listRecords"`, which automatically displays it. The `innerHTML` is a property that is used to access the text between the tags of an HTML element.

CHALLENGE 22.6

The challenge here is to retrieve the data stored in the previous challenge. To do this, you simply create the files in Figures 22.17 and 22.18 and place them in the appropriate folders in the WampServer, as described, again, in the previous challenge. If everything works properly, when you enter a postcode, the records with postcode that match it are listed in a table.

22.5 Optimizing Website Performance

Website performance generally revolves round how quickly a Web page downloads and renders completely, and a number of factors affect this. These include too many requests to the Web server, too many media objects (especially images), media objects that are too large, and large quantity of codes. While making too many requests to the server may be a less common practice, the use of large media objects, too many media objects, and large volume of codes is common. Quick page download and quick rendering times are crucial because they can determine whether or not visitors decide to stay and look at a website or whether they have good user-experience if, due to some circumstances, they must look at it. In other words, the success of a website can depend on it.

The main way to minimize page download time is to optimize the assets used in creating the page. These assets largely fall under **text-based**, **image-based**, and **font-based** assets. Their optimization involves, in the main, minimizing their size, which is achieved mainly through data compression, mentioned in Chapters 6 and 7. As you might have gathered from these chapters, compression is the process of encoding data using fewer bits and there are many compression techniques and algorithms. Also, the types used depend on type of asset, and different ones can be combined to achieve best compression. This section presents some guidelines that are based on Google's recommendations.

22.5.1 Optimizing Text-Based Assets

Text-based assets cover both the codes used to create pages and the textual content of the pages. The optimization of codes involves first minimizing their volume through a process known as **minification**, after which text compression is applied to the minified output and also textual contents. Minification is the principle of reducing by as much as possible the volume of codes, while still retaining their meaning. This is done by removing data that are unnecessary for codes to run, such as white spaces (spaces and tabs), comments, and structure. Figures 22.19 and 22.20 show the same code before and

```
<html>
  <head>
   <style>
    /* Comment */
    .home { font-size: 125% }
    .home { width: 50% }
   </style>
  </head>
  <body>
   <!--Comment -->
   <div>...</div>
   <!--Comment -->
   <script>
    runApp(); // Comment
   </script>
  </body>
</html>
```

FIGURE 22.19 Code before minification.

```
<html><head><style>.home{font-size:125%;width:50%}
</style></head><body><div>...</div><script>runApp();
</script></body></html>
```

FIGURE 22.20 Code after minification.

after it has been minified, in which the volume of the code is significantly reduced from about 400 to about 125 characters.

Although minification can be achieved manually, it is best automated and there are various tools, called **minifiers**, available on the Web that specialize in minifying different Web languages like HTML, CSS, and JavaScript, and they can be quite easy to use. Because minified codes are difficult to read, the usual practice is to not minify until the final stage of development when everything is working as intended and no further debugging is necessary. It is also recommended practice to keep the original unminified readable copies, in case changes are required later.

Applying compression to minified codes and normal textual content is typically done using GZIP compression, which can reduce text by up to 80%. All modern browsers support it and will automatically ask servers to use it on the resources it serves. A server usually needs to be configured to enable the use of GZIP. Your Web hosting company can duly advise you on the procedure.

22.5.2 Optimizing Image-Based Assets

There is no single best standard for optimizing all images, because different situations require different levels of optimization. For example, a quality that is acceptable for an icon is generally not for full-screen display. Also, there are multiple factors to consider, each of which might have more than one acceptable solution. For example, there are many different image file formats, each of which offers different capabilities, produces different levels of quality, and is suitable for different types of image contents. The following are some of the guidelines to keep in mind:

- **Use vector instead of raster images** wherever possible. This is because the quality of vector images is not affected by different resolutions and scaling (zoom) factors. This makes them suitable for situation in which an image needs to be delivered on different devices and different screen resolutions. Ideally, vector images should be produced (saved) using SVG and CSS, as this means, for example, that they can also be minified to further reduce their sizes.
- **Minify and compress SVG and CSS**: Because SVG and CSS images are produced using codes, they can be minified and also compressed using GZIP as described earlier in the text.
- **Use the most suitable raster image format**: Different raster image formats have different characteristics that make them suitable for different situations.

For example, some degrade image quality when they compress images while others do not. Similarly, some produce smaller file sizes than others at similar quality level. Some are also better for some types of image content than others. Most image editing programs allow you to choose from multiple formats and apply varying compression settings. You should reduce image size as much as possible without visible signs of degradation for optimum size.

- **Deliver images at the size they will appear on a page** instead of using HTML attributes or CSS properties to reduce them to the required size. This minimizes the amount of unnecessary pixels. For example, if you intend for an image to be displayed at 250×250 and you create it at 300×300, you will end up with 27,000 (i.e., $300 \times 300 - 250 \times 250$) unnecessary pixels.

22.5.3 Optimizing Web Font

The use of Web fonts in Web design is an increasingly standard practice because they largely eliminate the need for fonts to be installed in users' computers and provide a wide range of font options. The following are some guidelines for optimizing them:

- **Be conscious of font use**: Minimize the number of fonts and the number of variants of each font used on your pages to help faster download.

- **Breakdown your font resources**: To minimize the size of font files for a page and aid faster download of the page, **large font families should be broken into subsets**, so that only the glyphs necessary for the page are delivered. For example, if you have a page that uses multiple styles and weights from a font family, each can be specified separately. This can be done, as shown in Chapter 13, through using `unicode-range` with the `@font-face` at-rule and subsetting, based on **Unicode scripts** (e.g., Latin, Greek, and Cyrillic scripts).

- **Serve optimized font formats**: Provide each font used in WOFF2, WOFF, EOT, and TTF formats (again, as shown in Chapter 13), and ensure that EOT and TTF, which are not compressed by default, are GZIP-compressed.

- **Ensure the reuse of fonts between pages**: Make sure that font resources are cached for long enough to allow reuse. This is typically achieved through ensuring that the server is configured to instruct the browser correctly to do this when it serves its resources. This is usually done through: (1) using the **Cache-Control** HTTP response header to specify browser caching behavior, and (2) using the cache response directive, **max-age**, to specify for how long resources should be cached. Additionally, the **ETag** HTTP header is used to ensure that even if the time for which to keep a resource has expired, if it is the same as the browser is requesting, it is used and not downloaded again.

- **Give font loading high priority**: Typical browsers' default behavior is to delay the download of fonts until other critical resources for a page have been downloaded. This is known as the **lazy loading of fonts** can lead to the "blank-text problem" or "Flash of Invisible Text" (FOIT), where the browser renders a page briefly without the text, or "Flash of unstyled content" (FOUC), where a page appears briefly with the browser's default or fallback font before loading the external stylesheet and rendering the text in the correct fonts. Various ways of solving these problems are available on the Web and commonly involve scripting.

22.6 Useful Info

22.6.1 Web Links

SASS/SCSS: sass-lang.com, thesassway.com

LESS: lesscss.org

STYLUS: learnboost.github.com/stylus

JavaScript tutorial: javascript.com

PHP: secure.php.net

AJAX: developer.mozilla.org/en/docs/AJAX, api.jquery.com/jquery.ajax/

Server packages: apachefriends.org,wampserver.com

Part III

Web Design Principles and Practices

23

Design: The Fundamentals

23.1 Introduction

Visual designs are made up of different individual elements that range from text to static and motion graphics. When these elements are combined appropriately according to certain well-grounded principles, the result is a meaningful and aesthetically pleasing design. These qualities have been recognized to play a significant role in how positively people judge, for example, a website. This chapter discusses various factors and principles that can help in the creation of meaningful and aesthetically pleasing visual designs.

23.2 Learning Outcomes

After studying this chapter, the reader should:

- Understand the role of aesthetics in visual design.
- Know how various elements of visual design are used.
- Be aware of the principles that guide the meaningful use of visual design elements.
- Understand the role of grid systems in visual design.

23.3 Visual Aesthetics in Design

Visual aesthetics plays an important role in the way a design is perceived and, therefore, in its acceptance. This observation persists, irrespective of the medium on which a design is presented, be it paper or computer screen. For example, research over the years has suggested that aesthetics is closely linked to how usable users judge a website. It has also been found, together with other design attributes, to be crucial to how users perceive and learn information as well as how they judge the credibility of a website. Similarly, it has been found that the best predictor of users' overall impression about a website is its perceived beauty and such judgment is usually instant.

The aesthetics of a website has also been found to be a strong determinant of users' satisfaction and pleasure and therefore the judgment of whether or not a website is appealing and easy to use. For example, **harmonious designs** (i.e., those typically judged by users to have high aesthetic quality) engage users and give them the sense of order and visual balance, while disharmonious designs are often found to be uninteresting and chaotic. The implication from these research findings is that although aesthetics does not replace content or make bad content good, it goes a long way in determining whether or not a website gets a second look.

Many factors are said to contribute to the judgment of aesthetics. In their research papers, Moshagen and Thielsch, for example, define the following:

- **Colorfulness**, which is defined in terms of the selection, placement, and combination of colors, has been identified to be one of the four core dimensions of websites aesthetics. **Color schemes**, discussed in Chapter 9, are a major contributor to this.
- **Simplicity,** which relates to Gestalt's principle of using simple, easily meaningful, and well-structured form or layout to achieve a good design.
- **Diversity,** which relates to the quality of variety, creativity, novelty, visual richness, interestingness, and dynamics.
- **Craftsmanship,** which relates to whether a website is designed with skill and adequate consideration, using up-to-date technologies.

There is also an 18-item questionnaire or instrument called Visual Aesthetics of Website Inventory (**VisAWI**) by Moshagen and Thielsch, with which these factors can be measured to evaluate the aesthetics of a website. Some guidelines on how to address colorfulness and craftsmanship have already been dealt with in the previous two parts of this book. Colorfulness was addressed in Chapter 9 and craftsmanship in various other HTML and CSS chapters. Simplicity and diversity are looked at in this part.

23.4 Design Elements and Principles

Design elements are the building blocks of visual design, and the principles of design are like the instructions for using these elements to build a coherent visual design that can be perceived as a unified entity, irrespective of whether the design is of an art piece on canvas or screen. The principles of design are largely derived from the observed compulsion of the brain to seek meaning to any visual stimulus, even something as relatively small and seeming insignificant as a point or dot on a blank page. Similarly, if there is more than one point, the brain instinctively tries to connect the points to derive some meaning. The compulsion to connect parts in this manner is known as **grouping**, or the **gestalt effect**, and it is how we make out shapes in a seemingly chaotic world. It is also what makes it possible, for example, to convey the essence of a shape with the use of only a few strategically placed lines or dots instead of many.

The gestalt effect (or gestalt) is a central principle of the **gestalt theory** (developed in the 1920s in Germany), which when translated in relation to a design roughly maintains that the perception that is formed of a design due to the grouping of its elements is distinct from any meaning that can be derived from any of the design's individual elements alone, and only exists when a design is whole (or unified). The implication of this is that the gestalt effect, in essence, is something that exists only in an individual's mind and unquantifiable.

The theory also attempts to describe some laws (or principles) that the brain uses to group parts into a unified whole, whether these are basic elements of design like points and lines, or complex elements formed from these basic elements. These principles inform on how best to use and organize the elements of a design to improve the chances of producing the gestalt effect. They are discussed in this section, but the roles of the basic elements of design are discussed first.

23.4.1 Basic Elements of Design

The most common fundamental elements of design include point, line, shape, form, space, color, value, and texture. They are abstract, in that singly they seldom represent anything meaningful other than the perception of their shapes. However, they can be useful for performing various diverse functions in design and have application in Web design. This section shows examples of how they can be used.

23.4.1.1 Point

A point or a dot is a design element with a position but no extension. Although using it alone may provide little meaning but perhaps intrigue, it is often when different types of points are grouped that they can become very useful in creating a design. For example, they can be used to imply shapes, forms, and patterns, as well as direct attention. Image "A" in Figure 23.1 shows examples of how points can be used to create shapes. The point at the top left, in theory, should attract attention because it is relatively isolated. The point in "B" shows a point that is also being used to attract attention. In theory, it should attract attention because it is surrounded by angular shapes and of a significantly different color.

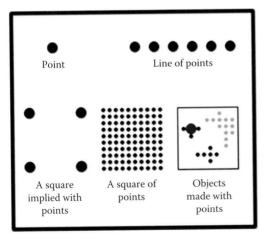
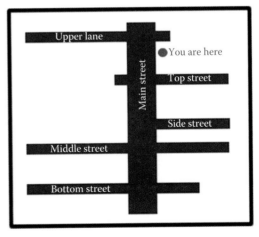

FIGURE 23.1 Examples of how points are used in designs.

CHALLENGE 23.1

Using HTML and CSS, create a line of six points as shown in "A" of Figure 23.1. Also, say how you would create from them the square of points shown in the image.

23.4.1.2 Line

Lines are one of the most basic, versatile, and commonly used elements of design, in that they are easy to produce, can be in many forms (e.g., straight, curved, and irregular), and used in the composition of almost any complex design. As a result they have many different functions in design, such as the following, which might give you some ideas:

- **Organizing, separating, and connecting objects**: Lines can be used to organize, separate, and link elements to indicate order. Figure 23.2 shows some illustrations.

- **Creating textures or patterns**: Figure 23.3 shows some simple patterns and textures. Textures or patterns may be used, for example, as background or bars in very subdued colors that do not interfere with the perception of foreground elements. Recall from Chapter 16 that patterns can be produced using CSS gradient properties.

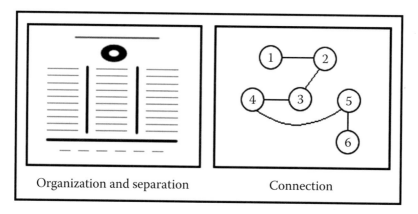

FIGURE 23.2 Use of lines for organization, separation, and connection.

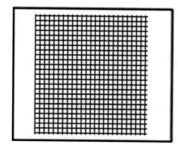

FIGURE 23.3 Examples of the use of lines in patterns and textures.

CHALLENGE 23.2

How would you subdue patterns when using them as background?

- **Guiding the eyes to a point of focus**: An actual or implied line can be used to lead the eyes to a feature in a design or an image that may otherwise be missed, especially in content presentation, as demonstrated in Figure 23.4.
- **Suggesting movement**: Oblique lines can be used to suggest movement or dynamism. Figure 23.5 gives an illustration.

FIGURE 23.4   Example of the use of line for directing attention. (Image from www.freeimages.co.uk.)

FIGURE 23.5   An oblique line being used to convey dynamism.

CHALLENGE 23.3

Why do the position of the bicycle and the orientation of the gray square in Figure 23.5 suggest dynamism?

- **Conveying specific feelings or moods**: The direction and orientation of a line can be used to imply certain feelings. For example, **horizontal lines** (as in shoreline) is believed to project rest, calmness, stability, openness, and quietude; **vertical lines** (as in pillars) can suggest power, strength, formality, height, dignity, restriction, and sometimes potential movement; **diagonal lines** (as in a slope) can suggest vitality, dynamism, and agitation; **curved lines** (as in human body) can suggest grace, beauty, elegance, movement, and sensuality; **sharp jagged lines** (as in cracked glass) can suggest violence or destruction; and **broken lines** (as in gaps) can suggest discontinuity. Using these different types of lines in an abstract design, for example, can help communicate specific feelings or moods. Figure 23.6 shows some illustrations. When lines are used to convey moods in Web design, they would usually be used in background image.

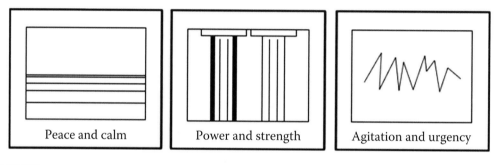

| Peace and calm | Power and strength | Agitation and urgency |

FIGURE 23.6 Examples of the use of lines for communicating feelings and tone.

CHALLENGE 23.4

State the mood typically associated with each of the following and how you would use lines to convey them:
- A Military website.
- A website for organizing rave parties.
- A website for bank or financing company.
- Cruise holiday.

CHALLENGE 23.5

Do a search with the term "mood lines" to see more about the use of lines for creating mood.

CHALLENGE 23.6

While lines can be used in setting the mood for a design, so can colors, as previous presented in Chapter 9. Bearing this in mind, state the colors you might use to compliment the use of the lines in the illustrations in Figure 23.6 to help strengthen the intended mood and also justify your choice.

- **Providing emphasis**: Underlining words in text gives them emphasis. Figure 23.7 shows the words "basic" and "versatile" emphasized.

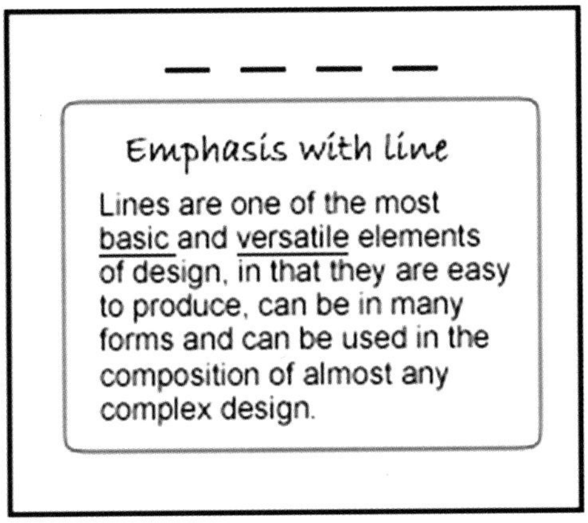

FIGURE 23.7   Examples of the use of lines for emphasis.

CHALLENGE 23.7

What is the possible problem with using underlining to emphasize a word on a Web page? If you just want to underline a word without giving it any further meaning that user agents will recognize, which HTML element and CSS properties would you use?

   Also, which other HTML elements and CSS properties underline words when used?

CHALLENGE 23.8

How can the choice of color used for underlining help minimize the possible problem posed by underlining words on a Web page?

CHALLENGE 23.9

The following are some other ways of using lines for emphasis, typically for headlines. They are called "breaking the line" and "flanking", respectively:

—EMPHASIS—   **EMPHASIS**

How would you create the two using HTML and CSS?

- **Defining shapes**: Lines are central to the creation of shapes, although shapes can also be created without lines. The types of shapes or designs that lines are used to create include logos and background graphics. Figure 23.8 shows some illustrations of the different roles lines play in creating shape.

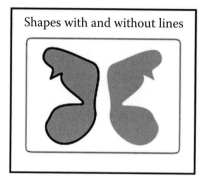 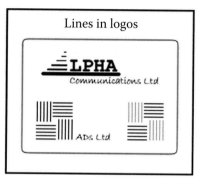

FIGURE 23.8   Examples of shapes created with and without lines.

CHALLENGE 23.10

If you have to use shapes in your design and you have the choice of delivering them in JPG or SVG formats, which would you use and why?

CHALLENGE 23.11

Like fashion, the use of shapes in Web design changes continually. To see a wide variation of how shapes are used and for inspiration, do a search with terms such as the following, as well as your own:

- Shapes used in Web design
- The use of squares in Web design

CHALLENGE 23.12

The design below was created using HTML and CSS border and flexbox properties. See if you can create it.

- **Decorating designs**: Lines can be used for beautifying a page or creating effects in various forms, including dashed and dotted lines. Figure 23.9 shows some examples. In the left design, lines are used to beautify the heading as well as depict shadows just by varying width and color. In the right design, lines are used for the hanging bar, the chains, the logo, and to border the page content.

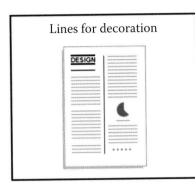
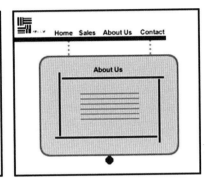

FIGURE 23.9 Examples of the use of lines for decoration and effects.

CHALLENGE 23.13

Do a search on the Web, using, for example, the term "lines in Web design" to see various examples of how lines are used.

CHALLENGE 23.14

Create the pattern below using HTML and CSS only.

CHALLENGE 23.15

Create a page design that is similar to the one below using HTML and CSS only.

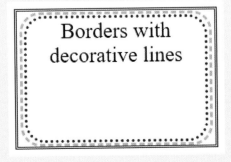

23.4.1.3 Shapes

A shape (flat figure) within the context of design elements is basically an enclosed space created as a result of the meeting of actual or implied lines. The three basic categories of shapes used in design are geometric, natural, and abstract. **Geometric shapes** are structured and include rectangles, circles, triangles, and polygons. **Natural shapes** (or organic shapes) primarily describe shapes that exist in nature, such as those of leaves. They can also be man-made; an ink blob, for example, is a natural shape. Natural shapes are typically irregular and/ or fluid at the edges. **Abstract shapes** describe approximated or stylized versions of natural shapes. Symbols on signs, such as the shape of a man or a woman used to identify toilets, fall under abstract shapes. Figure 23.10 shows examples of these different types of shapes.

Traditionally, geometric shapes, particularly those with straight vertical and horizontal lines, are more commonly used in screen designs than other types. This is mainly because squarish shapes tend to allow optimal use of space and facilitate the organization of elements. However, more rounded organic shapes do find applications in some types of websites, particularly in less formal websites, such as games and children's websites. Figure 23.11 shows some illustrations.

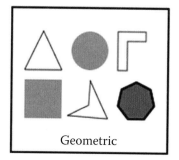

Geometric   Natural   Abstract

FIGURE 23.10   Examples of different types of shapes.

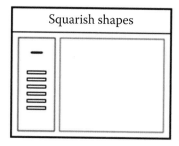
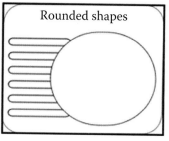
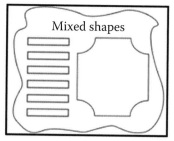

Squarish shapes   Rounded shapes   Mixed shapes

FIGURE 23.11   Varying uses of shapes in screen design.

CHALLENGE 23.16

Because design ideas continually change, the best way to know of the current trend is to explore the Web. So, do a search on the Web, using, for example, the term "shapes in Web design" to see various examples of how shapes are used.

CHALLENGE 23.17

In addition to the CSS properties presented in this book for creating shapes, more properties have since been released, but it was too late to include them in this book. Do a search for "CSS shape properties" to find out how they make it easier to create shapes.

23.4.1.4 *Size/Scale*

Visual size and scale exist together and are similar, but different. Whereas size describes the actual or usual physical dimensions of an element, scale describes the size of an element in relation to other things, including its actual physical size. Scale, in essence, is relative. Size and scale can be used to accomplish many goals in design, such as to emphasize the most important element, attract attention, create hierarchy (i.e., order of importance), create perspective, organize elements, contrast two elements (e.g., adding small text to a large element), and create interest and variety. Giving the right sizes to different elements of a design, such as sidebar, header, and the main content area, creates scale, which if right contributes to the achievement of the gestalt effect. Figure 23.12 shows the example of size and scale in use.

FIGURE 23.12   Size and scale being used to attract attention.

CHALLENGE 23.18

For which of the following types of websites would you consider the design concept in Figure 23.12 applicable, and why?

1. A website that provides services.
2. A website that sells products.
3. A website that sells books.
4. A slimming website.
5. A funeral home website.

23.4.1.5 Space

Space is the area on a page and there are two types from the point of view of design: negative and positive. **Negative space** is empty space and what a design would normally start with. Positive space is the space that contains an object. The ratio between the two is important in design. For example, a lot of negative space can make an object more conspicuous while too little can make a design appear cluttered and unattractive. Figure 23.13 illustrates negative and positive space.

Figure 23.14 shows how the ratio of negative and positive space can affect the look and feel of a design. Notice how more airy the one on the left is. With a little imagination, it is possible to see how a screen that looks like it would be more aesthetically appealing. Positive space is sometimes also referred to as **positive shape** and negative space as **negative shape**.

The other use of space in design is in depicting the illusion of depth. The main techniques used to achieve this include diminishing size and vertical position, overlapping, diminishing details, and linear perspective. Figure 23.15 shows some basic examples.

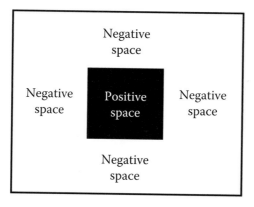

FIGURE 23.13   Illustrations of negative and positive space.

FIGURE 23.14   Effects of negative and positive space in design. (Image from www.freeimages. co.uk).

FIGURE 23.15 Illustration of the techniques used for depicting the illusion of depth in design: (a) Diminishing size and vertical position, (b) overlapping, (c) diminishing details, and (d) linear perspective.

Image A in the figure demonstrates the notions that the farther away objects are, the smaller they become and also that objects that are smaller and higher on the screen tend to be perceived to be farther away than those that are lower and bigger. **Image B** demonstrates that when an object is partially blocked by another, it gives the sense it is farther back than the one blocking it. **Image C** demonstrates that as objects move farther away, their details, such as color and value (i.e., tone), become less distinct both in relation to other objects and the background, making us perceive objects that are clear as being closer relative to those that are faded or indistinct. **Image D** shows that all lines will eventually come together at a point on the horizon (called the **vanishing point**) that is farther away. The technique is used to create a focal point in a design, where the most important object is placed. The lines used would usually be implied, using, for example, objects' alignment. Notice how in the illustration the eyes always seem to be led to the center back of the design by the lines. Any combination of A, B, C, and D can be used to produce an even stronger illusion of depth. Figure 23.16 shows an example of how overlapping is often used in a Web page to create the illusion of depth.

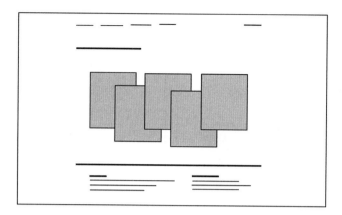

FIGURE 23.16   Overlapping being used to convey depth.

CHALLENGE 23.19

Using HTML and CSS, create four rectangles that are positioned and layered as shown in Figure 23.16.

23.4.1.6 *Hue and Value*

Value, as mentioned under the HSL (or HSV) color model in Chapter 9, refers to the relative level of lightness or darkness of a color. The lightest color has the highest value, while the darkest the lowest. So, light colors are sometimes called **high-value** (or high-key) colors, while dark ones **low-value** (or low-key) colors. Value is an important element in design and can be used to communicate various visual messages. **Gradation** in value, for example, can be **used to create the illusion of depth**, as should be evident in the use of CSS gradient properties in Chapter 16. Figure 23.17 illustrates this with two circles, one filed with plain color and the other with gradient.

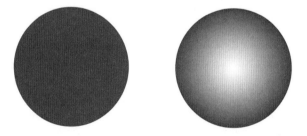

FIGURE 23.17   Example of the use of value for creating the illusion of depth.

CHALLENGE 23.20

Using HTML and CSS gradient properties, produce an effect similar to the one in the right image of Figure 23.17, filling the page with it so that it represents the background.

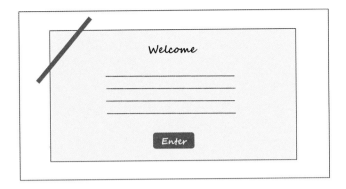

FIGURE 23.18   Value and emphasis.

Different values can also be **used to create contrast**. The farther apart the values are, the more pronounced the contrast produced. Contrast is especially useful for **creating emphasis** and **attracting attention**. For example, a light figure on a dark background is automatically emphasized, and vice versa. Figure 23.18 shows a design with different-value elements. The color of the button and the angular bar at top-left is red and that of the larger rectangle, which is light pink, was derived from adding high value to the red.

Another important role of value in design is its use in creating mood. In theory, lower values produce designs that are often described as somber and quiet designs, while higher values produce lighter, happier, more vibrant, more cheerful, or more playful ones.

CHALLENGE 23.21

How would you describe the mood projected by the design in Figure 23.18 and why? Also, whatever mood you determine it to project, how would you make it project the opposite?

23.4.1.7 Texture

Texture refers to the surface quality of an object. It is both visual and tactile. However, it is the visual dimension that is so far typically applicable in Web design. It can be described in various ways, including soft, rough, smooth, wavy, and patterned. When using texture in a design, the aim is to match it to the theme of the design. For example, a design about fashion might use the texture of fiber. It is important, of course, that a texture does not overpower the foreground elements. For example, overpowering text can compromise legibility. Figure 23.19 shows some textures as well as demonstrates the effects of overpowering textures. Notice how overpowering the textures are in the left illustration and how after they have been toned down the text is more legible in the right image. A better design also seems to have been produced.

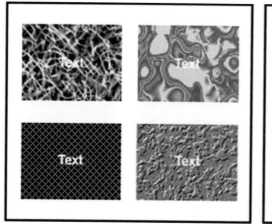 

Overpowering background   Subdued background

FIGURE 23.19   Examples of textures when they are overpowering and when they are not.

CHALLENGE 23.22

Which CSS properties allow you to create textures and patterns? Also, compare and contrast the method with using image editing programs?

23.4.2 Principles of Design

Any component of a design that can be separated and defined on its own is an element of the design; and the basic elements of design, such as dots and lines, can be organized to create a design that produces the gestalt effect that communicates a meaningful cohesive visual message. The principles described by Gestalt theory for achieving this effect are mainly balance, emphasis, rhythm, proportion, and unity.

23.4.2.1 Balance

Balance in visual design relates to the concept of visual equilibrium and refers to the way elements are distributed across a design and the perception of whether the design is visually balanced or lopsided around the pivot point of the design. Within the principle, every area of a design carries a **virtual weight** in terms of lightness or heaviness. For example, lighter colors appear lighter in weight than darker colors, neutral colors appear lighter than vivid colors, and transparent areas appear lighter in weight than opaque areas. One way to view a design when addressing balance is in terms of a set of scales or see-saw. Using the see-saw analogy, it can be imagined that a page is laid flat and balanced on a fulcrum and the various elements represent weights, as illustrated in Figure 23.20. The general idea is that a page is balanced if the total of the visual weights on one side of the fulcrum roughly balances out the total on the other side. This naturally takes into consideration the distance of each element from the fulcrum, just like with a see-saw. There are two main types of visual balance: symmetrical balance and asymmetrical balance.

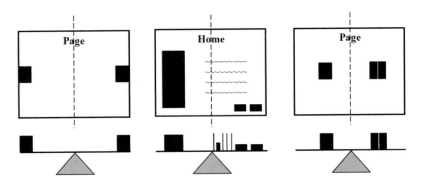

FIGURE 23.20 Illustrations of balance achieved in different ways.

Symmetrical balance (also known as **formal balance**) is when visual weight is equally distributed on either side of the central vertical axis of a design. It is achieved in two ways: pure symmetry and approximate symmetry. In **pure symmetry**, identical parts are distributed on either side of the central axis of a design. The design produced can be monotonous and uninteresting. In any case, this type of balance seldom lends itself to too many practical applications, as it is seldom possible to distribute elements identically about the vertical axis of a design. In **approximate symmetry**, the elements in the two halves of a design are varied but still similar. Ways in which this is done include varying value, texture, and shape. Designs that are balanced in this way are often more appealing and interesting. Figure 23.21 shows an illustration each of pure and approximate symmetry.

In contrast to symmetrical balance, **asymmetrical balance** (also known as **informal balance**) occurs when both sides of the central axis of a design are not identical but appear to have the same visual weight. This usually happens when several smaller elements on one side of the axis are balanced by a larger one on the other side, or smaller elements are positioned farther away from the center of the screen than a larger one. Figure 23.22 shows some examples.

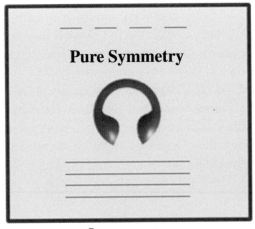

Pure symmetry

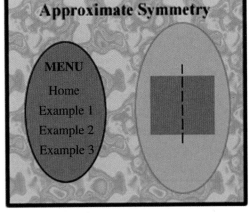

Approximate symmetry

FIGURE 23.21 Illustrations of pure and approximate symmetry.

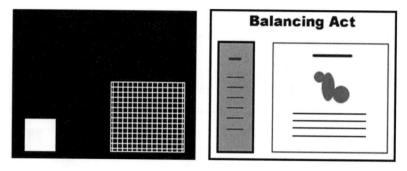

FIGURE 23.22   Illustration of asymmetric balance using density of objects.

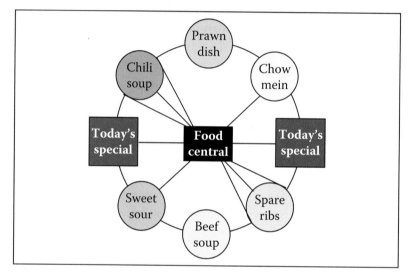

FIGURE 23.23   An example of radial balance.

Other types of balance that are not as commonly considered but might apply to a design are vertical and radial. **Vertical balance** is essentially balancing the visual weight on either side of the central horizontal axis (i.e., balancing the top part against bottom). Typically, the bottom would be visually heavier than the top. **Radial balance** is when elements are organized around the center of a design at equal distances. Figure 23.23 shows an example.

It is important for a design to be balanced, as off-balance (or discordant) designs can cause uncomfortable feelings, such as the feeling of motion. This does not mean, of course, that off-balance designs are prohibited in Web design. Sometimes it suits exactly the requirement of an application. For example, a design might be intended to project some artistic merits and be thought-provoking.

CHALLENGE 23.23

In what types of websites do you think off-balance designs might be applicable?

CHALLENGE 23.24

To see real world examples of the concept of balance in Web design, do a search on the Web, using, for example, the term "concept of balance in design" or just "balance in design."

23.4.2.2 Emphasis

Emphasis makes an element stand out and gives it importance (or dominance). This makes it attract attention. For this reason, emphasis is used to control the attention of the user. Commonly used techniques for implementing emphasis include contrast, placement, and isolation.

23.4.2.2.1 Emphasis through Contrast

Contrast causes an abrupt change in the continuity of a design and therefore in eye movement. The contrast may be due to change in any of various characteristics, including color, value, shape, orientation, and size. Figure 23.24 shows some examples. The design on the left shows emphasis through change in orientation, the middle design through change in color, and the design on the right through change in shape. By far the most powerful shape for producing contrast-based emphasis is a circular shape, mainly because most other shapes around us or in most designs are angular. For this reason, circular shapes can attract attention even without being filled with vivid colors or surrounded by white space.

Emphasis through contrast is especially invaluable for producing **visual hierarchy of importance** to aid the navigation of content. Visual hierarchy essentially controls what to look at first, second, third, and so on. It involves emphasizing important elements and organizing them logically and predictably to help guide viewers' eyes through content, so that they can view content the way intended. To implement visual hierarchy, content elements are identified based on their importance and then given emphasis accordingly, with the most important elements getting the most emphasis, the second important getting weaker emphasis, and so on. Hierarchy also makes content easily scannable. Other

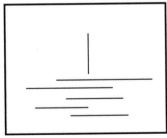
Change in orientation

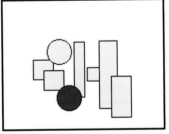
Change in color

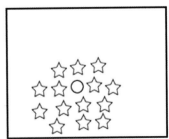
Change in shape

FIGURE 23.24 Illustrations of emphasis by contrast.

FIGURE 23.25   Illustrations of visual hierarchy.

principles used to make text scannable are discussed in Chapter 24. Figure 23.25 shows some examples of visual hierarchy application. In the left image, the eyes are likely to dart back and forth between the design elements. In the middle one, they are likely to be attracted first to the pepper, then the headline, then the footer; while in the third, they are likely to go to the headline, then to the pepper, then to the footer.

Figure 23.26 shows examples of visual hierarchy with simulated textual content. The image on the left represents a screen full of plain text; the middle represents the same text chunked up, with sub-section headings that have larger font size and bolder font style and text with jagged right edges; and the rightmost adds short text in the form of comments and excerpts from the main text. It also adds light graphics in the form of color blocks to provide more contrast.

FIGURE 23.26   Illustration of the effects of contrast on content presentation.

CHALLENGE 23.25

Using HTML and CSS, produce the layout shown in the rightmost image in Figure 23.26.

CHALLENGE 23.26

In the rightmost image of Figure 23.26, what do you recognize the hierarchy of importance to be? Also, give the reasons for your answer.

23.4.2.2.2 *Emphasis through Isolation*

When the element to which attention is to be attracted is placed some distance away from other elements and surrounded by ample space, this is known as creating emphasis through isolation. Figure 23.27 shows a couple of illustrations. The star and word on the right in the images certainly appear to have more importance, simply because they are isolated.

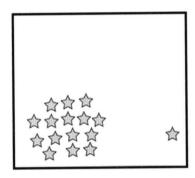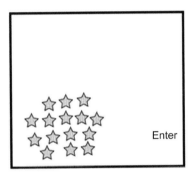

FIGURE 23.27   Illustrations of emphasis by isolation.

CHALLENGE 23.27

Which Web page do you think the design in Figure 23.27 will suit better: a home-page or any other page, and why?

CHALLENGE 23.28

In which of the following scenarios do you think it would be beneficial to use isolation for emphasis, and which element or elements would you isolate?

*   A page with a heading, sub-headings, and graphic illustrations that are cited in the text of the page.
*   A form with minimum number of fields, a form with average number of field, and a form with many fields. Each form naturally has a submit and a reset button.
*   A page where all elements hold similar level of importance.
*   A page of text with a heading and a block quotation to which you want to draw attention.
*   A page with an important paid advert.

23.4.2.2.3 *Emphasis through Placement*

Emphasis by placement is when an element is positioned such that it attracts attention. This is achieved in a number of ways. One way is to arrange an element so that other elements in a design point to it. This exploits the human tendency to look in the direction of a pointer or in the direction someone is looking. An element can also be placed in the center of a design, exploiting the human tendency to focus first on the center when a design is homogeneous; or it can be enclosed in a frame that is not so thick or whose color is not such that it overpowers the object. Figure 23.28 shows an illustration of each

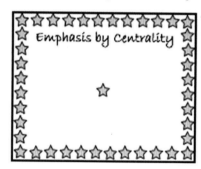 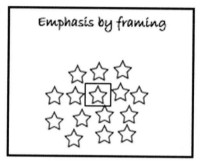

FIGURE 23.28   Illustrations of different types of emphasis by placement.

CHALLENGE 23.29

Again, which Web page do you think the design in Figure 23.28 will suit better: a homepage or any other page, and why?

CHALLENGE 23.30

Using HTML and CSS, how would you create a design similar to the one on the left in Figure 23.28? Also, how would you frame an element to give it emphasis similar to the way shown in the right illustration?

CHALLENGE 23.31

In which of the following scenarios do you think it would be beneficial to use placement for emphasis, and which element or elements would you isolate?

- A page with a heading, sub-headings, and graphic illustrations that are cited in the text of the page.
- A page where all elements hold similar level of importance.
- A text page with a heading and a block quotation to which you want to draw attention.
- A page with an important paid advert.
- The button for closing a pop-up window.

type. Other types of placements include objects overlapping or placing them such that they touch the outside edge of a design, thereby arousing curiosity.

23.4.2.3 Rhythm

Visual rhythm in design describes the timed, regular, or predictable occurrences of elements throughout a design. It is in essence the repetition of elements in a design. An advantage of visual rhythm is that it creates an easy path that the eyes almost instinctively follow. The movement of the eyes can be slow, connected, and flowing, or abrupt and dynamic, or circular, depending on the frequency of repetition, the types of repeated elements, and spacing. The repetition of similar elements or flowing circular elements produces a design that makes the eyes move through it in a connected flowing rhythmic fashion, while the repetition of unrelated elements produces a design that makes the eyes move in an abrupt and dynamic manner. Figure 23.29 shows some basic illustrations that communicate this general principle. Notice that each of the three designs has a different visual rhythm. Assuming they were producing musical beats, the rhythm they would generate would be different. Notice also that out of the three designs, "C" has the most pronounced accent. What this means is that if three different Web pages are designed to simulate the rhythm of each of the designs, the page design that simulates "C" would be the easiest to find items on, because the eyes will be guided from one point to another much more easily.

Rhythm is particularly important in long Web pages or when large amount of information is being presented. Too bland a rhythm can result in nothing standing out more than others, making it difficult for someone to locate things. This, in a sense, relates to the topic of emphasis through contrast discussed earlier. Similarly, too much rhythm can make a page look chaotic. The best approach is to design a page on the basis of how the information it contains is intended to be viewed. It may be that people are intended to read quickly through, or go from one important part to another in the first place and then read the less important parts if they wish. Figure 23.30 shows an example of rhythm being used in a Web page. It is designed to guide people to the important parts of the page. The page basically presents titles of articles and a brief description under each title. Notice how each article is presented using repeated patterns of color, text style, design elements, and alignment. Notice also how the different sections have different rhythm/ style but are not so different as to disrupt the overall feel or theme of the page.

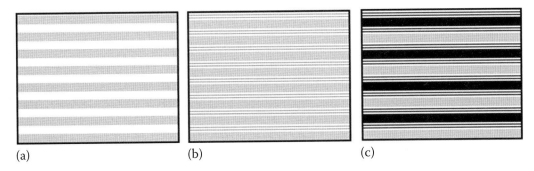

(a)   (b)   (c)

FIGURE 23.29 Illustrations of rhythm in design.

FIGURE 23.30 An example of how rhythm can be used in Web page design to guide the eyes (Image from www.digg.com).

CHALLENGE 23.32

Which of the patterns in Figure 23.29 does the rhythm in Figure 23.30 most suit and why?

23.4.2.4 Proportion

Proportion describes the relationship between the sizes of visual elements of a design as well as between the elements and the design as a whole. It is said to be good or harmonious when there is a correct or desirable relationship between the elements. To help produce designs with proportions that are considered harmonious, mathematically derived **grid systems** (or **grid theories**) have long been used by designers. The practice goes back thousands of years, and although it was originally used for technical designs, such as architectural designs, it has since been adopted and adapted in various areas of visual design, including photography, videography, graphic design, and more recently Web design. Grid systems (i.e., the ways grids are divided) vary widely. The two most commonly used are the **golden ratio** and **rule of thirds**. While these grid systems are more typically used in shot composition in photography, film, and art, they can sometimes find use in Web design, especially in content design. The grid layout model discussed in Chapter 20 is mostly concerned with the precise placement of elements rather than where best to place them for the purpose of aesthetics.

23.4.2.4.1 Golden Ratio

The golden ratio, which is also known by various other names, such as **divine proportion**, is one of the oldest and most commonly used grid systems in visual design. It was derived hundreds of years ago from the observation that a certain pattern or proportion ratio commonly occurs in natural designs, such as in horns, shells, and flowers, and because of this it is believed that it is probable that humans are genetically programmed to instinctively find it aesthetically pleasing. The value of the ratio, termed **phi**, is known to be 1.6180339 (approximately 1.618). The proportion between two geometric elements is in the golden ratio if the ratio of their sizes is equal to the ratio of the sum of their sizes to the size of the larger of the two. Using Figure 23.31 to illustrate, this means that **b/c = a/b**. As also shown in the figure, to achieve the ratio, the size of an element is simply divided by 1.618 to obtain the size for the larger part and this is then subtracted from the size of the element to obtain the size for the smaller part.

The most common evidence of the attempt to apply the golden ratio to design is in the form of the golden rectangle, in which the ratio of the larger part to the smaller part is in golden ratio. This is illustrated in Figure 23.32 with a horizontal length of 960 pixels, which is the width that is left to display a Web page at 1024×768 screen resolution in a typical Web browser, after the chrome (the edges of the browser) and space needed for the vertical scrollbar have been accounted for. Many Web pages are designed in this style or its variations.

Of course, the application of the golden ratio involves more than just dividing a rectangle into two aesthetically proportioned parts. Its application extends to using it to determine where to best place elements within a design to produce an aesthetically pleasing composition. This typically involves repeating the division process, starting

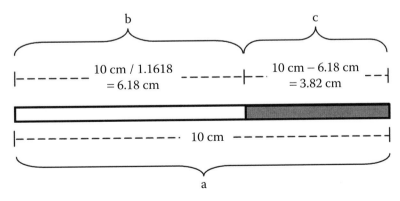

FIGURE 23.31   Illustration of the golden ratio.

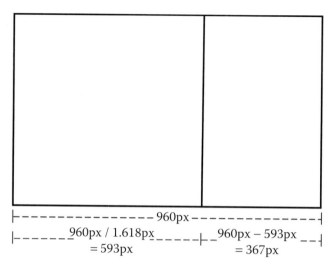

FIGURE 23.32   An illustration of golden ratio applied to 960px-wide Web page design.

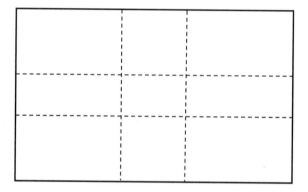

FIGURE 23.33   A phi grid derived from the golden ratio.

from every edge of the rectangle, so that a grid like that shown in Figure 23.33, known as the **phi grid**, is produced. It is believed that when the object of focus is positioned along a grid line or on the intersection of two grid lines, more tension and interest is created than simply placing the object in the center, thereby producing a more aesthetically pleasing composition.

Another interpretation of how the golden ratio should be used involves placing the **golden spiral** on a design and using it as a guide. The golden spiral, shown in Figure 23.34, is created through connecting the opposite corners of the sequence of squares produced through repeatedly applying the golden-ratio-division process to the smaller of the parts created after each process, until division is no longer practical. In any case, given its relative complexity and the fact that Web page design does not need to be perfect to the pixel, the strict application of the golden ratio is hardly necessary and generally not followed. It is often only used as a guide.

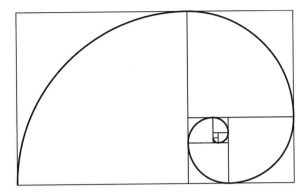

FIGURE 23.34   The golden spiral created from golden ratio application.

CHALLENGE 23.33

Use the search term "web design golden ratio" or something similar to see various uses of the golden ratio in designs.

23.4.2.4.2 Rule of Thirds

Like the golden ratio, the rule of thirds is hundreds of years old but still relevant. It is an easier system to apply in a design than the golden ratio, in that it involves just dividing a space, such as a screen, into thirds, vertically and horizontally; that is, into a 3 × 3 grid. As with the phi grid, it is believed that a design would be more appealing if the areas of interest in the design are located along the grid lines or at the intersections of the lines. Figure 23.35 shows the rule-of-thirds grid. Notice its similarity to the phi grid. Figure 23.36 shows an example of the grid being used for positioning content.

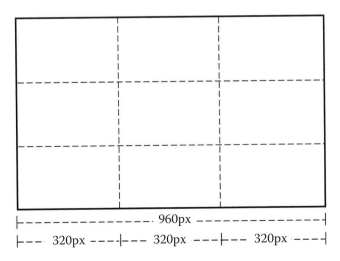

FIGURE 23.35   The rule of thirds grid.

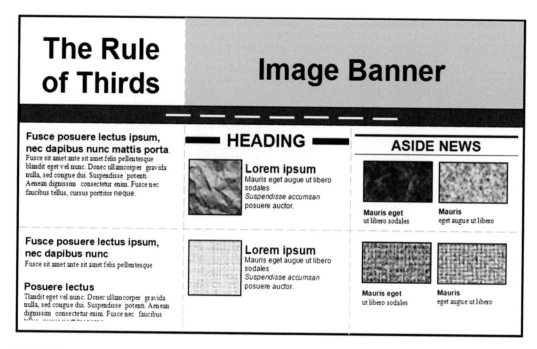

FIGURE 23.36   Using the rule of thirds grid as a guide.

CHALLENGE 23.34

Again, use the search term "web design rule of thirds" or something similar to see various uses of the rule of thirds in designs.

23.4.2.5 *Unity*

Visual unity is achieved when the various elements of a design, such as typeface, shape, color, texture, line, and space, agree and are in harmony with each other to produce a unified design (i.e., something that the eyes see and the brain likes). It is a very important goal, as it helps project the central theme of a design. It is an indicator that all the other design principles have been applied correctly in relation to each other. Without visual unity, viewers may miss certain elements of a design, or may not get its essence or connect with it. Unity is achieved using a collection of secondary principles, or methods, including proximity, repetition, closure, continuation, and alignment, which are discussed next.

23.4.2.5.1 *Proximity*

When elements are positioned close to one another, they project the sense of belonging together. This can also allow viewers to see a pattern, which can further enhance the connection with a design. To apply this principle effectively, related objects are placed closely together, as shown in Figure 23.37. Notice how the design on the right looks more compact and more structured. Many would see it to be more aesthetically pleasing.

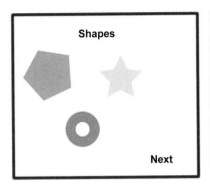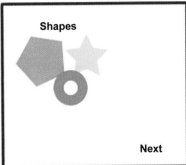

FIGURE 23.37 An illustration of the use of proximity to achieve unity.

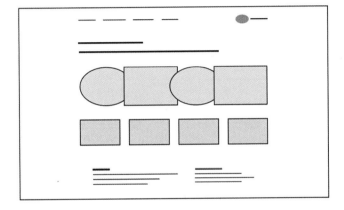

FIGURE 23.38 The proximity law used to group in a design.

In the design example shown in Figure 23.38, it is clear that it is the proximity between the elements of a group that causes the perception that they are in a group. Notice that even though the ovals and rectangles are of different shapes, their proximity to each other gives the impression they are in the same group. If all the elements in the design have been of equal proximity to one another, for example, it would be ineffective to use proximity for grouping and another technique will have to be used.

CHALLENGE 23.35

How many groups can you identify in the design in Figure 23.38 that you think are due to proximity?

23.4.2.5.2 Similarity

Elements that look similar tend to seem to belong together. Grouping based on similarity is done using three main properties: size, shape, and color/value. Figure 23.39 shows an illustration of each. Note that the proximity of elements to each other can affect the effectiveness of this principle. So if it is difficult to instantly group by size, color, or shapes respectively in the figure, it is possibly because the relevant elements

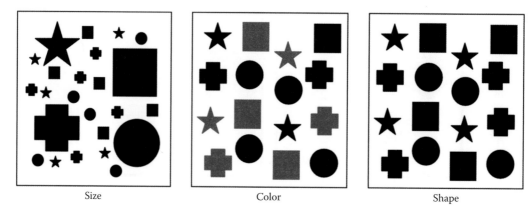

FIGURE 23.39   Grouping using similarity in size, color, and shape properties.

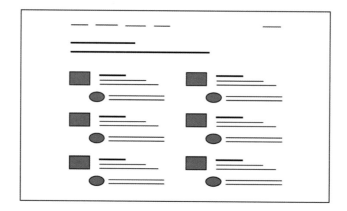

FIGURE 23.40   The effects of similarity in shapes on grouping in a design.

are too far apart. The degree to which elements that are supposed to be in a group are similar to the elements of other groups can also play a role, as does, for example, the orientation of elements.

Even when the proximity law is already used to group elements, the similarity law can still influence grouping. In Figure 23.40, for example, even though the grouping of the elements is informed by proximity between each rectangle and oval in a pair, all rectangles and ovals seem grouped by shape. For example, you would instinctively expect information with the rectangles to be of the same type, and likewise for the ovals. The use of the similarity law to group items is common with websites that sell products. It is what is at play, for example, when the products in a section of the screen are of similar sizes even when they are differently shaped.

CHALLENGE 23.36

In the middle and right examples in Figure 23.39, the property to use for grouping is not instantly perceivable, what would you do to make it clearer in each case?

CHALLENGE 23.37

In Figure 23.40, identify as many groupings as you can and state the property on which the grouping is based. Also, in what type of website can you see the layout applicable?

23.4.2.5.3 *Repetition*

Repeating elements, such as colors, shapes, textures, and lines, can create visual relationship between different elements. Typically, only the key elements of a design need to be repeated to bind the design together. This allows nonkey elements to be used to add variety, uniqueness, or character to a design to make it interesting. Repetition, of course, equals consistency. For example, consistency in theme across pages that deal with the same subject is a kind of repetition. Figure 23.41 shows a simplistic illustration. The design on the left has no repetitions and therefore looks less unified compared to the one on the right in which the key elements (i.e., the two sidebars and buttons) are identical.

23.4.2.5.4 *Closure*

Generally, complex objects are made up of smaller and simpler elements that the brain puts together as a single entity. For example, a face is a collection of different elements, including mouth, nose, ears, and eyes. The closure principle is based on the idea that if any of these elements is missing, the brain is capable of filling them in to complete a picture. In visual design, the use of the closure principle can make designs different and more interesting, provided care is exercised not to remove the vital parts of an object. Figure 23.42 shows two examples, a triangle and circle with missing parts. When the closure principle is used properly in a design, so that the arrangement of the elements that make up the design projects a discernible shape, it can help unify a design.

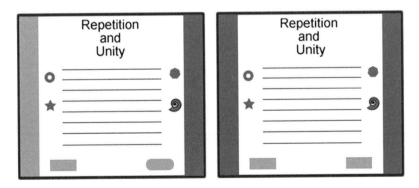

FIGURE 23.41 Illustration of how repetition can affect the unity of a design.

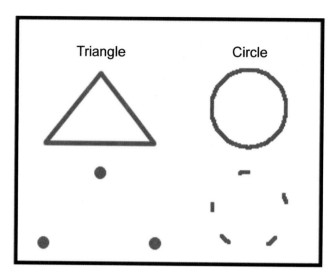

FIGURE 23.42 Illustrations of the idea of closure in design.

23.4.2.5.5 Continuity

The principle of continuity is based on the notion that when we perceive a path, we tend to continue looking along its direction, even when the path is intersected by another, until our attention is drawn by something more significant, or we have reached how far we can go in that direction. This is how when two lines intersect; we still can distinguish between them. In design, this means, for example, that if one element points to or overlaps with another, the eyes tend to continue on from the first element to the next, and so on. This tendency is usually exploited to direct a viewer's attention. Figure 23.43 shows an example of the continuity law being applied in the form of an arrow being used to direct attention to a piece of information that is important but could not be placed in a more noticeable area of the page because information about newer more important items need to be placed there. Because the continuity principle essentially involves connecting one element to another, it can also help in unifying a design.

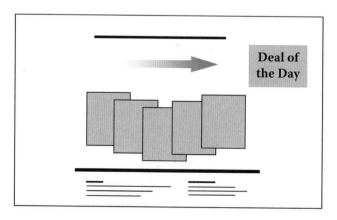

FIGURE 23.43 The continuity law being used to direct attention.

CHALLENGE 23.38

How do the rectangles in the example in Figure 23.43 convey the sense of continuity?

CHALLENGE 23.39

Again, in Figure 23.43, how else could the "Deal of the Day" sign be made to draw attention in terms of changing its property?

23.4.2.5.6 Alignment

The alignment law involves arranging elements so that their edges or centers align with those of other elements, creating more sense of harmony in a design. Figure 23.44 shows the difference good alignment can make. The design on the right certainly looks more unified and more professional because its elements are well-aligned.

Alignment can also be used in projecting a tone, as illustrated in Figure 23.45. Although there is nothing particularly wrong with the alignment of the elements of the design on the left, it is probably too symmetrical, too formal, and uninteresting. With a different alignment, plus an extra element to ensure balance, the design becomes a little more interesting and less formal, as shown in the design on the right.

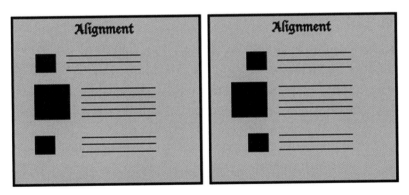

FIGURE 23.44   Illustration of the use of alignment in unity.

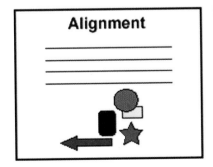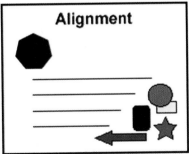

FIGURE 23.45   Illustrations of alignment.

CHALLENGE 23.40

Given the guidelines on unity, do you think that the design on the right in Figure 23.45 achieves unity, and why? If not, state how it might be made to achieve unity.

CHALLENGE 23.41

Which of the following design(s) do you think lack(s) unity/balance and why?

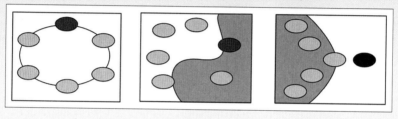

23.5 Useful Info

23.5.1 Web Links

Golden Ratio calculator: atrise.com, thegridsystem.org

Web usability guidelines: usability.gov, nngroup.com (Under "Articles") **Design examples, inspirations, etc.**: topdesignmag.com, inspirationti.me, webdesignledger.com, youthedesigner.com, creativebloq.com, veerle.duoh. com, usefulgraphicdesigntutorials.com, awwwards.com, webdesignerdepot. com, computerarts.co.uk, digitalartsonline.co.uk, design.tutsplus.com/tutorials, webdesignfromscratch.com

24

Designing for the Web

24.1 Introduction

The once totally desktop-centric approach to website design has changed a great deal since the emergence of mobile devices and the need to deliver websites on them to provide more convenient ways for people to access websites. However, many of the essential design features still remain the same and only their size change as necessary, as shown under responsive design in Chapter 21. This chapter discusses these features as they apply to websites in general and from the viewpoint of a standard screen size, while Chapter 25 deals with mobile design specifically.

24.2 Learning Outcomes

After studying this chapter, the reader should:

- Be aware of the importance of website credibility and the design factors that affect it.
- Know how to design the navigation and content components of a Web application.
- Be aware of what to consider when designing for different ages of users.

24.3 User Experience

User experience (UX) describes the experience of a user during interaction with a website, product, or service. Its study and design concern understanding users, for example, in terms of what they need, what they value, and their ability, including their limitations, all in combination with the content being delivered and the context within which user-interaction with the content occurs. Good user experience is known to:

- Improve how users perceive a brand.
- Increase conversion of visits to sales.
- Reduce customer dissatisfaction.
- Improve search engine ranking.
- Reduce costs of development and support, because it ensures a website is developed the correct way from start and reduces the amount of problems users have that require support.

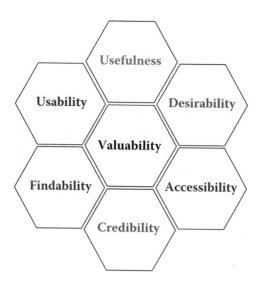

FIGURE 24.1   Adapted Morville's user experience honeycomb.

User experience is largely subjective, since it revolves around users' individual perceptions and responses to the features of a website, which can be different between users for the same website. However, it is still possible to design websites in ways that evoke similar feelings in most users, and this is the focus in the field of user experience. In order for a website to produce a meaningful and valuable user experience, the expectations of the user must be met at least the most basic level, without any fanfare or problems. Peter Morville visualizes the main factors that contribute to the achievement of this goal with a honeycomb, an adapted form of which is shown in Figure 24.1, followed by the general guidelines for addressing the factors in Web design.

- **Usefulness**: This represents how valuable users perceive the features, functions, and information provided to them. All information necessary for users to perform the tasks supported by a system should be provided, without unnecessary extras.
- **Usability**: The qualities that define the usability of a system are mainly **learnability** (ease of learning), **memorability** (ease of remembering how to use it), **effectiveness** (how effectively it can perform a task), **efficiency** (how quickly it can be used to perform a task), **errors** (number of errors, severity, and recoverability), **utility** (provision of useful functions), and **satisfaction** (how pleasant it is to use). To achieve these qualities, a website should be easy to use. Interaction techniques should be familiar and standard so that they match users' expectations. There should be no unnecessary actions or difficult processes that tax the memory, such as calculations or need to recall a lot of information. Errors should also be avoided. This is why proper testing (discussed in Chapter 26) is important. If errors occur, it should be easy to recover from them. Shortcuts should also be provided for frequently performed tasks, as should be feedbacks to communicate what is going on, to users to make them feel in control.

- **Desirability**: Design should be visually pleasing, easy to understand, minimal, and to the point. This includes using design elements, such as image, branding, or identity, in a way that evokes favorable emotion, or simply neutral emotion.
- **Findability**: It should be easy to navigate and locate content on-site or off-site. This means navigation should be intuitive and easy to understand. It should also be easy for users to find solutions to problems.
- **Accessibility**: Website should be accessible to users with disability so that they have similar experience as others. How this is done with respect to how the features of a website are implemented have been noted in various HTML and CSS chapters as appropriate.
- **Credibility**: Website should be such that users trust you enough to believe what you tell them. Because of the nature of a website to be used by total strangers who need to be convinced also by total strangers, being able to design a website in a way that effectively conveys credibility is especially important. Guidelines on this are presented in the next section.
- **Valuability**: Everything done should be toward making user experience a valuable one.

24.4 Website Credibility

The importance of the need for a website to project credibility cannot be over-stated, in that a website represents the first impression total strangers get about the owner of the site. This impression takes only a fraction of a second to form and used by visitors to make an instant judgment on whether or not to trust the owner and stay. The higher the level of credibility projected by a site the more likely visitors are to decide to stay longer. The decision to stay longer, in turn, translates into more exploration of the site, which has a higher likelihood of translating into business, whatever the form. This means that credibility is one of the key performance indicators of a website. The use of a single attribute to make an overall judgment about something in this way is sometimes known as the **Halo Effect**. An example of this effect is when the "Last updated" date is used to judge the reliability of the information on a website.

Web credibility is part of a broader area of study termed **captology**, which deals with how computers can be used as **persuasive technologies**. These are technologies designed to change attitudes or/and behaviors, without using coercion or deception. Persuasive technology, in turn, includes **Persuasive Web design**, which deals with how to design websites in a way that convinces visitors to stay on a site, believe it, and make decisions that are favorable to the site. More plainly, it is how to use design to help convert as many visits as possible into transactions. Techniques used to achieve conversion include, for example:

- Using relevant imagery to help people imagine how they might use a product to benefit themselves.
- Providing expected information, such as product or service information, cost and fees, and locating them where expected.

- Providing multiple ways of placing an order.
- Providing useful deeper content, such as reviews and testimonials.
- Providing encouragements, such as information about any rewards or discounts.
- Providing information about warranties/guarantees, if applicable.
- Providing FAQs (frequently asked questions) and answers to them.

While the broader notion of captology is yet to find a well-defined place in design, the notion of Web credibility is one that is already commonly applied in Web design. Various factors contribute to making a website credible. As mentioned in Chapter 23, visual aesthetics is an important one of these. It gives visitors a good feeling, which when they have they are more likely than not to judge a website positively almost instinctively. However, just good looks are not enough; there still has to be something meaningful and useful beyond this. Therefore, there are also operation-specific attributes that a website should have in order to further guarantee the enhancement of credibility. In addition to the guidelines discussed in Chapter 23 on visual aesthetics, this section presents others that can be used to enhance website credibility. They are summarized from findings from studies by the Nielsen Norman Group (NN/g), a group that researches user-experience, and Stanford's University's Stanford Persuasive Technology Lab.

24.4.1 Show Usefulness

Usefulness is defined as the combination of **utility** (i.e., whether the features needed are provided) and **usability** (i.e., how easy and pleasant the features provided are to use). A website should be useful by providing features that are typical for its type and the features should be easy to use. Typical features include search function, where applicable. Providing **user-specific information**, based on user's current search or/and previous interactions and transactions, may prove useful. This may be, for example, in the form of showing adverts to match, or suggesting items that the user may also consider, based on their current or past choices. It may also be in the form of listing items that others who made the same choice also chose. Amazon, for example, does this, as of time of writing. In contrast, attributes like **long download time** and **difficult navigation** certainly reduce credibility, as can unnecessary showing off of dazzling and fancy features. According to the NN/g, fancy features are one of the most common causes of long download time.

24.4.2 Show Professionalism

As well as paying attention to the elements that contribute to **visual aesthetics**, such as **good layout** and **high-quality images** for content, where applicable, and **clear navigation**, showing professionalism also involves doing various things, including showing expertise and avoiding **errors**. Website should **project expertise** by including elements to help convince visitors that its owners are experts in what they do. Elements necessary to do this depend on the relevant area. For example, credentials of owners could be provided. If the website (company) deals with or is associated with respected organizations, this should be mentioned. If website delivers information, then information should be provided about the sources of the information, such as in the form of citations and references. Links to sites that are not credible should be avoided. All types of **errors should be avoided** including design (e.g., image covering part of text), functional (e.g., a crash), broken links, and typographical and grammatical errors.

24.4.3 Manage Adverts Properly

Advertising is an important element of Web design because it is a money-making concept; as a result, most commercial websites carry one type of advert or another, including in the form of pop-ups and banners. However, **adverts seldom enhance user experience** and can put off users, as they are often a nuisance. According to studies, such as by the Nielsen Norman Group and Stanford University's Stanford Persuasive Technology Lab, advertising practices that annoy users include pop-up adverts; adverts not having a "Close" button or having one that is difficult to find; adverts covering most of the page or what users are trying to see; adverts flashing or floating across the screen; adverts automatically playing sound; adverts not saying what they are for and therefore making users click to find out; and adverts slowing page-download time. Especially bad for credibility, because they seem unprofessional and dishonest, are pop-up ads that try to trick users into clicking what looks like simple click-and-play games but are not games, and adverts disguised as normal links that end up generating pop-ups.

Usually, users feel annoyance toward both the advertisers and the websites that present them, so it is important for websites to consider the adverts they accept. In addition, accepting only adverts that are relevant to the theme of a website can reduce the probability of the adverts causing user dissatisfaction. It can also improve the chances of breaking through users' **banner blindness**, which is the habit of automatically ignoring adverts, or anything that resembles them or is next to them. If users know that what is being advertised matches their interests, they are likely to pay attention.

Too many adverts should be avoided and they should be **kept at the periphery** of a page where they are least likely to interfere with user experience. They should also **not be placed near important content**, as users may mistake content for adverts and ignore it. Similarly, **important content should not be kept in the outer area of an advert**, as users may not look beyond the advert. If an advert is not the last thing placed at the periphery, it should carry a label to indicate that it is an advert and not part of the content. Naturally, content should not look like adverts, otherwise they are likely to be ignored.

24.4.4 Show Trustworthiness

Many research studies, such as those by Nielsen, Molich, Snyder, and Farrell in 2000 and Fogg et al. in 2001, identify trustworthiness as an important component of website credibility. They also suggest that various things contribute to it, ranging from the knowledge that a website is of a real and legitimate business to the impression of how straightforwardly business is done. To show that a website is owned by a legitimate business, **contact information should be provided**, such as a physical address (including Google local map that shows the location, if possible), contact phone number, and e-mail address. Information that can also help where applicable includes showing **evidence of membership to a respectable organization** and providing the **photographs** of the business environment and of at least key employees.

To project trustworthiness in dealings with users, **detailed and useful information about transactions should be presented** as early as possible in the process, if applicable. For example, if delivery charges are involved, this should be stated clearly upfront, instead of waiting until after people have gone through the process of completing all forms, etc.; otherwise users may get the impression that a site is trying to corner them into buying at all costs. **Transaction security** and **privacy information**, such as credit card logos, should be clearly shown and there should be quick access to **clearly written terms and policies**, including assurance on how personal data will be used. Also **ensure that appropriate trust marks are displayed**, such as SSL (Secure Sockets Layer) sign for secured transaction, to assure users.

If it is software download service that is offered, download should not be described as free if it is not really free and people will be asked in the end to pay to make it work fully. If it is a **trial download**, this should be made clear from the start, as should the conditions of usage, such as time period and the level of functionality that will be available, if limited. Furthermore, a trial download should not be described as **free download**, since trial downloads are free to download, anyway. Saying that software is free download suggests that the software is free, rather than a trial version.

Where a website is selling products, the **products' photographs should be provided**, including shots that show the essential views, so that users can get a good idea of what they look like. Content should also be kept up to date, as missing or out-dated information can quickly put doubts in users' minds as to the reliability of a site. **Prices should be clearly shown** so that users can quickly use them to make decisions. For a site that provides information, **date of last update should be provided** so that users can determine whether or not the information on the site is still relevant. Also, providing **outbound links to other sites** can suggest that the owners of a site are well-informed about the service they offer. Linking a site to other sites is typically a sign that the site is not operating in isolation, has nothing to hide, and therefore may be trusted.

Users should also be provided with an effective description of a **site's purpose**. One way this is done is through the use of a **tagline on top of the home page**, which should be no more than a short and meaningful sentence describing what the company or organization does and what makes it unique among competitors. The "**About Us**" section can then provide more information. The "About Us" section basically should provide at least one or two paragraphs of information about the goals and accomplishments of the company or organization. Where it is not obvious how a website makes its money (i.e., if it is not through straightforward selling or advertising), information should be provided about this so that users do not get the impression the site has a hidden agenda. If there is a lot of information, then this can be categorized into groups (e.g., case studies and list of previous clients) and each group presented on a separate page. The "About Us" link can also be labeled "About <name-of-company>," such as "About GE," but ambiguous labels, such as "Info Center," should be avoided, as users might find locating it difficult. Also, **avoid claiming you are the best**, as people are unlikely to believe you anyway.

Simply state what you can do and have done. Having a **social media presence** can also help to show that there are real people behind a business.

Where there is registration involved, **early registration should be avoided**, as users tend to dislike or get suspicious of being asked to provide their details before they have had the chance to see any content or understand why their data is needed. Even the request for just an e-mail address can raise concerns and make users turn away if done before they have built a sense of trust in a site. Registration process should be deferred until the user has decided to commit. For example, for an e-commerce site, users should not be asked to register until they have browsed products or services, placed an order, and are ready to checkout. In addition, the process should be made as brief and easy as possible.

24.5 Designing Website Interfaces

The single overarching principle of user-interface design is that **a good interface is self-explanatory**, irrespective of type. Naturally, there are different types of Web interface designs and this is not surprising, given that a user interface is a representation of the functions offered by an application and there are different types of Web applications. In addition to this, target audience affects interface design, since different categories of users perceive things differently, have different preferences, and react differently to the same things. For example, Figure 24.2 shows two Web designs with the same basic layout but different styles to suit different target audiences. The one on the left (the less serious) is generally more suitable for children than the one on the right, which is more suited to adults. They are different in various ways, such as in color and shape. For children's designs, colors are usually more vivid and shapes are rounder and more playful, while for adults, colors are typically more subdued, shapes are more squarish, and layout is busier. Even then, there is no such thing as an interface that is suitable for all in any specific audience category, particularly when children are concerned, as different age groups prefer different types of interface designs.

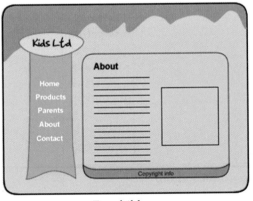
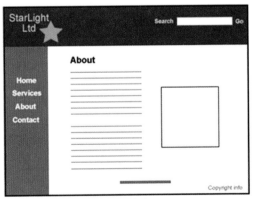

For children · For adults

FIGURE 24.2   Some comparisons between designs for children and adults.

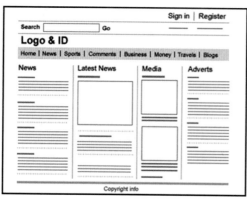
News website

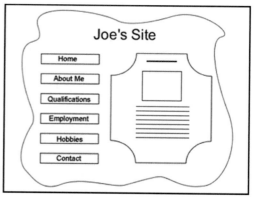
Personal website

FIGURE 24.3   Some comparisons between designs for different applications.

Similarly, Figure 24.3 shows two designs that are different because of the difference in application goals. The one on the left is more suitable for a news media website than the one on the right, which is more suitable for a personal website, or some alternative style website. The former is busier and more formal while the latter is more spacey and casual.

Irrespective of differences in higher-level features or characteristics, most Web pages, at least professional ones, can be said to comprise four main parts: header, footer, content area, and navigation. This has already been implied earlier in Chapters 2 and 19–21. The **header** is the graphic strip across the top of the page, the **footer** is the one that goes across the bottom, the **content area** is the space in-between, and **navigation** design is varied. Figure 24.4 shows the typical design components of a Web page. Within this design concept, there are myriads of variations. For example, links are embedded in content and

Header (logo, utilities, e.g., search, login, cart)		
Primary navigation (links to different pages)		
Secondary navigation (e.g., links to specific sections)	**Content area** (e.g., text, images, video, animation, and links to audio)	**Tertiary navigation** (e.g., blogs, comments, adverts, promotions, and links to external resources)
Footer/Miscellaneous information (e.g., links to terms, policies, and warrantees)		

FIGURE 24.4   Typical Web page design components.

various elements are placed in different areas. However, Web design can still be broadly categorized as comprising mainly navigation and content parts. An effective Web page design is therefore best achieved by addressing each area specifically, using the various design principles discussed so far to accomplish a design that is well organized, uses space economically, and communicates clearly at a level that matches users' capabilities.

24.5.1 Designing Website Navigation

There are various approaches to designing navigation in Web applications, but the mostly used is **persistent navigation**, which has its roots in GUI (graphical user interface) design where menus are displayed permanently and appear on every screen. One of the main advantages of this is that it creates consistency, which makes it easy for users to master an interface quickly. It enables recognizability, predictability, efficiency, and user empowerment. It enables **recognizability**, because things always look the same and users know where to find them; **predictability**, because things always work the same way and users know what to expect when they initiate an action; **efficiency**, because there is no wasting time constantly learning new features; and **user empowerment**, because users know they can rely on their past knowledge to plan a set of steps to achieve a goal. It gives the sense that they know what they are doing.

Like menus in traditional desktop GUI designs, navigation elements in Web design are distributed around the top, bottom, left, and right areas. Studies have shown that none of these positions holds any significant usability advantages over the others, as long as navigation components are clearly visible and consistently located. A combination of top, bottom, and left side is common in Web design, depending on the number of functions that need to be represented.

The exact types of navigation elements used in an application generally depend on the structure of the application and the functionalities it offers. For example, as illustrated in Figure 24.5, a Web application that has four pages and requires user-interaction to navigate them might have two elements to go to the next or previous page, if it has a **linear structure**, or four

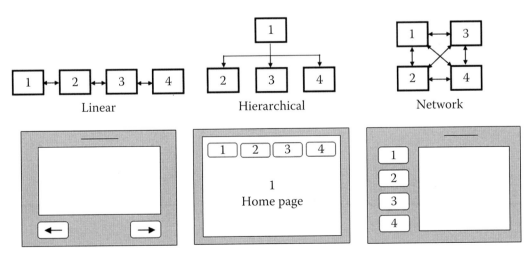

FIGURE 24.5 Examples of application structures and corresponding navigation elements.

elements, each for taking users to the corresponding page, if it has a **network structure**. For a **hierarchical structure**, the home page might have three elements for going to each of the other pages, each of which would have an element to go back to the home page. A hierarchical structure, of course, can be made to behave like a network if all navigation elements are persistent, in that users can navigate to any page from any other page.

In more complex Web applications than the examples, such as Google's on-line word processor, navigation may not only be to other pages, but may also involve opening new dialogue windows on top of the main window. The more pages or functionalities (options) an application offers, the more the number of navigation elements required in its interface. Where there are lots of elements, it is seldom practical to display all of them at once without compromising the usability of an interface, so, dividing them into groups is usually necessary. However, this can also result in a structure that contains **too many menu levels** that can make finding contents or functions confusing or frustrating. Generally, any structure that goes beyond the second level requires extra-careful planning from the beginning to reduce number of levels, if possible. In other words, the design on the left in Figure 24.6 is likely to be easier to use than the one on the right.

This means that a balance is important between having too many navigation elements on a page and a structure that is too deep. A balance might involve, for example, embedding a linear structure in a hierarchical structure. The fact that different navigation structures are best suited for different situations also helps toward reaching a balance. A linear navigation structure, for example, is adequate for presenting simple content or training materials and more suitable for children. In contrast, more complex content and more matured users benefit better from hierarchical or network structures, because these structures provide more options and flexibility.

As mentioned earlier, a combination of top, left, and bottom placement is the most common way of locating the menus for a website's navigation. When menus are located at the top area, they are usually placed in and/or closely under the header, and when located at the bottom, they are usually placed in the footer. Figure 24.7 shows an example of a permanent navigation design, identifying some standard navigation elements that are commonly included, such as application ID, links to all sections, a "you are here" indicator, utilities options, and a search facility.

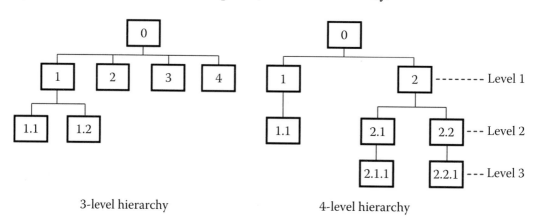

FIGURE 24.6   Illustration of different levels of hierarchical navigation structure.

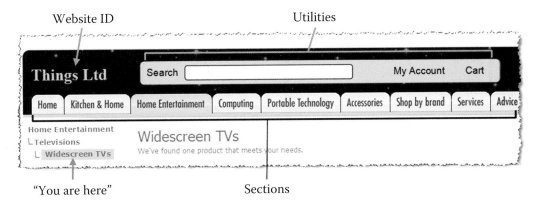

FIGURE 24.7   An example of permanent navigation.

- **Website ID**: This identifies the website and is typically in the form of a logo or name, or both, and placed at the top left area of the page/header in cultures that read from left to right, so that it is one of the first things users see. For a target audience that reads from right to left, placement would naturally be top right. Appearance should be different from the rest of the page, so that it can easily attract users' attention. When a logo is used and it does not indicate the name of the website, this should be provided clearly (typically in bold) below or on either side. Figure 24.8 shows some examples of the variations used. It is useful and standard practice to also make website ID a link to the home page, so that clicking it while on any other page takes users there.

- **Links to sections**: These are features that provide access to the sections available on a site and sometimes referred to as menus. They can be in a variety of forms; they can be buttons or hyperlinks and placed across the top of the page or vertically on the left or right side. A common convention when located in the top area is the use of **tabs metaphor**, such as shown earlier in Figure 24.5. Guidelines on the design of tabs are discussed later in the chapter. A link can lead directly to content or to further links, which can be presented, for example, through a **mega drop-down menu**, also described shortly. One of the links to sections (typically the first) should be to the home page, so that, in essence, every page has a link to the home page. For consistency, each link should also match exactly the name (title) on the page it leads to and the name should stand out clearly, be accurately descriptive of the page content, and positioned so that it is clear that it applies to the content of the page. Making a page name stand out can be achieved via

FIGURE 24.8   Examples of how the name of a site is used with a logo to form Site ID.

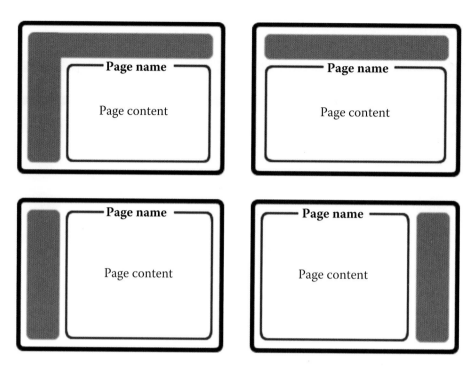

FIGURE 24.9   Illustrations of page name placement.

font style (typically bold), font size, or color. Figure 24.9 shows some examples. Although the positions of the names are centralized in the examples, placing a name at the top-left or top-right of a page can also be effective.

- **Utilities options**: These include essential facilities and information that are not part of the main content, such as Shopping Cart, Your Account, About Us, Contact Us, and Help. The types of utilities provided depend on type of application. They may be placed anywhere, but are typically placed at the top of the page to the right. Ideally, four to five should be displayed at once to ensure no item is difficult to find. Where there is not enough space to display all available utilities, the most frequently used can be displayed and others grouped under one option.

- **Search facility**: This feature provides means of searching the content of a site and is particularly essential where there is a lot of content and compensates for the tendency for complex navigation structures and content to lose users. It is placed near the top of the page, so that it is easy to see, and should be in the form of type-in text box, not a link to another page or a dialogue window, because users usually require immediate action. Also, a text box is what users are likely to look for when they want to do a search. The text box should be wide enough to contain a few words without scrolling, as scrolling makes it difficult for users to verify their input. It should also have at least an associated button for activating the search. The simple convention is a box, button, and the word "Search." The word "Go" is also commonly used on the button. Figure 24.10 shows some variations.

FIGURE 24.10   Examples of commonly used basic search conventions.

The use of fancy or unfamiliar words, such as "Find" and "Keyword Search" can be confusing, as they might make users wonder whether or not they represent the same as a normal search function. If a search of both a site and the Web is offered, any instructions to distinguish them should be short and straight to the point, such as shown in Figure 24.11.

To let users search only a specific section for a term, the search function can also include the **scope option**. Because of the tendency for users to miss the option, it is good practice to set default search scope to "All," as shown in Figure 24.11, so that the search is treated as normal. If scope option is offered, the section searched by a user should be stated clearly at the top of the result page. Advice should also be offered on the page on how to reduce scope when a search returns too many results. There seems no evidence that an **advanced search** feature is usually needed, since most users are unable to use it; but, if it is offered, it should be on a separate page, with a link to the page placed near the normal search function, such as "more" and "tips," as shown in Figure 24.12.

- **"You are here" indicator**: This feature is not strictly a component of navigation; rather, it is a piece of information to help users determine where they are within the hierarchy of a site. One way to make it perform this function effectively is through

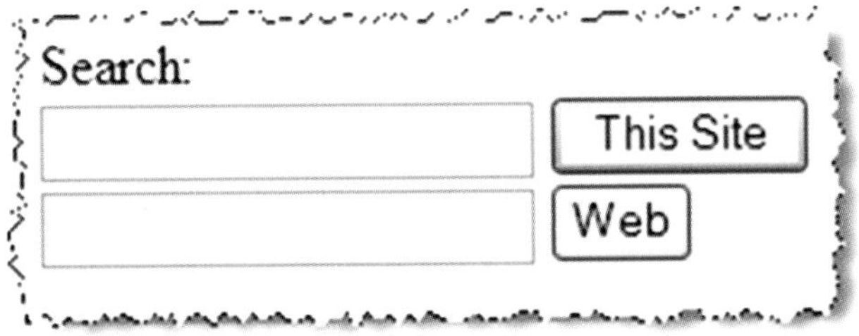

FIGURE 24.11   An example of how to provide simple search options.

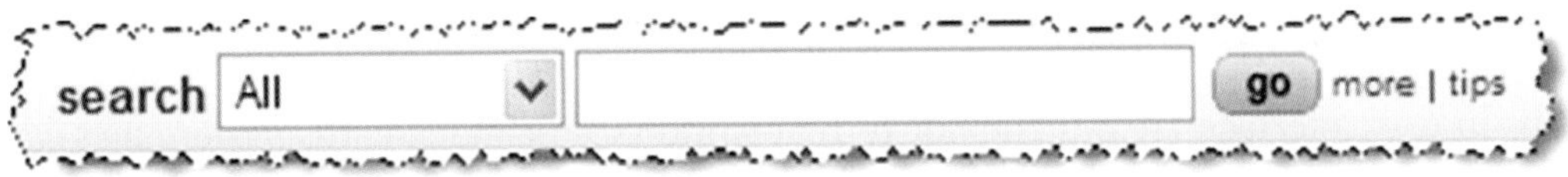

FIGURE 24.12   An example of how to provide search options.

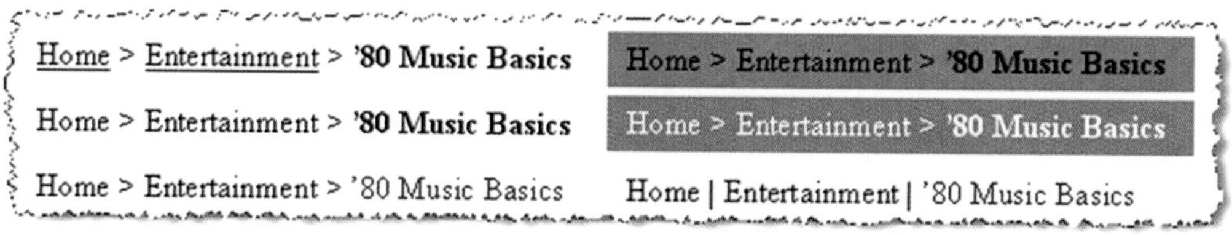

FIGURE 24.13   Examples of breadcrumbs designs.

highlighting the currently selected page in the navigation area, as well as ensuring that the item's description matches the name of the corresponding page, as shown earlier in Figure 24.6 with "Widescreen TVs" page. Highlighting can be achieved through different text or background color, text styling, such as bold text, and special characters (e.g., an arrow). **Breadcrumbs**, also known as **breadcrumb trail**, are a variation of "You are here" indicator and implemented in various ways. Like a "You are here" indicator, for breadcrumbs to be effective, they need to stand out, but without being overwhelming, since they only serve a secondary function. The **last item of the trail (i.e., the current page) should stand out** from the rest of the items in the trail. This can be achieved by using different font style (typically bold), different color, or negative contrast. Combining highlighting with **smaller but legible font size** can further ensure that a breadcrumb trail does not compete with primary navigation mechanism or content. Six different conventions are shown in Figure 24.13. As well as the types of separators (">" and "|") used in the example, other characters, such as "/" and ":", are commonly used.

   The individual items on a breadcrumb trail, except the last (i.e., active) one, should be active hyperlinks to the corresponding pages and **look clickable**; for example, they could be underlined or in a different color, typically blue. This provides additional means for users to navigate back. Again, the description of each item should match the name of the page to which it refers. To make the breadcrumb trail easy to find, it **should be placed in the top area of the page**, after the header and the menus, but before content. It can also be useful to place the phrase "You are here" at the beginning to help people who are not familiar with breadcrumbs understand its function.

CHALLENGE 24.1

Redesign the navigation interface shown earlier in Figure 24.7, including all the navigation features shown.

24.5.1.1 Tabs Metaphor

Tabs in user interface are a metaphor of real-world tabs or index cards system and can be effective for both organizing and navigating content. This is because they help users to quickly see the mix of content (sections) offered by a website and their positions within the content structure. Figure 24.6, earlier, shows an example of tabs in use. Like with any other interface component, for tabs to work well they need to be designed and used correctly. The following are some longstanding guidelines by the Nielsen Norman Group. While as much artistic freedom as required can be expressed, the principles should be followed to ensure good user experience.

- A Tab **should contain only one type of information**; so, tabs are best suited for when content can be broken up into distinct logical chunks that can fit under a tab each. This ensures both better usability and user experience than when users have to switch back and forth between tabs for related types of information.
- There should be **only one row of tabs**, as multiple rows make users jump from row to row, making them forget which tabs they have already visited. If there are too many tabs to fit in one row, then the simplification of design or the use of another navigation method should be considered. Also, **the single row of tabs should be placed at the top** where users expect them and can easily see them, not on the sides or at the bottom where they can be easily missed. Although it is not taboo to have tabs inside tabs; this can be difficult to implement in a way that does not confuse users.
- Tabs should look like the clickable versions of real-world tabs, and the **currently selected tab should appear different and "pushed out"** and be in front of the other tabs to make it easy to identify it as the selected one. This can usually be achieved by ensuring that the tab and its content area together represent one continuous space (i.e., connected) and the space is in a contrasting color to other tabs, as illustrated in Figure 24.14. If every tab is given a different color, the selected tab should have some characteristics that help to clearly distinguish it and its content area from the other tabs. This could be, for example, in the form of thicker boundaries and/or bold text for the tab label.
- The **unselected tabs should be clearly visible** and accessible and appear to be behind the selected tab.
- The **scope of the content area** of a tab should also be clearly defined so that users know what falls under the tab.

Good: Active tab stands out

Bad: Tab and its content area not continuous

Bad: Active tab does not stand out from other tabs

FIGURE 24.14 Illustrations of good and bad tabs designs.

- Each **tab should carry a short descriptive label** (between one and two words) that is not in all caps (to ensure legibility) and follows a capitalization convention, such as capitalizing only the first letter of a sentence, or using **headline-style capitalization**, in which the first letter of every word (except articles and prepositions) is capitalized. The labels of the **unselected tabs should always be clearly visible** to keep users mindful of other options available.
- When a new tab is selected, the corresponding panel should be **displayed instantly** in a fraction of a second.

CHALLENGE 24.2

Tabs used to be implemented mainly through creating the images for the tabs in an image editing program and then incorporating them in HTML. Now tabs can be done using HTML and CSS. Without necessarily implementing one, what do you imagine the implementation logic will be to implement one, given above guidelines; and which CSS properties do you think you might use?

24.5.1.2 Drop-Down Menus

In complex Web applications, there are usually many functions and therefore many options to present to the user. The way this presentation is done effectively is through **drop-down menus**. This is a menu that drops from the menu bar, or navigation bar (**navbar**), when the user activates a menu by, for example, pointing at it, clicking it, or touching it. Once activated, the menu remains open until further action is taken by the user. Such action could be the user choosing a menu item or clicking outside the menu. A drop-down menu is different from a **pull-down menu**, which is pulled down from the menu bar and remains that way until released. It is also different from a **pop-up menu**, which is displayed when the user operates, for example, the right mouse-button.

In order to ensure drop-down menus are easy to use, **good organization is important** and this is achieved by **logically grouping related options** under one menu and **ordering them**, using criteria like frequency of use, importance, sequence of use, relationship with other listed options, and/or alphabetical order. If the options under a menu can be further grouped, this should be done to reduce the length of the menu-items list. Every menu and sub-menu (sub-group) should be given a name that adequately describes what it offers.

How menu items are ordered and laid out in a drop-down menu also affects how easily users can work with them. The items are traditionally displayed vertically in a single column, and **left-aligned** (i.e., for left to right reading). This makes each new line start at the same vertical point and allows the user's eyes to move straight down the menu, thereby aiding scanning. According to the NN/g, to further facilitate scanning, menu items should also start with the **most information-carrying words** to quickly inform users as they scan. **Starting items with the same words should be avoided**, as this means users are forced to look beyond the first word to distinguish between the options.

Navbar

Top-level
option

Mega drop-
down menu

FIGURE 24.15 Example of a mega drop-down menu once in use at actionenvelope.com.

Combining **vertical and horizontal arrangements** can also be effective. It makes the menu more compact and also shows more items at a glance, thereby reducing reliance on short-term memory when users are comparing the items. As well as this, it allows for the use of icons, which can aid faster recognition of the functions of menu items. An example of the approach is the **"Ribbon" design** introduced with Microsoft Word 2007. In Web design, the "ribbon" design is generally known as **mega drop-down menu**. Figure 24.15 shows a smallish example.

To ensure that a drop-down menu behaves in a way that aids usability, **response time** when the cursor points to a menu should not be too slow or too fast. If it is too slow it will feel like users are not in control, and if it is too fast, there may be too much flickering when the mouse is moved across the navbar, which can affect some users adversely. The general guideline is that it should start displaying after the cursor has hovered over its label for about 0.5 seconds and finish displaying within 0.1 seconds of starting. It should then remain displayed for as long as the cursor remains on it and starts to close about 0.5 seconds after the cursor has moved outside it or its label (or the navbar).

CHALLENGE 24.3

What are the advantages and disadvantages of using mega dropdown menu?

24.5.1.3 Site Map

A site map is a form of table of contents and is typically most useful when a site is very large, or when content pages, such as archive pages, are not properly linked to each other. Since the primary reason people would refer to it is because they are lost and cannot find what they are looking for on the navigation, **it should add something extra**. This can be either in the form of a different navigation design or information that is capable of helping users. Its goal should be to provide the overview of the structure of a site at a glance, showing sections and sub-sections. It **should be static and simple**, with compact layout of links, and not be too long, so as to ensure that it does not discourage users. The **recommended length** is about two and half pages. Figures 24.16 and 24.17 show examples implemented reasonably well in different styles. Every item is a link, which when clicked takes users to the corresponding page. Other features that can

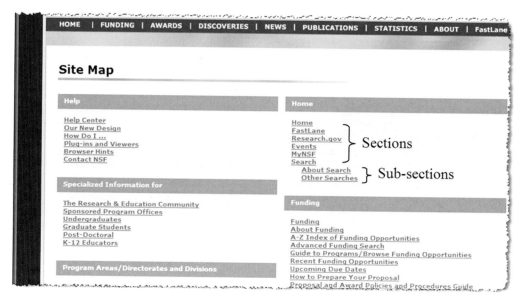

FIGURE 24.16   Part of the site map for www.nsf.gov.

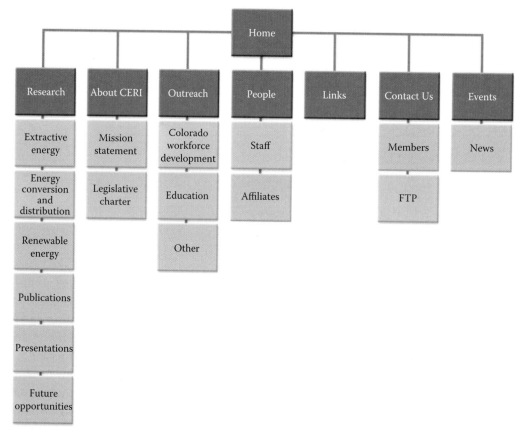

FIGURE 24.17   Graphical site map for www.ceri-mines.org.

be useful in a site map, if they can be added, include a "**You are here**" indicator and a distinction between visited and unvisited links. There are **various tools available on the Web** for generating site maps.

Another way a site map is used is for providing search engines information about the organization of the content of a site. **Web crawlers**, such as Googlebot and Bingbot, which browse the Web for the purpose of indexing it, read this file to more intelligently gather information about a site. A site map file can provide useful metadata about the pages and contents it contains. The metadata provided about a page could, for example, be the last time it was updated, frequency of update, and its relative importance to other pages. The metadata provided about specific types of content, such as image, video, and audio, could be type, license, and subject matter for an image, and include playing time and age-appropriateness rating for video.

CHALLENGE 24.4

Is a site map necessary for every website? Give reasons for your answer.

CHALLENGE 24.5

Why would the design concept in Figure 24.17 not be good for the www.nfs.gov website site map shown in Figure 24.16, considering only half of the site map is shown?

24.5.1.4 Footers

The footer of a Web page is like a supplement to the header and almost always has the same width to ensure uniformity. The underlying design is also similar to that of the header, particularly in color scheme, in order to maintain the site's design theme. It could, for example, carry a scaled-down version of the website ID. This is to maintain consistency and also distinguish it from the content area and attract users' attention. It can be very basic or contain a lot of information, including links to further information. Its purpose is to inform users and what is included in it to achieve this depends largely on the nature and content of website. For example, for a site that stores content primarily in sections and sub-sections, the footer may be in the form of just a site map with links to the sections and sub-sections, while for a site that sells something, it may be in the form of links to information to remind users of promotional items and its business policy. The following are some standard inclusions: date of the last update, copyright notice and links to copyright policy, terms and conditions of use, privacy policy (if customer information is gathered), contact us, delivery and return policy, FAQs and answers to them, text version of site (if available), the Webmaster's e-mail, and the site map. A call to action is also a common element placed in footer. This could, for example, be a call to join you on social media or sign up for something, such as a newsletter. Figure 24.18 shows a basic footer design.

FIGURE 24.18   An example of a Web page footer.

CHALLENGE 24.6

Do a quick search on the Web, using, for example, the term "website footer" to see different kinds of footers, observing how type of website influences the types of information included, as well as design.

24.5.2 Designing Content Area

The content area of a Web page is the space left to display content after the spaces for header, footer, and menus have been carved out. Its successful design requires effective presentation of all the elements that make up content, such as text information, images, illustrations, video, and animation. When treated and combined correctly, the impact of these elements can make a page design graphically interesting and motivating, as well as supportive of comprehension. The main goals of content design typically include grouping and clearly defining content pieces, prioritizing, directing users' attention, and engaging them. Some of the principles for achieving these goals are discussed here, including how to write effectively for the Web.

24.5.2.1 Homepage Content

The homepage of a website should be different from the other pages, but only slightly, since consistency in look and feel is essential between all pages to ensure unity. The distinction is necessary to enable users to easily recognize the page when they are there and can be achieved through either designing the content area differently from those of other pages (typically in terms of layout) or placing a unique and noticeable feature in the header that only appears when the homepage is displayed. One way the content area can be made different is by displaying images of products' examples or promotions, or news flash, depending on type of site. Any image or item used in the homepage in this way should have a link that leads directly to details about the product or item, rather than a page of category to which the product or item belongs. This is important because when people click a link to an item they expect to be taken to a page that gives them information about that exact item. The NN/g's website provides comprehensive lists of over a hundred usability guidelines for designing effective homepages that are worth looking through.

24.5.2.2 Content Display Size

Designing content size to suit screen display area is important, because when **content is too large for display area**, a design tends to look "un-unified" and unprofessional, because some parts are inevitably cut off. Not just this, users may be forced to scroll horizontally, which can be especially irritating and confusing, particularly as vertical scrolling may also be involved. Naturally, it may also mean that images cannot be viewed in their entirety at a glance, which can place extra demands on short-term memory and compromise user experience. Figure 24.19, for example, shows two screenshots of the same 640×480 px image displayed at different screen resolutions, making the image too big for the display in one. The one on the left, which is at 1024×768, requires both vertical scrolling, while the one on the right, which is at 1920×1080, requires no scrolling. Incidentally, on-line tools are available on the Web for checking how a page will be displayed in different screen resolutions.

What the demonstration in Figure 24.19 shows is that, although the space available for content is determined primarily by the amount left over after the header, footer, and menus have been taken care of, other factors like screen resolution also play important roles. Screen size, browser size, and printing width are also among these, all of which depend on the requirements of the target audience. This means that there is no single correct content size that suits all situations; hence **responsive Web design**, which was discussed in Chapter 21, and as noted there, if you want to rank high in Google, is recommended, because it is considered to satisfy user experience across multiple devices.

If you choose to develop a **non-responsive website**, then the general recommendation is to **optimize a page for the current most widely used screen resolution** as a compromise. World usage percentages for different resolutions can be found on the Web. On the other hand, if you know your audience well enough, you might optimize for them first, and then for others. When a page is optimized for a screen size, all important information is visible without scrolling and legible, irrespective of column width, and all page elements are displayed as intended. Of course, because **different operating systems and browsers use different amount of space** to display their native components, such as taskbar and browser chrome, pages optimized for specific size or sizes should also be tried on different systems. **Browser chrome** is the term used for the graphical framework and elements that frame the display area of a browser window and includes borders, title bar, menu bar, status bar, toolbar, and address bar.

In addition to display problems, **pages that are too wide also do not print very well**. For example, the right margin is usually cut off, or if the browser's "fit to page" function

1024×768

1920×1080

FIGURE 24.19 Screenshots of a big page displayed in different screen resolutions. (Image from www.freeimages.co.uk.)

is used, pages may not be legible, due to excessive reduction in font size. This means that pages that are likely to be printed, such as those containing large textual content, should be checked with at least international paper size standard (ISO 216).

24.5.2.3 Content Length

A Web page can be as short or as long as required. While a short page has the advantage of making all the contents of a page available instantly without further action by users, it is not always possible to break up a long page into shorter logical ones that fit into a page each. Also, long pages can be the easiest and quickest way to present most contents that occupy more than one screen-full. For example, instead of creating multiple pages, only one is created, and this is more straightforward to do and easier to maintain. Furthermore, only one download is required by users. One long page is also easier to print than many short ones, making long pages useful for presenting information intended for printing for off-line reading. Whereas scrolling used to be a source of usability problem, it has since become an accepted and expected method of interaction, no doubt largely because the mouse scrolling wheel and touch-screen swiping action have made the action much easier to perform. The following are some usability guidelines to consider when using long pages:

- There is really **no one page length that suits all**, as different types of websites call for different treatments and users tolerate different page lengths, depending on context. Some types of websites need be no more than three or so pages. Websites for which this is suited include those that present specific and predetermined amount of information. In contrast, a page that is presenting the result of a search or comments made by various users about the same topic can be as long as necessary and may even incorporate **infinite scrolling technique**, in which content is loaded continuously as the user scrolls down. Research shows that, generally, users are happy with a long page if it contains related information, such as a list of a type of product they are looking to buy. The implication of this is that the length of a page is usually best determined by the relevance of the information being presented on it. However, even when its use is suitable, infinite scrolling should be used with caution, because it can harm user experience when a page seems to go on forever.

- In some types of long pages, some kind of **within-page navigation aid** should be provided that can take users back to the start of the page. Examples of these types of pages include alphabetized lists, FAQs, and a page that has a table of contents at the start of it that leads to sections of the page. The navigation aid could be, for example, in the form of a "**jump to the top**" button or a link at the bottom-corner of the screen (e.g., bottom-right in left-to-right writing mode), where it is less likely to cause too much distraction. How this can be implemented and necessary design considerations can be found in Section 4.5.3 of Chapter 4.

- Pages that are too long can take too **long to download** as well as overwhelm RAM limitations, in some cases, resulting in the browser crashing, particularly when there are a lot of graphics. If there are a lot of graphics, it is reasonable to consider providing links to the images instead of displaying them. Alternatively, thumbnails could be used.

- The **most important content should be placed at the beginning of a page**, particularly if it is a homepage, so that it is "**above the fold**" (i.e., visible in the browser before the need to scroll; so, the "**fold**" is the bottom boundary of the initial screen of a page). This is important because studies (e.g., the NN/g) have suggested that many users rarely pay much attention to content beyond the initial screen-full. Another advantage of placing useful and relevant information above the fold, according to "**information scent theory**," is that it is likely to encourage users to scroll past the initial screen-full, with the hope that the information "**below the fold**" will be just as useful. Information scent is described as the degree to which it is possible for users to predict what will be found if they follow a path on a website. It is part of **information foraging theory** that relates the behavior of users when interacting with a system to that of animals hunting for food.

24.5.2.4 *Line Length*

Line length refers to the total **number of characters per line**. The general recommendation is between 45–75 characters, including white space, with the ideal being 66. Although up to 90 is considered acceptable, it is discouraged where deep comprehension is essential and should only be used for discontinuous text, such as bibliographies and footnotes. When line length is too long, it makes reading difficult. This is because human eyes can generally only span comfortably about 3 inches long of text at normal distance. Beyond this length, people have to use more of the muscles of the eyes and/or the neck to enable them to read an entire line and move to the beginning of the next. In addition to this, it makes it easy to get lost when seeking the beginning of the next line. As a result, the longer the length of text, the slower the rates of reading, comprehension, and retention. Lines that are too short can be equally difficult to read, particularly if they are so short that every other line is hyphenated. A length of 40–50 characters is recommended for columns in multi-column layouts.

24.5.2.5 *Content Layout*

Effective content layout requires attention to two main goals; one is to position elements such that the gestalt effect discussed in Chapter 23 is fostered, and the other is to position them such that important elements are not overlooked by users. As already discussed in Chapter 23, **aesthetics-related element placement** can be achieved using grid systems, such as golden ratio and rule of thirds. This means that only how to position contents to improve their chances of being noticed is discussed here. About this, various theories suggest that when people scan the content of a Web page, they tend to do so in particular ways. Although these theories do not offer exactly same observation of how people read a page, there are useful similarities in terms of how they describe human reading habits. Understanding these habits informs on where to place the most important elements on a page to improve their chances of being noticed. Some common theories are the Gutenberg rule, the z-pattern, and the F-shaped pattern; and although they do not suit every Web page design goal, they provide a useful starting point.

24.5.2.5.1 Gutenberg Rule

Gutenberg rule originated from printing, but is it also commonly adapted to screen content layout. The rule essentially divides a page into four quadrants, illustrated in the left image in Figure 24.20. The top-left is known as the **primary optical area**, top-right as the **strong fallow area**, bottom-left as the **weak fallow area**, and bottom-right as the **terminal area**.

According to the Gutenberg rule, when Western readers scan a page containing **heavy textual content** or **evenly distributed and homogeneous content** (i.e., content that does guide eye movement in anyway), they tend to start reading from the primary optical area, then move across to the right and down in a series of short sweeping movements until the terminal area is reached. Each sweeping movement is along what is termed **axis of orientation**, formed by a horizontal line created, for example, by aligned elements or lines of text, or by explicit segments like paragraphs. This reading behavior of going from top-left to bottom-right is attributed to what is termed **reading gravity**. It is considered that reading gravity virtually pulls the eyes from top-left to bottom-right of a layout. In addition to this basic reading behavior, it is believed that once the eyes have reached the terminal area, they then move upward to focus on the strong fallow area, after which they then generally either focus or not focus on the weak fallow area. The word "fallow," incidentally, describes inactivity, so, the word in this context means that the "fallow areas" do not see a lot of reading activity. In cultures that read from right to left, naturally, the reverse of the behavior described is likely to be the case.

What the Gutenberg rule roughly translates into is that when viewing a page the greatest attention is often paid to Area 1, followed by Area 4, then Area 2, and possibly

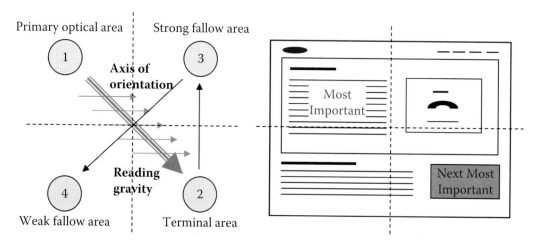

FIGURE 24.20 The Gutenberg diagram and an example of its application.

Area 3. A typical application of this to content layout is to place elements in these areas according to their importance. For example, most important elements (e.g., heading and high-value information paragraph) are placed in the top-left area, the next important elements in the bottom-right area, the next important in the top-right area, and the least important in the left-bottom area. Naturally, since the eyes pass through the middle on their top-left to bottom-right journey, any element placed in the middle is likely to receive some attention and also reinforces the pull of the reading gravity. A common practice is to place **elements that call for action** from users (e.g., download buttons, links, and relatively important images) in the bottom-right area. Of course, where a page does not contain heavy textual or evenly distributed and homogeneous content, the Gutenberg rule is unlikely to apply. In such cases, the characteristics of the elements of the design (e.g., weight and color) plus the layout and composition of the elements are more likely to direct the movement of the eyes. For example, if elements in the bottom-left area are visually emphasized they will probably attract more attention than elements placed in other areas.

However, it is worth noting that as of time of writing there seems no strong empirical evidence to support the usefulness of the Gutenberg rule in Web page layout, although a website (**optimisation-mavericks.blogspot.co.uk**) claims to have done tests whose findings do. They found that when the position of a product was rotated round the four quadrants defined by the rule, it received most attention in Area 1, followed by 2, 3, and 4. They also found that Area 2 is effective for placing call-to-action elements.

24.5.2.5.2 z-Pattern

The z-pattern theory suggests that when readers scan the content of a page, their eyes move from left to right across the top of the page, then diagonally to bottom-left, and then to bottom-right, following a path that describes a z-pattern, as illustrated in the left image in Figure 24.21.

Although like the Gutenberg rule there seems no empirical data to verify the effectiveness of the z-pattern theory, it is a relatively common belief. Its implication for content layout is that important elements should be located along the z-path. A typical application is to place elements that users are intended to notice, or might want to see,

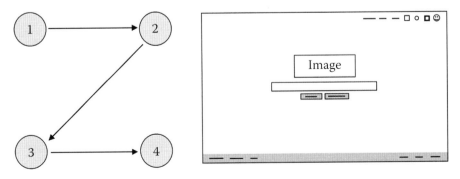

FIGURE 24.21 Illustration of the z-pattern and a rough example of its application.

first (e.g., logo, menu, and sign-on) across the top of the page; then the next important elements (e.g., image) in the middle, where they should catch users' attention as the eyes travel diagonally down to the bottom-left area, where some useful but not urgent information might be located; and then more information is located along the bottom (such as links to further information); and then at the bottom-right area, elements that call for users' action (e.g., download button) are placed. The right image in the figure shows an example application. Note that the example is actually the template for the Google page, which is not saying that the z-pattern is used. Indeed, it is not readily possible to determine which rule, if any, has been used for a layout until the level of importance the elements are supposed to have is known.

24.5.2.5.3 F-Shaped Pattern

The F-shaped pattern, according to Jakob Nielsen of the NN/g, describes the rough and general pattern followed by Western readers when reading Web pages. This is illustrated in Figure 24.22 and suggests that people tend to first read in a horizontal movement across the top of the page to the right, then move down a bit and do a shorter second left-right horizontal scan, after which, finally, the left side is scanned, sometimes fairly slowly, in a top-bottom vertical movement.

The essence of the patterns produced in Figure 24.22 is illustrated on the left in Figure 24.23. Applying the observation to content layout means that the higher-up information is on a page, and the more it is to the left, the more is the likelihood that it will be read. This naturally means that the most important information should be located in this area. For example, in the case of textual content, important information should be presented in the first one or two paragraphs and the start of sub-heads, paragraphs, and lists should contain information-carrying words that you want users to notice. Judging the design layout shown on the right in Figure 24.23 based on this

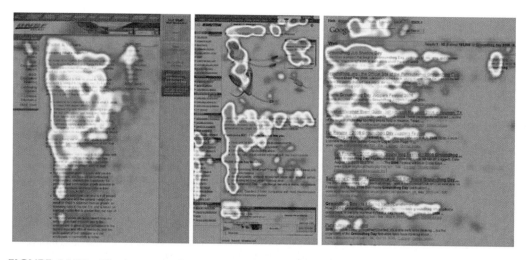

FIGURE 24.22 The heatmaps from tracking users' eyes while reading three Web pages. (From Nielsen, 2006, www.nngroup.com)

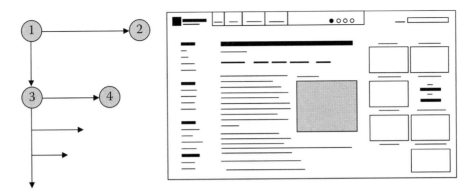

FIGURE 24.23 F-shaped pattern and a rough example of its application.

principle, for example, means that the designer deems the heading area most important and intends it to be read first, after which the next important areas are read accordingly. Worth noting is that the general area covered by the F-shaped pattern also resembles the scanning pattern some other studies refer to as the **golden triangle area**.

24.5.2.6 Managing Content Amount

Generally, the less content there is on the screen at one time (i.e., the more **white space** there is), the easier it is to organize the screen and achieve a good design. According to research, users typically only read 20–28% of the words on a Web page. What this implies is that **only about a third of display needs to be filled**. However, the amount of content presented on a Web page cannot be determined by this fact alone, as it also depends on other factors, such as type of site, aim of site, and the target users. This means that there is no one-size-fits-all solution. Often, the best solution is a compromise that suits the purpose of a wide range of users. A standard guideline is to **keep introductory text short** and simply state the purpose of the content of a page. If introduction is too long, users are likely to skip it, even if part of it provides useful information. If a long introduction is necessary to convey the true essence of the content, a link may be provided to a longer version. This principle of disclosing only limited information until more is required is known as **progressive disclosure** and it is the foundation of various content management techniques, including text collapsing, accordion, and carousels.

24.5.2.6.1 Collapsing Text Technique

The collapsing text technique enables some of the text to be hidden until requested by users, typically via clicking or touching. Figure 24.24 illustrates the use of a hyperlink in Windows help information system, which when clicked expands into more text. As is evident from the example, the text in the design is easier to read and the design is more visually appealing with minimal amount of text. Another way the text can be displayed when the link is clicked is in a pop-up window. The technique is typically implemented in Web design using JavaScript.

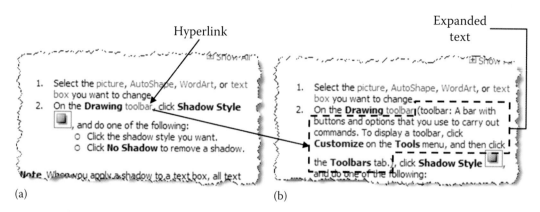

FIGURE 24.24   An example of a hyperlink used to reduce the amount of text displayed.

24.5.2.6.2 *Accordion Menus*

An accordion menu describes a vertical stack of headers, each of which when clicked expands to reveal the associated content or retracts to hide it. Figure 24.25 shows an example. The top illustration shows stack before any header is clicked and the bottom one after "Header 3" has been clicked. Notice the change in the arrow direction and the bar color after the header has been clicked.

Accordions can be used to shorten pages and so prevent or minimize scrolling as well as make a page neater by reducing the amount of text displayed at once. They can

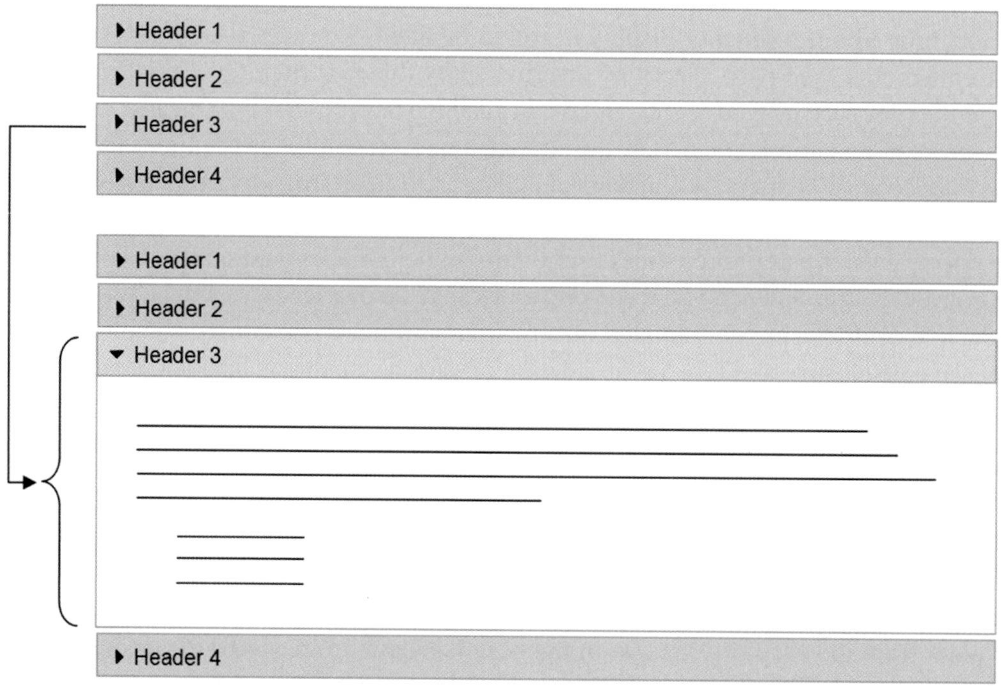

FIGURE 24.25   Illustration of an accordion menu.

also be used instead of **within-page links**, but this should be avoided, if possible, as studies have found that users tend to be confused when they click a link and it does not take them to a new page. There are also issues with the accordion technique itself. For example, having to click the headers to read their contents instead of just having all the contents at once to scan through can easily begin to feel like too much work. Furthermore, they only provide access to a bit of information at a time and, so, it can be hard, for example, to compare the content of one header with that of another, because users are likely to forget what they have read in one by the time they open the other, due to the limitation of short-term memory. Naturally, they require extra attention in order to make them accessible to those who do not interact with Web pages in the conventional ways. Printing the contents of pages that use accordions can also be tedious, in that the content of every header has to be printed separately. This means that if they are used, and a page is likely to be printed, a link should be provided to a separate file containing a full-length version.

24.5.2.6.3 *Carousels*

A carousel GUI essentially allows different pieces of content to occupy the same space at different times, typically in a cyclical manner, either through user-interaction or animation, so that after the last piece of content is displayed, the display starts again from the first. Usually, movement can be in left or right direction, or up or down, but not necessarily, as carousel designs vary widely. Manual navigation can be linear or nonlinear. Figure 24.26 shows some of the wide range of design concepts commonly used.

A carousel can be placed anywhere on a page. However, it is **typically placed near the top of the home page**, especially when used to present, for example, important information that a company wants users to see, such as the company's brand or mission, promotions, and services provided. If it is for the purpose of simply presenting content, such as a gallery of images or videos, then it can be placed wherever is relevant.

While carousels are **useful for saving screen space**, they do have drawbacks that should be considered before use. For example, research shows that **users tend to ignore them** for various reasons, such as because they mistake them for adverts, or simply find them frustrating to interact with, since they automatically rotate before users can read and digest their content. To make things worse, it can be difficult to figure out how to stop them. This essentially takes control away from the user and can cause bad user experience. Also, **animated carousels can be annoying**, since, like any animation, they persistently attract attention and can be continually distracting. Although static carousels do not have these drawbacks, **users can miss the point that they are a collection of images** and not know to look past the currently displayed frame, if there is no clear suggestion to do this.

An altogether different alternative to carousels that is less likely to be ignored is a static **hero image** (or **hero graphic**), which is basically a large image banner at, or near, the top of the home page. The recommendation is that a hero image should be

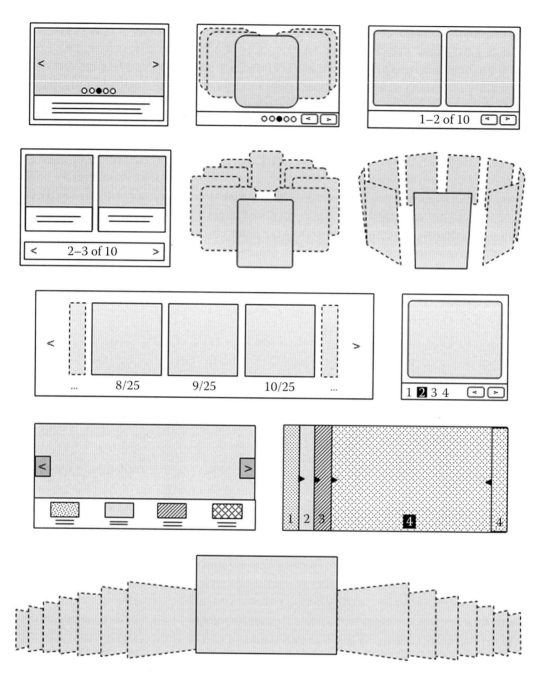

FIGURE 24.26 Examples of carousel designs.

designed to attract attention (e.g., via bold and complementary colors and font) and communicate clearly, using multiple media types, typically image and text, to provide the same information. Providing the same information via multiple channels can help improve the chances of quicker understanding. However, users can also ignore hero images, therefore it is recommended that important information presented in a carousel or hero image is also provided somewhere else.

24.5.2.6.3.1 Guidelines for Designing Carousels In order for the full benefit of carousels to be realized and for them not to cause usability or user experience problems, they have to be designed properly. The following are some guidelines:

- **Limit the number of frames/slides to five or fewer**, as users are unlikely to look at more than this, or remember what they have seen after five frames, due to the limitations of short-term memory. Of course, if there is a good enough indicator to help users determine what they have or have not seen, such as numbering or changing the appearance of what has already been seen, then this restriction may not be necessary.

- **All navigational aids need to be clearly visible and their function obvious** in order for a carousel interface to be easy to use. Basically, there should be a feature that informs of the **position of the currently displayed item** in the carousel and, ideally, also serves the role of **nonlinear navigational aid**. If this is not possible, the feature could just display the position of the current item and the total number of items, such as "2 of 20" and 2/20.

- **If carousel is auto-forward** (i.e., animated), the common behavior is for it to stop when the cursor enters the display area. Also, when users click on a navigational aid, this should be seen to indicate that they want to navigate the carousel manually and so the carousel should pause. It should continue to do so until the cursor is no longer in the navigation area, since users are likely to want to keep the cursor in the area while navigating the slides and spending variable times reading each one. They are unlikely to prefer clicking an aid to navigate to a specific slide and then moving the cursor to the display area each time to pause the carousel to allow them to read the slide's content.

- **Make text and images crisp-looking** to improve the chances that users will pay attention to them.

- **Keep information on each slide concise** to give users fewer reasons not to read it.

CHALLENGE 24.7

Visit a few websites that use carousels, of which there are many, and critically assess them, given the guideline above. Say how you can make them more user-friendly. If you do not know of any site with carousel, visit www.wta.com, which has one as of time of writing, or try any other tennis site, as these sites tend to use them.

NOTE: Creating carousels and accordions

Implementing carousels and accordions typically requires scripting or programming. However, there are numerous free tools for creating them on the Web. These tools are usually created using "**JQuery**," discussed in Chapter 19. A quick search for JQuery carousel on the Web should produce some useful and interesting tools.

24.5.2.7 Writing Content for the Web

Text is a very important component of content delivery, so, presenting it effectively can enhance content communication in many ways. Doing this, in turn, is influenced by many factors, including the extent to which it is scannable, style of writing, and use of correct grammar and spelling. These factors are discussed here.

24.5.2.7.1 Designing Scannable Text

According to studies by Nielsen Norman Group (NN/g), most Web users scan pages, picking out words and sentences here and there, rather than read it word by word. Given such findings, it is reasonable to design a page in a way that aids scanning in order to facilitate the reading of content. Text can be made more scannable in various ways, including the following:

- **Text can be broken up and section headings used**. Section headings should be short, meaningful, and bold in style. Bulleted or numbered lists can also be used, with the length of each list-item kept short. Each list-item should start with keywords, if possible. Where list-items are too short to be meaningful, more initial information can be provided by using **title-summary combination** for list items. Furthermore, the title, which should typically be bold, can be a link to more detailed information. Figure 24.27 shows this being used to good effects. Tables can also be used instead of lists.

The **summaries of articles should be provided** instead of the full articles. Users are more likely to cover more topics when summaries are provided than when a full article is provided first in which they are not interested. In other words, if they are not interested in the first summary, they are likely to go to the next one, and so on, whereas if they are not interested in the first full article, they are likely to abandon all available articles.

Some of the company's most established news sites include:

- inthenews.co.uk – all the latest breaking news, sport, business and entertainment from around the world, as well as in-depth features, film, music and book reviews and the latest scientific breakthroughs for those who want to keep fully informed of the latest developments.
- politics.co.uk – the foremost specialist political news site in the UK, politics.co.uk is targeted at politicians, journalists, academics, students and anyone with a general interest in politics.
- myfinances.co.uk – bringing you the latest news in personal finance, myfinances is

FIGURE 24.27 Example of the use of title-summary combination in lists.

- **Important words can be highlighted**, using, for example, variation in font style (e.g., bold) or color, as the eyes tend to stop on things that stand out.
- **Inverted pyramid style can be used**, as in journalism, in which content starts with conclusion before going into more details. In Web page terms, this translates into placing important facts near the top of a page so that users can find them quickly. Multiple theories and studies suggest this is a good idea.

EXAMPLE: Pyramid and inverted pyramid style

With pyramid style, you start with a foundation (an introduction) and gradually build up to a conclusion, as shown in the following structure:

1. Problem statement (Introduction to the problem)
2. Related work (Background to the problem)
3. Methodology (Solution proposals)
4. Results
5. Conclusion (Report of whether or not proposals solved problems)

The opposite is the case with **inverted pyramid style**, where conclusion is presented first and detailed information progressively later, as shown below:

1. Conclusion
2. Supporting information
3. Background and technical details

- **Fewer words can be used** than in printing without over-cutting or over-simplifying content. Alternatively, content that cannot be made concise without compromising the intended message can be provided in a way that is easy to print. Indeed, it is good practice to assume that users will print anything that is more than half a page.
- **Number of ideas per paragraph** can be limited to one, so that users can know just by reading the start of a paragraph whether or not the paragraph is of interest and whether or not to skip it.
- **Paragraph should be left-aligned** (or right-aligned for right-to-left writing mode) to facilitate reading, as justification causes irregular word spacing (spacing between words) that make reading difficult. See Chapter 14.
- **Grouping together of related information** can be used. This can be done, for example, by grouping under different headings; grouping by visual style (e.g., font style and color); or using clearly defined areas or nesting. Figure 24.28 shows some illustrations.

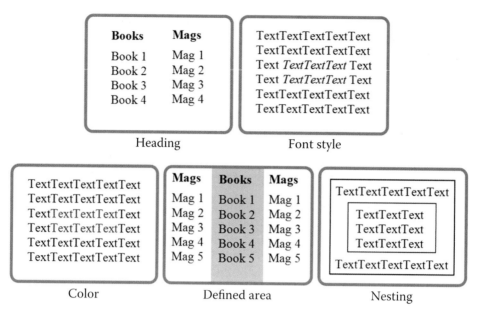

FIGURE 24.28   Illustrations of how grouping is used in making text scannable.

24.5.2.7.2 Style of Writing

Whether or not a style of writing is effective and helps readability depends on many factors, such as grammar, punctuation, the choice of words, spelling, and the length and structure of sentences. The following are some guidelines:

- **Sentence structure**: Sentences should be **simple and easy to understand**. The first two words, in particular, should be right, as **eye-tracking research** suggests that these are often what users see when scanning textual content. This means that using important keywords at the beginning of sentences, summaries, and in page titles are highly important design considerations. As well as making text highly scannable, using keywords helps **SEO** (Search Engine Optimization) effectiveness. Keywords can also help in the achievement of a high **GYM rating**. This is rating with Google, Yahoo, and Microsoft search listings. **Sentences should also be short**, as some users, particularly older adults, can have problems connecting with long complex text.

- **Using active and passive voices**: Where possible, active voice (i.e., "Actor does X to Object") should be used instead of passive voice (i.e., "Object has X done to it by Actor"). The reason for this is that active voice requires less thinking than passive voice to understand. Passive sentences that do not state the actor, such as, "Council taxes must be paid quarterly," can be even more difficult to understand. A better structure is "Tenants must pay council taxes quarterly." However, **passive voice**, too, has a role in some elements of content, such as titles, headings, summaries, bulleted lists, captions, blurbs, link text, and lead sentences. This is because it lets you start these elements with the most important words, which are often all users see when scanning Web pages. Another advantage of doing this is that it helps **SEO effectiveness**.

- **Using positive and negative statements**: Positive statements (e.g., "Do X") should be used instead of negative statements (e.g., "Avoid X") or double negative (e.g., "Avoid not doing X"). If you must use "avoid," then the user should also be advised on what to do instead.

- **Choice of words**: Speaking users' language helps the successful communication of a message and ensures, for example, that a Web page is found easily. This involves using words that are familiar and precise. **Familiar words**, for example, are what users are likely to use for search queries on the Web; and **precise words** improve the chances of a Web page being found. For example, someone searching for websites that sell affordable travel tickets is likely to use a phrase like "cheap travel tickets" than "competitively priced tickets." Similarly, most users are likely to use, for example, "deaf users" instead of a politically correct terminology like "audibly challenged users." If made-up words must be used, they should be supplemented with familiar words.

- **Variants of language**: Users notice the variant of language a website uses, such as whether a variant of English is British or American. They do this through things like spelling, terminology, slang, and currency. The recommendation is to use the language variant for where a website is based and use it consistently. For example, if a website is based in Britain, then British English should be used. Using American English, for example, might give the wrong impression. If nothing else, it might reduce credibility, as users might think that the site intends to deceive them. On the other hand, people do not mind dealing with a foreign site if the site can accommodate it, so, using local variant may not necessarily be automatically disadvantageous.

- **Writing numbers, in general**: The ways numbers are presented on Web pages are different from when presented in printed text. Some guidelines derived from various studies are presented here. Because important pieces of information need to stand out, often among a lot of words, the general guideline is that all numbers should be written in numerals, not words, even when a number is the first in a sentence or after a bullet point. Exceptions include when writing them in words reduces confusion or provides extra meaning.

  o **Writing big numbers**: Numerals should be used for numbers up to one billion, as too many zeros can be difficult to interpret. For example, "3,000,000" is better than "three million," while "three trillion" is better than "3,000,000,000,000." Alternatively, a combination of numerals and words can be used that involves using numerals for the significant digits and words for the magnitude (e.g., "25 billion" is better than "twenty-five billion" or "25,000,000,000"). In order to further help reading and understanding, commas should be placed after every three digits from the right, if there are over three digits, as in "there are 34,859 lines."

  o **Writing numbers in specific facts**: Numerals should be used for representing exact data (e.g., 3,924 items, 8.625, 0.25, 1/2 in, 1/2 a pint), as this communicates more credibility and typically suggests that someone knows what they are talking about. Where numbers do not represent specific facts or data, or are rounded, words should be used (e.g., "about half an inch" instead of "about 1/2 an inch," "thousands of people" instead of "1000s of people," "about 200 million people" instead of "about 200,000,000 people," and "tens of thousands" instead of "10s of thousands"). If users are unlikely to be familiar with a term, such as "trillion," it should be explained. Also, abbreviations for measurement units, such as those typically used in relation to computers, should be explained. For example, you might explain that "TB" means "terabyte" and that "1 TB" is equal to 1 trillion bytes.

- ○ **Writing Numbers with units and nouns**: A number should be joined to a unit of measure with a hyphen when the unit describes a noun (e.g., "a 6-foot tree," "9-year-old children," and "a 24-stone English man"). Abbreviations of units of measure should be singular (e.g., 2 cm, 2 kg, 2 min, instead of 2 cms, 2 kgs, 2 mins, respectively).

- ○ **Writing adjacent numbers**: When two numbers are next to each other, such as in "5 11-year-olds," to improve comprehension, one of them (typically the shorter) should be spelled (e.g., "five 11-year-olds" or "5 eleven-year-olds" or "5 eleven-year-old children").

- • **Writing microcontent**: Microcontent can be described as a short text that conveys what page content is about and includes page titles, headlines, and e-mail subject lines. To be effective, it should be in plain language and contain no puns, boastful subjective claims (such as "best ever"), or teasers that must be clicked in order to find out what content is about, as this can irritate users and even compromise credibility. Articles, such as "a" and "the," should not be used at the beginning of Web page titles (or e-mail subjects) in order to prevent a page from being listed, for example, under "T" or "A" with other pages that start with "The" or "A," which could be numerous. However, headings used within a page can begin with articles. It is also good practice to start microcontent with high-information-carrying words, such as the name of the company, person, or topic an article is about, in order to provide useful information. Basically, a headline should make sense alone. Finally, all page titles should not start with the same word, as this will make it difficult to differentiate between them when listed together. If necessary, common start-words should be moved to the end of the line, as shown in the box below.

NOTE: Moving common words to the back

Bad

Design Issues: User Interface
Design Issues: Web accessibility

Good

User Interface (Design Issues)
Web Accessibility (Design Issues)

24.5.2.7.3 *Writing for International Audience*

If a website intends to deal with users from all over the world or multiple countries, their characteristics should be supported by paying special attention to certain elements of content, such as presentation of measurements, dates, names, and addresses. Ideally, special sites should be created for various languages. However, this can add more cost than can be justified in terms of benefits. A less costly approach is to create just one site and test it on users from the relevant countries, although this too is relatively costly. A more typical approach is to simply aim to design a site that will be usable by as many international users as possible. Ways in which this can be achieved include **supporting variable spellings and formats for names** if the site requires information from users. For example, in some countries, people use only one name, so, making name fields mandatory when users only have one name may cause confusion.

The site should also **support different formats of representing a postal address**. For example, users should be able to place house number before or after street name, and postal codes or ZIP codes of variable lengths should be supported, as should variable formats of phone numbers. In addition, website's contact **phone numbers should be in numbers** rather than in letters, as not all countries include letters on their phone keypads. In particular, because different character sets are used in languages around the world, the site should support a multilingual character encoding system like Unicode (discussed in Chapter 3), so that characters are displayed correctly.

Other commonly used elements in websites that vary between countries are dates and units of measurement. Because some countries start dates with day and others, month, users can confuse the two. For example, 4/6 may be interpreted as "4th of June" or "April 6th." To avoid this, the **name of month should be spelt out** when displaying a date. Also, instead of asking users to type in dates, drop-down lists or a date picker (such as shown in Chapter 5) should be provided. Where measurements are involved, the various **units used around the world should be supported**. For example, dimensions should be supported in both **metric** (centimeters) and **imperial** (inches) systems and temperature in **Celsius** and **Fahrenheit**. If a site sells products that conform to varying world standards, such as electrical or media products, the standards supported should be made clear. For example, the voltage a device is designed to operate with (e.g., 110 or 220 volts) should be clearly specified.

24.5.2.7.4 *Writing Links*

The way hyperlinks are written and styled is important to how easy they are to use and user experience. The following guidelines can help in writing and styling them effectively:

- **Number of links**: This should be kept to minimum on a page, as too many can cause distraction, particularly as users tend to want to click them. If there are many supplementary resources, only important ones should be linked to from within main text. The rest should be placed at the bottom where they can be seen but do not cause distraction. If a link is to an external site, the content should be displayed in a new window, so as to ensure users do not lose the current site, as this can cause confusion and frustration. In particular, there should not be multiple links to the same destination, as it is likely that users will not realize that they actually lead to the same destination and end up wasting time trying them out, all of which can result in navigational disorientation.

- **Link color**: Different colors should be used for visited and unvisited links, as not knowing which links have already been visited can get users going around in a virtual circle. By default, modern Web browsers generally display unvisited links in blue and visited in purple. This convention should be maintained to prevent giving users the extra burden of remembering a different color scheme.

- **Link text**: When a link is used within a main text, the text used for the link, which is known as link text, should be descriptive and fit seamlessly into the meaning of the rest of the sentence. Rather than craft a sentence around a link, the sentence should be created as normal and then the link placed on the word or words that best describe the content to which users will be linked. This is illustrated in the following box.

NOTE: Using descriptive text in a document

Good

"Make links easier to use by *managing their placement* within a document so that they fit seamlessly into the context."

Bad

"*Click here* for more information about how best to place links within a document."

- **Link titles**: A description of where a link will lead should be provided when it is not obvious through link text or surrounding text, as this helps users to make better navigation decisions. A **link title** is the text that pops up when the cursor hovers over a hypertext link. The types of information a link title should contain include the name of the section in the current site (or the name of the site) to which the link leads, the kind of information that will be found at the end of the link, and any other useful information. A link title should not be too long (about 60 characters), and because different platforms and browsers display them differently, it is useful to try them out on different types.

24.5.2.7.5 *Writing FAQs*

For most websites that deal with customers, especially the general public, the FAQs feature is inevitable and a very valuable one for both the sites and the users. For the websites, it saves them from repeatedly addressing the same questions, thereby freeing them to more productively use their time. For the users, it provides quick, on-the-spot solutions to their concerns about which they would have had to e-mail or use other means of communication. FAQs would typically start life based on guessing questions that people are likely to ask and providing answers to them. Imagining being in the user's position can help with this. The initial effort can then be added to, based on the questions that users actually ask. Like any other content page, the FAQs page needs to be designed properly in ways that foster usability, good user experience, and accessibility. Many of the various design and writing guidelines already noted, such as proper structuring, the use of correct spelling and grammar, and conciseness, also apply to an FAQ page as appropriate. The following are more specific guidelines:

- **Organization**: If many, FAQs should be grouped into categories, if possible. A table of contents or menu can even be provided to make navigation easier. Most frequently viewed FAQs can also be placed in its own category.

- **Search function**: For a very long FAQs page, a search function for the page that is different from the search function for the entire website may also be useful, as it can make the page easier to use. If this is included, it should be titled appropriately so as not to confuse users. An example title is "Search FAQs page." Of course, where a page is too long and can be broken up logically into separate pages, then doing so should be considered. If this is not practical, then a link back to the top of the page, where there should be some sort of table of contents or menu, is an acceptable alternative. Refer to "Content length" earlier for how to deal with FAQs page that is too long.

- **Collapsible content**: Where space is limited, a common approach is to use collapsible content technique that works in a similar way as the accordion menu discussed earlier under "Managing content amount." In essence, the questions alone are displayed, and when a question is clicked, the answer expands out underneath it. If this approach is used, having an option (such as in the form of a checkbox) to show all answers should be provided for the benefit of users who might prefer, for example, to minimize the number of clicks.

- **Media**: If the answer to a question is better explained through the use of other media object types, such as image, video, or animation, then they should be used.

- **Readability**: Distinguish between questions and answers, such as making questions bold or using different colors. Placing "Question," "Q," "Answer," or "A" in front of questions or answers, even in bold, should be avoided, as it requires users to repeatedly look at the beginning of the text to check if they are reading a question or an answer.

- **Position**: The FAQs link should be located where it can easily be seen, typically in the header or footer.

- **Answer quality**: Answers should be direct, concise, and honest. This is just as important for credibility as various other factors.

CHALLENGE 24.8

A good exercise for knowing what is required for a good website design is see what bad ones look like. There are many of these and which they change over time, because some of the designers eventually realize the errors in their design. So, the exercise here is to search the Web for bad website designs. You could do this, for example, using the term "bad website examples." Most of the sites that showcase these bad websites do not say what is wrong with the designs. See if you can identify them, given all you have learnt so far. Also, pick one or two and try to redesign them.

24.6 Designing for Different Ages

A website that uses the various guidelines described so far in this chapter and various others would be suitable for most types of users, as the result would be a website that is easy to use and accessible. A website to which these guidelines are applied appropriately is likely to have, for example, a clean, well-laid out design, good graphics that are used appropriately (if graphics are used), and font-size that promotes legibility, all of which are favored by users of all ages. Where it is necessary to design an application for a specific age group, because only that group is going to use it, refinements need only be made in the form of adding features preferred by that group. The three main categories of users commonly distinguished are children, teenagers, and adults, each of which has sub-categories that have their own preferences. For example, children of age 3–12 years are typically further categorized into young (3–5), mid-range (6–8), and older (9–12) children. So, designing for different ages amounts to designing for all ages plus making necessary refinements. Table 24.1, adapted from studies by NN/g, shows some of the differences between children, teenagers, and adults in terms of their preferences.

TABLE 24.1

Preferences of Different Types of Audiences

	Children	**Teenagers**	**Adults**
Willingness to wait	Not patient	Not patient	Limited patience
Sweeping the screen for clickable elements	Liked	Not liked	Not liked
Multiple/redundant navigation schemes	Very confusing	Confusing	Slightly confusing
Reading	None (younger) A little (young) Scanning (older)	Do not like a lot of it	Scan

(Continued)

TABLE 24.1 (*Continued*)

Preferences of Different Types of Audiences

	Children	Teenagers	Adults
Typeface	Rounded, playful, sans serif typeface; Serif for reading applications; ample letter spacing and leading	According to application goal and theme	According to application goal and theme
Font size	12–24 pt, depending on age; larger points for younger ages	10–12 point	From 10 point; for older people: up to 14 or 16 point
Color	2–5-year-olds (primary colors and high contrast graphics)	According to application goal and theme	According to application goal and theme
Physical limitations	Slow typing/poor mouse control by younger children	None (unless disabled)	None; larger clickable areas for older or disabled users
Scrolling	Not liked (younger) Tolerate some (older)	Like a little	Like
Animation and sound effects	Like (particularly pre-literate)	Like a little	Usually dislike
Advertising and promotions	Like, but confuse them with real content	Appreciate if not overused	Dislike
Interactive features (e.g., games, quizzes, and forums)	Like them	Like them	May or may not like them
Age-specific design	Necessary (3–5, 6–8, 9–12-years old)	Seldom necessary	May be necessary for older people
Search feature	Used by older children	Mostly used	Mostly used

CHALLENGE 24.9

Select a children's site, such as www.funbrain.com, and describe how it can be redesigned for adult use.

24.7 Useful Info

24.7.1 Web Links

Web usability guidelines: usability.gov, nngroup.com (Under "Articles")

Web Design: topdesignmag.com, inspirationti.me, webdesignledger.com

Writing for the Web: ec.europa.eu/ipg

Site map generators: freesitemapgenerator.com, wonderwebware.com

Screen ruler: wonderwebware.com

Free website creators: wix.com, one.com

Screen resolution simulator: rapidtables.com

25

Designing for Mobile Devices

25.1 Introduction

The term "mobile devices" describes a broad range of handheld computer technologies from small- and big-screen smartphones to tablets. While many of the general guidelines discussed in previous chapters for designing websites for desktop are also relevant to these devices, the differences in screen sizes and capabilities between desktop computers and the devices make it necessary to design specifically for them. Whether you choose to design a website specifically for a type of mobile device or you choose to use a responsive design that adapts to different ranges of screen-size devices, you still need to be aware of how to design effectively for each class of devices; recall from Chapter 21 that it is necessary to specify the layout details for each of the relevant screen sizes, using CSS `@media` at-rule.

25.2 Learning Outcomes

After studying this chapter, you should:

- Be aware of the common design practices when designing for smartphones.
- Be aware of the issues to address when designing for tablets.

25.3 Designing for Smartphones

Standard Web pages (i.e., those designed for delivery on a desktop) typically do not display well on smartphones due to their small screen size. For example, elements may not appear where they are intended in relation to other elements, text or images may be cut off, and a link text may be wrapped over several lines, making it difficult to read. Essentially, a design may be ruined. Figure 25.1 shows an example of how a Web page designed for a wide, high-resolution-screen looks on a smartphone.

Whether the solution to the type of problem in Figure 25.1 is to design a website specifically for mobile phones or adopt a responsive design (discussed in Chapter 21), the challenges created by mobile phones' small screen sizes need to be addressed. In addition to this, the fact that mobile phone are not operated via mouse clicks but typically via screen touch creates another set of challenges in relation to designing for touch-screen

Desktop screen   Smartphone screen

FIGURE 25.1   A Web page on a desktop (left), smartphone (right). (Image from decembermarketing. com.)

interaction. For example, how big must touch targets be to accommodate the finger, and how do users activate functions as one would with a mouse click on standard desktop computer. How these challenges are met in mobile design, such as through gesture inter- action and how to design content for limited space are discussed.

25.3.1 Designing Content for Smartphones

The structure of content forms the basis of navigation structure. For this reason, the structuring of content is usually done first, as it results in the creation of catego- ries and sub-categories, which in turn translate into menus and menu items. The types of processes used to structure content, such as **card sorting**, are discussed in Chapter 26. The most important issue to consider when designing content for delivery on smartphones is limited screen space. Studies show that the small size of mobile phones compromise usability in various ways. One is that it makes comprehension of information more difficult than usual. For example, a message is often spread across multiple screens, requiring users to remember the content read in the previous screen and connect it to the one in the current screen to construct an understanding. This is often more than the highly volatile and weak human short-term memory can handle. Scrolling from one part of the screen to another to read the rest of a piece of informa- tion can also create the same problem. The problem gets even worse with horizontal scrolling. Having to go from screen to screen in order to see the whole of a piece of information also diverts users' attention from the primary task of constructing under- standing to the secondary task of looking for the rest of the information. All these mean that when delivering content on smartphones, **design should compensate for small screens** and prevent or minimize these problems. Some guidelines on how to achieve this are provided here.

25.3.1.1 Content Structuring

For a successful mobile version of a website or a mobile app, the core principle is to **keep content extremely compact but meaningful**, while also focusing users' attention on what is important, using, for example, highlighting. The first screen should provide just enough elements to communicate the desired message. If users will not miss an element if it is not there, then it should not be there. Supportive or detailed information should be placed on secondary screens and shown only when requested by users. This is known as "**progressive disclosure**" (i.e., the principle of revealing a little at a time). In practice, this translates into providing short outlines of secondary content on the first screen and the means of accessing the detailed version. Studies have shown that the less dense and more focused the first screen, the more the likelihood that people will try to read and not skip it. This almost always translates into more visitors for a site. Even secondary content, such as a menu, should be subject to progressive disclosure. Figure 25.2 illustrates the principle of progressive disclosure, using menu page and menu-item page designs. The design on the left reveals too much for a menu, resulting in a design that is too dense and uneconomical with space. The same content is broken up and spread across the middle and right designs. The middle displays only the headings as hyperlinks, allowing for the use of ample space. The design on the right shows what is displayed when the first item is activated.

Bad content structuring   Good content structuring

FIGURE 25.2   Illustration of a wordy content (left) and its presentation using progressive disclosure (middle and right).

CHALLENGE 25.1

What would you say are the problems with the design on the left in Figure 25.2?

25.3.1.2 Number of Columns

It is best to use a single column that spans the width of the screen. Content should expand downwards instead of across, as it is easier to scroll downward than sideways and users generally prefer it. Even though some smartphones like iPhone typically zoom out content so as to make it fit the screen, when this is done, text usually becomes illegible, requiring users to zoom in various parts of a page in order to make them legible. This is not easy and requires extra work and can result in bad user experience.

25.3.1.3 Amount of Text Entry

Entering text on smartphones is more cumbersome than doing so on a proper QWERTY keyboard. Typing speed is slow and the number of errors is comparatively high. For these reasons, the amount of text users are required to enter should be minimal. To minimize text entry, users might be asked to use PIN instead of password, which is usually required to be long for the sake of security. When an address is required, users should be able to enter just an address code (postcode or zip code), which the system then uses to fill in the rest of the address. Also, users should only have to enter their address once. The address should be stored and retrieved when required.

25.3.1.4 Registration

Like in regular websites, **early registration should be avoided** in mobile websites or apps. Making users go through any type of registration process (including providing just an e-mail address) on the first screen of an app, before they can see what an app is about and decide whether or not they find it valuable enough to commit, can be off-putting. This can be even more so than in regular websites, because of the extra effort generally involved in inputting text in mobile devices. Another off-putting feature is a splash screen. Although it may be novel the first time, it can quickly become a nuisance, in that it forces users to wait unnecessarily.

25.3.2 Designing Navigation for Smartphones

Once the process of structuring content is completed and done thoroughly, it is easy to design navigation structure, since it is just a matter of connecting the categories and sub-categories that have emerged during the structuring process and translating them into menus and menu items. Unlike with desktop screens, many menus cannot be displayed across the top of a smartphone screen. However, because interaction is touch-based with mobile phones and buttons or icons must therefore be larger to accommodate the finger makes this impractical in mobile interface design, which is also commonly known as "**mobile design pattern**." Instead the presentation of menus in mobile phones is based on variations of a few general design principles, such as using the whole screen (or most of it) to display menus, permanently displaying only core navigation aids at the top or bottom of the screen, and permanently displaying a master generic navigation icon, such as a "**three-line menu navicon**," previously mentioned in Chapter 21. Figure 25.2 has already shown a variation of placing permanent navigation at the top and bottom of the screen. Figures 25.3 and 25.4 show illustrations of the use of the whole screen to display menus and the use of a permanently displayed navicon, respectively.

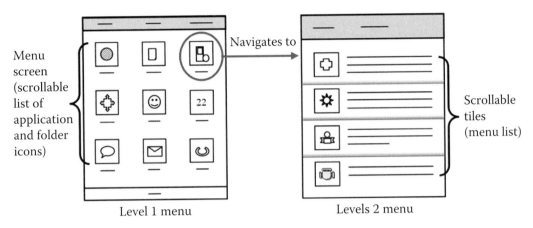

Menu screen (scrollable list of application and folder icons)

Navigates to

Scrollable tiles (menu list)

Level 1 menu

Levels 2 menu

FIGURE 25.3   Using the entire screen to display menus in mobile design.

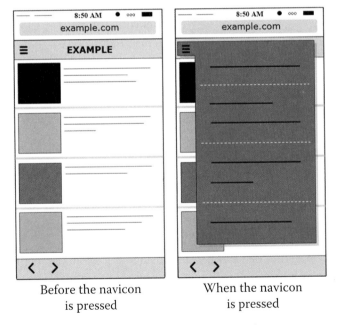

Before the navicon is pressed

When the navicon is pressed

FIGURE 25.4   Using the three-line menu navicon in mobile design.

CHALLENGE 25.2

It is impossible to cover all the variations and combinations of the principles illustrated in Figures 25.2–25.4. To get a better feel of mobile interface design, do a search on the Web for "mobile design patterns."

CHALLENGE 25.3

Design a mobile interface for a second-hand car sale company, assuming it sells different classes of vehicles, such as cars, vans, and trucks, and in different models.

25.3.2.1 Designing Touch Targets

Once navigation structure is established, navigation aids, such as buttons and icons, or touch targets, need to be designed. The designs vary, but the same best practices apply. All touch targets **should be big enough** to accommodate the size of a fingertip for easy touching or tapping. Making touch targets large enough to comfortably accommodate the fingertip contributes to good user experience, because it ensures that users can work as fast as they want without activating the wrong targets by mistake. According to Fitts' Law (discussed further in Chapter 26), the larger a target, the faster it takes to move from one point to the target. An implication of this, of course, is that the larger the target the less likely users are to worry about missing it and touching the wrong ones. For example, instead of requiring users to tap on just text or radio button, the surrounding area should be sensitive too to increase target size. **Touch targets should also not be too close to each other**, particularly if they are not big enough for the fingertip, otherwise users may end up touching the wrong target. An easy way to achieve these goals is to keep the amount of navigation options displayed simultaneously to minimum, so that there is enough space.

There is no one single recommendation for the size of a touch target, whether in centimeters or pixels. This is because different devices use different pixel sizes and different mobile platforms and manufacturers provide different recommendations. Also, different people have different finger sizes. In addition to this, different users screen-touch with different fingers; for example, some do with the index finger, while some with the thumb, which is bigger. There is, of course, also the question of whether there is enough space to make touch targets as big as possible. Here are some practical guidelines:

- Make targets the **average width of the index finger** if users are most likely to interact with an interface with the index finger or other fingers, but the thumb. This is between 1 cm and 2 cm, which is roughly **44–57 px** on standard resolution screens and **88–114 px** on high-density (retina) screens. Most mobile applications are interacted with using a non-thumb finger.

- Make targets the **average width of the thumb** if users are most likely to interact with the thumb, such as in games applications. This is about 2.5 cm (which is roughly **72 px**).

- If screen space does not allow making targets as big as the fingertip, the recommendations of the relevant manufacturer can be used; or the number of touch targets can be reduced to only very essential ones and navigation structure refined accordingly.

Touch-targets should also be clear and look touchable in order to promote **high discoverability**. The hover state is hardly useful on touch-screen and does not need to be implemented. Unless a server is able to automatically detect whether users are using a mobile or desktop device, it can be useful to provide a **clear direct link from the regular site** to the mobile site, and a **direct link from the mobile site to the regular site**. For a mobile application (mobile app), this is seldom a design concern, as there is usually no accompanying site to which to link.

25.3.2.2 Designing Touch Gestures and Animations

After navigation structure and touch targets have been designed, the touch gestures to be used with them, and the associated animations (i.e., transition effects), need to be designed. The use of finger gestures on mobile screens to activate specific functions is probably an inevitable invention, because it is intuitive, requires limited space to execute, and the same space can be used to execute different gestures.

Touch gestures can be divided into two components: the action of the finger on the screen, and the function it activates. These components are termed, for example, by Google as touch mechanics and touch activities, respectively. A "**touch mechanic**" can be a single tap on the screen and may result in any of multiple commands, such as to start or stop a process, depending on context. For example, it might be to start playing a piece of music when a media player is opened or to close a window when its corner is tapped. Similarly, a "**touch activity**" can be evoked via using a touch mechanic or a combination of touch mechanics. Good gesture interaction design should be about using gestures that are most intuitive and easy to learn, as this contributes to good user experience. For example, a gesture interaction design that requires users to flick up or down a Web page is likely more intuitive than one that requires them to flick from left to right or right to left. Similarly, requiring a combination of gestures for such a basic and frequent task is likely off-putting. A practical and safe starting point is to make use of commonly used gestures and the functions for which they are commonly used. These are listed in Table 25.1.

TABLE 25.1

Common Touch Gestures and Their Description

Gesture	Description and Common Usages
Tap	One finger taps the screen. For selecting an element.
Double tap	One finger taps the screen twice. For zooming in or out on content, or opening something, as in double-clicking.
Drag	One finger touches, moves relatively slowly, and lifts. For moving an object from one point to another.
Swipe (or flick)	One finger touches screen, moves quickly, and lifts. It is basically a quick drag movement. Used for functions like scrolling, rejecting, and panning in different directions.
Pinch closed	Two fingers with space between them touch the screen, move closer, and lift. Used for functions like zooming out and closing an opened object.
Pinch opened (spread)	Two fingers with no space between them touch the screen, move apart, and lift. Used for functions like zooming in and opening a closed object.
Press	One finger touches screen, waits, and lifts. Used for functions like selecting an element (e.g., a list item) and changing mode.

(Continued)

TABLE 25.1 (*Continued*)

Common Touch Gestures and Their Description

Gesture	Description and Common Usages
Press and drag	One finger touches screen, waits, moves, and lifts. Used for picking up and moving an object and selecting multiple items.
Press and tap	One finger touches the screen and the second taps it. Used for displaying menu. Equivalent to right-clicking.
Double-tap drag	One finger touches the screen, lifts, touches again, moves, and lifts. Used for zooming in and out.
Two-finger tap	Two fingers simultaneously tap the screen. Used for zooming out.
Two-finger drag	Two fingers touch the screen, move, and lift. Used for selecting multiple items.
Two-finger swipe (or flick)	Two fingers simultaneously touch the screen, move quickly, and lift. Used for panning and tilting.
Two-finger double tap	Two fingers simultaneously tap the screen twice. Used for zooming out.
Two-finger press and drag	Two fingers simultaneously touch the screen, wait, move, and lift. Used to pick up and move objects.
Rotate	Two fingers simultaneously touch the screen and simultaneously rotate about a point. Used to rotate objects.
3D-touch	This was introduced in iPhone 6S and 6S Plus and allows finger pressure on the screen to be incorporated into screen gesture interaction design. It can be combined with any of the other gestures.

The **animation component of touch gestures** helps give a touch activity feedback and more realism. Instead of the screen going directly from one state to another when a gesture is given, the states are animated, as discussed in Chapter 18. The animation can be a simple transition effect or a more elaborate and fancy animation. However, it is worth noting that fancy animations can become annoying after the initial fascination they provide. Figure 25.5 shows an illustration of the content of the screen changing from "1" to "2" after, for example, a swipe gesture, with the next content coming in from the right to cover the current one. The middle state represents the transition phase.

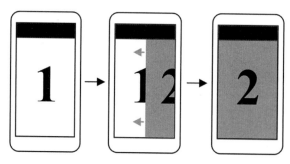

FIGURE 25.5   Illustration of transition between screens following a gesture.

CHALLENGE 25.4

Figure 25.5 shows an illustration of a screen content change after touch gesture. What sort of gesture would you design to initiate it and why?

25.4 Designing for Tablets

The screen sizes of tablets are unlike those of smartphones. They are larger and can be, as of time of writing, as big as 2048 × 1536 at 264 ppi or over. This means that they can display regular Web pages reasonably well. However, for websites to be actually usable on tablets, they need to support touch-screen operation. For example, touch-targets, such as link text and interactive features, need to be larger than normal to accommodate tapping and give the appearance that they can be activated.

What this means is that there are a number of options available for catering to the tablet audience:

1. You could design a tablet-friendly regular website that supports touch-screen interaction.
2. You could design a responsive website.
3. You could create a tablet application, which strictly is not a website.

Whichever you choose, the same general design principles are followed that facilitate touch-screen interaction as with smartphones, except that more content can be displayed at once on tablets. Here are some guidelines:

- Text should be larger to aid legibility. If possible, a function could be provided to allow users to control text size.
- Enough space should be provided around links, especially form controls and drop-downs like calendars, to aid accurate touch-selection.
- Like for other touch-screen devices, the hover state is not necessary and does not need to be implemented in tablet versions of websites.
- Standard navigation convention should be supported, including homepage-like features, search facility, back buttons, and touchable headlines, because users often desire them. In particular, users would rather have a regular table of contents that they could use to make a choice anytime than swipe through long lists of thumbnails (or popovers) to do it. Figure 25.6 shows examples of how standard navigation and menu presentation convention, such as drop-down menu, is implemented on tablet.

CHALLENGE 25.5

Do a search on the Web for tablet and iPad design patterns to see the broad varieties of design concepts and help formulate your own ideas.

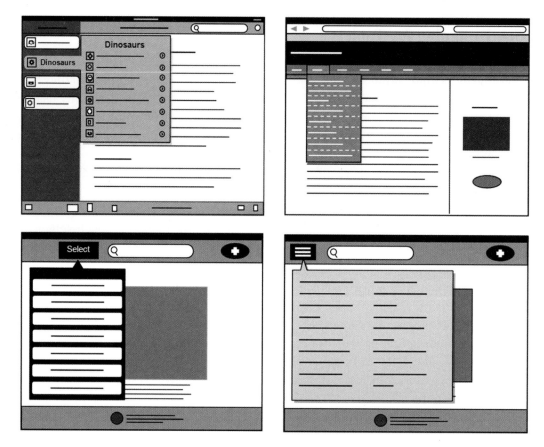

FIGURE 25.6   Examples of drop-down menu on iPad.

25.5 Useful Info

25.5.1 Web Links

Design usability: nngroup.com (under Articles)

Offering mobile-version of your site: company.skweezer.com

W3 Mobile web initiative: w3.org/Mobile

List of mobile emulators: mobilexweb.com (under Emulators tab)

Testing site for suitability for mobile: ready.mobi, responsivepx.com

Mobile emulator: mobilephoneemulator.com, ipadpeek.com, iphonetester.com, validator.w3.org/mobile

Part IV

Web Development Process

26

Web Development Process

26.1 Introduction

While a small website project that involves only one person and has no time constraint may not require a systematic approach for it to succeed, in large, complex Web projects that involve many people, including clients and users, a systematic way of working can mean the difference between success and failure. This systematic approach involves working in stages to ensure good understanding of the problem being solved, the proposed solution, and the requirements of the target users. This chapter explains the concept of systematic approach in Web development, using user-centered design (UCD).

26.2 Learning Outcomes

After studying this chapter, you should:

- be aware of the concept of user-centered development process and the tasks performed at each stage.

26.3 User-Centered Design Process

One of the first conceptual models for managing software development projects was software development life cycle (SDLC). It is a general model that is designed to impose structure on the way any type of software is produced and defines the phases of software development as Planning, Analysis, Design, Development, Testing, Delivery, and Maintenance. The idea is that by following these phases, the process of software development becomes more structured, more manageable, and less prone to failure. Various implementations of the concept have since been developed and most system development processes or models borrow in some way from it.

One of the significant failings of the SDLC concept is its lack of adequate attention to the users of the system being developed. Once the requirements for a system

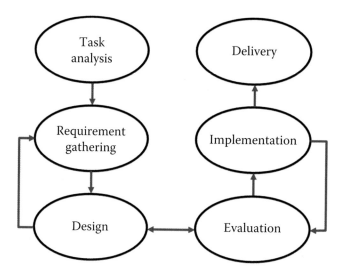

FIGURE 26.1　The stages of UCD.

have been gathered from them, they are typically not involved again until the end of the project during delivery. There is no paying attention to their feedback and characteristics all through the stages of development and using them to revise the system's design. This problem is what subsequent processes like the UCD process are designed to address. The UCD process combines the elements of sequential and iterative techniques, and is quite sympathetic to users and their needs. For example, it is based on the principle that a system should be made to work the way users want it to work rather than the other way around. Figure 26.1 shows one representation of the stages of UCD, which are Task Analysis, Requirements gathering, Design, Implementation, Evaluation, and Delivery. The rest of this chapter discusses the typical tasks involved within each stage.

26.3.1 Task Analysis Phase

Consider a commission to develop a Web application to assist a group of people in performing their daily tasks. The first process would be to understand what these people (the potential users) do and how they do it. Technically speaking, **task analysis** is conducted on what they do. There are different ways of conducting task analysis, each capable of providing different types of information, but all have the same aim of identifying a goal and the series of tasks necessary to accomplish it in order to develop an understanding that enables their modeling. Two common ones are **field studies** and **hierarchical task analysis**.

26.3.1.1 Field Studies

A field study essentially entails observing people working in their natural environment and gathering as much information as possible for analysis. Although it can also include the analysis of documents and conversations or interviews with participants, observation is the main activity and this is usually conducted quietly. Being quiet is especially important so as not to bias users or make them change behavior. The output from the process is a description of the tasks these people perform when undertaking their duties, and if a computer system already exists, a description of their interaction with it. Although the process does not provide all the requirements for a system, it does provide an initial indication of the possible direction for design. Because field studies can help identify potential sources of problems right from the start, it can help avoid the problems at a later stage when they are more costly to correct.

26.3.1.2 Hierarchical Task Analysis

Hierarchical Task Analysis (HTA) is a process in which a goal is progressively broken down into smaller parts, such as tasks, sub-tasks, and actions, until the smallest task is reached; hence, the term "hierarchical." The output from HTA can be in textual or graphical form. If in text, a hierarchical list of tasks is produced, along with a plan of the order in which they are carried out. Figure 26.2 shows an example of a graphical output for the typical tasks involved in cash withdrawal from an ATM machine. It is a commonly used example, because most people are familiar with the sequence of steps used for withdrawing cash from the ATM machine. It says the goal (i.e., 0) is to withdraw cash and the sequence is to perform task 1 and its sub-tasks (1.1 and 1.2), and then move on to task 2, and so on, until 5.2. A textual output is written just like a table of content.

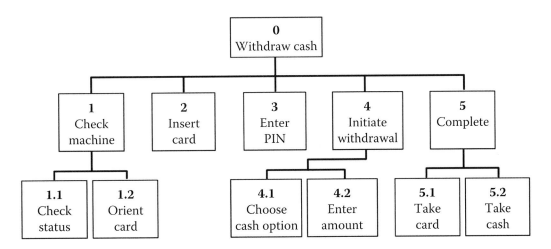

FIGURE 26.2   Task analysis for ATM cash withdrawal.

CHALLENGE 26.1

Produce Figure 26.2 in textual form. Just imagine you are producing a table of content and structure the steps accordingly.

26.3.2 Requirements-Gathering Phase

Having completed the necessary task analysis, the next phase is to gather requirements for the system you want to develop. These fall into two main categories: functional and usability. **Functional requirements** (i.e., what the system is required to do) are mostly derived from the HTA output, and **usability requirements** (i.e., the ease with which tasks can be carried out on the system) are derived from various other means, including interviews, questionnaires, observing users work in their natural work environment, and usability principles. Additional requirements may also relate to legal and ethical issues. These include, for example, whether or not copyright clearance for any media that will be used or compliance with any laws, such as data protection laws, are required. In all, the requirements should answer questions like what users' preferences are; what their skills and experience are; and what they need. These questions should also help determine the weaknesses and strengths of users, based on their skills and experience, all of which contribute to deeper understanding of what is expected of the new system, including what design options to consider.

As might be expected, finalizing requirements the first time this phase is undertaken is rare, particularly as users are not usually clear about what they require or how to describe it, or whether or not what they want is technologically feasible; so, this phase, like most after it, may have to be revisited many times. The output from it is a report, known as the **requirements statement**, which clearly lists both the functional and usability requirements for the new system. For each requirement, what is required is described, along with the rationale for it and a way of measuring it in the completed system. This measurement can be **quantitative**, that is, in the form of measuring something, such as number of keystrokes or screen-touches it takes to complete a task. So, for example, a metric might be that anyone should be able to complete a task in five keystrokes or screen-touches. The measurement can also be **qualitative**, that is, in the form of asking users to complete questionnaires, for example, about how satisfied they are with the color scheme of a screen. Web accessibility requirements, which can be derived from Web accessibility guidelines, would be part of what is included in the requirements statement. In some cases, it may be necessary to provide a justification for the need to address Web accessibility, in which case, a business case would need to be provided. However, this is usually only relevant in large projects for organizations. The business case for Web accessibility is provided by w3.org.

26.3.3 Design Phase

During this phase, the requirements in the **requirements statement** from the previous phase are translated into design. To accomplish this, information and requirements already gathered are categorized, typically using **card sorting** (explained shortly), and **prototypes** of various design ideas are created from the output and evaluated in the next phase to identify and correct usability problems. This design-evaluation process is repeated until all obvious problems are identified and fixed, at which point implementation of the design that is agreed on can commence.

26.3.3.1 Card Sorting

Card sorting is used to organize information in order to help design the information structure of a system. For a website, it helps inform on the content of pages and the connection between the pages. A **card sorting session** involves participants (who can be subject experts or novice users) organizing topics into categories in a way that makes most sense to them. They may or may not also be required to name the categories, with each category translating into a page. On large sites, the pages can also be grouped to create sections. Card sorting can be conducted using actual physical cards or pieces of paper, each carrying a separate topic, or any of the various on-line software tools can be used. The method is especially useful because it can help you understand what users expect from a site.

There are two main types of card sorting: open and closed. In **open card sort**, participants are required to sort information into categories and name the categories. This approach is usually good for determining how to best structure information to benefit users. In **closed card sort**, users are required only to group topics into a pre-defined set of categories. This is suitable for checking if the current information structure matches users' expectations. The two, of course, can be combined. Once categories and/or sections are determined, they are used as the basis for producing different design ideas, which are then visualized using prototypes.

26.3.3.2 Prototypes

A prototype is basically a rough version of a design idea that allows you to show the idea to users for consideration and constructive feedback before investing effort, time, and money in full development. No doubt it is easier and cheaper to make changes to a design idea early in development, when you are still planning and before any codes are even written, than after a site has been fully implemented. Prototypes ensure a product is produced that pleases the users and are typically high fidelity or low fidelity.

- **High-fidelity prototype**: These are computer-based and usually allow user interaction, for example, via mouse, keyboard, and/or touch. Because they are as close as possible to the intended design, they are considered the best for collecting accurate user-performance data, such as those that require responses from the system. They are also preferred when demonstrating design ideas to clients.

- **Low-fidelity prototype:** These are usually paper based and not interactive. They can be anything from hand-drawings on paper to printouts of diagrams. Because they are easy and cheap to produce, it is possible to create many alternative design ideas, thereby increasing the chances of arriving at the best possible design. Typical examples are flowcharts, wireframes, and paper prototypes, which are discussed next.

26.3.3.2.1 Flowcharts

Flowcharts have their origin in engineering and are visual representations of the flow of control (i.e., the steps involved in a process). They describe how things work and are like maps of events. They can be basic or very complex, depending

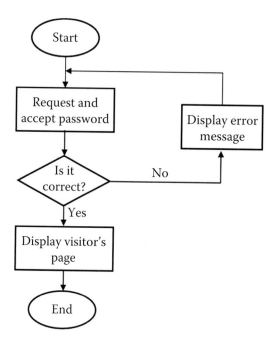

FIGURE 26.3   An example flowchart for a simple process.

on the complexity of the task being visualized. Figure 26.3 illustrates the concept. It visualizes a basic process in which the user is asked for a password. After it is entered, it is checked; if it is not correct, an error message is displayed and the user is asked for it again. The process is repeated until a valid password is entered, after which the user is allowed to go on to their page. The rectangles in the chart represent screens with messages and/or content for the user and can contain anything, including images, video, and animation. The diamond, known as **decision symbol**, indicates a decision-making process. The ovals are just terminals to indicate where a task starts and ends. There are various other symbols designed to communicate specific functions.

   A flowchart is used to visualize many different kinds of processes and often annotated in different ways, so there are various types, but the goal is the same and that is to clearly communicate the workings or structure of something so that everyone involved can create it and/or use it. In Web design, a flowchart can be as basic as a diagram showing how the pages of a site connect to each other. This is why it is sometimes referred to as a **sitemap** or a site's **navigational structure**. For a complex website, flowchart can also include script-generated pages and loops to illustrate paths of user-interaction or decisions. Path of user-interaction or decisions is also sometimes referred to as **user flow** or **user journey**. Figure 26.4 shows two different navigational structures for a basic personal website. The left design shows a **linear navigation structure** in which users can only go from a page to the one that is adjacent. The right design shows a **network navigation structure** that allows users to go from one page to any other. In either design, the site can be entered from any page just by, for example, typing the address in a Web

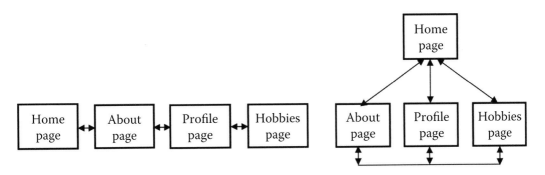

FIGURE 26.4 Two different navigation designs for the same site.

browser. Naturally, the design on the right makes more sense for a personal Website, as users are more likely to want to choose specific pages than navigate linearly.

In the example, if in order to go from the home page to any of the other pages a password is required, then how that process should work and the pages/messages that will be displayed are included in the flowchart. These could directly be part of the chart, or an appropriate symbol could be used to represent it and the full details presented separately.

CHALLENGE 26.2

The navigational structures in Figure 26.4 imply the types of navigational components or aids that each page on the site must have. State them. Also, produce a user flow chart for going from home page, to product page, adding a product to cart, and completing purchase.

26.3.3.2.2 Wireframes

A wireframe is a skeletal diagram, typically with no color or graphics, which is used to specify the details of everything that will enable a screen to be created as intended. These can include the layout of elements, color scheme, text color, font type, font size, media usage and intended treatments, and interactivity details, such as the description of actions possible from the screen. If videos or animations are involved, for example, the scripts to be spoken or used in voice-overs, if any, are included. Using the flowchart on the right in Figure 26.4 as reference, Figure 26.5 shows the wireframe of a possible design concept for the home page. The term **"storyboard"** is sometimes used to refer to a wireframe or a collection or sequence of wireframes.

CHALLENGE 26.3

Create the wireframe for the home page for the flowchart on the left in Figure 26.4, assuming you are presenting the same content as the wireframe in Figure 26.5.

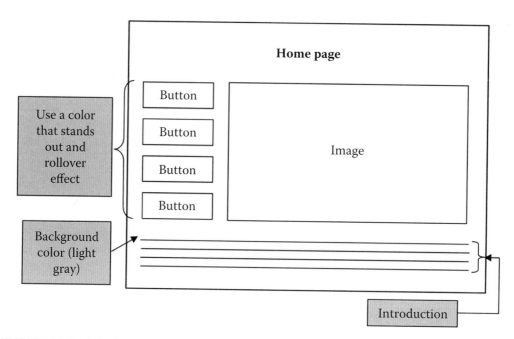

FIGURE 26.5   Wireframe for the home page design of the flowchart on the right in Figure 26.4.

26.3.3.2.3 Paper Prototypes

Paper prototypes are by far the quickest methods of collecting useful feedback on preliminary design ideas and information structure. They are straightforward to produce
and basically involve using pieces of paper to simulate a user interface. The pieces can
be stuck on one another, folded, and colored as necessary. The approach especially
fosters creativity in that it encourages the exchange of ideas between different people.
It is also cost effective, popular, requires no design or coding skills, and encourages
rapid design evaluation. Figure 26.6 shows a snapshot of an example of a paper prototype from an NNGroup paper prototyping training video.

FIGURE 26.6   An example of a mobile application paper prototype. (Image from nngroup.com.)

26.3.4 Evaluation Phase

Evaluation primarily serves the purpose of testing a website for various types of characteristics. It could be **formative** (i.e., conducted during development to ensure users' needs continually shape development) or **summative** (i.e., conducted after a site is completed to check if it meets set requirements). The two main types of summative evaluation are alpha testing and beta testing. **Alpha testing** is the first evaluation after completion and usually done to see that a site works under varying setups and conditions. The errors and usage problems recorded are then fixed, after which **beta testing** is conducted. This is typically done with a limited number of people from the intended users in the normal environment. The reasons evaluation is done include the following:

- Checking if a system performs efficiently or is not producing the expected results, perhaps due to incorrect logic in programming or misinterpretation of the system's requirements.
- Checking whether users find a system easy to learn and use, or like the way it works or looks in terms of aesthetics.
- Checking conformity to some standards, such as Web Content Accessibility Guidelines (WCAG).

Where a commercial site is involved, evaluation can also be a useful tool to find out from potential users how they would like the site to work, look, and feel when finished. In reality, **evaluation starts as soon as a project begins and design ideas are proposed**. Also, it does not have to be of the system being developed; it can, for example, be of an existing system or systems to garner ideas for a new one. Apart from testing that the functions of a website work as intended, **usability testing** is the most important evaluation activity in a development process and is part of the general **user experience testing**. Also important is website **accessibility testing**.

26.3.4.1 Usability Testing

Ensuring high-degree usability of anything designed to be used is important in order for the thing to be acceptable and popular. A website is no different. In the face of many competitions, a website that is not easy to use and does not give visitors user satisfaction and good user experience is most likely to lose out, because people will probably stop visiting it. Website usability testing is the evaluation of a site for the property of being easy to use. It involves measuring users' performance while they use the site to accomplish pre-determined tasks, or after they have accomplished the tasks. The primary aim is to determine whether users find the site usable for accomplishing the tasks for which it has been designed.

To conduct usability testing, users are given set tasks to complete and their performance and satisfaction level measured. Types of tasks can vary widely, ranging from reading from different types of interfaces with different color schemes or fonts to navigating content and searching for information. While these tasks are performed, performance data is collected in various ways, including through **interaction logging**

techniques (e.g., recording keystrokes, mouse-button clicks, mouse movements, or touches) and **video recording**. User-satisfaction data is collected using **query techniques** (e.g., interviews and questionnaires) in the form of asking users to rate their feelings on a scale, usually immediately after completion of tasks when feelings are still fresh. Performance is measured mainly in terms of two elements—time and number, such as completion time and the number of steps it takes to complete a task. Typical usability performance measures used in the evaluation of an application include:

- Time to complete a task.
- Time to complete a task after being away from an application for a specified time.
- Number of errors per task.
- Number of errors per unit of time.
- Number of navigations necessary to get to help information.
- Number of users committing a particular error.
- Number of users completing a task successfully.

Using combinations of these measures as appropriate, it is possible to evaluate the qualities that define the usability of a system, which are, as previously mentioned in Chapter 24, mainly **learnability** (ease of learning), **memorability** (ease of remembering how to use it), **effectiveness** (how effectively it can perform a task), **efficiency** (how quickly it can be used to perform a task), **errors** (number of errors, severity, and recoverability), **utility** (provision of useful functions), and **satisfaction** (how pleasant it is to use).

26.3.4.1.1 Usability Testing Methods

Website usability testing can be carried out in various ways. The following are some of the commonly used methods in computer application development, which naturally apply to Web applications.

26.3.4.1.1.1 Hallway Testing   This is a testing that is set up in an area of high pedestrian traffic and designed to test bystanders and passersby. It relies on people who have time to spare and are willing. It is especially suitable for websites intended for the general public, because it provides the opportunity to determine how usable the sites are to a large and diverse audience. To get the best results from the method:

- Choose an area that has heavy foot traffic and avoid scheduling tests during inconvenient hours or when there are major events going on.
- Use pleasant, outgoing, and determined greeters to identify and recruit test participants.
- Ensure that the objectives of the test are clearly explained to participants.
- Do not make a test last too long. The maximum time for an individual is 10 minutes.
- Reward volunteers, for example, with gratitude or gifts, such as sweets or pens.

26.3.4.1.1.2 Paper Prototype Testing Paper prototype testing entails testing paper prototypes described earlier under the Design phase. Usability testing with paper prototypes is usually iterative and one of the best methods for discovering potential usability problems with a design early. Finding problems as early as possible and addressing them can save a lot of time, effort, and money that would be lost if the design were developed and the problems found later. Another benefit of the technique is that it supports user involvement from an early stage.

Conducting usability testing on a paper prototype usually involves the **user**, a **facilitator** (who is a usability expert who records issues raised during the testing), **the design expert** (who understands the design being tested and quietly manipulates the paper prototype in response to the user), and **observers** (who are typically members of the development team, who observe and interpret the users' interaction with the prototype and take note). The total number of users tested, like in other usability tests, is about five, which, according to the Nielsen Norman Group, is capable of catching about 85% of usability problems.

To evaluate a paper prototype, the user is asked to touch the desired feature on the paper representation of a screen to simulate a click. When this is done, the design expert changes the paper interface accordingly to simulate screen response. For example, if it is an option to go to another screen, then the current page is replaced with the requested one. If it is a menu, then a piece of paper representing a drop-down menu is shown, and so on.

26.3.4.1.1.3 Usability Laboratory Testing (Controlled Testing) Controlled usability testing is conducted in a usability laboratory, or an environment that is similarly controlled, where users cannot be disturbed or interrupted. Such an environment would consist of the **testing room**, which is fitted with audiovisual facilities to record various interaction activities, including microphone to capture what is said and video cameras to record users' behaviors, such as movements and facial expression. These activities are watched on monitors in an adjacent **observation room** separated from the testing room with a one-way mirror that allows investigators to observe the participants. The downside is that this type of setup lacks the features and activities of a natural work environment. This means that findings from evaluations conducted in usability labs may not necessary hold when a system is used in a natural work environment where there usually are disturbances, such as interruptions and noise. Additionally, usability labs can be very expensive to run and maintain. A common alternative is to set up monitoring equipment temporarily in the relevant work environment. When this is done, a work environment is, in effect, temporarily converted into a usability lab. This is relatively less expensive and provides a more natural environment for users, making findings more accurate.

26.3.4.1.1.4 Walkthroughs In computing, walkthrough, usually called **code walkthrough**, is often used to describe the process of inspecting algorithms and source code to check if certain programming principles, such as coding style and naming conventions, are followed. In evaluation, walkthroughs seek to perform similar function, except that the aim is to identify usability problems. Essentially, experts use a system as if they are the intended users in order to identify usability problems. The most commonly used are **cognitive** and **pluralistic** walkthroughs.

In a **cognitive walkthrough**, experts explore various sequences of steps users are likely to go through to accomplish a task on a system to identify usability problems. The main aim is usually to determine how easy it is to use a system. Because of the exploratory nature of the technique, the checks performed revolve round determining, through asking questions, if a system supports exploratory learning. Basically, for each step taken to accomplish a task, an account of why the step facilitates or does not facilitate usability is provided. To conduct a cognitive walkthrough, four items are required:

1. A description of the prototype to be evaluated.
2. A description of a specific task that the intended users will perform on the system.
3. A complete list of the actions (i.e., steps) required to complete the task.
4. A description of the characteristics of the intended users, such as experience level.

Equipped with this information, an evaluator follows the sequence of actions listed in Item 3 above to accomplish the specified task and then gives an account of associated usability issues. In order to be able to give this usability account, the evaluator asks questions that include the following:

a. Will the action necessary to perform a task be obvious to users at that point? Will users know what to do to achieve the task?
b. Will users notice that correct action is available? Will they notice, for example, the button or menu item that they can use to perform the action?
c. Once users find the correct action, will they know that it is the one needed to complete the task?
d. Will users understand the feedback they are provided after the action is completed? Will they know that they have made the right or wrong choice?

The evaluator keeps records of what is good and which aspects of the design need refinement. A set of standardized forms may be used for this. One form, used as cover, might list the information described in Items 1–4 listed earlier as well as the date and time of the walkthrough and the names of the evaluators. For each action listed in Item 3, a separate form might be completed that provides answers to the questions in a–d. Any negative answers to any questions for any action are carefully documented on a separate form, including the details of the system, its version number (if applicable), the date of evaluation, the evaluators' names, and the description of the usability problem. Also normally included is the severity of the problem, such as the frequency of occurrence, its impact (whether it is easy or difficult to overcome), and its persistence (whether users will be repeatedly bothered by it). This information helps designers give priorities to the order in which problems are fixed. Systems that this technique is suited for include those that require complex operations to perform tasks. The downside is that it can be very time consuming and laborious, and requires a good understanding of the cognitive processes involved in completing a task.

In **pluralistic walkthroughs**, the same procedure is followed as in cognitive walkthroughs, except that it is done by a diverse group that includes users, interface designers, developers, usability experts, and management. All participants are asked by the coordinator to assume the role of a user. Bringing different types of participants together makes it possible to gather views from various perspectives, allowing for a greater number of usability problems to be identified. The method is particularly well suited for early development stages, enabling the discovery and resolution of usability problems quickly and early. Another advantage is that it makes developers more sensitive to users' concerns, which can be very useful where usability can make the difference between life and death. The method is accomplished through a sequence of steps:

1. Each participant is presented with a series of printed screens that are ordered in the same way that they would be displayed when users are performing specific tasks, and asked to write down, in as much detail as possible, the sequence of steps they would use to go from one screen to another; for example, "Press the up-arrow key four times, then press 'Enter'."

2. A discussion is held about the actions all participants have suggested. Usually, the representative users speak first, so that they are not intimidated by the experts' contributions. Next, the usability experts present their findings, and then the developers provide their comments, which would include the rationale for the design. The developers' attitude would be welcoming. If necessary, the coordinator presents the correct set of actions and clarifies any unclear situations.

3. All participants are asked to complete a brief questionnaire regarding the usability of the evaluated design.

4. Steps 1–3 are repeated for all screens.

CHALLENGE 26.4

Conduct a cognitive walkthrough for viewing the details of a camera at www.amazon.co.uk, without going on to buy it.

26.3.4.1.1.5 Expert Review—Heuristic Evaluation Heuristic evaluation involves different experts assessing a system independently for its compliance with recognized heuristics (i.e., usability principles and practices), with the aim of finding usability problems in the system. The elements evaluated can be user-interface elements, such as color scheme, menu, navigation structure, and dialogue boxes, or functional elements, such as speed of response and error recovery. Ten general principles (or rules of thumb) are defined by the Nielsen Norman Group (NN/g) that should be followed to ensure usability:

- **Visibility of system status**: A system should always inform users in good time about what is going on, using appropriate feedback, such as pop-ups and sound.

- **Match between system and the real world**: A system should communicate in the users' language, instead of in technical terms.

- **User control and freedom**: When users choose a system function by mistake, there should be a quick and clearly marked "emergency exit." Undoing and redoing actions should also be supported.

- **Consistency and standards**: The system should be consistent in behavior, both by itself and in relation to other systems like it. Users should not be made to wonder whether different words, situations, or actions mean the same thing. For example, the same words should always be used to describe the same situations and actions, and established ways of doing things should be consistently maintained.

- **Error prevention**: As well as providing appropriate error messages, a system should prevent errors from occurring to start with. For example, error-prone procedures, such as typing, should be replaced with less error-prone ones like drag-and-drop and users given the chance to confirm an action before committing to it.

- **Recognition rather than recall**: Objects, actions, and options should be made visible so as to minimize memory load and aid dialogue between the user and the system. For example, important information from one screen should be carried forward to the next, instead of making users remember it. Also, help information and instructions should be clearly visible and easily accessible.

- **Flexibility and efficiency of use**: A system should provide multiple levels or modes of interaction so that it can cater to both inexperienced and experienced users. This should also include user customization and the use of shortcuts that allow tasks to be accomplished in as few steps as possible.

- **Aesthetic and minimalist design**: Dialogues should contain only information that is relevant or often needed. Too much information makes relevant information harder to see and can also make presentation aesthetically less pleasing.

- **Help users recognize, diagnose, and recover from errors**: Error messages should be in plain and precise non-technical language, stating the problem and suggesting a solution.

- **Help and documentation**: Help documentation should be provided that is structured and easy to search, and provides concrete steps that can be easily followed, particularly for complex systems. Five basic types of help are identified that can be provided, based on the types of questions users typically ask during interaction: **goal-oriented** (What can I use this application to do?), **descriptive** (What is this or what does this do?), **procedural** (How do I perform this task?), **interpretive** (Why has that happened?), and **navigational** (Where am I?).

During evaluation, these heuristics are matched against the features and functions of a system. For example, in the case of a website, for the first heuristic, an evaluator might check whether it provides feedback when the cursor points at an interactive element (such as a button) and whether the feedback is visible enough to be easily noticed, and then repeat this with various elements of the site before moving to the next heuristic. The higher the number of evaluators involved, the higher the number of usability problems likely to be found. A disadvantage of heuristic evaluation method is that it is not always as accurate as expected.

CHALLENGE 26.5

In the case of a navigational button and an image, how would first heuristic on the list be satisfied, and what aspect of HTML and/or CSS can be used to achieve it?

26.3.4.1.1.6 Expert Review—Keystroke-Level Model Method   The Keystroke-Level Model (KLM) is one of evaluation methods known as predictive modeling methods. These methods involve experts using formulas (known as **predictive models**) to predict user-performance at completing various types of tasks on various systems. This means that they can be used, for example, to evaluate whether a system is performing to standard, or compare the efficiency of different systems at performing the same set of tasks, or compare and choose between different user-interface designs for a proposed system, such as in terms of the effectiveness of their layouts for performing the same task.

KLM is the simplest and the most commonly used of the predictive models and one of a class of predictive methods known as Goals, Operators, Methods, Selection (GOMS) rules. This is why KLM is also referred to as KLM-GOMS. It uses predefined classes of operators, each of which has estimated execution time assigned to it. This makes it possible to use the model to predict and compare the times it will take to perform a task on a system when using different sequence of actions. This is particularly useful for determining which of the different ways of performing a task is the most effective, or which design is most effective for performing a task. The original KLM defines the following six classes of operators and execution times:

- **K** For single key-press
  - Best Typist (135 wpm): 0.08 seconds
  - Good Typist (90 wpm): 0.12 seconds
  - Poor Typist (40 wpm): 0.28 seconds
  - Average Skilled Typist (55 wpm): 0.20 seconds
  - Average Non-secretary Typist (40 wpm): 0.28 seconds
  - Typing Random Letters: 0.50 seconds
  - Typing Complex Codes: 0.75 seconds
  - Worst Typist (unfamiliar with keyboard): 1.20 seconds

- **P**—For pointing the mouse to an object on screen: 1.10 seconds
- **B**—For button press or release (e.g., mouse): 0.10 seconds
- **BB** (or **P₁**)—for button click (e.g., mouse), that is, pressing and releasing: 0.20 seconds
- **H**—For moving hands from keyboard to mouse or vice versa: 0.40 seconds
- **M**—For mental preparation for performing an action: 1.20 seconds
- **R** (**R(t)**)—For system response, where the user has to wait when carrying out a task
- **T(n)**—For typing a sequence of n characters on a keyboard (**n × K sec**)

To use the model to evaluate a system, the evaluator first chooses a representative task and determines the different ways in which it can be completed, or how users might complete it. Next, any assumptions are listed. For example, if the task is to delete an item, assumptions might state whether or not the Trashcan (Bin) is visible on the screen and can be pointed to, and that only one item will be deleted. They would also include stating the start and end position for a task, such as whether the hand starts and ends on the mouse, and where the cursor will end up at the end of the task. Next, the sequence of keystrokes-level actions (i.e., instructions) for each approach, such as "Point to file icon" and "Press and hold mouse button," is listed, along with the corresponding operators, such as K and P. If necessary, operators are included for when users must wait for the system to respond, or have to stop to think. Next, the execution time for each operator is included and the total time calculated for each method. The one with the smallest execution time represents the most efficient method of completing the task. This procedure is repeated for all representative tasks. The following example is the sequence of operators required to accomplish the task of dragging a file icon to the Recycle Bin that is visible in Windows platform and the total execution time for the task.

1. Point to file icon (**P**)
2. Press and hold mouse button (**B**)
3. Drag file icon to Recycle Bin icon (**P**)
4. Release mouse button (**B**)
5. Point to original window (**P**)

Total execution time $= 3P + 2B = 3 \times 1.1 + 2 \times 0.1 = 3.3 + 0.2 = 3.5$ sec.

The main advantage of the KLM is that it allows decisions to be made about systems without the necessity for expensive procedures and the sometimes difficult task of conducting evaluation using users. The main downside is that the execution times used are only estimates that may not hold in real-life work environments. They do not, for example, make allowance for errors or various factors that influence user-performance when performing a task, such as fatigue, mental workload, and working style; nor do they make allowance for the fact that users do not always carry out tasks in a predictable sequential order. For these reasons and other limitations, predictive models in general are most useful only when tasks are short and clearly defined, with limited variations in the way they can be performed.

CHALLENGE 26.6

Conduct a KLM evaluation for accomplishing the task of selecting a file icon and pressing the Delete key to delete it, and then compare the result with the example above and state which one is the more efficient method. Remember to state any assumptions made.

26.3.4.1.1.7 Expert Review—Fitts' Law   Fitts' law is another predictive modeling technique used in usability testing. It is a law that suggests a relationship between the time required to move from one point to a target, the distance to the target, and the target's size. A useful piece of information from this is that the bigger a target, the more easily and more quickly it is to reach it, perhaps because people are more confident about their judgment and therefore more apt to advance more quickly than move at reduced speed. In essence, it provides the primary reason for why graphical user-interfaces with bigger buttons and icons are easier to use than those with smaller ones. The law is represented mathematically in various ways. Figure 26.7 shows an example of one of the simpler ones.

CHALLENGE 26.7

Given the message of Fitts' law, how might it help during design, even without engaging in formulas and calculations?

26.3.4.2 Evaluating Websites for Accessibility

Evaluation designed specifically to address accessibility is a relatively recent kind of evaluation, as accessibility is a more recent notion brought about by the popularity of the Web for delivering information to the general population by governments and organizations designed to help the general public. As with guidelines on how to implement

$$T = k \log_2(D/S + 1.0)$$

where
   T = average time taken to move the pointer to a target
   D = the distance from starting point to the center of target
   S = the size of target (normally measured in terms of its width)
   k = the speed of pointer; a constant of approximately 200msec/bit

FIGURE 26.7   Equation for Fitts' law.

Web accessibility, detailed recommendations on when and how its evaluation should be conducted are provided on W3C WAI's website. As a result, only summaries of the key elements are discussed here.

Evaluation of accessibility serves numerous purposes. One is to help identify during the development of a website any problems that might compromise accessibility. Another purpose is to determine conformance to Web accessibility guidelines, which may be proprietary, government guidelines (such as America's Section 508), or W3C WAI's WCAG. Evaluation of accessibility can also be to monitor an existing site on an ongoing basis to ensure accessibility is maintained. It is particularly useful when done throughout the development of a website, as it makes it possible to identify accessibility problems early when they are easier to correct or avoid.

The comprehensive evaluation of a website to determine whether it complies with all accessibility guidelines can be complex and time consuming. However, several automated and semi-automated tools are available that can speed up and facilitate the process. Unfortunately, though, these tools are usually not capable of checking all guidelines; therefore, manual evaluation by a knowledgeable human (ideally the author of the relevant website) is essential. Manual evaluation can help spot false or misleading results produced by automated tools and can also check compliance with guidelines that are better judged by humans, such as the use of clear and simple language, and ease of navigation. Naturally, evaluation can involve users as well as the use of some of the evaluation techniques previously discussed in this chapter. In particular, the involvement of people with disabilities is highly recommended where possible, as the concept of accessibility is largely about providing access to them. In addition, the involvement should be as early as possible to ensure a smooth and efficient development process.

Before evaluating a website for accessibility, a preliminary review is usually conducted to determine whether there are indeed any accessibility problems with the site. This is like the evaluation itself, but less rigorous; for example, only sample pages are reviewed. The output from the process is a report that (1) summarizes both positive and negative findings, and (2) recommends what needs to be done next (e.g., a full compliance test) and how identified problems can be resolved.

26.3.4.2.1 Evaluating a Website for Accessibility Conformance

Evaluating a website to determine whether or not it conforms to accessibility guidelines usually starts by disclosing the conformance level that the evaluation is targeting. This would have been determined through the preliminary review or some other means. Typically, all the pages of a site are evaluated. If this is not possible, then as many representative pages as possible are evaluated, using at least two different evaluation tools, since different tools tend to detect different problems. As well as evaluating a site for accessibility problems, the Web languages used to develop the site, such as HMTL and CSS, are usually validated to check whether they are used correctly, as this can affect how accessible a site is to assistive technologies, such as screen readers. These languages have been discussed in previous parts of this book and tools for validating their usage are available on the Web, some on W3C's site.

To conduct manual evaluation, each page being evaluated is checked against necessary accessibility guidelines in a range of graphical browsers (e.g., Internet Explorer, Chrome, Firefox, Opera, and Safari) running on different operating systems. To expose whether or not Web accessibility guidelines have been followed, the settings for the browsers or/and the operating systems are adjusted in ways that would normally create problems for people with disabilities, such as those with visual and auditory impairment. For example, in order to evaluate whether the guideline that says to provide equivalent alternative to non-text content has been broken, images might be turned off in the browsers to see if the text for every image is available and adequately describes the image. Similarly, to evaluate whether the guideline that says to provide equivalent alternative for time-based visual and auditory content has been broken, videos might be checked to see if they are captioned or subtitled correctly. Each page is also evaluated in specialized browsers, such as a **voice browser** (e.g., Natural Reader) or **text browser** (e.g., Lynx), to see if their outputs match those of graphical browsers.

As part of the evaluation, the textual content of each page is also usually checked for correct grammar and for whether the writing is clear, simple, and appropriate for the purpose of the website and the target audience. If dynamically generated pages are involved, then the templates, as well as the pages they generate, are evaluated. Finally, for each page or page-type evaluated, a summary is produced that includes:

- Any problems and good practices found, and the method used to identify them.
- Recommendations on how to fix the problems, how to extend the good practices identified to other parts of the site, and how to continually maintain the site.

Web accessibility evaluation tools, which can be off-line- or on-line-based, usually do not require much more than specifying the page to be evaluated, specifying the guidelines to check against, and initiating the process. They work in two main ways: one is to do accessibility checks on a page according to a specified conformance level and correct any accessibility problems that can be corrected automatically. The other is to do the checks and highlight any accessibility problems, so that they can be manually checked and fixed. Accessibility tools therefore present the result of an evaluation in various ways. For example, output could be in the form of a report that indicates, at the minimum, the problems found, conformance level used as reference, and which guideline has been broken. Figure 26.8 shows an excerpt of such a report from an on-line tool known as A-Checker, which allows WCAG and other Web accessibility guidelines (e.g., BTIV, Section 508, and Stanca Act) as well as HTML and CSS syntax to be checked.

Different tools offer different combinations of features that inevitably render them suitable or unsuitable for different situations. This means that careful consideration is necessary when choosing accessibility evaluation tools, so as to ensure that they are (1) suitable for the targeted stages of development, and the complexity and size

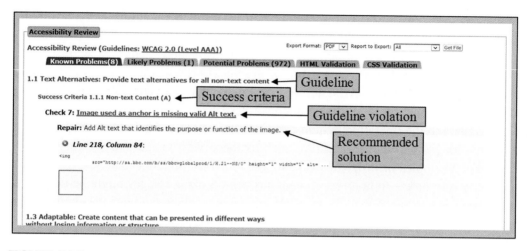

FIGURE 26.8 Part of an accessibility report, showing details of problems found and recommended solutions.

of website, (2) compatible with the host operating system, and (3) match evaluators' skills and knowledge.

CHALLENGE 26.8

Go to www.w3.org/WAI/ER/tools/complete.html, or search for Web accessibility evaluation tools, choose at least two tools, and use them to evaluate a simple Web page. Compare both tools in terms of features, ease of use, and usefulness of report output.

26.3.4.3 Evaluating Your Website for SEO

The **search engine optimization** (SEO) of a website is now a standard part of Web design and development and so has its own evaluation part. SEO evaluation is necessary to ensure that the best practices for optimizing a website have been followed and the website's interaction with users and search engines is as best as it can be. Following known best practices improves a website's visibility in search engines and makes it easier for search engines to crawl, index, and understand its content, which, as previously noted in Chapter 21, can translate into the website being placed at the top of search engines' organic (non-paid for) query results. This can, in turn, translate into increased traffic and increased conversion to sales. SEO is not some big undertaking, but mostly just doing the right things to improve user experience, that is, following the various guidelines already given in various chapters of this book. This is why SEO in principle revolves around what is best for the users of a website; for example, what they are likely to search for and how to make doing this as easy as possible for them. Getting this right will inevitably result in high SEO ranking on **search engine results pages** (SERPs). One of the ways of evaluating the SEO of a website is to check it against Google's SEO guidelines. A summary of the guidelines is presented here. Note that there are websites that offer SEO evaluation and **Google Webmaster Tools** are very useful too.

- **Use unique, accurate page titles**: Each page should have a unique title (implemented with the `<title>` element) that concisely and accurately describes its content and is not stuffed with keywords. The title is displayed in bold in search results and can help users determine quickly whether the content of a page is relevant to their search. See Chapter 2 for how to use the `<title>` element.

- **Use page meta-descriptions**: Each page should have a description (implemented with the `<meta>` element) that provides an accurate summary of the content of the page. The search engine might use it or part of it in the **snippets** it displays for the page in the search results. Meta-description can be any length but the recommendation is to keep it at a maximum of 155–160 characters, because search engines generally do not use more than 160. See the `<meta>` element in Chapter 2 for how to add meta-description.

- **Use microdata markup**: Microdata markup allows bits of data on a page to be specified and used by search engines to improve the presentation of the page in search results. You can find more information and examples on microdata on the Web.

- **Use easy-to-understand URLs**: To achieve this, have a structure that is logical and easy to navigate, and ensure that directories, sub-directories, categories, sub-categories, and files have meaningful names that accurately describe their contents. Use lowercase, because users expect this, and avoid the use of excessive keywords, as Google does not like this. **Breadcrumb links** (introduced in Chapter 24) can make a useful addition.

- **Use descriptive link text**: Link text should accurately and concisely describe the content to which the link leads and links should stand out so that they are easy to recognize. See Chapter 4 for more on links and the `<a>` element, which is the element used to create them.

- **Provide information about images**: Use descriptive but distinct and concise image filenames and **alt text** to provide accessibility and make appropriate engines recognize images easily. Also keep images in a common directory and use standard file formats. See the `<img>` element in Chapter 6 for how to add alt text, which is done with the `alt` attribute. Advanced Web authors also use **image sitemap** files (i.e., markup files that list locations of images) to provide information about images to search engines.

- **Use the heading elements for headings**: Use the `<h1>` to `<h6>` elements to give a hierarchical structure to the content of a page, but they should not be overused (because this can make understanding a structure difficult) or used for styling content. See Chapter 3 for how to use the elements.

- **Specify what not to crawl**: Indicate which parts of your site search engines should not crawl, using any of a number of methods. For example, you could use a **robots.txt** file, which is placed in the root directory, or "`noindex`" with robots in the `<meta>` elements. Google Webmaster Tools provides a **robots.txt** generator and Chapter 2 shows how to use the `<meta>` element.

- **Specify links not to follow**: You would do this if you do not want users to be linked to a site when they activate the link to it. This is done through setting the value of the `rel` attribute to "nofollow" in the `<a>` element, or using "nofollow" with robots in the `<meta>` element to apply it to all the links in a page. See Chapter 4 for how to use the `<a>` element and Chapter 2 for `<meta>`.

- **Check that your mobile website is indexed**: Ensure that your website is recognized by search engines so that it can be indexed. You may need, for example, to create a **mobile sitemap** and submit it to Google. How to do this can be found at Google Webmaster Tools.

NOTE: More on SEO optimization

For more detailed guidelines on how to optimize a website, you should get Google's "Search Engine Optimization Starter Guide," from where most of the guidelines derive. It is available at https://support.google.com/webmasters, as of time of writing.

26.3.4.4 Data Collection for Evaluation

Data collection is central to accomplishing evaluations. The three most commonly used are methods **data recording**, **query**, and **observation**, and it is useful if you are going to evaluate a website to know about them.

26.3.4.4.1 Data Recording

There are many types of data recording, the most common of which are note taking, photographs taking, audio recording, and video recording, each of which may be used alone or in combination with others. Each type of data recording has its advantages and disadvantages in terms of, for example, ease of use, usefulness of the data it provides, cost, and how obtrusive it is.

- **Note taking** costs the least and is the least obtrusive. It also presents the least complications technically to implement and is very flexible. However, it is difficult to listen, observe, and write at the same time, particularly writing as quickly as people talk. Also, what is recorded depends too much on the investigator's discretion, which may result in missing some important points just because they are deemed unimportant.

- **Taking photographs** is relatively easy, particularly with point-and-shoot cameras, but a photograph only captures the data of a moment in time, and it is not always easy to differentiate the data without annotation, which is often not possible to add until the photograph is out of the camera and in hardcopy, or transferred into a computer.

- **Audio recording**, also, is relatively easy to accomplish and does not have the speed limitation of writing. It also allows the investigator to concentrate on talking to the data provider, but transcribing audio data can be time consuming, particularly where quality is poor, either due to surrounding noise or poor recording level, or speech that is not clear. Even when content is clear, audio data tends to provide limited meaning and is often most useful when combined and coordinated with other types of data, such as notes and photographs.

- **Video recording** produces the most complete data because it captures real-life events (i.e., visual and audio data). However, it can be obtrusive, depending on setup, and is the most demanding to operate as well as the most expensive. It can also limit focus of investigation, since it forces the investigator to focus only on the area covered by the field of view of the camcorder, although using multiple camcorders can reduce this problem. Naturally, participants may also play for the camera, which can affect the reliability of data, especially if it is behavioral data that is being gathered.

Consequently, which data recording techniques are used, either singly or combined, depends on the prevailing situation. Where specific data is needed and can be comfortably written down, note taking may be adequate, while photographs are ideal for capturing the way objects look, including the environment, and may be used with note taking or audio recording to provide additional data, such as the contents of documents. Where it is important to observe how an operation is performed, video recording is ideal, as it provides both visual and audio record that can be analyzed over and over again.

26.3.4.4.2 *Query Techniques*

Query techniques, also known as **conversational techniques** or **verbal techniques**, involve asking users their opinions and can take various forms, such as through **interviews** and **questionnaires**.

26.3.4.4.2.1 Interviews   There are four main types of interviews: **unstructured**, **structured**, **semi-structured**, and **group interviews**. Which one is used is determined by a number of factors, such as the purpose of the interview, how much control is required on the scope, and at what point it is taking place in the development life cycle. For example, if what is required is for users to express their opinions freely about a product, then an unstructured interview would be the most suitable, whereas if what is required is feedback on a specific feature of a design, a structured interview might be used. Interview data can be in the form of interviewer's notes, video recording, or audio recording. Opinions and responses to open questions are **qualitative**, while responses to closed questions and responses that are in numbers, such as age, are **quantitative**. The following are the differences between the various types:

- **Unstructured interviews**: These are open-ended interviews in which the interviewer exerts minimum control on the scope and depth of response. Questions are open and designed to simply prompt interviewees to formulate and express their opinions freely. For example, the question, "What do you think about using the website?" prompts a general rather than specific response and is the type of question known as an **open question**. The response can be lengthy or brief and both interviewer and interviewee can control the direction of the interview. To ensure all relevant topics are addressed, it is common for the interviewer to have a list of such topics to use to steer the interview, if necessary. The main advantage of unstructured interviews is that they provide a lot of information that gives both deep and broad understanding of a topic. However, this can also easily be an issue, as such information may be difficult to analyze.

- **Structured interviews**: In structured interviews, questions are predetermined and specific, and designed to elicit specific types of responses. Typically, the questions are short and clear, and require the interviewee to choose from a set of responses, such as "I agree," "I strongly agree," and "I disagree." These types of questions are referred to as **closed questions**. Example usage of closed questions might be: "Which of the following colors do you like used for screen background: White, Red, Blue, or Black?" Every question is worded exactly the same way and asked in the same order for every interviewee. When working with children of pre-reading or early-reading age, how responses are designed is usually different. For example, if they are required to choose from options, such as Awful, Not very good, Good, Really good, and Brilliant, a **smiley-o-meter gauge**, shown in Figure 26.9, developed by Read, MacFarlane, and Casey in 2002, may be used. Structured interviews are typically used when quick responses are required and/or interviewees are in a rush or even mobile.

- **Semi-structured interviews**: These are part unstructured and part structured interviews, which means they can contain both open and closed questions. The interviewer typically has a set of questions that is used to guide the interview so that the interviewee does not digress or say too little. Normally, the interviewer starts with a closed question, and then guides the interview as desired. For example, the interviewer might first ask: "Which of the following colors do you like used for screen background: White, Red, Blue, or Black?," and then follow with the question on why a color has been chosen. In all, care is taken not to phrase questions in a leading way so as not to influence response.

    Awful   Not very good   Good   Really good   Brilliant

FIGURE 26.9   A smiley-o-meter gauge for use with children.

- **Group interviews**: A group interview typically involves an interviewer and a group of interviewees. An example of a group interview is a **focus group**, in which a number of people, commonly 3 to 10 of them, take part in a discussion that is facilitated by the interviewer (the **facilitator**) in a relaxed and informal environment. Typically, a simple question is posed, which is designed to create a starting point for a broader discussion, which the interviewer then mediates, ensuring everyone has their turn to voice their opinions. It is a flexible method that allows discussion to follow pre-prepared directions as well as unexpected ones, thereby possibly bringing out issues that might otherwise be missed. It is common practice to record these types of interviews and analyze them later; and even ask people to explain their comments later, if they are not clear. This form of interview is particularly useful when gathering requirements for a product that is going to be used by different groups of people for different purposes. One disadvantage is that social pressure within a group can inhibit some people's ability to speak their minds, which may limit the scope of the collected data.

26.3.4.4.2.2 Questionnaires   Questionnaires are similar to interviews, in that they use both open and closed questions, depending on the intended goal. However, with questionnaires, questions need to be more clearly worded, particularly as they are usually completed without an interviewer around to clarify any ambiguous elements. Questions also need to be specific and, if possible, closed, with a range of answers offered, just as described under structured interviews, including the "none of these" or "No opinion" option. Having questions and answers of this nature ensures that a questionnaire can be completed more accurately and collected data analyzed efficiently. Questionnaires are especially well suited for collecting data from a large number of people, because they can be distributed widely, even though different versions might be necessary for different populations of respondents. They can be used on their own or together with other techniques of data gathering, such as interviews, meetings, and observation. Because many people tend to be warmer to these other methods than to questionnaires, the benefits of questionnaires are attainable only when people are willing and able to complete them. If they are not, then a structured interview is usually used.

Questionnaires are typically divided into two general sections: the section that gathers demographic information about a respondent (e.g., age, gender, place of birth, and experience level in subjects) and the one that gathers the respondent's opinion about what is being evaluated. **Demographic information** is usually useful for putting questionnaire responses into context. For example, it can reveal that more females like something than males. Any of these sections, of course, can be further subdivided. For example, sometimes, a section for soliciting additional comments is added. A well-designed questionnaire should incorporate features that encourage respondents to complete it. For example, there should be clear instructions on how to complete it, and it should look good. This can be achieved via appropriate text styling, formatting, and ample white space. It should also be short: typically 10 to 15 questions long or less.

In order for responses to be as accurate as possible, the type of response allowed for a question must match the question. These response types are referred to as **response formats** and there are different types, each of which is suitable for a particular type of question. For example, an open question requires space for respondents to write (or type, in the case of on-line questionnaires), while a closed question requires a set of answers from which to choose. Questionnaire data can be in written form or in electronic form that is stored in a database. As with interviews, opinions and responses to open questions are **qualitative**, while responses to closed questions and responses that are in numbers are **quantitative**. The following are some commonly used response formats.

- **Ranges and check boxes**: These are commonly used to group quantities. Figure 26.10 shows an example usage. In this case, respondents are expected to be between the ages of 16 and 35. Notice that the ranges do not overlap, such as in 16–20, 20–25, as this can cause confusion. Notice, also, that the intervals are not equal and do not have to be. For example, the ranges in the figure could be Under 16, 16–35, and Over 35.

   Sometimes, ranges are combined with check boxes, as shown in Figure 26.11, which respondents tick, for example, instead of circling their selection. Naturally, check boxes are used in various other ways, such as to present yes, no, and don't know options.

   However, in on-line questionnaires, check boxes are used only when responders are required to make multiple choices. Where only one selection is required, it is **radio buttons** that are used, as shown in Figure 26.12.

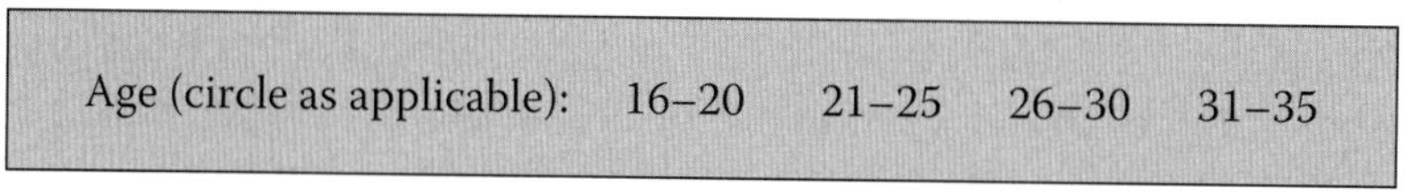

Age (circle as applicable):   16–20   21–25   26–30   31–35

FIGURE 26.10   Illustration of range response format.

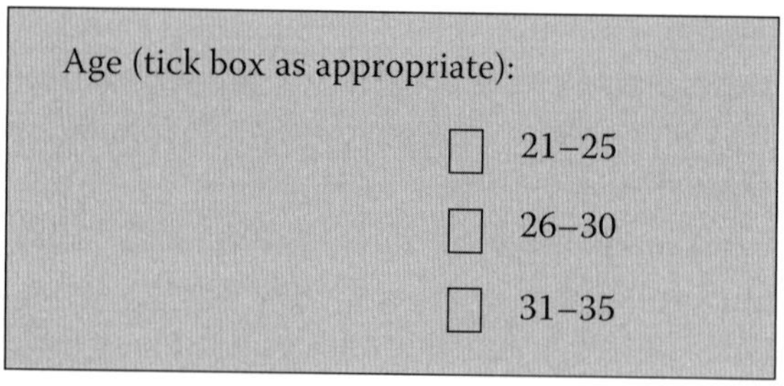

Age (tick box as appropriate):

☐   21–25

☐   26–30

☐   31–35

FIGURE 26.11   Illustration of check boxes response format.

☑ Surfing   ◯ 21–25
☐ Biking   ◉ 26–30
☑ Driving   ◯ 31–35

FIGURE 26.12   On-line use of check boxes and radio buttons.

- **Ranking**: In this method, respondents are asked to rank the items of a list based on some criteria. Figure 26.13 shows an example usage of ranking.

  In on-line questionnaires, input boxes may simply be provided for responders to type in their choices, or a dropdown list of numbers may be used. Scripting can be used to ensure that a ranking is used for only one item.

- **Rating scales**: A rating scale is basically a set of options that vary in degree, such as strongly agree, agree, undecided, disagree, and strongly disagree. These scales are well suited for getting respondents to make judgment about things. Two of the commonly used, Likert and semantic differential scales, are described here. **Likert scales** use a set of statements that describe levels of opinion, emotion, and so on. They are used for measuring strength of feelings, opinions, and attitudes, and because of this are commonly used to evaluate subjective measures (experience), such as user satisfaction with products. Figure 26.14 shows two different versions of Likert scale. A particular strength of Likert scales when they use numbers, as in the top example, is that they allow data to be recorded quantitatively, making it easier to analyze the data statistically.

  In contrast to Likert scales, **semantic differential scales** use pairs of words that represent extremes of possible options and respondents are asked to place a cross in one of the positions between the two extremes. Figures 26.15 and 26.16 show some examples with 7-point scales.

Instruction: Please rank the following Web sites based on how useful they are to you by putting a ranking after them (1 = most useful and 5 = least useful)

www.bbc.co.uk   www.abcnews.go.com   www.five.tv

www.itv.com   www.cbsnews.com

FIGURE 26.13 Illustration of ranking response format.

1) All text is readable (where 1 represents strongly agree and 5 represents strongly disagree):

1   2   3   4   5
☐   ☐   ☐   ☐   ☐

1) All text is readable:

Strongly agree   Agree   Neutral   Strongly disagree   Disagree
☐   ☐   ☐   ☐   ☐

FIGURE 26.14 Examples of Likert scale.

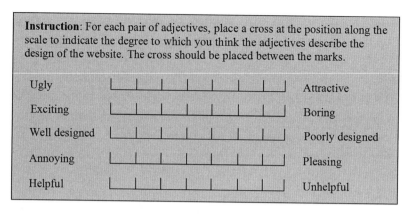

FIGURE 26.15   Example of semantic differential scales.

Instruction: For each pair of adjectives, circle the number along the scale to indicate the degree to which you think the adjectives describe the design of the website.

Ugly	1	2	3	4	5	6	7	Attractive
Exciting	1	2	3	4	5	6	7	Boring
Well designed	1	2	3	4	5	6	7	Poorly designed
Annoying	1	2	3	4	5	6	7	Pleasing
Helpful	1	2	3	4	5	6	7	Unhelpful

FIGURE 26.16   Example of number-based semantic differential scales.

Generally, rating scales use 7-, 5-, or 3-point scales, or a 9-point scale, as used by Questionnaire for user interface satisfaction (**QUIS**), a well-tried and tested tool for evaluating user satisfaction on various interface elements. The matter of which is the best is debatable. For example, while one argument states that scales with many points help people to discriminate better, another suggests that people might be incapable of accurately discerning between many points and therefore scales with more than five points can be unnecessarily difficult to use. Some recommend using a small number when possibilities are very limited. When it comes to the matter of **odd and even number of points**, both have positives and negatives. Mainly, odd number of points provides a central/neutral point, thereby providing respondents a way out, whereas even number of points forces them to make a stand, even when they are unsure. On-line rating scales typically use radio buttons, drop-down menus, and even sliders.

26.3.4.5 Observational Techniques

Like queries, observational techniques are used at various stages of website development to gather data. During the early part of design, they are used to study and understand the way users' perform tasks with an existing system to supplement the requirements-gathering process. Later in the development, they are used to investigate how users interact with a prototype. Observation can be **direct** or **indirect**. In addition, it can take place in the field, such as users' normal work environment, or in a controlled environment, such as a usability laboratory. It can also be obtrusive or unobtrusive. Data that are in the form of observer's notes, audio recordings, video recordings, photographs, and the description of behavior and task are qualitative data, while data that are in the form of numbers, such as time, are quantitative.

26.3.4.5.1 Direct Observation

In direct observation, the investigator observes users, in person or remotely (e.g., via closed-circuit television), as they perform their activities, either in the field or in a controlled environment. **Observing people in the field** is a very useful technique in evaluation, as it provides additional dimension of user-interaction data that interviews or questionnaires do not provide, such as information about social interaction and physical task performance, thereby filling in details that might otherwise be missed. For example, the observer is able to see why activities happen the way they do. However, in order for this type of observation to be as effective as it can be, it needs to be properly planned and conducted with care, otherwise too much irrelevant data might be produced.

In order to conduct productive observation, it is typical to use a framework to structure and focus the observation. A framework essentially provides a guide on what to look for during observation. Using it, while being flexible to any changes in circumstances, usually produces the best result. A framework can be basic for inexperienced observers, or detailed for experienced ones. A **basic framework** can be as simple as focusing on just who, where, and what; that is, who is using what, where they are using it, and what they are doing with it. A **detailed framework** focuses on many more items, such as details of the people involved, the activities they are taking part in and why, specific aspects of activities, sequence of events, what participants are trying to achieve, and what their individual and collective moods are.

As well as the use of a framework, another aspect of planning that can influence the outcome of observation is the choice of the **level of participation**. Two main approaches characterize this: passive observation and participant observation. In **passive observation**, the person conducting observation quietly observes and records the activities of the users. The level of participation is minimal, and so is the level of intrusion. However, because the observer is outside the observed situation, it can be difficult to capture enough details about users' activities, although this problem can usually be minimized by also capturing the situation in photograph and/or video and transcribing later to produce a highly detailed analysis, even though these are typically elements of indirect observation.

In contrast, observation may be from inside a situation, in which case, the evaluator, referred to as a **participant-observer**, plays the dual role of a participant and an observer; that is, he/she performs tasks with users while also observing. This type of observation, known as **participant observation**, is especially useful when it is difficult for users to express how they accomplish tasks, or when aspects of team performance are being evaluated to understand how members organize and perform their tasks. The main challenge of the approach is separating effectively the role of the participant from that of the observer and being able to give an objective report of the observation.

Other typical elements of planning include decisions about how data are going to be recorded and the strategy for interacting productively with the people being observed, particularly in terms of giving equal attention and consideration to everyone. Generally, asking questions is limited, as this can upset the natural flow of how users work and interact, which is typically one of the things that are observed. Observation notes are made during a session or as soon as possible after the session in order to avoid forgetting any details. Photographing and videoing can also be used.

When **observing children** with this technique, it is particularly important to blend in so as to capture as much of their natural behavior as possible. For example, the observer should dress informally and not stand around, so as not to look like a figure of authority. To blend in more, the observer might also engage themselves with an activity, such as using a tool, and be informal and playful when asking the children questions. Because note taking can introduce the sense of formality or being scored, the person asking questions is usually not the one taking notes, and any note taking is discreet.

Observing people in a controlled environment is markedly different from observing them in the field. It is usually used during the evaluation stage of the development life cycle and so the system being evaluated would have been developed with users. It is a more formal method than observation in the field and especially benefits from a pre-prepared script that states how a session should progress. The script typically contains how every participant will be welcomed and told the aim of the study, its duration, and their rights, such as the right to leave at any time during the evaluation session. As with observations in the field, data are recorded through note taking, photographing, and videoing, all of which are aimed at capturing users' interaction activities, such as those performed via computer keyboard and mouse. The equipment to be used for observation is normally set up prior to the session and arranged properly so that the required activities are captured.

An additional technique used during observation in a controlled environment is the **think-aloud technique**, which involves asking users to think aloud; that is, to say aloud what they are doing and thinking. It is designed to provide a window into what a user is thinking while interacting with a system instead of having to guess. However, the formal nature of controlled observations can also sometimes give some users too much of the sense of being watched, which may result in unnatural behavior.

26.3.4.5.2 Indirect Observation

Indirect observations are designed for when direct observations are not possible, such as when distance does not allow, or when they prove to be too obtrusive or too dangerous. The data collection techniques commonly used are video recordings, diaries, and interaction logs. **Video recordings** are done the same way as in direct observation by positioning video cameras as necessary to capture required activities, which are then analyzed later.

The **diaries technique** involves asking participants to keep a regular diary of the details of their interaction with the system being investigated. Examples of what is recorded include what they did, when they did it, how much time they spent on various activities, what they found hard or easy, and what their reactions were to the situation. A diary can be in any format, but having a standardized format for all users can be quite beneficial in terms consistency. It also simplifies storage into a database for analysis, if necessary. Although they are usually in text, the use of multiple media types is increasingly a possibility. Diaries are useful when conditions such as distance between participants or distance between participants and observers make direct observations impractical. They have the advantage of requiring very little in terms of resources, either in the form of equipment or personnel. The main disadvantage is that they rely too much on participants to be willing and reliable, although these problems can be minimized through providing incentives and making the diary-entry procedure itself easy.

Instead of relying on users to record their activities, the **interaction-logging technique** uses software to track and record users' activities as they interact with a system, and the data collected are analyzed later, using any of a number of tools designed to process and give meaning to large amounts of data, including visualization tools. Activities logged vary according to the goals of study but typically include mouse activities (i.e., movements and button clicks), key presses, number of times the help system is used, and amount of time spent using it. Where possible, audio and video data may also be recorded and synchronized with these activities to help to further understand user interaction with the system being evaluated. As well as its use in evaluation, this technique is used for **monitoring on-line activities of visitors** to websites, possibly for the purpose of improving the sites or evaluating the effects of some improvements. Naturally, collecting data on users' activities in this manner without their consent may raise some ethical issues, depending on what is collected. Unlike diaries, the interaction-logging technique is unobtrusive and can simply continue in the background.

26.3.4.6 Delivering an Application on the Web

Although a website can be hosted on a home computer, for serious websites, professional **Web hosting services** are used. These services may also be provided by Internet service providers (ISPs). A Web hosting service essentially enables anyone to make their Web applications accessible on the Internet via the Web. Four basic steps are typically required for publishing a website properly on the Internet: (1) registering a domain name, (2) choosing a Web hosting company, (3) linking the domain name with the Web host's Web server, and (4) uploading files to the Web server. The following are the details.

26.3.4.6.1 Registration of a Domain Name

The first task when registering a domain name is to decide a name and then check its availability; that is, whether or not it is already taken. This can be done through any of various sites, for example, **WHOIS** (www.whois-search.com). The domain name is simply entered and searched. It is typical to choose a name that is catchy, easy to remember, and relevant to the purpose of the site, particularly if the aim of the site is to attract as many people as possible. To be valid and usable, a domain name has to be registered, and there are numerous reputable companies available for doing this. Network Solutions is one of the first companies to offer domain name registration and remains a leading competitor as of time of writing. Many companies that offer domain names also offer Web hosting along with the facility for checking availability. One of the components of a domain name is **top-level domain** (TLD); that is, **.com**, **.org**, and so on, and one must be specified when registering. As well as generic ones like .com, there are also **country-specific TLDs**, such as **.co.uk**, **.co.in**, and **.jp**, which are for the UK, India, and Japan, respectively. Typically, payment is yearly for the privilege of owning a domain name and the cost varies depending on company and the required TLD. For example, a generic TLD is generally cheaper than a country-specific TLD.

26.3.4.6.2 Choosing a Web Hosting Company

Web hosting companies provide a wide range of services. Most offer these services in multiple packages, each with a different level of functionality and price. A quick search on the Web should reveal a myriad of packages, and which is suitable depends on the purpose of the website to be hosted. **For personal sites**, a basic account, which typically provides a free domain name, sub-domains, storage on the server, unlimited bandwidth, e-mail, and FTP, should be adequate. Free Web hosting provides similar facilities, except that they may also require that adverts appear on Web pages. **For professional sites**, additional facilities, such as database, blogging and graphs tools, and a website builder that can be used to create a site, are provided. For e-commerce sites, data backup, data restore, streaming, security protocols, such as **SSL** (Secure Sockets Layer) and **TLS** (Transport Layer Security), which encrypt data to prevent eavesdropping and data tampering, are provided, along with support for standard server-side scripting languages, such as JavaScript, Ruby, PHP, Java, and Python.

26.3.4.6.3 Linking Domain Name with the Web Server

Linking a domain name with a Web hosting account ensures that the request for the domain name connects a Web client (Web browser) to the Web server of the Web hosting company. Implementing this typically requires following step-by-step instructions provided by the Web hosting company. Once the process is completed, there is usually a waiting period (e.g., from 24 to 72 hours) for the various **name servers** located around the world that store domain names to be updated with necessary information, after which the domain name is available to the world.

26.3.4.6.4 Uploading Files to the Web Server

The final step in publishing a Web application is to upload the files that constitute the application, such as HTML and CSS documents, and associated files, such as media files, to the Web hosting server. The easiest way to implement this process is to use an

FTP program (FTP client), which allows files to be transferred to the desired directories on the Web hosting server, usually through dragging and dropping. Different file types are usually placed in different directories both to enhance their management and because they are required. The Web hosting company would normally provide necessary instructions. A requested media file from a Web server is normally downloaded, but can also be streamed, depending on the way it is requested from the server. However, for proper streaming, the use of specialized streaming technologies is required, which is usually an additional service from Web hosting services.

26.4 Useful Info

26.4.1 Web Links

Usability testing: nngroup.com/articles, usabilitygeek.com, usability.gov, usabilitynet.org

Web accessibility evaluation: wave.webaim.org, valet.webthing.com, achecker.ca, cynthiasays.com

Paper prototyping: paperprototyping.com

Flowchart creation tool: gliffy.com

27

Managing Web Development

27.1 Introduction

Essential to the success of any project, private or commercial, is how well it is managed at all stages, from the first meeting with a client to the final sign-off. The same is true for a website development project, and it is particularly so because of the different types of tasks that need to be juggled. This chapter discusses what the stages of a Web project entail.

27.2 Learning Outcomes

After studying this chapter, you should:

- Be aware of how Web development projects are managed.
- Know about Web project management phases.

27.3 Introduction to Web Development Management

Project management is essentially the organization and management of resources, including human resources, in a way that ensures the desired project quality is achieved, given a set of defined scope, time, and cost constraints, together known as the **triple constraint**. The relationships between quality and these constraints are illustrated in Figure 27.1.

What the quality-time-cost-scope relationship means is that if one factor changes, one or both of the others must be adjusted in order to maintain the same level of quality. Effective project management involves manipulating these factors to suit prevailing circumstances. For example, if the time available to complete a project is reduced, then cost must be increased to cover the increase in manpower and/or overtime that is needed in order to maintain intended quality. Similarly, the scope of the project may be reduced by prioritizing features and removing some of them, so that there are fewer tasks and fewer people needed. On the other hand, instead of spending more money to hire more people to reduce completion time, fewer expensive experts that are more efficient may be employed to finish the project more quickly.

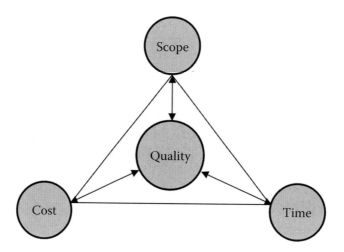

FIGURE 27.1   The triple constraint in project management.

Basically, project management ensures that the various elements that are essential for the success of a project are defined and managed correctly, and the criteria that broadly determine this success are primarily:

- Whether the client's requirements have been met.
- Whether the project is within budget.
- Whether the project is completed on time.

To ensure the accomplishment of these criteria, project management defines goals that are said to be **SMART** (i.e., **S**pecific, **M**easurable, **A**ttainable, **R**ealistic, and **T**ime-bound). These guidelines, which vary according to context, are used to set and assess project goals in order to maximize their chances of success.

A **specific goal** is one that is clear and precise rather than general. It addresses the "W" questions, which are what, where, why, which, who, and when of the goal. It should state what will be accomplished, where it is to be accomplished, why it needs to be accomplished (including, for example, the benefits it will bring), which requirements and constraints are considered, who will be involved, and when completion is expected. In some cases, goals may even be as concise as simply stating what is expected, when it is expected, and how much it will cost.

A **measurable goal** is one that has numeric or descriptive ways of measuring progress toward its achievement as well as its achievement. This is important in helping to stay on track and meet necessary targets. Measures can include quantity, quality, time, and cost. The typical questions to ask in relation to them include how much or how many, and how will we know when this is accomplished.

An **attainable goal** is one that is realistic and achievable, given available resources, such as timeframe, budget, abilities of team members, and control over prevailing circumstances. Evaluating whether a goal is attainable may also lead to the discovery of a more efficient way of achieving it. Typical questions to ask include "How can the goal be best accomplished?"

A **relevant goal** is one that is beneficial to the entity for which a project is being undertaken. It may also be linked to any other relevant goal. A typical question to ask is whether a goal benefits the entity in any way, directly or indirectly, presently or in the future, and whether the right people will handle it.

A **time-bound goal** is one that has a definite target date for completion as well as for each milestone in a project. This helps focus both individual and team effort on the completion of every milestone as well as prevent a project from slipping behind. Typical questions repeated for every milestone include how much work is required to achieve a goal and how much of it can be accomplished in a working day.

Once goals are defined, various project management tools and techniques are used to plan their achievement, as well as to monitor, control, and evaluate them. The types of goals defined and the difficulties they pose depend largely on the nature of the area of project. In Web projects, what can be straightforward managerial activities in other types of projects can become quite complex, because different media types are involved. This can mean that people from different disciplines are involved who are experts in their own rights, have different work practices, and more often than not have contrasting views of what constitutes appropriate interpersonal behavior. Additionally, the subject of quality control can be far from simple, particularly as there is no one right media quality, since whether or not a quality is suitable depends on several factors, such as media type and context.

Furthermore, where all media assets are not created in-house, there may be the issue of seeking out people to get their permission to use their works, and if a Web application is for use in some areas, this may require extending the scope of management. For example, if an application is for use in the area of marketing and business, this may mean that business and marketing elements need to be incorporated in managerial activities. Adding to this the increasing number of different technologies on which the same Web application can be delivered, such as Web, mobile devices, iPad, iTV, and kiosks, the difficulty of managing a Web project is further compounded.

CHALLENGE 27.1

In the triple-constraint model, describe what you consider represents quality in an interactive Web project.

27.3.1 Web Project Management Tools

There are numerous tools and techniques for making project management as easy as possible and the same tools are generally used in Web project management. They are usually visual, making them easy to use, and different types are used at different stages of a project to achieve different objectives. Essentially, some are best suited for planning and others for managing the management process itself. Four of the most commonly used are discussed here, and comprise **brainstorming** (for generating ideas), **work breakdown structure** (WBS; for describing a project's scope), and

critical path method (CPM) and **Gantt chart** (for describing scheduling and planning resources). While the CPM is good for developing and testing a plan for robustness, Gantt charts are better for quick communication of the scheduling for a project, because they show tasks-time relationship in a way that is easier to understand. Both can be produced manually or with software.

27.3.1.1 Brainstorming

Brainstorming is a random, free-thinking, but powerful technique for creating new ideas and solving problems. It is usually the **first important creative stage** of project management, but it can also be used at any stage of a project. Because it involves the people involved in a project working together, brainstorming also has the benefits of developing and motivating a team, as well as encouraging creative and free thinking. Although it is random, it is **important for it to be structured** and to follow brainstorming rules. The project manager, or a designated person, will usually ensure this. The rules are generally that all ideas are welcomed, and **no ideas should be criticized**; the more the ideas, the better it is; and everyone should try to build on the ideas of others. Ideally, the **number of participants should be less than 10** to ensure manageability. The participants should also be **diverse in background**, if possible, to broaden the scope of ideas, although it is important that they have some subject-matter expertise in order to facilitate manageability.

Brainstorming consists mainly of determining the aim of a session, conducting the session, and acting on the actions decided. The aim of a session would be to solve a problem, which would have been identified prior to the session. To start, the project manager ensures that everyone understands and agrees on the aim of the session and also knows the rules. The **aim should be kept simple** in order to ensure that the brainstorming does not get too unwieldy. It may also help to **present aims in question form**. To simplify an aim, it can be divided into smaller objectives, with time limits given to each. A session should not be too long, as this can be tiring and unproductive. If satisfactory ideas have not been found at the end of the set time limit, the session should be postponed and the participants encouraged to think about the problem at hand for the next session.

The brainstorming process itself involves recording ideas suggested at random by participants on something that everyone can see, such as a flip-chart or whiteboard, to ensure everyone knows what is going on and encourage full participation. At the end of the time limit, different colored pens are used to categorize, group, or connect the ideas as necessary to communicate the relationship between them. To help generate ideas, prompters, such as who, what, where, when, and why, may be used. The ideas gathered are then combined and refined, creating new headings or lists, where necessary. A skilled project manager would **ensure no ideas are dismissed outright**, so that no participants feel their ideas are unimportant, as feeling this way can have negative effects on motivation and team building. Next, the ideas or lists created are evaluated, ranked, and developed into a set of actions/options. How the actions are to be implemented, the appropriate timescale, and who will be responsible are then determined using other processes or tools. Brainstorming can also be individual if the project is not team based. One of the ways the outputs from brainstorming can be represented is with a **WBS**.

27.3.1.2 *Work Breakdown Structure*

A WBS is used to organize the elements of a project into a hierarchical structure, which can be represented diagrammatically or/and in a table-of-content (TOC) format. A WBS can be created using a template from previous successful projects, or from scratch, using brainstorming to identify the elements required for a project's main deliverables, and then grouping them, based on common characteristics, into phases, activities, and tasks that can be organized hierarchically. Alternatively, the major deliverables of a project may be identified first, and then each deliverable may be broken down into smaller more manageable components in progressive levels of detail, until there are only lists of individual tasks. Figure 27.2 shows a partially finished diagrammatic example, and Figure 27.3, the TOC format.

The output from a WBS is typically used to produce **scheduling charts** and **cost estimates**. For a complex project, a diagrammatic WBS is usually better suited for communicating its many elements than a TOC-format-based WBS, particularly to clients. On the other hand, a project team may prefer the TOC-format when implementing the tasks.

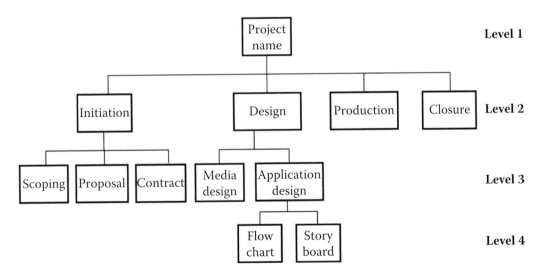

FIGURE 27.2   A partially completed WBS for a Web project.

```
1. Project Name
    1.1 Initiation
        1.1.1 Scoping
        1.1.2 Proposal
        1.1.3 Contract
    1.2 Pre-production
        1.2.1 Media Design
        1.2.2 Application Design
            1.2.2.1 Flowchart
            1.2.2.2 Storyboard
    1.3 Production
    1.4 Closure
```

FIGURE 27.3   A TOC-format version of Figure 27.2.

27.3.1.3 Critical Path Method

The CPM is a network model (a chart) that comprises a series of logical steps that represent the scheduling of the activities of a project. More specifically, it is a model that presents the list of the activities required to complete a project, the duration of each activity, and the dependencies between the activities. Using the model, it is possible to calculate the longest path of intended activities to the end of a project, and the earliest and latest each activity can start and end without extending the duration of the project. This path is known as the **critical path** and the activities on it, **critical path activities**. Any delay in a critical path activity will result in delay in the completion time of a project, whereas delay in activities outside a critical path will not. Knowing the activities that can or cannot be delayed gives you a better control of a project. For example, it enables you to concentrate resources on critical activities when there is the risk of a project overshooting deadline, or simply to finish a project earlier than planned. It is possible for a project to have more than one critical path.

The most common way of representing a CPM model as of time of writing is through an **activity-on-node diagram**, which has all but superseded an **activity-on-arrow diagram**, usually referred to as a Project Evaluation and Review Technique (PERT) chart. In the former, which is also referred to as **precedence diagram method** (PDM), information about activities is shown at the nodes, usually inside and around boxes, whereas in the latter, it is shown along the arrows that connect nodes. Activity-on-node network diagrams are generally easier to produce and interpret. However, the more information they are designed to communicate, and the more activities there are, the more complex they become. For example, determining just the critical path for the planned activities of a project requires simply making each activity a node, connecting them in the order they are to be done, and calculating the longest path from the start activity to the end activity. On the other hand, to provide additional information, more work is required. Examples of additional information might be **float time** (slack time) for any activity (which is the amount of time an activity can be delayed before it causes a project to be delayed), earliest start and finish, and latest start and finish.

Before a network diagram is produced, a list is typically created that comprises the information needed for the diagram, such as, for each activity, Activity ID, Activity name, earliest start time, duration, and the activities on which it is dependent. Producing the diagram is then just a matter of placing and arranging boxes that represent the activities in the order of precedence. Table 27.1 shows a list of activities for a small Web project, and Figure 27.4 shows the corresponding activity-on-node diagram. The duration (in weeks) for each activity is shown at the bottom of the box. The duration of each start-finish path is calculated by adding the duration of each activity on it, and

TABLE 27.1

Information About the Activities of a Project

ID	Activity	Week No.	No. of Weeks	Dependent on
A	Requirements gathering	Week 1	2	–
B	Application design	Week 3	3	A
C	Text design	Week 6	2	B
D	Image design	Week 6	3	B
E	Video design	Week 6	4	B
F	Integration	Week 10	5	C,D,E
G	Testing	Week 15	4	F
H	Delivery	Week 19	1	G

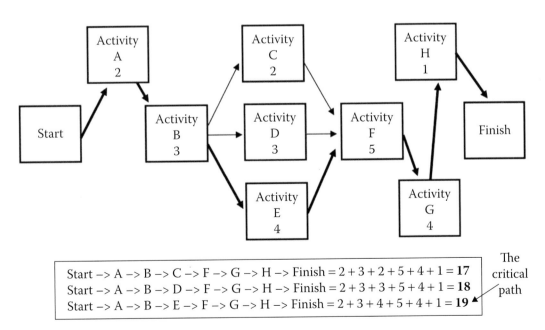

Start –> A –> B –> C –> F –> G –> H –> Finish = 2 + 3 + 2 + 5 + 4 + 1 = **17**
Start –> A –> B –> D –> F –> G –> H –> Finish = 2 + 3 + 3 + 5 + 4 + 1 = **18**
Start –> A –> B –> E –> F –> G –> H –> Finish = 2 + 3 + 4 + 5 + 4 + 1 = **19**

The critical path

FIGURE 27.4 A basic activity-on-node diagram of Table 27.1, showing the critical path in thick arrows and how it is calculated in the box underneath.

the path with the largest total is the **critical path**. The float/slack time for each activity can also be calculated. The float for every activity on the critical path is zero. For other activities, the total of the activities on a noncritical path is subtracted from that of the critical path, and the difference is the float for each activity on the noncritical path that is not on the critical path. For example, the float for "C" is 2 and that for "D" is 1. The start and finish boxes in the diagram are optional.

For a more advanced version of the diagram, the node boxes are divided into sections for presenting more scheduling information, such as the earliest and latest time an activity can start and finish. How this is done varies widely. Figure 27.5 shows the legend for the example that is used here and Figure 27.6 the activity-on-node diagram.

Earliest start and finish can be calculated using a technique known as **forward pass**, which involves the following:

1. The **earliest start** (ES) of the first activity in the critical path is 1, while the **earliest finish** (EF) of any activity is its ES plus its duration, −1. This means that, for Activity A (the first activity in the diagram), the ES is 1 and the EF is $1 + 2 - 1 = 2$.

Earliest start time	Duration	Earliest finish time
Activity ID or name		
Latest start time	Float	Latest finish time

FIGURE 27.5   A typical convention for a node-box.

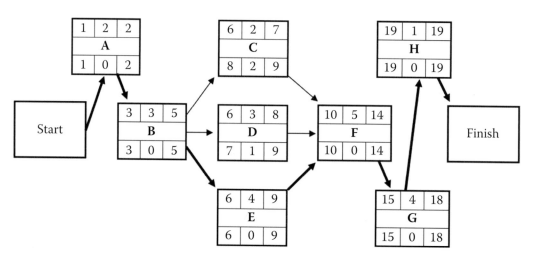

FIGURE 27.6   A more detailed version of the activity-on-node diagram in Figure 27.4, showing earliest start and finish, latest start and finish, and float (critical path is in thick arrows).

2. For the ES of the next activity, 1 is added to the EF of the previous one. This means the ES of Activity B is $2 + 1 = 3$, and the EF is $3 + 3 - 1 = 5$.

3. If an activity has more than one predecessor, the one with the latest EF is used, since the next activity can start only after the latest of the previous ones is completed. So, the ES for Activity F is $9 + 1 = 10$.

Similarly, latest start and finish can be calculated using a technique known as **backward pass**, which involves starting from the end of the critical path and working backward, as in the following:

1. The **latest finish** (LF) of the last activity on the critical path is the same as the EF. To calculate the **latest start** (LS), the duration of the activity is subtracted from the LF, and then 1 is added. This means that the LS of Activity H in the diagram is $19 - 1 + 1 = 19$.

2. For the LF of the previous activity, 1 is subtracted from the LS of the next activity, meaning that the LF of Activity G is $19 - 1 = 18$, and the LS is $18 - 4 + 1 = 15$.

3. After completely filling all the activities in the critical path, those in the next longest path that have not been filled are filled as described in 1 and 2, and so on, until all activities have been filled. For example, the next longest path in the diagram is "Start –> A –> B –> D –> F –> G –> H –> Finish," and Activity D is the only one that needs to be filled.

CHALLENGE 27.2

If you feel up to it, use the data in the table below to produce an activity-on-node diagram. Determine also the critical path.

ID	Activities	Week No.	No of Weeks	Dependent on...
A	Scoping	Week 1	2	–
B	Proposal	Week 3	2	A
C	Contract	Week 5	1	B
D	Content design	Week 6	4	A,B,C
E	Text design	Week 10	4	D
F	Image design	Week 14	4	D
G	Animation design	Week 18	8	D
H	Video design	Week 26	4	D
I	Integration	Week 30	8	E,F,G,H
J	Testing	Week 38	2	I
K	Delivery	Week 40	1	J

27.3.1.4 Gantt Chart

As should be evident from the example shown of the CPM, a network diagram is not quite intuitive to read and understand. In contrast, a Gantt chart is easier both to create and to interpret. People do not have to be trained to be able to understand them. To produce a Gantt chart, a list similar to the one earlier in Table 27.1 is created that comprises mainly activity ID and name, week number, and duration. The chart can then be drawn on a simple graph paper or created with dedicated software, into which the data is entered and the graph generated. A spreadsheet program, such as Microsoft's Excel, can also be used.

Figure 27.7, which is the Gantt chart version of the network diagram in Figure 27.4, was created using Excel by simply selecting the number of cells that match an activity's duration and coloring them. Activities in the critical path are in black and those not are in grey. No calculations are needed to determine slack times for activities that are not in the critical path; it is easy to see them. For example, Activity C has two extra weeks and Activity D, one week, before the next Activity (F) must start. The arrows linking the end of some activities to the start of others were drawn using normal drawing tools and indicate that later activities cannot be started until earlier ones have finished. This is known as **finish-to-start** (FS) dependency. However, although Gantt charts are easier to create and interpret than network diagrams, they can be more complex than shown here. They can be more detailed; activities can be broken down into sub-activities, weeks into days, and various more types of inter-dependencies between activities and constraints on start and end times can be incorporated. For example, as well as FS dependency, other types of relationship are possible, such as **start-to-start** (i.e., an activity can only start after another activity has started), **finish-to-finish** (i.e., an activity cannot finish until another has finished), and **complex** (i.e., there is more than one relationship between a pair of activities).

		01/08/11	08/08/11	15/08/11	22/08/11	29/08/11	05/09/11	12/09/11	19/09/11	26/09/11	03/10/
ID	Activity	Week 1	Week 2	Week 3	Week 4	Week 5	Week 6	Week 7	Week 8	Week 9	Week
A	Requirements gathering										
B	Application Design										
C	Text design										
D	Image design										
E	Video design										
F	Integration										
G	Testing										
H	Delivery										

FIGURE 27.7   Part of the Gantt chart for the information in Table 27.1.

27.4 Web Project Management Phases

Web projects present similar types of management issues as other types of projects. The same set of variables, which range from the look and feel of an application to schedule, cost, budget, and resources, are involved. Some of the most referenced texts on Web project management are those by England and Finney. In their books, Web project management is described as having four phases: preliminary, production, final sign-off, and archiving. Other models have described the phases in other ways, such as in terms of concept development, preproduction, production, testing, and archiving. However, irrespective of the number of phases, or the labels used, what is important is that the phases of management span the stages of Web development cycle; after all, Web project management is simply the management of the various activities of a Web production as well as the associated resources. For the purpose of discussion, the stages of Web development cycle are defined in this text as initiation, preproduction, production, and postproduction, and the management phases are matched to these stages accordingly, as illustrated in Figure 27.8.

27.4.1 Initiation Phase

The initiation phase of a Web project typically comprises the definition of the scope of the project, the production and tendering of the final version of the proposal, and the production and signing of the contract. It is the phase in which the initial important decisions are made, including whether or not a project should go ahead, if there had not been any preliminary process. It is where agreements and promises are made that give a project its goal. Although it is not where most of the hard work is done, it is a very important phase, in that getting it wrong can cause problems later in a project. Because of its pivotal position, all the key people in a project are usually present at the start of the phase, if not all through it. Usually everyone who will be using the system is involved at some point during the phase, if situation permits. It is particularly important to urge that end users are involved, as this can often give them the sense of co-ownership, thereby improving their willingness to cooperate.

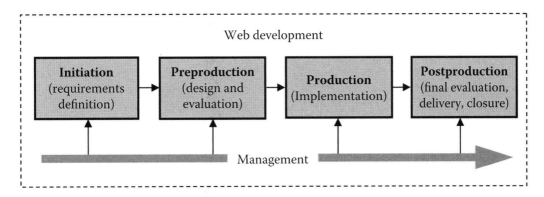

FIGURE 27.8   Project management running in parallel with development process.

27.4.1.1 Project Definition Process

The determination of a project's scope (also known as **scoping**) is the first main activity in the initiation phase and its overall goal is to gather enough information to facilitate the success of a project through researching the client, target audience, relevant content, and the marketing of the finished product, where applicable. Typical agenda includes determining the project's aims and objectives, determining the risks and possible difficulties, and laying down a road map for the project. As a Web project manager, your role in completing this agenda is very significant. You are responsible, for example, for identifying tasks, breaking them down, estimating the number of hours each task will take, determining staff and assets necessary for each task, and putting a cost to them. You can achieve all these usually through using different tools and techniques, such as meetings, discussions, and brainstorming sessions, including the techniques discussed in Chapter 26 that are used for evaluation, such as questionnaires. Combinations of techniques usually produce the most complete result, since different techniques have their pros and cons.

The scoping process should seek to extract as much information as possible to fulfill the project's objectives. Questions should be crafted to provide answers that can be used to determine the resources, cost, time, scope, and quality variables. They should seek to extract, for example, the problem you are trying to solve, business objectives (if any), target audience and its technological awareness, how much of each media object type needs to be used, whether there are existing contents and/or system, delivery platform, expected completion time, type of maintenance required, budget, and, where applicable, the contact details of the important people, such as those responsible for giving the go-aheads and sign-offs.

Of all scoping tasks, the costing of a project in the absence of all facts is often most difficult. It is often a guess, even if educated; therefore, the chances of under-costing are just as high as over-costing, depending on experience. It is usually prudent to work on the basis that a little more would be required of everything than has been calculated. If cost then turns out to be less, it would certainly be a pleasant surprise, especially for the client, where there is one.

To help structure and ease the process of costing, there are tools available to do the calculations. However, the tools cannot make decisions on how many hours a task will take, or the cost per hour. In theory, the more structured the scoping process, the more easily and more accurately tasks can be identified and a project appraised. Breaking down activities into smaller task units usually makes the allocation of resources, scheduling, and costing easier and more accurate, just as the use of charts and diagrams, such as described earlier in this chapter, can help present who is responsible for completing which tasks more clearly. A properly structured scoping process also ensures a structured output, which is essential for the production of a proposal.

27.4.1.2 Proposal Process

A project proposal brings together all the information gathered during the scoping process into a single cohesive document that communicates the goal of a project, without being too specific on the details of development, particularly as it can be difficult to be certain of everything at the initiation phase. The overall success of the document at communicating the intended message effectively depends on its content and the presentation of that content. The presentation component is the least challenging to attain and the principles that guide its success are not much different from those for producing readable content on the screen. Basic things such as **visual hierarchy** (using fonts appropriately) and leaving enough space at the margins to enable clients to write comments while reading a proposal can go a long way toward making a proposal inviting, and easy to read and work with, and so can the **inclusion of visuals** (such as graphs and charts) and **good quality print**.

Style of writing is also very important for easy understanding. A proposal should not be long when it can be **short and sharp**. Even when it has to be long, it should not be rambling, but direct to the point that is relevant. It should also be in **formal** and **"politically correct" language** that most people understand. For example, colloquial expressions or slangs should be avoided, as they are likely to be understood only locally or by a group of people. The use of "he" or "her" alone, too, should be avoided, because the person reading the proposal might be of the opposite gender and might feel alienated. The same goes for technological jargons. If they must be used, then they should be explained, for example, via footnotes or appendix. Above all, a proposal is a proposal, not a set of instructions, so it should be **advisory rather than prescriptive**. This helps ensure that clients get the sense that whatever decision they make is their own and you have not told them to do anything. To help further give clients the sense of having an option, it is usually useful to suggest more than one way of addressing their needs. Although this might require a little more work, it can add to the building of trust, in that it gives the impression that you are not trying to push any particular treatment(s) for your benefit.

A proposal can be of any size, ranging from just a few to hundreds of pages, depending on various factors, such as size, type of project, and whether you are competing with others for the same job and therefore need to include a lot of information to gain an edge. However, irrespective of its size or the type of information contained in it, it should normally convey clearly the following messages:

- The problem the proposed project will solve and/or the needs it will fulfill.
- Why you are qualified to do the project.
- What you are proposing to do to solve the identified problem or satisfy the clients' needs, including proposed timetable and costs.

Usually, these messages are most clearly communicated by breaking down a proposal into smaller, distinct, and appropriately headed sections. Figure 27.9 shows an example that covers many of the topics typically included in a Web proposal. If nothing else, it provides a possible starting point. What goes under each topic depends on various factors, such as size and type of project. The cover letter is not part of the proposal and is usually very short and seldom does more than simply drawing attention to the delivery of the proposal.

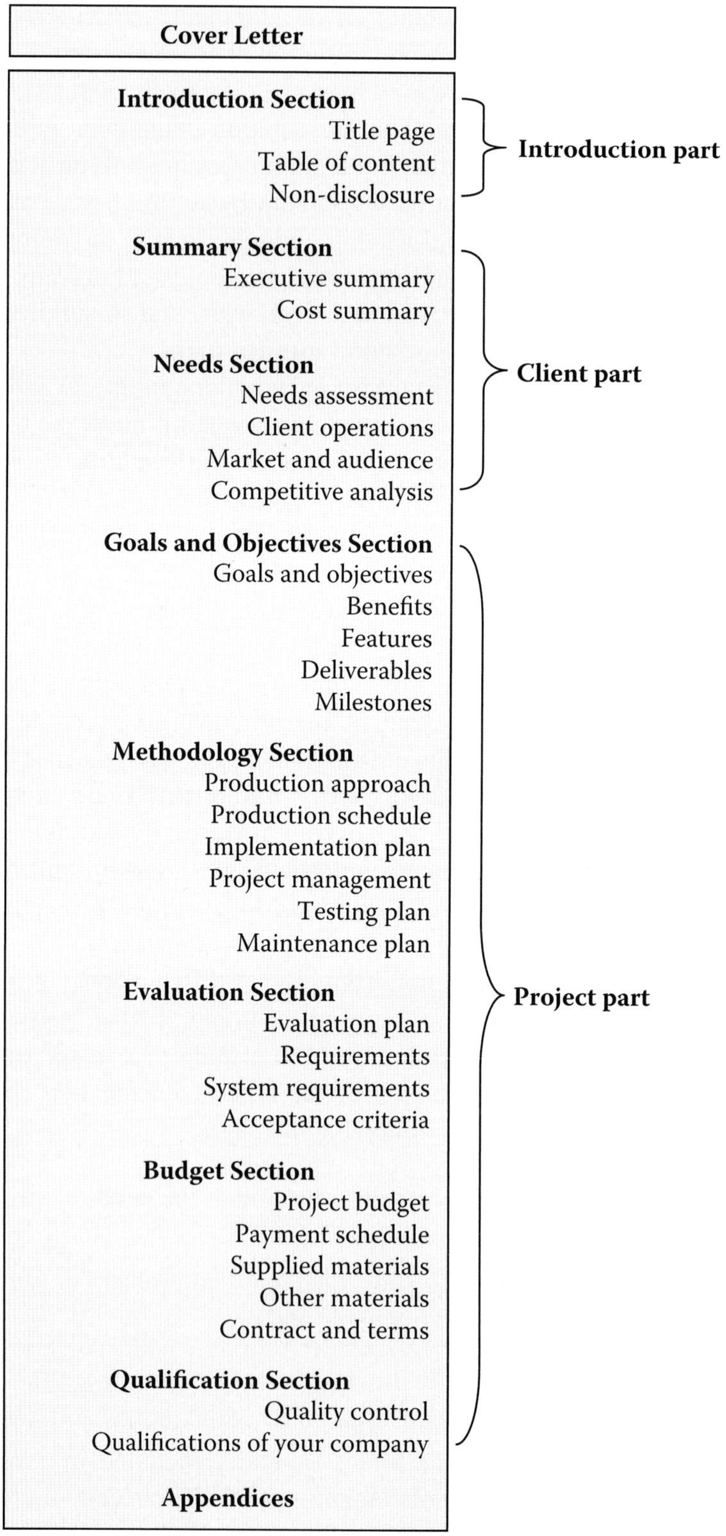

Cover Letter

Introduction Section
Title page
Table of content
Non-disclosure

⎬ **Introduction part**

Summary Section
Executive summary
Cost summary

Needs Section
Needs assessment
Client operations
Market and audience
Competitive analysis

⎬ **Client part**

Goals and Objectives Section
Goals and objectives
Benefits
Features
Deliverables
Milestones

Methodology Section
Production approach
Production schedule
Implementation plan
Project management
Testing plan
Maintenance plan

Evaluation Section
Evaluation plan
Requirements
System requirements
Acceptance criteria

Budget Section
Project budget
Payment schedule
Supplied materials
Other materials
Contract and terms

Qualification Section
Quality control
Qualifications of your company

Appendices

⎬ **Project part**

FIGURE 27.9   Example of a Web project proposal structure.

27.4.1.2.1 Introduction Section

The introduction section provides items that introduce the content of the proposal and its purpose. The **title page** ideally carries information such as name and address of developer, project title, date, the name and job title of the person for whom the proposal is prepared, the name and job title of the person that prepared it, the description of the project, and project number, if applicable. For easy scanning, the **table of content** should be divided into sections or parts that reflect the structure of the proposal. A **non-disclosure agreement** is included to prevent a client from disclosing the information contained in the proposal to other companies.

27.4.1.2.2 Summary Section

The summary section is the most-read section of a proposal because it gives a quick brief account of what a project is about. The **executive summary** describes, in simple language, the essence of a project and **cost summary** gives the cost totals, typically in the form of costs per group, followed by the project's total cost. It is common practice to include a disclaimer, at the end, to indicate that the costs are only estimates and not final.

27.4.1.2.3 Needs Section

The needs section is used to show the clients that you understand their needs and/or problems and know how to address them. It typically includes the understanding of how the client operates, as well as the description of its background, market, target audience's characteristics, competition, strengths, and weaknesses. In the case of the target audience's characteristics, for example, description might include size, demographics, why the audience is the target, and also how the proposed solution will be targeting it. The inclusion of some kind of justification for any proposed solution is also important to bring the client along. This might include, for example, how the proposed solution can give the client an edge over competitors, help the client survive possible adverse industry trends, and/or help productivity and profitability.

27.4.1.2.4 Goals and Objective Section

The goals and objectives section provides the objectives of the proposed project and how their achievement will be measured. Typically, the features and benefits that will be offered by the proposed system and how they will be achieved are described. The dates and description of milestones, including the start and acceptance dates of the project, and what will be delivered, are described, possibly also using diagrams, which may or may not be placed in the appendices. Any possible disruptions the implementation of the project will cause in the client's operations, and how these will be limited, are also useful additions. In all cases, it is important not to promise what is not certain you can deliver.

27.4.1.2.5 Methodology Section

In the methodology section, the phases of the proposed project are detailed. For example, the production processes that will be used to achieve the objectives of the project are described, including process model stages, details of human and other resources, marketing plan, legal matters, and constraints and their effects on the project, as well as how they will be managed. The conditions on which the content of the proposal is valid are also commonly stated. These may be, for example, that the proposal is accepted by a certain date, the clients play their parts (such as providing information and existing content on time), and external factors remain roughly the same all through the project (such as costs of sub-contracting). A list of identified risks may also be provided that describes the risks involved, what will be done to minimize them, and the contingency plan to address them, should they materialize. If this information is included, then it is useful for legal reasons to also include a caveat that makes clear that there are no guarantees that all risks have been identified, or that those identified are completely accurate.

The **testing plan** can include various testing information, including the types of tests that will be conducted, when during the development process they will be conducted, the tools that will be used, how any problems found will be reported, tracked, and resolved, and how re-testing will be carried out. The **maintenance plan** provides maintenance details, which can include the components that will require maintenance, how often the maintenance will be, estimate of the cost, and who will be responsible for providing it. Even if maintenance will be provided by the same company that develops a site, entering into a separate agreement is usually required.

Any other information relating to the processes and deliverables for a project are also provided in this section or, in some cases, the appendix, including the following:

- Description of how the existing content and any that is created will be used.
- Clear description of treatments proposed to match users' needs, along with the reasons behind choosing them; avoiding any attempts to impress.
- If applicable, an outline of unusual technical requirements needed for the delivery of size.
- If applicable, information relating to security, data management, regulations, permits, licenses, training plan, installation schedule, data recovery plan, and backup plan.
- If applicable, a list of the project team members, giving the names, roles, and responsibilities.

27.4.1.2.6 Evaluation Section

The evaluation section outlines the details of evaluation and describes how, when, where, and by whom the success of the project will be measured, including whether evaluation will be done all at once, or in stages, for example, in line with the project's milestones. Also included are the criteria against which the project will be evaluated, which are essentially the requirements on which the project has been based in the first place, such as functional requirements, contractual requirements, system requirements, document and training requirements, user-interface requirements, and performance requirements. Explanations about how deliverables will be assessed against these requirements and necessary contracts and agreements are provided. All stages of evaluation and their purpose are explained, including how data will be collected and analyzed, and how the results obtained will be reported.

27.4.1.2.7 Budget Section

Details of the cost summary presented in the executive summary section are provided here. Essentially, everything that is to be paid for by the client is itemized in this section, along with a simple justification, if possible. For example, the rationale for charging $100 for something might be that it is the standard cost. Providing such justification ensures transparency in costing, which in turn can translate into clients' trust. Importantly, a line should be included for hidden costs, such as costs of phone calls, postage of documents, report writing, consumables, and transport, which may easily accumulate during the course of a project. The same applies for contingencies to cover unforeseen circumstances that may call for more time and/or resources. As a rule of thumb, an amount of about 10%–15% is typically added for contingencies. If applicable, a detailed cost-benefit analysis may also be provided that gives some years' projection. This may show, for example, total costs, benefits in money and return of investment (i.e., "benefits in money" minus "total cost").

The **payment schedule page** provides mainly dates, amounts, and the criteria for payment. Staged payment is favored, for many reasons. For example, you might need the money to help progress the project. It is also an insurance against the possible event of the client ceasing trading before a project is finished, which might leave you with no payment for all the work that has been done, if this has not already been settled. Indeed, some companies might just refuse to pay. It is common for payments to be in thirds: one-third at the start of project (i.e., with the signing of the contract), another third at delivery, such as during alpha or beta testing, and the last third on final sign-off.

The **supplied materials** item specifies the materials to be provided by the client and can be in the form of a list of descriptions of the materials and their due dates, noting that it is the client's responsibility to provide them on time to avoid delays. The **other materials** item describes any equipment, materials, hardware, or software required for the project, stating which will be provided by the client and which will be provided by you, and also whether they are to be purchased or leased. If any materials will be cleared (licensed) for use on behalf of the client, this is indicated, and the cost included in the budget section. A **contract and terms** page is also typically included in this section if a separate contract is not presented elsewhere.

27.4.1.2.8 Qualifications Section

This section is used generally to describe why you think you are best qualified to achieve the objectives of the proposed project. This may be in the form of listing the client's needs outlined in the needs section and describing how you are qualified to satisfy each of them. The amount of information provided depends on different factors, such as scale of project. For example, for large projects, such as government projects, a lot of information is usually required, given that there usually are several companies bidding for the same project. The general aim is to communicate why you are unique for the project in question. In large and/or mission-critical projects, it may also be necessary to include description of any quality control measures in place to ensure that the project does not go wrong, stating if such measures comply with any recognized standards. Further information may be provided in the form of track record or history that provides evidence of your suitability for the project, including the description of past, similar, and successful projects, along with testimonies from past clients, references the client can contact, and even resumes of project team members, if known. In essence, any information that will instill confidence in the client about your capabilities is included.

27.4.1.2.9 Appendices

Any information that can help the client further understand the proposal, but cannot be included in the body of the proposal, is placed here. The information might include charts, testimonials, references, solicitor-checked warrantees and disclaimers, glossary, forms, lists of definitions, acronyms, illustrations, and short nontechnical description of relevant Web technologies. Again, the amount of information included depends on factors like the size and complexity of a project. The information is also usually referred to from the body of the proposal, and relevant proposal page numbers may be used with relevant information for better cross-referencing. Like the rest of the proposal, the content of appendix needs to be structured and formatted properly, using sectioning, spacing, and styling appropriately, to make it easy to scan.

27.4.1.3 Contract Process

A contract is a binding agreement between persons or parties, and can take many forms. It can be simple, complex, oral, or written. However, in formal business dealing, such as a Web project, it is usually written, for many reasons, some of which are to prevent any party denying, forgetting, or getting confused about their contractual rights or obligations. In a Web project, reaching the contract stage implies that the client has agreed with the content of the proposal. If there is a suitable **template contract** that contains regular clauses applicable to Web projects, then you need only to ensure that aspects relating to the present project are added, as well as seek the advice of a media lawyer for unusual circumstances that have not been encountered before.

During the process of drawing up a Web project contract, one of the first things to decide is whether the necessary contract terms and clauses will be included with the proposal, or put on a separate document and negotiated separately after the acceptance of the proposal. This is important, as the decision might influence the phrasing of the terms and clauses. **If the contract will be included in the proposal**, standard legal terms and clauses can simply be spelt out on a separate page and attached to the proposal, while also inserting at various relevant points in the proposal, appropriate terms and conditions. For example, on the Payment Schedule page, terms and conditions may be stated relating to the consequences of failure to comply with the payment schedule. **If the contract is separate from the proposal**, again, standard legal terms and clauses may be spelt out in a separate document, except that, in this case, project-specific clauses that reference various aspects of the proposal are also added. For example, a clause may be included in relation to, again, the Payment Schedule, stating the consequences of failure to comply.

A contract must be signed for it to be binding. In many cases where the contract and the proposal are separate documents, both are signed, but not always; all depend on factors such as the way the contents of the documents are phrased. This is one reason that the use of a lawyer is often well advised. Like with a proposal, there is no single correct way of structuring a Web contract, nor is there one correct set of information that is concluded. The following are some of the typical sections found in Web production contracts.

- **Recitals**: This is the typical preamble at the start of most contracts. It describes the intentions of the parties involved. For example, it says what services a developer provides and what service a client wants.
- **Definitions**: These are the definitions of the terms used in the contract.
- **Development, delivery of deliverables, and payment**: In this section, the details of the project are given. Examples include the description of the project in no more than two short sentences; statements that the developer or approved contractors will work and deliver deliverables according to specification, production schedule, and confidentiality agreements; statement that the client will pay according to the payment schedule; and statements relating to the maintenance and change policy. Naturally, there will be changes, particularly in large and/or complex projects, so it is common to devise ways of managing them than try to prevent them altogether. The relevant clause could state, for example, that when changes are required, their feasibility, cost, and effects on project schedule will be assessed. If the project will be delivered and/or signed off in stages, then a statement can be included to state the need to agree on who will be responsible, from both sides, for doing the signing-offs. The agreed names can be added to the proposal, where they can be changed during the duration of a project, if necessary.
- **Testing and acceptance**: This section presents clauses on the types of testing or evaluation that will be carried out and the responsibilities of the developer and the client, as applicable. Clauses may also cover policy regarding the reporting of errors that are found after the delivery of website. If applicable, there may be a statement on how long testing will go on after the delivery of the system before the final sign-off. The details of the testing plan would have been provided in the proposal.

- **Copyrights**: What all the parties concerned are entitled to, or not entitled to, is clearly outlined here. Examples include who owns the media produced and/or the generated codes, you or the client, and whether or not the clients may use the media produced for other purposes. In a small project, all that is usually required is a release form clearing you from any claims or demands resulting from the use of the media created. A release form for a photograph or a video, for example, can be as simple as shown in Figure 27.10.

- **Confidentiality**: In this section, terms are stated regarding what information can and cannot be shown to third parties. It is similar to the **non-disclosure agreement** that may be included in the proposal. The difference lies mainly in when either is signed. A non-disclosure agreement is signed with the tendering of a proposal and typically refers to the content of the proposal, whereas confidentiality agreement is signed after the proposal has been seen, and accepted, and therefore generally refers to what is disclosed during the project. Again, there is no one correct approach; a non-disclosure agreement signed when the proposal is tendered can be made to cover the entire project.

- **Warranties, Covenants, and Indemnification**: This section states the terms under which the developer and the client can enter an agreement, including the damages and costs, each party is secured against. Also, there are usually

---

Release Form

I, _____, hereby grant to _____, (here after referred to as "Photographer/Producer") the right and permission to use any photographs/video he/she has taken of me for any purpose and in any and all media now or in the future. I hereby grant to (Photographer/Producer) the right and permission to use my name in connection with the photographs if he/she so chooses.

I hereby release and discharge (Photographer/Producer) from any and all claims and demands arising out of or in connection with the use of the photographs/videos, including any and all claims for libel or invasion of privacy.

I am of legal age and have the right to contract in my own name. I have read the above and fully understand the contents. This release shall be binding upon me and my heirs and legal representatives.

_____
Printed Name
_____
Signature
_____
Date
_____
Witness

FIGURE 27.10   An example of a release form for a photograph or a video.

statements to say that the use, performance, and distribution of the product delivered by the developer will not violate the rights of any third parties, and that it is the clients' responsibility to properly license the content they provide. If the clients want to use other people's work in their content, then they must secure the rights for such usage and indicate in writing to you that they have done so. This indemnifies you from possible **secondary copyright infringement**. If you are licensing any content on behalf of the client, this responsibility is stated clearly also, along with how any incurred cost will be paid, if not included in the proposal under Project Budget and Cost Summary. For obvious reasons, some contracts may also include a clause freeing the developer from any responsibility regarding deficiency in performance due to influences that are not theirs, such as defective hardware or inadequate computer system setup.

- **Termination**: The circumstances under which a project will be terminated are described in this section, along with the subsequent actions to be taken, such as whether compensations will be made by one party to another and what will happen to the media assets already produced.

- **Miscellaneous**: Other clauses are included here. These include standard clauses, also known as **boilerplate clauses**, such as Force Majeure, to indemnify the parties involved. Other non-specific issues about a project can also be addressed.

NOTE: Addendum to a contract

After the contract is signed, it is not unusual, when it is necessary to make minor changes, to create an addendum to the contract, instead of reproducing the whole contract. This addendum is then signed by all parties involved.

Because a Web project can involve dealing with freelancers to complete parts of a project, such as video production, instructional design, and music production, it is sometimes necessary to also draw up contracts for these parties. Any formal agreements with such parties naturally happen after the main contract has been signed with clients, and it is clear the project is going ahead. Once all agreements are firmed, the project is moved on to the planning and designing phase.

CHALLENGE 27.3

Most Web development contracts contain clauses designed to protect developers from things that they have no control over. List the things that you think might be out of a developer's control during a Web project and therefore need to be addressed in a contract.

27.4.2 Preproduction Phase

This phase is where the project team is determined (if applicable) and the elements necessary for achieving the objectives of a project designed and/or gathered. The managerial tasks are to ensure that the right people are selected and the design of both media components and website satisfy the requirements that have been set out during the initiation phase. The sets of tasks include building the team, gathering content and getting clearances, designing the system, designing the media elements, selecting the production and development tools, and selecting types of testing, all of which are discussed next.

27.4.2.1 Project Team Selection

The first task required in putting together a team for a project is identifying the skills needed to fulfill the requirements of the project. Doing this requires you to have a clear vision of what a project entails, as well as a good understanding of the skills used in the various fields involved. This knowledge would also have been applied during the initiation phase to produce the estimates (e.g., schedule and cost) presented in the proposal. The mix of skills required would depend on many factors, some of which are content, media object types that will be used, best-suited integration tool, and project size. The challenge at this point is to match the skills required to personnel selection. How this is done, again, depends on various factors, such as your size, and whether or not you have dedicated staff with the skills required. For example, if you are a freelance developer with multiple skills, you may not need to put a team together, or might only need to contract out only a small part of the work. In contrast, a multi-staffed developer company may have full-time staff from which to assemble a **core team** (i.e., people that provide the core skills needed) and only need to bring in other people from outside, as required, to form an **extended team**.

For obvious reasons, core skills are usually matched with in-house personnel, where possible, before considering people from outside. For example, it tends to cost less. Recruiting outside personnel can be made especially easier if there is already a list of freelance developers that can be brought in, instead of using advertising or recruitment agencies, which often adds extra cost to the process. Typical core roles include Web designer/programmer and graphic designer. Extended roles include video personnel (e.g., director/producer, editor, and journalist), sound personnel (e.g., sound editor), animator, instructional designer, actor/actress (e.g., voice-over artist), proofreader, tester, and many more, depending on type of project.

CHALLENGE 27.4

Visit www.amazon.co.uk and list the roles you would require to build such a site, describing for what each role will be responsible.

27.4.2.2 Content Gathering and Clearance Process

The completion of the core team selection, if applicable, means that the crucial manpower is in place to start the development part of a project, which is started by first gathering and analyzing relevant existing assets. The task here is to ensure that the assets are provided in time by the person who would have been identified during the initiation phase. It is also to ensure that the assets are evaluated against project requirements, which may involve checking quality and whether or not any clearance (creator's permission to use asset) is needed, and has been acquired by the client, if applicable. The outcome of this process will largely influence the decision about which components need to be designed. For example, if the quality of an asset is not good enough, or it cannot be cleared for use in all the required territories, it means it has to be created or bought from royalty-free stock. For noncommercial projects, such as personal sites, there are many sites that offer free media as long as certain terms are followed, which is typically that a link is provided back to their sites.

Even if the client is responsible for clearing existing assets, it is your responsibility to ensure that they have been cleared properly, because rights clearance can be complicated. For example, clearances normally cover specific markets and territories; that is, they are cleared for specific purposes, audience types, length of time, and countries. For instance, clearance is usually for the whole world, since the Web is global. Most importantly, the clearance process should start as early as possible so as to prevent any delay. For example, sometimes, clearance may take long, either because the author of a media cannot be ascertained or found, or a publisher's licensing process is complex and lengthy. This can delay a project. Also, requests for clearances can sometimes be refused. If this is not realized as early as possible and fixed, it can disrupt a project. If it is realized early, necessary decisions can be made to drop the media concerned and clear another, or design a substitute, without any delay.

27.4.2.3 Website Design Process

Whether or not any significant designing has been undertaken before the preproduction phase of a project depends on the negotiating situation. If, for some reasons, it has been necessary to show some sort of prototype to the client before proceeding with the signing of the contract, then some designing activities would have been undertaken during the initiation phase. However, in most cases, the design phase is where serious designing work happens. The task is to ensure that an appropriate design concept is established that matches requirements and this should be done from the start, as problems are better and more easily solved at the early stage than later when they can cause serious disruptions, including termination of project.

It is important that the right design tools, such as wireframing and flowcharting (discussed in Chapter 26), are used and every design detail documented, following a predetermined format, in order to foster effective and consistent communication of design ideas within the project team, if there is one. Doing this also ensures that if any team member drops out, another person can easily pick up from where they left without serious disruption.

For a freelance developer, although the urge may be strong to skip the design phase and/or the use of visual techniques like storyboarding and move on to production, it is always advisable to suppress it, because not only does visualizing a design first on paper help spot any design short-sightedness that might prove costly later in development, but also outputs from such processes are part of the documents archived at the end of the project for future reference. The importance of archiving is discussed later in this chapter.

27.4.2.4 Media Objects Design Process

Designing the media objects needed for a website typically entails a variety of task sets, such as designing graphics, producing animation and video storyboards, determining the types of sounds required, and designing the content. The task here is to make sure that every component is designed to meet the project's specification. For example, in the case of sound, is it in mono or stereo, is resolution in 8, 16, or 24 bits, and is it CD quality? In the case of graphics, what resolution should be used? Similarly, for video, is it full-, half-, or quarter-screen in size; is color resolution in 8, 16, 24, or 32 bits?

The management of media components' quality is particularly important, as poor media quality can make an application appear unprofessional. Of course, good project management also includes knowing that high-quality media is used only when necessary. For example, images used for icons need not be of high quality, whereas images used for content must be of good-enough quality to communicate intended message effectively. The design of some media components may also require choosing between professional and non-professional production. For example, if a project requires an original piece of music, this would require professional-standard production, probably in a professional studio or a similarly equipped environment. Similarly, if a high-quality video is required, professional production may be considered.

Good management would also ensure that appropriate and consistent file formats and file-naming conventions are used to store files to facilitate the exchange of files between software tools. For example, a file could be named according to "screen number + whether an image is a button + if it is a button, the state it represents, and so on," representing each parameter with a number or letter(s), as appropriate; so that the image of a button that is depressed and on screen 2 might be coded as 2BD, where "B" stands for button and "D" for depressed. Something like this can prove very useful for troubleshooting and the effective management of changes during subsequent phases.

27.4.2.5 Media Production Tools Selection

Whether the selection of media production tools should come before or after the designing of media elements is debatable. One way of thinking is that knowing what is going to be created helps in the choice of the right tool to do it. The choice of these tools will usually be influenced by the operating systems running on the computers to be used for production. For example, there are some tools that are available on Microsoft's Windows but not available on Apple Macintosh or Linux, and vice versa.

However, most tools are increasingly available across main operating systems, and for tools that are not available on other operating systems, there are equivalent tools that offer similar functions.

27.4.3 Production Phase

The translation of the design to an actual system occurs in this phase, although it is not unusual for some minor adjustments to be made to some designs. In general, project management in this phase revolves mainly around managing content creation, content processing, and the creation of the designed website. **Content creation** and **content processing** (i.e., editing and adding effects to media) tend to happen together when content is newly created, whereas for existing content, only processing is usually needed. In either case, all outputs need to be checked against project specification. Where a team is involved, typically, the individual team members responsible for creating or processing any media component would be capable of doing this, but the project manager may be involved, or at least be aware of the outcome, either immediately or periodically. One way a project manager usually manages the outputs from the various media production activities is through using a database, not necessarily to store the media components, but to store their details, so that a search for the name of a file, for example, would provide all necessary information about it.

In comparison to other phases, more problems are likely to occur or surface during this phase, because translating designs to reality is often more difficult than generating them. Even though design would have been assessed for feasibility, unforeseen problems commonly surface, some of which can be so difficult to overcome. This means that the chances of a project starting to fall behind are greater during this phase and good management is needed to minimize them.

27.4.4 Postproduction Phase

Assuming website implementation is complete and the client still wants it because it has not gone ridiculously over deadline, the next set of tasks are final evaluation, delivery, final sign-off, clean-up, and archiving, all of which constitute the postproduction phase, which should not be confused with the same phase in media production, which comprises, for example, the cleaning up of media, editing, and addition of effects, which fall under the production phase here.

27.4.4.1 *Final Evaluation*

The evaluation plan outlined during the initiation phase would have been reviewed and refined before this point. You would also have ensured that the iterative evaluation of prototypes were carried out all through the development process, so that the final evaluation will just be about testing to see whether or not the site meets the overall project requirements. The evaluation is comprehensive. For example, testing is done on different systems and browsers (particularly major ones), different browser configurations, different Internet connection speeds, and different devices. All bugs, problems, and data from users are recorded and reported consistently, using the method that would have been specified under the evaluation plan in the proposal. This ensures that necessary corrections and changes are made in an organized way that is easy to monitor. After the initial corrections and changes, further tests may be done to find more functional problems, and this is repeated until there are no more obvious ones, at which point, the system is formally delivered and any subsequent problems are dealt with under the maintenance plan negotiated in the proposal.

27.4.4.2 Delivery and Final Sign-Off

For delivery, a domain account with adequate specifications is acquired, as discussed in Chapter 26. Delivery is also accompanied with well-written documentation that contains, for example, information on how to solve possible problems. Issues relating to the copyright of the media produced during the project are also dealt with. The types of rights issues that commonly arise in a Web project are discussed in Chapter 28.

The **final sign-off** is the formal indication that all the objectives of the project have been delivered, evaluated, and found by the client to be acceptable. The final payment will also usually occur at this point, if applicable. If a project is large, then there would have been prior **intermittent sign-offs** and they would also have been tied to payments. The maintenance plan is also implemented at this final stage. Where maintenance will be provided by a different company, necessary maintenance materials are transferred to them. If you will be taking on maintenance, a separate contract would usually have been signed. Irrespective of who provides maintenance, the contract does not usually start until after a grace period, during which any missed problems are fixed for free by the developer company, provided no other company has tampered with the product in the intervening time.

27.4.4.3 Closure

An orderly closure (i.e., cleanup and archiving) is important after a project has been completed, so that aspects of the project can be referenced quickly and easily in the future. This may be necessary for various reasons. For example, a completed project may be opened again in the future, either because a client is commissioning additional work or for maintenance purposes. It may also be because the elements used in the project need to be applied to a new project for someone else.

The orderly closure of a project involves various tasks, such as backing up all relevant files (more than once, if possible) in an orderly fashion and according to the predefined plan set out in the proposal, after which the originals are usually removed from the immediate work environment to make room for new projects. For extra security, backups are sometimes stored at different locations. To wrap up a project in a meaningful way, a **project review** or **retrospective analysis** may be done to consolidate the lessons learnt from the project and how they could be applied to future projects. If a team is involved, then this would be in the form of a final project meeting.

27.5 Useful Info

27.5.1 Web Links

Management tools: mindtools.com

Gantt tutorial: gantt.com

27.5.2 Free Software

Scheduling tool: Open Workbench (Win), GanttProject (*Win, MacOS*), Ganib (*Cross Platform*), xPlanner-plus (*Cross Platform*), jxProject (*Cross Platform*), OpenProj (*Cross Platform*)

Brainstorming tool: XMind (*Cross Platform*)

Some common tools for diagramming: Gliffy, Mockflow, iPlotz, Lovely charts,Mockingbird, Mocking builder, Pidoco, Lucid charts.

28

Introduction to Intellectual Property

28.1 Introduction

In order for the use of people's works to be legal, it is generally required by law to first get their permission. This permission could be for a fee or for free, depending on various factors, such as type of work, purpose of use, and even country. Intellectual property laws provide information to help determine in what situations permissions are required and from whom to seek them. Because interactive Web projects involve the use of multiple media types, some of which can be other people's works, and some of which are created in a project, each of which is protected in different ways by law and for varying durations, it is important for a Web designer to be aware of the different types of laws that govern the use of other people's works as well as the protection of those produced in a project.

28.2 Learning Outcomes

After studying this chapter, you should:

- Understand what intellectual property means and how it is protected.
- Know the general procedure for seeking permission to use others' works and dealing with an act of infringement.
- Be aware of the intellectual property in Web projects.

28.3 Intellectual Property

Intellectual property (IP) is a general term used to describe a creation of the mind (hence, intellectual) or a creative activity. A creation can be in various forms, including in the form of a written or recorded piece, design, invention, image, or even a name. Intellectual property enables those who have created any of these things to own them as they might own physical property. The term is also sometimes used to describe the various legal rights the creator of a piece of work has in the work. Typically, intellectual property law says that anyone who owns the intellectual property to a creation can control when, how, and where the creation is used and, if they choose to, do this in exchange for a reward. This means that not seeking the permission of an IP owner and therefore failing to give him/her the opportunity to exercise his/her rights is breaking the law.

Intellectual property laws are not readily straightforward to deal with. For example, how they are enforced vary widely from country to country. This is one reason various attempts have been made internationally to unify them. The establishment in 1967 of the **World Intellectual Property Organization** (WIPO) is one such attempt. The organization represents a forum for different member countries to create and unify rules and practices that ensure that the rights of creators and owners of intellectual property rights are recognized, protected, and rewarded worldwide.

Intellectual property covers numerous types of rights, which are commonly grouped into copyright and industrial property. **Copyright** covers the rights in both published and unpublished creative, intellectual, or artistic works, while **industrial property** concerns the rights in the category of creations relating to industrial products, the main ones of which are patents, designs, and trademarks, all of which are relevant in various Web projects, depending on the nature of project.

28.3.1 Copyright

Copyright is the exclusive right to determine what is done with a literary, musical, or artistic work. The owner of the copyright to a book, for example, has the exclusive right to reproduce, publish, sell, or distribute it. However, copyright only protects the form of expression of an idea, not the idea itself. The form of expression, in this case, relates to how elements such as words, musical notes, shapes, colors, and even inventions are arranged to create a unique piece. So, for example, a person cannot own the copyright to the idea of making people dance, but can own the copyright to a specific arrangement of musical notes that they have created to make people dance.

The concept of copyright has its roots in the advent, in the 1430s, of printing technology that made it possible for the first time to mass-produce and widely distribute literary works. Along with this, naturally, also came the practices of unauthorized reproduction and distribution of peoples' literary works. To control this, the **Worshipful Company of Stationers and Newspaper Makers** (also known as the **Stationers' Company**) was granted the monopoly of producing and distributing literary works around 1557. The way this worked was that the Stationers' Company bought manuscripts from authors and, after the sale, the company decided what to do with the manuscript and kept all profits from it. One of the side-effects of this practice was that authors had no control over what happened to their works, nor were they able to benefit financially as much as they should from them. The **Copyright Act of 1709** (also known as the **Statute of Anne**—named after Queen Anne of Great Britain who passed the act) was designed primarily to address this seemingly unfair situation and also serve as inducement to authors to produce more works, knowing that they would profit fairly from them. The act gave the exclusive right of printing literary works to authors and/or those authorized by them to do so.

This principle was then subsequently extended to other kinds of creative works. Not only this, different nations around the world came to introduce their own copyright acts, which were sometimes significantly different from one country to another. The first attempt to establish a framework to internationally harmonize these various acts was in the form of the **Berne Convention** for the Protection of Literary and Artistic Works in 1886. Several copyright conventions and treaties then followed, including the **Universal Copyright Convention** (UCC) of 1952, which was created as an alternative for countries that did not like the terms of the Berne Convention, and the **Rome Convention** for the Protection of Performers, Producers of Phonograms and Broadcasting Organizations of 1961. In essence, these conventions and treaties seek continually to refine and harmonize intellectual property laws, especially is relation to advances in technology, which often bring about new ways of expressing ideas and creativity, and new modes of communicating and distributing them.

Under the original Berne Convention, copyright protection extends to all original forms of literary and artistic works, irrespective of whether they are of good or bad quality. The Convention also lists various categories of works which member countries, and other countries, should protect under their copyright laws, most of which can be incorporated in a Web application in one form or another. They include the following, all of which can be relevant to Web projects, given the presence of the Web in businesses:

- Literary works (e.g., poems, theses, lectures, sermons).
- Musical works (e.g., musical compositions, including accompanying words).
- Dramatic works (e.g., plays, dances).
- Sound recordings.
- Cinematographic and other audiovisual works.
- Radio and television broadcasts.
- Artistic works (e.g., paintings, sculptures, drawings, logos).
- Lithographic works.
- Choreographic works (such as dance routines and ballet).
- Photographic works.
- Collections of literary and artistic works (such as encyclopedia).
- Translations and arrangements of literary and artistic works.
- Illustrations, maps, three-dimensional works, and so on.

While the Berne Convention focused on the outputs from the technologies of the time, which were analogue, subsequent intellectual property treaties extended copyright protection to different types of digital outputs. For example, the distribution of copyright materials over digital networks, particularly the Internet, is covered by the **WIPO Copyright Treaty** (WCT) and the **WIPO Performances and Phonograms Treaty** (WPPT), also sometimes referred to as the **Internet Treaties**. Also covered by some of these treaties is the copyright protection for the elements of intellectual creativity inherent in the uniqueness of the design, arrangement, or data selection process in a database. Essentially, **database rights** prevent acts like the removal and re-use of whole or substantial part of the contents of a database. This is without compromising the rights in the individual contents of the database.

Even Web productions are judged to involve creative effort and therefore deserving of copyright protection. Like for database rights, the rationale is that, although the individual components of a Web production are themselves creative works and are provided protection under copyright laws, putting them together in a unique way in a Web production can be regarded as an original form of expression of ideas and creativity. Some countries, including the UK, also grant a **right to copy-protected devices**. For example, a copy-protected device, such as CD, is protected against people copying its content, disabling the copy-protection mechanism, or making or selling devices, or providing services, to disable it. Copyright may even apply by virtue of publishing a work, whether in analogue or digital form. For example, **EU Directive 93/98/EEC** defines **publication right** for European Union members and gives copyright to the person who first publishes a previously unpublished literary, dramatic, musical, artistic, or cinematographic work after its original copyright has expired. Protection extends to 25 years, starting from publication.

All in all, the way the unification of rights through conventions and treaties works across countries is that countries that are signatories to them try to adhere to the framework set out, and the conventions and treaties, in turn, ensure that there is enough room for individual countries to incorporate their own additional protection terms.

28.3.1.1 When Copyright Protection Begins

In most member countries of the Berne Union, and many other countries, the instance a work is put into a tangible form—that is, into a form that can be heard, seen, or touched—the author automatically owns all copyrights in the work and any derivative works, unless, or until he/she disclaims them, or they expire. In some countries, such as the US, although copyright protection is automatic, a copyright has to be registered before an infringement lawsuit can be filed in court in the event of an infringement on the copyright. Registration is intended to serve as a public record of the facts about a copyright and can be used by an author as proof of copyright.

One of the ways the term "tangible form" can be explained is that you cannot, for example, own a copyright to a design idea you have in your head, even if you have told someone about it. You have to either put it on paper or in some other medium for it to be in tangible form. After the design is in a tangible form, you can put a **copyright notice** on it to show that you own the copyright. The common way to do this is to put "*Copyright ©*," year, and name at the bottom of the paper, or on the label of the recording medium, thus, *Copyright © 2016 Joe Smith*. The © symbol is known as the **copyright symbol**, but its use is not universal. For example, **(c)** and **(C)** are used in some countries. The notice means that the design was created in 2016 by Joe Smith. If later, in 2015, the design was modified, the notice can read "*Copyright © 2016, 2017 Joe Smith*" on the new version to show that the design was first created in 2016 and then modified in 2017. You probably have seen similar notices at the bottom of many Web pages. However, the © symbol is really not a legally recognized symbol. It is also not obligatory to put a copyright notice on a work for the work to be protected by copyright. It is good practice to use it, however, as (1) it serves to inform that the work is in copyright and of the owner, and (2) it deters infringement.

Where to put the copyright notice depends on whether or not a work is separable. In the case of a website, the notice can be placed on each page. In addition to the copyright protection, there are other rights protections. For example, for musical compositions, etc., there is, when sound recordings are involved, another type of right that relates to the sound recordings themselves. This is known as a **phonogram right**, which is a category of rights known as **related rights**, discussed later in this chapter. A phonogram right notice is commonly denoted by the "P in a circle" symbol: ℗. That is why notices containing both the © and ℗ symbols may be found on music CDs or vinyl records. Using the earlier example, commonly used formats include "*Copyright © 2016 Joe Smith,*" ℗ *2016 Joe Smith,*" and "*© & ℗ 2016 Joe Smith.*"

Naturally, for legal purposes, it is important to be able to prove that something was actually created when the creator said it was, and there are various ways this is done. The most common is for the creator to put the copy of the creation in an envelope, post it to himself/herself through registered or special mail, and then leave it unopened. The postmark serves as date of creation and therefore the date that copyright protection begins. This approach can be used for any type of work. For example, video, animation, software, or copies of working files and the final version could be put on a storage medium (e.g., CD, DVD, Blu-ray disc, or memory stick) and then copyrighted in this way. Copyrighting both copies of working files and the final version is necessary essentially to provide a progress history of a work and therefore better proof of ownership.

Additional statements can also be added to a copyright notice in the form of extended notice to specify exactly what is covered. This could be, for example, in the form of a simple statement, such as "*All rights reserved,*" or a description of how and for what a work may be used, or not be used, such as "*Permission granted to reproduce for personal and educational use only. Commercial copying, hiring, or lending is prohibited.*"

Another way a work may be copyrighted is registering it with a copyright service. In the UK, for example, there is the **UK Copyright Service**. When this is done, the work is given a **license number**. If a work is registered, a **notice of registration** can also be put with the work as a further deterrent from unauthorized usage. This notice can be put after or below the copyright notice, including the license number. Here is an example of a notice of registration: "*This work is registered with the UK Copyright Service. Registration Number: 12345.*" Depositing a work with a solicitor or a bank are also valid ways of proving copyright. Of course, as in posting such work to yourself, it needs to be sealed and left unopened. Keeping a track record of the development of a work, and leaving deliberate and unique signs or patterns in some types of works, such as computer programs, too, can provide additional proof, should it ever be necessary to make a claim.

28.3.1.2 Duration of Copyright

The duration of copyright is not indefinite and also varies from country to country, largely because, as mentioned before, different countries have differently crafted copyright laws. In countries that are signatories to the Berne Convention, and many other countries, the duration of copyright in a work is generally the **life of the authors, plus 50 years after their death**. The Berne convention also stipulates a framework for the duration of copyright for what were deemed unusual works, such as posthumous, anonymous, and cinematographic works, all of which may be relevant to Web production. The stipulations are for the following copyright durations:

- For a cinematographic work, 50 years from the time the work is created or, if the work is made public within that period, 50 years from the date the work is made public by the author.
- For posthumous work, if copyright exists at the death of author or at the death of the last author in joint authorship, but the work has never been made public, then copyright exists until the work is made public, plus 50 years from the date it is made public.
- For anonymous work, 50 years after the work is made public.
- For artistic work, a minimum of 25 years from the date of creation.
- For publication right, 25 years from the date of publication.
- For database rights, 15 years from the year it is made accessible to the public, or the time of modification.

Many countries' copyright laws typically specify longer periods than are described above. For example, in EU countries, US, and many other countries, copyright for most works extend until 70 years after the death of the author. The **EU Directive 93/96/EEC** extends the copyright protection for films (i.e., cinematographic and other audiovisual works) to 70 years after the death of the last of the director, the screenplay writer, the script writer, and the composer of the music specially written for the film. The same directive extends the protection for photographic works to 70 years after the death of the creator, except photographs that are taken automatically, such as passports, in which case, *sui generis* related rights may be applied. The term *sui generis* is a Latin expression that means "of its own kind" and *sui generis* rights are special types of rights.

Extending copyright protection for as long as possible after the death of authors is a very sensible thing, in that it enables the successors of copyright owners to benefit economically from the copyright. In all cases, when the copyright in a work expires, that is, when a work is **out of copyright**, the work goes **in the public domain**, and from there on, the public may use or exploit it without permission. However, a work can be in the public domain and yet not be out of copyright. This typically happens when the person who owns the copyright in a work puts the work in the public domain so that people can use it with or without conditions. The implication of this is that caution is necessary when using works in the public domain. In particular, it is important to be clear about any conditions attached to their use, such as whether they can be used where you want to use them, especially as a work may be out of copyright in one country and not in another. A common condition is for a work to be free to use for noncommercial purposes, but not for commercial purposes without explicit permission. The rule of thumb is to assume that a work is not completely free to use, unless you know otherwise.

28.3.1.3 *Rights Protected by Copyright Laws*

According to the Berne Convention, when authors are said to own the copyright in their works, this automatically means that they can use it as they wish, as long as it is done within the sense of what is legally permissible in the relevant society. This means, for example, that authors may not use their works to harm others, physically or otherwise. As well as granting them the rights to use their works as they wish, the Berne Convention grants to authors exclusive rights to permit others to use their work; and even more, any author from a country that is a member of the Berne Union has the same rights in other member countries as the nationals of those countries, including all the rights granted by the Berne Convention, if not already in the national laws.

The exclusive rights granted to a copyright owner have been designed with two main goals in mind. One is economic and the other is moral-based; so, rights generally fall under economic and moral rights.

28.3.1.3.1 *Economic Rights*

Economic rights are meant to enable authors to derive financial benefits from the use of their works. The activities prohibited without the permission of the author of a work include:

- Reproduction of the work in various forms.
- Distribution, sale, lending, leasing, rental, or any transfer of ownership of copies.
- Importation of copies. This is in order to protect the interest of the copyright owner in a particular country.
- Public display, performance, or broadcast of part or whole, or communication to the public, such as over the Internet. Even use in a private house is prohibited, if a substantial amount of people who are outside the usual circle of a family is present.
- Translation into other languages.
- Recitation or translation.
- Arrangements or adaptation, such as from novel to movies.

28.3.1.3.2 *Moral Rights*

Moral rights were not added to the list of rights until the Berne Convention for the Protection of Literary and Artistic Works of 1928. The concept emerged from continental Europe and is premised on the notion that a work is an extension of the author's personality and therefore the author has interests in how the work is used. Moral rights, therefore, enable authors to control how their works are used, so that the trueness, or essential quality, or meaning of the works is preserved, even when they no longer own the copyright. Essentially, authors have the moral rights to specify what may or may not be done to their works. However, unlike copyright, moral rights are not usually transferrable; only the author and his/her heirs can exert them. Four specific rights are protected under moral rights:

- The **right of attribution**, which gives the right to claim authorship, such as the right to be acknowledged or credited for a work when used, or when it appears in another work.
- The **right of disclosure**, which gives the author the right to specify when and how a work should be presented in public, including whether anonymously or pseudonymously (i.e., with a fictitious name).
- The **right of integrity**, which gives the right to prevent any treatment of a work, which might be derogatory to the work, or the author's reputation or honor, including destruction, mutilation, or distortion of the work.
- The **right to refuse attribution** for a work.

While most countries that are signatories of the Berne Convention recognize moral rights as part of copyright laws, or agree with the concept, the scope of implementation of moral rights varies across countries. For example, in US, there is no specific legislation for moral rights. Rather, they are covered under various laws, including copyright laws, and only visual arts, such as paintings and sculptures, are explicitly granted moral rights, through the **Visual Artist's Rights Act** (VARA). On the other hand, in the UK, moral rights are recognized, but not as strictly as in some other EU countries, such as France. Nevertheless, the UK copyright laws grant the authors of literary, dramatic, musical, and artistic works, and film directors, moral rights, although the owners can waive them, if they choose to do so.

As a Web designer, it is important to understand the implications of moral rights in Web design. Just because the authorization has been obtained to use a piece of work does not mean that it can be used in anyway. For example, a piece of music may not be mutilated or used in a context that may compromise the composer's position, such as combining it with degrading images or using it for some cause to which he/she is not sympathetic, without his/her consent. Whether you do these things or your website is intended to allow them to be done, you might be found to be infringing on the author's moral rights or aiding others to do so. The same is the case with the treatment of images. Even a treatment that seems as minor as coloring a black and white original image may result in an infringement of moral rights. This is why an author might want to know how a work will be used before granting permission. Some would even ask to provide a sample of how the work will be used; so, it is useful to be clear about how a media is going to be used when clearing it. In general, most authors are happy for their creations to be used, in return for license fee or just an acknowledgment, as long as the usage is in good light, or for a cause with which they empathize.

28.3.1.4 Limitations on Rights

Although copyright owners have the exclusive rights to say when and how their work must be used, there are circumstances in which there are limitations to these rights.

They are called **exceptions**. In copyright laws, limitations are classified mainly as **free use** (also known as fair use, fair deal, or fair practice) and **nonvoluntary licenses**, both of which are relevant in Web production.

28.3.1.4.1 Free Use

Free use limitation specifies that works can be used in certain circumstances without authorization from the authors and without compensating them, on the condition that (1) the use complies with the terms of **fair dealing**, (2) the use is appropriate and not excessive, and (3) the source of the material and the name of the author are mentioned. Circumstances where free use exception applies include:

- When part of a work, such as quotation or excerpt, is used in news reporting.
- When the use of a part of a work is incidental, such as when a protected work is unintentionally caught in the background of a private video shoot. Of course, if the video is to be made public, then the permission of the owner of the work may be needed; or the offending parts may be blurred or taken out, as commonly done in documentaries.
- When a work is used privately, or for educational or research purposes.
- When versions of a work, such as Braille or enlarged versions, are produced for use with the blind or visually impaired.

The free-use exception is designed generally to ensure that copyright laws are not so strict that they prevent the use of works, even when this is in the interest of the public, or cause people to be penalized unduly, say, for using something briefly in error. However, what is fair use can be difficult to determine sometimes, particularly when the rights protection given to works in digital form conflict with what traditionally is fair use. A common example is how creating a photomontage from image cuttings from different copyrighted works, such as magazines and newspaper, can be considered fair use, while scanning the same images and creating a photomontage in a computer may amount to an infringement of copyright.

In opposition to the restrictions imposed by copyright, including lack of clarity of fair use, and particularly **digital rights management** (DRM) that often disallows copying of any kind, certain nonprofit organizations have since emerged that provide alternatives to typical copyright laws. Their collective belief is that copyright tends to stifle creativity and adequate exploitation of people's works and there are many copyright owners who would like more people to make certain uses of their works without having to come to them for permissions, provided they comply with stipulated conditions of use, particularly the one that the works are not to be used for commercial purposes. The motto of these organizations, in general, can be said to be **Some Rights Reserved** rather than **All Rights Reserved** and the general aim is to communicate this principle to as many people as possible on behalf of willing copyright owners. Examples of these organizations are **Creative Commons**, **Free Art License**, and **MIT License**. These organizations promote the principle of **copyleft** or **share-alike**, which generally permits people to reproduce, modify, or distribute a work as long as any resulting work is made available under the same principle. So, rather than put the conventional copyright symbol on a work, an author who accepts this principle uses alternative symbols instead. For example, **CC** in a circle is used for Creative Common license.

28.3.1.4.2 Nonvoluntary License

Nonvoluntary license exception is so called because the authorization to use a work is not necessarily voluntary on the part of the copyright owner. It specifies that a work can be used in certain circumstances without the owner's authorization, just as in free use, except that payment is required to be made to the owner for the use. Circumstances in which this limitation applies include when a new technology has been invented that is important for providing essential services to the public and there are fears that the owner might refuse to grant permission to others to progress it. In such a case, the national legislator, or equivalence, might evoke the limitation. A good example of such a technology is the Internet, although the Internet was never copyright protected in the first place, since it began life as a government project.

28.3.1.4.3 Other Rights Exceptions

Other situations in which rights are limited or authors are compelled to relinquish their rights include employer-employee, contractor-subcontractor, and author-publisher situations, in which terms are usually included in contracts to stipulate or confirm who owns what rights. For example, in **employer-employee** situations, if the creator of a work is employed for the purpose of creating the work, then it is the employer who owns the copyright in the work. This is really a kind of **transfer of rights**. If this is not stipulated in employment contract, then the creator may own the copyright.

In contrast, in **contractor-subcontractor** situations, the subcontractor owns the copyright in the works created, even if he/she is paid for the work, unless otherwise stated in the contract. For example, if someone pays a photographer to photograph something for them, the photographer owns the copyright in the photograph and a reproduction without his/her permission is an infringement of copyright. This is why a photographer would typically give prints rather than film negatives (in the days of film-based photography) or digital files.

In **author-publisher** situations, although authors automatically own copyright, they may transfer it to a publisher they feel can better exploit their work on their behalf, in return for which they are paid money, known as **royalties**, according to how successfully the work is exploited. This is another form of authors transferring their rights and may be done in either of two ways: assignment or licensing. **Under assignment**, some or all rights covered under copyright may be transferred. When this is done, the party to which rights are assigned becomes the new copyright owner. In contrast, some countries only allow rights to be licensed. **Under licensing**, authors retain ownership but may transfer some rights to others to do specific things and for a specified amount of time. For example, the owner of the copyright in a novel can license the right to publish the novel to one party and the right to turn it into a movie to another. Of course, authors may also transfer all rights to one party under licensing, just as under assignment; the main difference is that it is not automatic.

28.3.1.5 Related Rights

Sometimes, in order for a creation to reach the form that can be published, other people are needed to contribute in the way of talents, and so on. For example, a person might write a play, but actors are needed to interpret and perform the play. While the writer owns the copyright in the play, related rights are designed to protect the elements of creativity that exist in the contributions of people, such as actors, who bring the play to life. The **Rome Convention** first recognized these rights, which were later extended to cover more acts by the Agreement on Trade Related Aspects of Intellectual Property Rights (**TRIPS**) and **WPPT**. Typically, those who are meant to benefit from these rights include performers, phonogram (music) producers, film producers, and broadcasting organizations in the form of performers' rights, phonogram producers' rights, film producers' rights, and broadcasting organizations' rights, respectively. As with copyright laws, there are limitations to these rights when protected works are used for purposes such as teaching, research, and private use, in which case, they are waived. Also, rights covered vary from country to country.

28.3.1.5.1 Performers' Rights

Performers' rights are different from Performing Rights, which are part of copyright law that allow authors to object to the performance of their work in public. Performers' rights allow performers to prevent people from doing certain acts with their performance without their permission, as well as the rights to be paid fairly when permission is given. These acts include the recording or broadcasting of their performance, the communication of their live performance to the public, the reproduction of the recordings of their performance, or the rental of such recordings. Some countries, such as EU countries, also grant performers the moral rights over whether or not their name should be associated with a performance, or to stop their performance from being adapted in a way they feel portrays them badly. According to TRIPS, the rights of performers are protected for a minimum of 50 years from the year of performance. In the EU, these rights are protected for 50 years from the year of performance or, if recorded, 50 years from the year the recording is published.

28.3.1.5.2 Phonogram Producers' Rights

Phonogram producers have the rights to prevent acts such as the unauthorized reproduction, rental, distribution, or importation of their recordings or copies, as well as the right to be paid fairly for the broadcast or communication to the public of their recordings, once they have been published. A phonogram these days generally refers to any audio recording on any of a variety of medium, including discs, tapes, and vinyl.

Typically, in order to protect a recording, all that is required is that each copy carries, as shown earlier, a **P in a circle symbol**, thus ℗, then the year of publication and the name of the owner of the producer's rights, not the name of the writer. The duration of producers' rights over a phonogram, according to TRIPS, is a minimum of 50 years from the year of its creation. In the EU, the duration is a minimum of 50 years from the year of creation, if unpublished, or 50 years from the year it is first published. In the US, the situation is more complex. For example, protection generally lasts for 70 years after death, except for "work made for hire," in which case, protection lasts for the shorter of 95 years after publication or 125 years after creation. A **"work made for hire"** is described as work created within employment or specially commissioned for use, for example, as part of other works, a translation, or an instructional text.

28.3.1.5.3 *Film Producers' Rights*

Film producers, just like phonogram producers, make creative decisions about productions; in this case, about the completion and quality of films. Accordingly, film producers have rights in the master copies of the films or other audiovisual works they have produced. The rights are similar to those of phonogram producers and can be used to prevent direct or indirect reproduction, distribution, rental, or public showing of the film. In the EU, the rights last for 50 years from the year a film is made or first released.

28.3.1.5.4 *Broadcasting Organizations' Rights*

Broadcasting organizations have the rights to prevent the re-broadcast, recording, or reproduction of their broadcast to the public where fees are charged. The duration for broadcasters' rights is a minimum of 25 years from the year of the first broadcast. In the EU, this duration is extended to 50 years.

28.3.1.5.5 Sui Generis *Database Right*

As well as copyright protection for databases, protection for them is extended in some countries. For example, **EU Directive 96/9/EC** extends protection to include *sui generis* database right, which recognizes the substantial investment made in the obtaining, verification, or presentation of the contents of a database and provides protection against their unauthorized extraction and re-use. The duration of the protection is 15 years, and for a dynamic database, the right is renewed each time substantial investment occurs. Even if a database does not qualify for copyright protection, it may still have this right. Of course, a database may also have both rights.

28.3.2 Industrial Property

Industrial property describes rights relating mainly to inventions, product designs, and unique marks or signs intended to distinguish products or services. Unlike copyright, some of these rights are not automatic and have to be registered for protection to take effect. Given that some aspects of Web design/development, such as a special algorithm for doing something, qualify for patent, it is useful for a Web designer/developer to be aware of this type of rights.

28.3.2.1 Patents

A patent is a set of rights designed to protect a new and useful invention by protecting features, such as what the invention does, how it does it, what it is made of, and how it is made. It is granted for only a period of time, in return for which inventors must disclose the details of their inventions to the public so that the society can benefit from it, either in its original or improved form. The requirements for granting patent and the extent of the rights granted vary widely from country to country, depending on national laws and international treaties. However, there are more similarities than differences.

Generally, in order for an invention to be considered worthy of patent, there must be the element of newness and human intervention. For example, digging up a substance that no one has ever seen before from the ground does not qualify as an invention. However, treating it with some chemicals and producing a new substance can be described as an invention. Some inventions do not necessarily solve any obvious problems, but are ideas or the representations of ideas. Indeed, according to patent law, an invention does not have to be in physical form for it to get protection. Consequently, there is more than one type of patent. The WIPO describes two types: product patent and process patent. A **product patent** might be, for example, for a new type of metal, while a **process patent** might be for a new process of producing a metal that is not necessarily a new metal. **In the case of a website**, the product is the website and process is the new and useful thing the website does. Google homepage design, for example, has a patent. Some countries describe their types of patent differently. The US, for instance, describes three types: **design** (e.g., website design), **utility** (what website does), and **plant** patents.

Unlike copyright, patent is not automatic. Patent law requires that an application is submitted to the patent office, along with a fee, providing the details of the invention and highlighting what is new about it by comparing it to anything that already exists in the relevant fields. The details must be such that they allow the production of the invention by others. The invention is then reviewed by qualified people. The preparation of an application for patent is an undertaking that requires the knowledge of the patent law, so, legal help is often essential. For an invention to qualify for a patent, it must meet certain set of criteria. This can be slightly different from country to country. For example, the EU only considers computer programs that are key to technical processes patentable, whereas in the US, patents can be granted to any type of computer program. However, in spite of the variations from country to country, the general requirements are that an invention must

- Be novel, that is, it must not have something already known in the relevant field. In order words, **prior art** must not exist.
- Be producible and of practical use, either to the general public or some industry.

- Show an inventive step that is not already known to people in the field.
- Be within the scope of subject matter the patent law of a country allows. Typically, it must not be in such subject matter as scientific or mathematical discovery, theory or method, literary, dramatic, musical or artistic work, medical treatment or diagnosis, some computer programs, animal or plant varieties, ways of doing mental acts, playing games or transacting business, or be anything that is detrimental to public order, morals, or health. This list is, of course, not exhaustive. Visiting a patent office or its website can usually provide a more detailed list. For example, information on UK's patent law is available on the Website of UK Intellectual Property Office.

Once patent has been granted to an invention, it becomes available to the public, and those who wish to exploit it commercially can do so, but not without the permission of the **patentee** (i.e., the patent holder). Typically, a patentee grants permission to use an invention, that is, licenses it, in return for royalty. This arrangement enables inventors to profit from their inventions, thereby encouraging more inventions.

Patent protection typically lasts 20 years, but in some countries, there can be additional terms. In the UK, for example, renewal is required every year after the fifth year for it to last the whole 20 years. Also, a patent is valid only in the country that granted it and, therefore, to protect an invention elsewhere, application has to be tendered there, or an international application may be put in under the **Patent Cooperation Treaty** (PCT), stating the countries in which patent is required. Application may also be put in under the **European Patent Convention**, stating the European countries required. A product can have multiple patents associated with it, each for a different component. A device like iPhone, for example, has many patents associated with it, including for the design of components, processes, and interaction models.

Once a patent expires, the patentee no longer has the rights to prevent people from exploiting the invention. The rights generally granted by patent law include:

- For a **product patent**, the right to prevent others from reproducing, selling, importing for sale, or using the product without the permission of the inventor.
- For a **process patent**, the right to prevent others from using, selling, or offering the process for sale; or importing for the purpose of using, selling, or offering for sale, products produced directly from the process.

Although these rights are there to be exercised at the discretion of a patentee, there are times when a patentee's decision to refuse license to others can be overruled, similar to nonvoluntary license in copyright. This is known as **compulsory license** and used by a government when licensing an invention is in the wider public or government interest. A patented medical invention that could be used to save people's lives, for example, is most likely a good candidate for compulsory licensing if the patentee refuses to grant licenses. Naturally, when a compulsory license is issued, the patentee is also rewarded adequately. In another kind of **patent law exception**, the owners of inventions, in certain cases, may not be legally qualified to patent their inventions. This applies when an invention is made by someone in the course of doing what they have been employed to do. In such a case, it is usually the employer who will file for patent and own the patent rights. Of course, an employer may also make a deal to give the inventor a percentage of royalties.

28.3.2.2 Industrial Designs

Industrial design describes the overall ornamental or aesthetic appearance of the whole or part of a useful product, while appearance derives from the characteristics of features such as shape, colors, lines, text, decoration, contours, texture, patterns, or materials, and any combination of these. It can be in the form of a three-dimensional product, or a two-dimensional pattern or logo to be displayed on it; and covers only the design, not the product. For example, it does not cover a mobile phone or its functionalities, but covers its shape and the color scheme used.

The visual design of a product is very important to the success of the product, particularly when there is competition. It could be what gives the product the necessary edge over other products that are just as functionally capable. One of the aims of industrial design protection is to protect this quality and reward its creators, thereby providing encouragement for investment in product design. This is why industrial design protection usually includes the condition that a design is useful in industry or reproducible commercially.

As with other types of rights, qualification criteria for industrial design protection and scope vary from country to country, and so, indeed, does the name. In the UK, for example, it is referred to as **design rights** and to qualify, a design must

- Be new or original; that is, not look like any existing designs in part or whole.
- Be for the purpose of beautifying only.
- Not be dictated by the function of a product; that is, it must be solely a design feature.
- Not be offensive or consist of protected emblems.

Provided qualification criteria are met, industrial design protection gives the owner of a design the exclusive rights to produce, import, sell, offer for sale, or hire products that use the design, as well as the rights to prevent others from doing the same without his/her permission. This protection applies in varying degrees, depending on whether or not a design is registered. For an **unregistered design**, protection is limited, lasting 10 years after its first appearance in the market, or 15 years after creation, whichever is earlier. It also does not protect two-dimensional aspects of a design and only grants exclusive rights for 5 years, after which the owner cannot refuse anyone a license. For a **registered design** (for which a fee is usually required), a wider range of features is protected and protection may last up to 25 years, provided registration is renewed every 5 years. On the other hand, in the US, for example, designs are protected under a different name, **design patent law**, and protection lasts 14 years from the date patent is granted.

28.3.2.3 Trademarks

A trademark describes a sign used to distinguish a product or service from the same types of products or services offered by other people and can be in the form of words or logo, or a combination of both. It may be placed on a product or/and its packaging, or on advertisements when used in relation to marketing. When used this way, it is sometimes referred to as a **service mark** in some countries, such as the US.

In order to be protected as a trademark, a sign or mark must be registered. This is not the same as registering a company with Companies House or registering a domain name, neither of which grants the rights to use a name as a trademark. Registering a trademark typically gives the exclusive right to use the trademark with relevant products or services and take legal action to prevent unauthorized use. A registered trademark symbol, ® (R in a circle), may be placed next to a registered trademark. A trademark must be registered for the symbol to be used with it. It is usually a criminal offence to use the symbol with an unregistered trademark. If a trademark is unregistered, only the ™ symbol, or the copyright symbol © (if protected by copyright), may be used with it. Also, legal action cannot be taken with an unauthorized use of an unregistered trademark the same way as with a registered trademark. Legal action can usually be taken only in an indirect way. For example, in some countries, this can be done only using common law action. In the UK, the **common law of passing off** is used, although such an action is usually difficult to win, as infringement is often hard to prove.

As well as making legal action easier to take, using a registered trademark symbol serves as a warning to people against using a trademark. However, not all signs are acceptable as trademarks. For a sign or mark to be acceptable for registration, it must meet certain criteria. For example, it must be distinctive and not describe any products, or services, or their characteristics (either in words or by shape). Furthermore, it must not contain a protected emblem, be offensive, illegal, or give the wrong impression of products or services. Being aware of these criteria is particularly useful to a developer in ensuring that the most appropriate trademark is produced, if required in a project. **A website name can be registered as trademark** in many countries.

28.3.3 Seeking Permission to Use People's Works

The failure to obtain permission before using a copyright-protected work can end up being much more expensive than the cost of obtaining one. Penalty can range from heavy fines to imprisonment in serious cases. Although fair use allows certain degree of use, this is unlikely to be adequate for most purposes in Web design projects. Who to obtain permission from depends on who owns the copyright in a work: the author or the publisher. Where there is one, the publisher is usually approached in the first instance. If the publisher is not responsible for giving the required permission, he/she should be able to point in the right direction.

Where it is an individual who owns the copyright in a work, he/she is approached for permission, typically in writing, and any agreement should be clear and also in writing. With website contents, the first point of contact is the person who owns the site, or the webmaster, if indicated. If it is a company website, it is possible that the webmaster will not be the one responsible for giving permission, but he/she should be able to point to the appropriate person. In almost all cases, information needs to be provided upfront about the media for which permission is sought and the intended usage in order to expedite the clearance process. Typically needed information includes:

- Name of author.
- Title of work.
- How work will be reproduced.
- Exact description of which part of a work is required.
- Details of any modifications intended.
- Description of the overall context. For example, if the work will be combined with other works, the percentage the licensed work will be of the overall work should be described.

In addition to this, a copyright owner may need to know if a work is to be used in a commercial product and, if so, the estimate of how many will be sold, and also for how long permission is needed and for which regions of the world. If permission is being sought to use a work on a product that is going to be sold commercially, then some payment may be required in the form of royalties on the quantity sold of the product. A flat fee is typical for noncommercial purposes. Any license agreement would state the terms and conditions of use, deviation from which will be an act of infringement and may end up being costly.

In some cases, **collective management organizations** can be used to obtain permission to use others' works. These organizations essentially give permission to use works protected by copyright and related rights on behalf of copyright owners and ensure that they receive payment for the use of their works. There are various types of these organizations, each involved in different types of works, such as musical, dramatic, and Web production. Most countries have at least one and there are some that operate worldwide. They are particularly useful when it is not possible to contact a copyright owner, or not practical for a copyright owner to grant permission, either because he/she is not available or requests are too many to handle.

28.3.4 Dealing with an Infringement

Different countries have different procedures for handling rights infringement, but the general principle is the same. It involves contacting the infringer, usually through writing, so that there is a record of the communication, and describing, politely and professionally, the nature of infringement, stating that the relevant work is protected by law and requesting that all offending materials should be withdrawn, stating a deadline for compliance. The correspondence should also state that you are seeking legal advice and prepared to take the matter further. If the infringement continues and/or you think you are entitled to some compensation, then the matter, with all available evidence, should be passed on to a solicitor. Evidence typically includes the infringing work, the infringed work, copyright registration (if there is any), any track record of the development of the work, and, of course, all correspondence with the infringer.

28.4 Intellectual Property in Web Design

A Web project probably involves more rights than any other type of project, given the many different media objects usually used. For example, in a typical Web project, such as one for a basic fan club website, rights may exist in the textual content, graphics used in the design of the pages, photographs, sounds, music, and video clips of the star, all of which usually require licenses before they could be used, if created by other people. Because there are moral rights in some works, the licenses also need to cover the way the works will be used, if they are going be used in an unusual way (such as combining them with contentious works or messages), or edited in ways that will mutilate them or alter their meaning. Of course, rights are also typically produced in a project, if works are created by the people in it, and the matter of who owns which rights need to be clarified, usually via the terms of employees' contracts. The following are some possible types of rights.

28.4.1 Rights in Text

Text is the most used media in Web design. While intellectual property rarely exists in its design, there is one in the literary work it is used to compose and this is protected. Consequently, if anyone's literary work is used word for word (e.g., copied and pasted), or translated into another language without permission, this may constitute both copyright and moral right infringement. In cases where free use exception is exercised, the amount used is limited and the text is enclosed in quotation marks as well as attributed to the author, thus:

> Copying and pasting an author's work without enclosing it in quotation marks and attributing it to the author is an infringement of copyright (James, 2000).

If a work is not copied word for word, but paraphrased, then, although no infringement has occurred, an offence called **plagiarism** may be committed if the amount paraphrased is large and there is no attribution to the author. It is also worth remembering that even if 70 years have passed since the death of the author of a literary work, this does not mean that the work is out of copyright. For example, there may be a translator of the work who is still alive and owns some rights.

28.4.2 Rights in Images and Photographs

Whether images are created with cameras or graphics programs, or started life in digital or analogue form, clearance is needed if they were created by other people. Even the scanning of images created by other people without permission may be an act of infringement. Although clients may have existing images or photographs, this does not mean they own the rights. If they do not, then permission must be sought from the creators to use the works in whichever ways are intended. Of course, where a company logo is created in a project, it must not be too similar to any existing logo design, as this is protected under copyright as artwork.

For some types of projects, such as personal, nonprofit website production, or sample use, including mock-ups, the use of free stock images is usually sufficient. However, although there is no need to ask for a license, it is important that the stipulated terms and conditions of use are complied with, otherwise this would constitute infringement. With some of these sources, all that is required is attribution, while with others, users are required to include a link back to the respective sites. This ensures that the websites are credited for the use of the graphics. Graphics from free-stock websites may also be used for commercial projects, in which case, a license usually needs to be purchased.

28.4.3 Rights in Music and Speech

There are many different rights in audio works and determining the correct licenses to obtain, and from where to obtain them, can be confusing, particularly as different types of uses require different types of licenses from different sources. For example, for a recorded tune, some rights are owned by the composer, some by the publisher, some by the producer of the recording of the tune, and some by the performer of the tune, if the recording is of a live performance of the tune. To complicate matters, some rights are regularly transferred between parties to maximize the exploitation of a tune. Essentially, on completion of a tune, composers usually license their copyright (but not moral rights) in a work to a publisher to exploit the tune on their behalf. The publisher then usually licenses the tune to a record company and/or broadcaster, which then records and/or broadcasts it, respectively. This means, in this case, that in order to legally use the tune in a Web application, for example, as background music, a license needs to be obtained from the composer or the publisher, whereas to legally make copies or sell the recording of the tune, it is usually the record company that has the right to give the permission.

The most common ways music is used in a Web project are as background music (for example, to enhance user experience) and in combination with visual content to communicate a message. These types of uses are different from when, for example, a website provides music download services (e.g., iTunes) or streaming services (e.g., Internet radios), in which case, a developer is unlikely to be involved in any licensing matters, as this is a business matter and does not involve the use of music in a project.

Where a tune will be used or synchronized with visual content, such as is done in motion picture, video, and commercial, a **synchronization license** is required from the composer or the publisher, which allows the re-recording of the tune and its use with a visual. If the tune is going to be performed live for the re-recording, then a **performance license** may also be required from the composer or the publisher. On the other hand, if an existing recording of the tune by a specific artist will be used, then, as well as a synchronization license, a **master recording license** is usually required from the owner of the master. If the existing recording is of a live performance, then a license may also be required from the performer, who usually owns the performers' rights. Where an audio recording is of spoken words only, permission is required each from the person who owns the rights in the speech, the recording, and the performing of the speech. If a live performance, whether of music or speech, is going to be recorded for use in an application, then permission is usually required from the performer, both to record and use the recording.

To make the acquisition of licenses more straightforward than chasing after rights owners, there are various **licensing agencies** (also called **copyright collectives**), from whom licenses can be obtained. These organizations perform the collective management of copyright and related rights for their members, who may be composers, performers, or publishers. They grant licenses, including compulsory licenses, to users and collect royalties on behalf of their members. Such organizations in the UK include PRS for Music, which deals with performance licenses, and the Mechanical Copyright Protection Society (MCPS), which issues copying licenses for a recording. In the US, they include the American Society of Computers, Authors and Publishers (ASCAP) and Harry Fox Agency, respectively. With most of them, only an on-line form needs to be filled to obtain most licenses.

28.4.4 Rights in Video and Animation

Like with audio, there can be multiple rights in video, depending on the type of video. For example, **for a video of someone**, there are rights in the performance and in the recording. This means that the permissions of both the performer and the person who did the recording are needed to use the video. If there is also an accompanying music in the video, then there are the usual rights in the music, as already described. **For a video of objects**, rights exist only in the recording, but permission might be needed to shoot the objects if they are other people's personal properties. If there is accompanying music or commentary, then, again, there are rights in the music, and the commentary is protected as literary work. With animation, there are rights in the whole animation piece as well as in any accompanying music or commentary.

The rights in both an animation and a video piece also apply to the individual images, since they are both essentially moving images or a series of images displayed at a certain speed. So, even if just a single image is used from a video or an animation clip, there may be copyright infringement, if done without permission. Of course, obtaining licenses to use a video is seldom as complicated as obtaining licenses in music, because the subjects in a video would often be required to sign a release contract that gives the videographer the right to use the video as deemed fit; so, videographers often have the right to give the permission to use the videos they have produced.

28.4.5 Rights in Codes and Database

The copyright in the source codes created in a project normally belongs to the developer, and it is also usually retained. This ensures that he/she can re-use the codes in other projects. Of course, he/she also needs to give the clients the permission to use the codes as well as access to them and other types of outputs from the project. This is so that, if desired, the clients can use other developers to make required modifications, instead of the original developer. These arrangements would have been made clear in the terms of the contract. Furthermore, in large projects where a system can last for very long time, in order to protect the interest of the clients, copies of codes are deposited with a third party, such as a bank, who can allow access to them in the event that the original developer has ceased trading.

If the application developed in a project is a media-rich Web application, the chances are that a database will be used to store the media files and scripts (codes) used for their selection, arrangement, and display. Any content that is protected by any rights will still be protected, even when stored in a database, and therefore, requires license before use. Permission is needed, too, before the content of other people's database or codes can be copied, adapted, or used.

Where original works have been produced in a project, including codes, database, and application design, it is important to contemplate how an infringement could be proven, and archive evidence accordingly. For example, as mentioned before, unique marks (e.g., deliberate mistakes in comments) may be placed in codes or somewhere in the database structure.

28.5 Industrial Property in Web Design

In most Web projects, only issues of copyright need to be dealt with, not those of industrial property rights, such as patents, designs, and trademarks. However, in some projects, industrial property rights may be relevant. For example, while trying to develop an effective process, a **unique algorithm** might be computed that is worth patenting. Some dating websites, for example, have their matching algorithm patented. This happened before with data compression algorithms for various media types. If you feel that your site will do something unique and groundbreaking, the next step should be to take legal advice, as patent applications are often complex. On the other hand, given that patent eventually expires and an idea becomes free for people to exploit as they see fit, if your idea is likely to be relevant and profitable for a long time (as, for example, Google's search algorithm is), it may be better to simply make the details trade secret and not patent the idea.

Where a project includes producing a trademark, caution would have been taken during design and production to ensure that it is not too similar to any pre-existing one, bearing in mind that even too much similarity in color scheme can constitute trademark infringement. Of course, trademarks are usually registered by the clients, not the Web designer.

28.6 Useful Info

28.6.1 Web Links

World Intellectual Property Organization: wipo.int
UK Intellectual Property: ipo.gov.uk
US copyright: copyright.gov
Creative Commons—Free use: creativecommons.org
Free software foundation: fsf.org
Free art: artlibre.org

Bibliography

Alsudani, F. and Casey, M. The effect of aesthetics on web credibility. In *Proceedings of the 23rd British HCI Group Annual Conference on People and Computers: Celebrating People and Technology*, 1–5 September 2009, British Computer Society, Cambridge, pp. 512–519, 2009.

Barr, C. *The Yahoo! Style Guide: The Ultimate Sourcebook for Writing, Editing, and Creating Content for the Digital World*. New York: St. Martin Griffin, 2010.

Bently, L. and Sherman, B. *Intellectual Property Law*. New York: Oxford, 2009.

Brinson, J. D. *Multimedia Law and Business Handbook*. Menlo Park, CA: Ladera Press, 1996.

Denzin, N. K. *The Research Act in Sociology*. Chicago: Aldine, 1970.

England, E. and Finney, A. *Managing Multimedia: Project Management for Web and Convergent Media: Book 1, People and Processes*, 3rd edn. Harlow, England: Addison Wesley, 2002a.

England, E. and Finney, A. *Managing Multimedia: Technical Issues, Book 2*, 3rd edn. Harlow, England: Addison Wesley, 2002b.

England, E. and Finney, A. *Managing Interactive Media, Project Management for Web and Digital Media*, 4th edn. Harlow, England: Addison Wesley, 2007.

Evans, P. and Thomas, A. M. *Exploring the Elements of Design*. NY: Cengage Learning, 2012.

Farkas, E. B. *Managing Web Projects*. Boca Raton, FL: CRC Press, 2010.

Fogg, B. J. *Persuasive Technology: Using Computers to Change What We Think and Do*. San Francisco, CA: Morgan Kaufmann, 2002.

Fogg, B. J., Marshall, J., Laraki, O., Osipovich, A., Varma, C., Fang, N., and Treinen, M. What makes Web sites credible?: A report on a large quantitative study. In *Proceedings of the SIGCHI Conference on Human Factors in Computing Systems*, pp. 61–68, ACM, ACM Press, Seattle, WA, 2001.

Haynes, R. *Media Rights and Intellectual Property*. Edinburgh, Scotland: Edinburgh University Press, 2005.

Lauer, D. A. and Pentak, S. *Design Basics*, 5th edn. Philadelphia, PA: Wadsworth Publishing, 2002.

Laurel, B. *The Art of Human Computer Interface Design*. Boston, MA: Addison-Wesley, 1991.

Lindgaard, G. Does emotional appeal determine the usability of websites. In *CYBERG '99*, Western Australia, 1999.

Lindgaard, G., Fernandes, G., Dudek, C., and Browñ, J. Attention web designers: You have 50 milliseconds to make a good first impression! *Behaviour and Information Technology* 25(2), 115–126, 2006.

Loranger, H. Accordions Are Not Always the Answer for Complex Content on Desktops. Nielsen Norman Group article. Accessed January 30, 2016. http://www.nngroup.com/articles/accordions-complex-content.

Loranger, H. and Nielsen, J. Teenage Usability: Designing Teen-Targeted Websites. Accessed January 30, 2016. http://www.nngroup.com/articles/usability-of-websites-for-teenagers.

Lutzker, A. *Copyrights and Trademarks for Media Professionals (Broadcast & Cable Series)*. Newton, MA: Butterworth-Heinemann, 1997.

Lynch, P. J. and Horton, S. *Web Style Guide: Basic Design Principles for Creating Web Sites*. New Haven, CT: Yale University Press, 2009.

Nielsen, J. *Designing Web Usability*. Thousand Oaks, CA: New Riders Publishing, 1999.

Nielsen, J. 113 Design Guidelines for Homepage Usability. Accessed January 30, 2016. http://www.nngroup.com/articles/top-ten-guidelines-for-homepage-usability.

Nielsen, J. *Usability Inspection Methods*. New York, NY: John Wiley & Sons, 2001.

Nielsen, J. Top 10 Guidelines for Homepage Usability. Accessed January 30, 2016. http://www.nngroup.com/articles/top-ten-guidelines-for-homepage-usability.

Nielsen, J. Information Foraging: Why Google Makes People Leave Your Site Faster. Accessed January 30, 2016. http://www.nngroup.com/articles/information-scent.

Nielsen, J. Avoid Within-Page Links, Nielsen Norman Group article. Accessed January 30, 2016. http://www.nngroup.com/articles/avoid-within-page-links.

Nielsen, J. F-Shaped Pattern For Reading Web Content. Accessed January 30, 2016. http://www.nngroup.com/articles/f-shaped-pattern-reading-web-content.

Nielsen, J. Children's Websites: Usability Issues in Designing for Kids. Accessed January 30, 2016. http://www.nngroup.com/articles/childrens-websites-usability-issues.

Nielsen, J. Website Response Times. Accessed January 30, 2016. http://www.nngroup.com/articles/website-response-times.

Nielsen, J. Scrolling and Attention. Accessed January 30, 2016. http://www.nngroup.com/articles/scrolling-and-attention.

Nielsen, J. Usability 101: Introduction to Usability. Accessed January 30, 2016. http://www.nngroup.com/articles/usability-101-introduction-to-usability.

Nielsen, J. Auto-Forwarding Carousels and Accordions Annoy Users and Reduce Visibility. Accessed January 30, 2016. http://www.nngroup.com/articles/auto-forwarding.

Nielsen, J. and Faber, J. M. Improving system usability through parallel design. *IEEE Computer* 29(2), 29–35, 1996.

Nielsen, J., Molich, R., Snyder, C., and Farrell, S. E-commerce user experience: Trust. Accessed January 30, 2016. http://www.nngroup.com/reports/ecommerce-ux-trust-and-credibility.

Norman, D. A. Emotion and design: Attractive things work better. *Interactions Magazine* 9(4), 36–42, 2002.

Pernice, K. Designing Effective Carousels: Create a Fanciful Amusement, Not a House of Horrors. Accessed January 30, 2016. http://www.nngroup.com/articles/designing-effective-carousels.

Pressman, R. *Software Engineering: A Practitioner's Approach*. New York: McGraw-Hill Higher Education, 2009.

Read, J., MacFarlane, S., and Casey, C. Endurability, engagement, and expectations: Measuring children's fun. In *Interaction Design and Children*, pp. 189–198, Amsterdam, the Netherlands: Eindhoven.

Shenkman, B. O. and Jonsson, F. Aesthetics and preferences of web pages. *Behaviour and Information Technology* 19(5), 367–377, 2000.

Sklar, J. *Principles of Web Design*. Boston, MA: Cengage Learning, 2009.

Smith-Atakan, S. *Human-Computer Interaction*. London: Thomson, Middlesex Press, 2006.

Tractinsky, N. Aesthetics and apparent usability: Empirically assessing cultural and methodological issues. Paper presented at Chi conference, 1997.

Tractinsky, N., Katz, A., and Ikar, D. What is beautiful is usable [Electronic Version]. *Interacting with Computers* 13(2), 127–145, 2000.

Williams, R. *The Non-Designer's Design Book*. Berkeley, CA: Peachpit Press, 2004.

Wixon, D. and Wilson, C. E. The usability engineering framework for product design and evaluation. In *Handbook of Human-Computer Interaction*, edited by Helander, M. G., Landauer, T. K., and Prabju, P. V., pp. 653–688, Amsterdam, the Netherlands: Elsevier, 1997.

Index

Note: Page numbers followed by f and t refer to figures and tables, respectively.